AMNESTY INTERNATIONAL REPORT 1998

This report
covers the period
January to December
1997

Amnesty International is a worldwide voluntary activist movement that works to prevent some of the gravest violations by governments of people's fundamental human rights. The main focus of its campaigning is to:

- *free all prisoners of conscience.* These are people detained anywhere for their beliefs or because of their ethnic origin, sex, colour, language, national or social origin, economic status, birth or other status – who have not used or advocated violence;

- *ensure fair and prompt trials for political prisoners;*

- *abolish the death penalty, torture and other cruel treatment of prisoners;*

- *end extrajudicial executions and "disappearances".*

Amnesty International also calls on opposition groups to halt abuses such as hostage-taking, torture and deliberate and arbitrary killings.

Amnesty International, recognizing that human rights are indivisible and interdependent, works to promote all the human rights enshrined in the Universal Declaration of Human Rights and other international standards, through human rights education programs and campaigning for ratification of human rights treaties.

Amnesty International is impartial. It is independent of any government, political persuasion or religious creed. It does not support or oppose any government or political system, nor does it support or oppose the views of the victims whose rights it seeks to protect. It is concerned solely with the protection of the human rights involved in each case, regardless of the ideology of the government or opposition forces, or the beliefs of the individual.

Amnesty International does not grade countries according to their record on human rights; instead of attempting comparisons it concentrates on trying to end the specific violations of human rights in each case.

Amnesty International has more than 1,000,000 members and subscribers in over 160 countries and territories. There are more than 4,300 local Amnesty International groups registered with the International Secretariat and several thousand professional and other groups, including over 3,400 youth and student groups, in more than 105 countries and territories in Africa, the Americas, Asia, Europe and the Middle East. To ensure impartiality, each group works on cases and campaigns in countries other than its own. Research into human rights violations and individual victims is conducted by the International Secretariat of Amnesty International. No section, group or member is expected to provide information on their own country, and no section, group or member has any responsibility for action taken or statements issued by the international organization concerning their own country.

Amnesty International has formal relations with the United Nations Economic and Social Council (ECOSOC); the United Nations Educational, Scientific and Cultural Organization (UNESCO); the Council of Europe; the Organization of American States; the Organization of African Unity; and the Inter-Parliamentary Union.

Amnesty International is financed by subscriptions and donations from its worldwide membership. No funds are sought or accepted from governments for Amnesty International's work investigating and campaigning against human rights violations. To safeguard the independence of the organization, all contributions are strictly controlled by guidelines laid down by the International Council.

AMNESTY INTERNATIONAL REPORT

1998

Amnesty International USA
322 Eight Avenue
New York, NY 10001

First published 1998
by Amnesty International Publications,
1 Easton Street, London WC1X 8DJ, United Kingdom

ISBN: 1-887204-13-X
AI Index: POL 10/01/98
Original language: English

Typesetting and page make-up by:
Accent on Type, 30/31 Great Sutton Street, London EC1V 0DX, United Kingdom

Printed by: John D. Lucas Printing Co., Baltimore, MD

Cover design: John Finn, Artworkers

Front cover photograph:
A boy outside a sugar cane refinery in southern India. © W. van Cappellen/Katz

Back cover photographs: (*from top to bottom*)
Graça Machel © AI
Daw Aung San Suu Kyi © Rex Features/Robert Service
Desmond Tutu © AI
(All are pledging to do everything within their power to uphold
the Universal Declaration of Human Rights, December 1997.)

This report documents Amnesty International's work and its concerns throughout the world during 1997. The absence of an entry in this report on a particular country or territory does not imply that no human rights violations of concern to Amnesty International have taken place there during the year. Nor is the length of a country entry any basis for a comparison of the extent and depth of Amnesty International's concerns in a country. Regional maps have been included in this report to indicate the location of countries and territories cited in the text and for that purpose only. It is not possible on the small scale used to show precise political boundaries. The maps should not be taken as indicating any view on the status of disputed territory. Amnesty International takes no position on territorial questions. Disputed boundaries and cease-fire lines are shown, where possible, by broken lines. Areas whose disputed status is a matter of unresolved concern before the relevant bodies of the United Nations have been indicated by striping only on the maps of the country which has *de facto* control of the area.

CONTENTS

APPENDICES

INTRODUCTION

All human rights for all

> **'All human beings, whatever their cultural or historical background, suffer when they are intimidated, imprisoned or tortured... We must, therefore, insist on a global consensus, not only on the need to respect human rights worldwide, but also on the definition of these rights... for it is the inherent nature of all human beings to yearn for freedom, equality and dignity, and they have an equal right to achieve that...'**
>
> The Dalai Lama, New York, USA, April 1994

It is 50 years since the Universal Declaration of Human Rights (UDHR) was proclaimed by the General Assembly of the United Nations (UN). Developed in response to the atrocities of the Second World War, the UDHR represented a collective determination never to return to those dark days. It was an important milestone in a discourse that stretches back through thousands of years of human history: what are the qualities that make us human and what rights, obligations and responsibilities do these create in our relationships with each other?

The UDHR sets out the human rights which are fundamental to the dignity and development of every human being. These range from economic rights, such as the right to work and to an adequate standard of living, to political rights, such as freedom of opinion, expression and association. They include civil rights, such as equality before the law, and social or cultural rights, such as the right to education and to participate in the cultural life of the community. The UDHR proclaims that all these rights belong to all people.

In effect, the UDHR was a promise made by governments to work towards a world without cruelty and injustice; a world without hunger and ignorance. Fifty years after its proclamation, how far have governments lived up to that promise? To what extent have the rights set out in the UDHR become a reality throughout the world?

Much has been achieved in the last half century. Struggles against colonialism and *apartheid* have changed the map of the world. Mass movements against race and gender discrimination have transformed societies. The rights enshrined in the UDHR have become a rallying cry for human rights defenders and ordinary people throughout the world. They have been elaborated upon and codified in international human rights treaties and declarations, as well as many national constitutions and laws. They have provided a foundation for UN and regional initiatives to secure peace and to reduce poverty, combat illiteracy and safeguard health.

But for most people the rights in the UDHR are little more than a paper promise. A promise that has not been fulfilled for the 1.3 billion people who struggle to survive on less than US$1 a day; for the 35,000 children who die of malnutrition and preventable diseases every day; for the billion adults, most of them women, who cannot read or write; for the prisoners of conscience languishing in jails in every region of the world; or for the victims of torture in a third of the world's countries.

'The Universal Declaration [of Human Rights] was adopted... only a few months after the first government which was determined to apply a policy of absolute apartheid came to power in South Africa. For all the opponents of this pernicious system, the simple and noble words of the Universal Declaration were a sudden ray of hope at one of our darkest moments.'

President Nelson Mandela of South Africa, January 1997

The UDHR's pledge of freedom from torture did not protect Juan and Marcos Zamora González, who were imprisoned and tortured in Mexico because of their peaceful campaign for their community's land rights. The UDHR's guarantee of the right to life was of little comfort to Lidiya Morozvona Puchayeva, whose 16-year-old daughter and three-month-old baby were shot dead by Russian troops as the family fled in terror from fighting in the Chechen Republic, part of the Russian Federation. The UDHR's promise of the right to seek asylum and of freedom from arbitrary detention has yet to help asylum-seekers arriving in Australia without a visa, who are automatically and arbitrarily confined in special detention centres.

As this report shows, governments around the world have failed to live up to their promises. This is nothing new. Driven by political expediency and self-interest, governments have long trampled on their citizens' rights in order to maintain power and privilege for the few. Constrained by difficult social and economic conditions, limited by weak or corrupt national institutions, governments have failed to implement their human rights commitments. What is relatively new, however, and deeply worrying for the human rights community, is that governments are mounting an increasingly concerted challenge to the concept that human rights should be universally and indivisibly applied.

For many years, particularly at the height of the Cold War, some governments have contested the human rights framework, arguing that it was developed and imposed to serve western policy interests. However, the conceptual challenge to human rights has grown in recent years, with a variety of governments and others arguing against universality, largely on cultural or religious grounds, and against indivisibility, largely on grounds of economic expedience.

© Santosh Harhare, Midday

A peaceful protest by women villagers against the construction of a power plant in May 1997 is broken up by police in Maharashtra, India. Hundreds of peaceful protesters, many of them women, were detained, harassed and ill-treated for objecting to the environmental and social damage caused by the project, a joint venture between three US multinational companies.

Universality and indivisibility

At the very heart of the UDHR is the principle that human rights are universal and indivisible, that **all** human rights should be enjoyed by **all** people.

In its preamble, the UDHR recognizes the "inherent dignity and the equal and inalienable rights of **all** members of the human family". Article 1 states, "**All** human beings are born free and equal in dignity and rights." More specifically, Article 2 proclaims, "**Everyone** is entitled to **all** the rights and freedoms set forth in this Declaration, without distinction of any kind".

By bringing together the range of human rights – civil, cultural, economic, political and social – the UDHR sets forth an **indivisible** as well as a **universal** body of rights. It enshrines the principle that human rights are interrelated, interdependent and mutually reinforcing. It recognizes that freedom from fear and freedom from want are two inextricably linked aspects of human well-being.

However, the geo-political global divide of the Cold War years allowed an artificial separation of two sets of rights. The two major human rights treaties deriving from the UDHR reflect this division: the International Covenant on Economic, Social and

Cultural Rights and the International Covenant on Civil and Political Rights. These two Covenants, however, affirm the indivisibility of the rights they enshrine, stating: "the ideal of free human beings enjoying freedom from fear and want can only be achieved if conditions are created whereby everyone may enjoy his economic, social and cultural rights, as well as his civil and political rights".

These principles have been repeatedly reaffirmed since the adoption of the UDHR, with governments from all regions of the world expressing formal support for universality and indivisibility.

In 1993, at the UN World Conference on Human Rights in Vienna, 171 governments adopted by consensus a declaration stating:

"All human rights are universal, indivisible and interdependent and interrelated... While the significance of national and regional particularities and various historical, cultural and religious backgrounds must be borne in mind, it is the duty of States, regardless of their political, economic and cultural systems, to promote and protect human rights and fundamental freedoms."

This affirmation has been echoed in other landmark declarations by the international community, such as those issued at the UN Summit for Social Development in Copenhagen in 1994 and the Fourth UN World Conference on Women in Beijing in 1995.

The challenge to universality

The universality of human rights has been increasingly challenged by governments and other groups on the grounds that local culture and tradition should take precedence.

In Asia, for instance, several governments argue that international human rights standards are based primarily on western concepts and are incompatible with Asian societies because they focus on individual rights. They point to crime, social problems and the breakdown of family and community structures as symptoms of excessive individualism in western societies. Asian people, they argue, place greater value on social harmony and are more inclined to sacrifice their self-interest for the good of the community.

Some African governments have put forward similar arguments, claiming that human rights in African societies exist to ensure the good of society as a whole; only through protecting the community can the rights of individuals be guaranteed. The African Charter on Human and Peoples' Rights lays particular emphasis on human duties towards family and society. The Rapporteur on the drafting of the Charter of the Organization of African Unity (OAU) noted that: "in Africa, man is part and parcel of the group, [and] some delegations concluded that individual rights could be explained and justified only by the rights of the community."

© Nigel Dickinson/Still Pictures

British police intervene during a non-violent protest on the planned site of a new road at Twyford Down in Hampshire. Protesters were demonstrating against the negative environmental consequences of the construction of the road. A number of protesters were allegedly ill-treated.

The universality of human rights has also been challenged by some governments which describe their rule as based on the Islamic faith. They have sought to justify systematic discrimination against women in countries such as Afghanistan, persecution of members of other religions in countries such as Pakistan, and judicial punishments such as floggings and amputations in countries such as Saudi Arabia, by referring to the holy scriptures of Islam. The effect is the institutionalization of human rights violations. In Saudi Arabia, for example, a man convicted of preaching Christianity was given 70 lashes in a prison courtyard in February 1997, in full view of other prisoners. He was barely able to walk as a result.

Many western governments in practice flout the principles of universality. The USA, for example, is reluctant to be bound by international human rights treaties that embody these principles. It stands virtually alone in not signing up to the UN Convention on the Rights of the Child. It is one of the few countries which has not ratified the Convention on the Elimination of All Forms of Discrimination against Women. Even when it has ratified international human rights conventions, it has often entered extensive reservations, refusing to be bound by many of the provisions within them.

Domestically, not all citizens are treated equally, even within states that proudly proclaim their commitment to human rights. In many western countries, criminals and those living on the margins of society are increasingly portrayed as subhuman, justifying the denial of fundamental human rights. Refugees, fleeing

© AI

The family of Consuelo Benavides Cevallos have fought a determined battle to ensure that the killing of their daughter while in the custody of Ecuadorian security forces is not covered up. They have faced repeated harassment and have had to sell their property to finance their quest for justice. In 1997 they won their struggle to have the case heard before the Inter-American Court of Human Rights.

from persecution, are castigated as people seeking unfair economic advantage and so refused their right to seek asylum.

Interpretations of human rights as overly individualistic, adversarial and detrimental to the community are misplaced. Human rights, by their very nature, are about what kind of society we live in – the quest for a just society in which all members are treated with dignity and respect. The goal is not unfettered individualism or anarchy: the rights of the individual can only be respected in a truly just society. If societies were as harmonious as some governments pretend, human rights would not be an issue. The standards only come into play because the rights of members of the community, or indeed whole sections of the community, are being violated, often solely on the basis of who they are or what they think.

Throughout the UDHR, rights are located in a group, community or social context. For example, Article 1 calls on all human beings to "act towards one another in a spirit of brotherhood" while Article 18 provides the right to hold beliefs either alone or "in community with others". Article 22 promises economic, social and cultural rights to everyone "as a member of society" and Article 29 states that "everyone has duties to the community in which alone the free and full development of his personality is possible".

As recognized by most human rights instruments, including the UDHR, rights must be exercised by individuals with a sense of duty and responsibility and, within strict limits, must give way to the larger good of society as a whole. International human rights standards were drafted by governments themselves, and they built in the restrictions they deemed necessary to be able to govern, including in situations of public emergency. These standards therefore reflect an ordered society, not unbridled individualism. As a result, although some rights are absolute and can never be suspended, such as the right not to be tortured, others, such as freedom of assembly, may be restricted in certain limited circumstances.

Challenges to universality also assume that cultural and religious perspectives are far more homogeneous than they usually are in reality. When certain political leaders speak of Asian values, they speak on behalf of a region that is incredibly diverse. More than half the world's population lives in Asia, speaking a multiplicity of languages and following a variety of religions. The Japanese car worker has little in common with the rice farmer from Bangladesh, be it language, religion or social norms. The same can be said for Africa, a vast continent with many disparate traditions. The Islamic world also offers great diversity in both theological interpretation and social models, from the secularism of Indonesia or Turkey to the theocracy of Iran or Saudi Arabia.

Arguments about culture and tradition often cloak political and economic interests. As one Asian commentator has put it: *"What makes it possible to imagine a uniform Asian perspective on human rights is that it is the perspective of a particular group – the ruling elites – that gets international attention. This elite group is united by their notion of governance and the expediency*

© AI

Khemais Chammari, a human rights activist and opposition member of parliament in Tunisia, was sentenced to five years' imprisonment in July 1996. He was released five months later, after national and international appeals on his behalf. In April 1997 his passport was returned to him and he was able to leave the country in order to attend a human rights conference in Malta.

of their rule... and their publicly expressed views on human rights divine from... the need to justify authoritarianism and occasional repression."

While Asian governments were preparing for the 1993 UN World Conference on Human Rights, a parallel gathering of Asian non-governmental organizations (NGOs) adopted their own statement, declaring that "human rights are of universal concern and are universal in value".

A similar conference of Arab NGOs expressed concern about the stress on regional particularities of culture and on national sovereignty in relation to human rights:

"*It was noted that several countries have used this 'excuse' to circumvent international scrutiny of their application of various instruments that deal with basic rights and freedoms... [The Conference] opposed such approaches if they were used to negate fundamental rights or lead to their abrogation."*

These are the words of the very people governments challenging universality purport to represent. Far from being alien and foreign concepts, human rights are crucially relevant to people in these societies and have given birth to a growing human rights movement.

Those that challenge universality also assert that because human rights – at least as expressed in current international standards – grew out of western liberal traditions, they are a tool of western domination and cultural imperialism in an unjust political and economic world order. They argue that the UN was predominantly western at the time of the adoption of the UDHR and that countries which have since signed up to the UN Charter and principles had no choice or bargaining power. This belies the many diverse traditions that feed notions of human dignity. All

Ruth Yudit Ortega Orozco, a student leader and human rights activist, was able to return to university in Mexico City in August 1997. In 1996 she was abducted, tortured and threatened with death by men believed to be connected to the Mexican security forces. Amnesty International appealed on her behalf, helping to ensure that repeated threats against her life have not continued.

© AI

cultures have moral codes regarding the standards of treatment that all people deserve. All societies have sought to define concepts of fundamental justice. The sacredness of life and human dignity and the importance of justice and fair treatment are consistent and recurring themes in all philosophical and religious traditions.

> **'You do not need to explain the meaning of human rights to an Asian mother or an African father whose son or daughter has been tortured or killed. They understand it – tragically – far better than we ever will. What they need, and what we must offer, is a vision of human rights that is foreign to no one and native to all.'**
>
> UN Secretary-General Kofi Annan, October 1997

It is true that the codification of the international human rights discourse has been stimulated by political and philosophical developments in the west over the past few centuries. As a result, the international language of human rights – the articulation of human rights concepts in international instruments like the UDHR – draws heavily on the language and concepts of western culture. It does not follow, however, that the underlying tenets are of restricted relevance. The terminology may be culturally specific, but not the principles themselves.

As Burmese opposition leader Daw Aung San Suu Kyi wrote in her book *Freedom from Fear*:
"It is difficult for the Burmese people to understand how any of the rights contained in the 30 articles of the UDHR can be seen as anything but wholesome and good. That the Declaration was not drawn up in Burma by the Burmese people seems an inadequate reason, to say the least, for rejecting it. If ideas and beliefs are to be denied validity outside the geographical and cultural bounds of their origin, Buddhism would be confined to North India, Christianity to a narrow tract in the Middle East and Islam to Arabia."

Culture is not static; it is constantly changing and evolving in response to interactions with other cultures. "Tradition" may have emphasized certain norms in the past, but this does not preclude tradition being reshaped by new realities. Sometimes cultural conventions are not only the justification for abuses but constitute human rights violations in themselves. In the case of women, for instance, what is termed "culture" or "tradition" often covers practices which restrict and damage women's lives. As Gro Harlem Bruntland, then Prime Minister of Norway, said, "violence against women, also domestic violence, can be said to be part of a 'cultural pattern' in most societies, including my own."

Female genital mutilation – the surgical removal of parts or all of the sensitive genital organs – is one of the most brutal manifestations of violence against women. It is generally performed on girls or young women by a traditional practitioner with crude instruments and without anaesthetic. The consequences for the physical and psychological health of women can be devastating, even life threatening. An estimated 130 million women and girls have been genitally mutilated. The practice occurs in many African countries, several countries in the Middle East and among minority communities in other parts of the world. There is a complex web of interrelated cultural factors behind female genital mutilation. It is seen by its practitioners as a necessary rite for initiation into womanhood and integration into the culture, without which a woman cannot marry.

The World Health Organization, the UN Children's Fund and the UN Population Fund declared in a statement on female genital mutilation in February 1996:

"It is unacceptable that the international community remain passive in the name of a distorted vision of multiculturalism... Culture is not static but is in constant flux, adapting and reforming. People will change their behaviour when they understand the hazards and indignity of harmful practices and when they realise that it is possible to give up harmful practices without giving up meaningful aspects of their culture."

The health and well-being of millions of young girls and women depend on such a reform of deeply rooted practices.

This does not mean imposing alien cultural values, or homogenizing the wonderful variety of collective human expression. Universality does not mean uniformity. The contribution of different cultures, at the local and global level, enriches our understanding of human rights. Indeed, in guaranteeing freedom of thought and belief, and freedom from discrimination on the basis of race, sex, language or other status, the UDHR serves to protect cultural and religious diversity.

The challenge to indivisibility

The nature of international relations has changed radically since the end of the Cold War. The accelerating globalization of the world's economy and the changing role of the state have led to a broad international convergence on political and economic matters. This has had a profound impact on the human rights debate.

Market-driven policies have been proclaimed as the formula for economic growth which will deliver fundamental economic rights. With economic development, the argument runs, will come greater civil and political freedom. While confidence in these arguments has been shaken somewhat by the recent economic downturn in Asia, they have become the prevailing economic orthodoxy. But while economic change has transformed the lives of millions, its dividends have not been evenly shared. The gulf between rich and poor has widened. Pressure upon resources and the environment has grown. Economic liberalization and structural adjustment policies have increased the marginalization of poor and vulnerable groups everywhere and contributed to further violations of their human rights.

Governments are resorting to authoritarian methods to maintain competitiveness and attract investment. Economic openness has not been accompanied by political reform – all too often, concepts of "good governance" promoted by international financial institutions and others as part of the new international economic order have focused more on the smooth operation of financial markets than on the fair and equitable treatment of people.

Many governments in the developing world insist on the primacy of economic growth which, they say, necessitates strong government and the subjugation of the individual's interests to those of the community. They argue that only when a country has attained a certain level of economic development can it afford the luxury of civil and political freedoms.

But economic growth is no guarantee of economic or social rights. Many governments in the developed world have dismantled elements of their welfare provision, justifying their actions on grounds of economic competitiveness. They have greatly reduced access to free education, health care and social security, leaving many homeless and hungry, even within the wealthiest nations.

In many ways, the challenge to the indivisibility of rights echoes the cultural challenge to universality outlined above. It shows that opposition to the legitimacy of human rights is ultimately about political and economic power, not cultural or religious values. It also highlights the intrinsic link between the universality and indivisibility of human rights. People cannot advance their economic, social and cultural rights without some degree of political space and freedom. Economic and social development, in practice, rarely benefits the poorest and most disadvantaged unless these groups are able to participate fully in their society, and to hold their government accountable by exercising freely their political and civil liberties. And people cannot

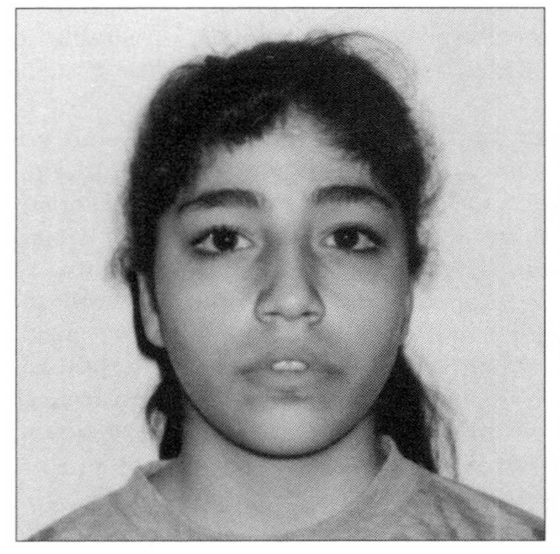

Sevgi Kaya alleges that she was tortured during detention at Istanbul Police Headquarters in 1996; she was just 15 years old. After Amnesty International members sent appeals to the Turkish Government on her behalf, trial proceedings began against five police officers in 1997.

© CINEP

Human rights defenders and environmental campaigners Elsa Constanza Alvarado and Mario Calderón were killed in May 1997 by gunmen believed to be members of a paramilitary group, operating with the tacit approval of the Colombian armed forces.

exercise their political rights or safeguard their civil freedoms if they are marginalized from society by poverty or their social position.

Poverty, in all its manifestations, is a grave violation of the economic and social rights enshrined in the UDHR. But the impact of poverty does not stop there: it makes people vulnerable to other human rights violations and limits their opportunities for redress.

Article 7 of the UDHR, for instance, guarantees that "all are equal before the law and are entitled without any discrimination to equal protection of the law", a principle enshrined in constitutions and legal systems the world over. But this basic civil and political right is compromised when economic and social rights are denied, skewing the legal system against the poor and socially marginalized groups.

In India, economic inequality is often exacerbated by rigid social hierarchies, in which the lowest castes or *dalits* face systemic discrimination and disadvantage. They have restricted access to education, live in segregated areas, work in poorly paid and socially stigmatized trades, and form the overwhelming majority of landless bonded labourers. In several parts of India, *dalits* are involved in conflicts with powerful local landlords over the use of land and resources. Often police, rather than upholding the law fairly and equitably, collude with landlords in abuses against *dalit* communities. Property is destroyed, false charges are registered, *dalits* are illegally detained and even tortured; yet the victims often lack the money, social position or political influence to defend themselves and seek redress. For example, Nisha Devi, an 18-year-old *dalit* woman, was partially stripped, pinned to the ground, beaten and kicked by four police officers who were looking for her brother-in-law. There were numerous witnesses. Nisha Devi reported the assault the next day, but it took police a further two weeks to file a report, and local police have since pressured her and her family to withdraw the complaint.

In the USA, whether or not the death penalty is imposed on a prisoner reflects their social and economic status to a chilling degree. Of the 432 prisoners executed in the USA since 1977, 44 per cent came from ethnic minorities. A black person convicted of killing a white victim is far more likely to receive a death sentence. One study of 10,000 homicides in Florida showed that a black person convicted of killing a white was 15 times more likely to be sentenced to death than a black who had killed a black. Many of the prisoners on death row were too poor to hire their own lawyer, and were inadequately represented by state-funded lawyers.

Girvies Davis, a young black man from Illinois, was executed in May 1995. He was arrested for armed robbery, but police claimed that he later gave them a handwritten note listing 11 murders he had committed. But Girvies Davis could neither read nor write. He admitted his involvement in the armed robbery, but consistently maintained that he had not committed murder. He claimed never to have seen his written "confession" until it was presented in court; it reportedly contained two different sets of "flowing" handwritten script. The prosecution later conceded that at least three of the murders to which Girvies Davis had allegedly confessed were committed by other people. Girvies Davis was tried by an all-white jury, after the prosecution challenged all potential black jurors without giving reasons. Girvies Davis was convicted and executed on the strength of a confession which he could not have written or read.

This pattern of social or racial discrimination is reflected almost everywhere the death penalty is used. In the Philippines, a May 1997 survey of the 325 prisoners on death row showed that the vast majority came from lower income brackets and around half had not received secondary education. The past few years have seen increased use of the death penalty in other countries of southeast Asia, with migrant workers especially vulnerable.

Just as economic and social disadvantage prevent people from exercising fully their civil and political rights, so too political repression obstructs people from defending and advancing their economic and social interests, or those of their community.

In Indonesia, for instance, the interests of the political and economic elite in holding down wages to maintain industrial competitiveness have led to sustained pressure on independent labour activism and trade union activity. Only the government-sponsored trade union federation is officially recognized, and members of independent unions face violence, intimidation and arrest. Dita Indah Sari, a leader of the non-governmental Centre for Indonesian Workers' Struggle, is among those who have worked steadfastly to improve workers' pay and conditions in Indonesia. She was arrested in July 1996 when she took part in a demonstration calling for a rise in the national minimum wage. The demonstration in the East Java town of Surabaya was entirely peaceful, yet it was blocked and violently dispersed by a heavy police and military force. Dita Indah Sari was later charged under Indonesia's draconian Anti-subversion Law and is serving a five-year prison sentence.

In many other countries, people defending their land, livelihood and resources have also faced violent repression by the state, often in the name of development. Leticia Moctezuma Vargas, a teacher and community worker in the Mexican state of Morelos, led a campaign against the development of a golf-course on land that her Tepoztlán community regards as sacred. The Tepoztlán community, and organizations working with the poor, peacefully protested against the environmental damage associated with this project, which is backed by a major development company, the state governor and the government. In April 1996 Leticia Moctezuma Vargas and her daughters joined a rally which was violently broken up by police. Many people were beaten, including Leticia and her children. Since this incident, she has received threats to her life, instructing her to "stop interfering in politics".

Governments around the world seek to justify violations of this kind in the name of development and economic competitiveness. They deny the indivisibility of human rights, claiming that if they concentrate on economic rights first, other rights will

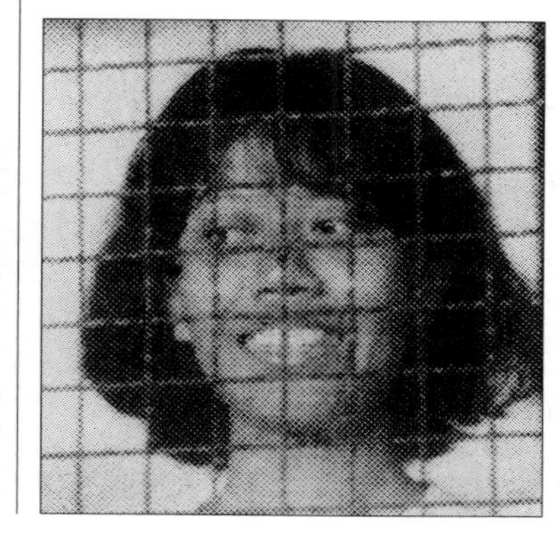

Dita Indah Sari, an Indonesian trade union activist, imprisoned for defending workers' rights.

Leticia Moctezuma Vargas, teacher and community activist, was beaten by members of the police and received threats against her life for defending indigenous land rights in Mexico during 1996.

© AI

surely follow. But economic growth does not necessarily translate into genuine human development. Development is a process embracing the place of individuals in civil society, their security and their capacity to determine and realise their potential. It is about the realization of human rights – *all* human rights. As the UN World Conference on Social Development in Copenhagen affirmed in 1995: "in order to promote development, equal attention and urgent consideration should be given to the implementation, promotion and protection of civil, political, economic, social and cultural rights." The UN Declaration on the Right to Development asserts that "the human person is the central subject of the development process", and that the purpose of development is "the constant improvement of the well-being of the entire population and of all individuals, on the basis of their active, free and meaningful participation". Individuals like Dita Indah Sari and Leticia Moctezuma Vargas should be able to participate in and seek benefit from the process of development without fear of intimidation, without fear for their lives.

Meeting future challenges

The urgent need for action to fulfil the promises of the UDHR is underlined by this *Amnesty International Report*. Its pages contain the stories of thousands of men, women and children whose lives have been wrecked by repression and cruelty. It demonstrates clearly that governments must be held to account, must shoulder their responsibilities, must implement in practice the promises they have made on paper. However, this report does not show only human suffering. It also reports on the efforts of human rights activists worldwide to prevent injustice and defend fundamental freedoms, despite the fact that human rights defenders themselves are increasingly targeted for repression. Amnesty International is proud to be part of this global movement for human rights, and is determined to do what it can in

© AI

Former prisoner of conscience, Vera Chirwa, addresses participants at the International Council Meeting (ICM) in Cape Town, South Africa, in December 1997. The ICM is the supreme decision-making body of Amnesty International.

defending the human rights movement and its achievements from threats, whether physical, political or ideological.

Today's human rights movement is richly diverse. The strategies adopted by human rights defenders around the world are just as varied. At its creation in 1961, Amnesty International sought to contribute to the ultimate goal of promoting the UDHR by mobilizing international pressure around a single, simple demand: that those imprisoned anywhere in the world for their beliefs should be freed immediately. Since then, Amnesty International's strategy has continually evolved and adapted to new realities. Its agenda has broadened gradually to encompass not just the plight of certain prisoners but a whole range of abuses of power, within and beyond the prison walls.

To promote the UDHR and defend the principles of universality and indivisibility in the next century, Amnesty International and the broader human rights movement of which it is part will need to rise to the challenges presented by a fast-changing world environment. Article 28 of the UDHR states that "Everyone is entitled to a social and international order in which the rights and freedoms set forth in this Declaration can be fully realized." Achieving such a world is the task before us.

We must face the shortcomings in our own ways of working, as well as the intransigence of governments. Among other things, this means addressing weaknesses in the international human rights framework and neglected aspects of our own agenda. It means considering changes in the nature of human rights violations and the contexts in which they occur. It means addressing the human rights responsibilities of people and institutions other than governments, and searching for more effective strategies for protecting human rights in armed conflict. It means finding new ways to disseminate the human rights message, to ensure that we relate to the realities of human experience, in all their variety.

The new directions in Amnesty International's work are aimed at enhancing its relevance and the effectiveness of its contribution to pressing contemporary human rights struggles. In December 1997 in South Africa, the International Council Meeting – Amnesty International's supreme policy-making body – took a number of decisions to ensure that the organization is a constructive partner in the worldwide endeavour to defend human rights in the years to come.

Amnesty International's effectiveness depends on its being able to mobilize a mass membership and the broader public into action around a focused, clear and coherent agenda. Amnesty International plans to review the coherence and relevance of its mandate, not in order to look inwards, but in recognition of the new human rights challenges confronting a changing world.

Addressing weaknesses in the human rights framework

In the 50 years since the declaration of the UDHR, the international (and regional) human rights framework has greatly expanded. Legally binding treaties have been drawn up which states have agreed to respect. Non-treaty standards representing the consensus of the international community have been adopted. The contract between the individual and the state has been gradually codified. However, progress in standard-setting has been uneven, leaving gaps and weaknesses. Among the several areas that have been relatively neglected are economic rights and women's rights.

Economic rights

The evolution of international human rights law saw an artificial and misleading separation of civil and political rights from economic, social and cultural rights, reflecting a world polarized by the ideological and strategic conflict of the Cold War. The end of the Cold War did not, however, bring consensus on human rights. The debate has been perpetuated in other forms, as reflected in divisions between developed and developing countries.

Undeniably, economic, social and cultural rights have received less attention from the UN and its constituent bodies. Standards in this area, and the mechanisms to implement them, are far less developed. As the Chairman of the UN Committee on Economic, Social and Cultural Rights, Philip Alston, argued in March 1997, "invisibility" rather than "indivisibility" is an apt description for this side of the human rights spectrum.

© REX FEATURES

Political violence in Algeria cost tens of thousands of lives during the year. Both government security forces and armed political opposition groups mercilessly tortured and killed unarmed civilians.

The assumption has been that civil and political rights could be defined by law and enforced in courts, since it is argued that they largely require the state to refrain from doing certain things to its citizens. By contrast, economic, social and cultural rights, it is argued, impose positive obligations on states which are not so susceptible to determination by the courts. They are more in the nature of calls on states to achieve certain goals, the argument runs, and the degree of the state's efforts to do so can neither be measured easily nor separated from the exigencies of circumstance. The International Covenant on Economic, Social and Cultural Rights obliges a state to implement these rights "to the maximum of its available resources", unlike the International Covenant on Civil and Political Rights which demands immediate implementation.

This argument is based on two misconceptions. First, it is wrong to argue that civil and political rights do not place positive obligations on states to take action. States have a duty not only to protect human rights, but also to promote them actively. For example, the prohibition on torture requires at the very least training of law enforcement officers and inspection of detention centres. Second, it is clear that many economic, social and cultural rights do have elements which can already, in the law and practices of some states, be invoked in court. For example, the new Constitution of South Africa guarantees the right to education.

It is striking how little effort has been made to provide meaningful administrative or judicial remedies to those whose economic or social rights have been violated. Even those governments which say they prioritize economic rights over civil and political rights have failed to support the development of standards or mechanisms which would enhance their population's enjoyment of these rights.

This can be seen in the painfully slow progress towards an Optional Protocol for the International Covenant on Economic, Social and Cultural Rights, which would provide a procedure for individuals to file complaints about violations of their rights to the appropriate expert UN body, similar to those which exist for the International Covenant on Civil and Political Rights and other international human rights treaties.

Addressing the imbalance between economic rights and other human rights is vital at a time when the debate over human rights is increasingly played out in the economic sphere. When governments fail to protect their citizens from the negative consequences of globalization, the need to protect and enhance economic rights becomes evident. The parallel imperative of ensuring that economic rights are not divorced from other human rights is shown each time that people are harassed, tortured and killed in the name of economic progress.

Amnesty International, with a mandate geared primarily to civil and political rights, has been a part of this imbalance. The very success of the organization in building a worldwide membership and raising its concerns among a wide public has been a factor in focusing attention on civil and political rights. Amnesty International is now engaging in broader human rights debates and seeks to promote the full spectrum of human rights in its campaigning and human rights education activities. However, this side of its work has remained relatively under-developed. Decisions taken by the 1997 International Council Meeting affirmed the need to explore ways of raising awareness of the full range of human rights, to provide more economic and social context in Amnesty International's reporting, and to make greater efforts to promote international standards and mechanisms protecting economic and social rights.

Women's rights

The UN Charter affirms the equal rights of men and women, and the UDHR states that everyone should enjoy human rights without discrimination on grounds of sex. However, the "gender blindness" of the international human rights framework has meant in practice that gross violations of women's rights have often been ignored and structural discrimination against women has not been challenged.

Many abuses are suffered only or primarily by women and girls. These range from female infanticide to the disproportionate malnutrition of young girls, from rape and mutilation to battery and murder. Countless women and girls die each day from gender-based discrimination and violence. Yet traditionally, such abuses of women's rights have been treated as separate from other human rights violations and taken less seriously by governments and NGOS.

Women's role in society often means that human rights violations have a disproportionate impact on them. Poverty and conflict affect women not only as individuals but also in their capacity as family carer. Women are more vulnerable to armed attacks on civilian targets because of their functions within the household and the community. To give just one example, women are the majority of those displaced by political violence in Colombia. Tens of thousands of peasant women, many of them recently widowed, have been forced to flee their rural homes, abandon their livestock and possessions and take precarious refuge in shanty towns around Colombia's cities.

There has been significant progress on women's rights, largely as a result of systematic campaigning by women's organizations over several decades. They have had to overcome entrenched obstacles. The interpretation of international human rights law has drawn a distinction between the "public" sphere of society – political, legal and social institutions – and the "private" sphere of the home and family. It has focused on the former, largely populated by men, and neglected the so-called "private" sphere in which women are traditionally enclosed. Doctrines of privacy and protection of the family, found in both international and national laws, have reinforced this artificial demarcation between "private" and "public" spheres.

This distinction has led to one of the most common misconceptions in the field of human rights – and one that has influenced Amnesty International. States have been held responsible only for violations that occur in the "public" sphere, but not for

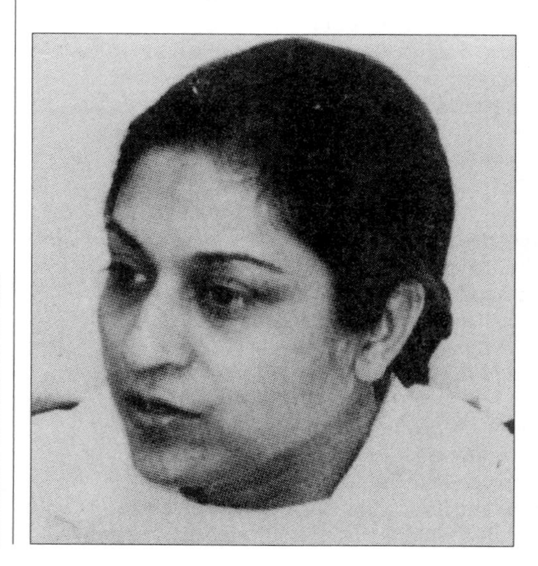

Amnesty International has been concerned over the years about the safety of Asma Jahangir, a human rights lawyer in Pakistan, who has faced grave danger for her work on women's and children's rights and the rights of minorities. She defended an illiterate 14-year-old boy sentenced to death for allegedly writing blasphemous words on the wall of a mosque. In 1997 she successfully defended a woman whose father sought to have her marriage declared illegal because she had married without his consent.

© HRCP

abuses that occur in the "private" sphere. As a result, many violations of women's rights have received insufficient scrutiny and concern. For example, the interpretation of the right to be free from torture has not encompassed violence against women in the family (such as domestic violence) and violence against women in the community (such as female genital mutilation).

In addition, the assumption that the condition of women in society is a product of inviolable social and cultural traditions has allowed states to repudiate accountability for violations of women's rights. Women's civil, cultural, economic, political and social rights have been systematically denied in the name of cultural values premised on unequal power relations between men and women.

One of the notable achievements of the UN World Conference on Human Rights in 1993 was its public endorsement of the message that the human rights of women are an inalienable, integral and indivisible part of universal human rights. At the Fourth UN World Conference on Women in 1995, the assembled governments incorporated the message that women's rights are human rights into the Beijing Declaration and Platform for Action.

Amnesty International is campaigning to promote the implementation of the Beijing Declaration and Platform for Action, particularly at the national level. At the international level, Amnesty International is calling for the integration of women's human rights into the work of the UN political and expert bodies that deal with human rights, and into the mainstream of all the UN's activities (see **Work with International Organizations**). Amnesty International is also working with women's groups and networks around the world for a strong Optional Protocol to the UN Convention on the Elimination of All Forms of Discrimination against Women, which would allow women to pursue complaints alleging violations of the rights contained in this treaty.

Amnesty International is also endeavouring to ensure that a gender-sensitive perspective is fully integrated into its own work. This involves examining the way its existing mandate has been interpreted, its research methods and its language. For example, in condemning the restrictions on women in Afghanistan, where *Taleban* edicts ban women from seeking employment, education or leaving home unaccompanied by a male relative, Amnesty International has extended its interpretation of "imprisonment" on grounds of gender.

Widening responsibility: government inaction

We cannot hope to achieve "a world free from fear" (the promise held out by the UDHR) as long as practices such as bride burning, child slavery, female genital mutilation, domestic violence and physical attacks on minority groups continue with impunity. These abuses demand attention because of their prevalence in today's world and their devastating effect on the disadvantaged.

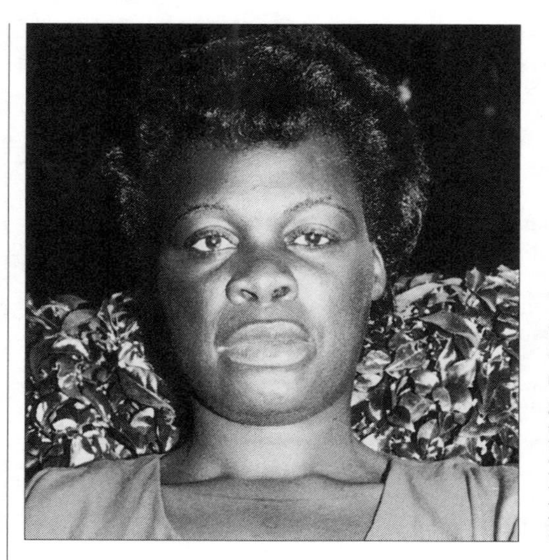

'Tsitsi Tiripano', a member of Gays and Lesbians of Zimbabwe (GALZ), which succeeded in opposing a government ban on their participation in the annual Zimbabwe International Book Fair. However, police did not protect GALZ members from attacks by an anti-gay group.

Recently developed international human rights standards affirm the responsibility of governments to prevent and punish such abuses when they are carried out by "private" individuals in the home or in the community.

When the state fails to protect its citizens from harm by others, it shares responsibility with those who commit the harm. Widening responsibility for the protection of human rights means focusing not only on what governments do, but also on what they fail to do to promote human rights and prevent violations.

In the past, Amnesty International has only addressed such "private" violence where there have been clear indications of the government's complicity or acquiescence, such as killings by "death squads" in Central America or by agents in the pay of private landowners in Brazil. At the 1997 International Council Meeting, the movement agreed to develop a more comprehensive framework for addressing abuses by "non-state actors" and to develop its expertise in this area by pursuing a number of pilot projects.

A recent program to counter female genital mutilation has been instructive, showing that Amnesty International has a contribution to make and pointing to the need to develop new strategies and techniques in close collaboration with the human rights defenders at the forefront of that struggle. Amnesty International activists in West and East Africa have developed a 10-point program for action by governments, based on their obligations under international human rights law. On its own, government action will not end the practice. Nevertheless, governments have it within their power to determine whether female genital mutilation will be eradicated within a generation, or whether millions more girls will pay the price of their inaction.

Widening responsibility: other perpetrators

Human rights are not the responsibility of governments alone. As the role of the nation state changes, governments no longer have a monopoly on political power. In many countries, armed conflict rages. In some, the state has entirely collapsed and competing warlords control a patchwork of territory. Influencing armed opposition groups to respect human rights is one of the pressing tasks of the human rights movement. Moreover, state policy is increasingly influenced by business corporations and international financial institutions in areas which have a profound impact on human rights. Encouraging the business community to play a positive role in promoting human rights is another challenge that cannot be ignored.

Business and economic institutions

The restructuring of the world economy has increased the influence of international financial institutions and global corporations. The UDHR calls on "every individual and every organ of society" to play its part in securing universal observance of human rights. Business interests and financial institutions are organs of society: they have an important part to play in the promotion and protection of human rights.

Amnesty International believes that businesses have a direct responsibility to ensure the protection of human rights in their own operations. Their workforces and clients are entitled to rights such as freedom from discrimination, the right to life and security, freedom from slavery, freedom of association, including the right to form trade unions, and fair working conditions.

Aleksandr Nikitin faces up to 20 years' imprisonment for publicizing the consequences of accidents on Russian nuclear submarines. He was released pending trial in 1996 and wrote to Amnesty International "I am convinced that the international attention and support, which you, among others, have initiated, will influence the further judicial proceedings in the case".

Dr Beko Ransome-Kuti, a Nigerian human rights defender and democracy activist, is serving a 15-year prison term for his human rights work on behalf of prisoners convicted in secret treason trials in 1995.

Particular care needs to be taken by companies making arms or other military or security equipment to ensure that their products are not used to violate human rights.

In addition, businesses have a responsibility to use their influence to try to stop violations of human rights by governments or armed political groups in the countries in which they operate. The silence of powerful business interests in the face of injustice is not neutral. When the world was campaigning to stop the execution of Ken Saro-Wiwa and his eight Ogoni co-defendants in Nigeria in 1995, Amnesty International urged the oil company Shell – one of Nigeria's most powerful investors – to intervene. The company insisted that it should not play a role in Nigerian politics. Yet companies like Shell regularly try to influence governments' tax and trade policies, their labour laws and environmental rules, and Shell itself has since spoken out publicly in support of human rights. Amnesty International believes that the business community has a responsibility to use its influence to promote respect for all human rights. Amnesty International has developed a checklist of human rights principles for companies, based on international law, for inclusion in company codes of conduct.

International financial and economic institutions such as the International Monetary Fund (IMF), the World Bank and the World Trade Organization (WTO) should also ensure that human rights are taken into account in the development of their policies and projects. Amnesty International is developing a lobbying program, calling on the World Bank, the IMF and the WTO to assess policies and programs in the light of the protection and promotion of all human rights; to support and build the institutions of civil society that stand as a bulwark against abuse of power by those in authority; and to speak out publicly when human rights are violated.

Human rights in armed conflict

Amnesty International campaigns against abuses by armed political opposition groups, urging them to respect human rights and abide by basic humanitarian standards. Many of the country entries in this report demonstrate how formidably difficult and increasingly important this is.

One of the most shameful aspects of contemporary armed conflict is the use of children as soldiers, primarily (though by no means exclusively) by armed opposition groups. Amnesty International's work on the forced recruitment of children by an armed opposition group in Uganda, the Lord's Resistance Army, illustrates the physical and psychological devastation caused. Many children are killed or maimed in the fighting. Others are subjected to brutalizing treatment, including gross physical and sexual abuse, in order to make them submit to authority. Just as traumatic, they are forced in turn to commit further abuses.

Amnesty International has decided to support international efforts to raise the minimum age of military recruitment to 18, as one important means of preventing the cycle of horror in which such children are trapped.

The media coverage of recent conflicts has brought home the terror of war and the fact that the brunt of suffering is increasingly borne by civilians – especially women and children. In 1997 the brutality of conflicts in Algeria and Central Africa shocked the world. A sense of powerlessness in the face of such recurring calamities has prompted Amnesty International, along with many others, to review its role in armed conflict situations and to search for creative strategies to prevent and respond to them. This search has led the organization to make changes in its mandate. These include a commitment to campaign against anti-personnel mines and other weapons whose effects are indiscriminate. In parallel with this, the organization opposes indiscriminate and disproportionate killings in armed conflict.

© AI

A drawing by one of the thousands of Ugandan children abducted and forced to become soldiers by the Lord's Resistance Army, an armed opposition group backed by the Sudanese authorities.

Disseminating the human rights message

One of the great challenges in the coming years is to articulate and disseminate the values of the UDHR in a culturally diverse form, without diminishing the concepts enshrined in it or the universality of their application. At the simplest level this means translating the UDHR into all the world's languages and making it available to the billions of people who do not know that it exists. More substantially, it is necessary to broaden consciousness and awareness of rights, drawing on different cultural, philosophical and religious traditions. Human rights will only come to life and grow in every community if they relate to the language and values of that community. Universality should benefit from diversity, not deny it.

Amnesty International is well placed to contribute to this effort as an international movement with members in more than 100 countries in every region of the world. In the year of the 50th anniversary of the UDHR, Amnesty International is campaigning to raise awareness and mobilize support. Its one million members are lobbying their governments, calling on them to rededicate themselves to the rights enshrined in the UDHR, and to live up to their promises in protecting those rights. They are asking ordinary people, community leaders, religious groups, business people and government leaders from all over the world to sign a pledge committing themselves to the UDHR. The world's largest book of signatures will then be presented to the UN as a demonstration of how much the people of the world value their human rights.

By showing the worldwide support for the UDHR, Amnesty International hopes to bring the document to life, to hold governments to account for the way they treat their people, and to support the work of hundreds of thousands of human rights defenders around the world. Many have paid with their freedom or their lives for their courageous stand in upholding the UDHR's ideals. We owe it to them to show that we value and support their efforts.

Amnesty International is asking people around the world to pledge: "I promise to do everything in my power to ensure that the rights set out in the Universal Declaration of Human Rights become a reality throughout the world." For its part, Amnesty International will do everything in its power to promote all human rights everywhere.

Making a difference

Amnesty International is guilty of "sloganeering, slanging off at people, abusing them", proclaimed the Australian Minister of Foreign Affairs, Alexander Downer. He continued: "It might make you feel good, but it doesn't achieve anything".

What sparked such remarks was Amnesty International's energetic campaigning in Australia as part of its work on the human rights of refugees worldwide, one of the organization's major campaigns of 1997. The Minister was particularly incensed at one of the campaign's reports, *Ethnicity and nationality: Refugees in Asia*, which exposed Australia's unfair treatment of asylum-seekers.

The Minister was wrong to believe that such campaigns achieve nothing. Even in his own country, his comments provoked the Senate to pass a resolution calling on him to "direct his energies to more vigorously tackle the [Indonesian Government's] human rights abuses in East Timor... and to review Australia's stance on East Timorese asylum-seekers". In October the Senate passed another motion noting Amnesty International's main recommendations on how Australia should improve its procedures for asylum-seekers.

© AI

Representatives of 201 student groups in Canada presenting more than 5,000 paper airplanes to the International Air Transport Association (IATA). Each airplane was a letter asking IATA members not to allow asylum-seekers to be forcibly returned to countries where they would risk human rights violations.

Other governments took positive steps during the campaign. The Hungarian Government proposed to introduce legislation that would remove the country's geographic reservation to the 1951 UN Convention Relating to the Status of Refugees, a reservation which has meant that Hungary only considers asylum claims from European refugees. The proposed law was still under discussion at the end of the year.

The campaign also had an immediate impact in Ukraine. In August members of Amnesty International in the country met Oleg Vladislavovich Shamsur, a senior official of the State Committee on Issues of Nationality and Migration, and raised the issue of Ukraine complying with its reporting obligations under the UN Convention Relating to the Status of Refugees. Oleg Shamsur expressed his positive attitude to Amnesty International's recommendations in its 1997 refugee campaign and said that he uses them in the Committee's work.

Progress was also achieved for some individual asylum-seekers featured in the campaign. At the beginning of 1997, for example, Mariam Azimi, an Afghan asylum-seeker, was hiding in a church in Norway fearing that she would be deported if she left the building. She was subsequently allowed to leave the church while her case was examined by an independent commission, and in July she was granted leave to stay in Norway with her children on humanitarian grounds. Soon afterwards she wrote: "This could not have been possible without the continued support from Amnesty International. I wish once again to thank you through this letter, even though I know it is not possible to express all my gratitude through a letter."

The campaign for refugees' rights highlighted the strength, diversity and imagination of the Amnesty International movement. In 1997 the million-strong force of Amnesty International members and supporters — people from all walks of life who refuse to

Aristeo Cervantes, aged five, and Renata Cervantes, aged three, signing a petition on behalf of refugee children, November 1997, in Mexico City, Mexico.

© AI

remain indifferent to the suffering of their fellow human beings — was active in 176 countries and territories of the world. In 105 of these countries and territories, they were organized in more than 4,300 local Amnesty International groups, over 3,400 youth and student groups, and several hundred professional and other groups. In 55 countries and territories the groups were coordinated by sections.

These activists mobilize their communities, put pressure on governments, support victims and their families, lobby for legal reform, and raise public awareness through the media and human rights education work. Alongside traditional campaigning methods such as letter-writing, each group looks for new and more effective ways of making their distinct contribution to promoting and protecting human rights. A group in a small village may focus on solidarity work with victims of torture in a faraway country. Children can give immense joy to prisoners and their families by sending drawings and cards. A group in a large town may organize joint initiatives with other non-governmental organizations (NGOs) to campaign on a particular human rights issue, or stage a concert to raise funds and promote awareness of human rights. Some members concentrate on public education, others work with sympathetic members of parliament to introduce laws to protect human rights. All these activities, as well as the policies and overall strategies of the movement as a whole, are decided by Amnesty International members themselves through internal democratic structures.

Amnesty International groups around the world mobilized in support of the 1997 campaign to raise awareness about the rights of refugees and the direct link between refugee movements and human rights abuses. Many materials were produced by Amnesty International's International Secretariat in London, United Kingdom, to help members achieve this goal. The main report, *Refugees: human rights have no borders*, provided detailed arguments on the international community's responsibilities towards refugees. A briefing, *Respect my rights*, and poster display showed the individual consequences of refugee crises, by allowing refugees to be seen and to speak for themselves. Five regional reports tackled some of the main refugee issues facing the world. In addition, Amnesty International worked with a Geneva-based NGO, the International Service for Human Rights, to publish a manual for activists using international human rights procedures to protect refugees' rights.

A novel aspect of the campaign, which began in March, was that each Amnesty International section was asked to decide when to launch the campaign in their country, and what issues were most appropriate to highlight. The Finnish Section, for example, launched the campaign in April and concentrated on nearby countries, such as the Russian Federation and the Baltic states. The Nepalese Section held actions every day in the month leading up to a peace march for refugees on 19 April. In June the Irish Section

© AI

A photo exhibition on the human rights of refugees organized in Amsterdam by members of the Dutch Section.

held its launch in Dublin town hall, hosted by the Lord Mayor of Dublin, and in Ghana the launch was attended by diplomats and representatives of the UN High Commissioner for Refugees (UNHCR) and NGOs. Even in Sierra Leone, where a violent coup had taken place within days of the planned launch, the section participated in the campaign, holding a press conference to mark the beginning of their activities on 20 June, Africa Refugee Day.

The diversity of issues affecting different countries was reflected in the range of activities that were organized. Members of the US Section marched to the Immigration and Naturalization Service headquarters in New Orleans to protest against US policy towards asylum-seekers. The march took the form of a New Orleans-style jazz funeral, commemorating those who have died at the hands of the state all over the world. The Austrian Section sent all members of parliament a negative reply to an asylum claim in Amharic, asking them to write an appeal in this language or in any of the official UN languages within two days. A letter was attached explaining that new immigration laws in Austria expect refugees to cope with just such a situation. The section also organized theatre productions in which prominent people read excerpts of negative asylum replies and reports from refugees in Austria.

The Japanese Section staged a concert featuring Yadranka Stojakovic, a well-known singer from Sarajevo. The concert was opened by discussions on refugee issues. During the campaign, the section held eight public lectures on refugee concerns, which will be collated and produced in book form. As a final event, the section held "walkathons" in Tokyo and Osaka under the slogan, "Walk for 27 million refugees worldwide".

Many other initiatives promoted the message that human rights have no borders. In Benin, Amnesty International members organized a television program on refugees which was broadcast on Africa Refugee Day. Their press conference included representatives of the refugee community in Benin and several NGOs. The same day, a feature program devoted to the campaign was shown on television in Côte d'Ivoire after the Africa regional report on refugees was launched in the country. The launch was covered by most of the local press and several international news agencies. On 22 June, the Nigerian Section staged a refugee charity musical concert with many top Nigerian musicians. The wide publicity surrounding the concert dramatically raised the profile of refugee issues in the country.

In Germany, a demonstration on refugee issues outside Schöneberger town hall in Berlin was featured by several radio and television stations. The Italian Section held concerts in Turin and Rome on the theme of refugees, and ran "human rights buses" around Turin and Milan. In Iceland, Amnesty International members ran a stall at a concert in May in Reykjavik, during which they collected signatures, including from the main band, urging the Icelandic Government to review the country's laws on refugees. In Cyprus, Amnesty International members organized a photo exhibition and showed Amnesty International videos about refugees.

Many Amnesty International sections exposed the level of popular opposition to government attempts to turn asylum-seekers away. Petitions with words to the effect of "I think my government should protect refugees' rights" were signed by more than 50,000 people in both France and Nepal. Petitions also won much support in Cyprus, Finland and the United Kingdom (UK). Dutch members lobbied the European summit meeting held in Amsterdam. They produced mock Euros (the new European currency), with "human rights have no borders" written around

A helping hand

Seven Iraqis who arrived in Australia by boat in December 1996 were held at Port Headland detention centre, 4,000 kilometres from Sydney or Melbourne where most refugee assistance groups are based. Their asylum claims were rejected the following May. In desperation they turned to Amnesty International's Australian Section for guidance and support. The section assessed their cases and addressed the arguments put forward by the authorities for rejecting the asylum claims. An appeal was lodged with the Refugee Review Tribunal, using the counter-arguments provided by the section. A couple of weeks later the Tribunal granted refugee status to all seven. The Tribunal made special mention of the information provided by Amnesty International.

The campaign's aim of raising awareness about refugees' human rights prompted the movement to develop new ways of reaching a wide audience. For example, several sections collaborated with advertising agencies. The Slovene Section secured free space on all major television and radio stations for advertisements. A radio spot produced by Bates advertising agency proved extremely popular in Africa. It was played, for example, by a South Africa-based pan-African radio station following a live interview on refugee issues. In the Netherlands, a television advertisement showed a Polaroid picture of refugees slowly developing. The text read: "Developing this picture took more time than they had to pack their things." The advertisement shown above was used in New Zealand. The Amnesty International interactive website created by Bates for the campaign (http://www.refuge.amnesty.org) won four media awards and was visited by tens of thousands of people between its launch in March and the end of 1997.

the edges, as well as mock passports stamped with "congratulations, you've got through".

The campaign had a direct impact at the UN. In October refugee coordinators and lobbyists from 10 Amnesty International sections converged on Geneva to raise Amnesty International's concerns about the human rights of refugees with the UNHCR Executive Committee. As a result, the Committee members were subjected to unexpected and unprecedented lobbying and media scrutiny.

Amnesty International also held an exhibition at the UN building in Geneva. The stand displayed publicity and campaign materials as well as press clippings to highlight the methods that Amnesty International members were using to campaign on behalf of refugees.

In recognition of the fact that the vast majority of the world's refugees are women and children, sections organized many activities to coincide with International Women's Day on 8 March and International Children's Day on 20 November, as well as during *AI week* — an Amnesty International week of action held annually in October. The Bermuda Section, for example, launched the campaign on International Women's Day with a lunch program entitled "Voices of Women". The 300-strong audience was treated to dramatic readings portraying five cases of refugee women, and a performance by female singers. The event made the front page of the country's main newspaper, and was reported on the radio and television. On International Children's Day, Amnesty International members around the world promoted six appeal cases featuring children, which were entitled "Don't Play with my Future".

Kenya action

Many of the collective taxis (*matatus*) that fill the bustling streets of Nairobi appeared to have a new logo in late 1997. They were adorned with blue and white stickers proclaiming, "Stand up for Human Rights, Justice for All". The stickers were produced by Amnesty International's Tanzanian Section, one of many collaborative efforts by Amnesty International members in Africa and elsewhere that helped make the 1997 action on Kenya such a success.

The Priority Action raised the profile of human rights issues in Kenya at a time when the country's future was being hotly debated. In the three months leading up to the action's launch in Kenya on 10 September, national and international pressure had been mounting on the Kenyan Government to review repressive legislation. In the same period, large pro-democracy rallies around the country were violently broken up by police, resulting in 15 deaths and many more injuries. In September the government finally agreed with opposition politicians a package of minimal reforms. These included removing sections of the Penal Code relating to sedition, restricting the power of local authorities to arrest and detain people, and repealing provisions for detention without trial.

© AI

The 5CS theatre company in Nairobi performing the play, *Dying to be Free*.

However, the reforms did not go far enough and many Kenyans believed that the government had been motivated by political expediency rather than by a genuine commitment to human rights. Indeed, as the reforms were being implemented, human rights violations continued. Police attacked opposition meetings and political violence escalated. Amnesty International's action on Kenya was therefore timely.

One of the key tools was Amnesty International's *Human Rights Manifesto for Kenya*, which was released in June during a visit to the country by Amnesty International's Secretary General. The manifesto, which sets out a practical and achievable program for legal and constitutional reform, gained the support of the national NGO Council, which represents 760 NGOs in Kenya, as well as many other important figures and organizations in the country.

Amnesty International's report, *Kenya: violations of human rights*, and a briefing, *Kenya: the quest for justice*, were produced and widely circulated. These highlighted the main human rights concerns in the country, including torture and killings by the police, the vulnerability of certain groups such as children and refugees to abuse by state officials, and repression of opposition activists. Five appeal cases highlighted the dangers faced by many Kenyans. One featured Juma Kiplenge, a 28-year-old lawyer, who had suffered repeated harassment because he took up legal cases for members of his Endorois community. He told Amnesty International that copies of his appeal leaflet were distributed widely. "Members of the Endorois community were extremely happy that somebody far away in a distant land knows and cared for us," he said. He added that the government's response was to reduce considerably the duration of custody for those arrested.

Several events held in Kenya highlighted the need for human rights reform. A play, *Dying to be Free*, was performed by the 5Cs theatre company in Nairobi and several other towns in September, and toured the country later in the year. The play, which was funded by the Dutch Section, aimed to encourage debate on the social and political abuse of power.

Workshops were organized to involve local activists. A workshop on women's rights brought together more than 30 women's NGOs in Kenya. Among the issues discussed were the harassment facing women human rights defenders, and legal and constitutional discrimination against women. An information technology and human rights workshop, which involved 20 participants from key NGOs and media institutions, focused on the use of information technology in developing human rights advocacy and campaigning.

Amnesty International sections and structures around the world participated in the action on Kenya. East African Regional Action Network groups in Finland, for example, sent letters and postcards to Kenyan human rights NGOs and activists, the Kenyan Embassy in Stockholm, and the Kenyan authorities. They also arranged information stalls and photo exhibitions in Finland, and sent money to support human rights activists in Africa.

Among many activities organized elsewhere were several widely publicized launches for the action and speaking tours involving Kenyan human rights activists. The sections involved

© AI

Amnesty International members at the launch of the Kenya action in Tanzania.

included those in Australia, Belgium, Denmark, Germany, Ireland, Norway, Sweden, Tanzania, the UK and the USA. Some of the results were impressive. The Australian Senate, for example, passed a resolution calling for "the setting of specific goals to safeguard human rights in Kenya and the sending of election monitors to Kenya with a strong human rights briefing to monitor, document and report on the elections... as well as to provide protection to local human rights election monitors".

Economic relations and arms sales

Amnesty International continued to develop its campaigning work to persuade governments and companies to use their influence on the authorities of countries with which they had economic and military-security relations to promote and protect human rights. Although Amnesty International takes no general position on sanctions or boycotts, the organization opposed in specific instances the transfer of military and security equipment, as well as of training and personnel, that could reasonably be assumed to contribute to human rights abuses.

For example, after serious human rights violations against demonstrators were committed by the Indonesian security forces using small arms and armoured vehicles, Amnesty International continued its campaign against the transfer of such equipment to Indonesia. The US Government reaffirmed its ban on the transfer of armoured vehicles, small arms and riot control equipment to Indonesia, but new contracts for the supply of armoured vehicles, water cannon, sub-machine-guns and sophisticated internal surveillance equipment to Indonesia were approved by the UK Government, and negotiations were proceeding for the supply of light tanks from Germany and of armoured vehicles from France. Even after the UK Government was persuaded to suspend or not issue export licences for some security equipment transfers to Indonesia, it stated in July that, "firearms training systems, unless they are specialized equipment for military training or for simulating military scenarios, do not require an export licence". In other words, it was feared that countries may simply switch orders for new military or paramilitary supplies from the army to the police. Meanwhile, the Indonesian authorities refused to allow independent human rights monitors unrestricted access to East Timor and other areas where military, security and police equipment has been misused.

Such inconsistencies in arms export controls and monitoring were also exposed in relation to Turkey. The UK provided about 80 per cent of the components for armoured patrol vehicles assembled in Turkey. These vehicles were used by gendarmes to patrol villages and towns in the security zones, yet the UK authorities did not consider the components to be military or paramilitary exports. Serious abuses involving armoured vehicles and small arms continued to be reported in Turkey. However,

On 10 December Amnesty International launched in South Africa a year-long campaign to raise awareness of and mobilize support for the rights enshrined in the Universal Declaration of Human Rights (UDHR). As part of this campaign, which coincides with the 50th anniversary of the UDHR, the movement began collecting signatures from people all over the world pledging that they will do everything in their power to ensure that the rights enshrined in the UDHR are realized. Among the first signatories were Daw Aung San Suu Kyi, Nobel Peace Prize laureate and leader of the major opposition party in Myanmar; Mary Robinson, UN High Commissioner for Human Rights; Graça Machel, wife of former Mozambican President Samora Machel and former UN Expert to Study the Impact of Armed Conflict on Children; and Archbishop Desmond Tutu of South Africa. The picture above shows members of the South Africa football team, *Bafana Bafana*, signing their pledge. Many people from all walks of life had signed by the end of 1997. They included Ian Roberts, a gay Australian rugby player; the Mothers of the Plaza de Mayo, who seek justice and truth in relation to "disappearances" in Argentina; and many leading state officials in Nepal, including the Inspector General of Police. Millions of people are expected to sign what will become the world's largest book of signatures, which will be presented to the UN as an expression of the commitment of people from all cultures to the promotion and protection of fundamental human rights. Amnesty International also launched a website (http://www.amnesty.excite.com) featuring information about the UDHR campaign.

© AI

Armoured personnel carriers supplied by the United Kingdom on patrol in Indonesia, where serious human rights violations continued.

arrests and exclusions of independent human rights monitors made it almost impossible to verify such reports.

The problem of human rights abuses being fuelled by arms, security equipment and mercenary inflows was stressed by Amnesty International's Secretary General when he addressed the UN Security Council in October 1997. He pointed out that analysing arms flows to areas of armed conflict can help determine responsibility for human rights violations and, if action is taken, abuses can be prevented. In view of the atrocities committed in the Democratic Republic of the Congo during 1997, the Secretary General urged the Security Council to follow up investigations into arms trafficking to the former Rwandese armed forces and militia. He recommended continued monitoring of transfers, particularly of light weapons, to the whole of Central Africa in order to encourage observance of international human rights standards and humanitarian law. Similar efforts, he said, could be made in relation to Afghanistan and other areas where armed conflict had fuelled human rights crises.

In May 1997 Amnesty International and other Nobel Peace Prize laureates launched an International Code of Conduct on Arms Transfers, which set out human rights and other international principles for the control of international arms transfers. Amnesty International sections and other NGOs subsequently promoted the Code around the world. The Code calls on every state to establish effective control of arms transfers based on:

- respect for a range of fundamental human rights based on international standards;
- respect for humanitarian law, especially Common Article 3 of

the Geneva Conventions;
- support for transparency and independent monitoring of arms transfers;
- the inclusion of light weapons, paramilitary equipment, technology and training;
- the inclusion of financial and logistical support for the transfer of such items;
- a commitment to support and expand the UN Register of Conventional Arms;
- an expanded role for the UN and other relevant intergovernmental organizations.

Fifteen former and current Latin American heads of state and two former US Presidents endorsed the Code. In June the US House of Representatives agreed a version of the Code which, if enacted, would mean that US military assistance and arms transfers would be provided only to states certified by the US President as democratic, protective of human rights and not involved in acts of armed aggression. However, countries that do not meet those criteria could still buy US weapons if the US President determines that there are national security reasons for allowing them to do so.

By late 1997 more than 600 NGOs had endorsed a European Union (EU) version of the Code. EU governments and many members of European parliaments expressed support for establishing harmonized arms control mechanisms based on eight criteria governing arms exports agreed by the Council of Ministers between 1991 and 1992. The criteria include "the respect of human rights in the country of final destination" and "respect for international law". Amnesty International sections in Europe joined coalitions of NGOs to press for a new EU arms control agreement based on this EU Code. The new UK Government offered to promote the EU Code and to seek a complete prohibition on the trade in equipment used for torture or other cruel, inhuman or degrading treatment. However, there was a danger that new proposals to implement the criteria would not be binding or comprehensive enough to stop unscrupulous arms dealers exploiting loopholes.

Torture using electro-shock stun weapons continued to be exposed by Amnesty International following the release in 1997 of its report, *Arming the torturers*, which contained the first worldwide survey of the problem. Appeals were made to the governments of the main countries exporting stun weapons — China, France, Germany, Israel, South Africa, Taiwan and the USA.

The use of other modern security technologies for human rights abuses — such as pepper spray in the USA and plastic bullets in Israel and the Occupied Territories, and the UK — was questioned by Amnesty International. Where police used tear-gas in confined spaces, such as in Kenya, Amnesty International called for a suspension of the supply of the gas until the authorities established safeguards against its misuse.

Amnesty International continued to develop its campaigning work to convince multinational companies and international financial institutions to use their influence to promote respect for human rights. At the World Bank and International Monetary Fund meetings in Hong Kong in September, Amnesty International urged these institutions to assess the human rights impact of their investments, to evaluate and monitor projects, to support policies and projects that foster the development of civil society, good governance and the rule of law, and to investigate thoroughly all human rights abuses alleged in connection with projects. Amnesty International highlighted the human rights abuses committed in the context of community protests against World Bank-sponsored projects in India. Vulnerable communities were subjected to excessive force and evictions from their homes by police while the companies and international financial institutions apparently took no action to help stem the abuses.

Many Amnesty International sections continued to develop approaches to multinational companies, encouraging a dialogue on promoting respect for human rights within the business community. Amnesty International was due to launch in early 1998 a set of human rights principles for companies based on the UDHR, core conventions of the International Labour Organisation and other key human rights standards.

Urgent Actions

"Words are too poor to express the gratitude and thanks of my mother for the return of her son, my wife for the return of her husband, and of my children for the return of their father... You were the only organization outside and inside the country (as far as I know) which raised its voice for the rights of citizens unjustly denied by the government in power."

This letter, received by Amnesty International in early 1997, was written by Timoshenko Pekmezi, who was sentenced in September 1996 to two years' imprisonment in Albania for conspiring to create a new Albanian communist party. The letter summed up some of the aims of Urgent Actions. In response to his case, Amnesty International had asked its members around the world to send letters and faxes to the Albanian authorities raising concerns about the fairness of his trial and fears that he was a prisoner of conscience. On 29 December 1996 Timoshenko Pekmezi was released by presidential decree, having served only three months of his sentence.

Urgent Actions are initiated whenever speedy action is required to protect anyone, anywhere in the world, from abuse of the human rights covered in Amnesty International's mandate. During 1997, 583 such actions were launched. In many cases, positive outcomes were achieved. For example, a blind Turkish lawyer, Eşber Yağmurdereli, who was arrested on 20 October, was facing 23 years in prison for a speech he had made in 1991.

"The fact that we are alive and safe is because of you." Reina Xiomara Zelaya wrote these words to Amnesty International after she and her three daughters (one of them, Johanna, is pictured below) were granted asylum in Sweden in February 1997. The family had fled to Costa Rica in early 1996 after receiving death threats in their native Honduras. In Costa Rica, the family reported continuing threats from the Honduran security forces. The Urgent Action network issued a number of appeals, asking the Honduran authorities to identify those responsible for threats against the family. The Costa Rican Government was asked to take steps to ensure the physical safety of Reina Xiomara Zelaya and her children.

Letters and faxes flooded the Turkish authorities in the following days, and on 10 November he was released. He wrote soon after: "Now I am out of prison but the restrictions on freedom of expression continue... Please send my thanks to your Urgent Action Network whose support I was aware of from first to last."

The sense of urgency is particularly keen when a prisoner is under the threat of torture or is facing execution. Several Urgent Actions were initiated during the year on behalf of prisoners in Israel, where the state officially sanctions torture during interrogation. The state's position makes Amnesty International's work against torture more difficult, but the feedback from lawyers and former detainees highlighted the importance of the efforts by the Urgent Action network. One letter received during the year from a Palestinian family said: "We would like to thank you and all your members through the whole world very much for all your help and support we got through the letters and faxes concerning our detained son Muhannad Abu Rumi... He received psychological courage and power when he knew that there were people out in the world who really care about prisoners and human rights..."

Another letter arrived from the mother of Sergey Vysochansky, who had faced imminent execution in Ukraine. She had been sure her son would die as the authorities were rushing through his case. After three rounds of Urgent Action appeals on Sergey Vysochansky's behalf, his sentence was commuted to 20 years in prison. His mother wrote: "Thank you for saving my son's life."

Karenni children from Myanmar in a refugee camp on the border between Thailand and Myanmar. In early 1997, following the forcible return of Karen refugees over the border, the Urgent Action network appealed to the Thai authorities not to force any more refugees back to Myanmar. The forcible returns subsided after the appeals. The Urgent Action network is increasingly engaging in such cases.

The wide range of human rights issues to which Urgent Actions respond has been highlighted by events in Mexico. After a peaceful demonstration in April 1996 by members of the Tepoztlán community in the state of Morelos against a golf-course development on land they consider sacred, Marcos Olmedo Gutiérrez was extrajudicially executed by the security forces and 34 community members were arrested. An Urgent Action was launched, and the 34 were released. They asked for their thanks to be passed on to those who had sent appeals. The Urgent Action network was reactivated in January 1997 when four community activists were arrested and held as prisoners of conscience. Appeals were rushed in: one of the activists was released within a few days, the other three were freed several months later. However, a teacher who had been arrested earlier, Gerardo Demesa Padillo, was sentenced in September to eight years' imprisonment. He remains a prisoner of conscience.

Brazilian land reform activist Diolinda Alves de Souza was released after an Urgent Action was issued objecting to her arbitrary arrest. She told Amnesty International in August that on the day of her release the prison authorities had given her a mass of letters. "I was curious to know who had written to me from abroad, and it was then that we saw that they were from Amnesty International."

Action Files

Wei Jingsheng, a long-term prisoner of conscience in China, was unexpectedly let out of prison in November 1997, the latest chapter in one of Amnesty International's oldest Action Files. He is 47 years old and has spent more than half his adult life behind bars.

Amnesty International groups in Japan, Sweden and the USA had been working for his release since 1979, when he was sentenced to 14 years' imprisonment for "counter-revolutionary" crimes. They raised his case with their governments and introduced his sister, Wei Shanshan, to officials, the media and NGOs in their countries.

Wei Jingsheng was released on parole in 1993 after serving his first sentence, but was arrested once again in April 1994 and held for nearly 20 months without charge. In December 1995 he was sentenced to a further 14 years' imprisonment for "engaging in activities in an attempt to overthrow the government". He has never used or advocated violence. His release, almost exactly 12 years before it was due, was the best possible reward for all the work done on his behalf by Amnesty International members and others. Soon after he was freed he explained to Amnesty International how he had learned about the support he was receiving and the effect it had: "A guard who never usually spoke to me struck up a conversation. We chatted casually for a bit and then I asked him very nonchalantly, 'I guess fewer letters have been coming for me lately, right?' The guard then looked at me and exclaimed incredulously, 'Fewer? Old Wei, you get **so** many letters!' When he finished saying this he realized what he had told me and suddenly stopped speaking and hurried out of the room... The mental inspiration this gave me greatly surpassed any small improvement in my living conditions."

Action Files are long-term human rights campaigning assignments given to local Amnesty International groups. A single group or a few groups in different countries work for the release of a prisoner of conscience, or for a victim of torture, or on any other concern within Amnesty International's mandate. Groups are encouraged to explore as many ways as they can to publicize the case they are working on and to put pressure on the authorities. They stage public events, such as exhibitions or a vigil; publish articles; work with other interested bodies, such as religious organizations and trade unions; or organize petitions and mass letter-writing or postcard campaigns.

The success of Action File activities cannot always be measured in terms of a release. Giving moral support is important too. In 1997, for example, a Nigerian prisoner of conscience was suddenly allowed to receive letters two years after being jailed. The first mail-bag contained a backlog of 9,000 cards and letters from members of Amnesty International and other organizations. The impact was enormous, especially as the

Wei Jingsheng at a press conference at Amnesty International's International Secretariat in London shortly after his release.

© AI

prisoner had been held in virtual isolation from the outside world and is forbidden from writing letters. A relative who can only manage to visit the distant prison occasionally is allowed short and closely supervised visits. In May 1997 the prisoner wrote to an Amnesty International member: "The warmth and care reflected in the large number of cards from [one particular country] has been overwhelming. I am deeply touched and very much encouraged by the realization that somewhere out there, someone cares. Now I can see the sun once again. I can hear the birds sing. The world is still a beautiful place! My profound gratitude to you members of Amnesty. What would the world be like without your caring and dedicated work?"

Action Files may last for many years, often until the case is resolved. There are currently more than 1,500 active Action Files naming over 4,000 victims of human rights violations. Sometimes, a file remains active for a period after a prisoner has been released to ensure that the prisoner remains safe. Such was the case for Adel Selmi, a Tunisian prisoner of conscience. He had been arrested in Tunisia during a holiday from his studies in France and was subsequently sentenced in 1994 to four years and two months' imprisonment for membership of an unauthorized political party. He denied any involvement with political groups. His Action File was taken on by groups in France and Norway. As a result of their activities, the university authorities in France sent Adel Selmi a letter in prison, and in December 1996 he was released early. The groups contacted him and carried on working on his case in 1997 as "aftercare". There was much celebration in September when Adel Selmi flew to Paris to resume his studies, where he was met at the airport by members of the French group.

Crisis response

The crisis in the African Great Lakes region persisted in 1997 and Amnesty International continued to use its crisis response mechanism to respond. The first challenge of the year came in January, when it appeared that the Tanzanian authorities were on the brink of forcibly returning thousands of refugees to Burundi. Amnesty International feared this would result in widespread killing of returnees by Burundi security forces. Amnesty International sections worldwide reacted immediately and protested to the Tanzanian authorities and other governments. UNHCR, which had been criticized by Amnesty International and others for its role in the expulsion of Rwandese refugees a month earlier, also opposed the expulsion of the Burundians.

As a result of members' activities, several governments expressed their concern. Amnesty International delegates, including former Canadian Foreign Affairs Minister Flora MacDonald, travelled to Tanzania. They met President Benjamin Mkapa, government officials and several foreign ambassadors. Amnesty International attracted front-page coverage in Tanzania and won assurances from the President that no more refugees from Burundi would be expelled under any circumstances. One Tanzanian newspaper printed in full Amnesty International's report, *Burundi: Leaders are changing, but human rights abuses continue unabated*.

Amnesty International also issued a report, *Great Lakes Region: Still in need of protection — repatriation,* refoulement *and the safety of refugees and the internally displaced*. This reinforced concerns increasingly voiced by development and

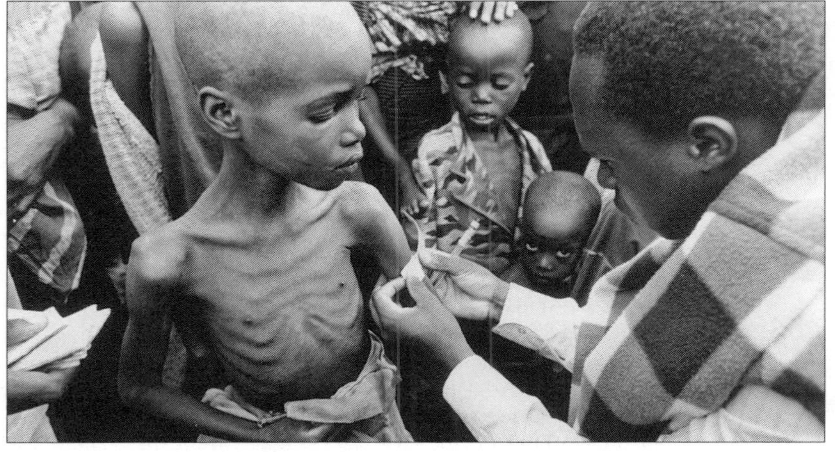

© UNHCR/R. Chalasahi

Rwandese refugees in Kasese camp, near Kisangani, Democratic Republic of the Congo (former Zaire)

humanitarian agencies in the region. The report repeated Amnesty International's criticisms of UNHCR and the international community. It appealed to governments hosting refugees from the Great Lakes region, the UNHCR and the international community to prevent further erosion of basic refugee protection principles in the region. Amnesty International sections, particularly in member states of the UNHCR Executive Committee, lobbied their own governments, reminding them of their responsibilities, such as providing more financial support for host states in the region. They also asked governments to refrain from promoting voluntary repatriation to Rwanda.

Other campaigning by Amnesty International focused on the unfair nature of trials starting in Rwanda against those accused of participation in the 1994 genocide, and on a new wave of human rights abuses in Rwanda following the return of hundreds of thousands of refugees. Amnesty International continued calling for UN action to investigate reports of atrocities in former Zaire by Zairian government forces, by the *Alliance des forces démocratiques pour la libération du Congo* (AFDL), Alliance of Democratic Forces for the Liberation of Congo, and by members of the former Rwandese government forces and militia. During 1997 the UN tried to undertake several such investigations, but the AFDL hampered these efforts by violent intimidation, delays and restricting access to areas where atrocities had allegedly taken place.

Amnesty International also responded to growing human rights crises in other parts of the world. As the coalition government in Cambodia became increasingly unstable during the first half of the year, Amnesty International sections were alerted to the potential crisis. As a result, they were able to react immediately following the violent removal from power of Cambodia's First Prime Minister in July. Sections lobbied their own governments and the Cambodian authorities, working on Urgent Actions and other documents produced by the International Secretariat. Amnesty International delegations visited Thailand to interview refugees from Cambodia, and Malaysia to discuss the human rights crisis in Cambodia with representatives of many governments attending the Association of South East Asian Nations (ASEAN) Regional Forum. A high-level Amnesty International delegation went to Cambodia at the end of August, at the invitation of the government, to discuss the issues of extrajudicial executions and torture of political prisoners that Amnesty International had documented since 5 July. The delegation was disappointed at the lack of cooperation from the government. A research visit to Cambodia at the end of the year revealed further information about extrajudicial executions. The delegate discussed the country's human rights problems with the Head of State, King Norodom Sihanouk.

In October, in response to the deteriorating human rights situation in Algeria and to the escalation of massacres of civilians and other human rights abuses, Amnesty International and three other international NGOs issued a joint international public appeal calling for action to be taken by the international community to address the plight of the Algerian civilian population. The joint appeal called for an international investigation to be carried out to ascertain the facts, examine allegations of responsibility in respect of the massacres and other abuses, and make recommendations for a long-term human rights plan to end the human rights crisis in Algeria. The UN Children's Fund (UNICEF) and several NGOs added their voices to the call for an international investigation and similar appeals were produced by a number of Amnesty International sections. In November Amnesty International launched a report on Algeria at the UN in New York, USA, where Amnesty International's call for an international investigation into the killings was presented to the media and government representatives. A short version of the report was issued to make the terrible facts known to as wide an audience as possible. Amnesty International sections in various countries organized or participated in actions, public meetings and demonstrations to express solidarity with the victims of the human rights crisis in Algeria.

On 9 October 1997 Amnesty International's Secretary General Pierre Sané led a delegation that visited death row in Texas, USA, to view prison conditions of the state's 440 condemned inmates. The delegation met three death-row prisoners, including Kenneth Ransom who was executed 19 days later. At a press conference shortly after the prison visit, Pierre Sané said: "We have witnessed how a deliberate policy aimed at dehumanizing prisoners is implemented coldly, professionally and heartlessly. The condemned await their deaths in rows of tiny cages reminiscent of the Dark Ages, their spirits are slowly broken. The conveyor-belt of death in Texas must be stopped." Thirty-seven prisoners were executed in Texas in 1997.

Mobilizing lawyers and health professionals

Lawyers and doctors have special skills to contribute to the defence of human rights and are active in human rights organizations around the world. Lawyers played a key role in creating Amnesty International and they have been among the founding members of sections in several countries. For many years Amnesty International has sought to involve legal and health professionals in its campaigning in order to bring their particular skills, expertise and influence to bear in relation to the protection of legal rights, the protection of the health and well-being of detainees and prisoners, and the documentation of abuses.

In January the health professionals' network continued a theme started in 1996 — the role of health professionals in the exposure of human rights violations. A report entitled *Kenya: Detention, torture and health professionals* discussed the use of torture in Kenya and the problems faced by doctors and other health professionals in exposing torture and defending the rights of prisoners. The report was widely distributed to doctors in Kenya by the Amnesty International network. In June a report,

Thirty delegates from Amnesty International sections and structures in all world regions, along with staff from the International Secretariat, gathered in London in April to discuss the movement's outreach work. Amnesty International's campaigning has at its core reaching out to engage key individuals, organizations or sectors of society in support of human rights and Amnesty International's concerns. It is an important means of strengthening Amnesty International's effectiveness and is undertaken by all levels and structures of the organization. Amnesty International's work with women's groups and organizations has developed greatly in recent years, as has outreach to the business sector. Campaigning on children's human rights has also been strengthened by the development of a specialized network within Amnesty International. Among other specialized networks are those that work on human rights issues of concern to lawyers, medical professionals and lesbians and gays.

Nurses and human rights, was published at the time of the International Congress of Nurses in Vancouver, Canada, to draw attention to the important role nurses can play in defending the human rights of patients and of the community. Throughout the year, the network took up numerous cases of detained health professionals, imprisoned women, victims of torture and human rights activists. It also acted in response to reports that Guatemala was preparing to use lethal injection to execute prisoners for the first time since replacing shooting as the execution method in 1996.

In 1997 lawyers campaigning within Amnesty International continued to draw on their own networks and associations to amplify the human rights message. Amnesty International lawyers' groups played a key role in all major theme campaigns during 1997, including Amnesty International's continuing campaign for a just, fair and effective international criminal court. They also contributed to numerous other Amnesty International campaigns, including support of the Draft Optional Protocol to the Convention against Torture and Other Cruel, Inhuman or Degrading Treatment or Punishment, and to appeals on individual cases in a number of countries.

Increasing the size of the legal network and in particular encouraging the establishment and development of lawyers' groups in under-represented regions have been high priorities. Amnesty International's global legal network at the end of 1997 had grown from 41 groups in 1995 to comprise lawyers' groups in 50 Amnesty International sections or structures in all five world regions. In October the international legal network held its fifth meeting of delegates from around the world.

Human rights education

"Education shall be directed to the full development of the human personality and to the strengthening of respect for human rights and fundamental freedoms."

Article 26, Universal Declaration of Human Rights

Amnesty International remains committed to developing awareness and understanding of international human rights standards as well as to promoting knowledge of the relevant national, regional and international mechanisms for protecting human rights. The ultimate goal is to encourage citizens and government leaders, groups and institutions, to adopt beliefs, behaviours and policies that will safeguard all human rights everywhere in the world. In line with this, during 1997 the organization's members around the world continued to press governments to integrate human rights concepts and information in all educational curricula. They also continued to design and implement innovative educational programs, often in collaboration with other NGOs and local or national educational authorities.

The forthcoming 50th anniversary of the UDHR offered educators within the Amnesty International movement an ideal opportunity to work closely with other NGOs and educational groups. In the USA, a new consortium, Human Rights USA, was formed. This brought together the Educators' network of the US Section; the Center for Human Rights Education of Atlanta, Georgia; the University of Minnesota Human Rights Center; and Street Law, Inc. of Washington DC. Funded by the Ford Foundation, Human Rights USA has three major components: national outreach in collaboration with other organizations working for social justice, intensive community and school-based education in four metropolitan sites, and a high-profile media campaign. The US Section also produced and distributed worldwide a human rights education manual for adults and children in preparation for the UDHR's 50th anniversary.

The Mauritius Section published their first resource book for human rights education, *Selected topics on human rights*. It will be used as a pedagogical support for their project, which involves 15 secondary schools. The project coordinator commented: "We are more than ever convinced that a human rights culture is essential in any democratic society and the more so in a multicultural country like ours... We hope that the human rights classes we are offering to sixth formers are but the start of a campaign to integrate this new subject into our formal curriculum."

© AI

Students from Bagabaga Teaching Training College in Tamale, northern Ghana, who participated in a human rights training program organized in the country by Amnesty International.

Working with the broader human rights movement

During the year Amnesty International entered many joint initiatives with other non-governmental organizations (NGOs). In one example, Amnesty International members from Botswana, Mauritius, South Africa and Zimbabwe participated in the Southern Africa Human Rights NGO Network (SAHRINGON) conference in Johannesburg, which was attended by about 80 representatives of NGOs from all southern African countries except Angola. The network agreed to lobby the South African Development Community (SADC) on human rights issues in the region.

In Taiwan, Amnesty International members worked closely with legislators who sponsored a motion on human rights education. The motion was passed by the Education Committee of the Legislative *Yuan* (parliament) towards the end of the year. It called for the promotion of human rights in schools, from primary level to high school, and for the UDHR to be included in the curriculum at all levels. The Taiwanese Section distributed many copies of a videotape about the UDHR, subtitled in Chinese, to legislators.

In August a regional meeting held in Querétaro, Mexico, agreed to develop a common, regional strategy for Amnesty International sections in Latin America to raise funds for human rights education. The meeting discussed the need for increased technical assistance and decided to disseminate information about their experiences in order to increase the impact of fundraising efforts.

Throughout 1997 work continued on Amnesty International's human rights education manual *First Steps*, which was produced for use in Eastern and Central Europe. Adaptations and translations into Albanian, Croatian, Polish, Russian, Slovak and Ukrainian were completed. Plans were made to translate the manual into Czech and Romanian.

In October Palestinian members of Amnesty International organized a workshop to draw up a national strategy for human rights education. The workshop aimed to support the integration of human rights concepts into Palestinian educational curricula and to encourage teachers, educators and advocates of human rights to be concerned about human rights education and to reinforce their commitment in this area. The Amnesty International Human Rights Education Campaign in Palestine was first established in 1994. The project is implemented in close cooperation with local institutions, both governmental and non-governmental.

The Hong Kong Section continued to make remarkable progress in its human rights education work. It has established an ongoing dialogue with the Department of Education on the question of civic education, which it hopes will broaden coverage of human rights issues within the curriculum. Inroads have been made within the community, especially with young people who are showing a growing interest in human rights.

In September a European regional conference of the UN Educational, Scientific and Cultural Organization (UNESCO) was held in Finland in the context of the UN Decade for Human Rights Education (1995 to 2004). Amnesty International was invited to give a presentation about its human rights education work. Participants at the conference concluded that work needs to be done to make human rights universally known, and to make sure that the underlying values of these rights and the means of protecting them are widely understood.

Human rights: an integrated approach

A role for human rights: development, peace and security, humanitarian action

The last decade has seen a remarkable recognition that the protection of human rights is a cornerstone of economic growth and development, political stability, maintaining peace and security, and humanitarian action. The end of the Cold War and of the great ideological divide that split the world for nearly 50 years, has created the potential for human rights to play a central role in world affairs. At the same time, we have seen some political challenges to the universality of human rights and attacks on the standards and mechanisms gradually built up over five decades to protect human rights. We have witnessed acts of "genocide", "crimes against humanity" and "war crimes" in places as diverse as Bosnia-Herzegovina, the Democratic Republic of the Congo (the former Zaire), Iraq and Rwanda. Never has there been such consciousness of the importance of human rights, nor such opportunities for human rights to be integrated into the overall approach of intergovernmental organizations.

The various UN world conferences in recent years have reaffirmed this trend. At the Vienna World Conference on Human Rights in 1993, 171 states said that "democracy, development and respect for human rights and fundamental freedoms are interdependent and mutually reinforcing". In Copenhagen at the UN World Conference on Social Development in 1995, states declared that "social development and social justice cannot be attained in the absence of peace and security or in the absence of respect for all human rights".

Human rights work in the conference rooms and corridors of the UN in Geneva is gradually being complemented by a human rights program of action in the field, at the UN headquarters in New York and in political and economic debates around the world.

UN agencies that have not traditionally seen the protection of human rights as part of their role are increasingly acknowledging and acting on these links. A notable example is the UN Children's Fund (UNICEF), which in 1996 changed its mission statement expressly to include the protection of children's rights, guided by the UN Convention on the Rights of the Child. This development has been reflected in some of UNICEF's programs in the field and

© UNICEF/94-1385/Little

Philippine children demonstrate their familiarity with the rights enshrined in the UN Convention on the Rights of the Child. UNICEF is increasingly being guided by human rights in its day-to-day development work.

in its advocacy work. During the year UNICEF released important statements about the abduction of children and their use as soldiers by the Lord's Resistance Army in Uganda, supporting an international investigation into massacres in Algeria, and calling for an end to female genital mutilation.

The UN Development Programme (UNDP) produced a policy paper in 1997 on human rights and sustainable development which commits the organization to promoting good governance and respect for human rights. During the year Amnesty International began discussions with both UNICEF and the UNDP about the role of human rights in their work. At the UN headquarters, the Departments of Political Affairs and Peace-keeping have already been responsible for deploying human rights officers in Angola, Bosnia-Herzegovina, Cambodia, El Salvador, Guatemala, Haiti and Liberia as part of post-conflict reconstruction and peace-building efforts.

The UN human rights program now has more staff working in the field than in its offices in New York and Geneva. The field work of those involved in human rights, development, politics, humanitarian action and refugee affairs has become increasingly interlinked and while much more is needed to improve the quality of coordination between them, joint strategies are being developed to coordinate their efforts and support each others' work.

This chapter looks at some of the milestones in the further integration of human rights into the UN during the year, such as the launch of a UN reform program, initiatives by the new UN High Commissioner for Human Rights and, in a first for the human rights movement, the address by Amnesty International's Secretary General to members of the UN Security Council. It also explores some of the set-backs and the continuing gap between rhetoric and reality.

UN reform package: integrating human rights

In July 1997 the UN Secretary-General, Kofi Annan, launched a package of UN reforms. It is a bold initiative which seeks to improve the coordination of the UN system; to clarify the functions of various agencies, funds and departments; and to create a new management structure. It foreshadows the shedding of 1,000 jobs, with savings going into a "dividend for development", and a loosening of bureaucratic procedures. The UN Secretary-General's report identifies five core areas of work for the UN: peace and security, development, economic and social affairs, humanitarian affairs and human rights. Human rights are identified as a "cross-cutting" activity, integral to all other areas. Despite some voices of dissent to the integration of human rights into all the activities of the UN, the reform package was endorsed by the UN General Assembly in December.

> **'During the cold war, peace and security tended to be defined simply in terms of military might or the balance of terror. Today... we know that lasting peace requires a broader vision, encompassing education and literacy, health and nutrition, human rights and fundamental freedoms.'**
>
> Kofi Annan, UN Secretary-General, October 1997

Integration is a key theme running through the reform program. UN field presences in a country will come together in a single building — UN House — under the unified leadership of a Resident Coordinator. The work of the UN Secretariat has been reorganized around the five core areas of work. The work on peace and security, development, economic and social affairs and humanitarian affairs is headed by a high-level Executive Committee for each area, which brings together the agencies dealing with these issues. Amnesty International welcomed the designation of human rights as an issue cutting across all other areas. Most importantly, the UN High Commissioner for Human Rights is able to participate in each of the four Executive Committees. This integration is intended to allow the role of human rights in supporting work in all core areas to be analysed and reflected in practical, cross-departmental projects. The UN High Commissioner's representation in New York has been strengthened with higher level staff, to ensure a more effective presence.

The UN reforms, the appointment of a new UN High Commissioner for Human Rights (see below), a UN Secretary-General who has strongly articulated the moral and human rights foundations of the UN's mission, the 50th anniversary of the Universal Declaration of Human Rights, and the 1998 review of implementation of the Vienna Declaration and Programme of Action have combined to provide unique opportunities for human rights activists.

Achieving proper integration, however, will be a long and slow process. Its success will depend on several factors. Human rights experts in the intergovernmental, governmental and non-governmental spheres must be willing to reach out and understand the language of development and humanitarian agencies and the constraints within which they work. At the same time, human rights protection must be based on the universal standards set out in the Universal Declaration of Human Rights and the treaties and non-treaty standards that have flowed from it. The perceived political constraints of other agencies must not lead to the watering down of human rights principles. The human rights movement will need to develop further its analysis of how human rights interrelate with political, security and economic agendas. It will need to show how keeping the peace requires the creation of institutions to strengthen human rights and civil society; how sustainable development is based on respect for all human rights; and how humanitarian action must ensure respect for human rights. Much more effort is needed in actively promoting ways of implementing and enforcing social and economic rights.

If the rhetoric of integration is to be translated into a reality, all departments, funds and programs of the UN need to look at how their own work could enhance human rights promotion and protection. Responsibility for this cannot be left entirely to the UN High Commissioner for Human Rights. The High Commissioner's resources are stretched too thinly to address properly

UN Secretary-General Kofi Annan launches the first stage of the UN reform program. A key theme of reform is the integration of human rights into all the UN's work.

© UN/DPI Photo by Evan Schneider

the human rights needs of post-conflict countries or development work. The UN Secretary-General will need to monitor progress closely to ensure that the culture of isolation is broken down and that human rights inform all areas of work.

UN High Commissioner for Human Rights: a catalyst for change

In March the first UN High Commissioner for Human Rights, José Ayala Lasso, resigned unexpectedly. He was replaced in September by Mary Robinson, former President of Ireland. In April, soon after the search for José Ayala Lasso's successor began, Amnesty International published a report, *Agenda for a new United Nations High Commissioner for Human Rights.* It highlighted the pivotal role of this post in championing all rights and bringing human rights into the mainstream of UN activity:

"Human rights issues have been ignored, downplayed, forgotten, silenced and overruled in the interests of so-called 'realpolitik'. Even within the human rights debate some rights have been marginalized within the small space allowed to human rights at the UN. The rights of women and indigenous peoples have never been properly supported; economic, social and cultural rights have been trumpeted with rhetorical rectitude by governments — but never properly tackled by the UN program... The new High Commissioner now has the chance to take the human rights standards and principles... and use them as an integral part of the UN's work on development, democratization, and the maintenance of peace and security."

The new UN High Commissioner started her term articulating clearly her role as a "catalyst... stimulating and coordinating" the integration of human rights into "the web of agencies tackling economic development, population activities, health, women and children, education, refugees and displaced persons" as well as those working on peace and security. She stated strongly her commitment to universality, putting greater emphasis on economic, social and cultural rights and women's rights, and her willingness to speak out publicly against abuses.

> **'I... intend to be a strong moral voice for the defence of the victims of oppression, discrimination, and exclusion — wherever they may be or whatever the violation.'**
>
> Mary Robinson, UN High Commissioner for Human Rights, at the UN General Assembly, November 1997

Mary Robinson started putting integration into practice by speaking at the Executive Committee of the UN High Commissioner for Refugees where she argued for more systematic and formal cooperation between the two offices at headquarters and in the field. She took steps to build on José Ayala Lasso's initiative in developing closer relations with the World Bank and development and humanitarian agencies.

© AI

The new UN High Commissioner for Human Rights, Mary Robinson, pledges to do everything within her power to uphold the principles of the Universal Declaration of Human Rights (UDHR) at Amnesty International's campaign launch in South Africa, December 1997. Early in her term of office, she emphasized the principles of universality and indivisibility: that all the rights enshrined in the UDHR should be enjoyed by everyone, everywhere.

The UN reform package merged the UN Centre for Human Rights and the UN High Commissioner into a new Office of the UN High Commissioner for Human Rights. It also asked the UN High Commissioner to look at how the human rights machinery — its political and expert bodies and mechanisms — could be made more effective. Amnesty International hopes that in developing these ideas the UN High Commissioner will give non-governmental organizations (NGOs) the opportunity to contribute their long years of expertise and practical experience.

Amnesty International encouraged the High Commissioner to be ready to confront governments when necessary. A tough stance is needed if governments refuse to cooperate with the UN human rights machinery; if constructive dialogue fails to lead to commitments and change; or if the situation in a country is rapidly deteriorating. In September the High Commissioner did help to break the silence about continuing massacres in Algeria when she said that such grave violations could not be considered an internal affair and that human rights know no borders. During a visit to Rwanda in December, she recognized the scale of the problems facing the government since the genocide of 1994, but nevertheless spoke bluntly about the government's responsibility for extrajudicial executions, prolonged arbitrary detention and inhumane conditions of detention.

Amnesty International also urged the new UN High Commissioner to ensure that human rights field operations were given the necessary financial support and guidance, and that their effectiveness was reviewed. The operations in Burundi and Rwanda had severely limited access to large parts of these countries, while the office in Colombia struggled with continuing

systematic violations of human rights (see **Colombia** entry). The Rwanda operation suffered a major set-back when five of its staff were extrajudicially executed in the southwest of the country in February. As part of a review of all UN human rights field operations, the High Commissioner announced in December that the Rwanda operation would be restructured, given a new leadership and more specialist expertise, and that she would examine how better to integrate human rights concerns into the full range of UN activities in Rwanda.

The role of human rights in building peace and security
Amnesty International's Secretary General, Pierre Sané, addressed members of the UN Security Council in September on human rights in armed conflict. It was the first time that a human rights organization had addressed members of the UN Security Council and it is hoped that this breakthrough will lead to presentations by other relevant organizations. "There is a tendency to see human rights work as somehow an obstacle to conducive political progress" in peace-making and peace-keeping, Pierre Sané told the ambassadors. He went on:
"... in fact human rights work can be part of the tool box needed to tackle emerging conflict and help the Security Council know what action might be taken to avert conflict. If the Security Council wants to grasp the causes of and solutions to armed conflict it should continue to pay greater attention to the human rights violations which lead to armed conflict, which fuel armed conflict, which can be a weapon of war within armed conflict, and which, if not addressed, will lead to further conflict and further threats to international peace and security."

Examination of human rights reports should be part of the process of preventive action and diplomacy. During an armed conflict, accurate and timely human rights investigations can dispel propaganda and rumours which only fan the flames of conflict. By understanding some of the causes of a war and the underlying grievances that fuel instability, the UN can go beyond *ad hoc* strategies that rely solely on emergency assistance projects and cannot resolve deep-rooted conflicts.

In March Amnesty International called on the UN Security Council to establish a Commission of Inquiry into the allegations of massacres of civilians in the conflict in eastern Zaire (now the Democratic Republic of the Congo). An investigation was initiated under the authority of the UN Commission on Human Rights. However, the *Alliance des forces démocratiques pour la libération du Congo-Zaire* (AFDL), Alliance of Democratic Forces for the Liberation of Congo-Zaire, which controlled the area, refused the mission access, claiming that one of the main investigators, Roberto Garreton, the UN Special Rapporteur on Zaire, was biased against the AFDL. The fate of the mission was sealed when the international community failed to give it strong political support. After further delays, the UN Secretary-General appointed his own investigative team in August, with the support of the Security Council. Despite several apparent agreements, it also faced hostility and obstruction from the new authorities in the Democratic Republic of the Congo and by the end of the year had made little progress (see **Democratic Republic of the Congo** entry).

Perhaps the most complex and difficult phase is peace-building after a conflict has formally ended. Raising human rights should not be seen as confrontational, an exercise that ought to be confined to the conference rooms of Geneva. On the contrary, the UN Security Council's work should be informed by the human rights dimension because the creation of a culture of respect for human rights should be seen as the cement which will help maintain lasting peace and prevent new cycles of violence. To achieve this requires a coordinated and integrated approach in which bilateral and multilateral aid, development and humanitarian agencies invest in nurturing civil society and in rebuilding the institutions that guarantee the rule of law. If such guarantors of human rights are strong, it is less likely that a country emerging from conflict will again descend into chaos. Such efforts often need to include the development of a fair and impartial judicial system, the creation of national human rights institutions, the rebuilding of the police and the military as entirely separate institutions, and the provision of human rights training.

'... today's human rights violations are the causes of tomorrow's conflicts'

Mary Robinson, UN High Commissioner for Human Rights, November 1997

At the end of 1997 the UN Secretary-General appointed a Special Representative for Liberia to take responsibility for post-conflict peace-building. Amnesty International has called for human rights to be at the centre of UN action on Liberia, given the appalling abuses committed over many years. In Angola the failure to appoint a head of the UN human rights operation by the end of the year also delayed the appointment of human rights monitors during a period when an effective human rights presence was vital.

Amnesty International has long urged that regional organizations should also take seriously how conflict resolution, regional stability and human rights are inextricably bound together. This was again illustrated by the crisis in Cambodia that started with the coup in July (see **Cambodia** entry). Speaking on the eve of the Association of South East Asian Nations (ASEAN) Regional Forum in Kuala Lumpur in July, Amnesty International argued that serious human rights violations in Cambodia during the year, including extrajudicial executions of political opponents, again thwarted the country's development, constrained its full participation in regional affairs and posed a threat to stability and security in the Asia-Pacific region:

"Far from being an 'internal affair', human rights issues directly engage the international responsibilities and national interests of other states. They belong squarely on the agenda of regional security discussions".

Long-standing human rights grievances are also among the root causes of massive refugee flows, armed conflicts and political instability in Africa. Human rights should, therefore, be at the heart of the political processes of the Organization of African Unity (OAU). In the past Amnesty International has pointed to the scant attention paid by the political bodies of the OAU to human rights issues and the lack of political and financial support for the African Commission on Human and Peoples' Rights (see *Amnesty International Report 1997*).

The OAU Council of Foreign Ministers and Assembly of Heads of State and Government, in Harare, Zimbabwe, in June was dominated by the coup in Sierra Leone, which was strongly condemned, and by the first official international appearance of Laurent Désiré Kabila, the new President of the Democratic Republic of the Congo. At the Harare meeting Amnesty International urged the OAU to support a program of reconstruction in the Democratic Republic of the Congo that would include rebuilding the institutions of the rule of law and reforming the police and military, to help prevent future cycles of human rights violations. However, many OAU member states felt constrained and in a weak position to raise human rights issues because of the OAU's silence for decades in the face of continuing human rights violations by the government of the former President of the then Zaire, Mobutu Sese Seko. The OAU did, however, clearly call on the Government of Burundi to disband the "regroupment" camps (see **Burundi** entry).

For many years the Organization for Security and Co-operation in Europe (OSCE) has espoused a progressive doctrine in which security, human rights and economic development unite to protect citizens in Europe from fear and instability. Unfortunately, enthusiasm in the early 1990s to develop detailed OSCE human rights commitments gave way to a gradual erosion of the central role of human rights. Amnesty International welcomed the first signs during the year of a new wave of possible reforms. With the appointment of a new Director for the Warsaw-based Office for Democratic Institutions and Human Rights came proposals to integrate human rights into the regular political and security work of the OSCE Permanent Council in Vienna — the heart of the OSCE — and proposals to reinvigorate the largely moribund biennial Human Dimension Implementation Meetings.

International justice: an international criminal court

Guaranteeing that justice will not be sacrificed for the sake of short-term political expediency is one way to integrate human rights into the process of post-conflict peace-building. In Amnesty International's experience, long-term reconciliation after an armed conflict is not possible unless justice is central to the search for peace. Sweeping aside the question of responsibility for atrocities during an armed conflict only leads to renewed cycles of violence and impunity. The urgent need for a permanent international criminal court was again highlighted during the year when speculation mounted that Pol Pot, former leader of the Khmer Rouge, might be delivered to a third country to be tried for crimes against humanity committed in the 1970s (see **Cambodia** entry). The Government of Cambodia formally asked the UN for assistance to bring Pol Pot and other former leaders to justice. Unfortunately, there was neither sufficient political will nor clear national legislation which would have allowed them to be tried by an individual state exercising universal jurisdiction or for an *ad hoc* international tribunal to be set up.

Nevertheless, the worldwide effort to establish a permanent international criminal court — the missing link in the interlocking chain of international justice in peace and war — has moved into a new phase. Since December 1996, when the UN General Assembly decided to convene a diplomatic conference in Rome in June 1998 to adopt a statute for such a court (see *Amnesty International Report 1997*), the question has no longer been "Will there be an international criminal court?", but "Will the court be independent, fair and effective?"

Throughout the year Amnesty International, together with more than 300 other members of the NGO Coalition for an International Criminal Court, urged governments to strengthen the draft statute for the court. In particular, NGOs participated actively in three separate preparatory meetings for the 1998 diplomatic conference which took place in February, August and December in New York. Before each session, Amnesty International prepared an in-depth analysis of the draft statute for government ministers and delegates, with specific recommendations for improvement.

Much progress has been made in reducing more than 300 pages of proposals to a manageable consolidated text for discussion at the diplomatic conference. In addition, there is an emerging consensus that the court will have jurisdiction over the "core crimes" of genocide, other crimes against humanity and serious violations of humanitarian law in both international and internal armed conflict; and possibly aggression.

Nevertheless, many other issues are still fiercely contested. How they are resolved will determine whether the court is an independent, fair and effective institution or, on the contrary, a set-back for international justice. For example, the permanent members of the UN Security Council (China, France, the Russian Federation, the United Kingdom and the USA) argue that they should each have a veto over any prosecution in a country that the UN Security Council is considering under Chapter VII of the UN Charter (threats to or breaches of international peace and security). Many other countries now agree with Amnesty International that, although the UN Security Council should have the power to refer a situation to the international criminal court for investigation, as this avoids further *ad hoc* courts and ensures that court orders can be enforced in any state, it should not have any power to prevent a prosecution.

Amnesty International has also argued that the prosecutor should be able to initiate an investigation based on information from any source, including victims and their families. This is no more than the power that the Prosecutor for the International Criminal Tribunals for the former Yugoslavia and Rwanda

> **'A window of opportunity now exists to bring a permanent international criminal court into existence before the turn of the century... Future generations will not look kindly upon us if we hesitate or fail in this task.'**
>
> South African Ambassador Khiphusizi J. Jele, speaking on behalf of the Southern African Development Community at the UN General Assembly, October 1997

already enjoys. Permanent members of the UN Security Council and some other countries argue that cases should only come before the court if a complaint is made by states or by the UN Security Council. However, many countries now agree with Amnesty International's position. Particularly significant has been the support from many states in Asia, Africa and Latin America for an independent prosecutor.

Other issues are likely to remain in the balance until the opening of the diplomatic conference in June 1998. Will the court follow all the internationally recognized standards for fair trial so that its verdicts are perceived by all to be just and fair? Will it have the broadest possible jurisdiction over genocide, crimes against humanity and serious violations of humanitarian law, including rape, forced prostitution and similar sexual abuse? Will the prosecutor be prevented from fulfilling his or her role by the requirement that the state which has custody of the suspect, the state where the crime occurred, the state of the victim's nationality and the state of the suspect's nationality must all have accepted the court's jurisdiction before an individual can be prosecuted? Will the court have an effective victim and witness protection and support program which requires each state party to be willing to receive its fair share of victims, witnesses and their families? Will the court receive long-term, secure financing through the regular UN budget?

The answers to these questions will depend to a large extent on the continuing efforts of the ever-growing NGO Coalition for an International Criminal Court, which Amnesty International helped to found. The NGO Coalition played a decisive role in the UN General Assembly's decision to convene the diplomatic conference in Rome in 1998. The UN General Assembly also decided that NGOs would be able to attend the plenary meetings and working group meetings in Rome, but not informal drafting groups. Representatives of some of the NGOs will be invited to address the opening and closing plenary sessions. Governments have recognized the importance of the comprehensive and detailed comments of NGOs on the draft statute and the rapid distribution of information about the preparatory process on the NGO Coalition's internet site <http://www.igc.apc.org/icc>.

Amnesty International members around the world have campaigned creatively for the court to become a reality. In Greece, a petition with 10,000 signatures was handed to the Prime Minister. Members in Togo were invited to meet the Minister of Justice for the first time ever, specifically to discuss the court. Press coverage and conferences were organized in Peru and Mexico. Portuguese language radio stations in Macao covered the story and quoted from Amnesty International documents. The campaigning will continue until a fair and effective court is established.

Integrating women's rights

Although the UN Charter proclaims the equality of women and men, it has taken almost five decades for the truth about the unequal position of women to reach the consciousness of UN bodies. Only in Beijing in 1995, at the Fourth UN World Conference on Women, were clear and detailed commitments made by states on a program of action to make women's rights human rights. Several steps have been taken in the UN itself to implement the Beijing Declaration and Platform for Action (see *Amnesty International Report 1997*). During the year Amnesty International stressed the importance of properly integrating a gender-sensitive perspective into statements, analyses, investigations and interpretations of international human rights law by the UN political and expert bodies that deal directly with human rights. It also focused on how to integrate the human rights of women into the mainstream of UN system-wide activity.

Individual leadership is vital in articulating what integration means and motivating others to work creatively to turn words into action. References to women's rights in the UN Secretary-General's reform package are sparse. Amnesty International encouraged the UN Secretary-General, the UN High Commissioner for Human Rights and the UN Special Adviser on Gender Issues, to use their moral authority and to implement practical programs for integration. The UN High Commissioner for Human Rights, for example, has been mandated by the UN Commission on Human Rights to ensure that all UN staff are given basic training in a gender-sensitive approach to human rights work and to review how her Office's technical assistance programs for governments — including projects aimed at law enforcement officials, judges and immigration officials — address the promotion and protection of women's rights. It is hoped that the UN Secretary-General will support the joint initiative, announced in April, by the World Health Organization, UNICEF and the UN Population Fund to "completely eradicate [female genital mutilation]... within three generations" and encourage other parts of the UN to work towards this goal.

For most of its existence the UN Commission on Human Rights effectively ignored the gender implications of its work. The work of the UN Special Rapporteur on violence against women, appointed in 1994, and calls by the Commission for its thematic and country experts to include gender-specific information in their reports have been welcome, although lack of resources for these experts has hampered progress. At the most basic level, however, the fact that fewer than 15 per cent of thematic and country experts of the Commission on Human Rights are women needs to be corrected, as does the under-representation of women on treaty bodies. Amnesty International called on all the thematic and country experts of the Commission on Human Rights to produce a report within the next five years on how human rights violations within their theme or country specifically affect women. The organization renewed its recommendation that pending widespread training of UN personnel in gender perspectives, teams investigating human rights violations should include a "gender adviser" with knowledge of the country being visited.

Experts sitting on UN treaty bodies, such as the Committee against Torture and the Human Rights Committee, should also ensure that their examinations of reports submitted by states include the impact on women of the obligations in the treaty. To do this some will need to consider how the rights in their treaty cover a range of gender-specific violations. The Committee against Torture, for example, should look at the definition of torture in relation to practices such as female genital mutilation, which the state has either failed to criminalize or has effectively condoned in state-run or state-licensed hospitals.

> **'Violence against women is a manifestation of the historically unequal power relations between men and women, which have led to domination over and discrimination against women by men and to the prevention of women's full advancement.'**
>
> Beijing Declaration and Platform for Action, paragraph 118

The 1993 UN Vienna Declaration and Programme of Action called on all states to ratify the UN Convention on the Elimination of All Forms of Discrimination against Women (the Women's Convention) by the year 2000. By the end of 1997, 162 states had done so. The 50th anniversary of the Universal Declaration of Human Rights provides an ideal occasion for the remaining 28 states to become parties. This would be a milestone in the promotion and protection of women's rights universally.

During the year Amnesty International also continued to work with women's groups around the world to create a procedure which would enable women to make individual complaints that their government had violated their rights under the Women's

Convention. Such a protocol to the Women's Convention, which would enable experts on the Committee for the Elimination of Discrimination against Women to hear such complaints, continued to be drafted by states. In December Amnesty International published a report, *The optional protocol to the Women's Convention: enabling women to claim their rights at the international level,* in which it made recommendations about how to ensure the protocol is effective.

Refugees and human rights: challenges to protection

The fundamental principles of refugee protection were challenged to an even greater extent in 1997 than in previous years. This led the human rights movement to argue even more strongly that human rights principles should guide refugee protection. There continued to be situations where the fundamental standards of refugee protection were not applied. For example, refugees from Rwanda and Burundi were subjected to, or under threat of, *refoulement* in the Great Lakes region of Africa and many were in danger of being killed in neighbouring countries. Rohingya asylum-seekers from Myanmar were at risk of *refoulement* from Bangladesh, and detention policies remained a concern in Australia and the USA. Asylum-seekers who had fled the violence in Algeria continued to have difficulty obtaining protection in many states in Western Europe, often because of those states' restrictive interpretation of the definition of who is a refugee.

Refugee protection was challenged not only in practice; the principles themselves were being questioned. The crisis in the Great Lakes region in particular has forced the international community to re-examine refugee protection. However, Amnesty International is concerned that instead of reaffirming the principles of protection, and exploring how they could be better achieved, the debate seems to be heading in the direction of undermining the principles themselves.

Amnesty International believes that now more than ever it is vital that human rights are recognized as the core of refugee protection and in 1997 it published a major report, *Refugees: human rights have no borders.* Upholding the rights of refugees cannot be seen in isolation from the broader campaign for human rights, and international human rights standards provide important guidance to support the protection of refugees.

The Executive Committee of the Programme of the UN High Commissioner for Refugees (UNHCR EXCOM) is the main international forum which develops standards of refugee protection. The conclusions of this annual intergovernmental meeting represent an important international consensus regarding current refugee-related issues, and carry persuasive authority as standards of refugee protection. In its meeting in October 1997, the UNHCR EXCOM initiated debate on the subject of "The Challenges of Repatriation". The definition of repatriation standards is widely recognized as one of the most important debates in refugee protection

© Howard J. Davies/Panos Pictures

Unaccompanied Rwandese Hutu children return home to Kigali, Rwanda, on board a cargo plane, with the assistance of the UN High Commissioner for Refugees and other international humanitarian agencies. The children had survived an armed attack in April on Biaro and Kasese refugee camps, in eastern Democratic Republic of the Congo, by the AFDL armed group, its allies and local villagers.

today. Amnesty International urged the member states of the UNHCR EXCOM to ensure that human rights safeguards are properly incorporated into the standards of repatriation so that all refugees are protected from *refoulement*. Amnesty International will continue to campaign for the principles of refugee protection to be upheld, and for the protection needs of refugees to be recognized as the central concern in establishing repatriation standards.

In addition to the refugee debates at the UNHCR EXCOM, international human rights mechanisms have evolved to play an important role in the monitoring of states' refugee policies. For example, the UN Human Rights Committee, in its examination of France's third periodic report in July, expressed concern regarding that country's restrictive interpretation of the definition of persecution for refugees, as it does not take into account possible persecution by non-state actors. The Committee also stated in April that Australia had contravened its obligations under the International Covenant on Civil and Political Rights by arbitrarily detaining a Cambodian asylum-seeker without providing for a real and not merely formal review of the detention (see **Australia** entry). The UN Committee against Torture also reviewed several individual communications brought forward by asylum-seekers.

In August, in a joint effort with the Geneva-based NGO, the International Service for Human Rights, Amnesty International published *The UN and refugees' human rights*, a manual for NGOs and others involved in refugee issues on how to use international human rights mechanisms to protect refugees. Amnesty International will continue to campaign to ensure that refugee issues are discussed in international human rights forums.

Accountability and *realpolitik* in UN political bodies

There is little point in integrating human rights into the activities of other parts of the UN if those UN political bodies which already have a mandate to deal with human rights do not discharge their basic duty to hold their peers accountable to international standards. The UN's record during the year was very mixed.

In the face of continuing gross human rights violations, both the UN General Assembly and the UN Commission on Human Rights showed themselves to be almost irrelevant to the protection of victims in Burundi, Rwanda and the Democratic Republic of the Congo.

The UN General Assembly was silent on the Democratic Republic of the Congo because *no* state would take a lead in preparing a resolution. States argued that the only relevant issue was cooperation with the UN Secretary-General's investigation team and that an agreement for access brokered by the USA had made such concern redundant. However, the continuing difficulties faced by the team were apparent. Beyond this, the UN General Assembly should have addressed broader issues such as the need for long-term investment in rebuilding the institutions which could restore the rule of law — one of the key areas in successful post-conflict peace-building. The UN General Assembly was also silent — for the second consecutive year — on the escalating abuses in Burundi, despite being presented with the facts by the UN's own human rights expert on the country.

At the 1997 UN Commission on Human Rights, Amnesty International urged states to tackle persistent, severe and systematic violations of human rights particularly in Algeria, Colombia, Indonesia and East Timor, Nigeria and Turkey.

Following Nigeria's failure to implement the Commission's 1996 resolution, Amnesty International welcomed the decision to appoint a Special Rapporteur to investigate the serious patterns of human rights violations in the country. Despite the pressure of regional solidarity and Nigeria's powerful position within the African group of states, some African states, such as South Africa, supported the 1997 resolution or abstained, ensuring its success.

Although Turkey escaped scrutiny yet again, intense pressure on the Turkish Government before and during the session did lead, a few months later, to a welcome invitation from the government to the UN Working Group on enforced or involuntary disappearances and the UN Special Rapporteur on torture to visit the country over a two-year period. Amnesty International was appalled, however, that the Working Group did not visit Turkey during 1997 and that the Turkish authorities did not agree on a date for a visit prior to the 1998 session of the Commission. The failure to visit in 1997 only added to the torment suffered by the families of the "disappeared".

© AP/Ricardo Mazalan

A soldier stands guard at the Pavarandó camp for the internally displaced in the Urabá region, Colombia, which houses several thousand of those displaced by the intensifying armed conflict. 1997 saw the establishment of an office of the UN High Commissioner for Human Rights in Colombia.

In a closely negotiated and carefully worded statement, the Chairperson of the Commission welcomed the opening of the UN High Commissioner for Human Rights' office in Colombia, but expressed concern about continuing widespread human rights violations and impunity in the country.

After three years of dithering, the Commission did send a clear message to the Indonesian authorities that they must act now to protect human rights in East Timor when it adopted the first resolution on this situation since 1993. The key, however, will be whether this resolution is followed up at the 1998 session.

Trade considerations and the political pressures of regional solidarity meant that most states avoided direct confrontation at the Commission. Dialogue and quiet diplomacy dominated, but all too often turned into silent diplomacy. The group of Western states revealed serious divisions in its ranks. A commitment to the ideals that the Commission should embody faded away in the face of potentially lucrative business deals. Several countries including Australia, Canada, France, Germany, Greece, Italy and Spain reversed their policy of previous years and refused even to co-sponsor the draft resolution on China. Yet again this draft resolution, with its mild censure of China's human rights record, was not even voted on after China yet again won a procedural motion.

© Cumhuriyet/Tarik Tinazay

Police assault students during the break-up of a non-violent student demonstration against educational fees in Ankara, Turkey. Systematic human rights violations in Turkey continue to be ignored by the UN Commission on Human Rights.

The Commission was once again entirely silent on gross human rights abuses by the security forces and armed political groups in Algeria. It was yet another "brick in the international community's wall of silence", said Amnesty International following the session. In October, after thousands more civilians were massacred, Amnesty International issued a joint call with three other NGOs for a special session of the UN Commission on Human Rights to be convened to establish an international investigation into responsibility for the atrocities in Algeria (see **Algeria** entry). Some governments argued that a special session of the Commission was inappropriate while the UN General Assembly was in session and could deal with the situation. Yet the atrocities were completely ignored by the General Assembly. Amnesty International's Secretary General, speaking at the launch of the organization's report on Algeria in November, told UN diplomats in New York that there was no other country where the violations were so extreme where there had been no international scrutiny let alone action — no visits by experts, no monitors, not even a resolution passed. He continued,

"Such indifference in the face of the daily slaughter becomes increasingly untenable, for it is an indifference that has contributed to a worsening of the situation by allowing impunity to prevail. In the absence of any concrete action, the condemnation of the violence and the expressions of regret for the loss of lives are sounding more and more like hollow rhetoric."

By the end of the year no steps had been taken to hold the special session of the Commission or to initiate an international investigation.

In a new and disturbing development two states denounced international human rights treaties which they had ratified. Jamaica announced it would withdraw from the Optional Protocol to the International Covenant on Civil and Political Rights (ICCPR). This withdrawal, effective as of January 1998, ends the right of individuals to appeal to the UN Human Rights Committee about violations of the ICCPR. Jamaica took this unprecedented step to make it easier to execute prisoners on death row (see **Jamaica** entry). North Korea (see **Democratic People's Republic of Korea** entry) claimed to have withdrawn from the ICCPR itself, although in an authoritative statement the UN Human Rights Committee explained that international law does not permit states to withdraw once they have ratified the ICCPR. Amnesty International was deeply concerned at these assaults on the international human rights system which would deprive citizens in two countries of the protection and rights they enjoy. The organization said it was imperative for states, UN human rights bodies and UN leaders to forcefully voice their opposition to such moves and dissuade other states from taking similar action.

COUNTRY ENTRIES

AFGHANISTAN

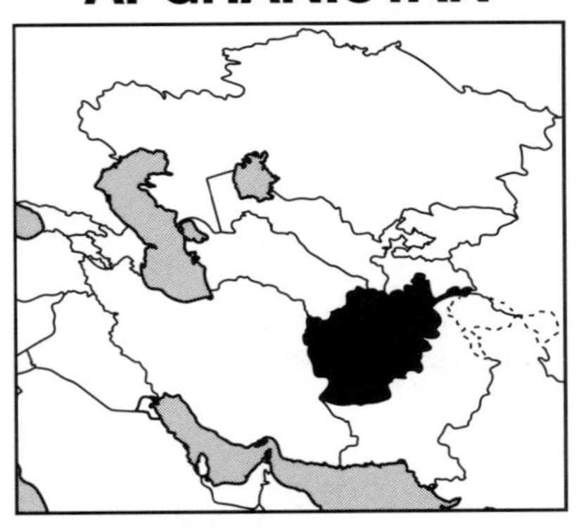

Thousands of people were reportedly detained for reasons of ethnicity or alleged un-Islamic behaviour. Tens of thousands of women remained physically restricted. Torture and ill-treatment, including beatings in public places, were widespread. Judicial floggings and amputations were carried out. Scores, possibly hundreds, of civilians were killed in massacres and deliberate or indiscriminate attacks on residential areas by different armed groups. Mass graves were discovered containing the bodies of *Taleban* militia members reportedly killed after being taken prisoner. More than six people were executed; some were reportedly stoned to death.

Continued armed conflict and security problems made information on human rights abuses difficult to gather and verify. The mainly Pashtun *Taleban* maintained their control over two thirds of Afghanistan, while the anti-*Taleban* alliance, comprising Tajik, Uzbek and Hazara armed political groups, held northern parts of the country. In May *Taleban* forces briefly captured the northern city of Mazar-e Sharif, but retreated in the face of an anti-*Taleban* uprising.

Hundreds of thousands of people were internally displaced or fled the country to become refugees. About 8,000 refugees fleeing to Turkmenistan in late June returned home after several weeks because of the severe shortage of food and drinking water and the harsh conditions they had to endure. Thousands of civilians, mainly Tajik, were reportedly forced from their homes by the *Taleban*, in some instances by the deliberate destruction of water supply and irrigation systems. Most forcible relocations took place in areas north of Kabul, the capital, including Jabol Seraj, Charikar and Gulbahar, where fierce battles between the *Taleban* and other forces raged throughout the year. Forcible relocations by other armed groups were reported in other areas, including the northwestern province of Badghis.

UN efforts to end the conflict and facilitate national reconciliation and reconstruction in the country remained stalled. In May Pakistan, Saudi Arabia and the United Arab Emirates recognized the *Taleban* as the Government of Afghanistan. Other countries continued to withhold recognition.

In October the UN Special Rapporteur on Afghanistan submitted his report to the UN General Assembly, in which he emphasized the need for the international community to safeguard basic human rights in Afghanistan and to adopt a principled approach of non-discrimination with regard to the constraints imposed on both women and men in the country.

Thousands of people were reportedly held for periods of up to several months on account of their ethnicity. Among these were around 2,000 Tajik and Hazara men rounded up from their homes in Kabul in July and held in various jails, including Pul-e Charkhi Prison in Kabul. Most of them were believed to be prisoners of conscience.

Tens of thousands of women remained physically restricted to their homes under *Taleban* edicts which continued to ban women from seeking employment, education or leaving home unaccompanied by a male relative. Other measures restricting women included the closure of women's *hammams* (public baths). Women were also barred from the streets for certain periods during the month of Ramadan.

Emma Bonino, the European Commissioner for humanitarian aid, was detained for several hours on 29 September by the *Taleban* after members of her entourage visiting Kabul took pictures of women.

Hundreds of women were beaten by *Taleban* guards in detention centres or in public places, including shops, streets and bus stops for defying *Taleban* edicts. For example, in May, five women employees of the aid agency CARE International were forced out of their minibus and publicly humiliated in front of a large crowd. Two of them were beaten despite having official documents allowing them to work.

Over 1,000 men were detained briefly and beaten for alleged un-Islamic behaviour or for not complying with policies which discriminate against women. In July alone, *Taleban* radio announced that some 700 men travelling from Kabul to Kandahar had been "punished in accordance with Islamic law for trimming or shaving their beards". Others beaten in public included taxi drivers for carrying women passengers, shopkeepers for selling goods to women, children for flying kites or playing other games in the street, and teachers for giving English lessons.

Torture and ill-treatment were widespread in jails and detention centres run by the *Taleban* and other armed political groups. Inmates, including elderly men and children, were reportedly beaten with steel wires, sticks and rifle butts. At times beatings resulted in death. Family members seeking to visit detainees were also beaten. Survivors of torture were often left with broken bones, bruises, or fractured skulls; some had serious burns resulting from fuel being poured on them and set alight. Eye-witnesses in Kabul saw men taken from the street and detained in metal transport containers, which are susceptible to extremes of heat and cold. Those who refused to enter were beaten.

Sentences of flogging continued to be imposed. In March, a three-man *Taleban* tribunal sentenced five Afghan prisoners to between nine and 29 lashes and one and a half months' imprisonment, and two Frenchmen to one month's imprisonment. The Afghan men, who were cooks, watchmen and drivers, and the two French aid workers were arrested in February for being in the company of women who came to a farewell lunch at a French aid agency, *Action contre la faim*. All prisoners were released at the end of their sentences; the floggings were carried out.

Several incidents of amputation were reported and it was believed that many more were unreported. In late 1996 a woman in the Khair-Khana area of Kabul had the end of her thumb cut off by the *Taleban* for wearing nail varnish. In April one man was reportedly punished for alleged theft in the southern Afghan town of Ghazni by having his hand and foot amputated. Local surgeons were reportedly ordered to carry out the punishment. The right hands and left feet of two men accused of armed robbery were publicly amputated in Urozgan Province in October.

Scores, possibly hundreds, of people were reportedly killed in deliberate or indiscriminate attacks by the warring factions, including during air raids and rocket attacks on villages and residential areas.

In May the bodies of 12 ethnic Hazara, reportedly all civilians, were found in a neighbourhood west of Kabul. They were believed to have been killed deliberately and arbitrarily by *Taleban* soldiers.

In September about 70 civilians, including women and children, were deliberately and arbitrarily killed by armed guards in Qezelabad village near Mazar-e Sharif. Survivors said the massacre was carried out by *Taleban* guards retreating from positions they had captured in the area, but *Taleban* officials denied responsibility for the killing. All of the victims reportedly belonged to the Hazara minority. Among the victims was a boy aged about eight who was reportedly killed and decapitated; other victims reportedly had their eyes gouged out with bayonets. Two boys aged about 12 were reportedly held by the guards and had their arms and hands broken with stones.

Over 20 mass graves were discovered in November near the city of Shebarghan in the northern province of Jowzjan. The exact number of those buried in the graves could not be established but most reports put the number at around 2,000. The dead were thought to have been among the *Taleban* militia reportedly taken prisoner after the *Taleban* entered the city of Mazar-e Sharif in May. They were alleged to have been killed deliberately and arbitrarily while in the custody of the forces of General Abdul Malik, an anti-*Taleban* military commander in control of the area at the time.

Several executions were reported and there was concern that prisoners of war throughout the country were at risk of execution. They included Ismael Khan, an opposition general and former governor of Afghanistan's western Herat province, who was taken prisoner in May and was believed to be detained in Kandahar. Four *Taleban* men accused of working with the opposition were publicly executed in Kabul in October.

Several people were reportedly stoned to death. In March a woman was reportedly stoned to death in Laghman Province in eastern Afghanistan after an Islamic tribunal reportedly found her guilty of adultery.

Throughout the year Amnesty International raised concerns about human rights abuses by all warring groups, including those against women. The organization published: *Women in Afghanistan: The violations continue,* in May; *Afghanistan: Continuing atrocities against civilians,* in September; and *Afghanistan: Reports of mass graves of* Taleban *militia,* in November. Amnesty International appealed to the countries which support the warring factions to shoulder their responsibility for human rights abuses in Afghanistan and to press armed political groups to respect human rights.

ALBANIA

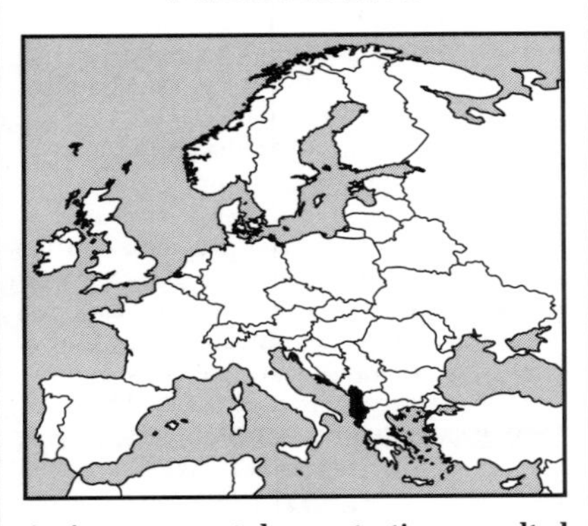

Anti-government demonstrations resulted in violent clashes with the police and the temporary collapse of government authority in most of the country. Demonstrators, journalists and bystanders were detained and ill-treated by police. Police were alleged to have shot demonstrators unlawfully. Most prisoners of conscience – both those detained during the year and those detained in previous years – escaped, were released or were pardoned. Political prisoners also escaped or were released. At least one death sentence was passed. No executions were reported to have been carried out.

Protests in a number of towns by people demanding the return of money they had lost in fraudulent savings schemes escalated into violent anti-government riots in January and February. Law and order broke down as the situation deteriorated, particularly in the south, amid widespread looting of military arms depots. As violence increased in February, nine people were killed in riots in the southern town of Vlora. Following these incidents, the government of Prime Minister Aleksander Meksi resigned and a state of emergency was declared on 2 March. On 3 March President Sali Berisha, of the Democratic Party, who had been in office since 1992, was re-elected by parliament. Opposition members boycotted the vote. As riots, demonstrations and disorder spread to the capital, Tirana, and other towns, those vocalizing their discontent demanded the resignation of the President as well as the return of lost money. International pressure led President Berisha to agree to an interim coalition government and early elections. An interim government led by opposition Socialist Party (SP) member Bashkim Fino governed until July.

The widespread lawlessness saw a mounting death toll from criminal killings and accidental shootings. By the end of the year some 1,600 people had been killed. Most of these deaths occurred between March and July. In response to the crisis, the UN Security Council authorized the dispatch of an Italian-led multinational security force, which was deployed from April to August to oversee relief efforts and the new elections.

Amid the disorder in the first half of the year, thousands of people fled abroad. Many of them were refugees fleeing serious human rights abuses and random violence; others were fleeing the economic chaos. In March around 59 Albanians died when the tugboat in which they were fleeing collided with an Italian naval ship which was attempting to stem the arrival of refugees (see **Italy** entry).

Elections held in June gave a clear majority to the SP. President Berisha resigned. The parliament elected SP member Rexhep Mejdani as President. Fatos Nano, an SP member and former Prime Minister, was appointed Prime Minister in July with a coalition government including members of other former opposition parties. In July the state of emergency was formally lifted.

Some prisoners of conscience were detained in connection with the crisis in the first part of the year. These included journalist Roland Beqiraj, who was held in Korça for at least 11 days in January and February and was allegedly beaten by police. However, the growing chaos resulted in the breakout or release in March of around one thousand prisoners. These included prisoners of conscience such as Fatos Nano (see *Amnesty International Reports 1995* to *1997*). He and approximately 50 other prisoners had been formally pardoned by President Berisha; another 600 convicted prisoners benefited from a separate Amnesty Law. The pardons and amnesties excluded some prisoners of conscience, for example, Idajet Beqiri, leader of the National Unity Party (see *Amnesty International Reports 1994* and *1997*). He had, however, escaped, and by the end of the year the police had not rearrested him or many of the other prisoners who escaped or were released during the height of the lawlessness.

In April charges of involvement in political killings, bombings and robberies against political prisoner Klement Kolaneci, son-in-law of former communist ruler Enver Hoxha, were dropped (see *Amnesty International Report 1997*). In October charges of "genocide" against former President Ramiz Alia were also dropped (see *Amnesty International Report 1997*).

As the demonstrations gathered pace in January and February there were increasing reports that uniformed and plain-clothes police officers, or civilians operating in groups linked to the authorities, were beating and detaining demonstrators, suspected demonstrators or opposition supporters. There were violent attacks on independent and opposition journalists, many of which were attributed to the authorities. These attacks took place in towns such as Vlora, which became the main focal point of the anti-government demonstrations, Berat, Fier, Korça and Tirana, as well as other towns. For example, in January B. Memushi alleged that he had been beaten by police in Vlora with a truncheon and chair leg, resulting in broken teeth and injuries to his genitals. He denied that he had even taken part in the demonstrations. In Berat, Vladimir Goxhi and others were treated in hospital after alleged beatings by police in detention. Relatives of other detainees who were held in the town were not promptly informed of their detention. In February journalists Roland Beqiraj (see above) and Alfred Peza were beaten by police in Korça and Fier respectively.

Six people killed during the February riots in Vlora were alleged to have been unlawfully killed by the state security police, who shot into crowds.

Despite an undertaking by Albania to the Council of Europe in 1996 to suspend executions, some death sentences were reported. For example, in October Myrteza Gjoka was sentenced to death for killing six members of his family. No executions were reported to have been carried out.

In February Amnesty International called on the authorities to maintain law and order in a manner in keeping with Albania's international human rights obligations; the organization expressed concern about reports of the ill-treatment of protesters and opposition supporters. It urged the release of those detained for the non-violent exercise of their right to freedom of expression and association, and for all other political prisoners to be granted a fair trial. In March, following the introduction of the state of emergency, Amnesty International reminded the authorities of the need to uphold at all times the right to life and the right not to be subjected to torture. It also criticized provisions in the legislation which authorized security forces to open fire to disperse crowds and to shoot without warning those failing to surrender weapons.

ALGERIA

Thousands of civilians, including hundreds of women and children, were killed in large-scale massacres committed in rural areas by armed groups. Thousands of people were killed by the security forces and state-armed militias; hundreds were reportedly extrajudicially executed. Hundreds of civilians were killed by armed groups which define themselves as "Islamic groups". Thousands of people, including prisoners of conscience and possible prisoners of conscience, were detained during the year; hundreds were charged under the "anti-terrorist" law. Thousands of people arrested in previous years were imprisoned after unfair trials. Scores of others continued to be held without trial. Torture and ill-treatment

continued to be widespread, especially during unacknowledged detention, and ill-treatment was reported in prisons. Several hundred people who "disappeared" after arrest by the security forces remained unaccounted for. Scores of people were abducted by armed groups. Scores of death sentences were imposed, most of them *in absentia*, and more than 600 people were under sentence of death at the end of the year. No judicial executions were reported.

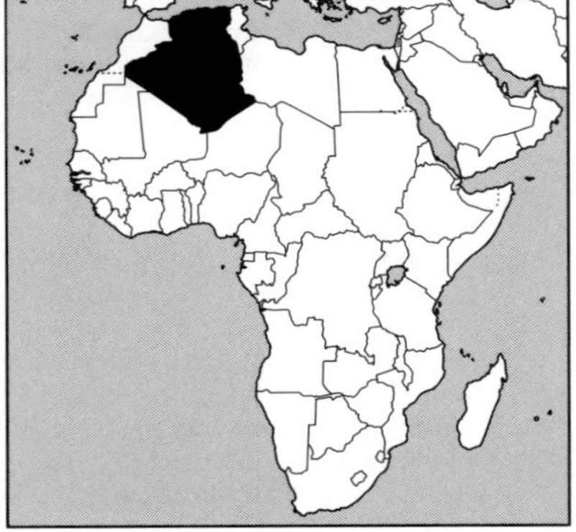

Legislative and local elections were held in June and October, respectively. The *Rassemblement national démocratique* (RND), National Democratic Rally, created in February by supporters of President Liamine Zeroual, took a lead in both elections. Opposition parties complained of widespread electoral fraud. In January Prime Minister 'Ahmed Ouyahia signed an executive decree legalizing the militias armed by the state, which had been in existence since 1994, and setting out a framework for their activities. The decree fell short of international standards governing the conduct of law enforcement officials, and did not provide essential safeguards contained in human rights standards, ratified by Algeria, designed to ensure both that militia members respect and protect human rights and that complaints of human rights abuses by militia members are adequately investigated. In practice militias routinely overstepped their self-defence mandate and carried out, or participated in, "anti-terrorist" offensive operations.

The state of emergency imposed in 1992 (see previous *Amnesty International Reports*) remained in place.

The UN Special Rapporteurs on torture, and on extrajudicial, summary or arbitrary executions were not allowed to visit the country.

The escalating political conflict resulted in some of the worst violence since the crisis began in 1992. Responsibility for individual human rights abuses was often difficult to verify, as security forces, militias armed by the state and armed groups defining themselves as "Islamic groups" often adopted similar patterns of conduct. Government restrictions on the news media and on the activities of human rights organizations, intimidation by the authorities of those trying to gather or communicate information about human rights abuses, and death threats against journalists by armed groups, severely restricted reporting of human rights abuses.

At least 2,000 civilians, including hundreds of women and children, were killed in large-scale massacres by armed groups in rural areas. The victims were slaughtered, decapitated, mutilated, shot, or burned alive in their homes. Most of the massacres took place near the capital, Algiers, and in the Blida and Medea regions, in the most heavily militarized part of the country. Often massacres were committed in villages situated close to army barracks and security forces posts, and in some cases survivors reported that army and security forces units were stationed nearby. The killings often lasted several hours, but the army and security forces failed to intervene to stop the massacres and allowed the attackers to leave undisturbed.

In August up to 300 people were killed in one night in Rais, south of Algiers. In September some 200 people were slaughtered in one night in Bentalha, also south of Algiers. Many of the victims were women, children and elderly people. Both villages were located near military barracks and security forces posts, but there was no intervention to stop the massacres.

The authorities blamed all the massacres on "terrorist groups", but there were allegations that some of the massacres had been committed by armed groups acting on instructions, or with the consent, of certain army and security forces units and paramilitary groups. No one was known to have been brought to justice for the massacres by the end of the year.

Thousands of people were killed by the security forces. Many were reportedly killed in military or security operations and in armed combat, although in the absence of independent sources it was not possible to establish the number or identity of those killed nor the circumstances of the killings. Hundreds were believed to have been extrajudicially executed when they posed no threat to the security forces and could have been arrested. Victims reportedly included people suspected of cooperating with armed groups, and extrajudicial executions often appeared to be used as an alternative to arresting and prosecuting known or suspected members or sympathizers of armed groups. For example, Rachid Medjahed, a former town council representative for the banned *Front islamique du salut* (FIS), Islamic Salvation Front, was arrested during an "anti-terrorist" raid in the capital, Algiers, in February and held in secret detention. His family only learned of his arrest when he appeared on television 10 days later and confessed to being the leader of the armed group responsible for the killing in January of 'Abdelhak Benhammouda, leader of the *Union générale des travailleurs algériens*, General Union of Algerian Workers. In April Rachid Medjahed's body was found, riddled with bullets, in a hospital in Blida. The authorities denied his death until May, when they said that he had died in February of bullet wounds sustained at the time of his arrest. However, when he appeared on television after his arrest he did not appear to be injured. No investigation was known to have been initiated into his death.

There were widespread reports of human rights abuses by militias armed by the state, which are known as "*groupes d'autodéfense*" ("self-defence groups") or "*patriotes*" ("patriots"). Militias were increasingly involved in military operations, and in some areas they had virtually replaced the security forces, organizing or participating in ambushes and "anti-terrorist" offensive military operations.

Armed groups which defined themselves as "Islamic groups" deliberately and arbitrarily killed hundreds of civilians and non-combatants. Some of the female victims were abducted and raped before being killed. In October, 16 children were killed on their way to school when the bus in which they were travelling came under machine-gun fire on the way from Sidi Selhane to Bouinan.

Scores of civilians were killed in bomb attacks by armed groups. In June some 20 people were killed and about 100 injured in three bomb explosions in public places near the capital in the space of three days.

Thousands of people, including prisoners of conscience and possible prisoners of conscience, were detained during the year. Many were charged with "security" offences while others were released without charge after periods of detention ranging from a few days to a few months.

Thousands of political detainees, including prisoners of conscience, arrested in previous years were sentenced to prison terms following unfair trials. Courts routinely ignored allegations by defendants that their confessions had been extracted under torture. In July prisoner of conscience Rachid Mesli, a human rights lawyer, was sentenced to three years' imprisonment following a trial which violated international fair trial standards. Rachid Mesli was found not guilty of the charges on which he was tried, but guilty of having "encouraged terrorism", even though this charge had not been brought against him during the trial and he had not had an opportunity to defend himself. The court also failed to investigate the abduction of Rachid Mesli in July 1996 and his allegations of ill-treatment during incommunicado detention (see *Amnesty International Report 1997*). The trial took place *in camera*. He petitioned the Supreme Court for review through the "cassation" procedure, which only looks at procedures and does not re-examine the facts of the case, and therefore does not constitute a full judicial appeal.

Although scores of political detainees arrested in previous years continued to be held without trial, a few were tried during the year. Nadir Hammoudi, an engineer detained since October 1992, was tried and acquitted in April but remained detained in connection with another case. 'Ali Zouita, a lawyer detained since February 1993, was tried on "terrorism" charges, acquitted and released. 'Abdelkader Hachani, a leading FIS figure detained since January 1992, was tried and sentenced to five years' imprisonment for a communique he had published in an Algerian newspaper in 1992. He was released immediately as he had already spent more than five years in detention (see previous *Amnesty International Reports*).

Prolonged incommunicado detention, well beyond the 12-day legal limit, was routine. Detainees were frequently held in unacknowledged detention for weeks or months. In July Messa'oud Ouziala, a kidney transplant surgeon, was abducted outside the Mustapha Hospital in Algiers. He was held in unacknowledged detention for two weeks and then released.

Torture and ill-treatment continued to be widespread, especially during unacknowledged detention. Methods included: the "*chiffon*" (tying the detainee in a horizontal position and pouring large quantities of dirty water and chemicals into the mouth, which is stuffed with a cloth, causing choking and swelling of the stomach); electric shocks to sensitive parts of the body; tying a rope around the detainee's penis and/or testicles, causing swelling of the genitals; suspension in contorted positions; cigarette burns; and beatings. For example, a 64-year-old woman arrested in May with two of her sons was reportedly partially undressed and beaten with a rubber hose and one of her sons was given electric shocks. Beatings and other ill-treatment were reported in several prisons. To date no judicial investigation is known to have been carried out into allegations of torture or ill-treatment.

Dozens of people "disappeared" after being arrested by the security forces and hundreds of people arrested in previous years remained unaccounted for. 'Aziz Bou'abdallah, a journalist with the Arabic-language newspaper *El-'Alam El-Siyasi*, was abducted from his home in April by three men who identified themselves as members of the security forces. He remained "disappeared" at the end of the year. Sa'ida Kherroubi was detained by security forces in Algiers in May when she went to bring food for her detained mother, and "disappeared" in unacknowledged detention for more than five months. She was then transferred to a prison and charged with having links with armed groups.

Some of the "disappeared" were reported to have died under torture or to have been killed in custody. The authorities denied that some of the "disappeared" had ever been arrested and claimed that others were killed by the security forces in combat, or while attempting to escape, and that some had been killed by "terrorist" groups. However, the authorities failed to provide any information to substantiate these claims. 'Allaoua Ziou, Djamaleddine Fahassi, Mohamed Rosli, Brahim Cherrada, Mohamed Chergui, Yamine 'Ali Kebaili, and 13 others who "disappeared" after their arrests in 1993, 1994 and 1995 remained unaccounted for. 'Ali Belhadj, a FIS leader arrested in 1991 and sentenced to 12 years' imprisonment in 1992, who "disappeared" in mid-1995 remained detained in a secret location (see *Amnesty International Report 1997*).

No further information could be obtained about Fou'ad Bouchelaghem, who had been arrested in June 1994 and reportedly shot dead by the security forces in detention (see *Amnesty International Report 1997*).

Scores of death sentences were imposed during the year, most of them *in absentia*, and more than 600 people were under sentence of death at the end of the year. In March the death sentence passed on Lembarek Bouma'arafi in June 1995 was upheld by the Supreme Court. He had been convicted of the murder in 1992 of President Mohamed Boudiaf in a trial which fell short of international standards for fair trial. He was detained in Blida Military Prison pending the outcome of his plea for clemency to the President. The moratorium on executions announced in December 1993 remained in force and no judicial executions were reported during the year.

In October Amnesty International and three other international non-governmental organizations – the International Federation of Human Rights, Human Rights Watch, and *Reporters Sans Frontières* – issued a joint appeal calling for a special session of the UN Commission on Human Rights to set up an international investigation into the human rights situation in Algeria (see **Work with International Organizations**).

In November Amnesty International issued a report, *Algeria: Civilian population caught in a spiral of violence*. The organization called for an international investigation to be set up to establish the facts concerning human rights abuses, examine responsibility for the violations and put forward a long-term plan to end the human rights crisis. Amnesty International condemned the massacres of civilians and other abuses and called on all parties in the conflict to stop targeting civilians. The UN Children's Fund (UNICEF) supported the call for an international investigation.

In most instances the government failed to respond on individual cases raised by Amnesty International. The organization was refused access to Algeria throughout the year.

ANGOLA

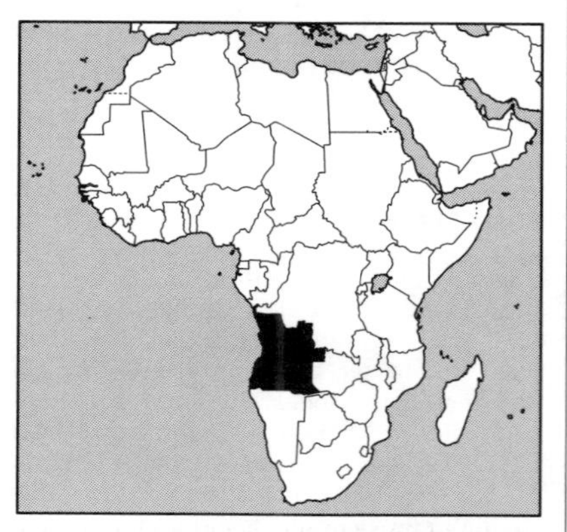

Severe beatings by police were commonplace. An investigation into the deaths of 10 prisoners was severely flawed. There were reports of extrajudicial executions. Both the government and the *União Nacional para a Independência Total de Angola* (UNITA), National Union for the Total Independence of Angola, killed unarmed civilians in contested areas of the country. UNITA held prisoners, including UNITA members suspected of disloyalty. An armed separatist group held hostages.

The implementation of the peace agreement signed in 1994 between the government of President José Eduardo dos Santos and UNITA, led by Jonas Malheiro Savimbi, continued despite delays and an outbreak of armed hostilities in mid-1997. In April parliament granted Jonas Savimbi the special status of President of the Largest Opposition Party. UNITA deputies took up the 70 National Assembly seats which the party had won in the 1992 elections and the Government of National Unity and Reconciliation was inaugurated. However, by the end of the year the UNITA leader had not taken up residence in Luanda, the capital.

In July the UN Angola Verification Mission (UNAVEM III) gave way to the UN Observer Mission in Angola (MONUA). During the year nearly 5,000 UN military personnel were withdrawn and about 100 more UN civilian police were deployed. Under MONUA, the Human Rights Unit (see *Amnesty International Report 1997*) with fewer than 20 staff was upgraded to a Human Rights Division with 55 staff. However, no new appointments were made during 1997. The MONUA Human Rights Division submitted 50 cases of human rights abuses which were reported to have occurred since September 1996 to the *ad hoc* group on human rights. This group had been established in December 1996 by the Joint Commission which implemented the peace agreement. The Joint Commission endorsed the group's recommendations. However, the Division did not inform the Angolan public of its assessment of the human rights situation or whether or not the parties to the peace agreement complied with its recommendations.

Progress in the demobilization of troops was slow and thousands of UNITA soldiers deserted the quartering areas. The formation of the *Forças Armadas Angolanas* (FAA), Angolan Armed Forces, ended in July with the incorporation of 10,899 UNITA troops, some 15,400 short of the total originally planned. In October UNITA demobilized 7,311 troops who had not previously been registered. More than 400 UNITA personnel were incorporated into the police force.

The confinement to barracks of the 5,000-strong paramilitary Rapid Intervention Police (PIR) was ended in October.

The extension of state authority to UNITA-controlled areas began in April, but broke down a few weeks later when political tension increased. In August UNITA, under international pressure, agreed to allow the process to resume. UNITA also agreed to provide details of its troop strength, including the previously unregistered diamond-mine police and Jonas Savimbi's bodyguard, and to turn its radio into a non-partisan station. It failed to complete these tasks and in October the UN imposed sanctions to forbid supply flights into UNITA areas and to prevent

UNITA representatives from travelling or operating offices abroad.

The conflict in the former Zaire affected the security situation in Angola. The Angolan Government sent military assistance to the opposition coalition which overthrew the Zairian Government. UNITA troops backed former President Mobutu Sese Seko. In late April UNITA troops who had been based in Zaire and Rwandese refugees, including former soldiers, fled the fighting in Zaire and crossed into Angola. In May heavy fighting broke out in the diamond-mining areas in northeastern Angola between government troops, including 400 PIR from nearby barracks, and UNITA forces. Clashes also occurred in other parts of the country. Both sides reportedly carried out forced conscription. Each accused the other of burning villages and killing unarmed civilians. At the end of the year 1,200,000 Angolans were internally displaced and 240,000 were refugees in neighbouring countries.

There was fighting in Cabinda, an Angolan enclave between the Republic of the Congo and the Democratic Republic of the Congo, formerly Zaire, where government forces faced armed factions of the *Frente da Libertação do Enclave de Cabinda* (FLEC), Cabinda Enclave Liberation Front. In October, thousands of government troops crossed from Cabinda into the Republic of the Congo, where both UNITA and FLEC factions had bases, and contributed to the overthrow of the government there.

The criminal justice system remained ineffective in many areas. The level of corruption and violent crime remained high, and poorly trained and ill-disciplined police were involved in both. Prison conditions were harsh. The Ombudsman's Office, provided for in the Constitution, had not been established and few non-governmental groups were involved in exposing human rights violations.

Roman Catholic priest Konrad Liebscher, who had been given a suspended one-year prison sentence in 1996 for carrying out an unauthorized demonstration (*see Amnesty International Report 1997*), had his conviction annulled in May. The Supreme Court found irregularities in the constitution of the court which tried him. It also determined that the act of driving a car bearing posters protesting against low salaries and other social problems did not constitute a demonstration.

Severe beatings by police were commonplace. Few prosecutions were reported of those responsible for beatings and other ill-treatment, and rape. Sometimes beatings were politically motivated, but most were linked to extortion, corruption and indiscipline within the police forces.

In March a group of men, some in police uniform, stopped a car driven by Miguel Filho, Secretary General of SINPROF, a teachers' union, and beat him. The men had been waiting for him to return from a meal with his guests, Norwegian participants in a trade union training seminar. They then drove off in Miguel Filho's car, taking with them one of the visitors whom they later released in another part of Luanda. Before this incident, Miguel Filho and other SINPROF members had received threats to their physical safety because of their trade union activities.

Military police embarked on what appeared to be an intimidation campaign in Cabinda city in July. They went into schools making students flee in the belief that they were to be forcibly conscripted into the army. Some were arrested and beaten and had to pay bribes to be released. After a subsequent protest demonstration, at least four students were arrested and beaten.

Other cases of ill-treatment by police included those of Inocêncio Victor, a civilian arrested and beaten by military police in January, and Lourenço Domingos dos Santos, a teacher, who was mistakenly arrested in March as an escaped prisoner and beaten. In June police arrested a young woman who had been selling ice near the Cathedral in Luanda. At the First Police Station they beat her for over 30 minutes with a piece of plastic hose-pipe. In October guests who spent three days at a hotel in Lubango heard the screams each day of someone being whipped in the next-door police station. In the same week, in Huambo a motorist saw police stop a passer-by, handcuff him and beat him on the head and shoulders with rifle butts, and in the Ilha area of Luanda, four police beat women market vendors and took their produce.

A commission of inquiry into the deaths of 10 UNITA members detained in Malange in November was seriously flawed. Twenty-three UNITA members had been arrested on suspicion of attempting to occupy the administrative offices in

Kangandala district. They were placed in a cell with 32 other prisoners. A commission of inquiry set up by the Interior Ministry found that the deaths occurred as the result of a fight among the prisoners and not, as had been alleged, as a result of torture or asphyxia. No autopsies were carried out. The inquiry did not conform to international standards of independence and impartiality nor did it follow internationally established methods of operation.

There were dozens of politically motivated killings and killings of suspected criminals by police and soldiers. In only one reported case was the suspected perpetrator arrested.

Many of the killings occurred in mid-1997, when political tension increased throughout the country. Soldiers killed unarmed civilians and burned their villages, particularly in the northeast. UNITA alleged that government troops had killed a number of individuals, including two traditional leaders, Dionisio Cassenha and Chissundaki, who were killed in Chitembo, Bie province, in July.

Three people who were reported to be UNITA supporters were killed and another injured in Huambo between June and August in attacks which appeared to be politically motivated. Detailed information on the killings and the identity of those responsible was not available, but there appeared to be no official investigations into these incidents. A former UNITA soldier who returned to Huambo in May was shot dead at close range several weeks later, as he arrived at his house in the São João area. A man known as Engenheiro Bango was shot and wounded near his home in June or July; he was reportedly subsequently shot dead while in hospital. José Luis Calúa, a taxi driver, was shot dead at close range by people waiting on the road where his passenger had asked him to stop. Another person survived an attempted killing. Virgílio Cavyli, who worked in the administration department of the Agronomic Research Institute, was shot through the jaw as he approached his house.

In Cabinda, suspected FLEC supporters were killed. Bernardo Kebeki was shot dead outside his home in Cabinda city by a man in plain clothes in August. A member of the security police arrested in connection with the death was later released uncharged. Following a FLEC attack in Cacongo district, soldiers reportedly arrested, beat, stabbed and shot dead Luís Nguba and Casimiro Dunge who had returned to the area after a hunting expedition.

Other killings apparently carried out by police included that of Tito Tomé, a market vendor, in Sambizanga, Luanda. He had been giving protection money to a group of men dressed in police uniforms and nylon stocking masks. In October he refused to pay and one night three men in police uniforms came into his bedroom and shot him dead. No investigation of the killing was carried out by police or other authorities.

Those responsible for the killings of Domingos Hungo, Ricardo Melo, and Adão da Silva in 1995 and António Casimiro in 1996 (see *Amnesty International Report 1997*) had not been brought to justice by the end of 1997.

Scores of people were detained by UNITA during the year, according to reports received by the MONUA Human Rights Division. Further details also emerged of prisoners detained by UNITA in previous years, some of whom seemed to have "disappeared". They included Edith Santos, who was held in southeastern Angola until 1992, and João Baptista Sikato, a teacher who was arrested in Andulo in 1996 and accused of being a government supporter. Manuel Pelágio Muhongo, a former student in a Catholic seminary in Huambo, was arrested on his way to visit relatives in Bailundo, a UNITA stronghold, in July 1996. He apparently "disappeared" shortly afterwards. Several people were reportedly beaten by UNITA personnel. They included foreign aid workers, UN personnel and government officials. Deliberate and arbitrary killings attributed to UNITA included 26 people killed in August, reportedly because they had expressed satisfaction at the impending arrival of government administrators in Chicomba, Huila province. Their bodies were discovered in a well in September. In 1997 UNITA reportedly admitted responsibility for the killing near Sanza Pombo, Uige province, in 1994 of more than 50 FAA soldiers they had captured in 1993.

FLEC factions also carried out abuses. These included the abduction of two foreign forestry workers in February by FLEC-*Forças Armadas de Cabinda* (FLEC-FAC), FLEC–Armed Forces of Cabinda, who initially threatened to execute the two men as government spies. They had not been freed by the end of the year.

In a report published in May, *Angola: Reconciliation and human rights – Amnesty International's appeal to the new government*, Amnesty International called for increased safeguards against human rights violations. The organization expressed concern about torture, ill-treatment and killings by police. It took up cases of human rights abuses by UNITA and appealed to FLEC-FAC to release its hostages. It received no replies. In October, two Amnesty International delegates visited Angola to participate in a human rights training seminar for UN civilian police, and to carry out research.

ARGENTINA

A prisoner of conscience remained imprisoned. Reports of torture and ill-treatment of detainees in police stations continued. Human rights defenders and journalists were subjected to death threats. There were reports of killings in circumstances suggesting possible extrajudicial executions.

Strikes and demonstrations against government economic policies took place throughout the year. Some became violent. Dozens of people were arrested and injured and at least one person was killed during clashes in the Federal Capital, Buenos Aires, and several provinces including Buenos Aires, Neuquén and Jujuy.

In November the UN Committee against Torture expressed concern about the increase in the quantity and gravity of abuses by police, which sometimes resulted in serious injuries or death, and at the discrepancy between the legal provisions for the prevention and punishment of torture and reality. The Committee pointed out the apparently recurrent pattern of police obstruction of judicial investigations into complaints of torture and ill-treatment, and the long delays in completing such investigations.

Legal initiatives taken in other countries to establish the fate of "disappeared" nationals in Argentina between 1976 and 1983 continued. The Argentine authorities refused to cooperate with Spanish court proceedings (see *Amnesty International Report 1997*). An investigation to find "disappeared" children was initiated by a federal judge in Buenos Aires. In July the non-governmental human rights organization *Abuelas de Plaza de Mayo*, Grandmothers of Plaza de Mayo, presented to the federal judge a list of 200 children abducted with their parents or born in captivity. A separate list of 40 cases was forwarded by the Under-Secretary of Human Rights. The abduction of children had been excluded from the Full Stop and Due Obedience laws and the subsequent presidential pardons of 1989 and 1990 which precluded investigations into "disappearances".

In October a federal judge accepted a petition submitted by non-governmental human rights organizations calling for an investigation of seven former high-ranking members of the army from past military governments, three government officials from the civilian government and several members of the judiciary, in connection with the fate of thousands of victims of past "disappearances".

One prisoner of conscience was held throughout the year. Fray Antonio Puigjane, a Franciscan friar, was sentenced to 20 years' imprisonment in 1989 (see *Amnesty International Report 1997*). In December the Inter-American Commission on Human Rights (IACHR) reported on the cases of members of the *Movimiento Todos por la Patria* (MTP), All for the Fatherland Movement (see *Amnesty International Reports 1990* to *1993*). The IACHR concluded that Argentina had violated the right to life of nine MTP members and the right to humane treatment of another 20, including Fray Antonio Puigjane. The IACHR recommended an independent complete and impartial investigation into events in January 1989, in order to identify and punish those responsible for the violations. It also recommended that those tried under Law 23.077 be given the right to appeal and to compensation.

Reports of torture and ill-treatment by police continued. Many of the victims were detainees held in police stations, often under provincial police by-laws and the Code of Misdemeanours. For example, in January Gabriel Gutiérrez was arrested by members of the 4th police station of Florencio Varela, Buenos Aires Province, accused of infringing police by-laws. He died four hours later, reportedly as a result of a severe beating. The case against the police accused of responsibility for his death was dismissed by the relevant judge.

Members of sexual minorities were reportedly ill-treated or tortured by police in Buenos Aires and the provincial cities of Rosario and Mendoza. There appeared to be a pattern of such incidents, although in most cases the names of victims were withheld because of fears for their safety. In February Adriana Cortés, a transsexual woman, was arrested in Mendoza, Mendoza Province, and taken to a police station. She was reportedly induced to have sex with a police officer in exchange for pain relief medication. After her release she filed a complaint and the police officer was transferred to another police station, but no further action was apparently taken.

Human rights defenders and journalists were subjected to attacks, harassment and death threats. In May the premises of the *Central de Trabajadores Argentinos*, Cutral-Co Argentine Workers' Centre, in Neuquén Province, where the local Human Rights Commission has its offices, were attacked with incendiary devices. The Human Rights Commission had called for an investigation into the killing of Teresa Rodríguez (see below).

At least 30 journalists were subjected to attacks, repeated death threats and intimidation. In several cases information received indicated the possible involvement or acquiescence of the security forces. In January press photographer José Luis Cabezas was killed in Pinamar, Buenos Aires Province; the investigation into his death was still pending at the end of the year. In February Santo Biasatti, a radio and television journalist, received anonymous death threats warning that he would suffer the same fate as José Luis Cabezas and that members of the provincial police would abduct him. Also in February Daniel Stragá, a journalist and human rights lawyer at the non-governmental organization *Coordinadora Contra la Represión Policial e Institucional* (CORREPI), Association against Police and Institutional Repression, received an anonymous telephone call threatening his life (see *Amnesty International Report 1996*). In June, three journalists were subjected to anonymous death threats and the sister of one of them, María José Fernández Llorente, was attacked in Palermo, a Buenos Aires neighbourhood, by three men who cut her hand with a knife. In each incident, the death of José Luis Cabezas was referred to. In most cases, police protection was granted but there was no progress in establishing who was responsible for the threats.

There were reports of killings in circumstances suggesting possible extrajudicial executions. CORREPI recorded 14 cases of killings known as "*gatillo fácil*" ("trigger-happy") during the year (see *Amnesty International Report 1996*). For example, in July a police officer killed a 15-year-old youth and wounded another in Santiago del Estero, Santiago del Estero Province, allegedly because they had stolen a poster from a shop. The police officer was charged with homicide and grievous bodily harm.

At least one person was killed and many injured in disputed circumstances during countrywide demonstrations. In April Teresa Rodríguez, a mother of three, was shot dead in the town of Cutral-Co, Neuquén Province, during clashes between demonstrators and members of the police and the gendarmerie. In May more than 80 people, including several children, were reportedly injured with rubber bullets and as a result of beatings by the gendarmerie during demonstrations staged by sugar workers in the locality of Libertador General San Martín, Jujuy Province.

Throughout the year Amnesty International expressed concern to the government about attacks and threats against journalists and human rights defenders and called for prompt, thorough and conclusive investigations. In May Amnesty International wrote to President Carlos

Saúl Menem, expressing concern at the killing of Teresa Rodríguez and the incidents in Jujuy and La Plata. No substantive response was received by the end of the year.

In November Amnesty International submitted its concerns about the use of torture and ill-treatment in Argentina to the UN Committee against Torture.

Also in November Amnesty International publicly called on the Argentine authorities to cooperate with proceedings initiated by Spanish courts into "disappearances" under past military governments of Spanish nationals and people of Spanish descent.

ARMENIA

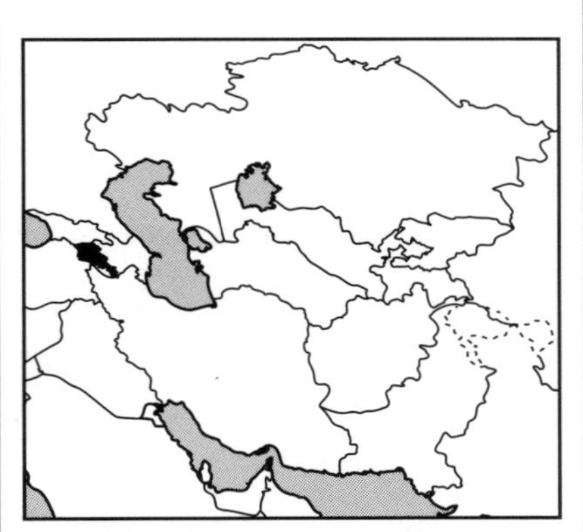

At least five men were reportedly jailed for refusing on grounds of conscience to perform compulsory military service. Over 40 political prisoners faced criminal proceedings that appeared to fall short of international fair trial standards. Allegations of torture and ill-treatment in detention continued. At least three men were sentenced to death. No executions took place.

Tension with neighbouring Azerbaijan flared up in April after a number of cross-border incidents in which soldiers from both sides were reported killed. President Levon Ter-Petrosyan and his Azerbaijani counterpart both reaffirmed their commitment to a cease-fire.

In April parliament passed in its first reading a new draft criminal code which abolished the death penalty for all crimes, whether in time of peace or war, and replaced this punishment with a maximum sentence of life imprisonment. However, the new code had not become law by the end of the year.

Military service remained compulsory for men aged between 18 and 27, and the lack of any civilian alternative placed conscientious objectors under threat of imprisonment. At least five men were imprisoned for refusing conscription on grounds of conscience. John Martirosyan, a Jehovah's Witness, submitted a statement in March explaining his religious objection to military service. In June his father went to the local enlistment office in Yerevan, the capital, to resubmit this statement, and was reportedly detained there illegally for a day in an attempt to force his son to present himself for military service. In September John Martirosyan was sentenced to 18 months' imprisonment for "evading regular call-up to active military service" under Article 75 of the Criminal Code.

Allegations continued that the trial of a senior member of the opposition Armenian Revolutionary Federation, Vahan Ovanessian, together with 30 others accused of attempting an armed coup (see *Amnesty International Report 1997*), fell short of international fair trial standards. Several witnesses testified, as many defendants had earlier, that they had been beaten or that their families had been threatened in order to coerce them into giving evidence against the accused. For example, Aghavni Karapetian, wife of defendant Gnel Ovanessian, testified in February that Interior Ministry employees from the Mashtots district of Yerevan had beaten her severely and that she subsequently miscarried. She said that her two sisters and disabled brother were also beaten. The trial ended in December: 28 defendants were convicted, including Tigran Avetissian, who was sentenced to death.

Similar allegations of ill-treatment were also made in a series of trials linked with events in September 1996, when opposition protests over disputed presidential elections turned violent. Twelve people stood trial in six separate hearings, and at least eight claimed that they had been beaten or threatened in order to extract confessions. At the first trial which began in February before the Supreme Court, for example, Abet Petrosian withdrew the testimony he had given in pre-trial detention, claiming that he had been beaten and that threats had been made against his wife and mother to force a confession. His four fellow defendants made similar allegations, although these were reportedly not investigated by the court as the judge considered there was insufficient proof (Abet Petrosian said that he was unwilling to name those involved in his ill-treatment for fear of reprisals against his family). The defendants were convicted but, like others subsequently sentenced in the series of trials, were given suspended sentences or released under an amnesty.

There were also allegations of torture and ill-treatment of criminal suspects. Manvel Virabyan, aged 17, was detained in April at his home in Yerevan by police investigating a robbery. He died in custody several days later, allegedly as a result of severe beatings and ill-treatment. His body was reportedly unrecognizable to his family. His mother also alleged that she dropped her initial protests when officials threatened another son.

At least three men were sentenced to death during the year, all for premeditated, aggravated murder: Tigran Avetissian (see above), and Arakel Gabrielian and Artur Kirakossian, who were convicted in October. At least one man had his sentence reduced on appeal. Armen Grigorian, one of three men sentenced to death after a political trial in 1996 (see *Amnesty International Report 1997*) had his sentence reduced to 15 years' imprisonment by the Supreme Court in July. No presidential commutations were reported, and by the end of the year there were at least 25 men on death row. No executions took place, as in previous years.

Amnesty International urged the authorities to release immediately and unconditionally all those imprisoned solely for refusing military service on grounds of conscience, and to enact legislation creating an alternative civilian service of non-punitive length together with a fair procedure in law for implementing it.

Amnesty International called for a judicial review of all political cases in which fair trial standards had allegedly not been met, and urged that all reports of ill-treatment be investigated impartially and comprehensively, with the results made public and those responsible brought to justice. Amnesty International also sought information on what steps had been taken to implement the recommendations made by the UN Committee against Torture in 1996 (see *Amnesty International Report 1997*). Commenting on allegations of ill-treatment, the new Procurator General told Amnesty International in November that he was constantly implementing measures to deal with the issue of torture, including by visiting places of detention; by setting up a confidential telephone line at the Armenian procuracy for those who wish to report abuses; and by issuing instructions to procuracy offices throughout the country to conduct objective, comprehensive criminal investigations of human rights abuses within strict time limits. With regard to specific allegations raised in political trials (see above), he stated that all the defendants had access to lawyers and that none had lodged complaints about their treatment at the time it was alleged to have happened.

The organization consistently urged that the death penalty be abolished and that all pending death sentences be commuted.

AUSTRALIA

The government moved to limit the effect of international human rights treaties. The UN Human Rights Committee found that Australia's policy of mandatory detention of asylum-seekers breached its obligations under international law. Ill-treatment by police was reported. An alarming rate of deaths in custody, particularly of Aboriginal people, raised concerns about possible ill-treatment.

Human rights issues were a major focus of public debate throughout the year. International human rights treaties, minority rights and the national human rights commission were attacked by politicians and influential individuals. While supporting the commission's international role, the government took steps to restrict its ability to fulfil its domestic functions, including a 43 per cent budget cut and plans for sweeping changes to its structure.

The Queensland State Government introduced legislation in March to ensure that all forms of torture were properly outlawed after a court found that no appropriate punishment existed for acts of torture which cause no bodily injury.

In April the Tasmania State Parliament repealed sections of the Criminal Code which allowed for up to 21 years' imprisonment for private homosexual acts between consenting male adults. The law had allowed for the imprisonment of prisoners of conscience (see *Amnesty International Reports 1993* to *1997*).

Electoral legislation which had led to the imprisonment of Albert Langer, a prisoner of conscience, during the 1996 federal elections remained in place (see *Amnesty International Report 1997*).

In February Australia's refusal to accept a binding clause on respect for "basic human rights as proclaimed in the Universal Declaration of Human Rights" caused the breakdown of negotiations with the European Union on a "Framework Agreement" (see *Amnesty International Report 1997*). Instead, both parties signed a non-binding political declaration affirming their commitment to human rights.

Draft legislation introduced in June would, if enacted, allow officials to disregard human rights treaties without fear of legal consequences. The Administrative Decisions (Effect of International Instruments) Bill 1997, first proposed in 1995, aimed to prevent a domestic challenge to an administrative decision on the basis that it violated a human rights treaty by which Australia was bound. The government argued that an Australian High Court decision in 1995 (known as the "Teoh decision") interfered with the proper role of Parliament in implementing treaties. The High Court had found a "legitimate expectation" that human rights treaties ratified by Australia should be considered by officials, even when they were not incorporated into local law. A formal government statement in February sought to invalidate the High Court's decision, and a final vote on the draft law was due in 1998.

The UN Committee on the Rights of the Child reviewed Australia's first report under the Convention on the Rights of the Child. The Committee expressed as its principal concern that in Australia the Convention does not give rise to legitimate expectations that administrative decisions conform with its provisions and that citizens have no right to bring a complaint in local courts on the basis of the Convention. The Committee recommended law reform initiatives to benefit children, and expressed concern about "the unjustified, disproportionately high percentage of Aboriginal children in the juvenile justice system" and the detention of child asylum-seekers.

People arriving in Australia without proper documentation, including those seeking asylum, continued to face mandatory detention while their claim was assessed, in clear violation of international human rights standards. Despite public perceptions, fuelled by politicians, that thousands of refugees were trying to enter Australia illegally, only 346 "boat people" arrived in Australia during the year, of whom 267 were returned, mostly within weeks.

In April the UN Human Rights Committee stated that Australia had breached the International Covenant on Civil and Political Rights by arbitrarily detaining a Cambodian asylum-seeker. He was detained for more than four years while pursuing his asylum claim and was denied the right to have his detention reviewed in court. In October the Australian Senate passed a resolution asking the government to respond to the Committee, to report on possible refugee policy changes to meet international human rights standards and to examine alternatives to the mandatory detention of asylum-seekers. In December the government rejected the Committee's views in a formal response and argued that such detention is not arbitrary because it is "lawful" under the Migration Act. In July, in an attempt to deter asylum-seekers from appealing against unsuccessful claims, the government introduced a fee of A$1,000 (US$740) for applicants whose claims were rejected both by immigration officials and the Refugee Review Tribunal.

There were reports that most "boat people" in the main immigration detention centre at Port Hedland, some 4,000 kilometres from Sydney, were initially placed in incommunicado detention. They were not informed of their right to claim asylum, to see a lawyer or to contact the Australian human rights commission.

In March police officers in Ipswich, Queensland, assisted by visiting US military police, were filmed by security video camera as they punched and kicked several Aborigines who were being held by other officers. Eye-witnesses alleged that police and security guards initially refused to call an ambulance for an unconscious man who had convulsions after an officer had flung him violently to the ground, handcuffed him and left him lying on the footpath.

In May the Human Rights and Equal Opportunity Commission reported on its national inquiry into the forced removal, under past government policies effective up to 1970, of tens of thousands of Aboriginal children from their families solely because of their race. The Commission found the policies had been "genocidal" and reported on the continuing effects of human rights abuses suffered by victims, including ill-treatment and restrictions on freedom of movement. The report stressed the link between the effects of the policies and current high rates of Aboriginal criminalization and deaths in custody. The government's response in December announced welfare and family reunion measures, but failed to comment on the Commission's findings that the policies had allowed for genocide, systematic racial discrimination and physical and sexual abuse of children.

At least 103 people died in custody or during police attempts to detain them, some of them in circumstances raising concern about lack of proper care amounting to ill-treatment. Of these at least 14 were Aborigines. Aborigines form two per cent of the population. In July ministers discussed the continuing high incidence of Aboriginal deaths in custody at a national summit meeting. Participants agreed on the need for action to address the problem, but failed to set binding targets. The Australian Institute of Criminology reported in July that the combined rate of deaths in custody of Aboriginal and non-Aboriginal people had increased to the highest level ever recorded.

In October a coroner found that conditions in a remote police cell on Bathurst Island "directly contributed" to the death of an Aboriginal man who was found hanging in the cell in May 1996. The coroner found that the filthy, unlit cell, in which points from which to hang oneself were easily accessible, "fell well short of and did not comply with the standards recommended by the Royal Commission into Aboriginal Deaths in Custody report" (see *Amnesty International Reports 1992* and *1993*).

There were new developments in cases from previous years. In September the Victoria state Supreme Court overruled a 1996 inquest finding that Colleen Richman, a mentally disturbed Aboriginal woman shot by police in September 1994, had caused her own death. A police officer had repeatedly fired at her after she did not respond to calls to put down a hatchet. Although three out of four bullets hit her in the back, the coroner had accepted police claims that they had shot her in self-defence.

In September the newly formed Anti-Corruption Commission in Western Australia decided to reinvestigate the death of Stephen Wardle, who died in police custody in February 1988 (see *Amnesty International Reports 1996* and *1997*).

In April Amnesty International published a report on police ill-treatment in Ipswich (see above), *Australia: Police brutality against Queensland Aborigines*. The organization also wrote to the government of Queensland, expressing concern that excessive force had been used in at least three of seven arrests during the incident. In his response, the Queensland Police Minister initially promised a "full response in due course", but in a second letter he declined to comment because of ongoing legal proceedings and a Criminal Justice Commission investigation into the incident. The Commission had not completed its inquiry by the end of the year.

Amnesty International issued a report in June, *Australia: Deaths in custody – how many more?* expressing concern about deficiencies in the prison and police custody system and highlighting the risk of death for Aborigines in prisons. In response, the government described the report as an important basis for discussion but did not comment on its contents.

In August Amnesty International welcomed proposals on human rights promotion in Australia's first White Paper on foreign policy, but criticized the lack of commitment to international human rights treaties.

In October the Foreign Minister dismissed an Amnesty International report, *Ethnicity and nationality: refugees in Asia*, mainly because of its comments on Australia's refusal to accept refugees from East Timor. The Minister's condemnation of Amnesty International prompted a Senate resolution which commended Amnesty International for its work and called on the Minister to address human rights violations in East Timor.

In December Amnesty International wrote to the Northern Territory authorities about a reported tacit acceptance by the government of cruel and inhuman punishment of Aboriginal people by other Aborigines under customary law.

AUSTRIA

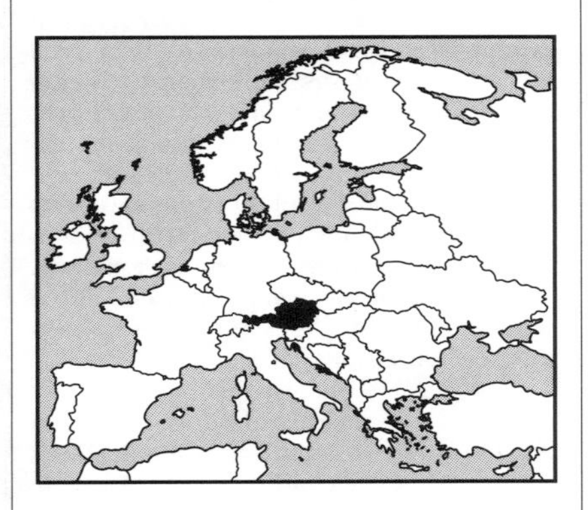

There were further allegations of ill-treatment of detainees by police officers.

In January it was alleged that Ewald Stattmann had been ill-treated the previous month, following his arrest in the town of Villach in southern Austria. According to reports, witnesses saw two officers beat Ewald Stattmann with rubber truncheons when they arrested him, and kick him while he was on the ground. Police sources were quoted as saying that Ewald Stattmann had attacked the arresting officers and had banged his head on the ground, and later against a wall at Villach police station, in an attempt to injure himself. Several hours after his arrest Ewald Stattmann was found unconscious in a cell at the station and rushed to hospital, where he underwent emergency surgery. His injuries included a fractured skull, cranio-cerebral trauma, a cerebral haemorrhage and multiple bruising.

In March Kureng Akuei Pac, a Sudanese diplomat, alleged that he had been ill-treated by police officers at a Vienna police station following an identity check in the centre of the city. According to the diplomat, after arriving at the station, officers pulled him by his tie into an interview room, punching him on the chin as they went. They then proceeded to strip him of his coat, tie, shirt and shoes and, prior to conducting a body search, asked him to remove his trousers. When he was refused permission to telephone the Sudanese Embassy from the station, Kureng Akuei Pac left the station to find a public telephone. He alleged that several officers went after him and pulled him back inside the station, hitting him several times on the back and upper arms. According to medical evidence Kureng Akuei Pac suffered bruising of the right shoulder and bruising and laceration of the lower lip.

In January a Vienna court found Violetta Jevremoviç guilty of attempting to resist state authority and of assaulting an officer (see *Amnesty International Report 1997*). She was sentenced to two months' imprisonment, suspended for three years. Her conviction for assault was overturned on appeal and referred back to the court of first instance.

In February the Austrian authorities informed Amnesty International that investigators had "not been able to find any objective evidence of criminal behaviour" by the officers alleged to have ill-treated Sabine Geisberger in November 1995 (see *Amnesty International Report 1997*). Sabine Geisberger had alleged that a Vienna police officer dragged her by the hair into the bedroom of her apartment and threw her into the corner of the room, where he repeatedly kicked her in the genitals. An examination performed the next day by a doctor from the gynaecological department of Klagenfurt Hospital had reported bruising to the rim of the pelvis, left thigh, and genitals.

In March Peter Zwiauer was acquitted by Schwechat District Court of charges of failing to comply with a call-up order, an offence which carries a penalty of up to one year's imprisonment (see *Amnesty*

International Report 1997). Peter Zwiauer had refused to report for military duty in May 1996 after his application to perform alternative service had been rejected on the grounds that it had not been submitted within the required time period. In acquitting him of the charges, pending appeal, Schwechat District Court ruled that "the accused could not be reproached for not knowing about the particular deadline... especially since the authorities made no particular efforts to inform the public about the regulation". Amnesty International had previously informed the Austrian authorities that if Peter Zwiauer was imprisoned as a result of his refusal on grounds of conscience to perform military service, the organization would consider him to be a prisoner of conscience and would call for his immediate and unconditional release.

In February Amnesty International called upon the authorities to carry out a prompt and impartial investigation into the alleged ill-treatment of Ewald Stattmann and urged that investigators pay special heed to the principles established in international human rights instruments regarding the use of force by law enforcement officials, and the medical care and supervision of detainees. In November the organization was informed that, according to the results of preliminary police inquiries, there was "no substantiated suspicion of police involvement" in the alleged ill-treatment of Ewald Stattmann.

In July Amnesty International asked the authorities for details of the reasoning behind the decision to discontinue the investigation into the alleged ill-treatment of Sabine Geisberger. The organization also expressed concern that criminal proceedings against Violetta Jevremoviç appeared to have been conducted with urgency while the investigation into her complaint of ill-treatment had still not been concluded more than a year after it had been submitted. Finally, Amnesty International called for a prompt and impartial investigation into the alleged ill-treatment of Kureng Akuei Pac. Amnesty International had not received any substantive reply to its inquiries by the end of the year.

In February Amnesty International published a report, *Austria: Conscientious objection to military service – a summary of current concerns.*

AZERBAIJAN

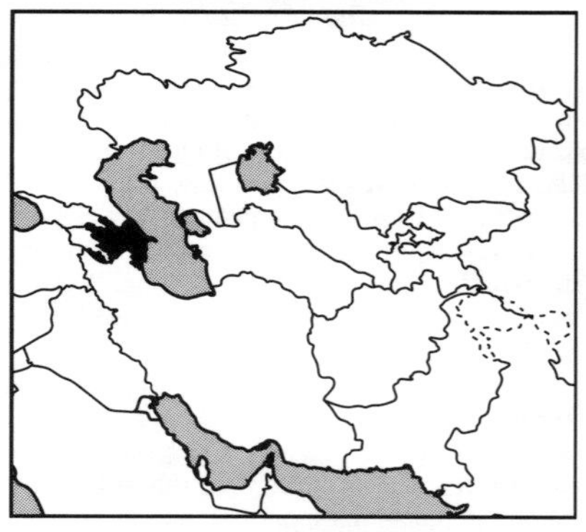

Around 20 possible prisoners of conscience were reportedly held solely on grounds of their ethnic origin in connection with the Karabakh conflict; about half were released in prisoner exchanges in the first six months of the year. Several groups of political prisoners were convicted in proceedings that reportedly fell short of international fair trial standards, mainly because testimony allegedly extracted under duress was allowed into evidence. There were numerous reports of torture and ill-treatment in detention. At least 16 death sentences were passed. No commutations were reported, but a moratorium on executions was announced officially.

President Heydar Aliyev met his Armenian counterpart in April as efforts to resolve the situation in the disputed Karabakh region continued (see *Amnesty International Report 1997*). In April and May more than 30 detainees held by Azerbaijan, Armenia and the self-proclaimed Nagorno-Karabakh Republic were released to mark the third anniversary of a cease-fire in the region.

In September the Speaker of Parliament announced that a moratorium on executions, in place since 1993, would be given legal force and would continue until the year 2010.

Among the detainees released by Azerbaijan in the prisoner exchanges of April and May were seven ethnic Armenians reportedly held as hostages on grounds of their ethnic origin, rather than on the basis of criminal charges. They included two women, Larissa Kirakosian and Irina

Kachaturian, and 15-year-old Armen Nersisian, detained the previous year (see *Amnesty International Report 1997*). All those released were said to be civilians, with no connection to the Karabakh conflict: Larissa Kirakosian, for example, alleged that she had been detained originally in Turkey while a tourist there, and subsequently handed over to Azerbaijan.

In the past, the Azerbaijani authorities have stated that ethnic Armenians suspected of, for example, complicity in terrorist actions have been taken to a special holding centre in the town of Gobustan and detained while their identity and reasons for travelling in Azerbaijan were confirmed. However, there were further reports of people continuing to be detained although no evidence of criminal activity had been found and no criminal charges were laid against them. For example, 18-year-old Artur Papayan was said to have been seized by Azerbaijanis in January while walking in Armenia's border district of Taushsky, and taken to Gobustan.

Several groups of political prisoners were convicted in proceedings that reportedly fell short of international fair trial standards, mainly because testimony allegedly extracted under duress was admitted as evidence. For example, at a trial of 37 members of the special police unit known as OPON, which ended in January, 24 of the defendants alleged that they had been subjected to physical or mental duress during the investigation period in order to extract testimony implicating them in a failed coup. Murshud Mahmudov stated that electric shocks had been applied to his ears. Abulfat Kerimov testified that he had been hung upside-down and beaten. A medical examination carried out at the request of defence lawyers showed that at least three of the defendants had sustained broken ribs, but it was not possible to establish the precise time or cause of the injuries. All the defendants were subsequently sentenced to long periods of imprisonment.

Numerous other allegations of torture and ill-treatment in pre-trial detention and police custody continued to be received; at least one person was said to have died as a result of such treatment. Samir Zulfugarov died in Semashko hospital in July, three days after his arrest on a charge of possessing drugs. The head of the anti-drug division at the Yasamalsky District Police Department had reportedly contacted the detainee's father to demand money for his release, and the father saw his injured son in a police cell. He had allegedly been severely beaten by police. A criminal case was instituted against one police officer but the outcome was not known at the end of the year.

There were proceedings in some other cases of alleged ill-treatment, but according to unofficial sources these rarely resulted in prosecution or imprisonment. In November 1996, for example, a criminal case was opened into the beating of journalist Taptig Farhadoglu, who reported that a man he subsequently recognized as a senior police officer had been among a group of men who beat him on the street in the capital city, Baku, that month. The case was reportedly closed in January by the Baku city procurator for lack of evidence, but reopened in April following wide protests. No further developments had been reported by the end of the year.

Two other journalists reportedly beaten by police officers in September also alleged that officials were reluctant to investigate. Zakir Jabbarly and Dilgram Bairamov were said to have been assaulted by three employees and the head of the Passport Department of Narimov District Police Station in Baku where they had gone to seek further information on the alleged illegal registration of residents at a hostel. Zakir Jabbarly was hospitalized; he reportedly lost consciousness and suffered from severe headaches and blood in his urine as a result of the attack. Dilgram Bairamov claimed that the district deputy procurator initially refused to open an investigation into the alleged beating.

At least 16 death sentences were reported to have been passed during the year, although the actual total was believed to be much higher. Among those sentenced to death was Karen Gevorkian, an ethnic Armenian, who was convicted in April of murder, espionage and sabotage by the Military Collegium of the Supreme Court. Karen Gevorkian was pardoned and released in the May prisoner exchange.

No commutations of death sentences were reported, and no executions took place. Over 100 men were believed to be on death row at the end of the year.

Amnesty International sought further information on possible prisoners of conscience, and urged the release of anyone held without charge solely as a hostage, or on grounds of their ethnic origin.

Amnesty International called for a judicial review of all political cases in which fair trial standards had allegedly not been met, and urged that all allegations of ill-treatment and torture by law-enforcement officials be investigated promptly and impartially, with the findings made public and any perpetrators brought to justice.

The organization welcomed the official moratorium on executions, urging that all pending death sentences be commuted and further steps be taken to abolish the death penalty completely.

BAHAMAS

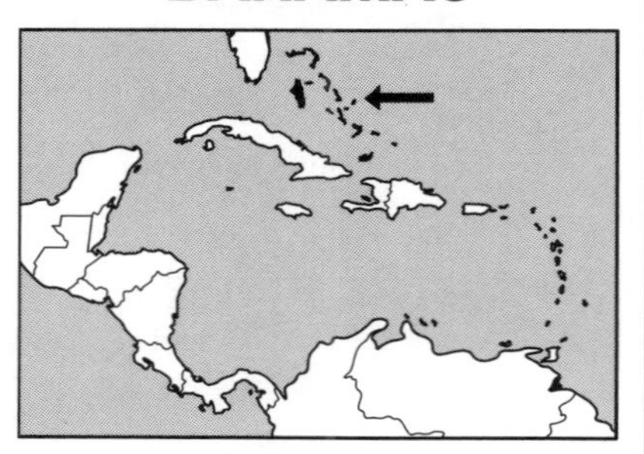

About 40 people remained on death row, including three who were sentenced to death during the year, but there were no executions. At least one person was sentenced to corporal punishment.

In elections in March, the Free National Movement party won 34 of the 40 seats in the House of Assembly. Hubert Alexander Ingraham remained as Prime Minister. Sir Lynden Pindling, who served as Prime Minister for 25 years following independence, stepped down as leader of the main opposition party, the Progressive Liberal Party.

In December the Judicial Committee of the Privy Council (JCPC) in the United Kingdom, the final court of appeal for the Bahamas, revised its 1996 ruling that executing a prisoner who had spent three and a half years or more under sentence of death would violate the constitutional prohibition against inhuman or degrading punishment (see *Amnesty International Report 1997*). The JCPC's ruling in December concluded that the guideline period should be extended to five years, in view of the Bahamas Government's undertaking to respect individuals' rights to petition the Inter-American Commission on Human Rights.

About 40 people remained under sentence of death. They included three men sentenced to death during the year. At least three men who had been imprisoned on death row for more than five years had their sentences commuted.

No executions took place during the year. Although dates were set for the execution of four prisoners – John Higgs, Brian Schroeder, Jeronimo Bowleg and Omar Hall – they received stays of execution.

Following a trial at which he did not have a defence lawyer, Cecil Musgrove was sentenced in May to six lashes of the cane and 10 years' imprisonment with hard labour. Corporal punishment was reinstated in the Bahamas in 1991 as a lawful punishment for males convicted of certain offences.

Amnesty International wrote to the authorities in May and October, expressing concern about the sentence of caning imposed on Cecil Musgrove.

Amnesty International urged the authorities not to execute John Higgs, Brian Schroeder, Jeronimo Bowleg and Omar Hall. In November Amnesty International urged the government to commute all death sentences, including those of prisoners who had spent three and a half years or more on death row. Amnesty International asked to be informed of any measures taken or contemplated to abolish the death penalty or restrict its scope, such as legislation to provide alternative penalties for murder.

BAHRAIN

Several hundred people were reportedly arrested during the year in connection with anti-government demonstrations. The vast majority of those arrested were Shi'a Muslims, among them prisoners of conscience, who were held for short periods and then released without charge. Eight religious and political leaders, all prisoners of conscience, remained held without charge or trial throughout the year. At least 36 political prisoners were

convicted and sentenced to prison terms by the State Security Court following unfair trials. Torture and ill-treatment of detainees continued to be reported and two detainees died in circumstances suggesting that torture or medical neglect may have contributed to their deaths. Three people sentenced to death in 1996 remained under sentence of death. Several Bahraini nationals were banned from returning to the country.

Widespread anti-government protests, which erupted in December 1994, continued during the year (see *Amnesty International Reports 1995* to *1997*). As in previous years, protesters demanded the reinstatement of the National Assembly, which was dissolved by the Amir, Shaikh 'Issa bin Salman Al Khalifa, in 1975; the restoration of the country's 1973 constitution; and the release of political prisoners. The authorities responded with mass arrests of protesters and other suspected government opponents, especially in the Shi'a Muslim districts of Jidd Hafs, Sitra and al-Sanabis. Several arson attacks targeted restaurants, hotels and shops resulting in the deaths of seven foreign nationals. Among them were four Indian nationals, including two children, who died in June when a shop was set ablaze in al-Manama.

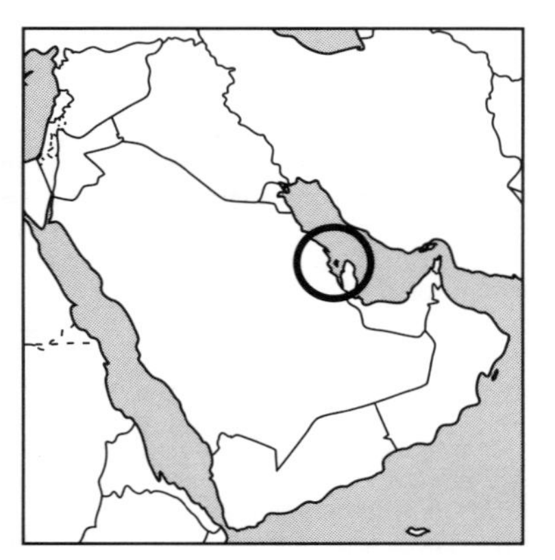

In August the UN Sub-Commission on Prevention of Discrimination and Protection of Minorities adopted a resolution and expressed its "deep concern about the alleged gross and systematic violations of human rights in Bahrain". It urged the government to comply with international human rights standards.

Several hundred people, mostly Shi'a Muslims, were reportedly arrested during the year in connection with anti-government protests. Most of them were detained for short periods and then released without charge. However, over a thousand detainees, including prisoners of conscience, were believed to remain held without charge or trial at the end of the year. Most were administratively detained under a state security law which permits the Minister of the Interior to detain individuals without charge or trial for up to three years. They included Shaikh 'Abd al-Amir al-Jamri and 'Abd al-Wahab Hussain 'Ali, who, along with six other prominent Shi'a Muslim religious and political leaders, were arrested in 1996 (see *Amnesty International Report 1997*). All eight were prisoners of conscience.

In February 'Ali Hassan Yusuf, a well-known Shi'a Muslim writer and poet, was arrested at his home in Jidd Hafs; he was a prisoner of conscience. His arrest and simultaneous dismissal from his job at the Ministry of Information were believed to be connected with the publication of a book of his poems entitled *Isharat* (Symbols), which was reportedly banned by the authorities for indirectly criticizing the government. He was released in April without charge or trial.

In March Sayyid Jalal Sayyid 'Alawi Sayyid Sharaf was arrested at his home in al-Duraz, reportedly on suspicion of transmitting information about the internal situation in Bahrain to persons abroad. He was believed to be held incommunicado in the al-Qal'a compound in al-Manama, where he was reportedly tortured during interrogation. By the end of the year, Sayyid Jalal Sayyid 'Alawi Sayyid Sharaf was said to be still held without charge or trial in al-Muharraq; he was reportedly allowed family visits.

A number of women were also arrested during the year in connection with the political unrest. In March four young women – Ahlam al-Sayyid Mahdi Hassan al-Sitri, Amal Ahmad Rabi', Maryam Ahmad 'Ali Bilway and Laila 'Abd al-Nabi Rabi' – were among a number of people arrested in the village of Sitra after participating in a non-violent demonstration held in commemoration of 'Issa Ahmad Qambar, who was executed in 1996 (see *Amnesty International Report 1997*). The four women, all prisoners of conscience, were released without charge or trial after having reportedly been held incommunicado for over two weeks at a police station in Madinat 'Issa. Scores of minors and children were arrested, the majority during anti-government demonstrations.

In March trials began before the State Security Court of 81 defendants on charges including involvement in an alleged Iranian-backed coup to overthrow the government, membership of a prohibited organization and illegal possession of firearms. The trials, which were held *in camera*, were manifestly unfair. Twenty-two of the defendants were tried *in absentia*. Thirty-six were convicted and sentenced to prison terms ranging from three to 15 years. They included Jassim Hassan Mansur al-Khayyat and 'Ali Kadhem 'Abd 'Ali al-Mutaqawwi, who were sentenced to 12 and 15 years' imprisonment, respectively, for their alleged involvement in a conspiracy with a foreign state to carry out acts hostile to Bahrain; and Ja'far Hassan Sahwan and Ghazi Radhi al-'Abed, who had been forcibly returned to Bahrain from the United Arab Emirates in 1996 (see *Amnesty International Report 1997*), and who were each sentenced to five years' imprisonment. The remaining 23 were acquitted. Most of the defendants had been arrested in early 1996 (see *Amnesty International Report 1997*), and had been denied access to relatives and defence lawyers until the start of their trials. Some of them were convicted on the basis of uncorroborated confessions which had reportedly been extracted as a result of torture.

There were continuing reports of systematic torture and ill-treatment of detainees arrested in connection with the political unrest, especially during the initial period of interrogation in the custody of police or security personnel when torture was commonly used to extract information from detainees. Methods of torture reportedly included severe and sustained beatings, suspension by the limbs, and enforced standing or sleep deprivation for prolonged periods. Two detainees died in circumstances suggesting that torture or medical neglect may have contributed to their deaths. In June 'Abd al-Zahra' Ibrahim 'Abdullah was among a group of demonstrators arrested in al-Sanabis. He was reportedly subjected to severe beatings following his arrest and held incommunicado in al-Qal'a Prison. A few days later, he was transferred to al-Salmaniya Hospital in al-Manama where he died. His body was later handed over to his family for burial. A spokesman for the Ministry of the Interior reportedly announced that 'Abd al-Zahra' Ibrahim 'Abdullah died as a result of a "blood disorder" following his release. It was reported, however, that his body bore visible marks of severe beating.

In the same month, Shaikh 'Ali Mirza al-Nakkas, a blind Shi'a Muslim cleric from Bilad al-Qadim, died in custody in al-Qal'a Prison, where he had been held incommunicado since his arrest in April, on charges of incitement against the government. His body was reportedly buried by the security forces on the same day. A spokesman for the Minister of the Interior was reported to have attributed the death of Shaikh 'Ali Mirza al-Nakkas to respiratory problems. However, there were reports suggesting that medical neglect may have contributed to his death. No official investigations into these deaths in custody or into reports of torture or ill-treatment of other detainees were known to have been carried out.

Three prisoners remained under death sentence at the end of the year. 'Ali Ahmad 'Abdullah al-'Usfur, Yusuf Hussain 'Abd al-Baqi and Ahmad Khalil Ibrahim al-Kattab were sentenced to death after unfair trials before the State Security Court in July 1996 on charges of carrying out a fire-bomb attack on a restaurant in Sitra, which resulted in the death of seven Bangladeshi nationals (see *Amnesty International Report 1997*). At the end of the year their death sentences were still pending ratification by the Amir.

Several Bahraini nationals who had spent some time abroad were forcibly exiled after attempting to return to the country. In September, for example, a Shi'a Muslim family of five was reportedly denied entry to Bahrain on their return from Iran, where they had lived since 1985. The family – 77-year-old Hajji 'Abd al-Hassan al-Seru and his four children, Baqir, Muhammad Jawad, 'Abd al-Hussain and Khadija – were reportedly held for five days at the airport where they were interrogated by security officials, had their family passport renewed and were then forcibly exiled to the United Arab Emirates.

During the year, Amnesty International repeatedly called on the government to release prisoners of conscience and carry out independent investigations into reports of torture and ill-treatment. It appealed for the commutation of the outstanding death sentences passed after unfair trials in 1996 and urged the government to halt unfair trials before the State Security Court and conduct a review of legislation governing this court in the light of international standards. The government responded by rejecting Amnesty International's findings and failed to address the organization's concerns.

In April Amnesty International submitted information about its continuing concerns in Bahrain for UN review under a procedure established by Economic and Social Council Resolutions 728F/1503 for confidential consideration of communications about human rights violations.

BANGLADESH

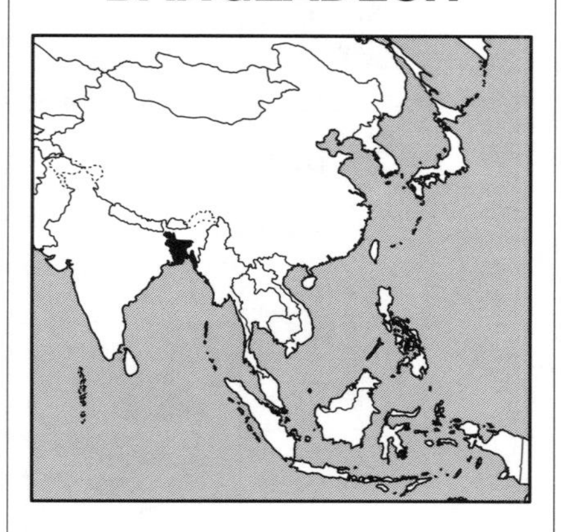

Several prisoners of conscience were among scores of political activists detained without charge or trial under the Special Powers Act (SPA). Police ill-treated demonstrators. Torture, including rape, was widespread and reportedly led to at least two deaths in custody. At least 33 people were sentenced to death and at least two were executed. Around 400 Rohingya refugees were forcibly repatriated to Myanmar from camps in Bangladesh.

The government of Prime Minister Sheikh Hasina Wajed took further preparatory measures towards the establishment of a national human rights commission. A draft bill was made public in December.

In the Chittagong Hill Tracts (CHT), talks between the government and tribal representatives to bring about a political solution to the long-standing conflict there resulted in the signing of a peace accord in December. Under an agreement between tribal leaders and government officials, the phased repatriation of around 50,000 refugees living in camps in India began in March and continued in November. Some 12,000 refugees had returned to the CHT by the end of the year.

As in previous years, political violence involving supporters of the main political parties – the ruling Awami League and the opposition Bangladesh National Party (BNP) – continued.

The trial of those accused of killing former President Sheikh Mujibur Rahman and his close relatives in a military coup in 1975 began in March. Of the 20 people charged in connection with the killings, five were in detention, one had been released on bail and 14 were being tried *in absentia.*

Several prisoners of conscience were among scores of people detained under the SPA which permits detention without charge or trial for an indefinite period. They included four senior members of the opposition BNP who were detained in March before a nationwide general strike. The four were held without charge until the High Court ordered their release in April. In an unprecedented judgment, the Court also awarded compensation to the prisoners after the authorities failed to demonstrate the lawfulness of their detention.

At least one political prisoner, Major Khairuzzaman, a former army officer who was arrested in August 1996 in connection with the 1975 killings, continued to be detained without charge or trial for over 18 months.

At least two people died in custody, reportedly following torture. One of them, Nuruzzaman Sharif, was arrested in June for illegally entering the Prime Minister's office in Dhaka. He died in police custody two days later. A post-mortem reportedly showed injuries consistent with torture. An investigation into Nuruzzaman Sharif's death by the Criminal Investigation

Department (CID) apparently found evidence implicating three police officers in murder and grievous harm. The CID were reportedly waiting for clearance from the public prosecutor before filing charges against the policemen, but it was not known if permission had been given by the end of the year.

Ill-treatment by police continued to be reported. Scores of demonstrators were beaten by police during a number of political rallies organized by opposition parties throughout the year.

At least three incidents of rape in custody by the security forces were reported during the year. In one case, in September, a woman was allegedly raped by a police officer in Rajshahi district after he had entered her home uninvited. Few of the officers responsible for rape in custody in this and previous years were brought to justice. In February, 18-year-old Shima Chowdhury died in Chittagong Jail where she was being held in so-called "safe custody" during an investigation into her alleged rape in police custody in October 1996 (see *Amnesty International Report 1997*). In July, four police officers accused of raping Shima Chowdhury were acquitted by a trial court in Chittagong. The judge reportedly criticized the prosecution for presenting a weak case. The government appealed against the decision, following an outcry from women's groups and human rights organizations. In August, three police officers were found guilty of the rape and murder of 14-year-old Yasmin Akhter in 1995 (see *Amnesty International Reports 1996* and *1997*) and sentenced to death.

In December, three prisoners died in Narayanganj district jail after falling ill while awaiting trial. Their deaths sparked renewed protests about prison conditions.

The whereabouts of Kalpana Chakma, a tribal women's rights activist who reportedly "disappeared" in the CHT in June 1996, remained unknown. A government-appointed commission of inquiry into the case was understood to have submitted its final report to the government in February, but its findings had not been made public by the end of the year.

In July the scope of the death penalty was widened to include the offences of airline hijacking and sabotage. At least 33 people were sentenced to death, all for murder. At least two people were executed.

In July a group of around 400 Rohingya refugees were forcibly returned to Myanmar from refugee camps in Bangladesh. Following protests by the UN High Commissioner for Refugees, the Bangladesh Government agreed not to return any more Rohingyas against their will, but stated that none of the remaining 21,000 refugees would be allowed to stay in Bangladesh permanently (see **Myanmar** entry).

Amnesty International appealed to the government to release all prisoners of conscience and urged that detainees arrested under the SPA be either charged with a recognizably criminal offence or released. In a report on the trial of those accused of killing Sheikh Mujibur Rahman published in May, the organization welcomed the investigation of past human rights violations and abuses, but called on the government to ensure that all trials conform to international standards for fair trial. In July Amnesty International published a report on the custodial rape and death of Shima Chowdhury and urged the government to strengthen institutional and legal safeguards to prevent similar human rights violations in the future.

BELARUS

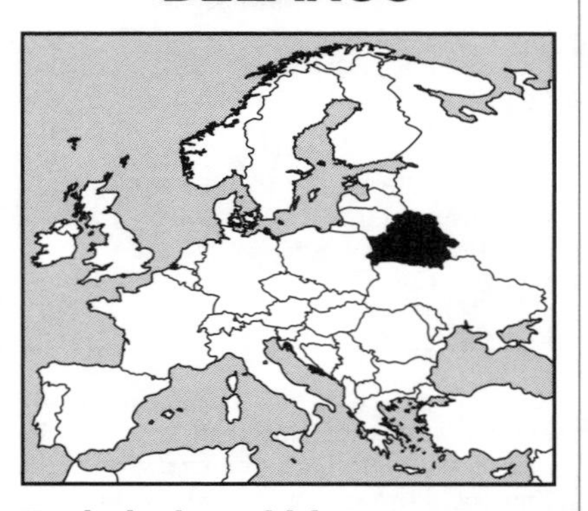

Hundreds of peaceful demonstrators were detained, including prisoners of conscience. Torture and ill-treatment by law enforcement officials were reportedly widespread. At least 17 people were sentenced to death and some 30 people were reportedly executed.

President Alyaksandr Lukashenka exercised total control over most aspects of government. The main law enforcement bodies – the Committee for State Security (KGB) and Ministry of Internal Affairs (MVD) – were both answerable to the President. The President used his constitutional powers to issue a number of decrees which violated constitutional guarantees for the protection of human rights. Decrees issued in March, May and October seriously restricted rights to freedom of expression and assembly; imposed further restrictions on detainees' access to legal assistance and resulted in a number of lawyers active in the defence of human rights losing their licences to practise; and provided for incommunicado detention of suspects for up to 30 days, in violation of national and international law.

In November, following a court decision, the authorities closed down *Svaboda*, the largest independent newspaper in Belarus, allegedly for printing two articles critical of the government.

Military service remained compulsory. A draft law proposing an alternative service of three years – twice the duration of military service – had been introduced for discussion in parliament in 1994. There are no provisions for conscientious objection in the 1996 Constitution.

At the beginning of January the Bureau of the Council of Europe's Parliamentary Assembly decided to suspend Belarus' status of special guest, stating that the 1996 Constitution was "illegal" as it "does not respect minimum democratic standards and violates the separation of powers and the rule of law".

In October the UN Human Rights Committee, examining Belarus' fourth periodic report on the implementation of the International Covenant on Civil and Political Rights, noted that the human rights situation in Belarus had deteriorated significantly since 1992. The Committee expressed concern at the number of crimes for which the death penalty is applicable and the high number of executions; allegations of ill-treatment by law enforcement officials during peaceful demonstrations, during arrest and in detention; the frequent use of weapons by police and other security officials; the severe restrictions imposed on the rights to freedom of assembly and expression; and reports of persecution and imprisonment of human rights activists by the authorities.

Prisoners of conscience continued to be detained during the year. Tatyana Protko, head of the Belarusian Helsinki Committee (BHC), a human rights organization, was detained in October by Ministry of the Interior officials and charged with obstructing the police; she had reportedly asked them to identify themselves. She was reportedly detained for researching the case of an alleged victim of human rights violations, and to prevent her from participating in the Belarusian non-governmental delegation to the UN Human Rights Committee the following week. She was a prisoner of conscience. She stood trial the following day and was released after the charges were dropped for lack of evidence.

Pavel Sheremet, bureau chief of Russia's public television station, *ORT*, Dmitry Zavadsky, a cameraman, and Yaroslav Ovchinnikov, the crew's driver, were detained in July in Minsk, the capital, for their professional, non-violent activities as media workers. All three were taken to a detention centre in Grodno, a town near the Lithuanian border. They were reportedly detained in connection with an unofficial visit they had made to the border between Belarus and Lithuania earlier in July, footage of which had already been shown on Russian television. The authorities had previously accused Pavel Sheremet of biased reporting. All three were released by 8 October. Two, Pavel Sheremet and Dmitry Zavadsky, were awaiting trial at the end of the year. According to reports, one of Pavel Sheremet's defence lawyers was stripped of his licence to practise, and the other withdrew because of threats to deprive him of his licence.

Hundreds of opponents of government policies, including prisoners of conscience, were detained and ill-treated during peaceful strikes and demonstrations throughout the year. Many of those detained were charged with administrative violations, fined and released. Others were released and were awaiting trial at the end of the year.

In March between 70 and 150 demonstrators were arrested following a peaceful rally against President Lukashenka in Minsk. Gennady Karpenko, Deputy Chairman of the Supreme Soviet of Belarus, and Yury Zakharenko, former Minister of Internal Affairs, were detained and accused of holding an unauthorized demonstration. Among those arrested was Gregory Kijko, an artist, who was reportedly beaten by police officers. He was at liberty awaiting trial at the end of the year.

Others arrested in March following demonstrations in other parts of the country allegedly included elderly people and young children who participated in a protest against plans to send certain students to perform their community service in areas of the country affected by the Chernobyl nuclear accident; and eight schoolboys reportedly arrested in the city of Kobrin and charged with organizing an unauthorized meeting after police broke up a peaceful march of a hundred schoolchildren protesting about a planned reduction in spring vacations.

In October Nadezhda Zhukova, an observer for the BHC, was assaulted and threatened in Minsk by unknown men believed to be connected to the police. As she left the building of the Leninsky District Court, where she had attempted to obtain information about the trial of Pavel Sivirinets and Yevgeny Skochka, two demonstrators arrested the previous day during a peaceful protest, she was approached by two men in plain clothes who told her that the two detainees were in police cars nearby. According to reports, two men got out of a car, grabbed her, hit her in the stomach, held a knife at her throat and took her to a nearby courtyard. There they took her BHC identity card from her bag and made threats against her and against other members of the BHC. The government delegation to the UN Human Rights Committee claimed that a criminal investigation had been opened into the case and that anyone found guilty would be brought to justice. However, no investigation was known to have been initiated by the end of the year.

Torture and ill-treatment of detainees in police custody and in pre-trial detention by law enforcement officials were reportedly widespread. Vera Glebova claimed that she was beaten by law enforcement officials from the Leninsky Department of Internal Affairs in Minsk in June, after being detained on charges of illegally trading cigarettes. Following the incident she was hospitalized for two weeks with serious injuries.

According to reports, the practice of *press-camera* (using prisoners, often those charged with or convicted of serious criminal offences, to control and ill-treat other prisoners) was common in a number of prisons and detention centres. Prisoner of conscience Pavel Sheremet stated that *press-camera* had been used in the pre-trial detention centre in the town of Grodno where he had been detained. No investigations were known to have been carried out into allegations of torture or ill-treatment.

According to official information provided to the UN Human Rights Committee, 17 people were sentenced to death in the first six months of the year. Among those sentenced to death were Igor Ganya and F. Verega, both citizens of Moldova, who were convicted of premeditated, aggravated murder in June. According to reports, some 30 people were executed during the year and at least 24 petitions for clemency were turned down by the President. The President was reported to have pardoned only one person facing the death penalty since coming to power in 1994. All 38 people sentenced to death in 1996 had been executed by the end of 1997.

Amnesty International called for the immediate and unconditional release of all prisoners of conscience, including any demonstrators detained solely for peacefully exercising their right to freedom of assembly, for prompt and impartial investigations into allegations of ill-treatment, and for anyone responsible to be brought to justice.

Amnesty International expressed concern for the safety of human rights defenders and called for them to be given all necessary protection.

Amnesty International called on the Government of Belarus to implement as a priority the recommendations of the UN Human Rights Committee. The organization urged the government to abolish the death penalty, and the Clemency Commission and the President to grant clemency and to declare a moratorium on executions.

BELGIUM

There were new allegations that members of the Belgian armed forces had tortured and ill-treated Somalis, including children, in 1993 while participating in the UN-authorized multinational peacekeeping operation in Somalia.

In March and April new information came to light about alleged human rights abuses carried out in 1993 by Belgian soldiers in Somalia. The military prosecutor's office immediately opened judicial investigations into the allegations.

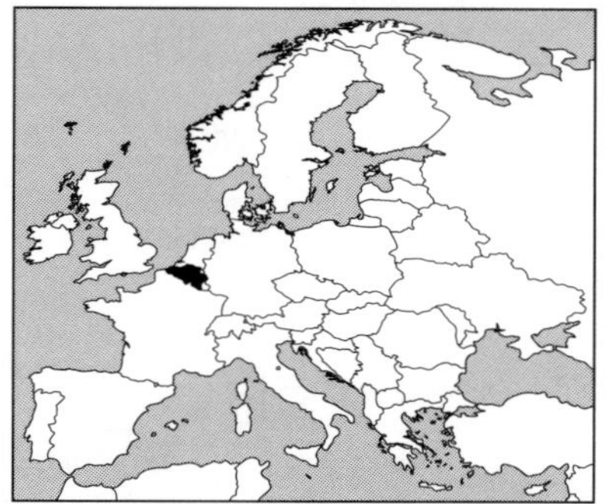

In June, two former paratroopers were tried by a military court on charges of assault and battery with menaces, committed on an unidentified Somali boy. Evidence at the trial included a photograph showing the boy being swung over an open fire by the accused. The paratroopers were acquitted, apparently on the grounds that there was no conclusive evidence that the boy had suffered actual bodily harm or had felt that his life was in danger. The military prosecutor appealed against the verdict, but the acquittal was confirmed in December. The trials of a sergeant accused of force-feeding a Somali child, a Muslim, with pork and salted water until he vomited; and of a sergeant major photographed urinating on the apparently dead body of a young Somali, were scheduled for September. In the meantime, however, further information about these and other alleged abuses by Belgian soldiers, came to light. All the court hearings were immediately adjourned in order to allow the military prosecutor's office to investigate this new information, which had been collected by a Somali human rights organization.

Other alleged abuses by Belgian soldiers were being investigated by the military authorities at the end of the year. They included the rape of a teenage Somali girl and the death of a child after 48 hours spent locked in a metal container in intense heat, without food or water.

The Minister of Defence ordered the General commanding the Belgian ground forces to carry out an internal investigation into alleged abuses by Belgian troops. In statements made in July and August, the Minister and the General announced that the inquiry had found that isolated, individual instances of human rights abuses by soldiers had occurred. They expressed concern about the presence within the army of "a small group of soldiers belonging to a political party holding extreme views" and the Minister advocated an independent inquiry on racism within the army. The statements also highlighted the need to improve army training – including the provision of more information on humanitarian law – and recruitment and selection procedures; to address excessive delays in disciplinary proceedings; and to tackle alcohol abuse. In September the General proposed specific reforms in some of these areas.

In July Amnesty International wrote to the Minister of Defence, expressing concern about the alleged human rights violations, welcoming the prompt opening of judicial investigations and asking to be informed of their outcome. The organization sought further information about several trials of Belgian soldiers which had taken place in previous years following a 1993 inquiry into alleged ill-treatment and unlawful killings by Belgian forces in Somalia, carried out by a commission comprising three army officers and a civilian assistant to the Minister of Defence (see *Amnesty International Report 1994* **Somalia** entry).

Amnesty International asked for the findings and precise terms of reference of the internal army investigation carried out in 1997. The organization inquired whether the authorities had considered holding a comprehensive inquiry, independent of the military, into alleged human rights abuses by Belgian troops in Somalia, in order to ensure a demonstrably impartial examination of the facts. No reply had been received by the end of the year.

BELIZE

A 16-year-old girl was allegedly raped and at least one man was ill-treated by police. A prison officer shot and injured a death-row prisoner in disputed circumstances. Two new death sentence were passed and seven men sentenced in previous years remained under sentence of death. One death-row prisoner was acquitted at a retrial. No executions were carried out.

In November two police officers were suspended pending investigation after they allegedly raped a 16-year-old girl in Punta Gorda police station.

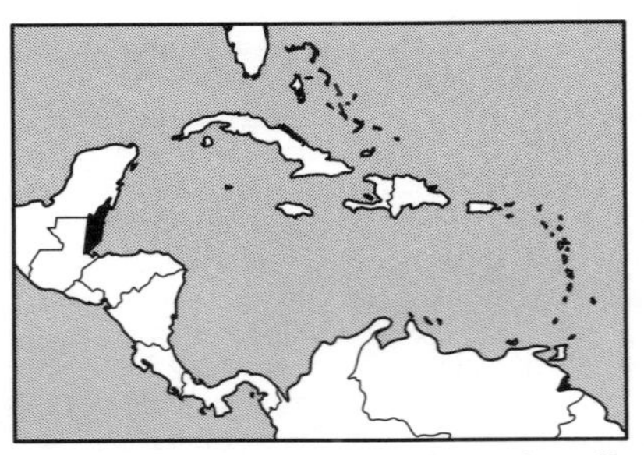

At least one man was subjected to ill-treatment by police. On 4 September convicted prisoner John Joy Hernandez was repeatedly flogged by a police officer while another held him down, after he had been recaptured following an escape attempt. One police officer was suspended from duty pending an investigation into the incident.

Prison conditions at Hattieville Rehabilitation Centre fell far short of the UN Standard Minimum Rules for the Treatment of Prisoners. A constitutional appeal on behalf of three death-row inmates – Pasqual Bull, Herman Mejía and Nicolás Antonio Guevara – arguing that such conditions constituted inhuman or degrading treatment or punishment and violated the Constitution, was still pending before the Supreme Court of Belize (see *Amnesty International Report 1997*). A similar appeal to the Supreme Court on behalf of Adolph Harris, and a petition by Wilfred Lauriano (see *Amnesty International Report 1997*) for leave to file a constitutional appeal to the Judicial Committee of the Privy Council (JCPC) in the United Kingdom, the final court of appeal for Belize, were adjourned pending the outcome of the joint appeal.

In August Wilfred Lauriano was shot in the back by a prison guard at the Hattieville Rehabilitation Centre. According to an official report, he had been attempting to escape with two other death-row inmates, Adolph Harris and Cleon Smith. However, Wilfred Lauriano stated that the shooting occurred as they approached the office of a senior prison officer to ask why they had been denied recreation periods for several days. When they disobeyed an order by an officer to turn back, the officer reportedly fired at both Adolph Harris and Wilfred Lauriano. A bullet hit Wilfred Lauriano, penetrating his lower back, and had to be surgically removed. The prisoners claimed it was obvious that they were not trying to escape as they were walking, not running, and were in their underwear. By the end of the year, no official investigation was believed to have taken place. Subsequent reports indicated that Wilfred Lauriano was returned to prison from hospital against the advice of doctors and that the medical care he received in the prison was deficient.

Two new death sentences were passed, both for murder. Cleon Smith was sentenced to death in April, and Norman Shaw in November. Both had appeals pending before the Belize Court of Appeal.

Seven men sentenced to death in previous years remained on death row. Apart from the constitutional appeals already mentioned, final appeals were pending before the JCPC on behalf of Dean Tillett (see *Amnesty International Report 1997*), whose appeal to the Belize Court of Appeal was dismissed in February; and Pasqual Bull and Marco Tulio Ibañez, who had both been granted leave to appeal to the JCPC in 1996 (see previous *Amnesty International Reports*).

In June Rupert Burke, convicted of murder in 1995 and sentenced to death, was acquitted at a retrial. In February the Belize Court of Appeal had found that the first trial had been prejudiced because the defendant's lawyer had given evidence in his client's defence. At the retrial the lawyer (no longer representing Rupert Burke) again testified that his client had been beaten by police to make him confess.

Amnesty International called on the authorities to investigate the beating of John Joy Hernandez and to bring those responsible to justice. It also urged the government to submit its second report to the UN Committee against Torture, which was due in 1992.

BHUTAN

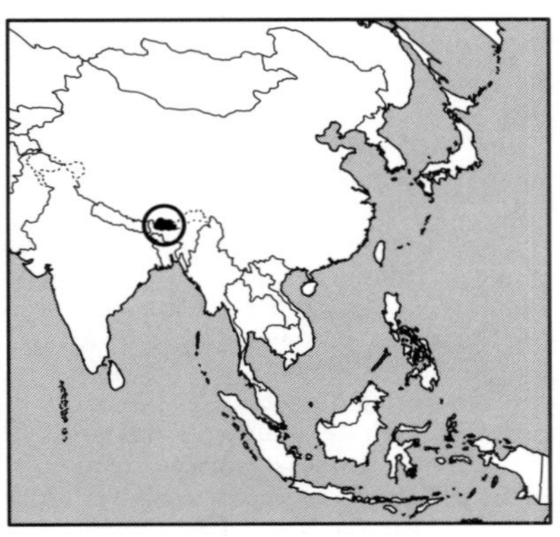

A prisoner of conscience remained held throughout the year. At least 150 possible prisoners of conscience were detained, many of them incommunicado, without charge or trial. Many were reportedly tortured or ill-treated by law enforcement officers. A Buddhist monk died in custody in disputed circumstances.

The Druk National Congress (DNC), a political organization set up in exile in Nepal, organized sit-ins, demonstrations and other campaigning activities, particularly in October, demanding a democratic system of government and greater protection of and respect for human rights.

In May a new extradition agreement with India, effectively providing for, among other things, extradition of anyone requested by either country, entered into force.

In July the National Assembly adopted a resolution authorizing the forcible retirement from civil service of relatives of people living in refugee camps in eastern Nepal.

A meeting of the foreign secretaries of Bhutan and Nepal was held in Thimphu in July to prepare for the eighth round of talks between the two governments on the fate of more than 90,000 people – mostly Nepali-speaking people from southern Bhutan – living in refugee camps in eastern Nepal (see previous *Amnesty International Reports*). No date had been fixed for the talks by the end of the year.

Tek Nath Rizal, a prisoner of conscience, spent his eighth year in prison (see *Amnesty International Report 1994*).

In April Rongthong Kunley Dorji, a Bhutanese national and leader of the DNC and of the United Front for Democracy (UFD), another political organization set up in exile in Nepal, was detained in India. He remained held at the end of the year awaiting the outcome of extradition proceedings to Bhutan. The charges featured in the arrest warrants issued by the Bhutanese authorities – the basis of the extradition request – appeared to be politically motivated. Rongthong Kunley Dorji had left Bhutan in 1991, shortly after being pardoned by King Jigme Dorji Wangchuck. He had been detained on treason charges and tortured by members of the Royal Bhutan Bodyguards.

At least 150 possible prisoners of conscience were detained. The arrests appeared to be part of a crack-down by the authorities on suspected DNC and UFD sympathizers. Many of those arrested were held in incommunicado detention without charge or trial. In October, in the immediate aftermath of a nationwide pro-democracy poster campaign, scores of suspected government opponents were arrested, mainly in eastern Bhutan, and held in incommunicado detention without charge or trial. A large majority of those detained were members of the Sarchop community. Among them were dozens of Buddhist monks and religious teachers. Kinzang Chozom, who was pregnant, was among those arrested and was not allowed to see her children. Other women were arrested, apparently in an attempt to force their husbands to give themselves up to the authorities.

Many of those detained on suspicion of being DNC and UFD sympathizers were reportedly tortured or ill-treated. In February, four DNC members – Taw Tshering, Tshampa Wangchuck, Tshampa Ngawang Tenzin and Chhipon Samten Lhendup – were held naked for one week in very low temperatures while in detention at Tashi Yangtsi prison in eastern Bhutan. In September Dorji Norbu, Kunga, Dorji Tshewang and Namkha Dorji were held in shackles and flogged daily at Pema Gatsel police station.

Gomchhen Karma, a Buddhist monk from Gomdar, Samdrup Jonkhar district, died in disputed circumstances at Korila, Mongar district, while in police custody in October. The government admitted he had been shot dead by the district administrator, but claimed that it had been an accident. However, an eye-witness alleged that the administrator shot Gomchhen Karma deliberately three times in the head.

Amnesty International continued to appeal for the immediate and unconditional release of Tek Nath Rizal; for pro-democracy supporters held in incommunicado detention to be released unless promptly charged with a recognizably criminal offence; and for fair trials for political prisoners. The organization also appealed for an immediate end to torture and ill-treatment by law enforcement officers. Amnesty International called on the authorities to guarantee immediate access to adequate medical care to Kinzang Chozom, in view of her pregnancy. The organization expressed its fears that, if returned to Bhutan, Rongthong Kunley Dorji might again be tortured.

BOLIVIA

Human rights defenders were subjected to threats and attacks. At least one person was allegedly the victim of an extrajudicial execution. Scores of peasants were detained for short periods. Torture and ill-treatment of detainees were reported.

In March Congress adopted Law 1768, removing the death penalty for the crimes of parricide, murder, treason and other crimes against the security of the state under the Penal Code and the Code of Penal Procedure, and providing instead for a penalty of 30 years' imprisonment without parole. This brought the penal laws into line with the Constitution, which does not provide for the death penalty.

In August former General Hugo Banzer of the *Acción Democrática Nacionalista* (ADN), Nationalistic Democratic Action, took office as President at the head of a coalition government, succeeding Gonzalo Sánchez de Lozada of the *Movimiento Nacional Revolucionario* (MNR), National Revolutionary Movement, following general elections in June. General Hugo Banzer had previously led a *de facto* government from 1971 to 1978.

In March the UN Human Rights Committee examined Bolivia's implementation of the International Covenant on Civil and Political Rights. In its recommendations the Committee urged Bolivia to investigate allegations of human rights violations, in order to bring to justice perpetrators of past and present human rights abuses.

The authorities continued to implement policies to eradicate coca-leaf crops agreed with the USA. There were confrontations between coca-leaf growers and combined police forces including the *Unidad Móvil de Patrullaje Rural* (UMOPAR), Mobile Rural Patrol Unit, in El Chapare area, Cochabamba Department.

Human rights defenders were the victims of threats and harassment. In January Waldo Albarracín, President of the non-governmental human rights organization *Asamblea Permanente de Derechos Humanos*, Permanent Human Rights Assembly, was abducted and tortured in La Paz by members of the police. He was blindfolded, beaten about the head, ears and testicles for several hours and threatened with death. He was subsequently taken to the headquarters of the *Policía Técnica Judicial*, Judicial Police, and placed in detention. He was taken to hospital on account of his injuries and later presented with an arrest warrant but not taken into custody. Waldo Albarracín had called for an investigation into deaths that occurred during a clash between miners and police in Potosí Department, in December 1996 (see *Amnesty International Report 1997*). He and his family were subjected to further threats and harassment during the year. The outcome of a parliamentary investigation into the attack on him had not been considered by the Chamber of Deputies by the end of the year.

In February Juan del Granado, President of the Human Rights Commission of the Chamber of Deputies, received anonymous telephone threats. He had publicly condemned the attack on Waldo Albarracín.

At least one person was allegedly the victim of an extrajudicial execution. According to reports, combined police forces of UMOPAR, the Ecological Police and the *Dirección de Reconversión de la Coca* (DIRECO), a government agency in charge of supervising coca-leaf eradication, were involved in an operation to eradicate coca-leaf crops in El Chapare region, Cochabamba Department. Alberta Orellana García, mother of seven children, was killed in Bajo Mariscal Sucre in April. She was reportedly on her knees begging the police not to eradicate her crop when she was shot dead by a member of UMOPAR.

Following her death, there were disturbances in which peasants attacked the DIRECO offices in the town of Eterazama and the police responded by firing on the crowd, allegedly indiscriminately, and by throwing tear-gas canisters. Six people were killed, including a member of UMOPAR. Freddy Rojas, a 22-month-old boy, died from tear-gas inhalation. More than 100 people were arrested and detained for short periods. Most of them were reportedly beaten, including Avelino Espinosa, leader of the Villa Tunari Peasants Federation, who was severely beaten by UMOPAR agents while being tied up. No investigation was initiated following a report on the incident by the Human Rights Commission of the Chamber of Deputies.

There was no clarification by the authorities of numerous cases of human rights violations committed between 1989 and 1993. The victims were political prisoners accused of participating in armed uprisings (see previous *Amnesty International Reports*).

In February Amnesty International wrote to President Sánchez de Lozada about the attack on Waldo Albarracín. In April the organization wrote to the President of the Chamber of Deputies asking for information about the investigation into the attack, but received no reply. In May Amnesty International published a report, *Bolivia: Undermining human rights work*, in which it urged the Chamber of Deputies to give prompt and serious consideration to the findings of the investigation into the attack on Waldo Albarracín.

In March Amnesty International submitted its concerns on human rights violations in Bolivia to the UN Human Rights Committee.

Amnesty International wrote to the President in April expressing concern about the deterioration of the human rights situation in El Chapare region and the events in Bajo Mariscal Sucre and Eterazama. The organization urged thorough and independent investigations. No substantive response was received from the authorities during the year.

BOSNIA-HERZEGOVINA

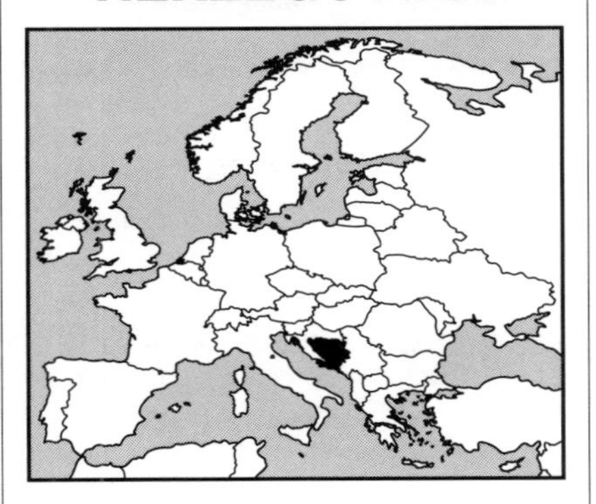

More than a million refugees and displaced persons were unable to return to their homes because of continuing human rights violations. Scores of people, including prisoners of conscience and possible prisoners of conscience, were detained on account of their nationality. Most were detained without charge or trial. Dozens of people charged with humanitarian law violations received unfair trials before courts in Bosnia-Herzegovina; trials of people from minorities within the separate political entities were also unfair. The whereabouts of more than 19,000 people, many of whom had "disappeared" in the custody of the police or armed forces, remained unknown. More than 100 people were ill-treated by police, and attacks on members of minorities appeared to be carried out with official acquiescence. At least one person was unlawfully killed by police. Scores of war crimes suspects remained at large.

Implementation of the 1995 General Framework Agreement on Peace (the peace agreement) continued, but animosity remained high between the Republika Srpska (RS) – the primarily Bosnian Serb entity – and the Federation of Bosnia and Herzegovina (Federation) – the Bosniac (Bosnian Muslim) and Bosnian Croat entity. Within the Federation the Bosnian Croat dominated authorities in some areas acted as a third territorial unit, and there was tension between the Bosniac and Croat-dominated authorities, particularly in the divided city of Mostar. The two entities, represented by a three-member presidency of Bosnia-Herzegovina chaired by President Alija Izetbegović, a Bosniac, with Bosnian Serb member Momčilo Krajišnik and Bosnian Croat member Krešimir Zubak, came to agreement on a number of issues. Other key issues such as citizenship remained unresolved until December, when the High Representative was granted authority to issue binding decisions.

The authorities on all sides stalled on implementing, and sometimes ignored, recommendations made by the civilian organizations and officials overseeing implementation of the peace agreement, such as the High Representative, the Organization for Security and Co-operation in Europe (OSCE), and the UN International Police Task Force (IPTF). This was particularly the case with regard to human rights issues. A new High Representative, Carlos Westendorp, took office in June.

A power struggle, which on occasion resulted in violence, erupted in the RS between Biljana Plavšić, President of the RS, and Momčilo Krajišnik after President Plavšić initiated investigations of high-level governmental corruption in June. Support for each leader was concentrated in the west and east of the RS respectively. President Plavšić dissolved the RS Parliament in July. In parliamentary elections in November no party won an absolute majority.

Municipal elections organized and monitored by the OSCE in September resulted mainly in victories for the nationalist parties. However, only 18 of 109 municipalities had been certified by the OSCE by the end of the year. Three municipalities, Srebrenica (RS), Vareš (Federation) and Žepče (Federation), did not meet at all. In many cases, lack of progress was due to political disagreement. However, in some cases elected councillors did not take up their seats for fear of violence or arrest if they visited the area (see below).

The authorities, in particular those in the RS and the Bosnian Croat dominated parts of the Federation, did not fully cooperate, and in some cases blatantly refused to cooperate, with the International Criminal Tribunal for the former Yugoslavia (the Tribunal). By the end of the year, 54 of 73 people known to have been indicted by the Tribunal remained at large; the majority were Bosnian Serbs believed to be living in the RS. Some of those indicted continued to exercise authority in a public capacity.

In April Zlatko Aleksovski (see *Amnesty International Report 1997*) was transferred to the Tribunal from Croatia and in October, after considerable international pressure on the Croatian Government, nine Bosnian Croat men surrendered themselves to the Tribunal. A 10th, Pero Skopljak, who had been arrested in Croatia in August, was also transferred to the Tribunal. In December he and two of the other Bosnian Croats were released after the prosecutor withdrew the charges on the grounds that there was insufficient evidence on which to try them. Charges against another Bosnian Croat were also withdrawn in December, when it was confirmed that he had died in October 1995. In July in the RS, the NATO-led Stabilization Force (SFOR) arrested Milan Kovačević and shot dead Simo Drljača while attempting to arrest him; both were Bosnian Serbs who had been secretly indicted by the Tribunal in March. Vlatko Kupreskić and Anto Furundžija, Bosnian Croats, were arrested by SFOR in the Federation in December. Anto Furundžija had been secretly indicted. However, despite these arrests and the apprehension of indicted Croatian Serb Slavko Dokmanović in Croatia by the UN forces serving there, states contributing to SFOR continued to defend their refusal to live up to their obligations under international law to seek and arrest all those indicted by the Tribunal.

In May the Tribunal found Dušan Tadić (see *Amnesty International Report 1996*) guilty on 11 of 31 counts of serious violations of humanitarian law and crimes against humanity. In July he was sentenced to 20 years' imprisonment. Both the defence and the prosecution appealed against the decision. Other trials continued throughout the year. In October the Appeals Chamber held that the 1996 plea of guilty by Dražen Erdemović (see *Amnesty International Report 1997*) was not fully informed and that the case must be sent back to a different Trial Chamber to permit him to enter a new plea.

Approximately 1.4 million people from Bosnia-Herzegovina remained refugees or internally displaced because it was still not safe for them to return to their homes or because they were prevented from doing so by bureaucratic obstacles. Approximately 110,000 refugees returned to Bosnia-Herzegovina, most of them to areas where their national group was now the majority. Germany forcibly repatriated more than 800 Bosnian refugees. Many other refugees who returned from countries which ended temporary protection for Bosnian refugees also did not return voluntarily and suffered, or were at risk of, human rights violations (see below). In some cases their repatriation prevented others from returning to their homes. At least half of the refugees who returned voluntarily or forcibly did not return to their pre-war homes and became internally displaced.

Human rights violations were widespread and occurred throughout the year. Most victims were members of minorities, although members of the political opposition were also targeted. Hundreds of homes were deliberately destroyed to prevent returns. Violent attacks by civilians on minorities, including displaced persons, were reported almost daily. The authorities frequently either encouraged or did little to discourage such attacks. In one incident, an 80-year-old Bosnian Serb died after he was severely beaten with sticks and stoned by a group of displaced Bosniacs in March. He was visiting a graveyard near Visoko (Federation) with his wife, who was also beaten.

In a few incidents large numbers of people were targeted. Violence against returnees was particularly severe in areas such as Doboj (RS) and the Šapna area (RS) when Bosniacs attempted to return to or repair their houses near the inter-entity boundary line. Scores of Bosnian Serb houses were also deliberately destroyed in Drvar (Federation). Displaced Bosniacs in the Sarajevo suburbs (Federation) violently attacked Bosnian Serbs who attempted to return to their homes; Bosnian Serbs who had remained in the area were also attacked throughout the year. In August Bosnian Croats attacked Bosniacs who had returned to villages near Jajce (Federation) (see below). Hundreds of Bosniacs were forced to flee again and many of their homes were burned. At the same time, in another village in the area, a Bosniac man was shot dead in his house. Some Bosniacs who had been forcibly expelled from Jajce but later returned found that fresh land-mines had been set around their homes.

Scores of people, including prisoners of conscience and possible prisoners of conscience, were detained on account of their nationality. Few were formally charged with offences, but in February a Bosniac in Teslić (RS) was sentenced to one month's imprisonment for singing "Islamic" songs; he was a prisoner of conscience. The various authorities continued to detain people from other national groups travelling through areas which they controlled (see *Amnesty International Report 1997*). Some were arrested on nationally defined war crimes charges, in violation of a procedure agreed with the Tribunal in 1996 whereby no one would be detained on such charges until their case had been reviewed by the Tribunal Prosecutor. Ivan Mijačević, a Bosnian Croat, was arrested in May while on the way to a cemetery in the RS and was charged with war crimes in connection with the bombing of Modriča (RS) in 1993. He was released in June, possibly in exchange for six Bosnian Serbs released from detention in Croatia several days earlier. In August a Bosnian Serb man imprisoned in Bihać (Federation) since October 1996 was released after the Tribunal found that the evidence upon which the authorities had attempted to bring charges against him was insufficient. Some councillors elected in the September municipal elections were threatened with arrest on war crimes charges, particularly in Brčko (RS), Srebrenica (RS) and Velika Kladuša (Federation), although their cases had not been reviewed by the Tribunal Prosecutor.

The various authorities exchanged dozens of prisoners, among them possible prisoners of conscience. For example, in August Federation authorities exchanged three Bosnian Serbs, two of them juveniles, for a Bosniac held by the RS; they may have been prisoners of conscience. Also in August, nine Bosnian Serbs detained in connection with the conflict, who had been held without trial since 1995 in Croatia, were released in exchange for nine Bosnian Croats convicted of common crimes in the RS (see **Croatia** entry).

In April the "Zvornik Seven", Bosniacs charged with the murder of four Bosnian Serbs in 1996 (see *Amnesty International Report 1997*), were found guilty by an RS court in a grossly unfair trial. All the men appeared to have been tortured in custody and were denied lawyers of their choice. Dozens of people tried in courts in Bosnia-Herzegovina for nationally defined war crimes did not receive fair trials. Among them was Miodrag Andrić, a Bosnian Serb sentenced in August to 20 years' imprisonment, who was not able to call witnesses from the RS to testify in his defence, thus violating his right to "equality of arms" in his defence.

Ill-treatment by the police was widespread, particularly where the detainee was a member of a minority. More than 100 people reported to international organizations that they were ill-treated by police. For example, a Bosniac man was beaten during his arrest in October in Sarajevo (Federation); he also claimed that he was handcuffed to a radiator overnight and coerced into signing a statement during interrogation. The authorities in the RS stalled in their investigations into the death in custody of Hasan Kovačević (see *Amnesty International Report 1997*). Police reportedly participated in attacks on minorities and returning refugees or displaced persons, including in Mostar (see below) and Jajce. In many cases the IPTF found that the police had not adequately protected civilians from these attacks.

According to the International Committee of the Red Cross the authorities clarified the fate of 500 missing people, but more than 19,000 people remained unaccounted for; many of them had "disappeared" or were otherwise believed to have gone missing after detention or abduction by the police or armed forces. Among the "disappeared" were Roman Catholic priest Father Tomislav Matanović and his elderly parents, who had been detained by police in 1995 (see *Amnesty International Report 1997*). The RS authorities failed to provide information on the case by October, in defiance of an order from the Human Rights Chamber, a national human rights body established under the Constitution, and at the end of the year the case remained unresolved. Exhumations carried out during the year by the local authorities and international organizations in some cases provided evidence that the victims had probably been deliberately and arbitrarily killed. At least four men who had "disappeared" were found alive. Two men of Arab origin "missing" for six months reappeared in January; they had been held incommunicado and without trial in Livno and Mostar by the Bosnian Croat authorities. In August, two Bosnian Serbs who had been secretly held in Zenica Prison (Federation) for almost two years (see *Amnesty International Report 1997*) were found there by the IPTF and released.

In February Bosnian Croat police officers in west Mostar (Federation) shot into a peaceful crowd of Bosniacs visiting a cemetery, killing Šefik Sulejmanović and injuring dozens of others. Other members of the crowd were beaten by the police. The Bosnian Croat authorities charged three officers with a minor offence and ignored calls from the High Representative for those responsible for the shooting and injuries to be properly brought to justice.

Despite commitments under the peace agreement, legislation permitting the death penalty remained formally in effect in both entities. No executions were known to have been carried out.

Amnesty International addressed the authorities in Bosnia-Herzegovina on several human rights issues and recommended to the international organizations implementing the peace agreement that they put human rights at the centre of their agenda.

In March Amnesty International published *Bosnia-Herzegovina: 'Who's living in my house?'* detailing the obstacles to the return of refugees and displaced persons. In December it published *Bosnia-Herzegovina: Righting the wrongs*, which called on states hosting refugees to extend their protection to all Bosnian refugees unable to return to their pre-war homes. Throughout the year Amnesty International called on SFOR to arrest those indicted by the Tribunal, and in October it issued a report, *Bosnia-Herzegovina: How can they sleep at night? Arrest now!*

BRAZIL

Hundreds of people were killed by police and death squads linked to the security forces in circumstances suggesting extrajudicial executions. Human rights defenders were threatened and attacked. Those responsible for human rights violations continued to benefit from impunity. Several people, including land reform activists, faced criminal charges which appeared to be politically motivated. Torture and ill-treatment by police were reported to be widespread.

On the first anniversary of Brazil's National Human Rights Program in May, President Fernando Henrique Cardoso installed a new National Secretariat for Human Rights within the Ministry of Justice. Legislative bills introduced by the government were under discussion which, if implemented, could reduce impunity for human rights violations. They included reform of the police, the criminal justice system and the judiciary, and the creation of a federal witness protection program.

In March the crime of torture was inserted into the penal code. Since 1989, when it ratified the UN Convention against Torture and Other Cruel, Inhuman or Degrading Treatment or Punishment, Brazil has not submitted any periodic reports, which are required under the Convention.

In December the Inter-American Commission on Human Rights published a report on its 1995 visit to Brazil, at the invitation of the Brazilian Government. The Commission noted a "wide gap between the constitutional, legislative and institutional structures that have been set up to defend human rights and the persistent abuses and absence of practical guarantees to uphold these rights in certain areas of society and the country." Brazil does not yet recognize the jurisdiction of the Inter-American Court of Human Rights which could consider individual complaints examined by the Commission.

Hundreds of people were killed by the police or by death squads linked to the security forces in circumstances suggesting they may have been extrajudicially executed. The number of fatal shootings by police in Rio de Janeiro state continued to rise following the state's decision in November 1995 to offer large pay rises to police agents involved in acts of "bravery and fearlessness". A report commissioned by the state legislature revealed that since May 1995 the number of deaths each month resulting from police action had doubled, and that 942 people had been killed by police between January 1993 and July 1996. The report also revealed that the majority of those killed had been shot in the head or back, which suggested that they had not been resisting arrest.

In January five criminal suspects were allegedly dragged from their houses, handcuffed and shot dead by civil police in Cavaleiro in the state of Pernambuco. Nineteen police officers were indicted on charges of homicide in February.

In July eight prisoners in Roger Prison in João Pessoa, Paraíba state, were extrajudicially executed by military police officers. The police stormed the prison before negotiations had been completed for the release of five hostages held by the prisoners. Autopsies on the eight prisoners revealed multiple stab wounds to the head and chest, indicating that police had tortured and killed prisoners after overpowering them. A number had had their throats cut, one had had an eye gouged out and his skull smashed, and another had been shot several times in the groin.

There were continued reports of violent attacks on indigenous communities and landless peasants in the context of land disputes. There was concern at the pattern of impunity for such attacks enjoyed by both police officers and gunmen, reportedly hired by local landowners, who sometimes cooperated with the police during evictions.

In September Teresa Pedroso was shot in the stomach by military police officers; she suffered a punctured intestine and spleen. She was shot when police attempted to disperse a group of landless peasants who were peacefully protesting about the government's agrarian reform policy by blocking a highway in Presidente Epitácio, São Paulo state. A police investigation was opened but no one had been arrested or charged by the end of the year.

In February eight members of the Landless Rural Workers Movement (MST) were shot and wounded on the São Domingos ranch in the Pontal de Paranapanema region, São Paulo state, by 12 gunmen attempting to evict an encampment of landless peasants. The son of the ranch-owner and four gunmen were arrested by the civil police and charged, but were then released and fled over the state border into Mato Grosso do Sul state. In August a group of gunmen fired on some of the 900 landless families who had been camped for four months near the Slaviero ranch in Querencia do Norte, Paraná state, killing José Arnaldo Santos. A police investigation was opened, but no one had been arrested by the end of the year.

There were fears for the safety of Nambikwara Indians in the Sararé area of Mato Grosso following the expulsion by federal police of some 8,000 illegal loggers and miners from the area; the authorities did not take adequate steps to protect the community following the expulsion or to prevent the loggers and miners from returning.

Death squads, often composed of off-duty police officers, continued to act with impunity in at least nine states. In the state of Mato Grosso do Sul in the border region with Paraguay, 87 death-squad killings were recorded by a local human rights organization in the first seven months of 1997 alone. Local human rights defenders received death threats following the discovery in October of clandestine graves containing the bodies of people allegedly killed by a death squad composed of police officers from the Frontier Operations Division. Edgar Lopes de Faria, a local radio journalist, was shot dead in October, allegedly because he had threatened to broadcast the names of those responsible for killings and "disappearances" in the area.

In June a public prosecutor and assistant lawyer in Espírito Santo state received death threats in connection with their investigations into the alleged death-squad activities of members of a police welfare organization, the *Scuderie Detetive le Cocq*.

Human rights defenders in the *Centro de Direitos Humanos e Memoria Popular* (CDMP), Centre for Human Rights and Collective Memory, in Rio Grande do Norte state received threats in connection with their investigations into a local death squad. An official investigation into the killing of Francisco Gilson Nogueira de Carvalho, a member of the CDMP, in 1996 (see *Amnesty International Report 1997*) was closed in September on the grounds of lack of evidence.

In July human rights defenders from the *Forum Permanente Contra Violência*, Permanent Forum Against Violence, and *Grupo Gay de Alagoas*, Alagoas Gay Group, in Alagoas state received death threats after pressing for an official investigation into the alleged extrajudicial execution of a transvestite and two homosexual men, and the alleged torture and ill-treatment in detention of three other transvestites, by civil police in June. In October, two environmental activists in Santa Catarina state received death threats in connection with their campaigning.

In April the first trial was held in Rio de Janeiro in connection with the Vigário Geral massacre in August 1993 in which 21 people were killed (see *Amnesty International Reports 1994* and *1997*). The first of the 48 military police officers charged with involvement in the massacre to be convicted was sentenced to 449 years' imprisonment. In November a second officer was convicted and sentenced to 441 years' imprisonment. However, the trial of the remaining officers had to be postponed after crucial ballistic evidence, which indicated the involvement in the massacre of a police officer who had previously been exonerated in February 1996, was delayed. A military policeman convicted in November 1996 in connection with the Candelária massacre in Rio de Janeiro in July 1993, in which seven street children and one youth were killed (see *Amnesty International Reports 1993* and *1997*), retracted his confession and was cleared of most charges at his automatic retrial in June. Trials in both cases exposed serious flaws in the investigation of human rights violations and the prosecution of those responsible. Vital evidence was withheld and witnesses were not adequately protected. By the end of the year some victims and relatives had still not received state compensation.

The 22 Rondônia state military police officers allegedly involved in the killing of 10 peasants in Corumbiara in August 1995 (see *Amnesty International Report 1996*) remained on active duty and had not been indicted by the end of the year.

In November Pará state military police officers were indicted on a charge of aggravated homicide as co-authors of the killing of 19 landless peasants in Eldorado de Carajás in April 1996 (see *Amnesty International Report 1997*).

Land reform activists continued to be held under preventive detention orders and to have politically motivated criminal charges brought against them. A possible prisoner of conscience was convicted of murder following an unfair trial. In June, José Rainha Júnior, a leader of the MST, was convicted of the murder in 1989 of a landowner and a military police officer in the state of Espírito Santo. He was tried in the rural municipality where the murders took place, and sentenced to over 26 years' imprisonment. The trial did not meet international fair trial standards. There were serious concerns about the impartiality of members of the jury, some of whom had personal connections with the murdered landowner, and there appeared to be no convincing evidence of his involvement in the killings. At the end of the year José Rainha Júnior was at liberty awaiting an automatic second trial. If the guilty verdict against him is upheld under similar circumstances and he is imprisoned, he would be considered a prisoner of conscience.

In February, five members of the MST in the Pontal de Paranapanema region of São Paulo state were, for the third time, placed under preventive detention orders on charges of "forming a criminal band". The federal Higher Court of Justice had ruled in 1996 that such a charge should not be used against those supporting land occupations (see *Amnesty International Reports 1996* and *1997*). Márcio Barreto, who was arrested under a preventive detention order, was released following a successful *habeas corpus* petition to the federal Higher Court of Justice.

Reports of torture and ill-treatment in police custody were widespread. Criminal suspects were routinely ill-treated by police. In February, 15-year-old Magnaldo de Aguiar was stopped in the street by military police in Recife, Pernambuco state. He was allegedly beaten and then thrown into a nearby tank containing an acid solution. He suffered third-degree burns on his face and lower body.

Ten military police officers were arrested following the showing on television in March of a video in which military police officers in Diadema, São Paulo state, were seen stopping and extorting money from motorists and torturing them. Jefferson Sanchez Capute was beaten with police truncheons on the soles of his feet. One man, Mario José Josino, was shot dead by police in his car. Ten police officers were arrested, charged and awaiting trial at the end of the year. Another video, broadcast in April, showed six military police officers beating criminal suspects in the Cidade de Deus area of Rio de Janeiro. Six officers were arrested and four expelled from the police force. In October Anali Filartiga Speratti and Evelio Miranda Barrios were arrested by police in Caçapava in São Paulo state, accused of sexual assault of minors. Evelio Miranda Barrios was allegedly beaten with rifle butts by officers at the police station, sustaining injuries to his head and face. Anali Filartiga Speratti was reportedly beaten by fellow detainees in the women's prison in which she was held, allegedly at the incitement of the police.

There were continuing reports of ill-treatment in prisons. In January around 80 women prisoners were beaten by guards in the Santa Rosa de Viterbo Prison in Altinópolis, São Paulo state, following a protest by inmates. One woman reportedly suffered a miscarriage and another sustained a broken arm. In March, 15 inmates at the women's prison in São Paulo city were beaten by guards; some women were reported to have vomited blood as a result of the beatings. Conditions of detention remained harsh in police stations and prisons, with severe overcrowding, poor hygiene and lack of medical care. Convicted prisoners continued to be held with remand prisoners in police stations owing to overcrowding.

Throughout the year Amnesty International called for investigations into human rights violations, including killings by police and police-backed death squads; attacks on indigenous communities and landless peasants; and torture and ill-treatment by law enforcement officials. The organization sent an observer to the first trial relating to the Vigário Geral massacre. It also participated in the second national human rights conference in May, and commented on the progress of the National Human Rights Program. Amnesty International representatives also met federal, state and municipal authorities during their visits to the country.

The organization published several reports, including *Brazil: Candelária and Vigário Geral – justice at a snail's pace*, in June; and *Brazil: Politically motivated criminal charges against land activists*, in August.

BULGARIA

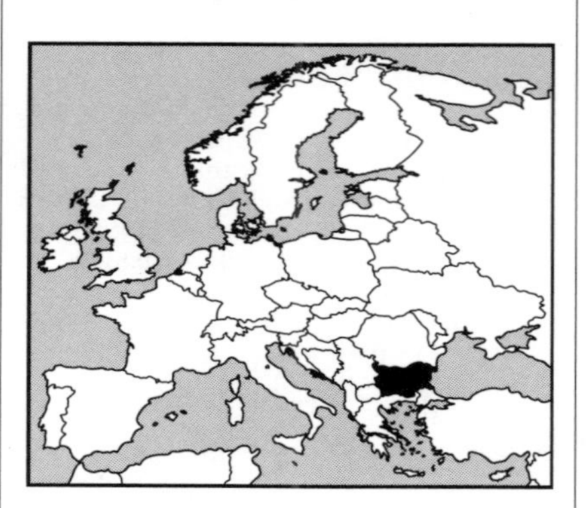

A conscientious objector to military service was imprisoned; he was a prisoner of conscience. There were widespread reports of torture and ill-treatment by law enforcement officials; many of the victims were Roma. At least five people reportedly died as a result of torture or ill-treatment. Shootings by police officers in disputed circumstances resulted in at least nine deaths. At least four people were sentenced to death. No executions were carried out.

Following the December 1996 resignation of Prime Minister Zhan Videnov, a member of the ruling Bulgarian Socialist Party, demonstrations calling for early parliamentary elections were held in January throughout the country. A demonstration in front of the National Assembly in Sofia on 10 January ended late at night with a massive police intervention. Nearly 300 people were injured as a result of ill-treatment by police. President Petar Stoyanov, who was inaugurated on 19 January, played a crucial role in preventing further violent clashes and in facilitating political negotiations between the Bulgarian Socialist Party and the opposition. An early election organized in April brought to power the Union of Democratic Forces, whose leader, Ivan Kostov, was appointed Prime Minister in May.

In March the government authorized publication of the report of the European Committee for the Prevention of Torture and Inhuman or Degrading Treatment or Punishment on its visit to places of detention in March and April 1995. The Committee concluded that detained criminal suspects "run a significant risk of being ill-treated at the time of their apprehension and/or while in police custody, and that on occasion resort may be had to severe ill-treatment or torture", and that conditions of detention in National Investigation Service facilities could be described as inhuman and degrading. The Committee expressed concern that two prisoners sentenced to death in Stara Zagora Prison had been held in isolation for several years in poor conditions and under an impoverished regime offering very little human contact.

Also in March the UN Committee on the Elimination of Racial Discrimination expressed alarm that the Bulgarian authorities had not been sufficiently active in effectively countering incidents of racial violence against members of minority groups, and seemed to have failed to investigate acts of violence promptly and effectively. In view of reported incidents of police harassment and ill-treatment against minorities, and particularly Roma, the Committee expressed concern that the training of law enforcement officials on the International Convention on the Elimination of All Forms of Racial Discrimination was insufficient, and recommended that the Bulgarian authorities take immediate steps to prevent and combat cases of excessive use of force by the security forces. It also recommended the establishment of an independent mechanism to monitor observance of human rights.

Dian Yankov Dimitrov, a conscientious objector to military service and prisoner of conscience who had been imprisoned in September 1996 (see *Amnesty International Report 1997*), was released in April. In December the government adopted a draft bill on alternative service. Certain of the proposed provisions were at variance with internationally recognized principles.

The government failed to initiate a revision of Article 148, paragraph 1, points 2 and 3 of the Penal Code, which appear to restrict the right to freedom of expression and to allow for the imprisonment of anyone who defames a public official. Separate criminal proceedings against journalists Valentin Hadzhiev and Mitko Shtirkov (see *Amnesty International Report 1997*) continued under this law throughout the year. Among other journalists prosecuted under the law were Karolina Kraeva, from Vratsa, charged in November. She had alleged in an article published in May that the local chief of police had intervened on behalf of a man ordered by the court to vacate her property. At the end of the year she was at liberty pending trial.

In January and February, six children and one 18-year-old died of malnutrition and hypothermia in the state-run Home for Mentally Handicapped Children in Dzhurkovo, when more than 80 children were left without adequate food or heating.

There were daily reports of torture and ill-treatment by police officers, but few investigations resulted in the prosecution of those responsible. No progress was reported in investigations into dozens of cases of torture and ill-treatment – many resulting in death – which had been reported in previous years. This illustrated the continuing failure of the authorities to conduct such investigations promptly and impartially. In November the National Police Directorate reported that it had received 74 complaints of ill-treatment by police since the beginning of the year, but claimed that in only 17 cases were there sufficient grounds for investigations to be initiated by military prosecutors.

Among cases reported during the year was that of Yanko and Elian Angelov. In September, in Plovdiv, four police officers apprehended the 16-year-old twin brothers on suspicion of theft. They reportedly drove them to a field outside the city where they kicked them and beat them with truncheons and a baton, only stopping when Elian Angelov suffered an epileptic fit. A forensic medical certificate issued by a military hospital established that both boys suffered multiple bruising to the head, back, chest and legs, and that Yanko Angelov also sustained a ruptured left ear-drum and broken jaw. An investigation was reportedly initiated but the results had not been made public by the end of the year.

At least five people reportedly died as a result of torture or ill-treatment. In January Stefan Stanev was arrested and taken to Popovo police station on suspicion of theft. Five hours later he was discovered dead in his cell. An autopsy reportedly established that he died from internal haemorrhaging caused by the fracture of three ribs which ruptured the lungs. The reported results of an official investigation – that Stefan Stanev had not been ill-treated, and that the fracture probably occurred when the arresting officer resorted to force in order to restrain him – contradicted an earlier police report that shortly following his arrest Stefan Stanev had been examined by a doctor, who found "no serious health problems". The investigation was reopened in April and the officer who arrested Stefan Stanev was subsequently charged with murder.

In March Georgi Byandov was reportedly severely beaten by police officers who questioned him following his arrest in Karnobat. He was later taken to Burgas hospital, where he died from head injuries apparently sustained in the beating. The Ministry of the Interior reportedly claimed that Georgi Byandov had resisted arrest, but that only his arm had been injured.

There were reports that officers ill-treated recruits during their compulsory military service. In February, in Aitos, Martin Argurov was allegedly punched and kicked by a sergeant when he failed to return a bullet after sentry duty. Martin Argurov was later treated for a broken jaw and other injuries. An investigation into the incident was initiated only 20 days later, as the commanding officer reportedly attempted to cover up the incident.

Roma, as in previous years, were particularly targeted for ill-treatment by police officers. Reports of racist ill-treatment in the region of Montana were illustrative of a country-wide pattern of ill-treatment. In June, at a public meeting with the local authorities, a representative of Amnesty International urged the Regional Police Directorate to suspend from duty two officers who were most frequently alleged to have been involved in ill-treatment incidents. The following day, one of these officers was among five police officers who reportedly beat Danail Nedkov Mladenov on the soles of his feet with a truncheon.

At least nine unarmed people were killed by police in disputed circumstances. Dozens of people were injured in other police shootings reported throughout the year. In one incident in May, Kolyo Todorov, a Rom, was shot by a police officer who observed him leaving the police station in Plovdiv, to which he had been brought on suspicion of theft. Kolyo Todorov died shortly after the incident. The Chief of the Regional Directorate of Internal Affairs reportedly stated that the officer had first fired a warning shot, and had acted legally in apprehending a criminal suspect. The results of an official investigation had not been made public by the end of the year.

At least four people were sentenced to death. In October the National Administration for Places of Detention reported that 16 people were under sentence of death. A moratorium on executions, imposed in 1990, remained in force.

In February Amnesty International expressed concern about six incidents of police shootings; five cases of alleged torture and ill-treatment by police officers, involving eight victims, two of whom died in suspicious circumstances; and the ill-treatment of hundreds of demonstrators in front of the National Assembly. In March Amnesty International expressed concern about the deaths in the Home for Mentally Handicapped Children in Dzhurkovo. Extreme neglect of those who are in the care of officials acting in a public capacity is considered by Amnesty International to amount to cruel, inhuman or degrading treatment. In July the organization wrote to the authorities concerning the ill-treatment of Roma in the Montana region. In October it published *Bulgaria: Growing incidence of unlawful use of firearms by law enforcement officials* and urged the authorities to investigate further incidents of police torture and ill-treatment. In December Amnesty International expressed concern to the President about the prosecution of Karolina Kraeva and urged him to initiate a revision of the law under which she was charged.

A response from the authorities in July stated that 12 children had died of pneumonia in February and March in Dzhurkovo, and that food supplies and the heating situation had deteriorated in the winter months, but failed to establish responsibility for allowing the situation to deteriorate to such an extent. The government also replied that investigations into five shooting incidents raised in February by Amnesty International had been suspended on the grounds that the conduct of the officers was permitted by the Law on National Police, which allows the use of firearms against suspects fleeing the scene of the crime. Amnesty International urged the authorities to revise this law to bring it in line with internationally recognized principles on the use of firearms.

BURKINA FASO

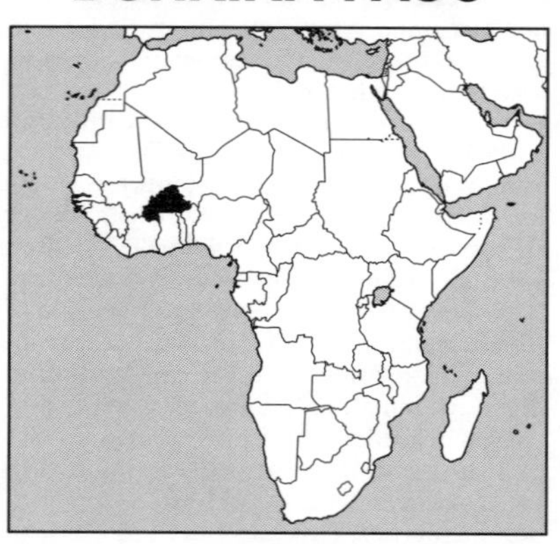

Dozens of students who appeared to be prisoners of conscience were detained briefly without charge. Some were ill-treated. There was no progress in bringing to justice those responsible for human rights violations in previous years.

Demonstrations early in the year by students at the University of Ouagadougou, the capital, in support of demands for improved conditions, resulted in the detention of dozens of students who appeared to be prisoners of conscience. On 31 January two student leaders, André Tibiri, President of the *Association nationale des étudiants burkinabè*, National Association of Burkinabè Students, and

Abou Dao, were arrested at their homes and imprisoned in Ouagadougou until 8 February. In early February students and school pupils peacefully demonstrating against the detention of their colleagues were arrested and held for three days. More students were arrested later that month; most were released without charge after a few days. In March the government announced that all students had been released.

Students arrested in early February were reported to have been beaten while held at the *Direction de la sûreté nationale*, the criminal investigation department of the police. Another student, Barthélemy Tenkodogo, was reported to have been abducted from the university in mid-February by unidentified armed men believed to be members of the security forces, put into the boot of a car and then beaten and abandoned several kilometres from Ouagadougou.

There was no official investigation into the death of a soldier who was killed in late December 1996 (see *Amnesty International Report 1997*). Sergeant Arzouma Ouédraogo, who had been among 25 soldiers arrested in October 1996 and accused of breaches of military discipline, died a few days after the release of the detainees was officially announced. Military authorities said that he had died in a road accident while being transferred from Ouagadougou to Gaoua, Poni Province. However, no details of the incident were provided and the exact circumstances of his death remained unclear.

The findings of official investigations into apparent extrajudicial executions in 1995 of seven men from Kaya Navio, Nahouri Province, and into the killing of two school pupils during a demonstration in 1995 at Garango, Boulgou Province, were still not made public (see *Amnesty International Reports 1996* and *1997*).

Amnesty International received no response to a letter to the government in January calling for a full and independent inquiry into the death of Sergeant Arzouma Ouédraogo.

BURUNDI

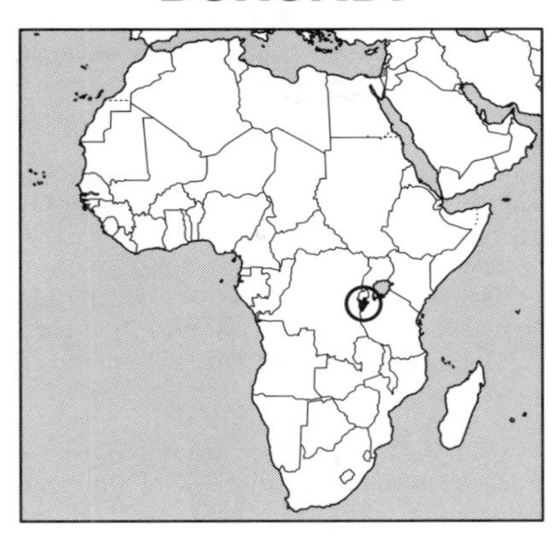

Thousands of unarmed civilians were killed by the security forces and armed opposition groups; hundreds were killed during the "regroupment" process. Government opponents and critics, including possible prisoners of conscience, were detained and sometimes tortured. Thousands of political prisoners were held without trial; others received unfair trials. Torture and ill-treatment were routine and lead to several deaths in custody. Several "disappearances" were reported. Six men were executed and more than 200 prisoners were under sentence of death. Scores of people were taken hostage by armed opposition groups.

Armed conflict continued between the Tutsi-dominated security forces and allied armed groups on one side and armed Hutu-dominated opposition groups on the other. Fighting was also reported between the main armed opposition group, the *Forces pour la défense de la démocratie* (FDD), Forces for the Defence of Democracy, the armed wing of the *Conseil national pour la défense de la démocratie* (CNDD), National Council for the Defence of Democracy, and the armed wing of the *Parti pour la libération du peuple hutu* (PALIPEHUTU), Party for the Liberation of the Hutu People. Attacks by armed opposition groups on Tutsi civilians or military positions provoked widespread reprisal attacks by the security forces against the majority Hutu population. Thousands of people were displaced by the violence and hundreds of thousands of already displaced people were unable to return to their homes.

Major Pierre Buyoya, who seized power in a military coup in July 1996 (see *Amnesty International Report 1997*), remained in power. Sanctions imposed by regional governments after the July 1996 coup were eased in April at a regional summit. The summit called for an international arms embargo on all protagonists and an end to "regroupment" camps.

Negotiations to end the conflict were repeatedly postponed. Secret negotiations between the government and the CNDD in Rome, Italy, resulted in agreement on areas for negotiation, although the reaction of some other political parties was hostile. Further progress did not appear to have been made by the end of the year. A meeting with government and military officials was held under the auspices of the UN Educational, Scientific and Cultural Organization in Paris, France, in September 1997; the *Front pour la démocratie au Burundi* (FRODEBU), Front for Democracy in Burundi, delegation was prevented from leaving Burundi to attend the meeting.

The National Assembly met, but was hampered by the continuing suspension of the Constitution, its lack of power to challenge government policies and actions, and by the absence of many members of parliament. Since 1993 many Hutu parliamentarians have been killed or forced to flee the country.

In March a new press law was passed restricting press freedom.

Relations with Tanzania deteriorated during the year. There were several incursions by the Burundi security forces into Tanzania, in which at least three Tanzanian civilians were killed.

In April the UN Commission on Human Rights adopted a resolution strongly condemning human rights abuses in Burundi and renewing the mandate of the UN Special Rapporteur on Burundi, but the government refused him access to the country and demanded that he be replaced. He was subsequently allowed to visit in December. In May the UN Security Council expressed concern about continuing instability in Burundi and called for a cessation of hostilities, unconditional negotiations and an end to the practice of "regroupment". A joint UN-Organization of African Unity (OAU) special representative for the Great Lakes was appointed in January. He visited Burundi in August.

Thousands of unarmed civilians, most of them Hutu, were killed by the security forces – sometimes acting in collusion with armed civilian Tutsi groups – and by armed Hutu opposition groups. Responsibility for specific incidents was often difficult to establish.

Many civilians were massacred during counter-insurgency operations by the army. For example, at least 19 people, mostly women and children, were killed by soldiers between 7 and 9 July in Isale district, Rural Bujumbura province. Soldiers reportedly visited the district several times over the two-day period, shooting and bayoneting those who could not escape and burning down houses, in reprisal for a land-mine explosion on 6 July which injured two soldiers.

In October over 200 people were reportedly killed in a series of massacres by the security forces, after the destruction of 16 schools in Rural Bujumbura province, attributed to the FDD. As many as 70 people were killed at Gitenga colline, Cabbies district, on 21 October. The following day, at Gihondo, Muhata district, at least 48 people were reportedly shot and killed and many others injured during a meeting to which they had been called by military officials.

In January, 126 refugees were handed over to the Burundi security forces by Tanzanian soldiers; 122 were shot dead shortly afterwards by members of the security forces. The Burundi authorities claimed that soldiers were overwhelmed by the numbers of refugees and panicked. Other sources indicated that the Burundi security forces systematically executed the refugees in small groups, accounting for the lack of wounded. In April, 10 soldiers were sentenced to between five months and 10 years for the killings by a military tribunal.

Detainees were extrajudicially executed by the security forces, including 35 people who were extrajudicially executed in the capital, Bujumbura, reportedly on the orders of a lieutenant at the *Brigade spéciale de recherches* (BSR), Special Investigation Unit. Their bodies were found close to Kanyosha market, near Bujumbura, in March. One of the victims was identified as Eliezer, a young man who had been arrested two days earlier and taken for questioning by the BSR.

Hundreds of unarmed Hutu were reportedly killed in July and August by members of PALIPEHUTU in Cibitoke and Bubanza provinces. The majority were reported to have been killed in Murwi commune, Bubanza province, because they were believed to support the rival CNDD. Scores of people, mainly Tutsi, were killed in attacks on camps for the displaced by armed groups. The FDD killed unarmed civilians, including at least 13 people in Nyanza Lac district, Makamba province, in July.

In several provinces where armed conflict was prevalent, large numbers of Hutu were forcibly relocated into "regroupment" camps – a military strategy which appeared to be designed to cut off support for armed groups. Hundreds of Hutu civilians were extrajudicially executed by the security forces during the "regroupment" process. For example, 57 people, including 21 children, were killed on 5 January in Rutegama district, Muramyva province. Hunger and disease were rife in the camps. Unlike the predominantly Tutsi displaced people's camps, the inhabitants were forcibly confined to the camps. Anyone not in camps in these areas was declared by officials to be a legitimate military target.

Extrajudicial executions, "disappearances" and ill-treatment by soldiers within the camps were reported. Hundreds of people were also killed and wounded in attacks on the camps attributed to PALIPEHUTU. In May, 63 people were killed during an attack on two "regroupment" camps in Cibitoke province attributed to PALIPEHUTU and members of the former Rwandese army. Towards the end of the year some camps were dismantled, although inmates were not allowed to return to their homes but were resettled along roads. Over 200,000 Hutu remained confined to camps at the end of the year.

Critics and opponents of the government were detained. Some of those held appeared to be prisoners of conscience, such as Solange Ndikumana, who was arrested in March and held for two weeks, apparently because she was found in possession of a letter criticizing Major Buyoya. FRODEBU Secretary General Augustin Nzojibwami was placed under house arrest in February, and subsequently transferred to Mpimba Central Prison and charged with distributing documents likely to incite civil war. His arrest appeared to be linked to his criticism of the government's "regroupment" policy. He was released a week later, although charges were not dropped. In September his car was fired on, reportedly by members of the security forces.

Several religious leaders, including the Reverend Emmanuel Ndayiziga, President of the Union of Baptist Churches in Burundi, and the Reverend Eliezer Ntunzwenimana, also of the Union of Baptist Churches, were arrested in March and April, apparently on suspicion of providing aid to Hutu armed groups. They appeared to have been targeted because of their welfare work among the local population. The Reverend Ndayiziga was released without charge after four days, but the Reverend Ntunzwenimana was held for 10 weeks before being released without charge and was reportedly unable to walk unaided as a result of ill-treatment.

Hundreds of people, mostly young Hutu men, were arrested on suspicion of having links with armed groups. Most were held without charge or trial and many were held initially in military camps where they were ill-treated. They joined more than 6,000 people, mostly Hutu, held in various prisons and detention centres, accused of involvement in massacres following the assassination of former President Melchior Ndadaye in October 1993 or of links with armed groups.

In January the authorities arrested former President Jean-Baptiste Bagaza of the *Parti pour le redressement national* (PARENA), National Recovery Party, and several leading members of *Solidarité jeunesse pour la défense des minorités* (SOJEDEM), Youth Solidarity for the Defence of Minorities. The arrests appeared to relate to their criticism of the government. Jean-Baptiste Bagaza remained under house arrest throughout the year, accused of illegal possession of firearms and subversive documents, before being charged, in December, with involvement in an alleged plot to assassinate President Buyoya.

In March several leading members of PARENA and SOJEDEM were arrested and reportedly tortured. One, retired Lieutenant-Colonel Pascal Ntako, died in detention in mid-May, after he was denied essential medical care. The detainees were charged with planning to assassinate President

Buyoya and tried before a military tribunal, the independence and impartiality of which were in doubt. The trials were continuing at the end of the year.

Trials continued of people accused of participation in the massacres and killing Tutsi civilians in 1993. Although the judiciary received UN assistance, the trials fell short of international standards for fairness.

Trials before the Supreme Court of around 80 people, both civilians and military, accused of participation in the October 1993 coup and the assassination of President Ndadaye started in May. Many prominent defendants, including François Ngeze, who appeared before the Supreme Court in October and November, remained at liberty. The Court had not reached a verdict by the end of the year.

In September a trial opened of 12 people in court and 11 *in absentia*, including the president of the CNDD, Léonard Nyangoma, charged in connection with land-mine explosions in Bujumbura. At least four had reportedly been tortured, including the Reverend Jean-Pierre Mandende who was beaten on his back and face during interrogation. The trial had not finished by the end of the year.

Michel Nziguheba, a journalist, was charged with "false report" and "prejudicial imputation" and sentenced to a total of five years' imprisonment after trials which may not have met international standards for fair trial (see *Amnesty International Report 1997*).

Torture and ill-treatment of detainees were routine in detention centres and prisons. Most detainees were tortured and ill-treated at the time of their arrest or during interrogation. In February the Executive Secretary of FRODEBU, Domitien Ndayizeye, was detained for five days and severely beaten. Three men held in an unofficial detention centre at Socarti military camp in Bujumbura reportedly died as a result of torture in May. One was the younger brother of "Savimbi", a prominent member of the FDD.

Seven children and one adult reportedly died as a result of suffocation and dehydration in Gatumba police station in October. They were among 10,053 people detained for two days in Gatumba as part of an operation to check identity cards.

Several people reportedly "disappeared", including FRODEBU National Assembly member Paul Sirahenda and his driver Hamissi Ndimurukundo who "disappeared" in August soon after being arrested by soldiers at Mutobo, Makamba province, near the border with Tanzania. Their burned-out car was later found, and officials claimed the two men had been killed by criminals. There were several reports, particularly from Bubanza and Karuzi provinces of apparent "disappearances" from "regroupment" camps.

Six people, including Firmat Niyonkenguruka (see *Amnesty International Report 1997*), were executed on 31 July, the first judicial executions since 1981. The six had been convicted of participation in killings in October 1993, after grossly unfair trials in which they did not have legal representation. At least one, Stanislas Mashini, a member of the *Rassemblement du Peuple Burundais* (PRB), Union of Burundi People, said he had been tortured to make him sign a false confession. Defence witnesses were excluded from trials, and despite the gravity of the charges, most trials lasted only a few hours.

At least 100 death sentences were passed during the year after similarly unfair trials, bringing the number of people under sentence of death to more than 200. Most had been convicted in connection with the massacres of 1993. Many, including Gordien Niyonzima, sentenced to death in April in Gitega, claimed to have been tortured to extract confessions.

Hundreds of thousands of Burundi refugees remained in Tanzania and Rwanda. Over 3,000 more returned from Rwanda, many apparently as a result of coercion, and several thousand were forcibly returned from Tanzania. The Burundi authorities repatriated hundreds of Rwandese refugees to Rwanda.

Scores of people were reportedly taken hostage by armed opposition groups and forced to accompany the armed groups, carrying provisions and ammunition.

Amnesty International repeatedly called on the authorities to investigate and bring an end to human rights violations, including extrajudicial executions, "disappearances", torture and ill-treatment by government forces. Amnesty International also called on the leaders of all armed groups to respect human rights.

In January Amnesty International published a report, *Great Lakes Region: Still in need of protection – repatriation,* refoulement *and the safety of refugees and the internally displaced*, calling on states in the Great Lakes region to halt the *refoulement* of refugees and appealing to the international community to provide the necessary assistance to ensure that the basic needs and protection requirements of refugees could be met. In July Amnesty International published *Burundi: Forced relocation – new patterns of human rights abuses*, calling for an end to the policy of "regroupment". The government responded that "regroupment" was spontaneous and for the protection of the population. It questioned Amnesty International's objectivity, but failed to address the human rights violations described in the report. In October the organization reiterated its appeals for durable and effective protection for refugees from Burundi, Rwanda and the Democratic Republic of the Congo in an open letter to several African governments.

CAMBODIA

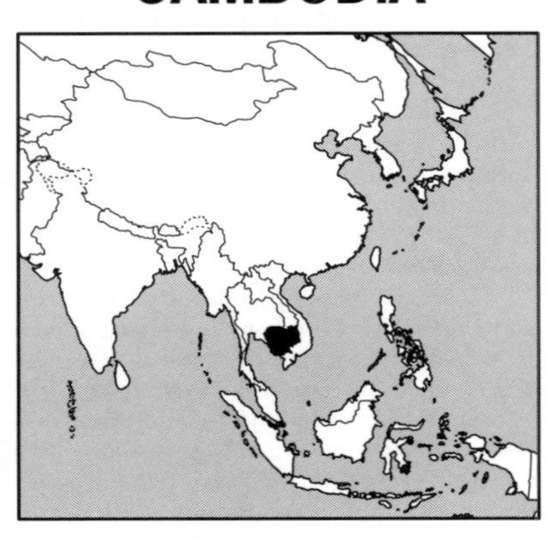

Scores of people were extrajudicially executed and hundreds detained without charge or trial following a coup in July. Dozens of the detainees were tortured. Prison conditions amounting to cruel, inhuman or degrading treatment were reported. At least 16 people were killed and scores injured in a grenade attack on an opposition party demonstration in March. An armed opposition group reportedly committed serious human rights abuses, including deliberate and arbitrary killings.

Low-level hostilities between the Royal Cambodian Armed Forces and the National Army of Democratic Kampuchea, commonly known as the Khmer Rouge, continued in the first part of the year. Political tensions between Cambodia's two Prime Ministers, Prince Norodom Ranariddh and Hun Sen, became increasingly acute as the year progressed. In February fighting broke out in Battambang province between forces loyal to FUNCINPEC (Prince Norodom Ranariddh's party) and those loyal to the Cambodian People's Party (CPP, Hun Sen's party). The tense political climate heightened with the news in June that the National Solidarity Party (NSP) – the latest name for the political wing of the Khmer Rouge movement – had overthrown their leader Pol Pot. In negotiations with a senior FUNCINPEC General, Nhek Bun Chhay, the Khmer Rouge leadership said they would hand Pol Pot over for trial in a third country, on charges relating to gross human rights violations during the period when the Khmer Rouge was in power in the 1970s. Since the split in the Khmer Rouge movement in 1996 (see *Amnesty International Report 1997*), both FUNCINPEC and the CPP had been attempting to attract Khmer Rouge defectors, in the run-up to elections planned for 1998.

On 5 July forces loyal to Hun Sen launched sustained and violent attacks against forces loyal to Prince Ranariddh in the capital, Phnom Penh. Prince Ranariddh was abroad at the time; many others followed him into exile, including politicians from FUNCINPEC, the Buddhist Liberal Democratic Party and the Khmer Nation Party (KNP). FUNCINPEC politicians who remained in Cambodia selected Foreign Minister Ung Huot as the new First Prime Minister, and his appointment was confirmed in a National Assembly vote in August.

Following the coup, Cambodia's planned entry into the Association of South East Asian Nations was suspended by the organization, and its seat at the UN General Assembly was left vacant.

In March the UN Special Representative on the situation of Human Rights in Cambodia submitted a report to the UN Commission on Human Rights, condemning continuing government and Khmer Rouge abuses. In September he made public a memorandum to the government about summary executions, torture and missing persons following the coup. In November the Special Representative submitted a report to the UN General Assembly, which adopted a resolution expressing grave concern about numerous instances of violations of human rights detailed in the Special Representative's reports. The resolution also requested that a group of experts be appointed to evaluate evidence about serious human rights violations committed in Cambodia while the Khmer Rouge was in power, with a view to addressing individual accountability.

Scores of people were extrajudicially executed following the CPP-led ousting of Prince Norodom Ranariddh and his supporters. Victims included senior FUNCINPEC military personnel, and those linked to them. Hor Sok, Secretary of State at the Ministry of the Interior and a senior FUNCINPEC official, who was close to Prince Norodom Ranariddh and General Nhek Bun Chhay, was arrested on 7 July while attempting to find a country which would offer him asylum. He was taken to the Ministry of the Interior compound and was executed later that day. His body was taken to a temple in Phnom Penh by uniformed, heavily armed men, who ordered an immediate cremation, although they did not have the necessary official permit.

General Krauch Yeuam, Under-Secretary of State at the Ministry of Defence and a senior FUNCINPEC member, fled Phnom Penh with Chao Sambath, a FUNCINPEC General, and a group of soldiers. They were captured by soldiers loyal to Hun Sen on 8 July in Kampong Speu province. The two were separated from their subordinates and were executed later that day. Krauch Yeuam's body was exhumed by human rights workers in October. His hands had been cut off and he had been shot dead. Chao Sambath's body was also exhumed in October. He too had been shot in the head. In addition to the known extrajudicial executions, dozens of people were hastily cremated in Phnom Penh in the immediate aftermath of the fighting, often without the necessary documentation. Some of them may have been extrajudicially executed. In spite of overwhelming evidence to the contrary, the government maintained that only one person – Hor Sok – was unlawfully killed, and that all other deaths around the coup occurred during the fighting.

Hundreds of people, mainly FUNCINPEC soldiers loyal to Prince Ranariddh, were detained in the immediate aftermath of the fighting. In Kandal province which surrounds Phnom Penh, more than 600 people were detained in different districts, while several hundred more were held in other provinces. The majority were released after short periods, although some were detained without charge or trial for weeks after the fighting. Access to some prisoners for human rights monitors was eventually granted by the Cambodian authorities, although not to all places of detention.

Dozens of those detained were tortured. Thirty-three FUNCINPEC soldiers captured in July by soldiers from Special Forces Regiment 911 were taken to the regiment's base at Kambol; they were detained for over a week in a small storage room, where they could not all sit down at the same time. The prisoners were taken out of the room for interrogation. Almost all were tortured by their interrogators to force them to confess to connections with the Khmer Rouge. The prisoners were variously blindfolded, beaten with belts, a wooden table leg and a plank, kicked, punched or had their hands crushed in a vice. They were threatened with death, with knives held to their necks or guns pointed at their heads. Prisoners detained by the military police at their headquarters in a Phnom Penh suburb were also beaten and tortured.

At least 16 people were killed and over 100 injured in March in a grenade attack on a peaceful, authorized KNP demonstration. The demonstrators were calling for reform of Cambodia's judicial system and the release from custody of senior KNP member Srun Vong Vannak, who was arrested and held in incommunicado detention in February on charges of murdering Hun Sen's brother-in-law, Koy Samouth, in November 1996. Demonstrators had gathered outside the National Assembly building when four grenades were thrown into the crowd. KNP leader Sam Rainsy escaped injury but one of his bodyguards was among the dead. Journalists gathered around Sam Rainsy were seriously injured and one, Chet Duong Daravuth, was killed. Heavily armed soldiers standing 200 metres behind the demonstrators allowed two people who were seen throwing grenades to run past them and escape, but prevented demonstrators from pursuing them. Police at the scene did not help the victims, some of whom lay dying in the sun for up to an hour. A team from the US Federal Bureau of Investigation visited Cambodia to investigate the attack, as a US citizen was among the injured. Its report was not made public, but a US newspaper claimed that it laid the blame for the attack on members of Hun Sen's bodyguard unit. Srun Vong Vannak was convicted of involvement in the murder of Koy Samouth after an unfair trial in September, on the basis of a confession obtained under duress while in incommunicado detention and later retracted. He was sentenced to 13 years' imprisonment. He appeared to be a prisoner of conscience. Two other men were convicted at the same time. They subsequently retracted their confessions which were obtained under similar circumstances. All three remained in prison at the end of the year.

There was no progress in calling perpetrators to account for human rights violations committed in previous years.

Prison conditions amounting to cruel, inhuman or degrading treatment were reported during the year. Prisoners frequently died in prison from untreated diseases, exacerbated by malnutrition and overcrowding. In one prison, shackling prisoners at night was standard practice to prevent potential escapes due to the dilapidated condition of the building. In Stung Treng prison, 10 prisoners serving long sentences were held in two metal cages, with inadequate light and ventilation.

Khmer Rouge forces were believed to be responsible for attacks on ethnic Vietnamese villagers in May in which at least three people were killed. In June Khmer Rouge Defence Minister Son Sen, his wife Yun Yat and 10 other people believed to include family members were shot dead, apparently on the orders of Pol Pot. Days later, Khmer Rouge radio announced that they had "brought the treason of Pol Pot to an end". On 25 July, a so-called "People's Tribunal" in the NSP stronghold of Anlong Veng denounced Pol Pot for ordering the death of Son Sen and sentenced him and three other men to life imprisonment. A foreign journalist who witnessed the event reported that the charges against Pol Pot related solely to his involvement in the killing of Son Sen and others in July, and not to the crimes committed when the Khmer Rouge was in power. Pol Pot and his co-defendants were not able to speak during the proceedings, which amounted to a public denunciation rather than a real trial. The fate and whereabouts of a British man and his Cambodian interpreter believed to have been taken hostage by the Khmer Rouge in March 1996 remained unknown at the end of the year.

In March Amnesty International published a report, *Kingdom of Cambodia: The children of Krang Kontroul – still waiting for justice,* about the killing of six children in 1996. In March and April the organization published reports about the grenade attack on the KNP demonstration and its aftermath, calling for those responsible to be brought to justice. In June Amnesty International called on the Cambodian authorities and the international community to seize the opportunity to bring to justice those suspected of responsibility for gross human rights violations in Cambodia during the 1970s.

In July the organization published *Kingdom of Cambodia: Arrest and execution of political opponents*, about human rights violations committed during and after the coup. An open letter was sent to Second Prime Minister Hun Sen in July, calling for improvements in the human rights situation. A planned visit to Cambodia to discuss human rights concerns with the government in July was postponed when the airport was closed following the coup. Amnesty International met the then Foreign Minister, Ung Huot, in Kuala Lumpur, Malaysia, at the end of July and presented him with a list of recommendations to improve the grave human rights situation in the country. Following an official invitation, an Amnesty International delegation visited Cambodia in September. In spite of the official nature of the visit, only one government minister met the delegation.

In October Amnesty International published *Kingdom of Cambodia: Time for action on human rights*, outlining the catalogue of commitments broken by the government and calling on the international community to maintain pressure on the authorities to improve the human rights situation and put an end to impunity.

There was little direct response from the Cambodian authorities. King Norodom Sihanouk acknowledged and thanked the organization for its work on Cambodia, but Second Prime Minister Hun Sen publicly condemned Amnesty International for its monitoring activities, while failing to address any individual cases of extrajudicial executions and torture.

CAMEROON

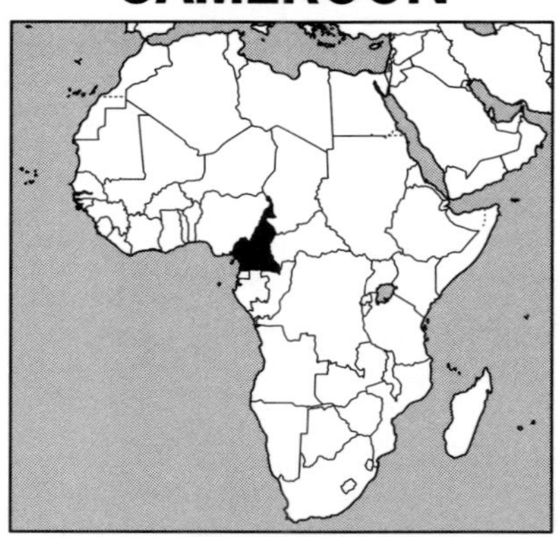

Hundreds of critics and opponents of the government, most of them prisoners of conscience, were detained. More than 60 political prisoners remained held without trial at the end of the year. Torture and ill-treatment remained routine and at least eight people died in custody from torture. Harsh prison conditions amounted to cruel, inhuman or degrading treatment. At least one prisoner was executed.

Legislative elections took place in May. In late March armed attacks in the English-speaking North-West Province, an opposition stronghold, led to several hundred arrests, predominantly of supporters of the Social Democratic Front (SDF), the main opposition party. The SDF accused the authorities of exploiting the insecurity to intimidate opposition supporters and prevent political activity before the elections. Both the SDF and another opposition party, the *Union nationale pour la démocratie et le progrès* (UNDP), National Union for Democracy and Progress, called for the elections to be annulled because of fraud. The ruling *Rassemblement démocratique du peuple camerounais,* Cameroon People's Democratic Movement (CPDM), of President Paul Biya, gained an absolute majority. International observers noted irregularities and intimidation and recommended an independent body, in place of the Ministry of the Interior, to oversee future elections. The SDF, UNDP and two other parties refused to contest the presidential election in October without an independent electoral commission and called for a boycott. President Biya was re-elected for a seven-year term. The opposition disputed the government's claim of high voter turnout. A new government formed in December included three UNDP members.

Legislation prohibiting torture was passed in January. It specified that torture is unjustifiable in all circumstances and that causing injury or death through torture is punishable by up to life imprisonment.

Four Rwandese nationals arrested in 1996 and accused of participating in the genocide in Rwanda, whose extradition had been requested by the International Criminal Tribunal for Rwanda, were extradited in January and the extradition of another two was authorized in November. Six others were released in February after a Court of Appeal ruled that there was insufficient evidence against them. (See *Amnesty International Report 1997.*)

Several hundred SDF members and supporters were arrested because of legitimate political activities. Saïdou Yaya Maïdadi, a prominent SDF member from northern Cameroon, was held for almost two weeks in Maroua, Far-North Province, in January. Although charged with contempt of the Head of State, he was not tried. Up to 50 SDF members and supporters were arrested in May and June and held for several weeks in South-West Province under legislation allowing administrative detention for renewable periods of 15 days. Hundreds of people were rounded up during the night by security forces in Douala and detained without charge for several hours shortly before the election results were announced on 6 June, in an apparent attempt to deter demonstrations.

Thirteen SDF supporters were arrested during a peaceful demonstration outside the Supreme Court on 6 June. Despite a legal limit of 72 hours' detention before referral to a judicial authority, they appeared before the Public Prosecutor five days later. They were charged with contempt of the Head of State and other offences, but subsequently acquitted.

Scores of SDF supporters were arrested around the time of the October presidential election. They included Konga Philip

Kuate, a prominent SDF official in Ebolowa, South Province. He was held briefly on 6 October and rearrested on 12 October, the day of the election, accused of distributing leaflets calling for a boycott. He was released uncharged a month later. At least 60 people were arrested in Santa and Ako in North-West Province. All were released without charge after several weeks.

Seven prisoners of conscience – UNDP members held since 1994 and sentenced to 10 years' imprisonment in 1996 – remained imprisoned until December, when they were released pending their appeal hearing scheduled for February 1998 (see *Amnesty International Reports 1995* to *1997*).

Up to 20 UNDP supporters were arrested in Far-North Province in October because of their boycott of the presidential election. Detained at a police station, they were escorted to the polling station and ordered to vote. They were released only after paying bribes to the security forces.

In February Abdoulaye Math, president of a non-governmental human rights organization, the *Mouvement pour la défense des droits de l'homme et des libertés* (MDDHL), Movement for the Defence of Human Rights and Liberties, was arrested when attempting to travel to the USA for a human rights seminar, shortly after organizing a conference on human rights abuses in northern Cameroon. He was charged with fraud and unauthorized selling of pharmaceuticals, although this charge was later dropped. He was released pending trial after eight days. Although the trial was scheduled for May, judicial authorities said that the case file had disappeared.

Journalists writing for independent newspapers were harassed and assaulted, convicted of criminal offences and imprisoned. Alain Christian Eyoum Ngangué, of *Le Messager,* was imprisoned in January at the Central Prison, New Bell, in Douala, after being sentenced to one year's imprisonment in October 1996 (see *Amnesty International Report 1997*). He was conditionally released in March. Evariste Menounga, chief editor of *L'Indépendant Hebdo,* previously detained without charge in late 1996, was arrested in March and imprisoned at the Central Prison, known as Nkondengui prison, in Yaoundé, the capital. Charged with inciting revolt and disseminating false news following an article about disaffection in the armed forces, he was convicted of the second charge only. He was released in May after receiving a six-month suspended sentence. Bosco Tchoubet, director of *La Révélation,* was arrested in April, following an article alleging that a government minister had established private militias, and charged with contempt and defamation. He was released in July after receiving a six-month suspended sentence. In late December the director of *Le Messager,* Pius Njawé, was imprisoned following an article which questioned President Biya's state of health. Five people who attempted to visit him in New Bell prison were also briefly detained.

In February Christian Mbipgo Ngah, a journalist working for *The Herald,* was arrested in Santa, apparently accused of criticizing the government and security forces. He was beaten for several hours at a gendarmerie headquarters before being released uncharged.

Shortly before the legislative elections, a UNDP delegation, including a former National Assembly member, Nana Koulagna, was attacked by the private militia of the traditional ruler of Rey Bouba in North Province; five people died in the confrontation. Nana Koulagna and 15 others were arrested, apparently accused of murder, but without evidence of individual responsibility for any death, and held at the Central Prison in Garoua. No member of the private militia was arrested. Although two were subsequently released, the others remained held and had not been charged by the end of the year.

In northern Cameroon, traditional rulers known as *lamibe,* often prominent members of the CPDM and acting with the tacit approval of the authorities, were responsible for illegal detention and ill-treatment of political opponents. There was no official investigation into human rights violations committed by them and their private militias. Some UNDP members who remained held illegally on the orders of the *lamido* of Rey Bouba had been held for several years. Three local chiefs from around Tchollirè arrested in 1996, apparently because they allowed UNDP members to live in the area, also remained held.

A former government minister and a close associate were sentenced to lengthy prison terms after an unfair trial. In April Titus Edzoa, Minister of Health, announced his resignation and intention to contest the presidential election. Security forces subsequently surrounded his home and his movements were severely restricted. In July he was imprisoned at Nkondengui prison, together with his presidential campaign manager who had been in police custody since May. Both men were charged with corruption and misappropriation of public funds. Their trial in October proceeded despite defence lawyers withdrawing in protest against being informed of the trial only 24 hours earlier. They were sentenced to 15 years' imprisonment. Appeals had not been heard by the end of the year.

Following armed attacks on several towns in North-West Province in late March, in which 10 people including three gendarmes died, up to 300 people were arrested. The attacks were attributed by the authorities to a group supporting independence for Cameroon's two English-speaking provinces. SDF supporters were arrested without evidence of involvement in the attacks. About 100 people were also arrested in South-West Province but later released.

Many of those accused of involvement in the attacks were transferred from Bamenda in North-West Province to Yaoundé. Almost 60 remained held at the end of the year, but none had been charged. They included members of the Southern Cameroons National Council (SCNC), which supports independence for the English-speaking community, and the affiliated Southern Cameroons Youth League. Five other SCNC members arrested in 1995 and 1996 in connection with a referendum on independence remained held without charge throughout the year (see *Amnesty International Reports 1996* and *1997*).

Many of those detained following the violence in North-West Province in March were tortured or ill-treated, both when arrested and subsequently at police stations and gendarmerie headquarters. At least five people died from torture, ill-treatment and lack of medical care. They included Emmanuel Konseh who died in late March after being severely beaten and stabbed with a bayonet, and Pa Mathias Gwei who, although critically ill following torture, was repeatedly denied medical treatment. He died in May within hours of being finally admitted to hospital. Ndifet Zacharia Khan was severely beaten following his arrest in Bamenda. He sustained serious injuries to his legs and buttocks; toes on both feet were amputated because of gangrene. During the arrests in North-West Province, civilians were beaten, kicked and humiliated and many incidents of rape were reported.

Opposition supporters arrested around the time of the presidential election were also tortured or ill-treated. SDF members Justin Pokam and Thomas Seme were reportedly beaten by police in Yaoundé. UNDP supporters in Far-North Province arrested for boycotting the election were publicly tortured by soldiers, including by being beaten on the soles of their feet.

Two young men died in police custody in Yaoundé in early November; one was tortured with a heated domestic iron applied to his genitals; the other was severely beaten. Action against those responsible for torture and ill-treatment was rare in the past, but in this case six police officers were arrested and charged with murder and complicity in murder.

Prisoners were regularly beaten and held chained in punishment cells without light, sanitation or water. In May a prisoner who attempted to escape, Ibrahim Mikila Bélédé, died after being severely beaten by prison guards at Maroua Central Prison. There was no investigation into his death. Also at Maroua Central Prison in May, a prisoner was reported to have been stripped and severely beaten by prison guards. When a member of the MDDHL intervened to protest, he too was beaten.

Prison conditions remained extremely harsh throughout Cameroon, with severe overcrowding, inadequate or non-existent sanitary facilities and seriously deficient health care and nutrition.

Several people were injured in incidents where the security forces apparently used excessive force. In early January, five women were admitted to hospital with injuries from beatings or gunshot wounds after gendarmes opened fire during the arrest of a traditional ruler in Fungom, North-West Province, in connection with a communal dispute. When women later protested against the gendarmerie's refusal to comply with a High Court order for release, more than 20 were injured, three of them seriously, after gendarmes opened fire.

In January a prisoner under sentence of death at Maroua Central Prison was reported to have been executed, the first known execution since 1988. Other executions also possibly took place during the year.

Twelve people from Equatorial Guinea arrested in September and at least two Chadians arrested in November were at risk of grave human rights violations if forcibly returned to their own countries. They remained held without charge at the end of the year; the reasons for their continued detention were unclear.

Throughout the year Amnesty International called for the release of prisoners of conscience and for other political detainees to be charged and tried, or released. It called for safeguards to protect all prisoners and detainees from torture and ill-treatment, for independent and impartial investigations into reports of torture and ill-treatment and for those responsible to be brought to justice. In September Amnesty International published a report, *Cameroon: Blatant disregard for human rights*, which made specific recommendations to the government to end human rights violations. It also called on the international community to scrutinize human rights in Cameroon and to press Cameroon to adhere to its human rights commitments. The government disputed the report but did not comment in substance. Amnesty International also called on the government not to forcibly return detained nationals from Chad and Equatorial Guinea and asked why they were held in detention.

CHAD

Scores of people were extrajudicially executed. Scores of suspected opponents and critics of the government, some of them prisoners of conscience, were detained without charge or trial. Human rights defenders and others received death threats from the security forces. Torture and ill-treatment were widespread. Prison conditions often amounted to cruel, inhuman or degrading treatment. Armed opposition groups were responsible for grave human rights abuses.

The forces of President Idriss Déby's government faced armed opposition, mainly in the south and east of the country, from the *Forces armées pour la République fédérale* (FARF), Armed Forces for the Federal Republic, the *Front national du Tchad* (FNT), Chad National Front, the *Front national du Tchad rénové* (FNTR), Renewed National Front of Chad, the *Armée nationale tchadienne en dissidence* (ANTD), Dissident Chadian National Army, and the *Mouvement pour la démocratie et le développement* (MDD), Movement for Democracy and Development. These armed opposition groups were responsible for serious human rights abuses against the civilian population, and the security forces committed grave human rights violations during counter-insurgency operations.

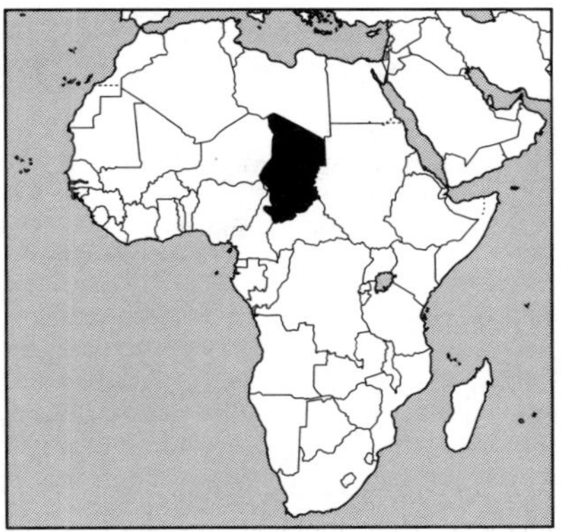

A peace accord was signed in April between the government and the FARF. It provided an amnesty to all members of the FARF and for the integration of its members into the army.

The UN Commission on Human Rights decided in April not to transfer consideration of the human rights situation in Chad from the confidential "1503 procedure" into the public procedure. The European Parliament passed a strong resolution on Chad in February, condemning the deteriorating human rights situation, calling on Chad to release all political prisoners, and urging European Union member states to ensure that military aid to Chad was not used to commit human rights violations. In November the African Commission on Human and Peoples' Rights examined the first periodic report of Chad.

Legislative elections took place in January and February, ending the transition period initiated in 1993. In March the *cour d'appel*, Court of Appeal, declared the majority of seats to have been won by the *Mouvement patriotique du salut* (MPS), the presidential party.

In February the government annulled the shoot-to-kill policy issued in 1996, which instructed members of the gendarmerie to extrajudicially execute people caught in the act of committing a crime (see *Amnesty International Report 1997*). However, this instruction was not followed by the security forces and scores of extrajudicial executions were reported. Between March and June, for example, at least seven suspected robbers were extrajudicially executed. In one case in the Ouaddai in June, two suspects were taken out of custody and killed by the security forces.

Suspected members of the opposition were also extrajudicially executed. In October the security forces shot dead several dozen people when they opened fire on people registering in Moundou in accordance with the peace accord signed between the government and the FARF. In the following days the security forces combed Moundou and neighbouring areas and extrajudicially executed many unarmed civilians whom they suspected of being FARF members. The victims included Laougoussou Nguirayo Etienne and Nguirayo Thimotée, respectively father and grandfather of the national executive secretary of the FARF, and Nanglar, aged 80, whose body was found in the Logone river.

A number of those killed were tortured by the "*arbatachar*" method, whereby the arms are tied behind the back in a painful position. Several mutilated and unrecognizable bodies were retrieved from the Chari and Logone rivers during the year: evidence indicated that the victims had suffered the "*arbatachar*" and had been extrajudicially executed by the security forces.

A man who escaped extrajudicial execution in January said he had been arrested by gendarmes in N'Djaména on suspicion of stealing a carpet. Ten days later he was taken from his cell and driven with two other prisoners to the River Chari. There, he said, gendarmes pushed them into the river, with their wrists and ankles bound. He survived because he managed to loosen his bonds, but believed the two others had drowned.

Scores of suspected opponents and critics of the government, including activists in non-governmental organizations and human rights groups, were detained without charge or trial. Some were arrested and held for short periods. Tohnel Doumro, an employee of *Secours catholique pour le développement* (SECADEV), Catholic Aid for Development, who had been arrested in November 1996 (see *Amnesty International Report 1997*), was released in February without charge. Mahamat Abdelhaq, chairman of the Abéché section of the *Association tchadienne pour la promotion et la défense des droits de l'homme* (ATPDH), Chadian Association for the Promotion and Defence of Human Rights, who had been arrested in December 1996 (see *Amnesty International Report 1997*), was also released without charge in February. However, he was warned by gendarmes that if he did not "keep quiet" he would be rearrested.

Firmin Nengomnang, a member of the *Ligue tchadienne des droits de l'homme* (LTDH), Chadian Human Rights League, was arrested in Moundou in December for a critical article published in July 1997 in the newspaper *Le Temps* about the commissioner of police of Moundou. Firmin Nengomnang had been assaulted, threatened with execution and beaten with rifle butts in February by members of Chadian security forces, including the commanding officer of the Chadian National Army at Penzengué in Logone Oriental. At the end of the year, Firmin Nengomnang was still held without charge and trial.

Following the October incidents in Moundou, at least 20 people were arrested in Moundou and N'Djaména. Some were released but at least five remained in detention at the end of the year. They were accused of "intelligence with the enemy". The people still detained at the end of the year included Danimbaye Kaïna Nodji and Souleymane Abdallah, the founder member of Alternative 94, a Chadian organization for political debate.

At least 20 political prisoners, including possible prisoners of conscience, arrested in previous years were in detention without charge or trial at the start of the year. Two of them were released and a few escaped from prison, but at least 10 remained in detention and were forcibly integrated into the army. Also held without charge or trial until they were forcibly integrated into the army were Etienne Tamlar, Valentin Djélassem and Moïse

Nodjimadji, who had been arrested in the two Logone regions between July and October 1995 on suspicion of collaborating with armed opposition groups.

Human rights defenders, including members of *Tchad Non Violence*, Chad Non-Violence, and the LTDH, as well as journalists, continued to be threatened by the security forces. Some, including Abdallah Issa Idriss, President of the regional branch of the LTDH at Faya Largeau, received death threats. Lazare Tikri Serge, General Secretary of *Tchad Non Violence*, was attacked in February by members of the *Agence nationale de sécurité* (ANS), National Security Agency.

In September Sosthène Ngargoune, President of the *Union des journalistes tchadiens*, Chadian Union of Journalists, was severely beaten by members of the security forces whom he was interviewing in the offices of the gendarmerie in Moundou. The attack was led by former members of the FARF who had been integrated into the army. They also threatened to kill human rights activists Dobian Assingar and Julien Beassemda.

Torture and ill-treatment by the security forces were frequently reported. Virtually all political prisoners and many criminal suspects were subjected to the "*arbatachar*", beatings and other forms of torture.

Information emerged about the death in custody of Mahamat Ahmat Hanat. He was reportedly tortured to death at the Fourth District police station in N'Djaména in November 1996.

Prison conditions remained so harsh that they often amounted to cruel, inhuman or degrading treatment. Three detainees who escaped from Faya Largeau said that they had been bound with chains for the first three months of their detention. They said that food was inadequate, sanitation virtually non-existent, and that they were forced to work for the French military aid mission at Faya Largeau.

Past cases of "disappearances" remained unresolved. There was no news of Mahamat Fadil, director general of the police under former President Hissein Habré, and two members of the MDD. The three men were arrested by officials in Niger and handed over to the Chadian authorities in November 1996. Nor was any information forthcoming about four people, including Ibrahim Souleymane, who "disappeared" in August 1996 after they were handed over to the Chadian authorities by the Sudanese authorities (see *Amnesty International Report 1997*).

Armed opposition groups committed grave human rights abuses. Several unarmed civilians, both men and women, were tortured by the FARF during the year. In February Joséphine Béasimbaye, Gabriel Yoramgam, Salomon Béaloum and Ibrahim Laoutoudji were tortured by members of the FARF. The same month Joseph Mbaïyaoel died of his injuries following ill-treatment by the FARF.

Members of the FARF also killed a number of unarmed civilians deliberately and arbitrarily. In February Laurent Beram and Bekande, from the village of Mbikou in Logone Oriental, were killed by the FARF. At around the same time Souleymane Ali, a cattle farmer from Donian, Logone Oriental, was also killed by the FARF. After the Moundou incidents in October, FARF members killed at least a dozen unarmed civilians and wounded several others.

In March Amnesty International published *Chad: Hope betrayed*, which documented systematic human rights violations and called on the Chadian authorities and the international community to improve the human rights situation in Chad. Amnesty International also called on armed opposition groups to take steps to end torture and deliberate and arbitrary killings.

Amnesty International urged the UN Commission on Human Rights to transfer consideration of Chad's human rights record to the public scrutiny procedure, but without success. The organization called on members of the international community to condemn military, security and police transfers that contributed to the continuation of human rights violations in Chad, and appealed in particular to the governments of the People's Republic of China, France and the USA regarding military equipment supplied by them which had aggravated the human rights situation in Chad.

In April Amnesty International representatives and other human rights activists met President Déby and urged him to promote respect for human rights in Chad.

CHILE

A new military petition to close all investigations into past violations was submitted to the Supreme Court. Human rights defenders received death threats. Reports of torture by members of the security forces continued to be received.

In June the Commission of Constitution, Legislation and Justice of the Senate presented a bill on detention of suspects which defines the crime of torture and sets sanctions. By the end of the year the bill was still being debated.

In March the Inter-American Commission on Human Rights (IACHR) made public a resolution of October 1996 concerning four cases of human rights violations committed under the military government of General Augusto Pinochet. The cases of Ricardo Lagos Salinas, Juan Aniceto Meneses Reyes and Pedro José Vergara Inostroza, who "disappeared", and of Juan Alsina, who was killed after being arrested by the security forces, had been closed by civilian and military courts by applying the Amnesty Law decreed during General Pinochet's government. The IACHR reiterated that the application of these amnesties constituted a violation of Article 1.1 of the American Convention on Human Rights. In its recommendations the Commission asked for domestic legislation to be adapted to conform to the provisions of the American Convention on Human Rights so that human rights violations by the *de facto* military government might be investigated and those found responsible effectively punished. It also recommended fair and effective compensation for the families of the four victims.

A bill calling for the abolition of the death penalty brought before the Senate was rejected in June.

In September the Military Prosecutor General presented a new petition to the Supreme Court requesting that it instruct all appeal courts and judges to close legal proceedings concerning hundreds of cases of human rights violations dating from the period of military government (see *Amnesty International Report 1997*). In October the Supreme Court rejected the request and recommended that courts and judges speed up all pending cases.

Death threats against human rights defenders attempting to uncover past violations committed under the military government were reported. In June, an anonymous caller told Sola Sierra, President of the *Agrupación de Familiares de Detenidos Desaparecidos,* Association of Relatives of Disappeared Prisoners, "now we are really going to kill you, you communist so-and-so". Another two members of the Association received similar threats. Police protection was granted after members of the Association made an official complaint before the Santiago Appeals Court.

Reports of ill-treatment and torture by security forces, including cases involving military conscripts, continued. Following the escape on 30 December 1996 of four political prisoners – all members of the *Frente Patriótico Manuel Rodríguez,* Manuel Rodríguez Patriotic Front – from the maximum security prison in Santiago, there were reports of reprisals, including ill-treatment of the remaining detainees. A number of prisoners were reportedly beaten by members of the *Grupo Especial Antimotines de Gendarmería,* the prison guards' anti-riot unit, during cell searches in January. Juan Aliste Vega, Oscar Cruces Espinoza, Carlos Gutiérrez Quiduleo, Carlos Plaza Villaroel and Juan Tapia Olivares reportedly sustained injuries following beatings. Marcos Andrade Sánchez was reported to be passing blood and to have wounds on his forehead, bruising all over the body and four loose teeth. According to reports, members of the anti-riot unit threatened further reprisals if the prisoners submitted complaints about the beatings.

In March human remains were found in a cave on Cerro de la Virgen in San

Felipe, V Region. They were later confirmed to be those of an 18-year-old military conscript, Pedro Javier Soto Tapia, who had been missing since December 1996. While serving his military service at the Yungay Regiment in San Felipe, Pedro Javier Soto Tapia had informed his parents that he had been subjected to ill-treatment and excessive punishment by his superiors. Claims by the military authorities that he committed suicide were strongly rejected by his relatives. During the investigation into the circumstances of his death, four conscripts were arrested and allegedly tortured during interrogation by army officials. The four – Johnny Pérez Torres, Andrés Serrano Leiva, Dagoberto Contreras Llanes and Guillermo Saavedra Aguilera – were arrested in April and accused of the killing. A parliamentary deputy complained publicly that the four had been beaten, verbally abused, deprived of sleep and threatened in order to extract confessions. Dagoberto Contreras' mother stated that her son had been beaten and was tortured with electric shocks. These allegations were categorically denied by the military authorities. By the end of May, the four conscripts had been released without charge owing to lack of evidence. There was no information as to whether an investigation was initiated into the complaints that they were tortured. The investigation into Pedro Soto Tapia's death had not been concluded by the end of the year.

In September it was reported that Alejandro David Uribe Sandoval, an 18-year-old mentally retarded criminal suspect, who was arrested in the locality of San Miguel by *carabineros* (uniformed police), was tortured. According to his mother, he was beaten, hooded and shot through the hands. He was taken by the police to an emergency care centre for medical attention and subsequently charged with assaulting a police officer by a military court.

In January Amnesty International wrote to the authorities expressing concern at reports of ill-treatment of political prisoners at the maximum security prison in Santiago. The organization asked that access be given to independent doctors to check the state of health of those held in isolation. Amnesty International reminded the authorities of the recommendation, made by the UN Special Rapporteur on Torture following his 1995 visit (see *Amnesty International Report 1997*), that detainees be given prompt access to medical attention as a preventive measure against ill-treatment. No reply was received. In March and April, Amnesty International expressed concern about allegations that Pedro Javier Soto Tapia had been ill-treated, and asked for a prompt and impartial investigation to officially identify the exhumed body and to establish the whereabouts of Pedro Javier Soto Tapia. The authorities replied that an investigation was taking place. Amnesty International expressed concern at reports that the four conscripts had been tortured. No information was forthcoming concerning these allegations. In June the authorities responded concerning five individual cases of torture (see *Amnesty International Report 1996*). The communication indicated that the allegations had been investigated by the *carabineros* and found to be unsubstantiated. No independent inquiry was known to have been carried out .

In November Amnesty International publicly called on the Chilean authorities to cooperate with the Spanish authorities in trials initiated by the Spanish National Court in connection with "disappearances" that took place under the military government.

CHINA

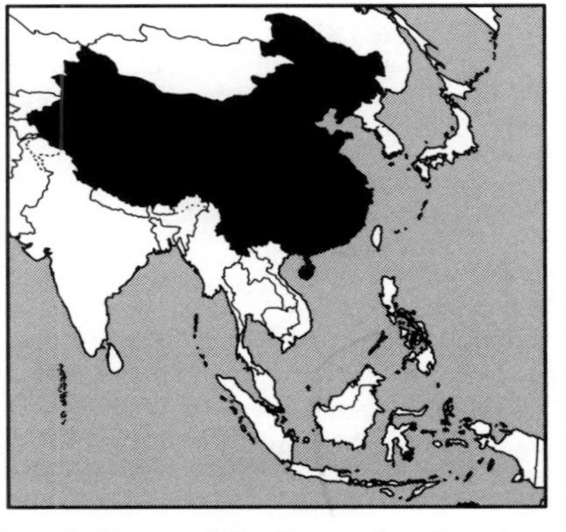

Hundreds, possibly thousands, of protesters and suspected opponents of the government were detained during the year, while thousands of political prisoners

detained in previous years remained imprisoned. Many were prisoners of conscience. Some were sentenced after unfair trials, others were detained without charge or trial. Torture and ill-treatment remained widespread. The death penalty continued to be used extensively.

In March the National People's Congress amended the Criminal Law. Although its most ostensibly political crimes of "counter-revolution" were repealed, they were replaced by a similar range of offences against national security. The amended law came into effect in October, but the cases of prisoners convicted of "counter-revolutionary" offences were not reviewed.

The 15th National Congress of the Chinese Communist Party, held in September, endorsed further economic reforms and resulted in some leadership changes. The Congress' report referred for the first time to the protection of human rights and stressed the need to "govern the country by law". In October the government published a paper on religion, acknowledging the principles on freedom of religion in international human rights instruments, but setting restrictions on authorized religious activities in China. At the UN Commission on Human Rights, China again blocked discussion on a draft resolution by moving a procedural motion to take no action. The UN Working Group on Arbitrary Detention visited China in October.

In October China signed the International Covenant on Economic, Social and Cultural Rights, but gave no indication of when it might ratify it.

Despite growing official acknowledgement of international human rights standards, serious human rights violations continued.

A crack-down on suspected Muslim nationalists, religious "extremists" and alleged "terrorists", which started in 1996, intensified in the Xinjiang Autonomous Region after ethnic protests and several bombing incidents attributed to underground opposition groups. In February anti-Chinese protests by Uighurs in Yining, western Xinjiang, turned into riots after clashes between police and local Muslims. At least nine people were killed and nearly 200 injured, although it remained unclear how many casualties resulted from rioting and how many from police action. Several hundred people were detained and at least 59 were subsequently tried for involvement in the protests. Their sentences were announced at "public sentencing rallies" held in Yining in April and July. Twelve of them were sentenced to death and executed, and 47 received sentences ranging from seven years' imprisonment to the death penalty suspended for two years.

Following the Yining riots, the authorities targeted "separatists", suspected nationalist sympathizers and members of unapproved religious groups in Yili and other areas of Xinjiang, leading to the dismissal of 260 grassroots officials and the closure of over 100 Koranic schools. Hundreds of people were reportedly detained, including 40 officially described as "core participants in illegal religious activities". Many were reportedly still held without charge or trial at the end of the year.

A crack-down on Tibetan nationalists and religious groups continued in the Tibet Autonomous Region (TAR). Official propaganda teams continued to carry out "patriotic education" in Tibetan monasteries and nunneries. Protests by monks and nuns who refused to denounce the Dalai Lama led to expulsions and arrests, while some went into hiding or fled the country to escape arrest. In February a group of nuns in Lhoka Choenkye county were reportedly detained for peacefully protesting when local government officials came to their nunnery to enforce a ban on pictures of the Dalai Lama. Taken to Nethang county prison, they were still reportedly detained several weeks later. In June Jampel Tendar, a monk at Gongkar Choede monastery, was reportedly detained for expressing support for the Dalai Lama when an official "re-education" team required monks to write statements denouncing him. He was reportedly beaten at the monastery and in detention centres in Tsethang and Lhasa. In June the TAR authorities reported that 98 people had been sentenced to prison terms in Tibet in 1996 for "endangering national security". They included 14 monks from Ganden monastery imprisoned for their involvement in clashes with government officials at the monastery in May 1996 (see *Amnesty International Report 1997*).

Protests by workers and farmers in various provinces led to arrests, but little information was available. In Sichuan province, at least nine people were detained in Mianyang in July for taking part in workers' protests against corruption among factory officials. Armed police broke up the protests, reportedly injuring scores of demonstrators and arresting dozens. Local officials later denied that any demonstrators had been injured, but confirmed that at least nine suspected "instigators" of the protests were detained. Li Bifeng, a dissident and former tax officer in Mianyang, who had issued a public appeal about the workers' protests, went into hiding in July to escape arrest. Several political dissidents were detained by police during the year in apparent attempts to intimidate or silence them.

State control over religious activities and harassment of members of unapproved Christian groups continued, although fewer arrests were reported than in previous years. Those detained included Xu Yongze, leader of the "New Born" Church, an evangelical group in Henan province. He was detained in March together with seven other Christians, and reportedly sentenced to 10 years' imprisonment in September for "disturbing public order". Su Zhemin, underground Roman Catholic Bishop of Baoding, in Hebei province, was reportedly arrested in October. He had been in hiding since a crack-down on Catholics in Donglu in May 1996 (see *Amnesty International Report 1997*) and had been imprisoned for his beliefs on several previous occasions.

Thousands of political prisoners detained without trial or convicted after unfair trials in previous years remained imprisoned. They included many prisoners of conscience serving long sentences for their part in the 1989 pro-democracy movement and others jailed for the peaceful expression of their beliefs. In January prisoners of conscience Hada and Tegexi, two ethnic Mongol intellectuals sentenced in 1996 to 15 and 10 years' imprisonment respectively (see *Amnesty International Report 1997*), had their appeal against their sentence rejected. According to official sources, at least 2,000 "counter-revolutionary" prisoners remained imprisoned and 200 monks and nuns were jailed in Tibet for activities "endangering national security". The true number of political prisoners was believed to be much higher. Many prisoners of conscience were serving terms of "re-education through labour", a form of administrative detention imposed by local government committees outside the judicial process. According to official sources, 230,000 people were detained without trial in 280 "re-education through labour" centres throughout the country for minor offences including prostitution, swindling and "other activities disturbing social order".

Around a dozen prisoners of conscience were released on parole or after their case had been reviewed or their sentences reduced. Others were released at the end of their sentence. They included Yu Zhenbin, an employee of the Qinghai provincial archives imprisoned since 1989, who was released in June after his 12-year sentence was reduced by four years, and Zhao Lei, held since 1993 in connection with the case of her husband Bao Weiji (see *Amnesty International Report 1994*), who was released in October after her six-year sentence was reduced. In a rare case, prisoners of conscience Tang Yuanjuan (see *Amnesty International Report 1992*) and Li Wei, both jailed since 1989, had one of their two convictions for "counter-revolutionary" offences quashed by a court and were released in July. In November Wei Jingsheng, China's best-known dissident, was released on medical parole and sent to the USA for medical treatment. He had spent most of the previous 18 years in prison.

Released prisoners of conscience continued to be subjected to police surveillance and harassment, and some were pushed into exile as a result. Bao Ge, a human rights activist from Shanghai held for three years in a labour camp (see *Amnesty International Report 1995*), was released in June. He was denied identity papers needed to find work and both he and his family were frequently harassed by police. He left China in November.

Political trials continued to fall far short of international standards, with verdicts and sentences decided by the authorities before the trial, and appeal hearings usually a mere formality. In April Chadrel Rimpoche, former Abbot of Tashilhunpo monastery, and two other Tibetans were tried in secret for communicating with the exiled Dalai Lama over the search for the reincarnation of the Panchen Lama. Chadrel Rimpoche was sentenced to six years' imprisonment for "conspiring to split the country" and "leaking state secrets", while his two co-defendants received terms of four and two years' imprisonment. The trial was closed to the public because it involved state secrets, according to official sources. No details of the proceedings were disclosed. In May a court in southern China sentenced Li Wenming and Guo Baosheng, two labour rights activists who had been arbitrarily detained for over three years, to three and a half years' imprisonment for "plotting to subvert the government". Their trial had started in November 1996 but was suspended after attracting the attention of the Hong Kong media. No independent observers were allowed to attend the hearings.

Torture and ill-treatment of detainees and prisoners held in detention centres, prisons and labour camps remained widespread, sometimes resulting in death. In October, for example, a common criminal prisoner at the Qingshan penal farm, Guangdong province, was reportedly beaten to death by two prison officers for failing to complete his daily assigned work. Between January and July, 300 to 400 cases of torture and ill-treatment were investigated by the procuracies, according to official sources, but the real incidence of torture was believed to be far higher. Few prosecutions for torture were reported. In a case publicized in February, four police officers were sentenced to prison terms of three to 11 years' imprisonment for torturing to death Lin Zhuhua, a bank robbery suspect in Jiangsu province. In October, two police commanders in Gansu province were given two-year suspended prison sentences for torturing three innocent suspects until they "confessed" to a murder. The suspects were sentenced to death on the basis of their forced confessions but a provincial high court ordered a retrial and they were later exonerated. Other reports of torture, however, were ignored by the authorities. In July, for example, Ji Xiaowei, a Hong Kong citizen sentenced to death in southern China for alleged drug-trafficking, claimed on appeal that he had confessed under torture during police interrogation. The appeal court ignored his claim and confirmed the death sentence. He was executed on 18 July.

Torture and ill-treatment of political prisoners held in various areas also continued to be reported. Liu Nianchun, a labour activist held in northeast China, was reportedly tortured with electric-shock batons by labour camp officials in May and placed in solitary confinement in harsh conditions after going on hunger-strike in protest at his imprisonment.

Prison conditions were often harsh, with inadequate food and medical care, and many prisoners suffered from serious illnesses as a result. Medical parole was rarely granted to political prisoners. Those denied medical parole included Chen Longde, a detained dissident crippled after jumping from a window to escape torture in August 1996 (see *Amnesty International Report 1997*). After several months in hospital, Chen Longde was returned to the Luoshan labour camp in December 1996 and required to work despite still suffering from his injuries and being unable to walk without crutches. In a public appeal to the authorities in October, his parents said they had unsuccessfully sought medical parole for him for over a year.

The death penalty continued to be used extensively to tackle growing crime resulting from economic and social changes. At least 68 criminal offences, many of them non-violent, were punishable by death. The suspended death penalty was abolished as a penalty for juvenile offenders when the Criminal Law was amended in March. Executions for fairly minor crimes, such as theft, continued during the year. Local media reporting of death penalty cases appeared to have been restricted. The limited records available at the end of the year showed that at least 2,495 people were sentenced to death and 1,644 executed. The true figures were believed to be far higher.

Those executed included at least 12 people accused of committing various offences during violent ethnic protests in February in Yining, Xinjiang Autonomous Region. Eight other people were executed in May in Urumqi, the regional capital of Xinjiang, for alleged terrorist activities, including bombings.

Amnesty International urged the authorities throughout the year to release all prisoners of conscience, ensure fair trials for other political prisoners, take steps to stop torture and executions, and review the use of the death penalty. In May Amnesty International held discussions on its concerns with a Foreign Ministry official and representatives from the China

Society for Human Rights Studies visiting Norway. Amnesty International published various reports during the year, including: in March, *People's Republic of China: Law reform and human rights*; in April, *People's Republic of China: The eighth anniversary of the 1989 massacre – those who have been silenced*; and in August, *The death penalty in China: Breaking records, breaking rules.*

COLOMBIA

Hundreds of people were killed by the security forces and paramilitary groups operating with their support or acquiescence. Many of the victims were tortured before being killed. Human rights activists were repeatedly threatened and attacked; at least 10 were killed. At least 140 people "disappeared". "Death squad"-style killings of people regarded as "disposable" continued in urban areas. Hundreds of people, including trade unionists, human rights defenders and social activists, were arrested and tried for political offences under procedures which fell short of international standards for fair trials. Armed opposition groups were responsible for numerous human rights abuses, including hundreds of deliberate and arbitrary killings and holding hundreds of hostages.

In March the UN Human Rights Committee issued a series of observations and recommendations which deplored the fact that gross and massive human rights violations continued to be committed in Colombia by members of the armed forces, the police, paramilitary and guerrilla groups. The Committee expressed deep concern about continued widespread impunity and about evidence that paramilitary groups received support from members of the military. It also considered that the legalization of armed vigilante groups known as *Convivir* would further aggravate the human rights situation. The Committee's recommendations included: that members of the armed forces and police accused of human rights abuses should be tried by independent civilian courts and suspended from active duties during the period of investigation; that support given by military personnel or security forces to paramilitary groups and operations should be investigated and punished; and that immediate steps should be taken to disband paramilitary groups.

In November the Constitutional Court ruled that the establishment of civilian vigilante associations was constitutional. The Court, however, warned that the *Convivir* should not be allowed to act as "death squads" nor to violate human rights. The Court ordered the *Convivir* to relinquish weapons whose use was legally restricted to the military which had previously been issued to them by the government.

The UN High Commissioner for Human Rights established an office in Colombia in April, with a mandate to assist the Colombian authorities to develop policies and programs for the promotion and protection of human rights, to observe violations of human rights in the country and to submit analytical reports to the High Commissioner.

In August Colombia acceded to the Second Optional Protocol to the International Covenant on Civil and Political Rights, aiming at abolition of the death penalty.

In September the government presented to Congress a draft bill to reform the Military Penal Code. The bill introduced important modifications to the Code including the specific exclusion from the military justice system of crimes not directly related to military service, including "torture, genocide, forced disappearance and any other crime which constitutes a serious human rights violation". Congress gave the bill preliminary approval in December. In November the government presented to Congress a draft bill which would incorporate the crime of forced disappearance into the Penal Code.

The bill establishes long prison sentences for the crimes of "disappearance", "genocide", physical or psychological torture and forming paramilitary organizations or "death squads".

There were renewed hopes for a peace process following the release in May of 60 soldiers captured by the *Fuerzas Armadas Revolucionarias de Colombia* (FARC), Revolutionary Armed Forces of Colombia, in an attack on a military base in Caquetá in August 1996. Ten marines captured by the FARC in Chocó department in January were released at the same time. However, government proposals to reactivate negotiations were rejected by the armed opposition and the long-running armed conflict continued to spread and intensify, particularly in the months preceding municipal and regional elections in October. In April the main armed opposition groups, the FARC and the *Ejército de Liberación Nacional* (ELN), National Liberation Army, announced their intention to sabotage the elections and launched a campaign of intimidation and attacks against electoral candidates designed to force their resignation. The national paramilitary organization *Autodefensas Unidas de Colombia* (AUC), United Self-Defence Groups of Colombia, threatened and killed candidates they believed to be guerrilla sympathizers. Over 40 mayoral and council candidates were killed by armed opposition and paramilitary organizations, and over 200 were kidnapped by the FARC and the ELN and held for days or, in some cases, weeks. Most were released unharmed but hundreds of candidates resigned. Two election monitors from the Organization of American States and a human rights official of the Antioquia regional government were among those kidnapped by the ELN. They were released after 10 days.

The principal victims of the spiralling conflict continued to be civilians, mostly peasant farmers living in areas whose control was disputed between the armed forces and their paramilitary allies, and armed opposition groups. The regions most affected included the departments of Antioquia, Bolivar and Cesar in the northwest, Chocó department in the west and Meta department in the east. Although the number of extrajudicial executions directly attributable to the armed forces continued to decline from previous years, there was a severe escalation in serious human rights violations carried out by paramilitary forces acting with their tacit or active support. Hundreds of civilians were extrajudicially executed and scores "disappeared" as paramilitary forces continued their campaign of territorial expansion in the northwest. Increasingly, army-backed paramilitary forces employed a "scorched earth" strategy, burning entire villages and displacing the inhabitants.

Over 200,000 people were displaced, principally from rural areas affected by the armed conflict. Most abandoned their homes after paramilitary attacks against their communities; others fled aerial bombardments by the armed forces or threats from armed opposition groups. Early in the year, the town of Ríosucio and surrounding villages in the north of Chocó department, near the Panamanian border, saw a massive displacement of civilians following sustained attacks by the paramilitary organization *Autodefensas Campesinas de Córdoba y Urabá* (ACCU), Self-defence groups of Córdoba and Urabá, aerial bombardments by the army and reprisal killings by FARC guerrillas. Several hundred refugees from Chocó department crossed the border into Panama, but were forcibly returned by the Panamanian Government, in collusion with the Colombian authorities, in breach of their international obligations. At least one returned refugee was later killed by paramilitaries.

In an attempt to escape the conflict, some communities in the northwest declared themselves "peace communities" and declared their neutrality in the conflict. However, killings of members of "peace communities" by paramilitaries and the FARC was reported throughout the year.

Scores of people were killed in July when the ACCU launched an offensive in FARC-controlled southeastern Colombia. Up to 30 civilians were tortured and killed during a five-day paramilitary incursion in the village of Mapiripán on the borders of Meta and Guaviare departments. In October the Procurator General opened disciplinary investigations against four military officers, including the commander of the army's 7th Brigade, for "negligence". Evidence had emerged that the paramilitary forces had passed freely through a military controlled airstrip, and that the army had failed to respond to repeated calls for help from authorities in the village during the attack. ACCU leader Carlos Castaño Gil announced in September that his forces would commit "many more Mapiripanes". In October another AUC paramilitary front, the self-styled *Contraguerrilla Llanera*, attacked and killed 11 members of a judicial commission and its security force escort in San Carlos de Guaroa, Meta department. Several others were seriously injured in the attack. In November ACCU forces launched attacks on FARC strongholds throughout the country, in which civilians were targeted and killed. In response to the massacres, in which at least 60 civilians died, the government announced the creation of a "special search unit" to combat the paramilitary organizations. However, by the end of the year little progress had been made in capturing and bringing to justice those responsible for the massacres. In December the Attorney General announced that there were 180 outstanding arrest warrants against paramilitary leaders.

Human rights defenders continued to face harassment, intimidation and violent assaults. At least 10 were killed. In May human rights and environmental activists Elsa Alvarado and Carlos Mario Calderón were shot dead by gunmen who broke into their home in the capital, Bogotá. Elsa Alvarado's father, Carlos Alvarado, was also killed and her mother seriously injured. Mario Calderón and Elsa Alvarado, both university professors, worked for the *Centro de Investigación y Educación Popular* (CINEP), Centre for Research and Popular Education. In October, four people were charged in connection with the killings.

Several members of CINEP and other independent human rights organizations, including Amnesty International, received repeated death threats. In July President Samper issued a directive recognizing the legitimacy of the work of human rights organizations and ordering national and regional authorities and the armed forces to cooperate with human rights defenders and to refrain from making statements of a threatening nature. Attacks against human rights defenders, however, continued throughout the year and little progress was made in most cases in identifying those responsible.

The killing of so-called "disposables" by police-backed "death squads" and urban militias linked to armed opposition groups continued in many cities and towns. Victims included vagrants, drug dealers and suspected delinquents. In May, three detainees – Juan Carlos Herrera, Fabián Gómez and Andrés Escobar – were abducted from the Valle de Lili juvenile detention centre in Cali, Valle del Cauca department, by heavily armed and hooded men. The three youths were forced into a car which was later found abandoned. Their whereabouts remained unknown. In May 1995, three detainees abducted from the Valle de Lili Centre in similar circumstances were later found shot dead. Two former police officers and two former Valle de Lili Centre employees were under investigation for the 1995 killings (see *Amnesty International Report 1996*).

At least 140 people "disappeared" after detention by the security forces or paramilitary groups. Trade union leader Ramón Osorio Beltrán "disappeared" in April in Medellín when he was seized, together with his young son, by heavily armed men. The boy was later released but the whereabouts of his father remained unknown. Ramón Osorio, a leader of the Agricultural Workers Trade Union and a member of the Colombian Communist Party, had been arrested in January together with four other people, and released in February because of irregularities in the arrest procedure.

Hundreds of members of human rights and social organizations and trade unionists were tried by the specialist regional justice system where procedures fell short of international fair trial standards.

In the vast majority of cases, those responsible for extrajudicial executions, "disappearance" and torture were not brought to justice. Military tribunals investigating abuses by army personnel persistently failed to hold those responsible accountable. In July, then army commander General Manuel Bonett Locarno acquitted retired army general Farouk Yanine Díaz on charges (originally brought by the civilian justice system) of creating paramilitary groups responsible for widespread human rights abuses. The Procurator General appealed to the Superior Military Tribunal to overturn the acquittal because the ruling had failed to take into account the evidence against Yanine Díaz. No decision had been announced by the end of the year.

In a landmark ruling issued in August, the Constitutional Court defined the limitations of military jurisdiction over crimes committed by military personnel. The Court concluded that human rights violations such as "disappearance", torture, murder and rape cannot be considered "acts of service" and should, therefore, fall within the jurisdiction of the civilian justice system. Commenting on the ruling, General Bonett said that the military jurisdiction was the "lifebelt" of the military and that "if society sends us to fight it has to give us legal protection".

In June paramilitary leader Fidel Castaño Gil was convicted and sentenced, *in absentia*, to 30 years' imprisonment for the "disappearance" and murder of 43 men from Pueblo Bello, Urabá, in 1990 (see previous *Amnesty International Reports*). Eleven members of Fidel Castaño's paramilitary organization were also convicted for the massacre, but only two were in custody. Fidel Castaño remained at large.

In September paramilitary chief Carlos Castaño (brother of Fidel Castaño) was charged with the murder of Senator Manuel Cepeda Vargas in 1994. Two army sergeants had been charged in 1996 in connection with the murder (see *Amnesty International Reports 1995* and *1997*). Carlos Castaño was not arrested and continued operating freely in heavily militarized areas of the country.

Armed opposition groups were responsible for numerous violations of humanitarian law, including hundreds of deliberate and arbitrary killings of civilians. In addition to politicians and electoral candidates (see above), victims included members of indigenous communities. Between July and September at least 20 members of the Koreguaje indigenous community were killed in the communities of El Cuerazo, San Luis and Aguas Negras, Caquetá department, reportedly by FARC guerrillas. In October, two members of the Emberá Katio indigenous community of Aguas Claras, municipality of Mutatá in Antioquia department, were also killed by FARC members. Father and son Mario and David Domicó were dragged from a meeting and shot dead. Several other members of the Emberá Katio communities were killed by the ACCU.

FARC guerrillas were also reportedly responsible for the killing of at least three members of the "peace community" of San José de Apartadó. Luis Fernando Espinoza, Fernando Aguirre and Ramiro Correa, were killed in October by members of FARC's 58 Front allegedly in reprisal for the community's refusal to sell food to the FARC. Thirty other members of the community were killed by ACCU paramilitaries after the community declared itself a neutral "peace community" in March.

In August the ELN abducted and killed Liberal Party Senator Jorge Cristo Shaiun in Cúcuta, Norte de Santander department. A unit of the ELN reportedly accepted responsibility for the murder and threatened to kill other political figures in North Santander. In September, five men were arrested and charged in connection with the killing of Senator Cristo.

Eleven-year-old twins Santiago Andres and Mario Alejandro López were killed in June when the ELN dynamited their parents' farmhouse in La Unión, Antioquia department.

At least 600 people were kidnapped and held hostage, principally by the FARC and the ELN. In addition to politicians and international observers, victims included landowners, business people and their relatives, judicial officials and journalists. Most were released alive, in some cases after months or years in captivity. Others were killed when ransom demands were not met or during rescue attempts by the security forces.

Amnesty International raised its concerns about Colombia at the UN Commission on Human Rights. These were addressed in a statement by the Chairman of the Commission which, while welcoming the opening of an office of the UN High Commissioner for Human Rights in Colombia, expressed deep concern at the persistence of thousands of violations of the right to life.

In October Amnesty International published a report, *Colombia's internally displaced: Dispossessed and exiled in their own land*, which documented the growing problem of civilians displaced by the armed conflict.

Amnesty International repeatedly called on the authorities to take steps to end widespread human rights violations, to disband paramilitary forces, to protect human rights defenders and to bring those responsible for abuses to justice. Amnesty

International condemned abuses committed by armed opposition groups and called for the release of people held hostage. The organization urged all parties to the conflict to observe basic humanitarian standards.

COMOROS

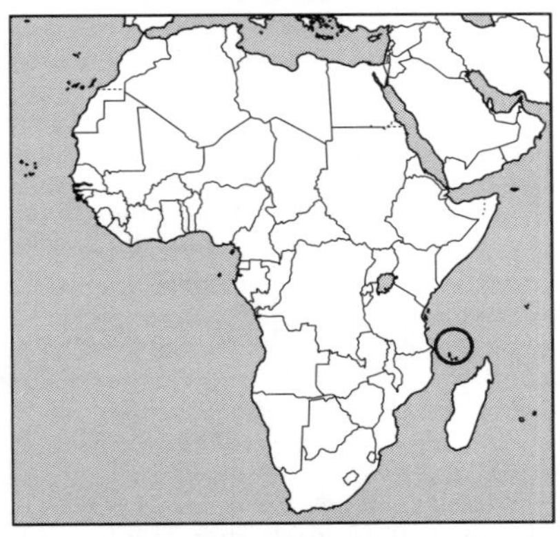

Several people were killed in possible extrajudicial executions by government troops dispersing political demonstrations. One person convicted of murder was executed. Two other people remained under sentence of death.

Social and political unrest resulted in the killing of civilians and government troops. Some of the deaths of civilians appeared to be possible extrajudicial executions. In January teachers and civil servants staged a series of peaceful demonstrations in Moroni, the capital, asking to be paid salary arrears and for their positions to be regularized. Thirty people were reportedly injured when the army used live ammunition to disperse one demonstration and 10 people sustained gunshot wounds. In the same month, members of the presidential guard destroyed shops and restaurants in Moroni in what the government said was a measure to enforce the Islamic law against alcohol. In March government soldiers fired into a crowd of unarmed demonstrators, killing four people and injuring 20 others, while breaking up a three-day strike on Anjouan Island. There was apparently no official investigation into the incident.

On 3 August a separatist movement on Anjouan island led by Said Mohamed Souef declared that it was no longer part of the Comoros islands, but rather part of the former colonial power, France. On 11 August another group of separatists announced the independence of the island of Moheli. In September the federal army crossed to the island of Anjouan to restore order, but clashed violently with groups of separatists. One civilian and three soldiers were reportedly killed.

In August a mediator from the Organization of African Unity was sent to the Comoros to negotiate between the political factions and to organize a conference to find "a consensual solution which respects the aspirations of all Comorians and maintain unity and territorial integrity". The conference took place in December, but no solution had been found by the end of the year.

In May Saidali Mohamed was executed by firing-squad after an Islamic court found him guilty of murder. As in the previous year when a man was executed for a similar offence, Saidali Mohamed was denied the right of appeal to a higher court and was not represented by legal counsel (see *Amnesty International Report 1997*). Mohamed Sahali and Youssouf Hamadi spent a second year under sentence of death.

Amnesty International condemned the increasing use of the death penalty and reiterated its appeal to President Mohamed Taki Abdoulkarim to commute all death sentences and to abolish the death penalty. Amnesty International expressed concern about the lack of fair trial safeguards for people accused of offences punishable by death. The organization appealed to the government to issue strict instructions to the security forces to prevent the ill-treatment of demonstrators and to prohibit the use of excessive force in law enforcement.

CONGO
(DEMOCRATIC REPUBLIC OF THE)

In the period before the change of government in May, scores of people, including prisoners of conscience, were detained without charge or trial, and the security forces tortured detainees and massacred unarmed civilians. Fifteen people were sentenced to death. Armed opposition

groups committed grave human rights abuses including thousands of deliberate and arbitrary killings. Rwandese refugees were missing after armed operations; many may have been killed. Under the new government, hundreds of suspected opponents were detained, mostly without charge or trial; some of them were prisoners of conscience. Torture and ill-treatment were widespread. There were reports of "disappearances" and hundreds of extrajudicial executions. One soldier was executed by firing-squad and 13 others were sentenced to death. The new authorities forcibly returned refugees to countries where they would be at grave risk of human rights abuses. Armed groups opposed to the new government also committed grave human rights abuses.

In the early part of the year armed conflict continued between the *Forces armées zaïroises* (FAZ), Zairian Armed Forces, and the opposition *Alliance des forces démocratiques pour la libération du Congo-Zaïre* (AFDL), Alliance of Democratic Forces for the Liberation of Congo-Zaire. The AFDL, with the support of Rwandese government and other forces, continued to gain ground from the east.

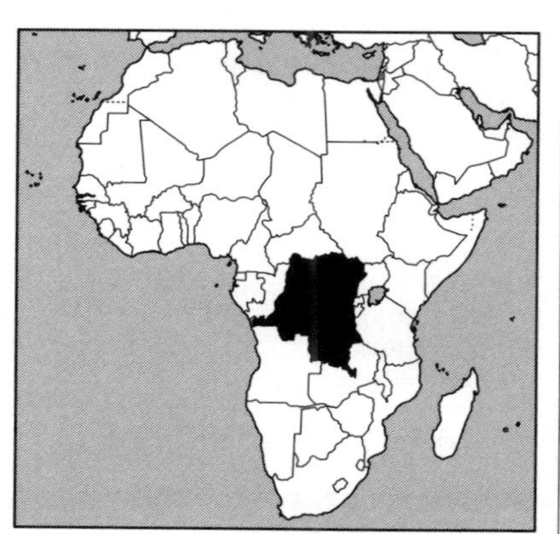

On 17 May the AFDL entered the capital, Kinshasa. Ousted President Mobutu Sese Seko left the country. A transitional government was named by the AFDL on 22 May and one week later AFDL leader Laurent-Désiré Kabila was inaugurated as President. The country changed its name from Zaire to the Democratic Republic of the Congo (DRC). The new government pledged to uphold human rights and to hold elections in 1999, but the Constitution was revoked. President Kabila was given wide-ranging personal powers, and political party activity outside the AFDL was banned.

Under the new government, armed conflict continued to be reported in the east of the country, with clashes taking place between the AFDL and armed opposition groups, including former members of the FAZ, members of the former Rwandese armed forces and Congolese armed opposition groups.

In late March the UN Special Rapporteur on Zaire led a fact-finding team to gather information about massacres during the conflict in eastern Zaire. Although the AFDL restricted his movements, the Special Rapporteur submitted a report to the UN Commission on Human Rights. On the basis of this report the Commission decided in April to send the UN Special Rapporteur on extrajudicial, summary or arbitrary executions and a member of the Working Group on Enforced or Involuntary Disappearances on a joint mission to eastern Zaire to investigate reports of violations of human rights and humanitarian law. The AFDL denied the mission access to the region and no investigation occurred. In August, after consultations with the UN Security Council and the new government, the UN Secretary-General sent his own investigative team to the country. The DRC Government persistently frustrated the team's efforts to begin investigations. The team's leaders were recalled to UN headquarters in October, but returned in late November to begin the investigation after an agreement was reached between President Kabila and the US Permanent Representative to the UN. In early December, after weeks of delay, the investigative team was deployed to Mbandaka in the northwest of the DRC. The team withdrew from the area in mid-December after it experienced hostile demonstrations and demands by local leaders to be paid before the investigation could begin.

In the period before the change of government in May, scores of detainees were held without charge or trial, including prisoners of conscience. Among them were Zairians of Tutsi ethnic origin, refugees, journalists and human rights activists. All were held in extremely harsh conditions and many were tortured.

FAZ soldiers looted, raped and killed with impunity. The victims included residents of towns and villages in the path of soldiers retreating from AFDL advances, people of Rwandese, Burundi or Ugandan origin, and refugees. Church, and international and national humanitarian aid workers were also targeted.

In January, 15 people were sentenced to death by court martial, joining scores already under sentence of death. No executions had been reported when the government fell in May, but it was unclear whether the sentences were upheld under the new government. Under the new government, one soldier was executed by firing-squad in October after a special military court found him guilty of killing a student in September. Eight soldiers convicted in September of attempted mutiny and five others convicted in December of violent offences, including criminal conspiracy, armed robbery and attempted murder, were under sentence of death at the end of the year.

While in opposition the AFDL committed gross human rights abuses in the territory under its control. It committed thousands, possibly tens of thousands, of deliberate and arbitrary killings of Rwandese and Burundian Hutu refugees and of Zairian Hutu. For example, on 25 February, several hundred Rwandese refugees, including eight Rwandese priests and three nuns, were reportedly killed in Kalima, two days after the town had been taken by AFDL forces.

Hundreds, possibly thousands, of Hutu refugees were reported to have been deliberately and arbitrarily killed in the South-Kivu region, particularly during February and March. Bodies were hidden in mass graves, or left by the side of roads. For example, scores of refugees were reportedly killed and buried in a mass grave at Mpwe, west of Shabunda, around March.

On 13 May some 800 refugees were massacred by AFDL soldiers at Mbandaka, Equateur region. Some of those killed were reportedly ordered to kneel or lie on the ground before they were shot or bayoneted to death. Others were killed when soldiers opened automatic fire on a group waiting for transport.

Tens of thousands of unarmed civilians, mostly Rwandese refugees, were missing after AFDL operations. It was feared that many may have been deliberately and arbitrarily killed or may have died from starvation and exposure.

As many as 40,000 refugees from Kasese and Biaro camps, south of Kisangani, went missing in April. The refugees had been fleeing westwards from refugee camps in Kivu, as the AFDL frontline advanced. On 20 April, six civilians were killed near Kasese camp; the killings were blamed by the AFDL on the refugees. Over the following days, international humanitarian organizations were denied access to the camps, which were reportedly attacked by AFDL combatants and armed civilians colluding with them. Local people reported seeing a bulldozer digging mass graves and burying bodies. By 23 April, Kasese and Biaro camps were entirely deserted. About 40,000 refugees were located by humanitarian workers in subsequent days but about 40,000 others remained unaccounted for. It was feared that many may have been deliberately and arbitrarily killed.

After the AFDL came to power, human rights violations persisted.

Hundreds of people were arrested and held without charge or trial under the new government; some of them were prisoners of conscience. Those held included human rights activists, journalists, members of opposition parties and people associated with the former government. Many detainees were held incommunicado, sometimes in private houses and other illegal places of detention.

Human rights activists were targeted for arrest and intimidation, including raids on their offices and death threats. Bertin Lukanda and Diomba Ramazani, leading members of a coalition of non-governmental organizations, were arrested in August on suspicion of collecting information about massacres for UN investigators. They were reportedly beaten severely. One of their colleagues, Dieudonné Asumani, was arrested in mid-August and accused of having sent information about their arrest to foreign organizations. Bertin Lukanda was also a member of a human rights group based in Kindu, known as *Haki Za Binadamu*, several of whose workers had been harassed and prevented from travelling around the country in previous months. They were all released in September.

Didi Mwati Bulambo, a human rights activist who had previously been arrested and ill-treated by President Mobutu's security officials, was arrested by AFDL soldiers on 23 August and held in a military barracks at Kamituga in Mwenga district of South-Kivu. He was denied access to legal counsel or to medical care until his release on 18 September.

Also arrested and held without charge were journalists critical of the AFDL, including Polydor Muboyayi Mubanga, editor-in-chief of *Le Phare* newspaper, who was arrested in September in Kinshasa. He was beaten by soldiers at the time of his arrest and was charged with "spreading false rumours and inciting ethnic hatred". The charge related to an article in his newspaper critical of President Kabila. President Kabila ordered his release in mid-November.

Supporters of opposition parties were arrested. For example, 15 members of the main opposition party, the *Union pour la démocratie et le progrès social*, Union for Democracy and Social Progress, were arrested at a peaceful demonstration in mid-August. They were reportedly tortured with electric-shock batons during interrogation and denied essential medical treatment. They were released on 14 October without having been charged or tried.

From June onwards, dozens of people associated with former President Mobutu's government were arrested. One of them, General Kikunda Ombala, appeared before Kinshasa Court of Appeal in December on charges of embezzlement of public funds and property when he was director of the Zairian Airways Agency and Air Zaire.

Torture and ill-treatment of detainees were widespread. For example, nine men arrested in Goma on 29 May and accused of armed robbery were repeatedly kicked and beaten with sticks and rifle butts. They were also burned when irons were welded round their arms and legs. Many former members of the FAZ taken into camps for retraining reportedly died after being beaten and deprived of food and medical care.

Women were reported to have been victims of torture, including rape, and to have been beaten on their breasts or otherwise ill-treated. A number of schoolgirls were reportedly raped by soldiers in August at Masambo, Rwenzori sub-district (*chefferie*), North-Kivu. Women dressed in miniskirts, trousers or leggings were targeted for torture or ill-treatment by AFDL soldiers in Kinshasa. For example, in May AFDL soldiers beat a girl wearing a miniskirt with a nail-studded piece of wood, and reportedly whipped another young woman 40 times.

The security forces repeatedly used violence, including lethal force, to disperse peaceful opposition demonstrations and meetings. For example, in July soldiers opened fire on a peaceful demonstration by the *Parti Lumumbiste Unifié* (PALU), United Lumumbist Party, in Kinshasa. At least one demonstrator, Kiambukuta Komisa, died as a result and six were severely injured. About 130 demonstrators were arrested. Soldiers also reportedly broke into the home of PALU leader Antoine Gizenga, where they reportedly stripped naked and whipped a number of PALU supporters.

"Disappearances" were reported. For example, 17 people reportedly "disappeared" in Rwindi, North-Kivu province, after being arrested on 26 May.

Extrajudicial executions by AFDL soldiers were reported in many parts of the country. In virtually all cases the authorities denied that the AFDL were responsible.

As many as 120 unarmed civilians were reportedly shot dead on 26 May by AFDL soldiers in Uvira. The victims were reportedly demonstrating against the killing the previous night of about 10 people by gunmen who local people suspected were members of the AFDL.

On 29 May a Save the Children Fund worker and four Rwandese refugees, including a child, were shot dead by AFDL soldiers in Karuba, west of Goma.

In early June about 40 Burundian former students from Bukavu University were reportedly bayoneted to death by members of the AFDL between Bukavu and Shabunda.

In late June about 60 Rwandese refugees, including children, were reportedly massacred by AFDL soldiers at Kavumu, Kivu. The victims were apparently on their way to Rwanda.

Between 2 and 5 August, AFDL soldiers were reported to have killed as many as 800 unarmed people in the villages of Wimbi, Alela, Abanga and Talama, which lie between South-Kivu and Shaba provinces on the shores of Lake Tanganyika. The soldiers reportedly came from the Shaba town of Kalemie, and were apparently searching for armed opposition groups.

In Kinshasa a number of former FAZ soldiers and criminal suspects were killed by AFDL soldiers. Some were mutilated and burned to death. Members of opposition political parties and students were also killed. For example, Freddy Manganzo Nzani, a university student in Kinshasa, was killed by an AFDL soldier during a demonstration in June. He was reportedly shot as he pleaded for his life.

The new government forced hundreds of refugees from Rwanda and Burundi to return to their countries, despite the fact that their lives would be at grave risk there. For example, on 4 September the government forcibly returned about 800 Rwandese and Burundian refugees in Kisangani to Rwanda. In protest, the UN High Commissioner for Refugees (UNHCR) suspended activities for Rwandese refugees in the DRC. On 3 October the government announced that it had returned 4,000 refugees to Rwanda, and ordered the UNHCR to stop its work in North-Kivu.

Armed opposition groups continued to commit human rights abuses including deliberate and arbitrary killings. Armed groups, including members of the former Rwandese army, former members of the FAZ, and members of an armed group known as the *mayi-mayi*, were reported to have killed members of the Tutsi ethnic group who had returned from Rwanda to North-Kivu in early 1997. Attacks on Tutsi civilians reportedly increased in the middle of the year after Tutsi were appointed to replace local government officials from rival ethnic groups in Kivu.

Amnesty International appealed repeatedly to the government of President Mobutu, to the AFDL, and to the government of President Kabila to respect human rights. In February it published *Zaire: Rape, killings and other human rights violations by the security forces*. In March it published a memorandum to the UN Security Council appealing for a commission of inquiry to investigate reports of atrocities in eastern Zaire.

In August Amnesty International submitted a memorandum to President Kabila proposing measures to foster the rule of law. The government turned down a request by the organization to visit the country.

In December Amnesty International published *Democratic Republic of the Congo: Deadly alliances in Congolese forests*, which detailed continuing mass human rights violations since March, including some carried out by Rwandese government forces.

CONGO
(REPUBLIC OF THE)

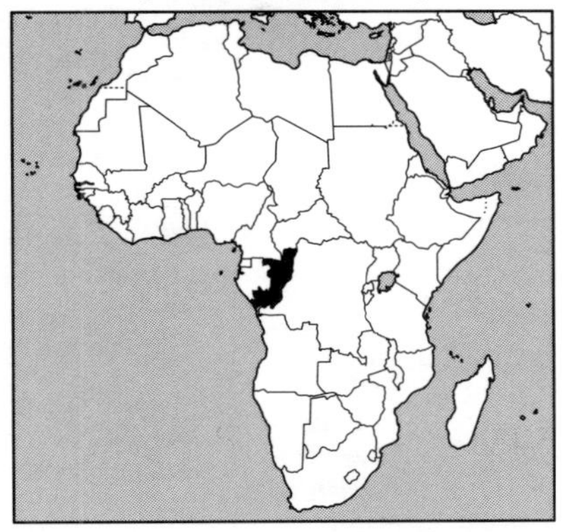

Thousands of civilians were killed in fighting between government troops allied with armed civilian militias on the one side, and militiamen belonging to an armed opposition group on the other. Both parties were responsible for torture and deliberate and arbitrary killings. Most victims were targeted because of their ethnic identity.

Political violence erupted after two years of relative stability (see *Amnesty International Reports 1996* and *1997*) and led to the overthrow in October of President Pascal Lissouba's government by militias loyal to former President Denis Sassou Nguesso.

The fighting began in June, some weeks before the presidential election. President Lissouba accused his main challenger for the election, Denis Sassou Nguesso, of staging a coup. He in turn accused the President and his allies of fomenting violence to force the postponement of the election in order to stay in power.

Despite several cease-fires and draft accords put forward by an International Mediation Committee chaired by Omar Bongo, President of Gabon, negotiations failed because there was no agreement on whether or not President Lissouba's mandate, due to end in August, should be extended. The fighting ended in October, when Denis Sassou Nguesso took power as President with the help of Angolan soldiers. He announced a transition period leading to presidential elections and promised that opposition parties would not be excluded from the election process.

From August to October, the UN Security Council called several times upon all parties to ensure the safety of the civilian population and the safe and unrestricted delivery of humanitarian assistance.

Thousands of unarmed civilians were killed during the fighting, mostly in Brazzaville, the capital. Both sides used heavy weaponry, particularly multiple rocket launchers, as a result of which at least half a million people sought refuge, notably in Congo's second largest city, Pointe-Noire. The violence increased in September when President Lissouba's mandate formally came to an end. Government forces carried out helicopter bombardments just north of Brazzaville, resulting in many civilian casualties, especially among displaced people. Unidentified fighters also launched shells across the river Congo to Kinshasa, capital of the Democratic Republic of the Congo, killing more than 20 people and prompting fears that the conflict might spread beyond the country.

Most human rights abuses were committed by armed militias allied to each of the two sides. Most government troops left the army to join militias linked to their own ethnic groups. Both the militias allied to the ruling *Mouvance présidentielle*, Presidential Tendency (known as "Zoulous"), and those loyal to Denis Sassou Nguesso (known as "Cobras"), terrorized Brazzaville, looting and killing or expelling people not belonging to their ethnic group. For several weeks the capital was in chaos and the bodies of dead fighters and civilians were left on the streets for days.

The level of violence made it difficult for human rights organizations to carry out independent investigations or to confirm who was responsible for individual killings of civilians, many of whom were targeted on account of their ethnic origin. In Brazzaville, militiamen of both sides set up barricades and road-blocks and stopped civilians to check their identity cards. People who did not have one were asked to speak in their first language in order to find out their ethnic group. Many members of the ethnic group of the opposing side were immediately killed. Killings on ethnic grounds also took place at various railway stations between Brazzaville and Pointe-Noire. People from the north who were Mbochis, the ethnic group of Denis Sassou Nguesso, were pulled off the train by "Zoulous" militiamen and killed or taken away in trucks to unknown destinations. Most of them remained unaccounted for at the end of the year.

Among those killed were women, children and sick people. In June "Zoulous" militiamen killed a boy who was coming back from school, apparently only because he lived in Poto Poto area, where many people from the north lived. "Zoulous" militiamen also occupied a hospital in Brazzaville in June in order to install heavy arms and to shell enemy positions. The militiamen killed some of the patients, because of their ethnic group, and expelled the rest.

Militiamen loyal to Denis Sassou Nguesso – "Cobras" – were also responsible for human rights abuses. In June men accused of being spies were given five minutes to explain themselves and were then summarily executed with a bullet in the chest or in the head. On 8 June "Cobras" detained 10 people, including two women. The women were tortured and the eight men were killed. On 15 June, three people were killed in Poto Poto because they were speaking in Kituba, the language of the southern part of the country, which is supposedly loyal to Pascal Lissouba. Also in June, volunteers working for the Congolese Red Cross were killed in Ouenze, a neighbourhood of Brazzaville, because they were suspected of supporting Pascal Lissouba.

When President Nguesso took power in October, scores of people suspected of being loyal to the former president were extrajudicially executed. The victims included the father and mother of Jean Sylvestre Souka, former director general of radio and television in Congo, who were extrajudicially executed in Mfilou, Brazzaville. Jacques Robert Kimpo, former Ambassador to Egypt, was arrested with seven other people in October, one of whom was released. The remaining seven people were extrajudicially executed by "Cobras". Gabriel Matsioana, a former Minister of the Environment, and Lieutenant Mikabou were also extrajudicially executed. In Pointe-Noire, women were raped and people suspected of being supporters of Pascal Lissouba were tortured and killed. Angolan soldiers who supported the "Cobras" also killed civilians, including Fabrice Koubaka, a pupil at a secondary school in Pointe-Noire, who was shot dead in front of his house.

Scores of people were arrested after President Sassou Nguesso took power. Some, including Pierre Kibamba, former Director General of Customs, and Ngono, a former bank official, were released without charge after one month's detention. Others remained in detention without charge or trial at the end of the year. They included Jacques Mounda Mpassi, former Minister of Youth, who was arrested in Pointe-Noire in November while trying to leave the country, and Albert Moungoundo, an executive member of the *Convention des démocrates pour l'union et la République*, Convention of Democrats for Unity and the Republic.

Amnesty International delegates visited Congo in June to interview Rwandese refugees coming from former Zaire and to investigate human rights violations in Congo. Because of the fighting, the delegates had to leave the country earlier than planned.

COSTA RICA

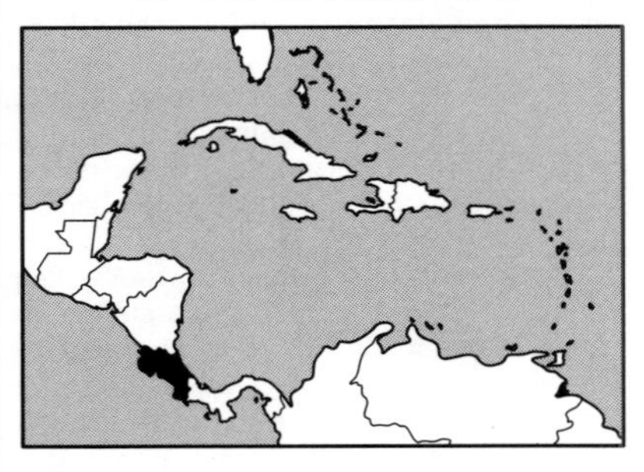

There were reports of ill-treatment by police and security guards during evictions of peasants from disputed lands. Former law enforcement personnel charged with responsibility for a death in custody in 1993 received suspended sentences and were released. A Honduran refugee fled Costa Rica following intimidation, apparently by members of the Honduran security forces.

In July and August, police and armed security guards operating under licence of the Ministry of Public Security, and private armed guards reportedly ill-treated peasants and destroyed homes, possessions and crops – during evictions from disputed lands in Sarapiquí, Heredia department. The evictions were carried out even though a court case was pending and an interim stay order had been issued. Similar allegations of abuses by such units during previous evictions in which peasants were reportedly shot and wounded, remained unresolved (see *Amnesty International Report 1997*).

In June, seven former agents of the *Organismo de Investigación Judicial* (OIJ), Judicial Investigation Unit, charged in connection with the death in custody in 1993 of William Lee Malcolm, a minor, were cleared of homicide and aggravated illegal arrest. The former agents were found guilty of abuse of authority, given suspended sentences and released. William Lee Malcolm had allegedly been tortured while in custody, and deprived of the rights to have his detention communicated to a competent court and to have a lawyer present during interrogation.

Honduran refugee Reina Xiomara Zelaya González fled Costa Rica, with her two daughters, following continued threats and intimidation, apparently from the Honduran security services. She had fled to Costa Rica in 1996 following a series of similar death threats (see *Amnesty International Report 1997*). In February Reina Xiomara Zelaya was granted permanent residence in a European country.

CÔTE D'IVOIRE

Dozens of students were arrested and three were sentenced to terms of impris1onment; all were considered prisoners of conscience. Twenty opposition party supporters arrested in November 1995, including possible prisoners of conscience, remained in jail without trial throughout the year. There were reports of beatings by the security forces; one person died, apparently as a result. At least one person died in custody. One person was sentenced to death but there were no executions.

In March Côte d'Ivoire acceded to the (first) Optional Protocol to the International Covenant on Civil and Political Rights (ICCPR).

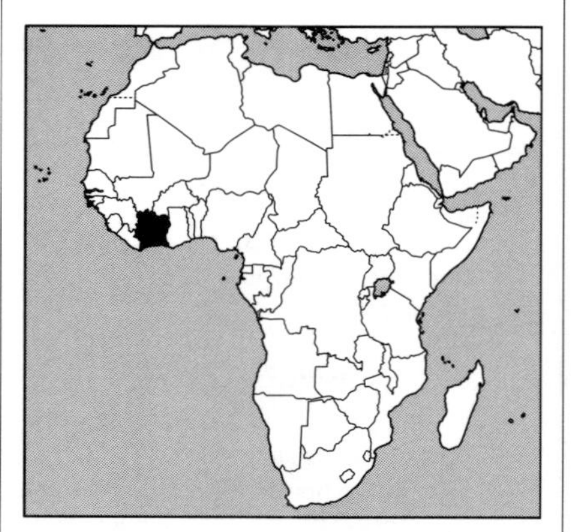

In January, three leaders of the *Fédération estudiantine et scolaire de Côte d'Ivoire* (FESCI), Ivorian Federation of Students and School Pupils, Picas Damané, Charles Blé Goudé and Sylvanus Goré, were sentenced to two years' imprisonment; they were prisoners of conscience. They had been arrested two weeks earlier in the office of the Minister of Security where they had been invited to discuss student grievances. They were convicted of inciting violence under a law, commonly called the "anti-riot law", which allows anyone who calls or leads a gathering to be held accountable for any violence which subsequently occurs.

Dozens of FESCI members were detained for short periods during the first half of the year. FESCI was officially legalized again in October. In January and February at least 20 students were arrested, including Guillaume Soro Kibaforé, Secretary General of FESCI. All were considered to be prisoners of conscience imprisoned solely because of their membership of FESCI, which the government claimed had been banned. All had been released by the end of February, after receiving a presidential pardon.

Twenty opposition party supporters, including possible prisoners of conscience, arrested in connection with the political unrest that followed the presidential elections in October 1995 remained in detention without trial in Gagnoa prison throughout the year (see *Amnesty International Report 1997*). They were among the 100 detainees accused of looting camps belonging to the Baoulé ethnic group, of which President Henri Konan Bédié is a member, during the October 1995 election period. This period saw the development of ethnic tension between Baoulé villagers and the majority ethnic group, the Bétés, to which Laurent Gbagbo, leader of the opposition *Front populaire ivoirien*, Popular Ivorian Front, belongs. Most of these detainees were provisionally released, but 20 remained in detention without trial at the end of the year.

Seven officers accused of plotting a coup were released in March and expelled from the army. They had been arrested in November 1995 and held without trial in incommunicado detention for 17 months (see *Amnesty International Report 1997*).

There were further reports of beatings by police officers. Student activists belonging to FESCI continued to be harassed and ill-treated by the security forces. During a raid on Abobo campus in Abidjan, the capital, in January, Akpélé Akpélé Marcellin, a student, died apparently as a result of beatings by members of the security forces. The then Minister of Security refused to open an inquiry into the causes of his death. In April a FESCI meeting at the Bouaké campus was broken up by members of the security forces who beat and otherwise ill-treated the students. One of the students, Estelle Zézé, who had asthma and was suffering from the effects of tear-gas, was severely beaten on the legs by members of the security forces while she was lying on the ground.

Two journalists working for the newspaper *La Voie*, were beaten by members of the security forces. In February, Félix Teha Dessrait was beaten by the police when he arrived at the police station to check whether Guillaume Soro Kibaforé (see above) was detained. In May, Daniel Opeli was severely beaten by police officers after identifying himself as a journalist while covering a story on a FESCI meeting in Abidjan.

At least one person died in custody. Djahi Djié Bruno died in February in the Gagnoa prison, apparently as a result of harsh prison conditions. He was the seventh detainee arrested after the October 1995 presidential elections to die in prison after months of detention without trial (see *Amnesty International Report 1997*).

One person was sentenced to death, but there were no executions. In June, Diomandé Hamadou was sentenced to death after being convicted of murder.

In March, Amnesty International called on the authorities to accede to the Second Optional Protocol to the ICCPR, aiming at the abolition of the death penalty.

CROATIA

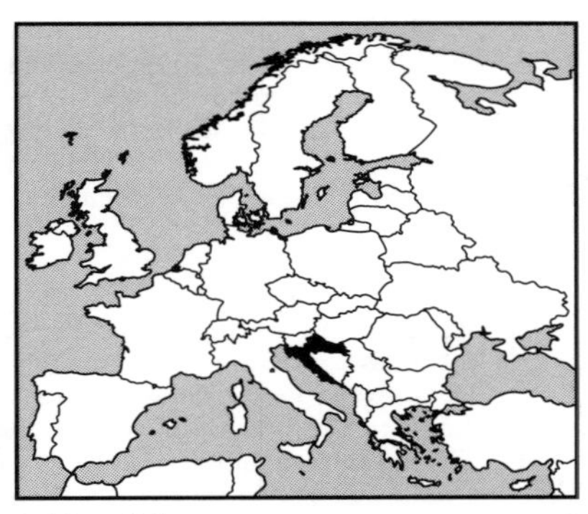

Critics of the government were prosecuted on criminal charges. At least 12 trials in national courts for war crimes appeared to be unfair. There were reports of ill-treatment by police. Attacks on Croatian Serbs, particularly in the Krajina territory, continued with impunity and the authorities deliberately resisted the return of Croatian Serbs to their homes. Although hundreds of cases were resolved, the fate of thousands of people who "disappeared" remained unclear.

The UN Transitional Administration for Eastern Slavonia (UNTAES) oversaw the reintegration of the last remaining rebel Croatian Serb area to Croatian authority. In July UNTAES' mandate was extended until January 1998, although it only had executive authority over the region until October. After that, the area was returned to Croatian control. In August William Walker replaced Jacques Klein as the UN-appointed Administrator for UNTAES.

In April elections were held for municipal and county assemblies and for the upper house of parliament. The ruling party *Hrvatska Demokratska Zajednica*, Croatian Democratic Union, regained control of the upper house and almost all the 21 county and municipal assemblies. In Eastern Slavonia, where elections were organized by UNTAES, Croatian Serbs won 11 of 28 municipalities. President Dr Franjo Tudjman was re-elected in elections held in June.

In April, under pressure from UNTAES and the UN High Commissioner for Refugees (UNHCR), the Croatian authorities agreed to a formal procedure for registering and administering the return of displaced people. By establishing joint working groups, the agreement allowed potential returnees to register their desire to return, and established procedures to ascertain the status of their houses. By the end of the year, approximately 2,500 refugees and displaced people had returned to Eastern Slavonia and approximately 9,000 from Eastern Slavonia to the Krajina. However, about 300,000 Croatian Serbs remained refugees in the Federal Republic of Yugoslavia and some 40,000 to 50,000 Croatian Serbs remained refugees in Bosnia-Herzegovina. There were violent attacks on returnees (see below), which the authorities claimed were due to procedures not being followed, but there were no provisions to protect returnees within the agreement, nor was it known whether the authorities had plans to protect those who had returned to the Krajina. Croatian Serbs in Bosnia-Herzegovina were prevented by administrative obstacles from returning to Croatia.

In June the mandate of the Organization for Security and Co-operation in Europe (OSCE) Mission in Croatia was extended until the end of 1998. The mission was reinforced by additional personnel to monitor human rights, particularly of Croatian Serbs. The monitors also observed the extent of Croatia's implementation of its commitments regarding the return of refugees and displaced people.

Also in June, Croatian Serb Slavko Dokmanović was arrested with the support of UNTAES personnel and transferred to the International Criminal Tribunal for the former Yugoslavia. He had been secretly indicted by the Tribunal in April 1996 for crimes related to the killing of approximately 260 men who had been taken from a hospital in Vukovar, Croatia, in 1991. His defence challenged the legitimacy of his arrest, which took place when he travelled to Eastern Slavonia from the Federal Republic of Yugoslavia for a meeting with

UNTAES. Four other Croatian Serbs known to be indicted by the Tribunal remained at large; two of them were believed to be in the Federal Republic of Yugoslavia and the other two in Republika Srpska, the Bosnian Serb entity of Bosnia-Herzegovina. Croatian authorities also failed to cooperate fully with the Tribunal by arresting indicted Bosnian Croat suspects in Croatia and transferring detainees to the custody of the Tribunal (see **Bosnia-Herzegovina** entry).

Croatia ratified the European Convention for the Protection of Human Rights and Fundamental Freedoms in November. Croatia had signed the Convention in November 1996 when it was admitted to the Council of Europe (see *Amnesty International Report 1997*).

As of April, more than 80,000 refugees from Bosnia-Herzegovina remained in Croatia. In addition, approximately 17,500 Bosnian Croats and approximately 3,000 Croats from the Federal Republic of Yugoslavia had obtained citizenship and settled in Croatia. Many of the Croat settlers were encouraged to move into houses owned by Croatian Serbs in the Krajina as well as in Bosnian Croat areas of Bosnia-Herzegovina. In some cases, housing appeared to have been deliberately allocated to refugee families when it became known that the owners' return was imminent.

Croatian Serbs, human rights defenders and critics of the government were the most common targets of a range of human rights violations committed throughout the country. Journalists and open critics of the government faced criminal charges, sometimes solely for expressing their opinions. In May a Zagreb court upheld an appeal by the state prosecutor against the acquittal of Viktor Ivančić and Marinko Čulić, editors of the independent weekly *Feral Tribune*, who had been charged with "slandering or insulting" President Tudjman in 1996 (see *Amnesty International Report 1997*). The first hearing of a retrial was opened in December, but adjourned. In August a prominent human rights activist, Ivan Z. Čičak, gave an interview in *Feral Tribune* in which he alleged that President Tudjman had discussed the partition of Bosnia-Herzegovina at a meeting with Serbian President Slobodan Milošević in 1991. He faced charges of "spreading false information" with the intention of causing alarm among a large number of citizens, which may be punished by up to six months' imprisonment. The leader of an opposition political party, Dobroslav Paraga, faced similar charges for making the same allegations in the independent newspaper *Novi List*. If found guilty and imprisoned on these charges, all four men would be prisoners of conscience.

The Croatian authorities released 18 Bosnian Serb prisoners of war, all of whom had been detained in Croatian prisons, including the "Lora" military prison in Split, after the cessation of hostilities. They included nine who were released in August in exchange for nine Bosnian Croats convicted of common crimes in Republika Srpska (see **Bosnia-Herzegovina** entry). All 18 had been detained since at least 1995 and at least one of them had been imprisoned since 1994 (see **Bosnia-Herzegovina** entry).

Trials and appeals continued in many cases of Croatian or Bosnian Serbs charged with war crimes committed in Croatia and Bosnia-Herzegovina. In at least 12 cases the fairness of the proceedings was in doubt. For example, in December one Croatian Serb was sentenced to three consecutive terms of 20 years' imprisonment. For two of the three sets of charges against him, he appeared to have been convicted solely on the basis of an uncorroborated confession made in 1993 and which he had withdrawn claiming that it had been made as a result of ill-treatment. For the other set of charges, witness testimony was reportedly contradictory and the judge added to the court record information not provided by the witnesses.

Unofficial sources in Serbia claimed that more than 100 Croatian Serbs remained imprisoned for war crimes committed in Croatia and Bosnia-Herzegovina.

There were reports of ill-treatment by police. The victims included human rights defenders, journalists and members of minorities. Vjekoslav Magaš, a representative in Eastern Slavonia of the *Hrvatski Helsinški Odbor*, Croatian Helsinki Committee, was assaulted by an off-duty police officer in April. The officer reportedly hit and punched Vjekoslav Magaš and threw stones at him as he tried to get away.

The authorities continued to fail to protect Croatian Serbs who had remained in the Krajina following offensives in 1995 by Croatian armed forces (see *Amnesty In-*

ternational Report 1997). They continued to be attacked by civilians, sometimes accompanied by police and soldiers. Croatian Serb refugees and displaced people who tried to visit or return to their homes in the Krajina were also attacked. In May, after a group of 10 displaced people returned to their homes near Hrvatska Kostajnica, a crowd of about 150 Bosnian Croat refugees armed with sticks and poles, went on the rampage. They systematically identified houses owned by people who had remained in the area during its occupation by Serb forces, primarily Croatian Serbs, then ransacked them and assaulted the occupants. Dozens of people were beaten during the initial mob attacks and in isolated assaults over following days. Mirko Knežević, who was 60 years old, died in hospital apparently as a result of beatings. National and local officials tried to justify the actions of the rioters, and 10 people were charged only with "participating in a gathering which committed a criminal act", despite the availability of witnesses to specific assaults.

Croatian Serbs, both returnees and those who had stayed in Croatia since 1995, came under attack in other towns in the Krajina, including Kistanje, Drniš, and Golubić. In Eastern Slavonia, those responsible for attacks on Croatian Serbs were not brought to justice. For example, in December a man arrested for a deliberate grenade attack which resulted in the death of one man was charged with a minor offence and released.

A number of land-mines or booby traps were placed in homes and other areas which had previously been cleared. For example, in April a man was killed in an explosion when he disturbed a haystack on his farm near Udbina. In the same area that month, a 67-year-old man was injured by a booby trap in a field near his house, and a woman was seriously injured by explosives placed under a plank in her garden.

The Croatian authorities supplied some information about criminal investigations into offences in the Krajina committed between August 1995 and April 1997 (see *Amnesty International Reports 1995* and *1996*). However, it was not possible to ascertain from the information provided whether human rights violations had been investigated or whether those responsible had been brought to justice. Many serious cases remained outstanding.

Of more than 2,000 people still missing as a result of the armed conflict in Croatia, many were believed to have "disappeared". Hundreds of cases were resolved, primarily through the identification of bodies exhumed from mass graves by the Croatian authorities or the International Criminal Tribunal for the former Yugoslavia. Among them were Siniša Glavašević, Branimir Polovina and scores of others who had been taken from a hospital in Vukovar and detained by Yugoslav National Army troops in November 1991 (see **Yugoslavia** entry, *Amnesty International Report 1992*). However, there was little progress in establishing the whereabouts of Croatian Serbs who "disappeared" during the armed conflict in 1991 and 1992 and during the military offensives in 1995.

At least 15 people, primarily from the Middle East, were detained in a "reception centre for foreigners" near Zagreb, apparently in contravention of international standards. At least three men were held for 12 months before being released and others remained in detention at the end of the year.

Amnesty International addressed the authorities on a variety of concerns including the protection of Croatian Serbs in the Krajina, freedom of expression, the protection of asylum-seekers, and the ill-treatment of Croatian Serbs, human rights defenders and others. The organization also stressed to the authorities that those responsible for war crimes should be brought to justice, but in fair and impartial trials. The organization also issued recommendations to the OSCE regarding the human rights aspects of its mission. In many cases, the authorities responded but failed to address fully Amnesty International's concerns.

CUBA

Hundreds of political prisoners detained in previous years and convicted after unfair trials remained imprisoned. Many were prisoners of conscience. Scores of dissidents suffered short-term detention and harassment and several were forced into exile. There were frequent reports of ill-treatment, in some cases amounting to torture, resulting in at least one death.

Prison conditions sometimes constituted cruel, inhuman or degrading treatment. At least five unarmed civilians were shot dead by law enforcement officials in disputed circumstances. No executions were reported but several men remained under sentence of death.

The government of President Fidel Castro justified suppression of political dissent on the grounds that the country continued to face hostility from the US Government, including a 35-year-old trade embargo which had been extended in 1996 by the Helms-Burton Act (see *Amnesty International Report 1997*). Cubans were encouraged to sign a declaration of loyalty to the government in support of Law 80 passed in December 1996, which made it illegal for anyone in Cuba to collaborate directly or indirectly in favour of the application of the Helms-Burton Act.

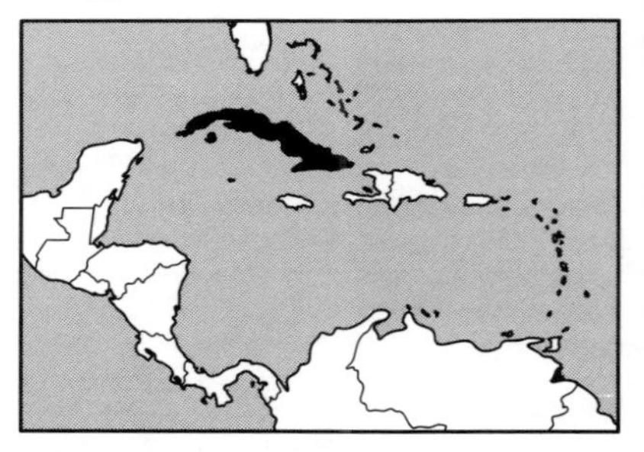

Between June and October, several bomb explosions took place in tourist locations in Havana, the capital, resulting in one death and several injuries. The authorities said they had proof that people based in the USA were behind the explosions. In September a Salvadoran citizen said to be linked to Cuban exiles was detained in connection with several of the bombings and charged with offences that carried a possible death sentence. However, he had not been tried by the end of the year. In November a US citizen, Walter van der Veer, who had been detained in 1996, was tried in a military court on state security charges, including "the promotion of armed action against Cuba", and sentenced to 15 years' imprisonment.

A revised version of the penal code came into effect in August. None of the offences frequently used to stifle dissent were changed and the death penalty was maintained as the maximum punishment for a wide range of crimes.

The government continued to deny the UN Special Rapporteur on Cuba access to the country. In November the UN General Assembly again overwhelmingly condemned the US embargo. Also in November the UN Committee against Torture expressed concern, *inter alia*, at the failure of the Cuban authorities to establish a specific crime of torture as required by the UN Convention against Torture and Other Cruel, Inhuman or Degrading Treatment or Punishment or to respond to specific torture allegations. It also expressed concern about "certain nebulous offences", such as *desacato* (disrespect), *resistencia* (resistance) and *propaganda enemiga* (enemy propaganda), because of the space they provide "for misuse and abuse", and criticized the absence of specific training about the Convention for law enforcement personnel and others. The Committee made a series of recommendations, including calling on the authorities to address urgently complaints of torture or ill-treatment and to permit human rights organizations to visit the country.

In the absence of official data and given the severe restrictions on human rights monitoring, it was difficult to estimate how many prisoners were held for political reasons. However, several hundred prisoners of conscience, as well as several hundred prisoners convicted of serious state security offences, many after unfair trials, were believed to be imprisoned.

Scores of members of unofficial groups working in the field of civil and political rights, and journalists working for independent press agencies, were detained for short periods. A few were held for several months, sometimes without access to a lawyer, before being released with threats that if they did not give up their activities or leave the country, they would face long-term imprisonment. Many were also subjected to other forms of intimidation, including organized *actos de repudio*, acts of repudiation, during which they were verbally abused and sometimes physically assaulted by government supporters for being "counter-revolutionaries".

Several of those detained were brought to trial or remained in detention awaiting trial. They included the following prisoners of conscience.

Héctor Palacio Ruiz, a political activist arrested in Havana in January after criticizing President Castro in a German television interview, was sentenced in September to 18 months' imprisonment for showing disrespect towards President Castro.

Nestor Rodríguez Lobaina and Radamés García de la Vega, President and Vice-President respectively of *Jóvenes por la Democracia*, Young People for Democracy, who in 1996 had both been subjected to sentences of "restricted liberty" and "confinement" for their advocacy of university reform (see *Amnesty International Report 1997*), were rearrested and sentenced to custodial sentences during 1997. Nestor Rodríguez Lobaina was sentenced to 18 months' imprisonment in April for "disrespect" and "resistance" and Radamés García de la Vega was sentenced to 18 months' "correctional work with internment" for "disrespect".

Dr Desi Mendoza Rivero, President of the *Colegio Médico Independiente de Santiago de Cuba*, Santiago de Cuba Independent Medical Association, was arrested in June in Santiago de Cuba. He had accused the authorities of covering up the extent of an epidemic of dengue fever in statements to foreign news media. He was tried in November on charges of using the mass media to spread "enemy propaganda" and sentenced to eight years' imprisonment.

In July, four members of a dissident study group were arrested after issuing a critique of a document disseminated for the Fifth Congress of the *Partido Comunista de Cuba*, Cuban Communist Party, which was due to be held in October. By the end of the year, the four – Félix Bonné Carcasés, René Gómez Manzano, Vladimiro Roca Antúnes and Marta Beatríz Roque Cabello – were still in detention awaiting trial.

In October several members of the unofficial *Partido Pro Derechos Humanos en Cuba* (PPDHC), Party for Human Rights in Cuba, in Santa Clara were detained after starting a fast in protest at the arrest of fellow PPDHC member Daula Carpio Mata. She was subsequently sentenced to 16 months' "correctional work with internment" for *atentado* (assault), on the grounds that she had verbally intimidated an official at an earlier trial, a charge for which there was no credible evidence. Eight of the protesters were sentenced to 18 months' imprisonment or "correctional work" after being found guilty of "associating with others to commit a crime" and "disobedience". Most of them continued their fast and some of those who were due to report for correctional work did not do so on health grounds. By the end of the year five PPDHC members, three of whom, including Daula Carpio Mata, were in prison, were reportedly very weak.

Several journalists working for independent press agencies, including Olance Nogueras (see *Amnesty International Report 1996*) and Héctor Peraza Linares (see below), left the country after being repeatedly detained and warned they would face imprisonment if they did not leave or give up their activities. At least one political activist left the country under similar circumstances.

A few prisoners of conscience were released. They included lawyer Leonel Morejón Almagro, who was released in May (see *Amnesty International Reports 1996* and *1997*). At least three prisoners of conscience were released early on condition that they leave the country.

At least five convicted political prisoners, including two prisoners of conscience, were brought to trial for showing disrespect to prison officials and given additional sentences of between three months and four and a half years' imprisonment. In at least one case, the prisoner was unable to consult his lawyer before the trial.

Trials in political cases again fell far short of international standards of fairness. Defendants in cases heard by municipal courts, often only hours or days after arrest, sometimes had no legal representation. Detainees held under investigation on state security charges often had only very limited access to lawyers while in pre-trial detention and were sometimes subjected to psychological pressures. Journalist Héctor Peraza Linares of *Habana Press*, who was detained in June and held for three months by State Security in Pinar del Río before being released, was unable to consult his lawyer who was also denied access to his client's case dossier.

There were frequent reports of beatings by police at the time of arrest and by prison guards in detention centres, as well as isolated reports of torture, resulting in at least one death.

In January several prisoners in Ariza Prison, Cienfuegos, were reportedly injured when prison officials attacked them with bayonets, sticks and tear-gas after they protested at a prisoner being beaten. After complaints by relatives, several senior prison officials were reportedly replaced.

In September, three political prisoners held in Guantánamo Provincial Prison – Nestor Rodríguez Lobaina (see above), who had recently been on hunger-strike, Jorge Luis García Pérez (known as "Antúnez") (see *Amnesty International Report 1994*) and Francisco Díaz Echemendía – were reportedly beaten and kicked, while handcuffed, by over 20 prison guards and then held naked and in darkness in a bare rat-infested punishment cell. They had reportedly founded a political prisoners' organization in the prison. In November the sister of "Antúnez", who was prevented from visiting her brother in October and told that he was on hunger-strike, lodged an official complaint about his ill-treatment.

Heriberto Véliz Ramos, who had been detained in March for common crimes, reportedly died as a result of severe beatings while he was held in a police station in Manzanillo, Granma province. Relatives, who claimed that his body showed signs of injuries, were informed by Interior Ministry officials that he had died of a heart attack. There was no further information.

Prison conditions appeared to deteriorate and in some cases, especially in punishment cells, constituted cruel, inhuman or degrading treatment. Conditions were undoubtedly exacerbated by economic pressures, including the effects of the US embargo on the availability of medicines and equipment. However, there were reports that medical attention and food were often deliberately withheld as a punishment.

At least five people died after being shot by security personnel in disputed circumstances. They included three men caught stealing from state-run farms and Reinaldo Rodríguez Puentes, who died in March. Officers of the *Policía Nacional Revolucionaria*, National Revolutionary Police, reportedly continued to fire at him and beat him while he was lying on the ground pleading for his life after being wounded by an earlier gunshot.

There were no reports of executions during 1997 but news was received of the execution in December 1996 of Francisco Dayson Dhruyet, who had been convicted of murdering his wife. Unconfirmed reports indicated that his alleged confession some four years earlier may have been obtained as the result of torture. Humberto Real Suárez (see *Amnesty International Report 1997*), who had been sentenced to death in 1996, had still not had his appeal heard by the People's Supreme Court by the end of the year. The fate of at least seven other men sentenced to death in previous years remained unknown.

Throughout the year Amnesty International appealed to the authorities to release all prisoners of conscience; to grant full judicial guarantees to those facing trial for politically motivated offences; and to cease using punitive and coercive measures, including the practice of forcible exile and patterns of harassment, against those seeking to exercise peacefully their rights to freedom of expression, association and assembly. It called for all prisoners to be allowed nutrition, medical care and hygiene in keeping with the standards of the general population and for independent and impartial investigations into allegations of torture or ill-treatment. On the third anniversary of the sinking of a tugboat in July 1994, in which at least 35 people died (see *Amnesty International Reports 1995* and *1997*), the organization again called for an independent investigation. No replies were received from the authorities.

DENMARK

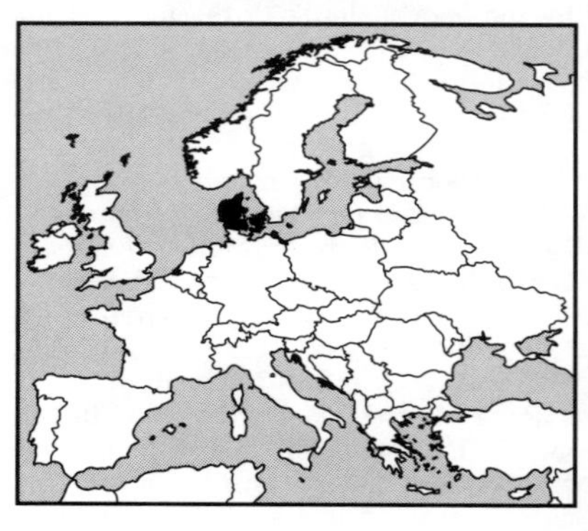

There were further developments concerning alleged misconduct by police in previous years.

In April the European Committee for the Prevention of Torture and Inhuman or

Degrading Treatment or Punishment published a report on its visit to Danish police establishments and prisons in 1996. The Committee made a number of recommendations concerning policing and respect for the rights of detained and imprisoned people, including those held in solitary confinement and subject to pre-trial restrictions.

In May the UN Committee against Torture examined Denmark's third periodic report on its implementation of the Convention against Torture and Other Cruel, Inhuman or Degrading Treatment or Punishment. The Committee recommended that the government make torture, as defined in the Convention, a distinct crime under Danish law and consider incorporation of the Convention into domestic law. It also recommended abolition of solitary confinement in all but exceptional circumstances, and in particular during pre-trial detention. It expressed concern about police treatment of detainees and about methods of crowd control, including the use of dogs, and recommended that the state ensure that detainees' allegations of ill-treatment be handled by independent bodies.

In January the Ministry of Justice informed Amnesty International that, while it regretted "the entire course of events in connection with the arrest" of Vietnamese national Chi Dung Nguyen "on grounds which subsequently proved to be mistaken" and that "the situation evolved in such a way that in the conduct of his arrest [he] was subjected to considerable use of force", it had not found grounds for action against the police officers involved. The Regional Police Complaints Board had, however, found grounds for believing that officers had hit him with batons while he lay handcuffed on the ground (see *Amnesty International Report 1997*).

In October the Regional State Prosecutor decided not to bring charges against the officers involved in the arrest and restraint of Nigerian national Veronica Ngozi Ugwuoha (see *Amnesty International Report 1997*). Although the Regional Prosecutor had concluded that Veronica Ngozi Ugwuoha's leg must have been broken during her arrest, he found that it could not be proved with certainty whether her injuries were sustained in the course of her interaction with a police officer when they both fell, or with another officer who unsuccessfully tried to grab her leg, or with a third officer who restrained her in a manual leg-lock. The Regional Prosecutor also decided not to criticize any officers for the approximately six-hour delay in calling a doctor to attend to Veronica Ngozi Ugwuoha, who was subsequently hospitalized for 10 days and underwent surgery. The Regional State Prosecutor found no grounds for criticism in relation to accusations of racist remarks, as none of the officers admitted to making or hearing such remarks during the arrest. Appeals to the Director of Public Prosecutions were pending at the end of the year.

In December the government agreed to pay Gambian national Babading Fatty full and final compensation for physical and psychological injuries suffered as a consequence of his detention and ill-treatment in 1990 (see previous *Amnesty International Reports*).

At the end of the year the latest investigation was continuing into the violent demonstration in the Nørrebro area of Copenhagen in May 1993 which culminated in police firing over one hundred shots in disputed circumstances. During the demonstration police officers were injured and at least 11 people were wounded by police bullets (see *Amnesty International Reports 1994* to *1997*).

Amnesty International expressed concern that the Regional Police Complaints Board's decision in the case of Chi Dung Nguyen had been overridden, and at the Regional State Prosecutor's decision in the case of Veronica Ngozi Ugwuoha. The organization also inquired about the measures being taken to implement the recommendations of the European Committee for the Prevention of Torture and Inhuman or Degrading Treatment or Punishment and the UN Committee against Torture.

DJIBOUTI

Fourteen government opponents forcibly returned from Ethiopia were detained on charges of armed conspiracy. Several other government opponents were harassed; some faced apparently politically motivated criminal charges and an opposition leader was detained for two

weeks. Five prisoners of conscience imprisoned in 1996 were released. Several suspected rebel supporters were briefly detained; some were reportedly tortured or ill-treated.

Following the parliamentary elections in December, the ruling *Rassemblement populaire pour le progrès*, People's Assembly for Progress, headed by President Hassan Gouled Aptidon, returned to power. In a new alliance with the former Afar opposition *Front pour la restauration de l'unité et de la démocratie* (FRUD), Front for the Restoration of Unity and Democracy, it won all 65 seats, defeating the two other permitted opposition parties. The 1994 peace agreement between the government and FRUD remained largely in force despite some fighting between government troops and a FRUD armed faction in the second half of the year.

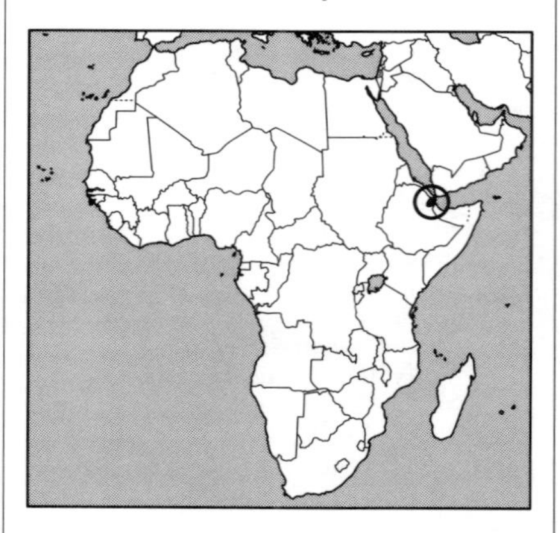

Five government opponents deported from Ethiopia (see **Ethiopia** entry) in September were immediately arrested on their return to Djibouti and later charged with armed conspiracy, attempted assassination and criminal association. They included Mohamed Kadamy Youssouf, a FRUD representative, his wife Aicha Dabale Ahmed, a relief agency employee and possible prisoner of conscience, and Ali Mohamed Maki, a FRUD military commander. Aicha Dabale Ahmed, who was pregnant, was at first refused medical treatment but was later transferred to hospital and, in December, to house arrest. Nine other FRUD exiles in Ethiopia were deported later in the year and detained and charged in Djibouti with similar offences. All were still held under judicial investigation at the end of the year.

Ahmed Daher Farah, a leader of the opposition *Parti du Renouveau Démocratique*, Party for Democratic Revival, was detained for two weeks in October and charged with political offences. Other government critics were charged with criminal offences, including Aref Mohamed Aref, a human rights lawyer. None had been tried by the end of the year. The charges appeared to have been politically motivated.

Five prisoners of conscience imprisoned in August 1996 (see *Amnesty International Report 1997*) were released in January after serving six-month sentences for defaming the Head of State. The five – who included Moumin Bahdon Farah, a former Foreign Minister, and Ismail Guedi Hared, former director of the President's cabinet – remained barred from political office for five years. Three were members of parliament; their imprisonment and subsequent exclusion from the elections were strongly criticized by the Inter-Parliamentary Union's Human Rights Committee.

Several suspected rebel supporters were detained for some days after a FRUD rebel attack in Obok district in early September. Some were reportedly tortured or ill-treated in military custody.

Amnesty International criticized the ban from political office of the five released prisoners of conscience. It appealed for humane treatment and fair trial for the exiles forcibly returned from Ethiopia, and in particular for Aicha Dabale Ahmed to receive all necessary medical treatment. In October Amnesty International wrote to the Minister of Justice questioning the charges brought against Aref Mohamed Aref and Ahmed Daher Farah, but received no reply.

DOMINICAN REPUBLIC

Thousands of people were arbitrarily detained for short periods, including prisoners of conscience and possible prisoners of conscience. Reports of torture and ill-treatment continued to be received. Some 30 people were shot dead by police in disputed circumstances.

In June a delegation of the Inter-American Commission on Human Rights (IACHR) visited the country. While recognizing the efforts of the government to improve the prison system through the establishment of the Commission for the Reform and Modernization of Justice, delegates criticized the severe overcrowding and poor conditions in prisons and the excessive slowness of the justice system. Following the IACHR visit, the authorities announced plans to relieve overcrowding in prisons and to expedite the processing of detainees' cases.

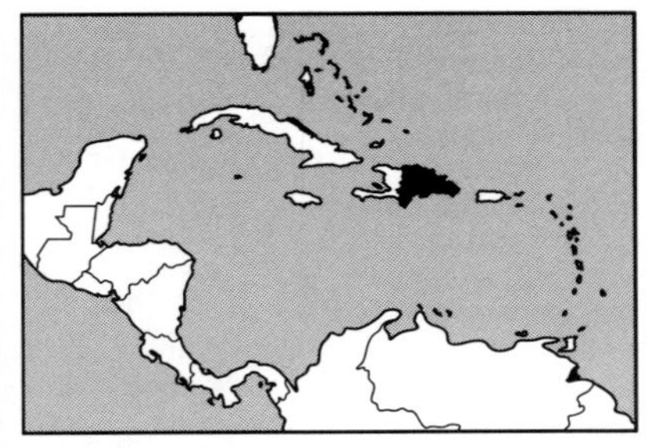

Throughout the year the government of President Leonel Fernández faced widespread protests about economic and social issues. Among the measures taken by the authorities to deal with the increasing unrest was the transfer of 7,000 military personnel to the police and the creation of an elite riot squad. Members of human rights organizations trying to document human rights violations faced harassment and, in a few cases, imprisonment.

Thousands of demonstrators were arbitrarily detained for short periods during the year. In October and November at least 500 members of popular organizations, including human rights defenders, were rounded up by police in advance of a general strike in November. Several of those detained were believed to be prisoners of conscience. They included Danilo de la Cruz, a member of the *Comité Dominicano de Derechos Humanos* (CDDH), Dominican Human Rights Committee, who was detained by police in November while he was observing a peaceful demonstration in Capotillo, Santo Domingo. He was held incommunicado for seven days in a cell at the National Police Palace and questioned under torture (see below) about his human rights activities before being charged with "defamation" and released on bail. Another CDDH leader, Abel Rojas, was arrested in November accused of killing a youth during the general strike. In December, following a *habeas corpus* petition, he was released for lack of evidence. However, it was not clear whether the authorities intended to appeal against the ruling.

The mass repatriation of Haitians living in the country continued throughout the year and resulted in widespread detentions of anyone suspected of being Haitian, including Haitians living in the country legally, and several black Dominicans. There were also some reports of ill-treatment by Dominican soldiers.

Reports of torture and ill-treatment by the security forces continued. In November Danilo de la Cruz (see above) was reportedly handcuffed and hung by the wrists from an iron tube on three consecutive days, causing serious injury to his arms, wrists and fingers. Kennedy Vargas, a journalist detained overnight in November, was reportedly beaten while held handcuffed in a rat-infested cave at the Support Unit of the armed forces. The Armed Forces Ministry later denied he was ill-treated. Other victims included minors and journalists.

No further news was received of the investigation into the torture of four prisoners at Plan Piloto police station in Santo Domingo in August 1996 (see *Amnesty International Report 1997*).

The judicial investigation into the "disappearance" of Narciso González in May 1994 continued, but had not concluded by the end of the year (see previous *Amnesty International Reports*).

Many people were reportedly injured and some 30 killed by the security forces in disputed circumstances, some in the context of popular protests, prison disturbances or alleged armed confrontations. In many cases, excessive force appeared to have been employed by security officials and several of the killings appeared to be possible extrajudicial executions. In January Manuel Mancebo, who was unarmed, was reportedly shot five times by police as he lay begging for his life. In February Ilex Actoin, a Haitian, was reportedly shot dead by two police officers because he refused to pay a bribe to avoid deportation.

In April six people, including three retired army generals, were indicted for murder after the authorities reopened the judicial investigation into the extrajudicial execution in 1975 of journalist Orlando Martínez Howley, who was killed after he criticized the then President, Joaquín Balaguer, in his newspaper column.

Between August and November the police authorities announced the dismissal of over 200 police officers for committing serious offences. It was not clear how many of the offences involved human rights violations, or whether charges had been brought against any police officer alleged to have committed such violations.

Amnesty International continued to call for a thorough and independent investigation into the "disappearance" of Narciso González and sought information about the legal situation of several possible prisoners of conscience. The organization also urged the authorities to conduct full and impartial investigations into several cases of people shot dead by police in disputed circumstances and into allegations of torture.

ECUADOR

One prisoner of conscience was detained for four weeks. Torture and ill-treatment continued to be reported. Five "disappearances" and at least six extrajudicial executions were reported. The authorities failed to clarify and bring to justice those responsible for past human rights violations.

In February, following a general strike against the government's economic policies in which police reportedly shot dead a student, the National Congress removed President Abdalá Bucaram Ortiz from office on grounds of his "mental incapacity". Vice-President Rosalía Arteaga assumed the presidency, but a week later Fabián Alarcón Rivera, President of the National Congress, was sworn in as interim President.

In January the National Congress approved a law regulating the work of Ecuador's first ever *Defensoría del Pueblo*, Office of the Ombudsman, and in April an Ombudsman was appointed to head the Office (see *Amnesty International Report 1997*). However, in June the Ombudsman resigned in protest at Congress' decision to end his four-year term of office in August 1998 and because the authorities had not made sufficient resources available for the Office to be effective. By the end of the year the Ombudsman had not been replaced.

In May the government held a national plebiscite in which the electorate ratified the naming of Fabián Alarcón as interim President and approved the establishment of a National Assembly and the "depoliticization of the administration of justice". In December the 70-seat National Assembly, elected in November, initiated its deliberations on reforming the Constitution.

In November the Constitutional Tribunal decriminalized homosexual acts between consenting adults by removing Article 516 of Ecuador's Criminal Code, on the grounds that the Article contravened the Constitution.

In April the Inter-American Commission on Human Rights (IACHR) published a report on the human rights situation in Ecuador. The IACHR acknowledged steps taken by the authorities to strengthen the protection of human rights but expressed concern that the authorities were failing to comply with certain standards enshrined in the American Convention on Human Rights. In November the Inter-American Court of Human Rights ruled that Ecuador had violated the rights of Rafaél Iván Suárez Romero in contravention of the Convention. The Court concluded, among other things, that Rafaél Suárez had been arbitrarily detained and held incommunicado for 36 days, was denied a fair trial and judicial protection, and was subjected to cruel, inhuman and degrading treatment. The Court had not opened trial proceedings on the Consuelo Benavides case by the end of the year (see *Amnesty International Report 1997*).

Prisoner of conscience Diego Ordóñez Ortiz, Secretary General of the National Union of Workers of the Ecuadorian Institute of Social Security, was detained in

Quito, the capital, in September. He had been arrested following allegations that a strike led by him and several other trade union activists infringed articles in the Criminal Code relating to the halting of public services. He was released after four weeks in detention following a successful petition to the High Court. However, the judge ruled that the case file on Diego Ordóñez Ortiz be kept open pending further investigations into the accusations against him.

Cases of torture and ill-treatment continued to be reported. In March Aníbal Aguas, a merchant, died while in police custody in the town of Machala, province of Los Ríos. According to a police report, Aníbal Aguas died as a result of knocking his head against a patrol car as he was being placed in the back seat. However, relatives claimed he died after being driven away and tortured. A civilian examining judge initially ordered the detention of four policemen implicated in his death, but later released three of them and referred the case to a police court. A police examining judge then ordered the release of the fourth policeman. A petition filed before the Constitutional Tribunal to have the case transferred back into the jurisdiction of the civilian courts remained pending at the end of year.

In March armed police entered the García Moreno Prison in Quito and assaulted several inmates using sticks and pipes. The authorities claimed the police were responding to a prison uprising. However, the prisoners claimed the incursion and abuses occurred after they started a peaceful hunger-strike.

Five men reportedly "disappeared" following detention. Ángel Heriberto Hinojosa "disappeared" in January following his abduction near Quito by a uniformed policeman and two civilians. He was bundled into a red car with no number plates. The incident was witnessed by a friend of the victim who managed to escape. In May Marco Bienvenida Palma was reportedly detained in the city of Manta, Manabí province, by military intelligence agents investigating the sale of weapons. His family claimed to have received information that he was later seen in the Ministry of Defence. Jeremías Ramírez, a Colombian national, and two unidentified friends "disappeared" after being detained in Quito in July by men who identified themselves as members of the police. Following the filing of successful *habeas corpus* petitions, the municipal authorities ordered the immediate release of Marco Bienvenida Palma and Jeremías Ramírez. However, the Secretariat of the Armed Forces and the police denied having detained them. The whereabouts of all five men remained unknown at the end of the year.

At least six men were reported to have been extrajudicially executed. In one incident, the authorities initially claimed that Vicente Vargas, Carlos Obregón and Juan Jiménez were shot dead by police while attempting to escape from a prison in the city of Guayaquil in January. However, after a video was broadcast on national television showing the police capturing the fugitives, human rights defenders claimed all three were extrajudicially executed. Four policemen were investigated by a civilian court on charges of homicide, but subsequently the case was transferred into the jurisdiction of a police court. By the end of the year those responsible for these killings, and that of José Miguel Manrique Morales, whose case was also transferred into the jurisdiction of the police courts (see *Amnesty International Report 1997*), had not been convicted.

Hundreds of cases of human rights violations documented in previous years remained unresolved and those responsible were not brought to justice. The Truth and Justice Commission and the congressional commission, mandated in September 1996 with investigating past human rights violations, had ceased functioning by the end of President Bucaram's administration. The failure of both commissions to publish any findings consolidated the impunity surrounding hundreds of cases of torture, "disappearances" and killings (see *Amnesty International Report 1997*).

Amnesty International appealed to the authorities, including the Ministers of Government and Police and of Foreign Affairs, to clarify the whereabouts of those reported to have "disappeared". The organization did not receive replies to any of these appeals.

In March Amnesty International called on the authorities to conduct an independent inquiry into allegations that the police had assaulted prisoners in the García Moreno Prison, and to make the findings public. The authorities replied in April claiming that an inquiry had been conducted which indicated that the prisoners had not been ill-treated. However, the report of the inquiry was not made public. In August the organization publicly stated that referring the case of the death in custody of Aníbal Aguas to a police court ran counter to a recommendation made to the Government of Ecuador by the IACHR that such cases be "submitted to the ordinary courts". In October Amnesty International called for the immediate and unconditional release of prisoner of conscience Diego Ordóñez Ortiz.

EGYPT

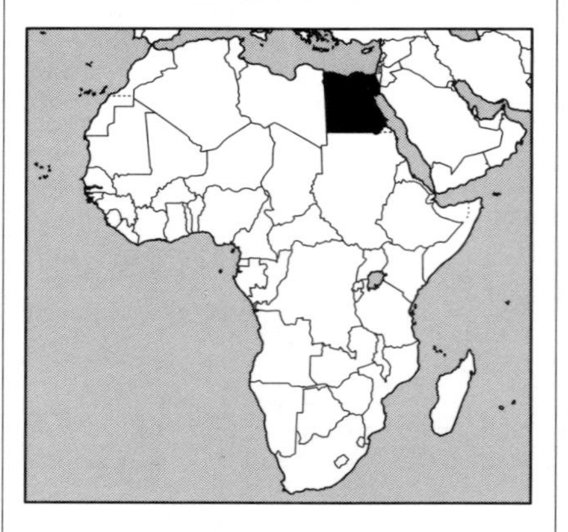

Hundreds of opponents of a new agricultural law, including prisoners of conscience and possible prisoners of conscience, were detained without charge or trial. Scores of prisoners of conscience were held, including 58 sentenced to prison terms by the Supreme Military Court in previous years. Thousands of suspected members or sympathizers of banned Islamist groups, including possible prisoners of conscience, were held without charge or trial; others were serving sentences imposed after grossly unfair trials before military courts. Torture and ill-treatment of detainees continued to be systematic. At least 55 people were sentenced to death and at least 24 people were executed. Armed opposition groups committed grave human rights abuses, including deliberate and arbitrary killings of at least 100 civilians.

Violent clashes continued between armed Islamist groups and the security forces, particularly in the Minya Governorate in Upper Egypt, resulting in dozens of casualties on both sides.

In February the People's Assembly overwhelmingly approved a decree issued by President Hosni Mubarak to extend the state of emergency for another three years. It had been in force without interruption since October 1981 (see previous *Amnesty International Reports*). In June an administrative court in Cairo, the capital, overturned a decree issued in July 1996 by the Minister of Health banning female genital mutilation from being carried out in state hospitals. The court ruled that the ban was unconstitutional. The government appealed against the court's verdict and in December the Supreme Administrative Court (State Council) upheld the decree issued by the Minister of Health. In October a controversial new agricultural law (Law 96 of 1992) came into effect after a five-year grace period accorded to tenant farmers. The law permits landowners to raise rents and evict tenant farmers, abolishing the provisions of the 1952 agrarian reform law which guaranteed security to farmers on rented land.

Prisoners of conscience and possible prisoners of conscience were among hundreds of people detained throughout the year in connection with opposition to Law 96. Dr Ahmad al-Ahwany, a professor of nuclear physics at Cairo University, was arrested in April and held in Istiqbal Tora Prison, reportedly on charges of planning to distribute documents "damaging to the public interest". The real reason for his detention appeared to be that he was found in possession of a bulletin critical of the new law. He was held for one month. Sayyed Ahmad al-Tokhi, a lawyer at the Egyptian Organization for Human Rights, was arrested in August and held in al-Mahkoum Prison in Tora and then in Mazra'at Tora Prison in connection with his peaceful opposition to Law 96. He was released in October. At the end of the year at least 150 farmers continued to be held without charge or trial for staging public protests against the law and at least 20 had been killed in violent confrontations between farmers and security forces and also between farmers and landowners.

Other prisoners of conscience held during the year included scores of youths, all reported fans of western rock music, who were arrested in January and accused of membership of a satanic cult and of practising satanic rituals. All had been released without charge by March.

In March, five students at Cairo University were arrested, reportedly after taking part in a peaceful demonstration in protest at Israeli settlement activities in the Israeli Occupied Territories. They were detained for up to a month before being released without charge.

In May a Cairo Appeal Court upheld a sentence of one year's imprisonment and a fine handed down in 1992 on writer 'Ala' Hamed for publishing a book entitled *al-Firash* (The Bed) which discusses sex (see *Amnesty International Reports 1992* and *1993*). Charges against him had included producing and possessing "printed materials of an indecent nature which encourage immorality". 'Ala' Hamed was arrested and imprisoned in Mazra'at Tora Prison and then transferred to al-Qatta Prison, north of Cairo, before he was released in August pending a final ruling in his case by the Court of Cassation.

In August, 34 alleged members of the Muslim Brothers, among them teachers, engineers, students and a doctor, were arrested and reportedly accused of membership of a banned organization, planning to recruit students as new members and possession of anti-government printed material. All had reportedly been released by the end of November.

Seven prisoners of conscience sentenced to three years' imprisonment by the Supreme Military Court in August 1996 (see *Amnesty International Report 1997*) continued to be held in Mazra'at Tora Prison. Fifty-two of the 53 prisoners of conscience sentenced to up to five years' imprisonment by the Supreme Military Court in November 1995 (see *Amnesty International Reports 1996* and *1997*) also continued to be detained; one of the 52, Hilmy Mostafa Mohammad Hammoud, aged 76, was pardoned by President Mubarak on health grounds in January. He had served more than 13 months of his three-year sentence of imprisonment with hard labour.

The 57 alleged members of a Shi'a group arrested in October 1996 (see *Amnesty International Report 1997*) were all released in February.

Thousands of suspected members or sympathizers of banned Islamist groups, including possible prisoners of conscience, were held without charge or trial under emergency legislation. Others had been acquitted by military or (Emergency) Supreme State Security courts, but remained in detention. For example, 'Abd al-Mun'im Gamal al-Din 'Abd al-Mun'im, a freelance journalist arrested in February 1993, had been acquitted of charges of membership of a banned Islamist group by a military court in October 1993 (see previous *Amnesty International Reports*), but remained held in al-Wadi al-Gadid Prison at the end of the year. At least 53 lawyers remained in detention at the end of the year. Most of them had been held for up to seven years without charge or trial (see *Amnesty International Report 1997*), but four – al-Shazli 'Obeid al-Saghier, Radhwan al-Tuni, Mostafa al-Sayyid and Khalaf 'Abd al-Ra'uf – were arrested in June and allegedly accused of membership of *al-Gama'a al-Islamiya* (Islamic Group). They and 61 others were being tried by a military court at the end of the year on charges of planning to assassinate a civilian judge and other officials, and membership of an unauthorized organization.

Scores of alleged members of Islamist groups were unfairly tried by military and (Emergency) Supreme State Security courts during the year. For example, 97 alleged members of *al-Gama'a al-Islamiya* were tried in summary proceedings in July and August by a military court. Charges against them included planting bombs, killing the deputy head of the State Security Investigations Department (SSI), Ra'uf Khayrat, possession of explosives, and membership of an unauthorized organization. Gihan Ibrahim 'Abd al-Hamid (see *Amnesty International Report 1997*) was sentenced in September to 15 years' imprisonment with hard labour. Four of her co-defendants were sentenced to death.

Torture of political prisoners continued to be systematic in the headquarters of the SSI in Lazoghly Square in Cairo, SSI branches elsewhere in the country, police stations and sometimes in prisons. The government failed to implement the recommendations made by the UN Committee against Torture in its report published in May 1996, particularly the need to set up an independent investigation machinery to examine allegations of torture.

The most common torture methods reported were electric shocks, beatings, suspension by the wrists or ankles, burning with cigarettes, and various forms of psychological torture, including death threats and threats of rape or sexual abuse of the detainee or female relatives. Lawyers and local human rights groups lodged hundreds of complaints of torture with the Public Prosecutor's Office. No information was made available regarding any investigations into the allegations.

Hamdein Sabbahi, a journalist, Mohammad 'Abdu, a veterinarian, Mohammad Sulayman Fayyad and Hamdi Haykal, both lawyers, were arrested in June in connection with their non-violent opposition to Law 96. The four prisoners of conscience were held in Tora Penitentiary where they were allegedly kicked, beaten with a stick and whipped for hours. Amal Farouq al-Maas, who was tortured during her detention in 1993 and 1996 (see *Amnesty International Report 1997*), continued to lodge complaints against the officers she alleged had tortured her. However, no thorough and impartial investigation into these allegations was apparently conducted.

Thousands of detainees continued to be held in prisons where conditions amounted to cruel, inhuman or degrading treatment. Detainees in al-Wadi al-Gadid Prison near the town of al-Kharga, in the desert southwest of Cairo, were reportedly denied adequate medical care. For example, Mostafa Thabit Bayyoumi, a lawyer detained without charge or trial since 1994, was denied medical treatment for his circulatory and spinal problems. His family reported that when they visited him in prison in May he had to be carried to the prison's waiting room and was unable to speak or move.

Several people who reportedly "disappeared" after arrest in previous years remained unaccounted for. They included shopkeeper Nabil Mohammad 'Ali Hassan al-Battugi, who reportedly "disappeared" after his arrest by SSI officers in Bani Sueif in July 1996, and Sayyid 'Ali Ibrahim who "disappeared" following his arrest in Abu Qerqas in Upper Egypt in September 1995.

The death penalty continued to be used extensively. At least 55 people were sentenced to death, including four *in absentia*. Thirteen of them were civilians sentenced by military courts, two *in absentia*, after grossly unfair trials, and five others, two *in absentia*, were sentenced by (Emergency) Supreme State Security courts, which allow no appeal. At least 37 people were sentenced to death for murder by criminal courts. At least 24 people, including 20 sentenced in previous years, were executed. In October, four people were executed. They had been sentenced to death by a military court in January in a case involving 19 defendants – 18 Egyptians and a Palestinian – all alleged members of *al-Gama'a al-Islamiya*. Charges against them included planting bombs in two cinemas in 1993 and killing an SSI officer. Death sentences passed by military courts are subject only to review by the Military Appeals Bureau, a body composed of military judges which is not a court, and ratification by the President. As far as Amnesty International knows, all death sentences passed by military courts since 1992 were confirmed by the Bureau and ratified by the President.

Armed opposition groups committed gross human rights abuses, including deliberate and arbitrary killings of civilians. Bomb and firearm attacks were carried out by banned Islamist groups, particularly *al-Gama'a al-Islamiya* and *al-Gihad* (Holy Struggle). At least 100 unarmed civilians were killed by armed men believed to be members of *al-Gama'a al-Islamiya* during the year. In February, 10 civilians, all Coptic Christians, were killed by four armed men, believed to be members of *al-Gama'a al-Islamiya*, in an attack on a church in the village of Abu Qerqas in Minya Governorate. In March, 13 civilians, including at least nine Coptic Christians, were killed by armed men, believed to be members of *al-Gama'a al-Islamiya*, in two separate attacks on civilians in 'Ezbet Dawud and Naga' Hammadi, both villages situated in Qena in Upper Egypt. In November, 58 foreign tourists, including at least 33 Swiss, and two Egyptians were killed in an armed attack at a tourist site near Luxor. The six gunmen who carried out the attack were later killed. *Al-Gama'a al-Islamiya* claimed responsibility for the massacre.

Dr Nasr Hamed Abu-Zeid remained under threat of death from *al-Gihad* (see *Amnesty International Reports 1996* and *1997*). He and his wife, Dr Ibtihal Younis, continued to live abroad.

Amnesty International repeatedly appealed to the authorities to release prisoners of conscience and criticized the long-term detention without charge or trial of political detainees. The organization called for an end to trials of civilians before military courts and for political prisoners to be given fair trials. It also called for the immediate implementation of safeguards to stop torture and ill-treatment of detainees, and for urgent, thorough and impartial investigations into allegations of torture and "disappearances". Amnesty International called for death sentences to be commuted and for the abolition of the death penalty.

In July an Amnesty International observer attended sessions of the trial of 97 alleged members of *al-Gama'a al-Islamiya* before the Supreme Military Court.

In March Amnesty International published a report, *Egypt: Women targeted by association*, which highlighted the human rights abuses suffered by some Islamist women as a result of their relationship to alleged members of banned Islamist groups. By the end of the year, the government had not responded to human rights concerns raised by the organization.

Amnesty International condemned the deliberate and arbitrary killing of civilians by armed opposition groups and called on them to put an end to such killings.

EL SALVADOR

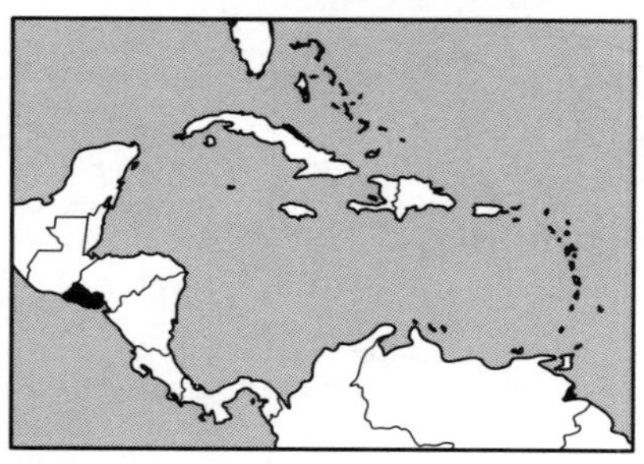

At least five people died in circumstances suggesting that they had been extrajudicially executed. Human rights defenders were threatened. The reintroduction of the death penalty was not pursued.

Elections in March for the Legislative Assembly resulted in the ruling *Alianza Republicana Nacionalista* (ARENA), Nationalist Republican Alliance, losing its majority and gains for the *Frente Farabundo Martí de Liberación Nacional* (FMLN), Farabundo Martí National Liberation Front, the main opposition party.

In April the Legislative Assembly approved a Penal Code and Penitentiary Law which complemented the Procedural Penal Code approved in 1996 (see *Amnesty International Report 1997*). The Penal Code created new offences such as torture and enforced disappearance, and stated that these crimes would not be subject to statutes of limitations. The Codes were due to come into effect in January 1998.

In July the UN Verification Office (ONUV) in El Salvador, the last UN body overseeing the implementation of the peace process, was closed. In August the final report on the UN's direct presence in El Salvador stated that changes to the military forces had transformed them into a professional body functioning according to the mandate given them by the peace accords. The report welcomed advances in establishing a new Supreme Court of Justice, but regretted the slow progress in the purging of dishonest or incompetent judges and judicial officials as provided for in the peace accords. The report also urged the implementation of recommendations towards national reconciliation, such as compensation for victims of human rights violations.

At least five people were reported to have died in circumstances suggesting that they had been extrajudicially executed. Various groups, including the church, claimed that clandestine armed groups within the police force were operating as "social cleansing squads", targeting members of juvenile gangs and criminal suspects. There were investigations by the authorities in some cases, but in many others there was none.

In February, during the election campaign, Moisés Cano Reyes was killed instantly when a group of up to 12 men dressed in black, wearing face masks and carrying M-16 guns, revolvers and grenades, opened fire on a group of people socializing in Nejapa, Cantón Calle Vieja, San Salvador department. Pedro René Ardón Peña was injured and died later as a result of his injuries. Two other people were injured. All those killed or injured were FMLN members. By the end of the year, no one had been brought to justice for these deaths. Other FMLN members were attacked during the election campaign, including a deputy and a candidate for the National Assembly. Those responsible were reported to have been members of the ruling ARENA party.

In April, 16-year-old Alexander Alberto Guillén and Jaime Ernesto Molina Rivas were shot dead in Colonia Carlota, barrio San Jacinto, San Salvador, and Víctor Baldemar Orellana was seriously wounded. According to witnesses, three men carrying firearms, with their faces covered and wearing military boots, emerged from a car with tinted windows and approached a group of six young men on a street corner. Three ran away and the other three were searched at gunpoint, then shot. Two weeks earlier, a patrol of the *Policía Nacional Civil* (PNC), National Civil Police, had approached and searched the group in the same place and told them they should not gather in groups. The methods and appearance of the attackers suggested that they were members of illegal groups operating either from within the security forces or in close connection with them. Although dozens of PNC agents were arrested and charged with crimes or abuse of authority, the institutional changes called for in the peace accords appeared to be some way from full implementation. Many cases involving PNC members were not properly investigated.

In May José Rodolfo García Avendaño died after being kicked and beaten by a group of policemen in Ilobasco. José García, a manual worker, was standing with a group of other men outside a house when a group of about 15 policemen – in uniform and civilian clothes – ordered them to raise their arms for a search. All but José García, who was slightly drunk, obeyed. He told the policemen he had done nothing wrong and was going away. The group of policemen threw him to the ground, kicked him and beat him with gun-butts. They then left José García unconscious on the ground. He was taken to hospital, where he died two days later. Five policemen were arrested a few days after his death.

Proceedings in the case of Francisco Antonio Manzanares Monjaraz, an FMLN member killed in October 1996, made progress. He claimed to have been under surveillance in the weeks before he was killed by eight heavily armed men in Colonia Satélite de Oriente, department of San Miguel (see *Amnesty International Report 1997*). In October 1996 a PNC sergeant was charged with premeditated murder and a PNC agent with complicity. In October 1997 the First Criminal Court of San Miguel ruled that there was evidence of a plan to kill Francisco Manzanares, that he had been under surveillance and that the killing had been political. The Court changed the charge of premeditated murder against the PNC sergeant to one of complicity and the PNC agent was charged with premeditated murder. In October organizers of an event in San Miguel to commemorate the first anniversary of the killing of Francisco Manzanares were allegedly followed and placed under surveillance by members of the PNC.

In November Dr Victoria Marina Velásquez de Avilés, National Human Rights Procurator, received anonymous telephone death threats. Since taking office in 1995, Dr Velásquez de Avilés had received several death threats and threats against her daughters (see *Amnesty International Report 1997*). By the end of the year there had been no investigations into any of the threats.

As a result of ARENA losing its majority in the National Assembly, the President of the Assembly's Commission on Legislation announced in April that ARENA would not seek ratification of a motion to reintroduce the death penalty (see *Amnesty International Report 1997*). ARENA officials made it clear, however, that the party had not abandoned its intention to reinstate capital punishment.

In March Amnesty International wrote to President Armando Calderón Sol to express its concern about the attack on FMLN members in late February, and other apparently politically motivated attacks. It called on the government to take the necessary measures to guarantee the safety of political activists and asked for information about the investigation into the incident and measures to bring those responsible to justice. Amnesty International reiterated its concern about illegal armed groups and the impunity they had enjoyed for many years.

Amnesty International called on the authorities to guarantee the safety of those working on the case of Francisco Manzanares. Amnesty International also expressed concern about the continuing death threats against the National Human Rights Procurator and called for an immediate, impartial and thorough investigation into those threats, for those responsible to be brought to justice, and for immediate and effective measures to ensure her protection.

Amnesty International welcomed the decision not to pursue the reintroduction of the death penalty and urged the government to take steps to sign and ratify the Second Optional Protocol to the International Covenant on Civil and Political Rights, aiming at the abolition of the death penalty, and the Protocol to the American Convention on Human Rights to Abolish the Death Penalty.

EQUATORIAL GUINEA

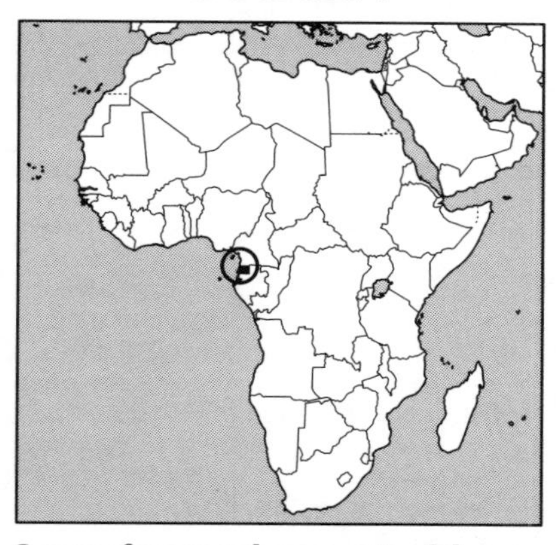

Scores of suspected opponents of the government were detained and held without charge or trial, for periods ranging from a few days to several months. At least 150 appeared to be prisoners of conscience. Torture and ill-treatment were routinely used and one prisoner reportedly died as a result. Two people were sentenced to death but there were no executions.

In February President Teodoro Obiang Nguema Mbasogo publicly announced that several measures would be adopted to put an end to human rights violations in the country, without specifying the nature of these measures. He also acknowledged that some military and security officers were "systematically violating human rights", and announced that perpetrators would be held responsible and punished.

In April the government and some opposition parties signed a National Pact, but one of the main opposition parties, the *Convergencia para la Democracia Social* (CDPS), Convergence for Social Democracy, was excluded from these discussions. In May the authorities claimed to have discovered a plot to overthrow the government by the leader of the *Partido del Progreso* (PP), Progress Party, Severo Moto. Severo Moto was tried *in absentia* in August and sentenced to 101 years' imprisonment on charges of plotting against the government and attempting to kill President Obiang. The authorities also announced that they were going to ban his party.

In April the UN Commission on Human Rights examined the report of the UN Special Rapporteur on Equatorial Guinea who had visited the country in December 1996 (see *Amnesty International Report 1997*). The Commission called upon the government to implement the recommendations made by the Special Rapporteur, including those aiming to put an end to arbitrary arrests and torture.

Scores of government opponents were arrested throughout the year, including at least 150 prisoners of conscience. Most of those detained were arrested for peaceful political activities. Some were held for organizing an unauthorized meeting, others for criticizing the government or for being members of parties which had not been legalized. Most were held for some days or weeks without charge or trial. No one was brought to trial but some were restricted to their villages after their release.

Political repression increased sharply after the discovery in May of an alleged plot by the PP leader, Severo Moto, to overthrow the government. Dozens of PP members were detained, despite the fact that there appeared to be no evidence of their personal involvement in the alleged plot. Most were held for some days or weeks and none was tried or charged. José Ekang Nangomo, leader of the PP in Gabon, and Francisco Edù, both arrested in July, were held until December.

Several members of the Bubi ethnic group, the indigenous population of Bioko Island, were arrested for allegedly belonging to the Movement for the Self-determination of Bioko Island (MAIB), a non-violent political party which had not obtained legal recognition. Antolin Banch, arrested in January for possessing copies of the MAIB newspaper, *O Bojuelo*, was released without charge in December. Silvestre Orichi, a senior member of the MAIB detained because a Bubi flag was found at his home, was still held at the end of the year.

In November, two members of the opposition party *Fuerza Demócrata Republicana* (FDR), Republican Democratic Force, which had not yet been legalized, were arrested by the Gabonese security forces in Libreville, Gabon. Felipe Ondó Obiang and Guillermo Nguema Ela were transferred the same day to Malabo, Equatorial Guinea, in the plane of the President of Equatorial Guinea. The arrests were carried out shortly after the arrival in Libreville of President Obiang for the ACP-EU (countries of the African, Caribbean and Pacific–European Union) summit. They were released one week later but were not allowed to leave Equatorial Guinea.

Many detainees appeared to have been ill-treated or tortured in order to force them to pay heavy fines or to join the ruling *Partido Democrático de Guinea Ecuatorial* (PDGE), Equatorial Guinea Democratic Party. In August, two members of the FDR – Sinecio Ngua Esono and Francisco Abeso Mba – were held for three weeks in a container in the Bata harbour where they were severely beaten.

In September several members of the CDPS, including six women, were held in Akurenam because they were preparing to welcome their leaders with songs. The women were stripped and severely beaten. They were released one month later without charge or trial after paying a heavy fine.

One person died, reportedly as a result of torture by the security forces. In January Evaristo Abaga Ndongo died after reportedly being beaten by police at the time of his arrest and in the vehicle that transferred him to Evinayong. As a result, he lost consciousness and was later taken to hospital, where he died shortly after arrival. No post-mortem appears to have been carried out and his family was told to bury the corpse without delay. Three weeks later, a military court convicted two police officers of responsibility for the death of Evaristo Abaga Ndongo and sentenced them respectively to prison terms of 10 and 20 years.

In October Matías Evung was sentenced to death after being found guilty of ritual murder. He appealed, and was provisionally released pending the appeal decision. In November Teófilo Ntutume Abogo was sentenced to death for murder.

In July Amnesty International published a report, *Equatorial Guinea: An opportunity to put an end to impunity*, in which it called on the authorities to act against impunity with no exception and in compliance with international standards. In October Amnesty International expressed concern about the increasing number of opposition party activists arrested and tortured for their peaceful political activities, and called for the unconditional release of all prisoners of conscience. The organization also strongly protested against the fact that one of its staff members, who was due to take part in a research visit to Equatorial Guinea in September was refused access to the country by the authorities. The organization said that the authorities were trying by that means to hide information on the human rights violations committed by the security forces.

ERITREA

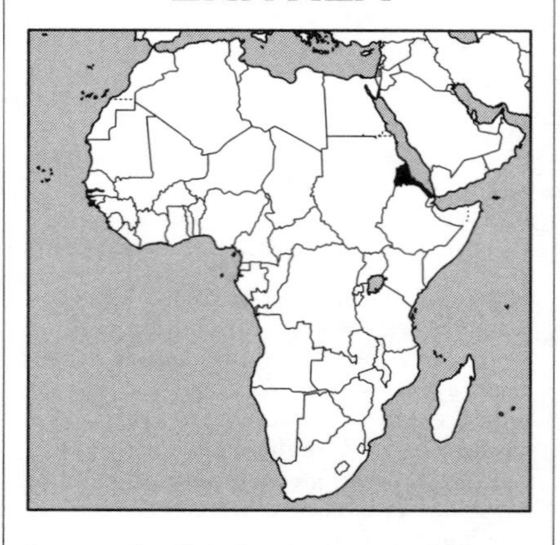

Scores of political prisoners, including a prisoner of conscience, were detained without charge or trial. Up to 100 political detainees arrested in previous years remained imprisoned, some following unfair trials. At least a dozen prisoners who "disappeared" in previous years were feared to have been extrajudicially executed.

Eritrea's first Constitution since independence in 1993 entered into force in May. It recognized the right to be brought to court within 48 hours of arrest and to petition for *habeas corpus,* but did not mention the right to legal defence representation. It did not recognize the right to conscientious objection to military service. It imposed restrictions on human rights and allowed for derogations in a way that contravenes basic international and regional human rights standards. The death penalty was retained, although it had not been used since independence.

Eritrea was one of only two African states not to have ratified the African Charter on Human and Peoples' Rights.

Elections to six new regional assemblies were held early in the year. Elections to a new National Assembly were scheduled for 1998. A new Penal Code, Criminal Procedure Code and Labour Law were being drafted during 1997.

The government headed by President Issayas Afewerki and the People's Front for Democracy and Justice, the only permitted political party, continued to face armed opposition from the Eritrean Islamic *Jihad*, and Abdallah Idris' faction of the Eritrean Liberation Front (ELF), both based in Sudan. Relations with Sudan were tense, each government supporting the other's opponents. The territorial dispute with Yemen over the Red Sea Islands went to an international arbitration tribunal.

Prisoner of conscience Ruth Simon, an Eritrean journalist working for the *Agence France Presse* (AFP) news agency, was detained in April because of an article claiming that President Afewerki said in a seminar that Eritrean troops were assisting Sudanese opposition forces in Sudan, a statement which the President denied. She was detained without charge or trial, at first in an undisclosed prison, and later under house arrest.

During the year scores of government opponents or suspected rebel supporters were reportedly detained incommunicado without charge or trial, often in secret. They included numerous Muslims suspected of links with the Eritrean Islamic *Jihad*, and others suspected of supporting the ELF.

Up to 100 members of the armed forces, and officials, of the previous Ethiopian administration detained since 1991 remained held; many of them were serving prison sentences imposed in 1996 after secret and unfair military trials (see *Amnesty International Report 1997*). One of them, Ajal Abdulrahman, a former assistant governor of Eritrea, died in prison in January after six years of incommunicado imprisonment.

At least a dozen opponents of the government who "disappeared" in previous years were feared to have been extrajudicially executed. Some had been abducted from Ethiopia and Sudan. The Eritrean authorities repeatedly denied that they had been detained (see *Amnesty International Report 1997*).

Human rights abuses, including arbitrary killings of civilians, were reportedly committed by all parties to the continuing conflict between government troops and opposition forces of the Eritrean Islamic *Jihad* and a faction of the ELF.

Amnesty International appealed for the immediate and unconditional release of Ruth Simon, and for all other political prisoners to be promptly and fairly tried. It urged the government to establish impartial inquiries into the reported "disappearances" and to allow all detainees regular access to their families and lawyers.

ETHIOPIA

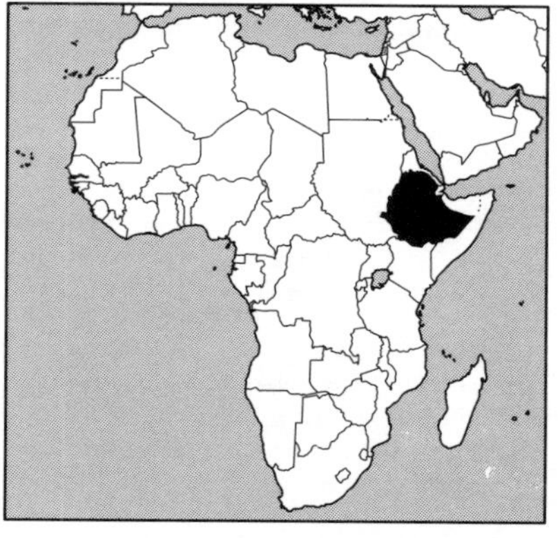

Hundreds of critics and opponents of the government were arrested, including prisoners of conscience. Some were tried but most were detained without charge or trial. Thousands of political prisoners arrested in earlier years remained in detention without charge or trial. The trial of

46 former government members continued and preliminary trial proceedings started against over 2,000 other former government or party officials. Torture of government opponents was reported, as well as "disappearances" and extrajudicial executions. Several death sentences were imposed by courts but no executions were reported.

Prime Minister Meles Zenawi's government continued to face armed opposition throughout the year, particularly from the Oromo Liberation Front (OLF) in the Oromia region and the Ogaden National Liberation Front (ONLF) in the Somali region. There were several violent clashes in the Amhara region and certain other regions, some involving opponents based in Sudan. There were also several bombings in Addis Ababa, the capital, Dire Dawa and Harar, causing civilian casualties. Ethiopian troops crossed into Somalia's Gedo region to suppress the *Al-Itihad* (Islamist) armed opposition group based there which had claimed responsibility for bombings in Ethiopia.

Ethiopia remained one of only two African states not to have ratified the African Charter on Human and Peoples' Rights.

Dozens of journalists from the independent press in Addis Ababa were arrested for criticizing the government and held under the Press Law (1993), which penalizes offences such as "publishing false information in order to incite war and unrest". They were prisoners of conscience. Arega Wolde-Kirkos of *Tobia* newspaper was arrested in January but provisionally released after eight weeks. Tolera Tessema of *Medda Welabu* newspaper was arrested in April and sentenced to one year's imprisonment. Solomon Namara and Tesfaye Deressa of *Urji* newspaper were arrested in September, provisionally released but rearrested in October. Their first arrest was for criticizing conditions in a hospital in Addis Ababa, the second seemed to be for questioning the official account of the killing of three alleged OLF members (see below).

Two *bahtawi* (independent hermit preachers) were arrested in January in connection with a petition which was presented to the Patriarch of the Ethiopian Orthodox Church at St Stephanos Church in Addis Ababa by a hermit who was shot dead by police. The two detained hermits, Gebre-Meskel Haile-Meskel, director of a humanitarian organization, and Sofonias Gume, were kept in prison until December despite earlier court orders for their release. They were prisoners of conscience.

Hundreds of members of the Oromo ethnic group (or "nationality") were detained during the year and accused of involvement with the OLF. Wako Tola, a schoolteacher in Addis Ababa, and Worku Mulata, an engineer working for an Oromo community project, were detained in February and accused of links with the OLF. Wako Tola died in custody on 30 March. Worku Mulata was still detained without charge at the end of the year. Both were prisoners of conscience. Some 20 prominent Oromos in Addis Ababa were detained in early November and accused of involvement with bombings, allegedly carried out by three captured OLF fighters, in Addis Ababa and Dire Dawa earlier in the year. Among the detainees were seven officials of the Human Rights League, a newly established Oromo human rights organization, who were prisoners of conscience. They included Beyene Abdi, aged 72, a former parliamentarian and retired judge; Beyene Belissa, a telecommunications manager; Gabissa Lemessa, an accountant for Save the Children Fund and former prisoner of conscience and torture survivor in the 1980s; and Addisu Beyene, General Secretary of the Oromo Relief Association, which had earlier been closed down by the government. In December they were charged with armed conspiracy.

Over 200 university students were detained in Addis Ababa in March after a peaceful demonstration which the government declared illegal. They were supporting protests by peasant farmers whose land had been confiscated because of their association with the former government. The students were all released without charge by May.

Among hundreds of people arrested in the Somali region on account of suspected links with the ONLF were three former district governors – Bashir Sheikh Abdi, Mohamed Ahmed Sheikh Abdi and Yusuf Muhumed Moallim. They were detained in April in Dire Dawa and were still held incommunicado and without charge by the end of the year.

Scores of Ethiopian Somalis, as well as refugees from Somalia, were detained without charge or trial for alleged involvement in bombings attributed to Somali opponents. Dr Umar Elmi Duhod, a British citizen, was detained in Harar in February with other guests at a hotel which was bombed. He was held without charge for six weeks. In December, 14 alleged members of *Al-Itihad* were charged with these bombings.

Some political prisoners detained in 1996 or earlier (see *Amnesty International Report 1997*) were released during 1997. They included journalists such as Terefe Mengesha and Solomon Lemma, who served prison sentences imposed in 1996. Numerous other journalists arrested in 1996 and 1997 were provisionally released. Abate Angore, an official of the Ethiopian Teachers Association (ETA), was freed in March. Some OLF suspects were released, including Bayera Mideksa, a pharmacist imprisoned since 1992. Among some ONLF suspects released were Ali Bashe Abdi and nine other members of the Somali region Assembly who were detained in 1996. Muhyadin Muftah, a leader of the armed opposition Afar Revolutionary Democratic Unity Front, who had been forcibly returned from Djibouti in 1996, was released in mid-1997. Svetlana Mamedova, a naturalized Ethiopian citizen of Georgian origin, was released and deported in June after a total of nearly three years' detention without charge in connection with a business case involving the government.

The former vice-president of the Somali region, Ahmed Makahil Hussein, a prisoner of conscience arrested in 1995, was provisionally released in December, pending his appeal hearing. He had been convicted of armed conspiracy and sentenced to seven years' imprisonment with hard labour in a summary and unfair trial in Jijiga in May. He had been refused legal defence rights and there was no credible evidence against him.

Thousands of political prisoners held since 1996 or earlier, some possibly prisoners of conscience, remained in detention, mostly without charge or trial. Most were held in regional prisons and accused of being members or supporters of armed opposition groups. They included Mengesha Dogoma, a southern politician held since 1992; two female Oromo folksingers, Baharsitu Obsa and Shabbe Sheko, arrested in 1996; Hussein Ahmed Aydrus and other ONLF suspects forcibly deported from Djibouti in 1996; Abdullahi Haliye and two other ONLF members deported from Somaliland and held in Harar prison at the end of the year despite a court order for their release in May; and Mohamoud Muhumed Hashi, a prisoner of conscience, former university lecturer and vice-chairman of the Ogaden Welfare Society, who was detained again in November 1996, a few months after being released from two years' detention without trial. Suspected members of other clandestine opposition groups, such as the Ethiopian People's Revolutionary Party, also remained in detention without charge or trial.

In four long-running trials of government opponents (see *Amnesty International Report 1997*) there was concern whether defendants were receiving fair trials. In the trial of Professor Asrat Woldeyes, chairman of the All-Amhara People's Organization, and 31 others, charges against seven defendants were dropped in mid-trial. However, the judges continued to accept several defendants' earlier admissions of guilt despite their retractions and claims that they had made them as a result of torture. Asrat Woldeyes and other defendants appeared to be prisoners of conscience.

Some charges were dropped in the armed conspiracy trial of Taye Woldesmayat, a former university professor and chairman of ETA (which the government was seeking to close down), and five other defendants. However, the judges appeared to accept the main prosecution evidence from a former defendant in the trial. The defendants appeared to be prisoners of conscience.

Another armed conspiracy trial continued of 38 Muslim leaders, mostly members of the Supreme Islamic Council, including *Imam* Mohamed Ahmed Wale and Mohamed Abdu Tuku, a professor of engineering. All appeared to be prisoners of conscience. The prosecution brought no substantial evidence that they had instigated violence at the Anwar mosque in 1995 when government troops killed at least 31 people. The court dropped all charges against 32 of the defendants, including Mohamed Abdu Tuku, in November.

The trial in Ziwai of more than 285 armed members of the OLF detained since 1992 was adjourned for most of the year.

The trial for genocide of 46 members of the former military government (known as the *Dergue*) headed by Mengistu Haile-Mariam, which began in 1994, was still continuing in the High Court. By the end of the year over 400 prosecution witnesses had testified to the former government's 17-year record of extrajudicial executions, "disappearances", war crimes, torture and arbitrary detentions.

In February the Special Prosecutor's Office announced that 2,246 other officials of the former government were still detained and had all been charged. Their names and charges were not disclosed but they were gradually brought to court and informed of the charges. Some preliminary trial proceedings started. They were charged in groups, mostly with genocide. A further 2,952 former officials were charged *in absentia*, and the prosecution said it would seek the extradition of those who had fled abroad.

There were new allegations of torture, "disappearances" and extrajudicial executions during the year. Torture was widely reported against suspected OLF and ONLF members, including Wako Tola (for whose death in police custody there was no inquest) and Worku Mulata (see above). The students arrested in March, who included a blind law student, Ishetu Aleme, endured harsh physical exercises and severe punishments which amounted to torture. Beyene Belissa (see above), an amputee, was deprived of his walking stick for several days while detained.

Reports continued to be received of "disappearances" of government opponents, allegedly arrested by the security service and taken to secret detention centres. Some later reappeared in official prisons or police stations. However, the fate of many who had "disappeared" in previous years – including Mustafa Idris, Yoseph Ayele Bati, Deeg Yusuf Kariye and Tsegay Gebre-Medhin (see *Amnesty International Report 1997*) – remained unknown.

Extrajudicial executions by the security forces were widely reported from areas of armed conflict, particularly in the Oromia and Somali regions. In Addis Ababa on 8 May, Assefa Maru, an official of ETA and a board member of the Ethiopian Human Rights Council, was shot dead by police. Police claimed he belonged to a clandestine armed opposition group and was escaping arrest, but eye-witnesses reported that he was shot dead without any attempt to arrest him. Three alleged OLF members, including Terefe Qumbi, a senior court official, were said by the police to have been killed in a shoot-out in Addis Ababa on 8 October, but they appeared to have been extrajudicially executed after arrest.

Several death sentences were imposed by courts but no executions were reported. In April the Supreme Court upheld death sentences imposed on three Egyptian nationals convicted of attempting to assassinate the Egyptian President and of killing two police officers in 1995 (see *Amnesty International Report 1997*).

Five exiles from Djibouti were arrested in Addis Ababa in September and nine others later in the year. They were immediately handed over to Djibouti, where they were detained and charged with political offences (see **Djibouti** entry).

Amnesty International appealed to the Ethiopian authorities to release prisoners of conscience, end arbitrary detention, and ensure that trials of political prisoners were not unfair or unduly protracted. It called for all allegations of human rights violations, such as torture, "disappearances" and extrajudicial executions, to be investigated impartially and thoroughly and for those responsible to be brought to justice. It urged the government to consider abolition of the death penalty. The authorities denied that violations had occurred or made no response. Amnesty International's researcher, excluded from visiting Ethiopia since 1995, continued to be denied access to the country, but two other Amnesty International representatives were able to visit Ethiopia in July.

FRANCE

Criminal proceedings were under way against conscientious objectors to the national service laws. Measures of administrative detention continued against some political refugees. There were reports of fatal shootings, ill-treatment and rape by law enforcement officers. Officers involved in cases of fatal shootings or ill-treatment in previous years were, after long delays, brought to justice; they were acquitted or sentenced to nominal terms of imprisonment.

Parliamentary elections were held in May and June, as a result of which the leader of the Socialist Party, Lionel Jospin, became Prime Minister of a broad left coalition government, which included members of the Communist Party and the Green Party.

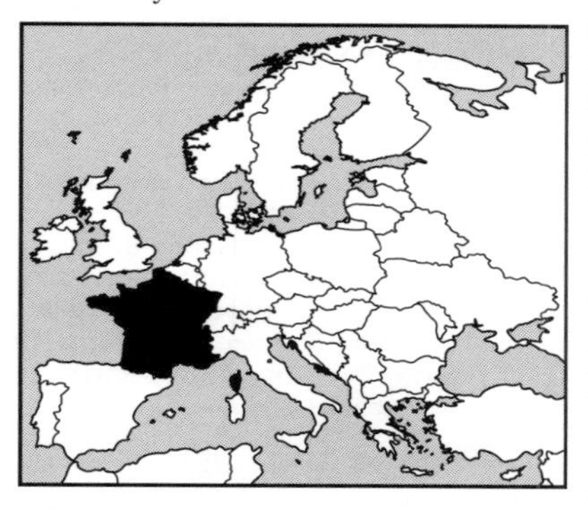

In July the UN Human Rights Committee considered the government's third periodic report on its implementation of the International Covenant on Civil and Political Rights (ICCPR). The Committee was "seriously concerned" by the number and gravity of the allegations it had received of ill-treatment by law enforcement officers of detainees and others, including unnecessary use of firearms resulting in a number of deaths. It underlined that the risk of such ill-treatment was "much greater in the case of foreigners and immigrants", and expressed concern that in most cases there was little, if any, investigation of complaints of such ill-treatment by the internal administration of the police and the National Gendarmerie. This resulted in "virtual impunity". The Committee also expressed concern at the "failure or the inertia of prosecutors in applying the law to investigating human rights violations where law enforcement officers are concerned and at the delays and unreasonably lengthy proceedings in investigation and prosecution of alleged human rights violations involving law enforcement officers."

Among the Committee's recommendations were that France establish an independent mechanism to receive and deal with individual complaints of ill-treatment by law enforcement officers, and that it introduce a comprehensive course in human rights at all levels of their training. The Committee additionally expressed concern that the powers, as a military corps, of the National Gendarmerie were wider than those of the police when operating in a civilian public order situation, and urged that steps be taken to modify or repeal the decree of July 1943 which greatly increased the powers of the gendarmerie in the use of firearms. Another subject of concern was the continued application of the "anti-terrorist" laws, which provide for a centralized court whose prosecutors have special powers of arrest, search and prolonged detention (up to four days) in police custody, and where the accused do not have the same rights in determination of guilt as in the ordinary courts.

At the end of the year the "*loi Chevènement*", a new law on immigration that proposes an extension of the right of asylum, was continuing its passage through the French parliament. Meanwhile, large numbers of Kurdish refugees fleeing Iraq were still being intercepted on the frontier between France and Italy and immediately returned across the border. Over 4000 were reported to have been intercepted by police since January.

There was still no right to claim conscientious objector status during military service and the alternative civilian service available to recognized conscientious objectors remained, at 20 months, twice the length of ordinary military service. In September the new government submitted to parliament a bill reforming compulsory national service. It replaced a similar bill put forward by the previous government (see *Amnesty International Report 1997*). The law, definitively approved by parliament in October, provided for the suspension by the end of 2002, via a phasing-out process, of compulsory national service, and its replacement with a compulsory one day's instruction in defence issues.

Criminal proceedings were pursued against conscientious objectors refusing to conform to the national service laws, with the exception of Jehovah's Witnesses (see *Amnesty International Report 1997*). The proceedings resulted in prison sentences, usually suspended. Objectors sentenced to periods of detention remained at liberty while awaiting the outcome of appeals lodged with higher courts.

Measures of administrative detention continued against some political refugees. For example, a refugee and member of an illegal opposition party in Tunisia spent a fourth year under a form of administrative detention (*assignation à résidence*). Salah Ben Hédi Ben Hassen Karker, a leading member of the Tunisian Islamist party *Ennahda* (Renaissance) had, in his absence, been sentenced to death in Tunisia and was recognized as a political refugee by the French authorities in 1988. A former Interior Minister issued an expulsion order against him in 1993 but no country would accept him. Salah Karker, who was transferred from the Haute-Loire region to that of Alpes-de-Haute-Provence in 1995, denied being in any way connected with terrorist activities and had won a number of actions for defamation against magazines and newspapers that reproduced accusations by the Tunisian Government that he belonged to a "terrorist organization". He has not been charged with any criminal offence within France.

There were further allegations of ill-treatment, rape and shootings and killings of unarmed people by law enforcement officers. Four Bordeaux police officers were detained in June while under investigation for allegedly "abusing their authority by rape and complicity in rape". An officer called to the scene of a traffic accident and reportedly finding a woman driver to be drunk, was said to have told her that no charges would be brought if she agreed to sleep with him and his colleagues. Several days after the accident he allegedly called at her home, hit her with a truncheon and raped her. The woman lodged a complaint with the police complaints authority, the *Inspection générale de la police nationale*, in which she claimed that some days later the police officer returned, this time with his colleagues, and a gang rape took place. The four officers, who were taken into custody at the request of the public prosecutor of Bordeaux, and placed in isolation, denied the charges.

In October an Egyptian architect was reportedly assaulted and had his leg fractured by four plainclothes police officers in a case of mistaken identity. Ahmed Hamed was visiting France with his mother, a patient at the American hospital in Neuilly, when he was approached by the officers in a launderette. He was reportedly handcuffed and forced towards a waiting car. Resisting what he believed to be a kidnapping, he was violently kicked and his leg was consequently broken. Ahmed Hamed was held in custody for 10 hours, after which he was admitted to hospital. He underwent several operations. The Interior Minister ordered that an administrative inquiry into the case be opened.

There were several reports of fatal shootings by police officers during the year. In one incident in December Fabrice Fernandez died instantly when shot in the jaw while handcuffed and under interrogation at a Lyon police station. An officer allegedly fired the fatal shot with a confiscated shotgun. According to the Lyon public prosecutor, Fabrice Fernandez had been arrested with two others by officers of the *Brigade Anticriminalité* (BAC), Anti-Crime Brigade, following a disturbance when a shotgun was fired into the air. The police officer who allegedly fired the fatal shot was suspended from duty, detained and initially charged with manslaughter. The charge was almost immediately increased to murder by the investigating judge. The police officer, who was reported to have already been suspended for assault, later offered his resignation from the police force. Following the death there were riots at La Duchère, the poor inner-city area of Lyon where the death occurred. The Interior Minister stated that: "use of a gun against a handcuffed man without checking whether or not it is loaded is absolutely unacceptable."

Violent disturbances also took place over several consecutive nights at Dammarie-les-Lys (Seine-et-Marne) following the death of 16-year-old Abdelkader Bouziane, who was reportedly shot in the neck by a police officer after trying, with friends, to drive through a police road-block.

A number of police officers and gendarmes were brought to trial in connection with cases from previous years of fatal shootings or ill-treatment. A large proportion of the cases concerned refugees, immigrants and people of non-European ethnic origin. In February the Bordeaux Court of Appeal upheld the four-month suspended prison sentence against a BAC officer for beating Didier Laroche with a truncheon (see *Amnesty International Reports 1995* and *1997*).

In May a police officer was given a 10-month suspended sentence and fined for assaulting Sikh refugee and asylum-seeker Gurnam Singh at the police station in Bobigny in 1996. Two other officers were given a 15-month suspended prison sentence and fined for forging the station records to make it appear that Gurnam Singh had been legitimately detained within their area of authority.

In June three officers were sentenced to 18 months' imprisonment, 15 of which were suspended, and to five years' disqualification from serving in the police force in connection with the assault on Sid Ahmed Amiri, a national of France and Algeria, during a "preventive action" in Marseille (see *Amnesty International Report 1996*).

In October, after continual delays and procedural irregularities, Rhône Court of Assizes sentenced a police officer to a five-year suspended prison term for the fatal shooting of Mourad Tchier, a youth of Algerian origin, in 1993 (see *Amnesty International Report 1997*). In November a gendarme who shot and killed Franck Moret in 1993 (see *Amnesty International Report 1997*) was discharged by the correctional court in Valence. The prosecution, and relatives of Franck Moret appealed against the judgment. Also in November the family of Ibrahim Sy, who was shot dead by a gendarme in 1994 (see *Amnesty International Reports 1995* and *1997*), appealed to the Court of Cassation after the Rouen Court of Appeal confirmed the decision of the investigating judge that there were no grounds for prosecution.

An appeal against a similar decision in the case of Todor Bogdanović, an eight-year-old Rom from Serbia who was shot dead by border police near Sospel (see *Amnesty International Report 1996*), was lodged with an appeal court in Aix-en-Provence in December. The court overturned the decision, rejecting a plea that the police officer had acted in legitimate self-defence, and referred the case to the Court of Assizes on a charge of manslaughter. In July experts on the UN Human Rights Committee had specifically referred to the death of the Romani child when expressing concern not only at the treatment and expulsion of refugees but at what appeared in this case to be an arbitrary and reckless use of firearms.

Amnesty International continued to express concern that, because of its punitive length, civilian service did not provide an acceptable alternative to military service. The organization was also concerned that there was still no provision for conscientious objection developed during military service. It reiterated its belief that conscientious objectors to military service should be able to seek conscientious objector status at any time.

Amnesty International wrote in December to the Interior Minister, urging him to give prompt and thorough consideration to lifting the orders of *assignation à résidence* and expulsion from Salah Karker if no charges were to be promptly brought against him. The organization explained that it considered people to be detained not only when they were incarcerated but when their freedom of movement was severely restricted. It expressed concern that decisions taken on appeals by Salah Karker against expulsion and *assignation à résidence* had not been open to scrutiny in a court of law.

The organization sought information from the authorities about the progress of investigations into incidents of shootings, killings, ill-treatment and rape, and in July submitted information about a number of its concerns on France to the UN Human Rights Committee.

The case of Todor Bogdanović featured in the Amnesty International Week campaign to raise awareness about refugees and the specific needs of child refugees. The organization pressed, among other things, for a full and fair investigation into the disputed circumstances of the child's killing and for the officer to be brought to justice.

GAMBIA

At least 14 prisoners of conscience were held for short periods. Some were tortured. Eight military detainees were held without trial. A death in custody and possible extrajudicial executions in previous years remained uninvestigated. Four prisoners were sentenced to death, but their convictions were quashed on appeal.

In January Colonel (retired) Yahya Jammeh's party won a majority in the parliamentary election, which completed the return to civilian rule. The new Constitution came into force. However, some legislation which violates basic constitutional provisions for human rights was not repealed. For example, the National Intelligence Agency (NIA), which has far-reaching powers of arrest (see *Amnesty International Report 1996*), continued to operate and the three political parties which had existed before the military coup of July 1994 remained banned. Also, all individuals who had been president, vice-president or a government minister during the 30 years before the military coup were forbidden from engaging in political activities.

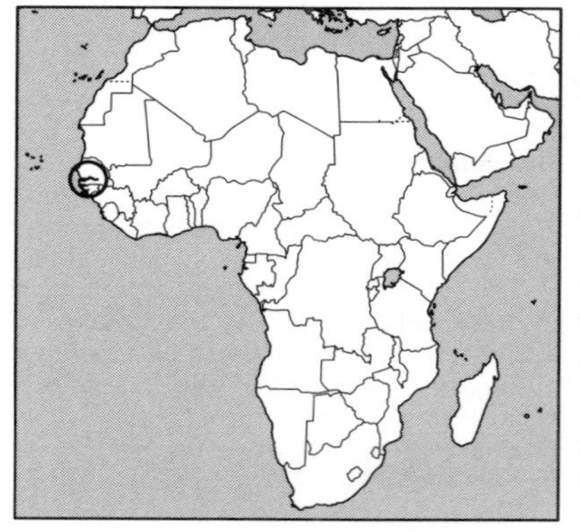

Journalists continued to be harassed and restrictive legislation introduced in 1996 remained in force. Decrees 70 and 71, for example, modified the Newspaper Act by greatly increasing the fines for any contravention of the Act. In January, three foreign nationals, all employed at the *Daily Observer* newspaper, were deported. In November the newspaper's editor-in-chief, Ellicot Seade, of Ghanaian nationality, was expelled. Other journalists were arrested (see below). The authorities tried unsuccessfully to ban an independent radio program which reviewed the print media and to prohibit the state media from broadcasting programs critical of female genital mutilation. This prohibition was lifted after national and international pressure.

At least 14 prisoners of conscience, mostly members of the United Democratic Party (UDP), the main opposition party, were held for short periods. The ill-treatment and short-term detentions faced by its supporters since the UDP's formation in September 1996 continued. In March, three UDP members were arrested at their leader's house. Demba Kanyi, Musa Kanyi and Ba Sorie Ceesay were held for a few days without charge or trial. Demba Kanyi was reportedly beaten and injured and other UDP members were also beaten by the police. In June, eight UDP members were arrested at the party's first regional constituency congress in Brikama when police intervened claiming that the meeting was illegal. The detainees were eventually taken to NIA headquarters in Banjul, the capital, where they were tortured (see below). They were released on bail after several days. The one woman arrested and tortured, Sarjo Kunjang Sanneh, had previously been held from December 1996 until February.

Pa Modou Faal, Secretary General of the Gambia Workers Confederation, was arrested by NIA agents and held for 26 hours in April as he was about to travel to Libya.

In July Alhaji Yorro Jallow, a local journalist for the *British Broadcasting Corporation*, and Alieu Badara Sowe, a freelance journalist, were held for five days' questioning after they reported that a prison riot had taken place in the capital's Mile Two Prison.

In February, 11 possible prisoners of conscience were released. Three of them, Pa Sallah Jagne, Ebrima Chongan and Kebba Dibba, all former members of the security forces, had been held since July 1994 (see previous *Amnesty International Reports*). Charges against them were finally dropped in April. Others released included Lamin Waa Juwara, a former independent member of parliament held without charge since February 1996.

Eight military detainees arrested in July remained held without trial. Three had been arrested at the time of an armed attack on the military post of Kartong, near the border with Senegal. The other five were extradited from Senegal and arrested on their return. All had apparently participated in an alleged coup attempt in November 1994.

Several cases of torture were reported; one detainee died in custody. Yaya Drammeh had been held at Mile Two Prison since an attack by armed men on the Gambia's second largest military camp at Farafenni in November 1996. The government stated that he died of a blood disorder, but sources at the hospital claimed he was vomiting blood, could not speak and had injuries to the genitals when he was brought to hospital three days before he died.

In June the eight detained UDP members were tortured by the NIA. The victims spoke to the press immediately after their release and showed evidence of injuries sustained as a result of being beaten with heavy whips while being forced to crawl on their hands and knees before security officials. There were also allegations that a water cannon had been used on them and that one man, Doudou Sanyang, had been burned on his genitals. In response, the Attorney General stated that the allegations of torture would be fully investigated. However, no investigation had been started by the end of the year.

New reports emerged that three UDP supporters who were among scores beaten by soldiers on Denton Bridge and in a military barracks in September 1996 died as a result of their injuries.

There were no investigations into suspected extrajudicial executions in previous years (see *Amnesty International Reports 1996* and *1997*).

In June, four men were sentenced to death by the High Court on charges of treason, following an armed attack on Farafenni military camp in November 1996. The convictions were quashed on appeal in October. However, the four remained held and were believed to face new charges. These were the first death sentences passed since the penalty was reintroduced in 1995.

In June Amnesty International urged the government to allow Sierra Leoneans fleeing their country as a result of a military coup in May to disembark from their boat to claim asylum. They remained at sea in hazardous conditions for several days before being allowed ashore. In July Amnesty International appealed to the authorities not to carry out death sentences. In December Amnesty International published a report, *The Gambia: Democratic reforms without human rights*. It reported on human rights violations during the election period and since the transition to civilian rule. It called on the government to end arbitrary detention of prisoners of conscience, stop torture, abolish the death penalty and organize investigations into human rights violations.

GEORGIA

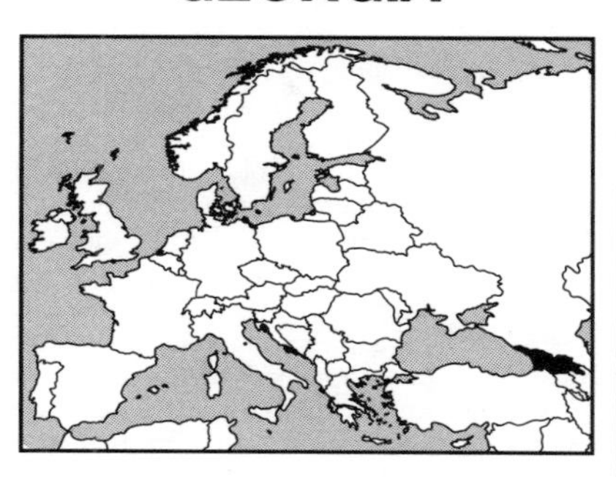

Several conscientious objectors were reportedly imprisoned. Further cases of torture and ill-treatment in custody were alleged. All death sentences were commuted and the death penalty was abolished for all crimes. In the disputed region of Abkhazia, several ethnic Georgian civilians were allegedly deliberately and arbitrarily killed by Abkhazian security forces. Around 14 people were on death row. Some 200,000 ethnic Georgians displaced by the conflict continued to face obstacles to their return.

In April the UN Human Rights Committee reviewed Georgia's initial report under the International Covenant on Civil and Political Rights. Among other things, the Committee expressed deep concern about the torture of detainees, including the use of torture to extract confessions, and deplored the fact that such acts usually went unpunished, causing a lack of confidence in the authorities which deterred victims from lodging complaints. The Committee was also deeply concerned about prison conditions, which it described as "disastrous", and noted with disquiet that some court proceedings had not met international fair trial standards.

The Committee's recommendations included filling the post of Public Defender as soon as possible; continuing efforts towards abolition of the death penalty; undertaking systematic and impartial investigations of all complaints of torture and ill-treatment, bringing those responsible to justice and compensating victims; systematically excluding confessions obtained under duress; and reviewing all convictions based on confessions allegedly extracted under torture.

The post of Public Defender, established under the 1995 Constitution specifically to monitor the defence of individual rights and freedoms (see *Amnesty International Report 1996*), was filled in October.

In November parliament abolished the death penalty for all crimes.

The situation in Abkhazia remained tense. The mandate of the UN Observer Mission in Georgia (UNOMIG) was renewed, as was that of the peace-keeping force from the Commonwealth of Independent States. In August President Eduard Shevardnadze met the head of the *de facto* Abkhazian authorities as part of ongoing efforts to resolve the region's political status. A Georgian partisan group named the "White Legion" continued to claim responsibility for armed attacks on Abkhazian targets.

By the end of the year parliament had still not considered a draft new bill on a civilian alternative to compulsory military service, to replace a 1991 law which had not been put into practice. Young men objecting to military service on grounds of conscience continued to face imprisonment for refusing their call-up papers. Several such prosecutions were believed to have taken place during the year, but details of individual cases were difficult to obtain. Officials reported that Kakhaber Galashvili, a Jehovah's Witness, had been released from an 18-month prison sentence imposed in July 1996 for refusing conscription on religious grounds.

There were further reports of torture and ill-treatment. In September, for example, a young woman was reportedly raped by several police officers after she went to Marnueli police station in order to take a meal to her husband, who was being held there on a charge of murder. The procuracy instituted criminal proceedings, but the police officers were said to have gone into hiding and it was not clear if any charges had been brought by the end of the year.

At least two law enforcement officials were imprisoned following prosecutions connected with the torture or ill-treatment of detainees. Gela Kavtelishvili, former deputy head of the Interior Ministry's Department to Combat Drugs and Drug-Trafficking, was sentenced to four years' imprisonment in May for, among other things, using electric shocks on a suspect while investigating a murder (see *Amnesty International Report 1997*). Another Interior Ministry official was also sentenced to four years' imprisonment, following the death from head injuries of David Amashukeli in December 1996 (see *Amnesty International Report 1997*). P. Bezhanishvili was found guilty of striking David Amashukeli several times around the head with a truncheon after an altercation in the street.

Between January and June at least three death sentences were commuted, including that passed on political prisoner Badri Zarandia who had been sentenced in 1996 after a trial which appeared to fall short of international standards (see *Amnesty International Report 1997*). By the end of the year all death sentences had been commuted: 54 men under sentence of death had their sentences commuted to 20 years' imprisonment in July and the last death-row prisoner had his sentence commuted following the abolition of the death penalty in November.

Several ethnic Georgian civilians were allegedly deliberately and arbitrarily killed by Abkhazian security forces. In February, for example, Vazha Dzandzava was said to have died in the village of Chuburkhinji after being beaten to death by Abkhazian police who accused him of illegally possessing a weapon.

In September the *de facto* Abkhazian authorities stated that there were 14 men on death row at that time, mostly convicted of premeditated, aggravated murder, but that there had been a *de facto* moratorium on executions since 1993.

Many of the estimated 200,000 ethnic Georgians displaced by the conflict in Abkhazia continued to face obstacles to their return, on what appeared to be grounds of their ethnicity and suspected political sympathies. In July the UN Security Council again condemned the obstruction of their return, and urged the *de facto* Abkhazian authorities to accelerate significantly the process of voluntary return without delay or preconditions, and to guarantee the safety of those who had already returned spontaneously.

In April Amnesty International informed the UN Human Rights Committee of its concerns in Georgia. The Committee addressed many of these in its recommendations to the government.

Amnesty International continued to call for a judicial review of all political trials in which confessions had reportedly been obtained under duress, and for a full, prompt and impartial investigation into all allegations of torture and ill-treatment in custody, with the results made public and the perpetrators brought to justice. It welcomed the commutation of all death sentences in July, and the complete abolition of the death penalty in November.

Amnesty International urged the *de facto* Abkhazian authorities to ensure the safety of all residents, regardless of their ethnic origin, by, among other things, instigating prompt, impartial and comprehensive investigations into all instances in which Abkhazian forces were alleged to have deliberately and arbitrarily killed civilians. Officials informed Amnesty International in September that they instituted a criminal investigation in each such case, but that the security situation made it difficult to identify the perpetrators. The organization urged the *de facto* Abkhazian authorities to commute all death sentences, and to take steps towards abolition of the death penalty. Amnesty International also urged them to take all appropriate and timely measures to ensure the voluntary return of refugees and displaced people, under conditions in which their safety, and the safety of those who had already spontaneously returned, could be guaranteed.

GERMANY

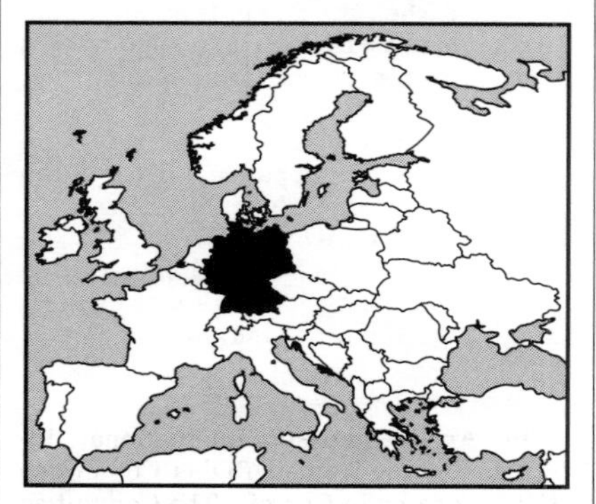

There were further allegations of ill-treatment of detainees by police officers.

In May the German Government rejected the recommendation made by the UN Human Rights Committee in November 1996 that "independent bodies [be established] throughout the territory of the State Party for the investigation of complaints of ill-treatment by the police" (see *Amnesty International Report 1997*), stating that it saw "no need for additional measures for regulating the investigation and prosecution of [such] allegations".

In July the government published the report of the European Committee for the Prevention of Torture, a committee of experts set up under the European Convention for the Prevention of Torture and Inhuman or Degrading Treatment or Punishment, on its visit to Germany in April 1996, together with the interim report drawn up in response by the German authorities. The Committee reported hearing during its visit "a certain number of allegations... of the use of excessive force by police officers at the time of apprehension. The most common forms of ill-treatment alleged by detained persons were blows and kicks received after they had been restrained and placed on the ground at the time of their apprehension". The Committee also reported meeting numerous detainees during its visit to police establishments who "apparently had not been informed of their rights... or of the basic rules applicable in the place of detention in which they were held", and repeated its recommendation, first made in 1991, that detainees be given a form, at the very outset of their custody, informing them of their rights.

During 1997 there were further allegations of police ill-treatment of foreigners, including asylum-seekers, and members of ethnic minorities.

An Israeli national alleged that in January a group of men he believed to be "neo-Nazis" chased him through Frankfurt railway station and then beat and kicked him after he fell to the ground. The men, who were dressed in civilian clothing, handcuffed him and took him to a police station where he learned that they were police officers. Following an identity check he was released from custody. According to medical evidence, the Israeli's injuries included multiple bruising of the arms, back and chest. He was later informed by the Frankfurt prosecuting authorities that he was under investigation for violently resisting police attempts to check his identity, for attacking the officers involved, and for calling them "Nazis". Both this investigation and the one into his alleged ill-treatment were discontinued in October.

Algerian asylum-seeker Nasr B. alleged that in March Berlin police officers violently twisted his arm behind his back, pushed him to the ground and kicked him on the head and body after he protested to them about being falsely accused of a street mugging. Medical evidence showed that Nasr B. had suffered a fracture of the right arm and multiple bruising. He also alleged that the officers subjected him to racist insults. Nasr B. was later informed by the Berlin police that he was under investigation for resisting police officers and for using insulting behaviour. His criminal complaint of ill-treatment was rejected in December.

In July Iranian refugee Homayoun Ghaleh alleged that a Dortmund police officer hit him on the head with a service radio and then struck his head on the ground after he intervened during an identity check on two of his cousins and a third youth. According to medical evidence his injuries included bruising of the forehead, crown of the head and cheekbone. The police officer involved denied ill-treating Homayoun Ghaleh and filed a complaint against him for resisting his authority and for assault.

Decisions were reached by prosecuting and judicial authorities on a number of cases of alleged ill-treatment by police in previous years.

In January the Berlin prosecuting authorities rejected Mustafa K.'s complaint that he was beaten, kicked and subjected to racist insults during a police search of his flat in July 1996 (see *Amnesty International Report 1997*). Mustafa K., who suffered bruising of the ribs and multiple bruising of the face, wrist, shoulders and arms, was himself charged with one count of assault and one of attempted assault, and with resisting officers in the exercise of their duty. An application by Mustafa K., a German national of Turkish origin, for a judicial review of the prosecuting authorities' decision not to charge the officers was later rejected on procedural grounds.

In February a Frankfurt court halted the trial of a doctor charged with "failing to render assistance" to Nigerian Kola Bankole and ordered the accused to pay DM 5,000 (US$2,700) to a charitable organization. Rejected asylum-seeker Kola Bankole died in 1994 after being bound and gagged by Federal Border Guard officers and injected with a sedative by the doctor when he physically resisted attempts to deport him from Frankfurt am Main airport (see *Amnesty International Report 1996*). None of the officers were charged in connection with Kola Bankole's death.

In May the trial took place of two officers accused of ill-treating Ahmet Delibas (see *Amnesty International Report 1997*). Ahmet Delibas, a Turkish national, alleged that the officers strangled him and punched him in the face in the back of a police car following his arrest outside a club in Hamm in North-Rhine/Westphalia in October 1995. Medical evidence showed that he had suffered serious injuries, including a fracture of the left cheekbone, and separate fractures to both eye sockets. Ahmet Delibas was himself accused of participating in an assault on one of the officers outside the club prior to his arrest. The court heard both cases simultaneously and found one officer guilty of negligent assault and fined him DM 4,500 (US$2,500). The second officer, and Ahmet Delibas, were acquitted of the charges against them.

In June a Hanover police officer was acquitted of causing the death of Halim Dener in June 1994 through negligence (see *Amnesty International Report 1995*). The court found that Halim Dener, a 16-year-old Turkish Kurd, had been accidentally shot when the officer tried to put his service revolver back in its holster after it dropped to the ground following a struggle with the youth.

In July Hidayet Secil was fined DM 450 (US$250) for resisting police officers in the performance of their duty, and for assault. Hidayet Secil's own complaint that the same officers had ill-treated him during his arrest in July 1995 had already been rejected (see *Amnesty International Report 1997*).

In September, two Frankfurt police officers were charged with assaulting Mohamed Z. (see *Amnesty International Report 1997*). In the same month the Bremen prosecuting authorities rejected a criminal complaint of assault made by Aliu Bo in April 1996 (see *Amnesty International Report 1997*).

At the end of the year the trial continued of four Bernau police officers charged in February 1995 with ill-treating Vietnamese detainees in their custody in 1993 and 1994 (see *Amnesty International Report 1995*). It had opened in January 1996. Four other officers were acquitted of the same charges in September.

Throughout the year Amnesty International expressed concern to the authorities about fresh allegations of ill-treatment brought to its attention and called for them to be investigated promptly, impartially and thoroughly. In most cases, the organization received confirmation from the authorities that investigations were in progress.

In April Amnesty International expressed concern to the Berlin authorities that the allegations of ill-treatment made by Mustafa K. had not been subjected to an impartial examination. The organization's criticisms were rejected by the Berlin prosecuting authorities in June. In the same month Amnesty International expressed concern to the Brandenburg authorities about delays in examining allegations against eight Bernau police officers accused of ill-treating Vietnamese detainees in their custody. In July the Brandenburg Justice Minister reported that a number of factors had contributed to the delay in proceedings, including the fact that some witnesses had since left the country and had to be summoned to appear in court.

In June Amnesty International urged the Federal Minister of the Interior to instigate a full and impartial inquiry into the role and accountability of all agencies involved in the deportation process, following the death of Kola Bankole and the end of trial proceedings against the doctor involved in the attempt to forcibly deport him. No reply had been received by the end of the year.

In July Amnesty International published a report, *Federal Republic of Germany: Continuing pattern of police ill-treatment,* which detailed allegations received between April 1995 and April 1997 that police officers had used excessive or unwarranted force in restraining or arresting people, or had deliberately subjected detainees in their custody to cruel, inhuman or degrading treatment or punishment. The vast majority of the alleged victims were foreign nationals, including asylum-seekers, or members of ethnic minorities.

In a letter accompanying the report sent to Chancellor Helmut Kohl and to the heads of government of the 16 federal states, Amnesty International stated that the allegations it had documented provided further evidence of a clear pattern of abuse. Amnesty International also expressed concern to the authorities that in many cases criminal investigations into allegations of police ill-treatment had not been carried out promptly, impartially and thoroughly. Amnesty International called upon the federal and state governments to establish permanent, independent oversight bodies with the responsibility and authority to maintain statistics on complaints about ill-treatment by officers and on their outcome; conduct their own investigations into such complaints and recommend whether criminal and/or disciplinary charges should be brought against any of the officers involved, and whether compensation should be awarded to any of the complainants; and to perform a continuous assessment of the measures adopted by the police authorities to prevent the use of excessive force or deliberate ill-treatment. In its letter to Chancellor Helmut Kohl, Amnesty International also expressed concern at the German Government's rejection of the UN Human Rights Committee's recommendation that independent bodies be established for the investigation of complaints of ill-treatment by the police. The organization stated that the refusal to implement this recommendation was inconsistent with Resolution 1996/22 of the UN Commission on Human Rights, adopted on 19 April 1996, urging "all States Parties whose reports have been examined by treaty bodies to provide adequate follow-up to the observations and final comments of the treaty bodies on their reports". By the end of the year Amnesty International had received no substantive response from the federal authorities. Only four of the 16 state governments replied to the organization's call for permanent, independent oversight bodies; all rejected it.

GHANA

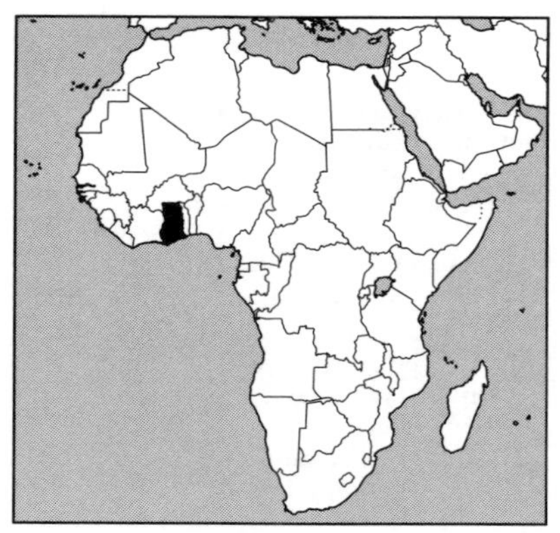

At least 13 possible prisoners of conscience, arrested in previous years, remained imprisoned throughout the year. Dozens of suspects were reportedly ill-treated following rioting in November. At least three prisoners were sentenced to death; none was known to have been executed.

In March the Supreme Court ruled that legislation providing for up to 10 years' imprisonment for false reporting likely to injure the reputation of the government was not in contravention of the right to freedom of expression contained in the 1992 Constitution (see *Amnesty International Report 1997*).

In April the government rejected some of the findings of the Commission for Human Rights and Administrative Justice (CHRAJ), established in 1993 to investigate and remedy human rights violations against senior government officials investigated for corruption. In June the government sought a ruling in the Supreme Court to stop the CHRAJ from ordering redress in cases of arbitrary dismissal by the previous, military government. Transitional Provisions inserted in the 1992 Constitution by the outgoing military government gave immunity from prosecution to officials in the two military governments headed by Flight-Lieutenant (now President) J.J. Rawlings after coups in 1979 and 1981. No ruling had been given by the end of the year. The Supreme Court had still given no date for hearing an application made by the CHRAJ in early 1996. The government had challenged the powers of the CHRAJ to investigate allegations that the government was involved in the killing of five demonstrators in Accra in May 1995. Armed government supporters were alleged to have killed the protesters during a demonstration against tax rises. By the end of the year, there had still been no thorough and impartial investigation into these allegations.

The government ignored calls by Ghanaians for independent investigations to determine whether excessive force had been used in several incidents in which at least four people died. These included a demonstration in Kumasi in March in which two protesters were reportedly shot in the back of the head by police using assault rifles. In October at least one teenager was reportedly shot dead by police during rioting in Nima, in Accra, the capital. In Akwatia, Eastern Region, in November, a police officer and one other person were killed in disputed circumstances when police tried to disperse a crowd protesting about the arrest of criminal suspects. In December, one man died when police tried to prevent a crowd forcibly releasing suspects arrested after clashes between Muslim groups in Wa, Upper West Region. The government said that police and troops had come under attack and had used lethal force only when other methods of crowd control had failed to disperse protesters.

In October, Kwesi Biney, a journalist, and Frank Awuah, circulation manager of the *African Observer* magazine, were detained for two days before being released to await trial on charges of criminal libel. They and two others not in court were alleged to have defamed a government minister.

At least 13 possible prisoners of conscience remained imprisoned throughout the year. Defence lawyers for Karim Salifu Adam, a leading member of the opposition New Patriotic Party (NPP), protested after he was sent for retrial on treason charges in July without their knowledge. He was still awaiting judgment after a trial by a specially appointed High Court in which all the evidence had been heard by November 1996 (see *Amnesty International Reports 1995* and *1997*). Judgment was due to be given in January 1997, but was postponed repeatedly because of the ill health and subsequent death of one of the judges. Karim Salifu Adam alleged that he had been charged with treason because he had refused to implicate opposition leaders and neighbouring governments in a fictitious coup conspiracy. His allegations that he was tortured while in incommunicado and illegal detention after his arrest in May 1994 were not thoroughly and impartially investigated.

The treason trial of five other possible prisoners of conscience – Sylvester Addai-Dwomoh, Kwame Alexander Ofei, Kwame Ofori-Appiah, Emmanuel Kofi Osei and John Kwadwo Owusu-Boakye – started in July, when they were brought before a specially appointed High Court in Accra. They had been arrested in September 1994 and accused of plotting to overthrow the government (see *Amnesty International Reports 1995* and *1997*). The trial had not finished by the end of the year.

At least seven political prisoners convicted of treason in the 1980s remained in prison. Their trials by Public Tribunals did not meet international standards of fairness because the Tribunals were not independent of government control. However, the prisoners were unable to appeal against their convictions or sentences because of the immunity provisions in the 1992 Constitution.

Hundreds of men were arrested in November following rioting in Akwatia and some were reported to have been beaten or otherwise ill-treated by police during transportation to Accra. Most were subsequently released without charge, but about 60 were charged with murder and reportedly held in cramped and insanitary conditions in one small cell at police headquarters in Accra.

At least three death sentences were imposed following murder convictions by the High Court: in Sekondi in March, and in Kumasi and Sunyani in May. Appeals had not been heard by the end of the year. No executions were known to have taken place.

In February, 22 prisoners had their death sentences commuted under a clemency measure announced in August 1996. They included two political prisoners, former Captain Adjei Edward Ampofo, who had been convicted *in absentia* of involvement in an attempted coup in 1983 and arrested in 1986; and former Sergeant Oduro Frimpong, whose death sentence, imposed in 1985 after a trial *in camera* for involvement in an alleged coup plot in 1984, and reportedly upheld on appeal, had not been confirmed by the government. The CHRAJ reported in 1996 that 292 prisoners under sentence of death were being held in harsh and overcrowded conditions.

GREECE

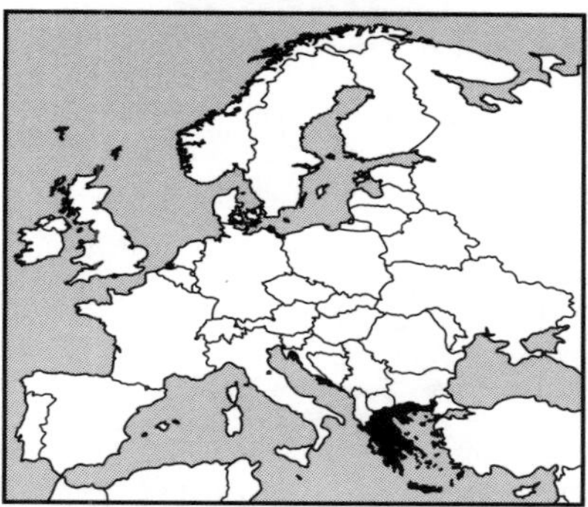

New legislation was introduced recognizing the right to conscientious objection. However, about 250 conscientious objectors to military service on religious grounds were imprisoned. All were prisoners of conscience. Legal proceedings continued in the case of 11 people prosecuted for peacefully exercising their right to freedom of expression.

In May Greece acceded to the International Covenant on Civil and Political Rights and its two Optional Protocols.

In June Parliament adopted Law 2510/97 on conscription, which includes a provision for alternative civilian service. The law states that conscientious objector status and alternative civilian service or unarmed military service are available to conscripts declaring themselves opposed to the personal use of arms for fundamental reasons of conscience based on religious, philosophical, ideological or moral convictions. However, the length of the alternative civilian service remains punitive, being 18 months longer than military service. The provisions for alternative service can be suspended by a decision of the Ministry of Defence in case of war and conscientious objectors performing alternative civilian service will be incorporated into the compulsory unarmed military service. The law does not recognize the right to develop conscientious objection during military service. Conscientious objectors who carry out trade union activities or participate in a strike during the period of alternative service will have their right to alternative civilian service or unarmed military service revoked and have to serve the remaining part of their service in the army. As the provisions relating to civilian service were not due to come into force until January 1998, conscientious objectors who refused to perform military service in the meantime still faced prison sentences of up to four years. During the year about 250 Jehovah's Witnesses were serving prison sentences for exercising their right to conscientious objection on religious grounds.

Legal proceedings continued in the case of 11 people prosecuted for peacefully exercising their right to freedom of expression. In March Hara Kalomiri's conviction for "founding and operating a place of private worship for a Buddhist community in Chalkidiki without government permission" (see *Amnesty International Report 1997*) was confirmed on appeal in Thessaloniki; her sentence was reduced to two months' imprisonment suspended for three years.

The appeal hearing of six members of the *Organosi gia tin Anasingrotisi tou Kommounistikou Kommatos Elladas*, Organization for the Reconstruction of the Communist Party of Greece, due to take place in September 1997, was postponed until January 1998 (see *Amnesty International Report 1997*).

In October Vasilis Romas, Costas Tasopoulos, Petros Vasiliadis and Pavlos Voskopoulos, members of the ethnic Macedonian minority party *Ouranio Toxo* (Rainbow) stood trial in Florina charged with violating Article 192 of the penal code. They were accused of "causing and inciting mutual hatred among the citizens" by hanging up a sign containing the words "Florina Committee" in both Greek and Macedonian, outside their Florina office in September 1995. The indictment stated that the use of the Macedonian words "*Lerinski Komitet*" "provoked and incited discord among the area's citizens [who] justifiably... identify these words with an old terrorist organization of Slavic-speaking alien nationals which was active in the area".

Amnesty International received information from the authorities about cases of alleged torture and ill-treatment and of excessive force by law enforcement officials which the organization had raised in 1996. In January Amnesty International was informed that the death in custody of Lütfi Osmance (see *Amnesty International Report 1997*) in January 1996 was due to "pathological reasons". The authorities stated that an administrative investigation had revealed as "groundless" allegations that the detainee had been ill-treated. Lütfi Osmance died in a police station in Athens where he was taken after being discharged from hospital. According to an autopsy report his head and face bore marks of beating – injuries not observed when he was treated in hospital. In December Amnesty International asked the authorities how they explained the apparent contradictions in the medical evidence surrounding the death of Lütfi Osmance. The organization also expressed concern that it had still not received information on numerous cases of alleged torture, ill-treatment and excessive use of force by law enforcement and prison officials which it had raised in previous years.

In July the Ministry of Public Order informed Amnesty International that an administrative inquiry had concluded that police officers who took part in a raid on a Romani camp in Aspropyrgos, near Athens, in February 1996 (see *Amnesty International Report 1997*), had acted with "excessive zeal" and had ill-treated residents of the camp. According to the authorities, disciplinary measures had been taken against the police officers responsible and against senior officers in charge of the operation. The Ministry also gave information about two other cases raised by the organization in 1996. An administrative investigation had concluded that Mohamed Farhank Amin, an Iranian national, had not been ill-treated following his arrest by police officers in Athens in October 1996, but had broken his kneecap after he fell trying to escape from officers. A trial was pending in the case of a police officer who shot and killed an Albanian national during an operation to round up illegal migrants in Skala, Oropos, in January 1996 (see *Amnesty International Report 1997*).

Throughout the year Amnesty International urged the authorities to immediately and unconditionally release all conscientious objectors and to review the length of the alternative civilian service with a view to bringing it into line with international standards and recommendations. The organization stated its belief that the right to perform alternative civilian service should never be derogated from, even in time of war or public emergency, and that conscientious objectors should have the right to claim conscientious objector status at any time, both up to and after entering the armed forces. It called on the authorities to modify the new law accordingly. In December Amnesty International was informed by the Office of Prime Minister Kostas Simitis that in the opinion of the government, the new law was adequate to safeguard the right to conscientious objection, but that "the experience which practical application of the law provides may lead to possible improvements in the legislation".

In October Amnesty International expressed concern to the authorities that the prosecution of the four Rainbow members was inconsistent with Greece's obligations under Article 10 of the European Convention for the Protection of Human Rights and Fundamental Freedoms, which guarantees the right to freedom of expression. The organization informed the authorities that if any of the men were imprisoned, it would consider them prisoners of conscience and call for their immediate and unconditional release. In October Amnesty International was informed by the Ministry of Justice that the trial of the men had been postponed until September 1998.

GUATEMALA

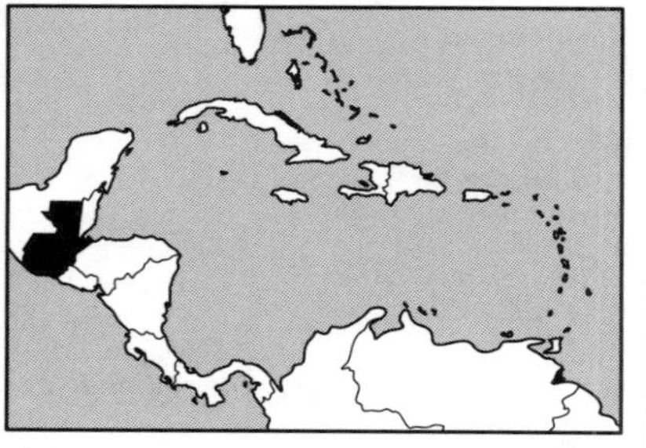

There were continued reports of torture, "disappearances" and extrajudicial executions by members of the security forces and armed groups reportedly backed by the government. Few of those responsible for past human rights violations were brought to justice; most continued to benefit from impunity. People from many sectors of Guatemalan society, including human rights defenders, continued to be threatened and harassed. Seven people were believed to be under sentence of death at the end of the year; some were at risk of imminent execution.

In December 1996, a Final Peace Accord agreed between the government and the armed opposition *Unidad Revolucionaria Nacional Guatemalteca* (URNG), Guatemalan National Revolutionary Unity, officially ended the civil conflict, which had extended over 36 years. This marked the start of an agreed timetable for bringing into effect all previous agreements between the two parties, negotiated under the aegis of the UN over several years. These covered numerous topics including human rights, the identity and rights of indigenous peoples, social and economic issues, procedures for resettling and protecting those uprooted by the armed conflict, the incorporation of the URNG into civil society and the role of the army in a democratic society. Prior to the signing of the Final Peace Accord, only the Global Human Rights Accord of 1994 had come into effect and its implementation had been monitored by the UN Verification Mission to Guatemala (MINUGUA).

In August the Commission for Historical Clarification, agreed under the accords, began clarifying "human rights violations and acts of violence... linked to the period of armed conflict". There was concern that various clauses in the accords on historical clarification and on the incorporation of the URNG into civil society, and in the Law of National Reconciliation approved by Congress in December 1996, could be construed so as to virtually assure impunity for the perpetrators of past human rights abuses.

A new police law was passed in February. It did not exclude former security force agents responsible for past human rights violations from joining the new *Policía Nacional Civil* (PNC), National Civil Police, which began functioning in mid-July. The government failed to dissolve the *Estado Mayor Presidencial*, Presidential Guard, an army intelligence unit linked to the office of the president. Over the years, this unit had frequently been implicated in human rights violations (see *Amnesty International Report 1981*) and its dissolution had been called for in the accords.

The justice system remained weak. The closure of military barracks, the formal termination of civil defence patrols, and the fact that the new PNC was not expected to be fully operational until 1999 resulted in parts of the country being left without a police force. High rates of violent crime, including kidnappings, "social cleansing", attacks on street children and lynchings were reported. It was often difficult to determine if specific crimes were instigated or carried out with the direct participation, complicity or acquiescence of present or former security force personnel or their civilian adjuncts.

In some areas, people responded to the increasing crime rate by taking the law into their own hands, lynching suspected petty criminals and others. In response, President Alvaro Arzú Irigoyen announced in July that various military bases closed under the previous administration were being reopened to control the violence.

At least 66 people were reportedly extrajudicially executed during the first half of 1997. Among them were Tomás Alonzo Sequen and his son, Roque Jacinto Alonzo Quisque. They were shot and killed in their home by a hooded man in army uniform in March, apparently because of their role as indigenous community leaders in Chimaltenango department. They had also been members of the Permanent National Commission on Land Rights, created by indigenous groups within the framework of the peace accords.

Despite the call in the Socio-Economic Accord for the creation of a new commission to resolve land disputes, on several occasions the government resorted to forced evictions, resulting in several deaths and injuries. In August at least two peasants died while being forcibly evicted from disputed lands in Sayaxché, El Petén department.

Several people were reported to have "disappeared". Controversy continued over the "disappearance" of Juan José Cabrera ("Mincho"), a former URNG combatant, in October 1996. He was allegedly arrested along with Rafael Augusto Valdizón Núñez ("Isaías"), another URNG combatant, by the Presidential Guard, which was pursuing those responsible for the abduction in August 1996 of 86-year-old Olga Alvarado de Novella. Several days after the alleged arrests the government and the URNG exchanged "Isaías" and Olga Alvarado de Novella. No mention was made of "Mincho" and both parties continued to deny that he had been captured and even that such a person had existed. In April, a MINUGUA report concluded that both "Isaías" and "Mincho" had been captured by the Presidential Guard, and that "Mincho" had probably been killed at the time of his capture. The government denied these accusations.

There were further reports of torture during the year. In March three trade unionists at an assembly plant in Guatemala department – Eswin Rocael Ruíz Zacarías, Edwin Tulio Enriquez García and Belarnino González de León – were taken from the plant by heavily armed men in plain clothes to a local police station where they were reportedly kicked, beaten and subjected to near-asphyxiation while being interrogated about a robbery at the plant. Those responsible for the torture had not been brought to justice by the end of the year.

Most of those responsible for past human rights violations continued to benefit from impunity. However, proceedings against a number of officials believed to have ordered a number of highly publicized abuses continued their slow progress through the courts. In 1993 a sergeant in the Presidential Guard was sentenced to 25 years' imprisonment for the 1990 killing of anthropologist Myrna Mack. However, the sergeant's three military superiors had still not been brought to justice for ordering her murder (see *Amnesty International Reports 1991* to *1995*). In August the Constitutional Court found that a 1996 Supreme Court decision, which effectively vacated the indictment and all proceedings against the three men, had violated due process and the original indictment and investigation were reactivated. In November, in separate proceedings, the Supreme Court turned down the defendants' appeal against the decision of a lower court which had ruled that they were ineligible for amnesty under the Law of National Reconciliation, as the killing of Myrna Mack was not related to the armed conflict and thus not covered by the law.

Information came to light in July that four police officers who kicked 13-year-old street child Nahamán Carmona López to death in 1990 had been released in 1996 after serving six years of their 12-year prison sentences. The street children's organization which brought the prosecution against the police had not been informed of the releases, as required by law, nor had the compensation awarded at the original trial been paid to the victim's family.

In July the former Minister of the Interior, his Vice-Minister and the former Chief of the National Police – the direct superiors of the police who carried out a crowd control operation which led to the death of student Mario Alioto López in 1994 – were sentenced to prison terms for second degree murder. Mario Alioto López died in police custody after having been shot and then beaten by policemen during a student demonstration. It was the first time that high-ranking government officials had been held responsible for acts carried out by forces formally under their command. However, in October an appeal court overturned the officials' convictions on the grounds that they had not been directly or indirectly involved in the student's death. A policeman who had beaten Mario Alioto López when he was already unconscious was convicted in July; his sentence was subsequently reduced to 10 years' imprisonment for second degree murder, on the grounds that he had not intended to cause the student's death. Two judges who had originally found the senior officials guilty reported that they had received death threats for having made the ruling.

There was some progress in initiating legal proceedings and investigations into some of the worst massacres carried out during the military's counter-insurgency campaign of the early 1980s, such as those at Dos Erres in El Petén department, Cuarto Pueblo in El Quiché department, and Rabinal and Río Negro in Baja Verapaz department. However, those involved in the exhumations of mass burial sites, of which there were an estimated 500 throughout the country, continued to be intimidated, threatened and harassed, apparently by those seeking to prevent responsibility for the massacres from being established, such as former military commissioners and local civil patrol members. The government maintained that both institutions had been disbanded, but former agents of both organizations continued to be named as perpetrators of ongoing abuses.

In September for example, unidentified men repeatedly came looking for Marlon García, a photographer with the Guatemalan Forensic Anthropology Team at his hotel in Izabal department. The team had recently begun to exhume a mass grave believed to contain the remains of as many as 100 Kekchí inhabitants of Panzós, Alta Verapaz department, killed by soldiers in 1978, apparently under the orders of a local landowner with whom the villagers were in dispute over land (see *Amnesty International Report 1979*).

In other areas, including San Andrés Sajcabajá, El Quiché department, where exhumations began in April, members of CONAVIGUA, the indigenous widows' organization, were harassed and threatened because they had witnessed massacres in the area or were pressing for exhumations of their relatives from mass graves. Again, the threats were believed to have come from former military commissioners and members of the local civil patrols.

Judicial investigations into the Xamán massacre of 1995 – in which 11 returned refugees, including two young children, were killed by soldiers – were obstructed. Witnesses and lawyers were threatened and evidence was reportedly tampered with (see *Amnesty International Reports 1996* and *1997*). Inquiries into the death of politician and newspaper publisher Jorge Carpio Nicolle, who was extrajudicially executed in 1993 along with three others (see *Amnesty International Reports 1994* and *1997*), also continued to be blocked by judicial manoeuvres and intimidation of judicial personnel assigned to the case.

Seven people, including three former national police officers, were known to be under sentence of death at the end of the year. Manuel Martínez Coronado, sentenced to death in October 1995 for multiple murder, exhausted all legal remedies available to him and was at risk of becoming the first person to be executed by lethal injection in Guatemala. The method of execution was changed to lethal injection following national and international revulsion when Guatemala's first executions in 13 years were broadcast live on

Guatemalan television in 1996 (see *Amnesty International Report 1997*).

In June the Constitutional Court turned down the appeals of three former policemen sentenced to death in May 1996 for murder and attempted murder. A key witness in the case was killed in October, and the public prosecutor handling the case reportedly sought asylum abroad after receiving death threats.

In March Amnesty International called on the UN Commission on Human Rights to renew the mandate of its Independent Expert on Guatemala. However, in April, in the context of determined opposition from the government, the Commission decided not to extend the mandate of the Independent Expert.

In April Amnesty International published a report, *Guatemala: State of impunity,* which included a 35-point program to end impunity and human rights violations. An Amnesty International delegation visited the country and presented the report to Guatemalan human rights groups and officials; representatives of intergovernmental bodies and agencies, including MINUGUA; and to government officials, including the Ministers of Defence and the Interior, the Attorney General and the President of the Presidential Commission on Human Rights. By the end of the year various government officials had failed to fulfil specific undertakings made to Amnesty International's delegation to provide detailed responses to the report.

GUINEA

Possible prisoners of conscience were detained during the year. Two prisoners detained without trial in previous years, one a possible prisoner of conscience, were released. Four opposition party members sentenced to prison terms were released on appeal. Death sentences were apparently commuted.

In July a permanent State Security Tribunal was established by presidential decree. The Tribunal contravenes Article 80 of the Constitution guaranteeing the separation of powers. Headed by the President of the civil and penal division of the Supreme Court, the Tribunal is responsible for hearing cases which threaten the internal and external security of the state. All eight members of the Tribunal were appointed by presidential decree, and a military commander regarded as very close to President Lansana Conté was appointed to the post of solicitor. There is no right of appeal against the decisions of the Tribunal.

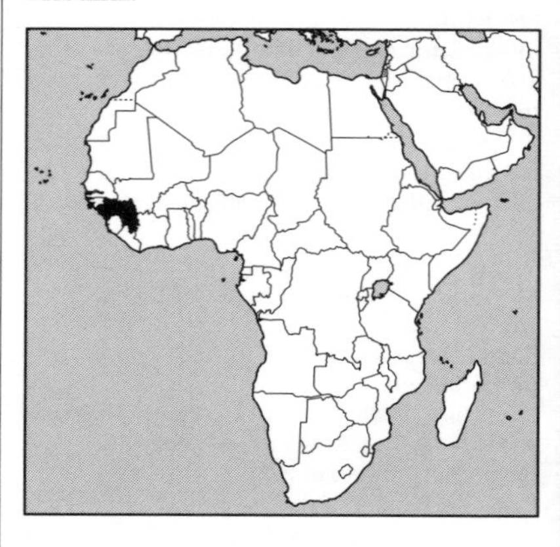

Three journalists were arrested in Conakry, the capital, and held for at least three weeks. Publications director Ousmane Camara and editor-in-chief Louis Espérant Célestin of the independent newspaper *L'Oeil* were arrested in August. The arrests followed a complaint by the Minister of Justice in connection with two articles published in June and July which criticized him. The two journalists were charged with spreading false information and defamation, and were provisionally released after two weeks' detention in Conakry Central Prison. Louis Espérant Célestin, an Ivorian national, was expelled from Guinea in December after his newspaper reported an opposition press conference. He was accused of "inciting violence and rebellion".

Foday Fofana, a Sierra Leonean journalist for *L'indépendant* and *British Broadcasting Corporation* correspondent, was arrested in October after he tried to interview a military commander at Alpha Yaya Camp in Conakry. He was accused of "attempting to threaten the security of the state" and was still held without trial at the end of the year.

Moussa Traoré, a supporter of the opposition *Rassemblement du peuple de Guinée* (RPG), Guinean People's Rally, who had been sentenced to three years' imprisonment in October 1996, continued to be held in Kindia Prison (*see Amnesty International Report 1997*). He was a possible prisoner of conscience.

Two prisoners detained in previous years were released without charge during 1997. Amadou II Diallo, detained since October 1992, was released in June (see *Amnesty International Reports 1996* and *1997*). Mamadou Diaby, an RPG member and possible prisoner of conscience arrested in 1996, was released in October (see *Amnesty International Report 1997*). It emerged that Banjou Oulén Oularé, an RPG official, had been released in December 1996.

Soldiers arrested in 1996 after mutinies in Conakry remained in detention charged with treason. They alleged that they had been held in a secret detention centre and tortured before being handed to the judiciary. No date for their trial had been set by the end of the year (see *Amnesty International Report 1997*). Their cases were transferred from the Assize court to the State Security Tribunal.

Three members of the RPG – Saloum Cissé, Madame Keita (*née* Bintoubé Camara) and Louceni Condé – who were arrested in November and December 1996 (see *Amnesty International Report 1997*) were brought to trial in June. They were charged with holding meetings, acts of violence, assault and battery, destruction and damage of public property. Sékou Tatia Combassa, another member of the RPG, arrested in June, was tried at the same time on the same charges. All four were sentenced to two years' imprisonment and a fine; they were released in November by the Court of Appeal.

Conditions of detention remained harsh and humiliating for all prisoners, and often constituted cruel, inhuman or degrading treatment. In Nzérékoré Prison, detainees were shackled every night. The authorities justified this as a measure to prevent escape. Prisoners suffered from lack of food and medical care.

In July Amnesty International received information that a death sentence passed on Sergeant Sékou Bangoura had been commuted to life imprisonment (see *Amnesty International Report 1997*). Although no official confirmation was received from the authorities on other death penalty cases, it appeared that all death sentences had been commuted.

GUYANA

Two people were executed and about 24 people remained under sentence of death. There were reports of ill-treatment by police and of fatal shootings by police in disputed circumstances.

Following the death in March of President Cheddi Jagan, his widow Janet Jagan was appointed Prime Minister, replacing Samuel Hinds, who was sworn in as interim President. Following elections in mid-December, Janet Jagan was sworn in as President; claims of irregularities resulted in a legal challenge, public protests, demands for scrutiny of the results and calls for new elections.

Michael Archer and Peter Adams were hanged in August. The executions were carried out with no advance public notification. The two men, arrested in 1987 and sentenced to death for murder in January 1991, alleged that incriminating statements used at their trial were obtained as a result of ill-treatment by police.

About 24 people were under sentence of death, including at least one person who was sentenced to death during the year. They included Abdool Saleem Yasseen and Noel Thomas (*see Amnesty International Report 1997*), whose petitions to the UN Human Rights Committee were pending. Dates were set for the execution of Raymond Persaud and "Paulo" Rampersaud, but both men received stays of execution pending the outcome of a constitutional appeal.

Reports of ill-treatment by police continued. In January Shawn Samuels was injured when he was reportedly forced into a truck by police and then beaten.

There were further reports of shootings of criminal suspects by police in disputed circumstances. Adam Hescott was shot dead by police in August after escaping from a prison where he was held awaiting trial. Eye-witnesses alleged that he was shot and wounded by police who apprehended him, then shot dead at point-blank range by another officer while being escorted to a police vehicle. An inquest was pending at the end of the year.

The trial of a police corporal charged with manslaughter in connection with the fatal shooting in 1996 of Jermaine Wilkinson (see *Amnesty International Report 1997*) remained pending. The officer was released on bail in January after a committal for murder in the same case was quashed by a court.

Conditions of detention and imprisonment remained overcrowded and complaints about poor sanitation and lack of adequate medical treatment were received. Following disturbances and escapes, in August the government appointed a Ministerial Committee to investigate prisons.

Amnesty International wrote to the government expressing deep regret at the executions of Michael Archer and Peter Adams. It urged the government to commute all death sentences and to take steps to abolish the death penalty.

Amnesty International expressed concern about fatal shootings by police in disputed circumstances, including the case of Adam Hescott. In view of increased reports of the use of lethal force by police, Amnesty International urged the government to review the use of force and firearms by law enforcement officials and to examine the existing regulations and training. Amnesty International repeated its request for information on cases of deaths in custody in previous years.

In November Amnesty International wrote to the government expressing concern about allegations of ill-treatment, including the cases of Shawn Samuels, Bonitus Mark Winter and Tulsie Persaud and others it had previously raised with the authorities. Amnesty International also expressed concern about human rights violations described in a report issued in September by the Amerindian People's Association, the Guyana Council of Churches and the Guyana Human Rights Association. Amnesty International urged the government to initiate investigations into all allegations of ill-treatment and fatal shootings by law enforcement officials, to bring to justice those responsible and to pay compensation to the victims or their families. Amnesty International asked to be informed of the results of the government's investigation into prisons and urged the government to submit its overdue reports to the UN Human Rights Committee and the Committee against Torture.

HAITI

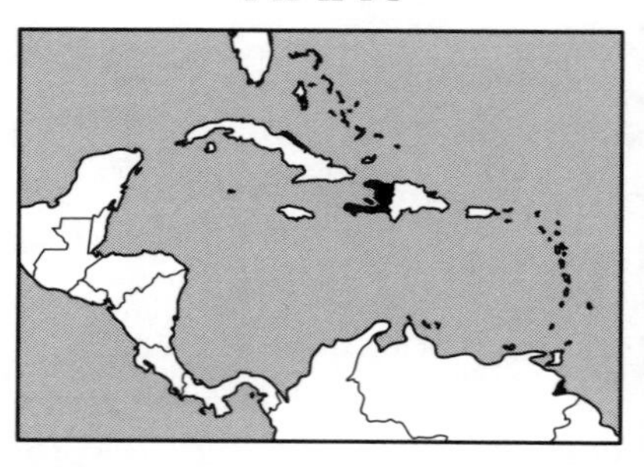

Little progress was made in bringing those responsible for human rights violations to justice. Investigation and trial procedures continued to fall short of international standards. Most people detained in 1996 accused of plotting to overthrow the government were released without charge, but others remained in detention without trial. Four others were arrested on similar charges during the year. There were frequent reports of ill-treatment and some reports of torture. At least two people died in detention. More than 20 people were shot dead by police in disputed circumstances, in some cases suggesting possible extrajudicial execution.

The government of President René Préval faced a serious political crisis after Prime Minister Rosny Smarth resigned in June in protest at the outcome of senatorial elections in April. The majority party in parliament, the *Organisation politique Lavalas* (OPL), Lavalas Political Organization, alleged that two seats won by candidates from the *Famille Lavalas*, Lavalas Family, the party of former President Jean-Bertrand Aristide, had been won fraudulently and called for the resignation of the Permanent Electoral Council. Divisions within the Lavalas movement, which had brought both President Préval and his predecessor to power, increased and by the end of the year President Préval had been unable to nominate a new prime minister acceptable to a majority in the parliament. The political crisis led to severe delays in parliamentary business including the passage of the judicial reform bill which had been introduced in 1996 (see *Amnesty International Report 1997*). Nevertheless, a report prepared by the *Commission préparatoire à la réforme du droit et de la justice en Haïti*, Preparatory Commission for the Reform of Law and Justice in Haiti, proposing a 10-year plan of action, was presented to the Minister of Justice in December.

The mandate of the UN Transition Mission in Haiti (UNTMIH), formerly the UN Support Mission in Haiti (UNSMIH), ended in November. The UN Security Council voted to replace it with a 300-strong UN Police Mission in Haiti (UNPMIH), which was mandated to remain in the country until at least May 1998. Some 500 US troops remained in the country under a separate bilateral agreement. In December the joint Organization of American States/ UN International Civilian Mission in Haiti (MICIVIH) was mandated by the UN General Assembly to remain in the country until 31 December 1998.

Several violent attacks on political figures, including the murder of parliamentary deputy Louis Emilio Passé in October, gave rise to speculation that at least some of the attacks might have been politically motivated or even perpetrated by government employees, although little concrete evidence of this came to light. However, three prison guards were being sought in connection with the killing of the deputy. One was detained but had not been brought to trial by the end of the year.

In September President Préval announced the imminent establishment of a committee to follow up the recommendations made by the *Commission nationale de vérité et de justice* (CNVJ), National Commission of Truth and Justice, in its 1996 report relating to human rights violations carried out between 1991 and 1994 under the *de facto* military government of General Raoul Cédras (see *Amnesty International Report 1997*). However, by the end of the year the committee did not appear to have been set up. There were reports that some of those who had given evidence to the CNVJ were facing intimidation from those named as responsible for human rights violations and that some of the latter were posing as victims in order to gain access to information for the purposes of retaliation.

In November the *Office de la protection du citoyen*, Citizens' Protection Office, established under the provisions of the 1987 Constitution to protect individuals against all forms of abuse from state employees, opened for the first time. Within the first two weeks, dozens of complaints, including allegations of ill-treatment, had reportedly been received.

Little progress was made in bringing those responsible for human rights violations, past or present, to justice. The ongoing failure of the government to take prompt and effective steps to address serious deficiencies in the justice system remained the greatest obstacle to overcoming impunity. Although a few alleged perpetrators of human rights abuses under the *de facto* military government of General Raoul Cédras were brought to trial, most were acquitted, usually for lack of evidence. For example, there were public protests in Jacmel in September when a former soldier was acquitted. He had been court-martialled in 1993 and sentenced to 15 years' imprisonment for the murder in 1993 of Marie Delaine Nicolas, who had refused his advances, but his original conviction had never been confirmed by the army high command. The prosecution had failed to produce any evidence or witnesses and there were allegations that the jury contained several former soldiers. In such cases, witnesses were generally reported to be reluctant to testify for fear of reprisals.

Preparations continued for the trial of several people accused of involvement in the massacre of some 50 people in Raboteau, Gonaïves, in 1994 (see *Amnesty International Reports 1995* to *1997*). The trial was expected to take place in early 1998. Further arrests were made and by the end of the year 22 people were in custody facing several charges, including murder. In March one of the accused escaped from custody during a court hearing related to the case and was not recaptured. Three prison guards, who were detained and accused of complicity in the escape, were later released but dismissed from the prison service.

Investigation and trial procedures for all detainees, including some detained on suspicion of having committed politically motivated offences, fell short of international standards and long delays in bringing detainees to trial resulted in severe overcrowding in the prisons. In November 1996 the government had set up a special commission to find ways of speeding up the judicial process and as a result of the commission's recommendations, many cases were reviewed and some detainees released. Most of those detained during 1996 on suspicion of plotting against the authorities were released. They included all but one of those arrested in August 1996 at the offices of the political party *Mobilisation pour le développement national* (MDN), Mobilization for National Development, who had spent almost a year in detention without trial (see *Amnesty International Report 1997*). However, a few, including former General Claude Raymond and Evans François, brother of Michel François, the former police chief under the military government, remained in detention and had not been tried by the end of the year.

In November, four people were detained, accused of plotting against the government. They included former police chief and presidential candidate Léon Jeune. Despite indications that his arrest had been planned, he was allegedly arrested *flagrante delicto* after police fired on his house without warning. Both Léon Jeune and his chauffeur, Lony Benoit, were beaten and detained. Following legal challenges to the procedures followed to detain the two men, they were released on bail in December. The other two were believed to remain in detention.

There were frequent reports of ill-treatment and some reports of torture carried out by members of the *Police nationale d'Haïti* (PNH), Haitian National Police. MICIVIH reported that in the first five months of the year it had received allegations from over a hundred individuals that they had been beaten by police officers.

In February Léonel Saintjuste required hospitalization for his injuries after he was reportedly beaten in Gonaïves police station. In May, as a result of an investigation by the Police Inspector General's Office, a policeman suspected of carrying out the beating was suspended. It is not clear whether any further action was taken.

In September a policeman was arrested in the capital, Port-au-Prince, accused of torturing a man detained on suspicion of theft by beating and kicking him and burning him on the buttocks, neck and stomach with an iron. The Police Inspector General's Office was also reportedly investigating allegations that in September a man suspected of participating in a "popular justice" killing had been beaten with cables and batons and had his arm broken in Gros Morne police station.

In October, two gang leaders were reported to have died following a shoot-out with police in Port-au-Prince. However, subsequent reports indicated that the two men had been beaten to death in Delmas police station. An official investigation was reportedly still under way at the end of the year.

In November the PNH director denied allegations that Léon Jeune and Lony Benoit (see above) had been beaten when they were arrested. It was not clear whether an official investigation was ordered.

The PNH were also reportedly responsible for over 20 fatal shootings, some of which may have been extrajudicial executions. In February Nicholas Métellus, a pawnbroker, was shot dead in the town of St Marc. According to witnesses, Nicholas Métellus, who was reportedly unarmed, was shot without warning inside his home by a police officer. The shooting occurred while police were seeking to arrest protesters who had been throwing rocks at them. A police inquiry was opened into the killing but the outcome was not known at the end of the year.

In September a police patrol in Port-au-Prince reportedly shot and killed a suspect after he had been arrested and handcuffed. An investigation was reportedly opened into the incident and the officers involved were suspended.

Although official investigations were opened by the police authorities into most reported cases of ill-treatment, torture and fatal shootings and several of those responsible were removed from their posts, only a few were detained and charged and few, if any, were brought to trial. A police report on the killing of at least eight people in Cité Soleil in March 1996 (see *Amnesty International Report 1997*), although reportedly completed, was never made public.

Little progress was made in investigations into killings of government opponents in suspicious circumstances in the previous two years. A man said to be an auxiliary of the *Unité de securité presidentielle*, Presidential Security Unity – the body which is responsible for the personal safety of the President and which was reorganized during 1997 – whose arrest was being sought in connection with the killing of MDN members Antoine Leroy and Jacques Florival (see *Amnesty International Report 1997*), was reportedly shot dead by police in a shoot-out in Léogane in December.

In February an Amnesty International delegation visited the country and met government officials. While welcoming the serious efforts being made by the Justice Ministry to prosecute those responsible for the Raboteau massacre, the delegates expressed concern that such efforts did not appear to extend to other cases, either past or present. They also urged the authorities to speedily implement the recommendations of the CNVJ, including the much needed reform of the justice system and the question of compensation for victims of human rights violations which occurred during the period of the *de facto* military government of General Raoul Cédras. In November the organization wrote to President Préval calling for an independent investigation into the reported ill-treatment of Léon Jeune and Lony Benoit and seeking clarification of their legal situation and the procedures followed to arrest them. It also urged the President to ensure that all security personnel were held accountable for their actions.

HONDURAS

Human rights defenders continued to be threatened and attacked. Children, especially street children, were subjected to human rights violations, including rape, by members of the security forces. There were allegations of torture in prisons. Prison conditions amounted to cruel, inhuman or degrading treatment or punishment and led to several prison riots. Eleven people, including indigenous leaders and peaceful demonstrators, were killed in circumstances suggesting that they were extrajudicially executed. Efforts to end impunity for past human rights violations made little progress.

The ruling Liberal Party won elections in November. Carlos Flores Facussé was elected President.

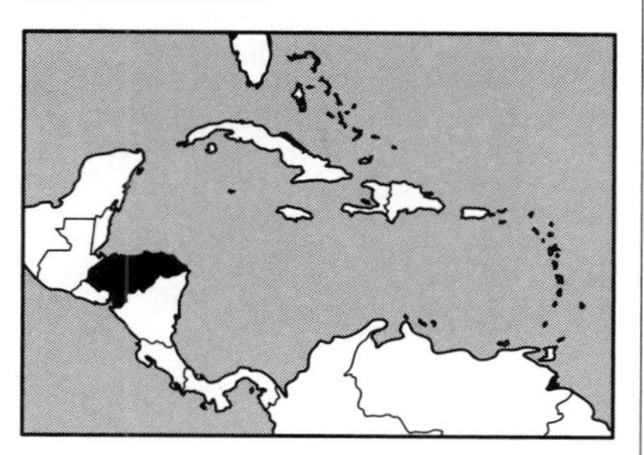

In October the process of transferring the police force from military to civilian control began.

Indigenous people staged massive demonstrations during the year demanding land rights and investigations into the murder of several of their leaders.

A series of bomb attacks continued (see *Amnesty International Report 1997*). Among the targets were the National Congress, the law courts in San Pedro Sula, facilities of the Public Ministry and private enterprises. No group claimed responsibility for the attacks and there were no official investigations.

In August Honduras ratified the International Covenant on Civil and Political Rights.

Human rights defenders were threatened and attacked. Bertha Oliva de Nativí and Liduvina Hernández, leading members of the *Comité de Familiares de Detenidos Desaparecidos en Honduras* (COFADEH), Committee of Relatives of the Disappeared in Honduras, received several anonymous telephone death threats. In August there were reports that the homes and offices of Dr Ramón Custodio López, President of the *Comité de Defensa de Derechos Humanos en Honduras* (CODEH), Committee for the Defence of Human Rights in Honduras, were under heavy surveillance by security forces. In September Benigno Ramírez García, a human rights defender working with the poor in San Pedro Sula and Yoro, was wounded and his three-year-old son Edwin was killed by three men carrying automatic weapons who opened fire on his truck. Benigno Ramírez was trying to mediate between two parties in a land dispute. One of the parties to the dispute, a former member of military intelligence, was suspected of being behind the attack. No investigation had been carried out by the end of the year. The National Human Rights Commissioner, Dr Leo Valladares Lanza, and one of his regional Deputy Commissioners also received death threats.

Children, especially street children, continued to be victims of human rights violations. In March, a 16-year-old street girl was raped by a member of the *Fuerza de Seguridad Pública* (FSP), Public Security Force, in a police station in Tegucigalpa, the capital. In June the policeman was arrested and charged with rape.

In February the Second Criminal Court confirmed the decision of the Appeals Court to revoke the 16-and-a-half-year prison sentence imposed on a military officer for the rape and killing of Riccy Mabel Martínez Sevilla in 1991 (see *Amnesty International Reports 1994* and *1997*). However, the Court increased the sentence on the second officer from 10 to 15 years' imprisonment.

In May the First Court of Appeals confirmed a six-year prison sentence on two members of a Honduras Army Battalion who raped an 11-year-old street girl, Martha María Saire, in 1994 (see *Amnesty International Report 1995*).

Allegations of torture within prisons were confirmed by a senior doctor in the central penitentiary. He submitted a complaint to a court alleging that penal authorities and prison guards were torturing and ill-treating prisoners and calling for an investigation. No investigation had been started by the end of the year.

There was widespread rioting in prisons, leaving at least two prisoners dead. In August prisoners burned down several prisons and there were mass escapes from prisons in different parts of the country. The riots were sparked by massive overcrowding, insanitary conditions and poor food.

In a pattern consistent with previous years, 11 people were killed in circumstances suggesting that they had been extrajudicially executed. Leaders of indigenous groups were among the victims. Some killings were reportedly carried out by landowners (or on their orders) with the complicity of local authorities and military personnel, in the context of disputes over land and natural resources.

In April Cándido Amador Recinos, General Secretary of the General Council of Assessment for the Development of Indigenous Groups in Honduras, and Ovidio Pérez were killed in Copán Ruinas, Department of Copán. Both were members of the Chorti indigenous group. Other possible victims of extrajudicial executions during the year were: 17-year-old Manvil Pinace, a member of a community organization protesting at evictions, in April; Jesús Álvarez Rochez, leader of the Garífuna community, and Jorge Manueles, a Lenca, in May; Adán Romero and Pedro Ramos, of the Tolupan indigenous group, in August; and Jorge Castillo and Julián Alberto Morales, members of the Garífuna indigenous group, in October. In the previous decade about 30 members of indigenous groups involved in defending their rights had been murdered. Investigations were carried out in only one case – that of Cándido Amador Recinos, which had not yet reached any conclusion – and no one was brought to justice.

In April José Cristino Díaz Herrera and 15-year-old Wilmer Alexander Vásquez were killed when members of the police and army violently dispersed a group of peaceful demonstrators in El Paraíso, Department of El Paraíso. According to eyewitnesses, Wilmer Vásquez was kicked in the head after he had been shot and was lying on the ground. In August a police officer was charged with his murder and arrested.

Judicial proceedings for past human rights violations made little progress. Thirteen out of 19 military officers, charged in 1996 for the "disappearance" and killing of Adán Avilés Fúnez and Amado Espinoza Paz in 1982 (see *Amnesty International Report 1997*), were in hiding. Two of the 19 were arrested and four gave themselves up to judicial authorities. Proceedings against these six officers were in progress, but the case against the other 13 was stalled. Similarly, there was no progress in bringing to justice those responsible for past "disappearances", including the temporary "disappearance" of six students in 1982 (see *Amnesty International Report 1997*). At least three former members of the security services, considered to be important witnesses in these and other cases against high-ranking military officers accused of human rights violations, were killed during the year by unidentified men.

Investigations into the killing of Miguel Angel Pavón and Moisés Landaverde in 1988 made some progress. Miguel Angel Pavón was regional president of CODEH in San Pedro Sula. Initial judicial investigations established a link between his murder and evidence he had given to the Inter-American Court of Human Rights on "disappearances" in Honduras in the early 1980s, implicating high-ranking members of the government and military (see *Amnesty International Reports 1989* to *1991*). In July 1996 the *Dirección de Investigación Criminal*, Directorate of Criminal Investigations, appointed two investigators to the case. They submitted their report in March 1997, which confirmed the identity of a lieutenant and a civilian already suspected of carrying out the killing. However, charges had not been brought by the end of the year.

Amnesty International called on President Carlos Roberto Reina and other government authorities to initiate prompt, full and independent investigations into the killings of indigenous leaders and to bring those responsible to justice. The organization urged the government to comply with agreements signed with indigenous peoples and called for immediate measures to ensure the safety of indigenous people in Honduras. Amnesty International also called on the authorities to investigate the killings in April when the police and army violently broke up a peaceful demonstration. Amnesty International also urged the authorities to guarantee the safety of human rights defenders.

HONG KONG

On 1 July the People's Republic of China resumed sovereignty over Hong Kong after over 150 years of British colonial rule. Amid concern over revisions to civil liberties laws, peaceful protests continued. Three court cases collapsed amid evidence of torture or ill-treatment by police. The Chinese Government announced that it would submit reports to the UN on the implementation of the International Covenant on Civil and Political Rights (ICCPR) and International Covenant on Economic, Social and Cultural Rights (ICESCR) in Hong Kong.

On 1 July Hong Kong became a Special Administrative Region (HKSAR) of the People's Republic of China, with a Basic Law setting a legal framework for maintaining a "high degree of autonomy". As resolved by the National People's Congress (NPC) in 1994 (see *Amnesty International Report 1995*), the existing Legislative Council (Legco) elected in 1995 was disbanded and replaced by a Provisional Legislative Council (PLC) chosen by a selection committee of 400 appointees for which there was no provision in the Basic Law (see *Amnesty International Report 1997*). Meanwhile a special Reunification Ordinance provided for continuity in the civil service and judiciary, and for all incumbents eligible for office under the Basic Law to be reappointed.

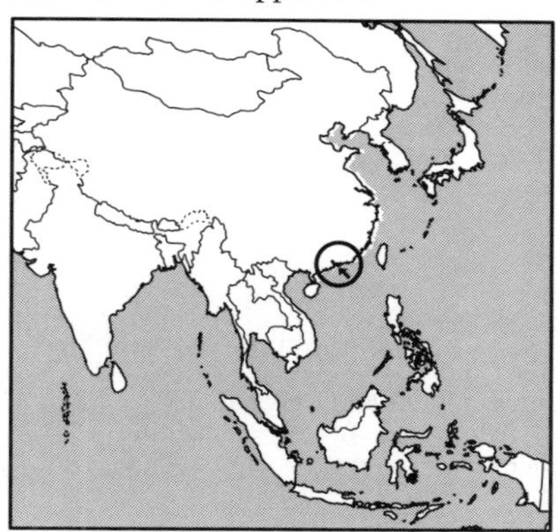

Controversy over the legality of the PLC continued throughout the year, with court cases unsuccessfully challenging both its validity and whether laws that it enacted violated the Basic Law. These cases raised questions about the solidity of key Basic Law principles, including guarantees for human rights. In July the Court of Appeal opined that the PLC was valid and held that its own powers to interpret the Basic Law did not extend to challenging the validity of the NPC's decisions.

New elections were set for May 1998 under substantially amended electoral laws which cut the franchise by an estimated 2.5 million in "functional constituencies". In local and regional councils, government appointees were reintroduced.

In February the Standing Committee of the NPC resolved that sections of the existing Bill of Rights, and of the Societies and Public Order Ordinances, contravened the Basic Law and therefore should not be adopted as laws of the HKSAR. The Chief Executive Designate issued a consultation document proposing major revisions to the Societies and Public Order Ordinances. These threatened civil liberties protected under the ICCPR and provoked an outcry. The proposals were substantially modified, but the amendments passed by the PLC on 1 July still allowed for the deregistration or prohibition of societies and empowered the Commissioner of Police to prohibit peaceful public gatherings or processions, "where he reasonably considers such prohibition to be necessary in the interests of national security". National security was loosely defined as "safeguarding of the territorial integrity and the independence of the People's Republic of China". Administrative guidelines for the police specified that intervention on national security grounds was appropriate if a public meeting or procession was advocating separation from the People's Republic of China, including advocacy of the independence of Taiwan and Tibet. Under the ICCPR, national security cannot be invoked to justify restrictions on freedom of expression and association except in serious cases of military or similar threat to the entire nation.

In June, during an attempt by the outgoing government to legislate on National Security offences as required under Basic Law Article 23, legislators deleted existing treasonable offences and narrowed the crime of sedition. However, by the end of the year the HKSAR government had not signed into operation either these changes, or a law regulating government interception of communications. In June the outgoing government also "localized" into domestic law the British Official Secrets Act. Legislators failed in their attempts to liberalize its definitions of espionage and unlawful disclosure.

Before being disbanded on 1 July, Legco also finalized much civil liberties legislation through private members' bills. Some of these were subsequently suspended and substantially repealed by the PLC. Trade unionists complained to the International Labour Organisation (ILO) that the PLC's repeal of amendments to employment and trade union laws violated ILO conventions on freedom of association and the right to organize. An amendment to the Bill of Rights, stating that the Bill's guarantees applied to all pre-existing legislation, whether relied upon by the government or private individuals, remained suspended at the end of the year.

Peaceful demonstrations over these and other national and international issues continued throughout the year. Inconsistent official statements gave rise to concern about how the amended Public Order Ordinance and the new crimes introduced by the PLC of desecrating the national and regional flag might be used against peaceful protesters. Demonstrators and the press complained at the designation of special protest zones and heavy-handed policing during the annual meeting of the International Monetary Fund and the World Bank in September, after which five demonstrators were charged with disorderly conduct and assaulting police. Police had greatly outnumbered protesters, allegedly cordoning them off from public view and easy contact with the media. Four activists, including members of the April 5th Action Group, awaited trial at the end of the year on multiple charges after demonstrations in the PLC chambers in July and September over the freezing of labour laws.

In June the police set a target of the year 2000 to implement reforms in the treatment of arrested suspects in response to a 1992 report by the Law Reform Commission. Measures included clarifying powers of stop and search, stipulating limits to and review of detention without charge, and progressively introducing video recording of interviews with suspects.

Concerns about police procedures and the treatment of detainees re-emerged in November when Chan Kwok-keung was shot dead at Aberdeen Police Station by an officer who had apprehended him for failing to provide an identity card during a routine inspection. The officer was charged with murder. The police authorities revealed that the officer had received psychological counselling from 1994 to 1996, and began a review of the management of "health-impaired" officers.

In February, August and November, three court cases collapsed following evidence that the police had used torture or ill-treatment to extract confessions. Two cases involved members of Kowloon East

Regional Crime Squad; medical evidence reportedly substantiated allegations of water torture.

On 23 June the government withdrew in its final stages a bill intended to provide a statutory basis for the Independent Police Complaints Council, an appointed civilian body which monitors and reviews investigations by police into complaints against fellow officers. Legislators' amendments would have given the Council independent investigative powers, a reform which was specifically recommended for Hong Kong by the UN Human Rights Committee in 1995.

In June, three inmates at Lai Chi Kok Reception Center were convicted of the manslaughter of a cellmate in April 1996. Remand prisoner Wong Hang-Kwok died after being beaten in an argument over cleaning duties. During the trial it was alleged that the defendants were favoured prisoners given informal supervision duties by the prison guards, and that the victim had been beaten for ignoring the defendants' orders. A guard had been alerted by his screams, but left when the defendants claimed to be playing. In September PLC members expressed dissatisfaction with the results of an internal investigation which found that this was an isolated incident, where a clash of personalities had been aggravated by overcrowding; one member blamed the system of supervision, recommending that it undergo a comprehensive, independent review. Throughout the year the government acknowledged that overcrowding, particularly in remand centres and women's prisons, was a serious problem which prison redevelopment plans alone would not resolve.

In the period before 1 July, many asylum-seekers from the People's Republic of China who had been permitted to remain in Hong Kong were granted asylum in third countries. Forced and voluntary repatriation of Vietnamese asylum-seekers continued throughout the year. Several groups of asylum-seekers mounted successful legal challenges against the flawed refugee determination procedure and their continuing detention. At the end of the year, 1,213 Vietnamese refugees remained in Hong Kong with little chance of resettlement overseas. In August the PLC passed a motion urging the abolition of Hong Kong's port of first asylum policy; the government was due to report on a wide-ranging policy review in 1998.

In June, as requested by the UN Human Rights Committee in November 1996, the British Government tabled its last report on the implementation of the ICCPR in Hong Kong. In November, after many years of uncertainty, the Chinese Government announced that it would submit reports to the UN on the implementation of the ICCPR and ICESCR in Hong Kong. The reports would be prepared by the HKSAR government, which stated that the established practice of public consultation would be maintained.

An Amnesty International delegation visited Hong Kong in February to discuss human rights protection and promotion following Hong Kong's return to Chinese sovereignty. A report, *Hong Kong: Human rights, law and autonomy – the risks of transition,* recommended that the incoming HKSAR government move quickly to secure the future of legal safeguards for freedom of expression and association, protect the independence of the judiciary and clarify laws governing the military garrison in Hong Kong. In April Amnesty International published its submission to the consultation process initiated by the HKSAR Chief Executive-Designate on proposed changes to the Bill of Rights and legislation governing public order and societies. In late June visiting Amnesty International delegates issued a list of human rights benchmarks for Hong Kong after the handover. Amnesty International's regional office in Hong Kong continued to monitor developments throughout the year and to maintain contact with the HKSAR authorities.

HUNGARY

There were reports that detainees were ill-treated by police officers.

In February, five police officers arrested Z.Z. and eight others, including two minors, in the centre of Szombathely on suspicion of theft. Most of those arrested were Roma. The officers allegedly called the detainees "stinking Gypsies". One officer reportedly knocked Z.Z. to the ground, and pressed a gun against his head. Police officers reportedly continued to beat Z.Z., both on the way to the police station and during questioning, until he vomited blood and lost consciousness for a short period. Police officers reportedly threatened to beat the other detainees if they did not sign statements incriminating Z.Z. and, when they refused, officers allegedly assaulted two of them. All the detainees were released later the same day; Z.Z. received medical treatment for injuries he had suffered as a result of the ill-treatment.

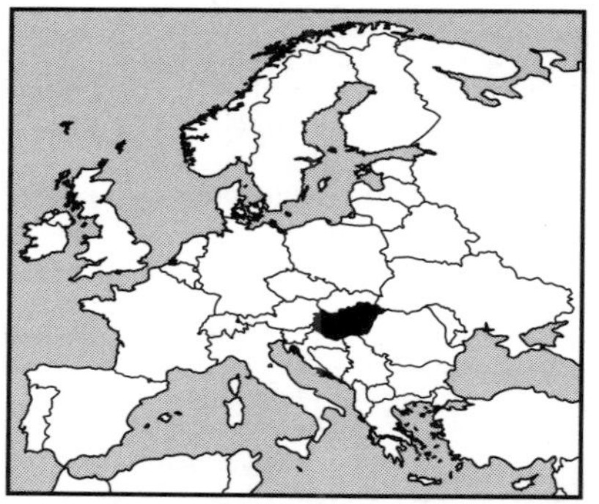

In May several police officers asked Monika Gölös and András Reichart to leave a public park in Budapest. When Monika Gölös complained that they were being addressed rudely, the officers reportedly sprayed them with tear-gas. They were then handcuffed, kicked and punched and taken to the First District Police Station for an identity check. They were held there for three hours and repeatedly beaten by police officers.

In July in the ninth district of Budapest, two police officers stopped László Máté for an identity check. When he asked to be released, the police officers reportedly twisted his arms behind his back, handcuffed him, pushed him to the ground and then repeatedly beat and kicked him. Melinda Vári-Nagy, a friend of László Máté, asked the police officers to stop the beating. She was also handcuffed and the couple was taken to the Ninth District Police Station. László Máté was beaten in the police car by the officer sitting next to him. At the police station he was kicked and punched in the face causing him to lose consciousness for a short period. After his release he was admitted to a hospital for three days for treatment of injuries suffered as a result of ill-treatment. According to a medical certificate, Melinda Vári-Nagy sustained bruises on her thigh and around her wrists.

In October, three representatives of the Hungarian Helsinki Committee, a non-governmental human rights organization, visiting the lock-up of the Sixth District Police Station in Budapest, saw two police officers beating a handcuffed man. The officers repeatedly punched the detainee on the head and, after pushing him to the ground, kicked him several times in the abdomen. Shortly afterwards, the human rights monitors observed four other officers push another detainee to the ground. A sergeant then stepped on his head. Both detainees were Ukrainian nationals who were released the following morning, but whose identity the police refused to disclose.

Investigations into these reports of ill-treatment were initiated but their results were not known by the end of the year. In May and November Amnesty International urged the Chief Public Prosecutor to ensure that these investigations were carried out promptly and impartially, the results made public and those responsible brought to justice.

In February Amnesty International received information from the Chief Public Prosecutor about investigations into incidents of police ill-treatment reported to the organization in 1996 (see *Amnesty International Report 1997*). Concerning the case of Hamodi Ahmed, an investigation against officer C.B. was dismissed because of lack of evidence. Another investigation in the same case against unknown police officers was also dismissed "as the identity of the offender could not be established". The official reply did not give substantial grounds for such decisions and although Amnesty International asked for full reports of the investigations into Hamodi Ahmed's complaint, these had not been received by the end of the year. In the case of István Nagy, the initial investigation was dismissed in December 1996. In January, following an appeal, the Chief Public Prosecutor ordered an additional investigation which was suspended in May because of lack of evidence and because "it was not possible to establish the identity of the perpetrator".

INDIA

Thousands of political prisoners, including prisoners of conscience, were arbitrarily detained. Torture and ill-treatment were endemic, leading to at least 300 deaths in custody. Prison conditions amounting to ill-treatment were common. "Disappearances" continued. Hundreds of extrajudicial executions were reported. At least 40 people were sentenced to death and five executions were carried out. Armed political groups committed grave human rights abuses, including torture, hostage-taking and killings of civilians.

The year ended with a caretaker government headed by Inder Kumar Gujral, who had been appointed Prime Minister in April after the near collapse of the ruling coalition government. Public controversy about corruption continued, and former Prime Minister Narasimha Rao faced trial on several related charges.

In October the government signed the UN Convention against Torture and Other Cruel, Inhuman or Degrading Treatment or Punishment.

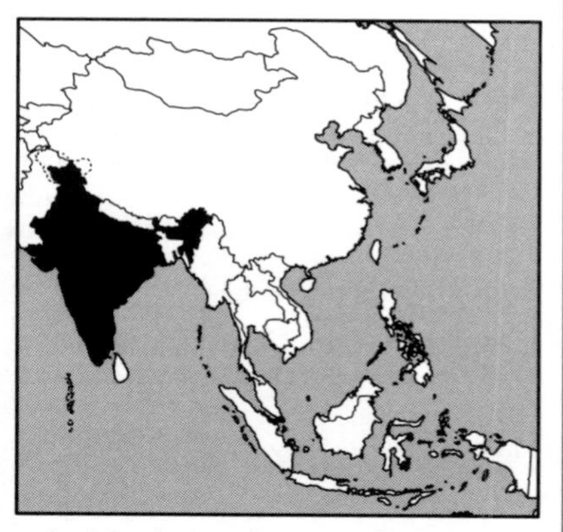

In July the UN Human Rights Committee recommended that India remove restrictions on the National Human Rights Commission (NHRC) which prevent it from investigating complaints of human rights violations by the armed forces, and abolish the requirement that central government approve prosecutions of members of the security forces. The Committee also expressed concern at the widespread use of preventive detention, notably under the provisions of the National Security Act and the Jammu and Kashmir Public Safety Act. The Committee recommended "the early enactment of legislation for mandatory judicial inquiries into cases of disappearance and death, ill-treatment or rape in police custody". It also highlighted discrimination faced by women and vulnerable groups such as Scheduled Castes, Scheduled Tribes, backward classes and ethnic and national minorities.

At the end of 1996, the Supreme Court issued a landmark judgment establishing requirements to be followed during arrest and detention to prevent abuse. During 1997, several state governments announced that they were in the process of implementing these measures.

In November the Supreme Court upheld the constitutionality of the Armed Forces (Special Powers) Act – which gives the security forces powers to shoot to kill with virtual impunity – after hearing petitions filed in 1980 and 1982.

The NHRC continued to monitor human rights abuses and raise concerns on a broad range of human rights issues. By the end of the year human rights commissions had been set up in three more states – Jammu and Kashmir, Punjab and Tamil Nadu. However, the state commissions were prevented by their mandates from investigating violations by the armed forces. In Tamil Nadu, the designation of sessions courts as special human rights courts under the Protection of Human Rights Act, 1993, came under scrutiny in the High Court, which set parameters for human rights cases to be tried in such courts and ordered that they be given powers to award compensation.

Armed conflict between government forces and armed political groups continued in various parts of the country, including Jammu and Kashmir, the northeastern states and Andhra Pradesh. Allegations that so-called "renegades" (armed groups cooperating with security forces) were responsible for abuses in Jammu and Kashmir continued. In Bihar, armed groups with links to state officials and political parties were involved in several violent attacks on rival political groups and their alleged supporters. Children and women were among those killed.

Thousands of political prisoners, including prisoners of conscience, were arbitrarily detained. Among them were human rights defenders. Hundreds of peaceful protesters, many of them women, were detained, harassed and ill-treated in the Ratnagiri district of Maharashtra for protesting against the construction of a power plant by the Dabhol Power Company – a joint venture between three US multinational companies.

Preventive detention provisions in state and central legislation continued to be used widely. For example, in Tamil Nadu alone, around 2,000 *habeas corpus* petitions were reportedly filed each year for the release of men and women detained under state legislation allowing detention without trial for 12 months.

In August, four human rights defenders and journalists were arrested in Assam, after speaking out against the granting of increased powers to the armed forces in Assam and against government corruption. They were repeatedly charged with having links with an armed opposition group and publishing statements issued by such groups. Three of them – Ajit Kumar Bhuyan, Lachit Bordoloi and Prakash Mahanta, all members of the human rights organization *Manab Adhikar Sangram Samiti* (MASS) – were subsequently charged under the National Security Act, which allows for preventive detention without trial on loosely defined grounds of national security.

In Jammu and Kashmir, leaders of the All Party Hurriyat Conference (APHC) – which comprises some 30 groups opposed to the accession of Jammu and Kashmir to India – were increasingly subjected to arbitrary detention and harassment. In November scores of activists were arrested and detained under preventive detention provisions of the ordinary criminal law while peacefully protesting against human rights violations. Some were still in detention at the end of the year.

Torture, including rape, and ill-treatment were endemic throughout the country. Victims included suspected political activists, criminal suspects, members of vulnerable groups, and those defending economic and social rights. In February, seven men who had been detained by police for several days were admitted to a hospital in Rajkot, Gujurat state, with serious eye injuries. Police officials had apparently rubbed a medicinal balm and chilli powder into their eyes. According to reports, the detainees had been ordered to strip and slap one another before being thrashed with belts. Investigations into the incident were continuing at the end of the year.

There were increasing reports of rape by members of the armed forces. In September, an 18-year-old girl was allegedly raped by soldiers during a search operation in her village in Assam. Doctors confirmed that she had been raped. No action was known to have been taken against the alleged perpetrators. Rape by the police continued. In October Jasbir Kaur was reportedly raped in her husband's presence by four police officers in a police station in Hoshiarpur, Punjab. In September a court in Tamil Nadu convicted six police officers of raping a woman, Padmini, in June 1992. She had been raped in front of her husband, who later died after torture (see *Amnesty International Report 1993*).

At least 300 people were reported to have died in custody; at least 94 of them in police custody in Jammu and Kashmir between January and March. In August, 14-year-old Ramesh and his 12-year-old brother were taken to the police station in Chennai, Tamil Nadu, on suspicion of stealing a bicycle. When their father pleaded with police to release them, he and his sons were severely beaten. Ramesh's younger brother was subsequently released but Ramesh's body, with his head severed, was found later on a nearby railway track. An investigation was continuing into the incident.

Many prisoners and detainees continued to be held in conditions amounting to cruel, inhuman or degrading treatment. Severe overcrowding, lack of medical facilities, poor sanitation and ill-treatment by prison staff were reported. However, NHRC recommendations calling for reform of prison legislation were not implemented (see *Amnesty International Report 1997*).

"Disappearances" continued to be reported and the fate of hundreds of people who "disappeared" in previous years remained unknown. In September the Supreme Court ordered compensation for the mothers of two young men who "disappeared" along with one other in Manipur 17 years earlier. Thokchom Lokendra Singh, Kangujam Loken Singh and Kangujam Iboyaima Singh were arrested by army personnel in September 1980. Their fate remained unknown and no action was taken to bring those responsible for their "disappearance" to justice.

The Jammu and Kashmir Home Minister told the state assembly in April that since 1990, 454 people had "disappeared" in the state. Hilal Ahmed Khan, a student detained without charge in Jammu and Kashmir by security forces in August, was handed over to police who released him. Security forces immediately rearrested him and took him to Bagat Kanipora camp, but later denied holding him. His whereabouts remained unknown at the end of the year.

In April an investigation ordered by the Jammu and Kashmir High Court into the abduction and killing of Jalil Andrabi, a lawyer and human rights activist (see *Amnesty International Report 1997*), identified a major in the Territorial Army as responsible. By the end of the year police had failed to arrest him.

Investigations continued into the alleged extrajudicial execution of hundreds of young men who "disappeared" in police custody in Punjab between 1980 and 1994, and the illegal cremation of their bodies. The Supreme Court directed the NHRC to examine "related issues", including compensation for the victims' families. However, at the end of the year, the NHRC's role was challenged in the Supreme Court by the central government, thereby delaying progress in investigations. The fate of Jaswant Singh Khalra, a human rights activist who "disappeared" in 1995 after filing a petition in the Supreme Court about the cremations, remained unknown (see *Amnesty International Reports 1996* and *1997*).

Extrajudicial executions continued to be reported from Jammu and Kashmir, states of the northeast, Andhra Pradesh and other parts of the country. At least 159 people suspected of being armed political activists were reportedly killed in Andhra Pradesh during the year, and at least 70 people were killed in so-called "encounter" killings between the Bombay police and armed criminal suspects between January and October.

In March the NHRC requested all state governments to ensure that all deaths as a result of "encounters" with police be investigated by an independent agency. The request resulted from NHRC investigations in 1995 into a few of the hundreds of alleged extrajudicial executions by police in Andhra Pradesh in recent years.

Chandrashekhar, a student activist, and Shyamnarain Yadav, a political activist, were shot dead in March while addressing a meeting in Siwan, Bihar. Reports indicated that the killers were linked to the victims' political rivals and to government officials. An investigation into the killings by the Central Bureau of Investigation (CBI) was continuing at the end of the year.

In April the singer and poet Gaddar, who had been active in protests against police killings of suspected *naxalites* (members of an armed left-wing group), was shot and seriously wounded outside his house. The police denied any involvement in the shooting. However, human rights activists alleged that an organization called the "Green Tigers", which claimed responsibility for the attack on Gaddar and subsequent attacks on members of the Andhra Pradesh Civil Liberties Committee (APCLC), was used as a cover by Andhra Pradesh police for illegal activities.

In July, 10 members of a *dalit* community (disadvantaged group determined by caste hierarchies) were killed and 14 injured when the police in Mumbai opened fire on a protest against the desecration of the statue of a *dalit* leader. A judicial inquiry was continuing by the end of the year.

At least 40 people were sentenced to death and five executions were carried out. Two *dalit* men sentenced to death in 1995 in Andhra Pradesh continued to await a decision on mercy petitions presented to the President in September 1996.

Armed political groups committed grave human rights abuses, including torture, hostage-taking and killings of civilians. In July Sanjay Ghosh, a social and environmental activist, was seized by the United Liberation Front of Assam (ULFA) on the island of Majuli in central Assam, accused of being an agent of the intelligence services. His fate and whereabouts were unknown at the end of the year.

Scores of people, including civilians, were killed by armed political groups in Jammu and Kashmir. Victims included politicians, journalists and members of the Hindu minority. In March, seven Hindu men were killed in Sangrampura in Budgam district. Unidentified armed men reportedly surrounded their homes at night, ordered them out and shot them dead. In May Ghulam Rasool Wani, a leader of the National Conference political party, was kidnapped by unidentified armed men and shot dead near his home in Kaskot in the Banihal area of Doda district. Civilians were also killed in apparently indiscriminate attacks. For example, in March a car bomb explosion in a crowded bus station in Jammu killed 16 civilians and injured 70.

Amnesty International published a number of reports, including: *India: Jammu and Kashmir – remembering Jalil Andrabi*, in March; *India: Official sanction for killings in Manipur*, in April; *India: The "Enron project" in Maharashtra – protests suppressed in the name of development*, in July; and *India: Appeal to armed opposition groups in Jammu and Kashmir to abide by humanitarian law*, in August.

In July Amnesty International submitted a detailed analysis of the implementation of the International Covenant on Civil and Political Rights in India to the UN Human Rights Committee.

In May, August and September Amnesty International delegates visited India and met government officials and representatives of the NHRC. At the time of the annual meetings of the World Bank and International Monetary Fund in Hong Kong in September, Amnesty International highlighted cases from India which demonstrated the use of repressive measures to facilitate projects funded by international financial institutions.

INDONESIA AND EAST TIMOR

At least 300 prisoners of conscience were detained. Forty-one were sentenced to prison terms and at least 40 others were on trial or awaiting trial or had been threatened with charges at the end of the year. Hundreds of people, including possible prisoners of conscience, were briefly detained without charge or trial. At least 208 political prisoners sentenced in previous years, many of them prisoners of conscience, remained imprisoned. At least 65 political prisoners received prison sentences after unfair trials. Torture of detainees continued and resulted in several deaths. In East Timor, "disappearances" continued. Dozens of people were killed by members of the security forces in suspicious circumstances. Previous cases of "disappearances" and extrajudicial executions remained unresolved. At least 33 people remained under sentence of death. There were no executions. An armed opposition group committed deliberate and arbitrary killings.

In May the ruling party, *Golkar*, won its sixth term of office in elections marked by violence. Presidential elections were scheduled for March 1998. The government faced continued armed opposition from groups seeking independence in East Timor, Irian Jaya and Aceh. Access by international and domestic human rights monitoring organizations to East Timor and Indonesia remained restricted.

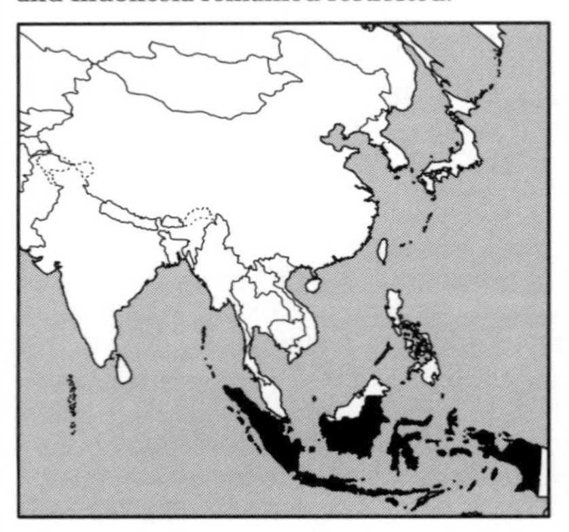

The UN Secretary-General appointed a Personal Representative on East Timor who visited Indonesia and East Timor in March and December. In January, following a visit to Portugal to interview East Timorese refugees, the UN Special Rapporteur on torture reported that there were continuing credible allegations of torture and ill-treatment in East Timor. By the end of the year, the Special Rapporteur had not received an invitation from the Indonesian Government to visit Indonesia and East Timor. In April the UN Commission on Human Rights adopted a resolution reiterating concern about the human rights situation in East Timor and calling on the Indonesian Government to take steps to implement recommendations contained in earlier resolutions and Chairman's statements, to release East Timorese political detainees, to invite the UN Special Rapporteur on torture to East Timor and to allow for a program officer of the UN High Commissioner for Human Rights to be located in Jakarta with unhindered access to

East Timor. In June the International Labour Organisation's Committee on the Application of Standards expressed concern about continuing restrictions on freedom of association for workers in Indonesia.

The National Commission on Human Rights (*Komnas HAM*) conducted investigations into land and labour disputes, allegations of ill-treatment and unlawful killings. In September *Komnas HAM* announced that of 241 complaints submitted to the authorities since the beginning of the year, only 28 had been resolved. There were no indications that the government had implemented *Komnas HAM*'s recommendations in relation to a raid on the Indonesian Democratic Party (PDI) headquarters in July 1996 and no information on the fate of 16 people still believed missing as a result of the raid (see *Amnesty International Report 1997*). *Komnas HAM* began operations in Dili, East Timor, but its ability to effectively monitor and investigate human rights violations was restricted by extensive military surveillance in the territory. Its Dili office was believed to have intervened in only one alleged "disappearance" in East Timor and was not known to have published any findings on any other investigations it may have conducted. *Komnas HAM* continued to call for the repeal of the Anti-subversion Law.

At least 300 prisoners of conscience, including labour and political activists, were detained during the year. In March, three members of an unofficial political party, the United Democratic Party, including former member of parliament Sri Bintang Pamungkas, were arrested. Two were released after several weeks, but Sri Bintang Pamungkas was charged with subversion and his trial began in December. Sri Bintang Pamungkas was also serving a 34-month prison sentence for insulting the President (see *Amnesty International Report 1997*).

Fourteen student activists linked to the People's Democratic Party (PRD), which was blamed by the authorities for riots in Jakarta in July 1996, were convicted of subversion and expressing hatred towards the government and sentenced to prison terms ranging from 18 months to 13 years (see *Amnesty International Report 1997*). The nature of the charges and the apparent lack of evidence linking them to any violent criminal activity indicated that the 14, including PRD leader Budiman Sudjatmiko, were convicted solely for their peaceful political activities. *Komnas HAM* condemned the use of the Anti-subversion Law against the 14. In September, the government banned the PRD.

The trial of independent labour leader Muchtar Pakpahan, begun in December 1996, was repeatedly postponed because of his ill health. Muchtar Pakpahan remained in custody and began serving a four-year prison sentence reimposed by the Supreme Court, despite the Court's own quashing of the conviction in 1995 (see *Amnesty International Reports 1996* and *1997*). In July Aberson Marle Sihaloho, a member of parliament and supporter of ousted PDI leader Megawati Sukarnoputri, was convicted of insulting the Head of State and sentenced to nine months' imprisonment.

Andi Syahputra, who was arrested in October 1996 in connection with the printing of an independent magazine (see *Amnesty International Report 1997*), was convicted in April of insulting the President and sentenced to 30 months' imprisonment; the charges against Dasrul, who was arrested with Andi Syahputra, were dropped and he was released.

Several people were taken into custody in connection with parliamentary and presidential elections. In January, four students were arrested in Central Java for advocating an election boycott. Three other students, arrested in Jakarta, were accused of expressing hostility towards the government and inciting others to break the law for writing graffiti supporting an election boycott in March.

In February Slamet Bibit and Faud Chafidin, arrested in April 1996, were each sentenced to two years' imprisonment for exposing election irregularities during the 1992 general election. In September Wimanjaya Liotohe, who nominated himself as Vice-President for the 1998 elections, was arrested on charges of insulting the President. His trial had not begun by the end of the year.

In East Timor at least 10 prisoners of conscience continued serving sentences of up to life imprisonment. At least 18 people were sentenced to prison terms for their non-violent activities in support of independence. Seventeen youths were convicted of expressing hatred towards the government during a demonstration in Dili in March and sentenced to terms of imprisonment of up to one year. Also in March, João do Rosario Rangel Pires was sentenced to one year's imprisonment for insulting the President after he displayed a cartoon of President Suharto with human bones in his mouth.

Hundreds of people, including peaceful activists, were subjected to short-term, arbitrary detention; many were held incommunicado. Twenty-six people were held in custody for three days following a labour rights training workshop in Lampung, South Sumatra. It was not clear whether they would face charges. Hundreds of people were arrested in East Timor following armed attacks by the resistance during the general elections. Most were arrested without warrants and released shortly afterwards. Many were denied access to independent lawyers while in custody. At least 50 people were being tried at the end of the year. In Aceh, dozens of individuals were arrested in connection with alleged links to the armed separatist group *Aceh Merdeka*. Several were held incommunicado in military custody.

At least 208 political prisoners, many of them prisoners of conscience, continued to serve prison sentences imposed in previous years after unfair trials, for links with armed resistance or secessionist groups in East Timor, Irian Jaya and Aceh, and with Islamic and political movements. At least 13 prisoners convicted of involvement in a coup attempt in 1965, remained imprisoned; many were prisoners of conscience and all were imprisoned after unfair trials. All were elderly and most were suffering from serious ill health. Five had been under sentence of death for over 25 years. In May Sukatno, one of the five, died after a long illness.

At least 65 political prisoners were sentenced during the year, most after unfair trials. Three men were sentenced to prison terms ranging from 12 to 33 months for advocating an Islamic state. At least 15 people were facing trial for their alleged connection to armed separatist activities in Aceh, including six charged with subversion. Their trials began in September and were continuing at the end of the year.

Torture and ill-treatment of detainees, including criminal suspects, continued and sometimes resulted in death. In June *Komnas HAM* stated that some of the 184 people arrested in connection with rioting in Banjarmasin, South Kalimantan, in May had been beaten by police. In September Dani Kuswardhani died in police custody in East Jakarta. The police reported that he was found hanged in police custody, but his family claimed that he had bruising on his back and that his fingernails had been removed. In June, Komaruddin died after he was beaten by four policemen following his arrest in Ujung Pandang. Few investigations were known to have taken place into allegations of torture and ill-treatment.

In July a police lieutenant was jailed for nine months and 10 days after being found responsible for the death from torture of Tjetje Tadjudin in October 1996 (see *Amnesty International Report 1997*). The police officer reportedly admitted during his trial to having beaten Tjetje Tadjudin and subjected him to electric shocks.

There were continuing reports of "disappearances" in East Timor. João Baptista "disappeared" following his arrest in May by the military. He was accused of having links with the armed resistance. By the end of the year, his whereabouts remained unknown.

There were reports of extrajudicial executions of alleged members of *Aceh Merdeka*. Abu Salam, who was alleged to have been involved in a bank robbery reportedly carried out by *Aceh Merdeka*, was shot dead by soldiers in March in North Aceh. He was believed to have been unarmed at the time. In July Muhammad Thaib was shot dead in Pidie, Aceh, by 10 unknown men wearing uniforms and believed to be linked to the military.

There were reports of extrajudicial executions in East Timor. It was not possible to confirm many of the allegations because of restrictions on access for human rights monitors. In February Fernando Lopes died after he was shot in Dili during a curfew, allegedly by members of the armed forces. Fernando Lopes was believed to have been deliberately targeted by the military because of his alleged links with the resistance.

Despite statements by the national police authorities that there was no policy to shoot alleged criminals on sight, several criminal suspects were shot dead by police in suspicious circumstances, prompting concern that they may have been unlawfully killed. More people were shot dead by police in Jakarta in the first six months of the year than during the whole of 1996. In February the East Java military authorities stated that criminals who ignored official warnings would be shot on the spot.

Previous reports of extrajudicial executions and "disappearances" remained unresolved. In November the prosecution dropped charges against Dwi Sumarji. He had been accused of the murder in August 1996 of journalist Faud Muhammad Syarfuddin who was killed, allegedly because of his investigations of local government corruption (see *Amnesty International Report 1997*). Dwi Sumarji had been held incommunicado by the police who offered him bribes to confess to the killing. It was not clear if the police were continuing to investigate the death of Faud Muhammad Syarfuddin. In September the police announced that the investigation into the murder in 1993 of labour activist Marsinah (see *Amnesty International Reports 1994* to *1996*) was closed owing to lack of evidence, despite earlier statements from *Komnas HAM* that individuals other than those originally tried for her murder, and ultimately acquitted, were involved in her death.

At least 33 people remained under sentence of death at the end of the year. Six people were sentenced to death during the year, including Second Lieutenant Sanurip, a member of the Special Forces Command, convicted in April by a military tribunal of murdering 16 people in April 1996. Evidence of his state of mental health was ignored during his trial. Two East Timorese men were sentenced to death in December after being convicted of murder, separatist activities and illegal possession of firearms. They were the first East Timorese to be sentenced to death since Indonesia invaded East Timor in 1975. No executions were carried out.

There were reports of deliberate and arbitrary killings by the East Timorese National Liberation Army, *Falintil*. The majority of the reports could not be verified because of restrictions on access for human rights monitors imposed by the Indonesian Government. In May an alleged informer, Miguel Baptismo da Silva, and his wife, Du-Lequi, were shot dead by the armed resistance in Baucau.

Amnesty International repeatedly appealed for the immediate and unconditional release of prisoners of conscience, for the review of cases of political prisoners imprisoned after unfair trials, and for urgent steps to be taken to end torture, extrajudicial executions and the use of the death penalty.

Amnesty International published *Indonesia: The Anti-subversion Law – a briefing* in February; *Indonesia: The PRD prisoners – a summary of Amnesty International's concerns* in October; and *East Timor: Truth, justice and redress* in November.

In a statement to the UN Commission on Human Rights in April, Amnesty International included reference to its concerns in both Indonesia and East Timor. In an oral statement to the UN Special Committee on Decolonization in June, Amnesty International described its concerns regarding East Timor and called for the establishment of human rights monitoring and investigative mechanisms.

Amnesty International publicly condemned deliberate and arbitrary killings by *Falintil*.

IRAN

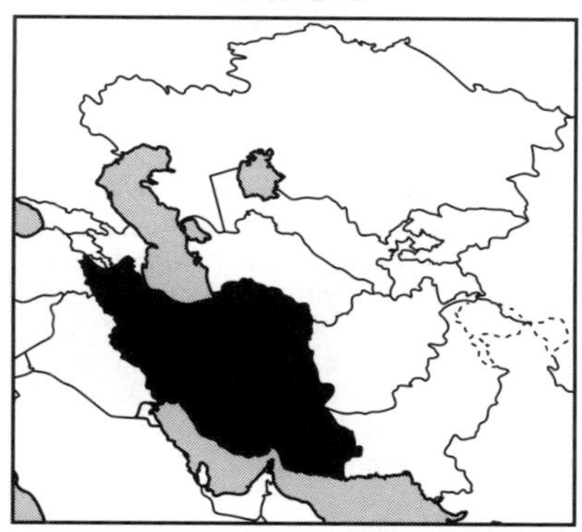

Hundreds of political prisoners, including prisoners of conscience, were held. Some were detained without charge or trial; others were serving long prison sentences imposed after unfair trials. Torture and ill-treatment continued to be reported. Judicial punishments of flogging were carried out. Several "disappearances" and possible extrajudicial executions were reported. At least 143 people were executed, including possible prisoners of conscience, and an unknown number

remained under sentence of death, some after unfair trials.

In May Hojjatoleslam val Moslemin Sayed Mohammad Khatami was elected President. In his first press conference, he was reported to have said: "We hope to gradually witness a more legal society... with more clearly defined rights and duties for citizens and the government".

The government continued to face armed opposition from the Iraq-based People's Mojahedin Organization of Iran (PMOI) and organizations such as the Kurdistan Democratic Party of Iran (KDPI), Arab groups in Khuzestan, and Baluchi groups in Sistan-Baluchistan.

The UN Special Representative on the Islamic Republic of Iran stated in his report to the UN General Assembly in October that "There are certainly many areas in which change is required in order to meet existing international norms and... to respect the freedom and dignity of the Iranian people". He noted the apparent continuing sharp increase in the use of the death penalty and called on the government, "as a matter of urgency", to reverse this trend.

Incidents of civil unrest were reported in several parts of the country. In February scores of oil workers were arrested, following apparently non-violent protests in Tehran, the capital, over pay and conditions. Most were later released, but two oil workers died in custody and several dozen oil workers, and up to 50 workers from the food and textile industries who were arrested subsequently, were believed to remain in detention at the end of the year.

Prisoners of conscience held during the year included at least 12 members of the Baha'i religious minority, four of whom were under sentence of death. In January the Supreme Court confirmed the death sentences against Dhabihullah Mahrami and Musa Talibi. Reports suggested that although they had been charged with apostasy, they were convicted of espionage (see *Amnesty International Report 1997*).

Faraj Sarkouhi, a magazine editor who "disappeared" for about seven weeks in 1996 (see *Amnesty International Report 1997*), was released from unacknowledged detention in December 1996 and re-arrested at the end of January 1997. He was tried *in camera* in September by a Revolutionary Court in Tehran on charges of spreading "propaganda against the Islamic Republic of Iran", and was sentenced to one year's imprisonment. He was a prisoner of conscience.

Grand Ayatollah Hossein Ali Montazeri was reportedly arrested in mid-November by the security forces, after making a speech which apparently criticized the leadership of Iran and which provoked widespread demonstrations against him in several cities. He was believed to have been held under house arrest in Qom for several years (see *Amnesty International Report 1997*). After his arrest, his son was reported to have been badly beaten and his offices ransacked, allegedly by the security forces. By the end of the year, there was no indication of his whereabouts nor any details of the charges against him.

Ebrahim Yazdi, leader of the Iran Freedom Movement, an opposition group, was reportedly called for questioning by revolutionary prosecutors, then arrested and taken to Evin prison. The day before his arrest, Ebrahim Yazdi had signed a petition in support of Grand Ayatollah Montazeri. He was released on bail in late December. Akbar Ghanji, publisher of the literary magazine *Rah-e Now* (the New Way) and a member of the Iran Freedom Movement, was reportedly arrested in December. He remained held without charge at the end of the year.

Shi'a religious leaders opposed to government policies, and scores of their followers, continued to be detained. Most were possible prisoners of conscience. Some were held without trial; others were imprisoned following unfair trials. At least three Grand Ayatollahs were believed to remain under house arrest, including Grand Ayatollah Sayed Hassan Tabataba'i-Qomi, who was reportedly denied access to medical treatment for heart disease. Ayatollah Ya'sub al-Din Rastgari also reportedly remained under house arrest (see *Amnesty International Report 1997*).

Several followers of Grand Ayatollah Sayed Mohammad Shirazi were detained during the year. In January Sheikh Mohammad Amin Ghafoori, a well-known religious figure and writer, his wife, and Sayed Hossein Fali were arrested in Qom. There were reports that they were beaten during arrest and tortured in detention. Sayed Hossein Fali was reported to have been released in June. Sheikh Mohammad Amin Ghafoori was said to have been sentenced in July to two and a half years' imprisonment by the Special Court for the Clergy, whose procedures fell far short of international standards. In October, five other followers of Grand Ayatollah Shirazi, including Reza Sultani, were reported to have been arrested and they remained held incommunicado at the end of the year.

Seven students arrested in November 1995, apparently on account of their links with Grand Ayatollah Shirazi (see *Amnesty International Reports 1996* and *1997*), were released in June. However, two of them, Aman Allah Bushehri and Sheikh Mohammad Qahtani, were reportedly rearrested in July and August respectively.

Several followers of Grand Ayatollah Shirazi were released during the year, including Mohammad Fazel Mohammad al-Saffar and Mohammad Ghaffari, who were conditionally released in January.

Members of minorities continued to be arrested. For example, Dimitri Bellos, a church worker, was reportedly arrested in August in Isfahan, days before he was due to leave Iran, and held incommunicado until October when he was reportedly allowed one family visit. He was reported to have been conditionally released in December pending further inquiries.

Other political prisoners, arrested in previous years and held without charge or trial, included scores of people arrested following demonstrations in Tabriz (see *Amnesty International Report 1997*) and hundreds of others arrested on suspicion of offences such as espionage, "propagating pan-Turkism" or "counter-revolution".

Political prisoners continued to be unfairly tried (see previous *Amnesty International Reports*). Detainees were reportedly denied access either to any legal counsel or to a lawyer of their choice, despite legislation providing for the right to legal representation. Trials before special courts, such as the Special Court for the Clergy, fell far short of international standards.

Political prisoners serving long prison terms after unfair trials included supporters of the PMOI; at least 10 members of the *Mohajerin* movement (followers of Dr 'Ali Shari'ati); members of left-wing organizations such as the *Tudeh* Party, *Peykar*, and factions of the Organization of People's Fedaiyan of Iran; supporters of Kurdish groups such as *Komala* and the KDPI; and supporters of other groups representing ethnic minorities such as Baluchis and Arabs.

Former Deputy Prime Minister 'Abbas Amir Entezam, a possible prisoner of conscience, who had been held in a government-owned house in Tehran (see *Amnesty International Reports 1996* and *1997*), was reportedly told in May that he was free to leave the house.

Reports of torture and ill-treatment continued throughout the year. Most of the detained followers of Grand Ayatollah Shirazi, including the five arrested since July, were reportedly tortured. Methods included beatings, severe burns, electric shocks, sleep deprivation, threatened executions and threats to relatives.

At least two people arrested following the protests by oil workers in February (see above) were reported to have died in custody as a result of torture. Hashem Kameli, who was said to suffer from a heart condition, reportedly died as a result of torture. Gholam Barzegar reportedly died after being beaten with rifle butts by Revolutionary Guards. No independent investigations were known to have been carried out into these deaths or into deaths in custody in previous years.

Judicial punishments amounting to torture, cruel, inhuman or degrading punishment, including flogging and stoning, continued to be imposed. Sentences of flogging were reported for a wide range of offences, sometimes in conjunction with prison sentences or the death penalty (see below).

"Disappearances" continued to be reported. Morteza Firouzi, the editor of *Iran News*, "disappeared" for over 10 weeks following his arrest in June. In November an Iranian newspaper reported that he had been arrested on espionage charges. The whereabouts of 'Ali Tavassoli, who went missing in Azerbaijan in 1995, remained unknown (see *Amnesty International Reports 1996* and *1997*).

Several people were killed in circumstances suggesting that they may have been extrajudicially executed. In February the body of Abraham Zalzadeh, a magazine editor, was found, reportedly with multiple stab wounds. His magazine, *Me'yar*, was said to have been forced to close after it published an article criticizing the government. Reports suggested that he may have been arrested and killed by members of the Iranian secret service.

The authorities apparently failed to investigate his death.

Further evidence emerged that the Iranian authorities were responsible for the killings of Iranian dissidents, both inside Iran and abroad, in previous years. In April, four men were convicted by a German court of killing three leaders of the KDPI and an interpreter in the *Mykonos* restaurant in Berlin in 1992. The court found that the killings had been ordered by Iran's political leadership through a "Committee for Special Operations", whose members were reported to include the Leader of the Islamic Republic, the President, the Minister of Information and Security and other security officials. The Iranian authorities continued to deny involvement in the killings.

The trial in Turkey continued of two men accused of killing a PMOI member in Turkey in 1992 on the orders of the Iranian authorities (see *Amnesty International Reports 1993* and *1997*).

The threat of extrajudicial execution continued to extend to many Iranian nationals abroad, as well as to non-Iranians. Prominent individuals and institutions in Iran, including the head of the 15 Khordad Foundation, Ayatollah Sheikh Hassan Sanei, continued to call for the death of British writer Salman Rushdie and to offer rewards for his killing (see previous *Amnesty International Reports*). The UN Commission on Human Rights, in its resolution on the situation of human rights in Iran, called on the government *inter alia* to "provide satisfactory written assurances that it does not support or incite threats to the life of Mr Rushdie". The government failed to condemn, or put an end to, such threats.

The death penalty continued to be used extensively. As in previous years, it was imposed for a wide range of often vaguely worded offences – including political offences and those relating to freedom of belief – sometimes after unfair trials. Some executions were carried out in public. At least seven people, including five women, were sentenced to death by stoning; three men and three women were reportedly stoned to death in October in Khazar Abad. At least 143 executions were reported, although the real number was believed to be considerably higher.

Hedayatollah Zendehdel and Abolghasem Majd-Abkahi, who were sentenced to death in July 1996 after an unfair trial on mainly political charges, were reportedly hanged in January. There were unconfirmed reports that Sheyda Khoramzadeh Isfahani, the wife of Abolghasem Majd-Abkahi, was executed in September. Of the four others tried in the same case, one, 'Alireza Yazdanshenas, was executed and three were sentenced to long prison terms and to 110 to 200 lashes (see *Amnesty International Report 1997*).

In August Zoleykhah Kadkhoda was reportedly arrested, charged with having sexual relations outside marriage, and sentenced to death by stoning. She was buried up to her waist in a ditch and stoned within 24 hours of her arrest. She was reportedly confirmed as dead by doctors, but revived in the morgue and was taken to hospital. There were reports that she could face execution if she recovered. The outcome of her appeal for clemency was not known at the end of the year.

Gholamreza Khoshrou Kouran Kordieh, who was convicted of multiple kidnap, rape and murder, was publicly hanged from a crane in Shahrak Rah-Ahan in August after receiving 214 lashes.

Also in August, Mohammad Assadi, a lawyer sentenced to death in March after an unfair political trial, was executed. The UN Special Representative stated in his report to the UN General Assembly (see above) that he deplored the failure of the government "to respond to his request for full details of the charges brought against Mr Assadi and the conviction entered against him, and its refusal to grant clemency in a case that, according to the information available to the Special Representative, may have involved no serious criminal activity".

Amnesty International repeatedly called for the unconditional release of all prisoners of conscience; for a review of legislation which allows for the imprisonment of prisoners of conscience; and for a review of the cases of political prisoners, so that those unfairly tried or held without trial could be promptly and fairly tried on recognizably criminal charges or released.

The organization called on the authorities to ensure impartial and thorough investigations into allegations of torture, "disappearances" and extrajudicial executions, and to bring those responsible to justice. It also appealed for cruel, inhuman or degrading judicial punishments and death sentences to be commuted. In an open letter, Amnesty International urged the President to give urgent consideration to the patterns of serious and widespread human rights violations.

Amnesty International continued to investigate reports that some opposition groups were holding detainees.

In May Amnesty International published *Iran: Eight years of death threats – Salman Rushdie*, and in June *Iran: Human rights violations against Shi'a Religious leaders and their followers*.

Amnesty International received some replies from the authorities on individual cases, but these failed to address the organization's serious concerns and its delegates continued to be denied access to the country.

IRAQ

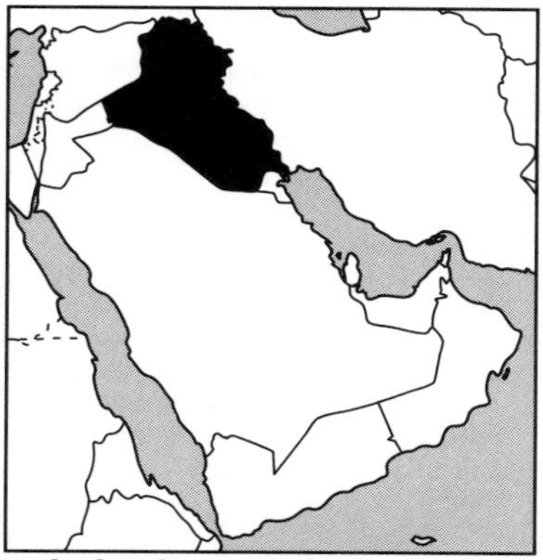

Hundreds of suspected government opponents, including possible prisoners of conscience, were reportedly detained without charge or trial and tens of thousands of others arrested in previous years continued to be held. Hundreds of executions were reported during the year, some of which may have been extrajudicial executions. Death sentences continued to be imposed. Torture and ill-treatment continued to be widespread. The fate of thousands of people who "disappeared" in previous years remained unknown. Human rights abuses by Kurdish political groups, including "disappearances", arbitrary arrests and extrajudicial executions, were reported in areas of Iraqi Kurdistan under Kurdish control.

Economic sanctions imposed on Iraq in 1990 by UN Security Council resolutions remained in force. In June the UN Security Council renewed an agreement, first implemented in December 1996, allowing Iraq to sell oil worth US$2bn every six months and to use the proceeds for humanitarian purposes. Two "air-exclusion zones" over northern and southern Iraq continued to be imposed. In October the Iraqi Government barred US members of the UN Special Commission (UNSCOM) from inspecting weapon sites in Iraq. In November the UN Security Council passed Resolution 1137 imposing an international travel ban on all Iraqi officials who block UN weapon inspections. At the end of November UNSCOM resumed its weapon inspections.

In May Turkish government forces entered parts of northern Iraq in pursuit of members and fighters of the opposition Kurdistan Workers' Party (PKK). Military clashes broke out and forces of the Kurdistan Democratic Party (KDP) took part in support of Turkish forces. Serious human rights abuses were reported in the city of Arbil (see below). By the end of June most Turkish forces had reportedly pulled out but they re-entered the area in September. By the end of the year, thousands of Turkish troops remained deployed in northern Iraq.

In October heavy fighting broke out in the Kurdish-controlled provinces between the forces of the KDP and those of the Patriotic Union of Kurdistan (PUK), in breach of a cease-fire agreement signed by the two parties in October 1996 (see *Amnesty International Report 1997*). During the clashes thousands of people were reportedly forcibly displaced.

In April the UN Commission on Human Rights adopted a resolution condemning "the massive and extremely grave violations of human rights and of international humanitarian law by the Government of Iraq" and extended for a further year the mandate of the UN Special Rapporteur on Iraq. In October the UN Human Rights Committee considered the fourth periodic report submitted by Iraq on its implementation of the International Covenant on Civil and Political Rights (ICCPR). The Committee noted that the impact of UN sanctions caused "suffering and death in Iraq and especially to children". In its concluding observations, it regretted that the government's report did not address the actual state of implementation of the ICCPR and that many of the questions relating to allegations of human rights violations in Iraq were not answered. The Committee also expressed its deep concern about reports received from many sources concerning the high incidence of human rights violations in Iraq.

Widespread arrests of suspected government opponents, including possible prisoners of conscience, continued to be reported during the year. In June hundreds of Shi'a Muslims were said to have been arrested by the security forces in Karbala' during processions celebrating a religious anniversary; scores of others were shot dead (see below). Most of those arrested were reportedly transferred to Baghdad and al-Hilla, although their fate and exact whereabouts remained unknown at the end of the year. Among those reportedly arrested were Sa'd Dawud Muhammad, 'Alia' 'Abd al-Kadhim, Jassim Sarsuh Hussain and Kadhimiya Muhammad 'Ali.

Scores of people, including women, were reportedly killed and hundreds of others injured when the security and intelligence forces clashed with hundreds of Shi'a Muslims from al-Basra participating in an annual religious procession to the Shi'a holy shrines in Karbala' in June (see above). The security forces reportedly opened fire indiscriminately on the crowds. Among the victims were 'Abbas 'Ali Mazhar, Sahira Muhammad 'Ali, Talib Dawud Muhammad, Zahra Hashim 'Abbas and 'Udai Ra'uf Sultan.

Hundreds of prisoners and detainees were executed during the year, although it was not possible to determine the exact number; some may have been extrajudicially executed. For example, in the period between July and October, at least 14 officers of the intelligence, special and security forces, and former members of the *Ba'th* Party were executed for involvement in a coup attempt and on charges of plotting to assassinate President Saddam Hussain. Among those executed were 'Ali Hassan 'Alyan al-Samarra'i and Ahmad Taha al-'Azzuz, both former leading members of the *Ba'th* Party, Brigadier-General Fauzi Mahmud al-Samarra'i, Brigadier-General Faruq Falih al-'Ali and Colonel Ahmad 'Abd al-Wahab al-'Ubaidi. Six of the victims had been arrested in December 1996 and reportedly tried and convicted by the special court of *al-Mukhabarat al-'Amma* (General Intelligence Services) in Baghdad. No details of the trial procedures followed in their case were available.

Hundreds of convicted political prisoners were said to have been executed in Abu Ghraib and al-Radhwaniya Prisons near Baghdad; some of them were reportedly awaiting their release after having served their prison sentences. Among them was Ahmad Nur al-Din, a member of a Turkman party from Kirkuk. He had reportedly been arrested by government forces when they and KDP forces entered Arbil in August 1996 (see *Amnesty International Report 1997*) and sentenced to life imprisonment. In July his family in Kirkuk was reportedly instructed by the security forces to collect his body from Abu Ghraib Prison. In November the authorities reportedly ordered the execution of hundreds of prisoners, most of whom were members of opposition groups, who had been sentenced to death or to life imprisonment. Among the victims were Jamil Nur al-Din 'Allawi, Fu'ad Ramadhan Karim and Hassan Salih Abu al-Quba.

In July a group of six people, including a woman, were sentenced to death by hanging on charges of organized prostitution and smuggling alcohol to Saudi Arabia. They were convicted by the special court at the Ministry of the Interior in Baghdad, which allows no appeal to a higher court. At the end of the year it was not known whether they had been executed. In December Ghalib 'Ammar Shahab al-Din, a Jordanian national, was sentenced to death on charges of smuggling car parts, but it remained unclear whether his sentence had been commuted by the end of the year.

In December four Jordanian nationals – including two brothers, Sa'id and Salah Yusuf 'Ali al-Dawji, Walid Muhammad Tawfiq Nuseirat and Rizq Bishara Rizq – were executed in Baghdad. They had been convicted of smuggling car parts and sentenced to death in October by the special court at the Ministry of the Interior. A fifth Jordanian national, Muhammad 'Ali Muhammad Salih al-Sabah, was also executed in December. He had reportedly been sentenced to death in June 1995 on charges of murder.

Torture and ill-treatment continued to be widespread. Torture methods included the use of electric shocks on various parts of the body, pulling out fingernails, setting dogs on detainees and severe stretching of arms and legs.

The fate of thousands of people who "disappeared" in previous years remained unknown. They included hundreds of suspected members of opposition groups and their relatives who were arrested when Iraqi government and KDP forces took control of Arbil in August 1996; thousands of Shi'a Muslims arrested in the aftermath of the March 1991 uprising; more than 600 Kuwaiti and other nationals arrested by Iraqi forces during the occupation of Kuwait in 1990 and 1991 and believed to be held in Iraq; an estimated 100,000 Kurdish civilians who "disappeared" in 1988 in the so-called "Operation Anfal"; and thousands of Shi'a Muslim Arabs and Feily Kurds who were arrested on the basis of their Iranian descent during the 1980-1988 Iran-Iraq war (see previous *Amnesty International Reports*). Victims included 33 members of the Yazidi community who were arrested in July 1996 in Mosul; Mohammad Rashid Tuzlu, General Secretary of the Turkmeneli Party, who was arrested along with other party members in September 1996 in Arbil; and three brothers, 'Imad, 'Adil and 'Atif 'Abd al-Hussain 'Ushair, who were arrested in 1981 because of their Iranian descent. During the year further "disappearances" were reported but it was not possible to ascertain the number.

Human rights abuses were reported in Kurdish areas under the control of the two main political groups, the KDP and the PUK. In January Ahmad Sharifi, an Iranian national and a former member of the Iranian opposition Organization of Iranian People's Fedaii Guerrillas (Minority), "disappeared" after he was arrested in his home in Sulaimaniya, reportedly by members of the PUK security forces. His fate remained unknown at the end of the year. In February two members of the Assyrian community, Lazar Mati and his son Havel Lazar, were deliberately killed when a group of armed men stormed the KDP-controlled Asayish Prison in Shaqlawa where the two men had been detained. No investigation was known to have been carried out into the killings nor into the apparent failure of the authorities to protect the prisoners.

In May armed clashes broke out in Arbil between KDP and PKK forces in the wake of Turkish government troops' incursion into Iraqi Kurdistan (see above). KDP forces launched attacks on several PKK offices in the city as well as in the suburb of 'Ain Kawa. Scores of people were killed and, according to unconfirmed reports, 28 PKK members, including four women, were taken prisoner by KDP forces and executed. The women were said to have been raped before being killed. Television reporter Bekir Dogan, a Turkish national, was reportedly among several people arrested during the same period when armed men, believed to be members of the KDP security forces, entered the Mesopotamian Cultural Centre in Arbil. At the end of the year his fate and whereabouts remained unknown.

During the year, Amnesty International appealed to the Iraqi Government to halt human rights violations, including the detention of prisoners of conscience, arbitrary arrests and incommunicado detention of political suspects, unfair trials, "disappearances" and executions. The organization also asked the authorities to conduct a full investigation into the execution by government forces of suspected members of opposition groups arrested in Arbil in August 1996 (see *Amnesty International Report 1997*).

In October Amnesty International published a report, *Iraq: "Disappearances" – unresolved cases since the early 1980s*, in which it appealed to the government to put an end to "disappearances" and to clarify the fate of hundreds of thousands of people who had "disappeared" since the early 1980s.

In September Amnesty International sought further information from the government about six people sentenced to death and appealed for commutation of their sentences. In its reply, the government stated that the six defendants had received a public trial in accordance with Iraqi laws, that they had confessed to the charges of "alcohol smuggling, white-slave trade and practising prostitution in Saudi Arabia", and that they had been allowed access to a court-appointed lawyer. However, the government failed to indicate whether the defendants had been allowed the right to appeal against their convictions and sentences before a higher court.

In November the organization received a response from the government to the *Amnesty International Report 1997*. The government dismissed the information contained in the report concerning extra-judicial executions and torture as "a repetition of previous allegations and lies made by the organization in its previous reports, which are exaggerated and lack accuracy and objectivity". Regarding the expansion of the scope of the death penalty to include new criminal offences (see *Amnesty International Report 1995*), the government stated that Amnesty International failed to take into account the exceptional circumstances resulting from UN sanctions imposed on the country, which necessitated the adoption of deterrent punitive measures to combat rising crime.

Amnesty International continued to express concern at human rights abuses by the KDP and the PUK. The organization raised the case of Ahmad Sharifi on a number of occasions with the PUK leadership, who promised to look into it. However, no response had been received by the end of the year. Reports of deliberate killings of PKK detainees in May in Arbil were raised during a meeting between Amnesty International and a KDP official and the organization's concerns were conveyed to the KDP leader, who issued a statement in May rejecting allegations that detainees were killed or raped in KDP custody. In July the organization received a letter from the KDP leader stating that the case of Bekir Dogan had been investigated and no person of that name had been arrested. However, no details of the investigation were made available.

ISRAEL
(STATE OF)
AND THE OCCUPIED TERRITORIES

At least 1,200 Palestinians were arrested on security grounds. At least 1,900 administrative detention orders were served; 354 Palestinians remained administratively detained at the end of the year. Prisoners of conscience included some administrative detainees and three conscientious objectors. At least 60 Lebanese nationals, including 23 held without charge or trial, or after expiry of their sentences, were held in Israel; a further 150 Lebanese nationals were held without charge or trial in Khiam detention centre in South Lebanon. Other political prisoners included more than 2,500 Palestinians sentenced in previous years. At least 1,450 Palestinians were tried in military courts whose procedures fell short of international fair trial standards. Torture and ill-treatment of detainees during interrogation continued to be systematic and officially sanctioned; beatings of Palestinians by members of the Israeli security services were reported. At least 18 Palestinians were killed in circumstances suggesting that they may have been extrajudicially executed or unlawfully killed. A total of eight houses were destroyed or sealed as punishment. Palestinian armed groups opposed to the peace process deliberately and arbitrarily killed at least 28 civilians.

The Israeli redeployment from Hebron, which had been scheduled to take place in 1996, took place in January. Israel withdrew from 80 per cent of the city. The Israeli Government under Prime Minister Binyamin Netanyahu authorized further building of Jewish settlements; the authorization to build on Jebel Abu Ghnaym/Har Homa in East Jerusalem provoked violent demonstrations.

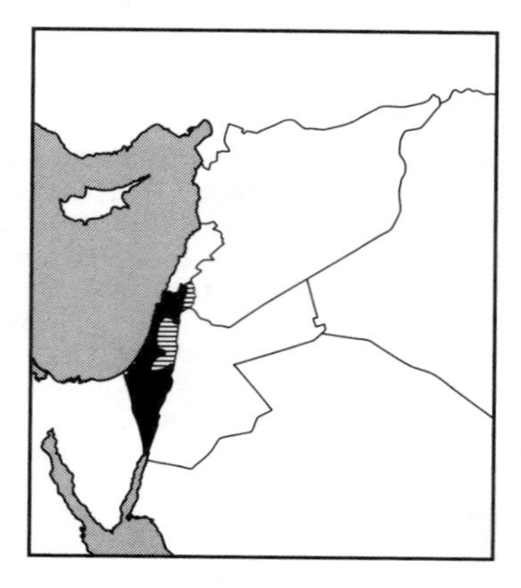

The Israeli Government made extensive use of border closures especially after suicide bombings (see below). Palestinians from the West Bank without Jerusalem identity cards were consistently prevented from travelling to East Jerusalem. Inhabitants of areas under the sole jurisdiction of the Palestinian Authority (see **Palestin-**

ian Authority entry) were frequently forbidden from entering areas partly or wholly under Israeli control.

A draft law which would have defined most activities of the Israeli Defence Force (IDF) as "combatant activity", thus invalidating the majority of victims' claims for compensation, passed its first reading in the *Knesset* (parliament) in July.

The UN Special Rapporteur, appointed pursuant to Commission on Human Rights resolution 1993/2 A "to investigate Israel's violations of the principles and bases of international law", visited areas under the jurisdiction of the Palestinian Authority but was denied access to members or officials of the Israeli Government.

In May the UN Committee against Torture considered the special report requested from Israel in November 1996 (see *Amnesty International Report 1997*). The Committee stated that methods of interrogation used by Israel constituted torture as defined in Article 1 of the Convention against Torture and Other Cruel, Inhuman or Degrading Treatment or Punishment, and requested Israel to cease such practices immediately. The Committee asked Israel to submit its second periodic report by September, but the Israeli Government had not submitted any further report by the end of the year.

At least 1,900 administrative detention orders were served; 354 people remained in administrative detention at the end of the year. Administrative detainees were denied the right to a fair trial, and detention orders were frequently automatically renewed. Detainees boycotted appeal hearings between August 1996 and September 1997 in protest against the apparently automatic rejection of appeals and the denial of the detainees' right to know the evidence against them. Prisoners of conscience included Wissam Rafidi, a journalist detained since August 1994, who was serving his 10th detention order at the end of the year. Ahmed Qatamesh remained in prison for a sixth consecutive year (see *Amnesty International Report 1997*). Two women were administratively detained, including 'Itaf 'Alyan, one of the prisoners released in February (see below); she was rearrested in October and served with a three-month administrative detention order. She remained on hunger-strike for 40 days in protest at her arrest. Marwan Ma'ali, arrested in August, committed suicide in Megiddo Military Detention Centre in September. Psychiatrists in the detention centre had reportedly diagnosed him as depressive with suicidal tendencies and recommended his release or hospitalization, and an Israeli human rights organization had described his isolation cell as "unsuitable for habitation by any human being". Nevertheless, his administrative detention had been extended for five months shortly before his suicide.

Prisoners of conscience included at least three conscientious objectors and a Syrian student. Yuval Lotem, a conscientious objector, was sentenced to 28 days' imprisonment in July for refusing to serve as a guard of administrative detainees in Megiddo Military Detention Centre. He was released in August. Ilham Abu Saleh, a student at Damascus University from the Golan Heights, was arrested in August and accused of "endangering state security" by spying for Syria. She denied the charge, which appeared to be baseless. She was not allowed to meet her lawyer or family until just before her release on bail 13 days later. No trial had been held by the end of the year and Ilham Abu Saleh remained under house arrest.

More than 60 Lebanese nationals remained imprisoned in Israel. At least 23 of them were held under administrative detention orders or after expiry of their sentences, including 21 who appeared to be held as hostages in exchange for the release of, or information about, Israelis killed or missing in action in Lebanon. Husayn Fahd Daqduq was arrested in Lebanon in April 1987, transferred to Israel, and sentenced to 18 months' imprisonment for "illegal military activities". By the end of the year he had been detained nine years beyond the expiry of his sentence. Shaykh 'Abd al-Karim 'Ubayd and Mustafa al-Dirani, abducted from Lebanon by Israeli forces in 1989 and 1994 respectively, had access to lawyers for the first time since their arrest. However, they continued to be denied access to the International Committee of the Red Cross (ICRC), as did Husayn Mikdad, a Lebanese national detained since May 1996 when a bomb he intended to use exploded prematurely in his hotel room. At least 150 prisoners remained held without charge or trial at Khiam detention centre in an area of South Lebanon controlled by the Israeli army (see **Lebanon** entry). Prime Minister

Netanyahu offered to exchange detained Lebanese nationals for the body parts of one of the 12 Israeli soldiers killed in action during an Israeli commando attack in Lebanon in September.

A total of 31 Palestinian women political prisoners were released in February in the context of peace accords. Shaykh Ahmad Yassin, the leader of *Hamas*, an Islamist opposition group, serving a life and 15-year sentence imposed in 1991, was released in September in exchange for Israeli intelligence agents arrested in Jordan for the attempted murder of Khaled Mesh'al, a leader of *Hamas* living in Amman (see below). A total of 20 Jordanians, including common law prisoners, and 50 Palestinians sentenced for offences such as shooting at cars or carrying arms, were released in connection with this exchange in October. At the same time President Ezer Weizman pardoned three Israeli Jewish political prisoners and reduced the sentences of four others; all had been convicted of killing Palestinians. Those released included two men sentenced to 10 years' imprisonment in 1993 for killing a Palestinian in Jerusalem in a grenade attack.

More than 2,500 Palestinians sentenced in previous years for political offences, following trials which fell short of international fair trial standards, remained in prison. At least 1,450 Palestinians were brought to trial before military courts for offences such as plotting to carry out "terrorist" attacks or stone-throwing and sentenced to up to life imprisonment. The trials did not meet international standards for fair trial; confessions, often extracted under torture, frequently formed the main evidence against the defendant.

Mordechai Vanunu remained held in solitary confinement for the 11th successive year. He had been abducted in Rome by Israeli agents and sentenced *in camera* for treason after revealing information about Israel's nuclear capability (see previous *Amnesty International Reports*).

Torture and ill-treatment of Palestinians continued to be systematic and officially sanctioned by secret guidelines allowing the General Security Service (GSS) to use "moderate" physical and psychological pressure. The ministerial committee overseeing the GSS continued to extend, for three-month periods, authorization to the GSS to use "increased physical pressure". Violent shaking (*tiltul*), which had caused the death of a detainee in 1995, was also allowed with the authorization of the head of the GSS. The High Court of Justice continued to sanction the use of physical force amounting to torture in interrogations of Palestinians, by rejecting court injunctions forbidding the use of physical force.

For instance, Ayman Kafisha was arrested in April on suspicion of involvement in the *Hamas* March suicide bombing which killed three civilians. He was held in Shikma (Ashkelon) Prison where he was tortured, including by being violently shaken and systematically deprived of sleep. The High Court of Justice rejected a petition requesting an interim injunction against the use of physical force during interrogation.

Palestinians were frequently beaten and violently ill-treated at check-points, demonstrations or immediately after arrest by the security services. For example, in July Muhammad Salah was stopped at a check-point when returning to al-Khader from East Jerusalem. He was beaten by border police, kicked all over the body and left in a ditch. He sustained injuries including a broken nose and a wound which needed five stitches. Muhammad Salah filed a complaint, but no action was known to have been taken by the end of the year.

At least 18 Palestinians were shot dead, mostly during demonstrations or at check-points, by members of the security services. Most of those killed appeared to have posed no danger to the security services. For instance, Ibrahim Tawfiq Abu Rutayna, aged 14, who was deaf and mute, was shot in June by IDF soldiers guarding Morag settlement in the Gaza Strip, apparently when he failed to stop following a shouted warning. He died in July in the Shifa' Hospital in Gaza. In September, two members of *Mossad*, the Israeli intelligence service, attempted to extrajudicially execute Khaled Mesh'al, a *Hamas* leader, in Amman, by injecting him with poison. Members of the IDF who carried out unlawful shootings were allowed virtual impunity. Three members of an undercover unit training in a Palestinian village beat to death Muhammad al-Hilu after shooting him in the leg. An IDF inquiry stated that the soldiers' lives were in danger; this did not appear to be the case.

Sa'id Badarneh, who had been sentenced to death in 1994 on charges including plotting a suicide bombing, was retried in February and sentenced to life and 15 years' imprisonment on the same charges (see *Amnesty International Reports 1995* and *1996*).

The Israeli army destroyed or sealed eight houses in Surif and al-'Asira al-Shimaliya belonging to people alleged to have been involved in suicide bombings, or their relatives, as punishment. House owners had the right to appeal to the High Court of Justice but no appeal was successful.

Palestinian groups opposed to the peace process, such as *Hamas*, carried out deliberate and arbitrary killings of civilians in Tel Aviv and Jerusalem in March, July and September; 28 people were killed and more than 200 wounded. For instance, in September, three suicide bombers exploded bombs in quick succession in Jerusalem, killing three people, including two schoolgirls, and injuring 150 others.

In April Amnesty International published a report, *Israel/Occupied Territories: Administrative detention – despair, uncertainty and lack of due process.* In July it published *Israel/South Lebanon: Israel's forgotten hostages – Lebanese detainees in Israel and Khiam detention centre.* Amnesty International made frequent calls for an end to torture and submitted its concerns on torture in Israel to the UN Committee against Torture. It also called for an end to the demolition or sealing of houses as punishment. The organization urged the immediate and unconditional release of prisoners of conscience and the release or fair trial of administrative detainees. Amnesty International expressed concern over the health of Mordechai Vanunu and Avraham Klingberg, a 79-year-old physician with chronic heart problems, held in secret incommunicado detention for 10 years after his arrest in 1983 on charges of spying for the former Soviet Union (see previous *Amnesty International Reports*).

In an oral statement to the UN Commission on Human Rights in March, Amnesty International stated that the effective legalization of torture by Israel undermined the fabric of international human rights protection.

Amnesty International condemned the deliberate and arbitrary killing of civilians by armed opposition groups and called on such groups to observe fundamental principles of humanitarian law.

ITALY

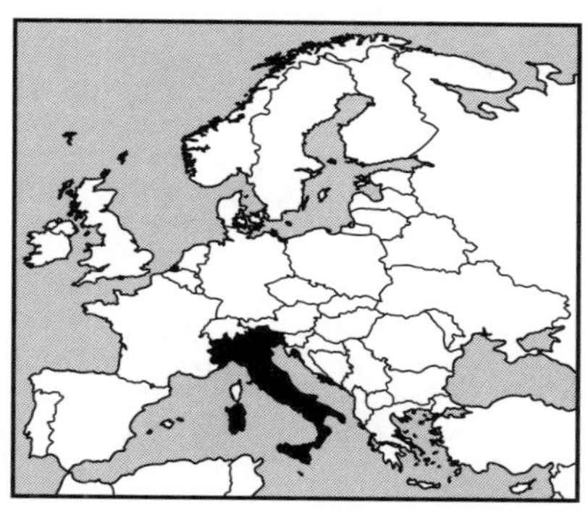

There were allegations that members of the Italian armed forces had tortured, ill-treated and unlawfully killed Somalis in 1993 and 1994, while participating in a UN-authorized multinational peace-keeping operation. There were new reports of ill-treatment by law enforcement and prison officers. Over 3,000 Albanians were forcibly returned to Albania where they risked serious human rights violations. Three people accused of a politically motivated murder were imprisoned after possibly unfair trial proceedings.

In January the Senate approved a bill reforming existing legislation governing conscientious objection to compulsory military service (see *Amnesty International Reports 1989* to *1997*). At the end of the year the bill was still awaiting approval by the Chamber of Deputies where its progress was delayed by over 2,000 amendments presented by opposition parties.

The findings of a 1995 visit of inspection by the European Committee for the Prevention of Torture and Inhuman or Degrading Treatment or Punishment to various places of detention and the government's interim response were published in December. The Committee stated that a "considerable number" of detainees in Milan and "many" in Rome had alleged ill-treatment by law enforcement officers, particularly police officers and, to a lesser extent, *carabinieri* officers. Further allegations had been heard in Naples and Catania. The Committee repeated the conclusion of its 1992 visit that detainees "and particularly foreigners and/or people arrested in connection with drugs-related offences, run a not inconsiderable risk of being ill-treated". It also reiterated its main recommendations on safeguards against ill-treatment and called on the government to establish an independent inquiry into the treatment of detainees by Milan police.

The Committee expressed particular concern about the persistence of severe prison overcrowding and stated that overcrowding in San Vittore prison had worsened since 1992, when overall conditions of detention already amounted to "inhuman and degrading" treatment. It stated that a "large number" of Poggioreale prison inmates had alleged ill-treatment by prison officers. After visiting Spoleto prison, it expressed concern that the so-called "Article 41-bis" regime applied to certain prisoners held in connection with organized crime, by combining extreme isolation from the outside world with frequent transfers, could cause irreversible mental damage. It said that one of the regime's "undeclared" aims might be to induce collaboration with the judicial authorities through psychological pressure.

Between June and August, a number of former Italian paratroopers made public allegations, sometimes supported by photographic evidence, that in 1993 and 1994, while serving as part of a UN peace-keeping operation in Somalia, they had witnessed colleagues torturing and ill-treating Somalis. In some cases the treatment was said to have resulted in death. Similar allegations were made by Somalis and by Somali human rights monitors. One former paratrooper said that Italian troops based at Johar camp kept Somali prisoners tied up in the sun, deprived them of food and water, and subjected them to blows, cigarette burns on the soles of the feet and electric shocks; some were thrown against razor-wire fences.

In early June the government announced that the army had opened an internal administrative investigation into the conduct of Italian armed forces in Somalia and that the military prosecutor's office in Rome had opened judicial investigations into specific alleged human rights violations. Some cases were subsequently referred to civilian prosecutors for further investigation. In mid-June a Ministry of Defence decree established a five-member Government Commission of Inquiry, led by Ettore Gallo, a former Constitutional Court president, into the conduct of the Italian troops. The Gallo Commission, accompanied by members of the magistracy, gathered information in Italy, Ethiopia and Kenya. It interviewed 141 people, including a small number of Somalis, but did not visit Somalia.

In its August report the Gallo Commission described evidence of ill-treatment at Johar camp. It also examined eight specific episodes of alleged human rights violations. It considered credible allegations that soldiers had subjected a Somali man to electric shocks; that four soldiers had gang-raped a Somali woman, after one of them had beaten her semi-conscious; and that a group of soldiers had raped another with a pistol flare. All three episodes were already under judicial investigation, as was the alleged rape and murder of a 13-year-old Somali boy by an army major. However, the Commission did not consider the allegations in the last case nor the allegations of ill-treatment and unlawful killing made in three others to be credible.

The Commission concluded that the overall conduct of the Italian troops in Somalia had been good; that specific violations had been carried out at the level of the ranks; that lower-ranking officers had sometimes participated actively or passively and had failed to exercise proper discipline. It concluded that senior professional officers were apparently not "directly involved" in the violations and that a "stretched" line of command had made failure to report violations to them inevitable.

The Commission urged the military authorities to upgrade human rights training for conscripts. It recommended that in future, peace-keeping troops should be accompanied by magistrates and experts on international and national human rights standards.

Within days of the report being lodged, new information came to light about further human rights violations by Italian troops in Somalia, accompanied by claims that high-ranking army officers had been aware of them and had not intervened to prevent them. The Minister of Defence asked the Gallo Commission to reopen its inquiry. It reconvened in September but its investigations were reportedly hampered because it did not have access to a substantial part of the new evidence. The new evidence was being investigated by the military prosecutor's office, and so was subject to judicial secrecy.

Further allegations of ill-treatment by law enforcement officers were reported throughout the country. The most common complaints were of beatings with truncheons and repeated slaps, kicks and punches, frequently accompanied by racial abuse. According to official statistics, 170 penal proceedings were opened during 1996 against police officers accused of ill-treatment or other offences against personal liberty or dignity. Fifty-five formal complaints were lodged against *carabinieri* officers between June 1995 and November 1996, resulting in 64 penal proceedings: the vast majority were still pending a decision. Judicial proceedings relating to alleged ill-treatment by law enforcement and prison officers were frequently delayed.

Trial proceedings against Secondigliano prison officers in connection with the alleged systematic ill-treatment of inmates in 1992 and 1993 (see *Amnesty International Reports 1994* to *1997*), had still not concluded by the end of the year. In January an appeal court acquitted Marcello Alessi of insulting a prison officer during an incident in San Michele prison in 1992 (see *Amnesty International Report 1997*) but confirmed his conviction for assaulting the officer. The joint trial of the officer charged with causing Marcello Alessi bodily harm and of Marcello Alessi, again charged with insulting the officer during the 1992 incident, was due to open in December, but was postponed until March 1998.

In February the Supreme Court annulled the suspended prison sentences passed by an appeal court in 1996 on four Palermo police officers, in connection with the torture and death of Salvatore Marino in 1985, and ordered their retrial (see *Amnesty International Reports 1986* to *1991*). The joint trial of two police officers charged with causing Grace Patrick Akpan serious injuries, insulting her, threatening her and abusing their powers in February 1996 (see *Amnesty International Report 1997*), and of Grace Patrick Akpan on charges of refusing to identify herself to them, and of insulting, resisting and injuring a police officer, opened in February. It was immediately postponed until October 1998. In September the Ministry of Justice stated that the Public Prosecutor's office attached to the Rome Tribunal had requested that no criminal action be taken against police officers whom Edward Adjei Loundens had accused of ill-treating him in 1995 (see *Amnesty International Report 1997*). There was no indication of what investigations the prosecutor had carried out into the alleged ill-treatment.

In March, in response to a sudden influx of over 13,000 Albanian asylum-seekers (see **Albania** entry), the government issued a decree offering temporary humanitarian protection. However, it excluded from such protection Albanians deemed a danger to public security, including those suspected of involvement in the organization of illegal immigration, prostitution, arms and drug-trafficking. Over 3,000 Albanians were reportedly summarily excluded and forcibly returned under these provisions. The Italian navy also patrolled the sea between the two countries, attempting to intercept and stem the arrival of asylum-seekers by boat.

In January, following a Supreme Court decision, Ovidio Bompressi, Giorgio Pietrostefani and Adriano Sofri began 22-year prison sentences for participation in the killing of Police Commissioner Luigi Calabresi in 1972. The criminal proceedings against them had opened in 1988 after Leonardo Marino, a former member of the 1970s extra-parliamentary left-wing group *Lotta Continua* (Continuous Struggle), confessed to a series of robberies and said that he had driven the assassin's get-away car in 1972, that Ovidio Bompressi, a prominent group member, had been the assassin and that Adriano Sofri, the group's leader, and Giorgio Pietrostefani, one of its committee members, had been the instigators. The four were first sentenced by an assize court in 1990 but a further six trials followed: three at appeal court level, including one which acquitted them, and three at Supreme Court level, including one which annulled a guilty verdict. Leonardo Marino was not imprisoned after the January Supreme Court decision. As a *pentito*, a person benefiting from remission of sentence in return for collaboration with the judicial authorities, he had received a reduced sentence of 11 years' imprisonment in 1990 and by 1995 had also benefited from the statute of limitations. He had previously spent some three months in detention. In December the three prisoners applied for a judicial review of their case.

Amnesty International was concerned about the length and complexity of the judicial proceedings and about several other aspects which raised serious doubts about their fairness. These included the extent to which the final verdict relied on the uncorroborated evidence of a *pentito* whose testimony was revealed during the proceedings to contain contradictions and inaccuracies. In addition, key material evidence was destroyed or disappeared, in one instance five months after the opening of the criminal proceedings against the three prisoners.

In March, noting the inability of the Albanian Government to ensure the protection of all its citizens, Amnesty International called on the Italian authorities to abide by their international obligations not to forcibly return people to a country where they risked serious human rights violations.

In June Amnesty International wrote to the Ministers of Justice and Defence welcoming the prompt opening by the military authorities of inquiries into alleged human rights violations by Italian troops in Somalia and asking to be informed of their outcome. It also called for a comprehensive inquiry by a judicial body independent of the military authorities, to ensure a demonstrably impartial investigation, and urged the establishment of an effective complaint mechanism for Somalis alleging human rights violations by Italian soldiers. It subsequently welcomed the establishment of, and provided information to, the Gallo Commission. In July Amnesty International recommended that those investigating the human rights violations carry out on-site investigations in Somalia as soon as possible.

In September the Minister of Justice informed Amnesty International that criminal courts in Livorno and Pescara had initiated five proceedings against Italian soldiers in connection with various offences, including sexual assault of Somali women, deliberate infliction of injuries leading unintentionally to the death of Somali citizens and the infliction of ill-treatment and physical injuries. No information was supplied by the Minister of Defence.

In March the organization drew Prime Minister Romano Prodi's attention to successive Amnesty International reports detailing its concern about allegations of ill-treatment, sometimes amounting to torture, inflicted by law enforcement and prison officers. The organization also sought information about any steps already taken, or envisaged, to implement the recommendations made to the government by the UN Committee against Torture in 1995 (see *Amnesty International Report 1996*). In September the Prime Minister forwarded a Ministry of Justice document providing information on the status of investigations or trial proceedings in a number of cases of alleged ill-treatment documented in Amnesty International reports.

JAMAICA

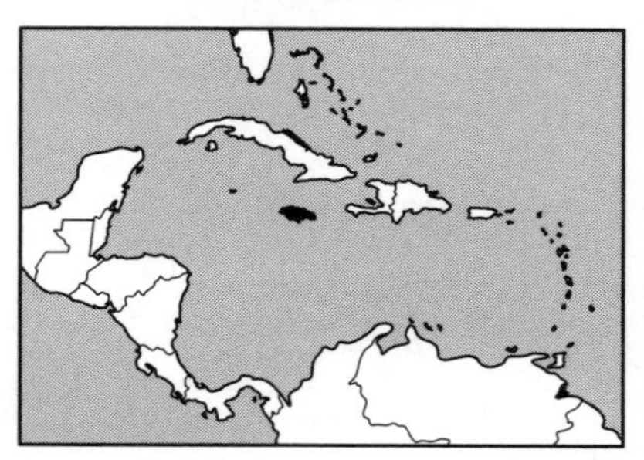

About 47 people, including at least five sentenced during the year, were under sentence of death. A prisoner was flogged. There were reports of ill-treatment. There were reports of fatal shootings by law enforcement officials in disputed circumstances.

P.J. Patterson was sworn in as Prime Minister following elections in December in which his party, the People's National Party, won a third successive term of office.

In August the government issued instructions which impose time limits on petitions by death-row prisoners to the UN Human Rights Committee and the Inter-American Commission on Human Rights.

According to these instructions, the government can execute a prisoner, even while a petition is still pending, if the time limits are not met by the prisoner or the international body considering the petition. In October the UN Human Rights Committee stated that these unilaterally imposed time limits could not be invoked as justification for any measure that would deviate from the International Covenant on Civil and Political Rights (ICCPR) or requests by the Committee for interim measures of protection.

In October the government informed the UN Secretary-General that it was withdrawing as a State Party from the Optional Protocol to the ICCPR, with effect from January 1998. Following this unprecedented withdrawal, the UN Human Rights Committee will no longer have jurisdiction to consider communications from individuals who allege that the government has violated rights guaranteed by the ICCPR.

Also in October, the UN Human Rights Committee examined Jamaica's periodic report of measures taken to implement the ICCPR. The Committee expressed "utmost regret" at the government's denunciation of the Optional Protocol and affirmed that the government remained bound by the provisions of the ICCPR and was still required to implement the Committee's recommendations in individual cases. The Committee expressed concern about a number of issues, including ill-treatment and deaths in custody; the "alarmingly high incidence of the use of firearms" by law enforcement officials; issues related to the administration of justice, including prolonged detention, the current state of legal aid representation and delays in judicial procedures, particularly in capital cases; corporal punishment; and prison conditions. It recommended that the government investigate all incidents of use of firearms by law enforcement officials and deaths in custody and that the results of these investigations, and of those into allegations of ill-treatment, be widely disseminated. It also urged the government to monitor the availability and quality of legal aid representation; closely observe standards related to pre-trial detention; ensure effective redress without reprisals to detainees and prisoners alleging ill-treatment by police and prison guards; and repeal legislation permitting corporal punishment. Many of these recommendations were consistent with concerns raised by Amnesty International.

About 47 people, including at least five sentenced during the year, were under sentence of death. No one was executed but warrants of execution were read for six men – Christopher Brown, Lansford James, Leroy Lamey, Neville Lewis, Samuel Lindsay and Henry McKoy. All were moved to death cells adjacent to the gallows to await imminent execution. Their executions were stayed because each filed a petition for relief.

For the first time in over 20 years, a person was whipped by court order. In February Errol Pryce was blindfolded, stripped below the waist, strapped to a barrel and flogged six times, reportedly in the presence of numerous prison staff.

There were reports of ill-treatment in prisons. In March death-row inmates were reportedly beaten by prison guards at St Catherine's District Prison, following an escape attempt by four prisoners under sentence of death. Some required hospital treatment for their injuries. In addition to contraband, prisoners' legitimate property – including legal documents, bedding and toiletries – were confiscated by prison staff and burned.

Prisoners, including death-row inmate Samuel Lindsay, were reportedly taunted and subjected to death threats by prison guards.

In August, 16 prisoners died and about 40 others were injured during disturbances in St Catherine's District Prison and Kingston's General Penitentiary. The disturbances reportedly started after guards walked out of the prisons in protest at the Commissioner of Corrections' announcement of his intention to distribute condoms to guards and prisoners, in an effort to control the spread of HIV/AIDS. Among those killed by other prisoners were prisoners who were targeted because they were homosexuals, and others, like Dennie Chaplin, who were known to be at risk. Twenty-five prisoners were charged in connection with the deaths. Among the injured were eight prisoners, who were reportedly shot by law enforcement officials. Although the report of the Board of Enquiry set up to investigate the incident had not been published by the end of the year, its preliminary findings reportedly included that prison guards had been inadequately trained and equipped to handle prison disturbances.

In November more prisoners were killed during further disturbances at Kingston's General Penitentiary and there were reports that many prisoners suffered injuries, including bone fractures, after beatings by prison guards.

Conditions in some police lock-ups, places of detention and prisons were so overcrowded, insanitary and so poor overall that they amounted to cruel, inhuman or degrading treatment or punishment.

There were reports of fatal shootings by law enforcement officials in disputed circumstances. In April Rohan Fraser, who was reportedly wanted by the police, was shot and killed by police in Tivoli Gardens, a community in West Kingston inhabited predominantly by members and supporters of the Jamaican Labour Party, one of the opposition parties. Initial police reports allegedly indicated that he was shot after he had aimed a gun at police, who were searching a house. Eyewitnesses, however, reported that he had his hands in the air when he was hit by 18 bullets fired by police. Three officers were later charged in connection with the killing.

Rohan Fraser's death sparked demonstrations in Tivoli Gardens. On the day before and on the day of Rohan Fraser's funeral in May, there were violent clashes and exchanges of gunfire with the security forces in Tivoli Gardens. While much of what happened on these two days is in dispute, it is not disputed that, in the course of these clashes, shots were fired from a defence force helicopter and many shots were fired into houses inhabited by people who were reportedly not involved in the violence. As a result, several people were injured and three women and a six-year-old boy were shot and killed. The boy was killed when a bullet entered his room through a window and struck him in the head as he was jumping on his bed. According to reports, one woman was shot on her way home from a shop, one was shot on her way home from Rohan Fraser's funeral and one was killed when a bullet entered her home. Despite calls for a commission of inquiry, the Prime Minister reportedly concluded that the police should investigate. The findings of the police investigation had not been made public by the end of the year.

Amnesty International wrote to the authorities after warrants of execution were read, urging the Governor General to exercise the prerogative of mercy and to ensure that no executions were carried out, and urging the government to take steps to abolish the death penalty. Amnesty International welcomed the setting up of the inquiry into incidents which culminated in the deaths and injury of prisoners in St Catherine's District Prison and Kingston's General Penitentiary in August. It called on the authorities to initiate full and impartial inquiries into the reported beatings of death-row prisoners in St Catherine's District Prison in March, and into the killings and beatings of prisoners in Kingston's General Penitentiary in November. It also called on the authorities to take steps to protect prisoners from ill-treatment; and to bring to justice those responsible for ill-treatment. In July the organization expressed concern about reports that prisoners had been taunted and threatened by guards. In October Amnesty International published a report, *Jamaica: A summary of concerns – a briefing for the Human Rights Committee*. This report expressed concern about Jamaica's failure to fully guarantee the rights enshrined in the ICCPR. It highlighted concerns about death sentences being imposed after trials which fell short of international standards; the lack of legal aid to death-row prisoners filing appeals to the highest court and constitutional motions; and the instructions imposing unreasonable time limits for the completion of death-row prisoners' petitions to international human rights bodies. The report also highlighted concerns about corporal punishment; ill-treatment; killings by law enforcement officials in disputed circumstances; conditions in jails and prisons; and laws punishing consensual sexual acts in private between adult males. The organization expressed concern that the government's denunciation of the Optional Protocol to the ICCPR could cut off an avenue of international scrutiny for redress of human rights violations in Jamaica and that this unprecedented step could undermine the system of international human rights promotion and protection; it urged the government to reverse its decision.

JAPAN

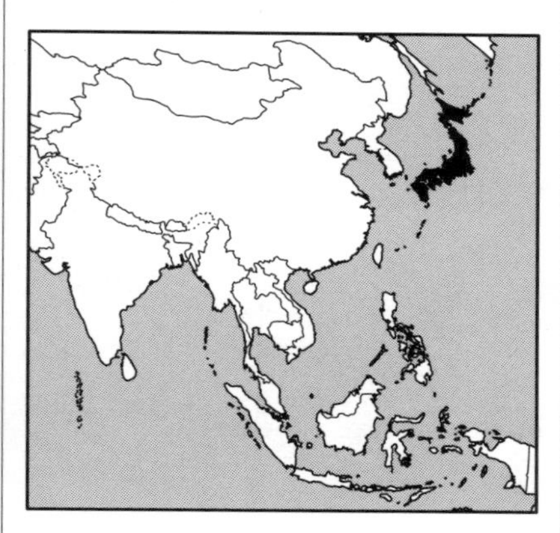

One possible prisoner of conscience was held. There were renewed reports of ill-treatment of detainees, including foreign nationals held in prisons and immigration detention centres. An Iranian man died in suspicious circumstances. Four prisoners were executed.

Prime Minister Hashimoto Ryutaro reshuffled his cabinet in September after his Liberal Democratic Party (LDP) regained an absolute majority in the *Diet* (parliament), following defections to the LDP by members of opposition parties. The government's stated aim of reforming the structure of government appeared to be stalling in November, following the economic downturn affecting much of south-east and east Asia. Japan continued its efforts to gain permanent membership of the UN Security Council.

The issue of compensation for former "comfort women" (women forced into prostitution by the Japanese army during the Second World War) remained unresolved. Few of the women accepted "atonement" payments from a non-governmental fund, with most continuing to demand that the Japanese Government accept responsibility for having forced them into prostitution, and that the funds disbursed be from official rather than private sources.

One possible prisoner of conscience was held for three months. Li Song, a Chinese pro-democracy activist, was detained on 4 June and released in September following the imposition of a suspended prison sentence for "resisting arrest". Li Song was detained as he was driving towards the site of a planned demonstration in Tokyo to commemorate the 1989 Tiananmen incident in Beijing, China, after allegedly attempting to drive through a police road-block. Li Song and other activists contended that, after his car hit a police barrier, he had been dragged out, beaten and kicked by police officers.

Prisoners and detainees in police custody were often subjected to arbitrary punishments, which frequently amounted to cruel, inhuman or degrading treatment or punishment. For example, in January Hoshino Fumiaki, serving a life sentence in Tokushima Prison, ended a four-month period of solitary confinement for breaking a prison rule in August 1996. According to his wife and his lawyer, he was punished because he had washed his foot without permission one evening, after having inadvertently stepped on a cockroach in his cell, and because he did not immediately obey a guard who ordered him to stop washing his foot. As a result, he was given a 20-day term of detention in a "punishment cell" in which he had to sit all day without moving; this was followed by four months in solitary confinement.

Foreign nationals in prisons and detention centres were also subjected to harsh rules which resulted in ill-treatment. For example, Kevin Mara, a US national imprisoned in Tokyo's Fuchu prison in connection with a drugs offence, was punished with solitary confinement on at least three occasions for minor breaches of prison rules. In one instance in 1993 he was accused of failing to keep his eyes closed, as regulations require, before starting a meal. Following his decision to sue the prison authorities for ill-treatment, he had been placed in continuous solitary confinement in 1996, and remained there throughout 1997. He was released in December after completing his term. His lawsuit seeking compensation from the authorities had not concluded by the end of the year.

Yu Enying, a Chinese national, remained in detention throughout the year in harsh conditions together with her one-year-old child and elderly mother. She was arrested in January 1996 in connection with an alleged false marriage declaration, and sentenced to a suspended term of imprisonment in May 1997. After the trial all three were immediately transferred to Nagoya Immigration Detention Centre pending deportation, on the grounds that Yu Enying's visa had expired while they were awaiting trial. They were first held in Nagoya Immigration Detention Centre, where they were kept in an insanitary and overcrowded cell, and Yu Enying was reportedly denied essential medical care. In June they were transferred to the East Japan Immigration Detention Centre in Tokyo, where their health reportedly continued to deteriorate as the three of them were held in a cell apparently intended for only one person. Applications by Yu Enying for provisional release had not been answered by the end of the year.

There was one death in suspicious circumstances of a foreign national held in an immigration detention centre pending deportation from Japan. Mousavi Abarbekouh Mir Hossein, an Iranian national, died suddenly in Kita-ku Immigration Detention Centre in Tokyo in August. His neck was broken. He had been detained there in July pending deportation to Iran. According to immigration officials, he was reprimanded after a cigarette lighter was discovered in his cell; this allegedly led to a scuffle with eight officers, who covered his head with a blanket. Officials claimed that he died after banging his head on the concrete floor. No investigation was known to have been held into the circumstances surrounding his death.

Four prisoners were executed in one day in August. They included Nagayama Norio, arrested for murder when aged 19, who had spent 28 years in prison before his execution in Tokyo and had become a renowned author. He was first sentenced to death in 1979 but the sentence was reduced to life imprisonment in 1981. In 1983, however, the Supreme Court ordered a revision of his trial, which led to his death sentence being reinstated. Kanda Hideki, convicted of murder in 1986, was executed in Tokyo after he had withdrawn an appeal against his death sentence. A married couple, Hidaka Nobuko and Hidaka Yasumasa, were executed in Sapporo. They had been sentenced to death in 1987 for murdering a coal miner's family. Like Kanda Hideki, they had withdrawn their appeal against their death sentences. According to their lawyers, they withdrew the appeal because they expected their sentences to be commuted before the death of Emperor Showa in 1989. They attempted to seek commutation again after Emperor Akihito assumed the throne, but this was rejected on the grounds that they had withdrawn their earlier appeal.

Official secrecy continued to surround the executions, and the government did not confirm the identity of those executed. As in previous years, neither the prisoners nor their relatives and lawyers were given advance notice of the executions. However, the Minister of Justice, following the precedent he set in 1996, confirmed to the press after the executions that he had signed four execution orders.

In September the Nagoya High Court overturned the death sentences passed by a Nagoya area district court on Yamaguchi Masuo and Nitta Sadashige, jointly accused of murder. The High Court ordered a retrial because the lower court had unlawfully appointed the same lawyer for both defendants, therefore giving rise to a conflict of interest for the lawyer in determining the two men's respective roles in the murder. Their retrial had not concluded by the end of the year. At the end of the year at least 50 prisoners were under sentence of death whose death sentences had been finally approved by the Supreme Court.

In August Amnesty International condemned the execution of four prisoners and called for the *Diet* to open a debate on the use of the death penalty in Japan. In June representatives of Amnesty International visited Japan to investigate conditions of detention and in November the organization issued a report, *Japan: Ill-treatment of foreigners in detention*, summarizing reports of ill-treatment against foreign nationals detained in prisons, police custody and immigration detention centres. The report set out detailed recommendations aimed at preventing the recurrence of ill-treatment. In written comments on Amnesty International's report, the government questioned some of the organization's views, provided further information on some individual cases, but stopped short of endorsing Amnesty International's recommendations.

JORDAN

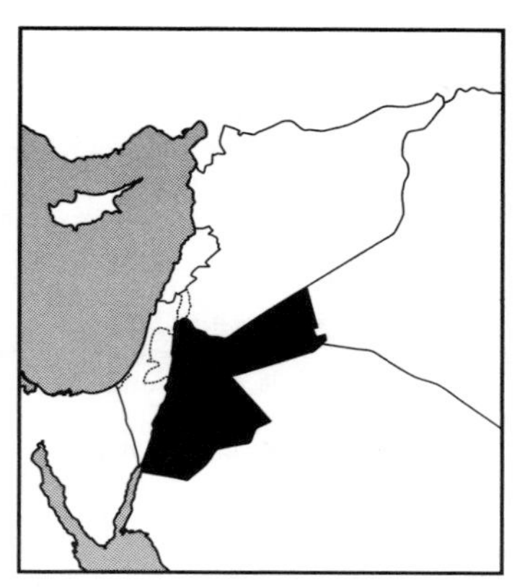

Five prisoners of conscience arrested in previous years continued to be held. About 350 people, including prisoners of conscience, were detained for political reasons during the year. Approximately 50 people were sentenced following trials before the State Security Court, some of which failed to meet international fair trial standards. There were reports of torture or ill-treatment of detainees arrested for common law offences, particularly during incommunicado detention. At least 11 people were executed and 21 others were sentenced to death.

'Abd al-Salam al-Majali became Prime Minister in March following the resignation of 'Abd al-Karim Kabariti. Elections, held in November, were boycotted by the Islamic Action Front, the main opposition party, in protest at what it said was the erosion of parliamentary authority. Seven other parties also boycotted the elections. Supporters of the government won a majority of seats in the new parliament. No woman was elected.

In May amendments to the Press and Publications Law were introduced shortly after a speech by King Hussein bin Talal in which he severely criticized the Jordanian press and accused newspapers of basing stories on false information. The new law limited even further the freedom of the press, forbidding publication of anything "which includes false information or rumours which relate to the general interest, or government institutions or its workers". Weekly newspapers had to increase their capital to 300,000 dinars (approximately US$420,000) or cease publication. The police reacted strongly to protest demonstrations by journalists, reportedly beating and kicking protesters and hitting them with batons. In September the government suspended 13 newspapers because they were unable to raise the required capital within the three months laid down by law; other newspapers, including the satirical journal *'Abed Rabbo*, ceased publication because they feared the effect of heavy fines.

Prisoners of conscience arrested in previous years who remained in detention included 'Ata' Abu'l-Rushta, spokesperson for the *Hizb al-Tahrir fi'l-'Urdun* (LPJ), Liberation Party in Jordan – a party seeking to re-establish the Islamic Caliphate – who was serving a six-month sentence for membership of an unlicensed organization after having completed a three-year sentence for an interview published in 1995 in the journal *al-Hiwar* (see *Amnesty International Report 1997*). 'Abdallah Bani 'Issa, editor of *al- Hiwar,* was sentenced in January to six months in prison for publishing the interview. However, he was not detained pending appeal, and the Court of Appeal overturned the conviction in April. Four members of the LPJ sentenced in previous years for distributing leaflets remained in prison as prisoners of conscience (see *Amnesty International Report 1995*).

About 350 people, including prisoners of conscience, were detained for political reasons during the year. Many were members of Islamist or other radical groups opposed to the peace treaty with Israel. Other prisoners of conscience were detained for articles or lectures critical of the government. Most were released without charge or trial. They included Ramadan Hassan Jilad, a teacher of religious sciences in the Jerash Mosque who was arrested in May and detained for three weeks. Twelve students from Amman University were also arrested in May for taking down a portrait of King Hussein from a room where they were holding a meeting. They were held for up to eight days before being released without charge.

Ibrahim Ghoshe, a spokesperson for the Islamist group *Hamas,* was arrested in September after suicide bombings in Jerusalem (see **Israel and the Occupied Territories** entry). He was held for 14 days without access to his family and lawyers before being released without charge.

A number of prisoners were released in January and February in the second batch of releases under the royal amnesty granted in November 1996 (see *Amnesty International Report 1997*); however, none was being held for political offences. A total of 20 Jordanians held in Israeli prisons were released in October in exchange for Jordan's release of Israeli intelligence agents involved in the attempted killing of Khaled Mesh'al, a leader of *Hamas* living in Amman.

Approximately 60 political prisoners sentenced, often following unfair trials, for violent activities in previous years also remained in prison. Some 50 people, about 20 of whom had been arrested in previous years, were tried for political offences before State Security Courts which were invariably composed of military judges; some trials failed to meet international fair trial standards. Some of those sentenced by the courts for political offences were prisoners of conscience. For example, Jubra'il Hassan was sentenced to 13 months' imprisonment in October for membership of the LPJ and for distributing illegal pamphlets. Others brought before the State Security Court included 'Ikrimeh Mahmud, Yusef Ahmad and 'Ali Muhammad Mustafa. They were convicted of plotting acts of "terrorism" and possession of illegal land-mines; they pleaded guilty to the latter charge only. They were sentenced to death in February; the sentence was immediately commuted to life imprisonment.

A Jordanian soldier, Ahmad al-Daqamsa, who killed seven Israeli schoolgirls and wounded five others by automatic gunfire in al-Baqura Island in March, was found guilty of unpremeditated murder and sentenced by a military court in July to life imprisonment with hard labour.

In March the Court of Cassation ratified the State Security Court verdicts in the *Bay'at al-Imam* (Allegiance to the Imam) case, involving 10 members of an Islamist group sentenced to up to life imprisonment on charges including manufacturing explosives, and in the case of Salem Bakhit and Ahmad Khaled, sentenced to life and 10 years' imprisonment for attacking a French diplomat (see *Amnesty International Reports 1996* and *1997*).

There were reports of torture and ill-treatment of common law detainees at the hands of the Criminal Investigation, Preventive Security and Metropolitan Police. For example, in July five men involved in a razor attack were allegedly beaten with cables and hoses by members of the Criminal Investigation in Jebel Hussein Police Station in Amman; two were beaten while suspended in contorted positions. They were released on bail after eight months in detention without trial.

Samer Khazer died after being beaten by members of the Criminal Investigation at his home in Zabda al-Wasatiya in June. The police stated that he had resisted arrest but statements by the family and villagers suggested that no serious attempt was made to arrest him. No independent inquiry was held into his death.

Muntasser Rajab Abu Zayd, who was allegedly tortured and ill-treated in order to extract a confession which reportedly formed the basis of his conviction for murder (see *Amnesty International Report 1997*), was executed in June. No investigation had been initiated into the allegations of torture or ill-treatment.

At least 10 other people were executed. Among the women executed were Amira Salem and 'Aidah Hussein, who were hanged at Swaqa Prison in June. They had been convicted of killing the husband of Amira Salem who was said to have regularly abused her. Those sentenced to death were reportedly not informed of their execution until about 15 minutes before it took place. A total of 21 people were sentenced to death for murder during the year. They included eight people from Amir al-Iraq convicted by the Criminal Court of killing two members of another family in a quarrel. One death sentence was overturned by the Court of Cassation.

In correspondence with the government Amnesty International responded in detail to criticisms by the authorities of the *Amnesty International Report 1997* received in December 1997. The organization continued to raise concerns about the use of the death penalty and urged the government not to forcibly return asylum-seekers to Libya or Iraq.

KAZAKSTAN

There were further allegations of torture and ill-treatment in police custody and in prisons. Prison conditions amounting to ill-treatment continued to be reported. Fifty-six death sentences were passed. Eight death sentences were commuted and at least 35 executions were carried out.

In July President Nursultan Nazarbayev signed into law a new Criminal Code to take effect in 1998. The new Criminal Code reduced the number of crimes which carry the death penalty and decriminalized homosexual acts between consenting adult men.

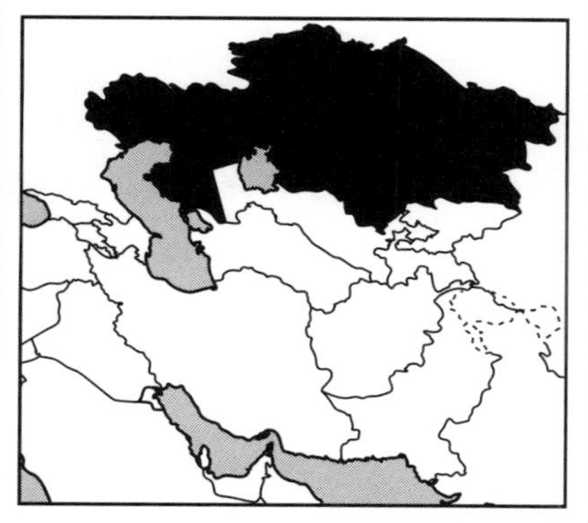

In February Zhurmabek Busurmanov, the First Deputy Chairman of the Presidential Human Rights Commission, accused three non-governmental human rights organizations based in Kazakstan of having links with international organizations whose aim was the "destabilization" of the country. This raised serious doubts about the Commission's willingness or ability to uphold fundamental human rights. Following international condemnation of his unjustified criticism of the three human rights organizations, Zhurmabek Busurmanov was reported to have been reassigned to other duties.

There were further allegations of torture and ill-treatment during the year. Yevgeny Tarasov, who was arrested in November 1995 in Pavlodar and charged with murder, alleged that while in the custody of the Pavlodar police he was beaten with truncheons, tied to a central heating radiator, and forced to wear a gas mask with the air supply switched off until he lost consciousness, in order to extract a confession. Despite his allegations of torture, the confession was accepted as evidence at his trial. He was convicted and sentenced to 10 years' imprisonment. The Supreme Court upheld the sentence in April. No investigation was known to have taken place into his allegations.

Criminal proceedings were reportedly dropped against law enforcement officials accused of beating Valery Zippa so severely during interrogation in 1994 that he required surgery to remove his spleen (see *Amnesty International Report 1997*). The authorities failed to provide information about the findings of the investigation into the alleged beating.

Poor prison conditions amounting to ill-treatment continued to be reported. There was continued concern over allegations of deliberate ill-treatment and poor conditions in a juvenile penitentiary, LA-155/6, in the capital, Almaty (see *Amnesty International Report 1997*). The government stated that there was no evidence of "cruel treatment, torture [or] ill-treatment" at the penitentiary, and asserted that "within the limits of present lack of material, financial and medical resources the prisoners in the colony LA-155/6 are treated in accordance with the labour-reform laws of the republic". However, it later reported the establishment of a program to provide the necessary technical, medical and social support to penal institutions.

The number of death sentences imposed during the year showed a marked decline over previous years, and in capital cases courts were reported to be more readily exercising the option of imposing a long custodial sentence rather than the death penalty. Fifty-six death sentences were passed and eight appeals for clemency were granted. However, at least 35 people were executed. Oleg Gorozashvili was executed in April, despite appeals for a stay of execution to allow an investigation into allegations that there had been serious investigative and judicial errors in his case, and an undertaking by the authorities that the execution would not take place until the allegations had been thoroughly investigated.

Amnesty International wrote to the President expressing concern at statements by Zhurmabek Busurmanov which criticized human rights organizations, and calling on him to condemn unjustified criticisms of human rights defenders by state officials.

The organization sought information on whether the new Criminal Code would decriminalize homosexuality and stressed that it regarded people imprisoned for homosexual acts between consenting adults in private as prisoners of conscience.

Amnesty International wrote to the authorities raising its concerns about allegations of ill-treatment and poor prison conditions.

The organization continued to call for the commutation of all death sentences and the abolition of the death penalty.

KENYA

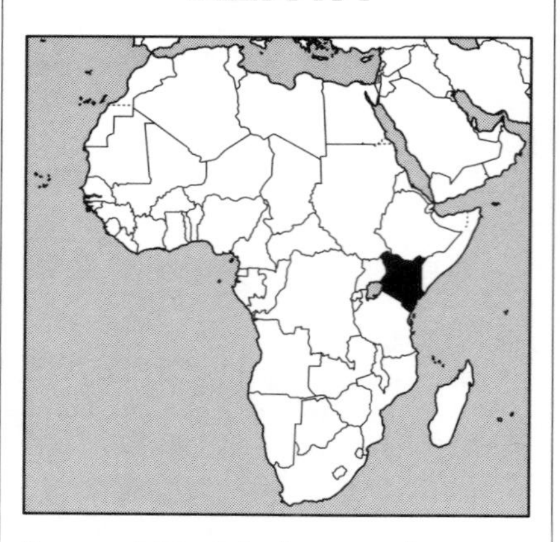

Human rights defenders, pro-democracy activists and journalists were harassed, detained or ill-treated for non-violent activities. Police officers routinely beat criminal suspects, apparently causing a number of deaths in custody, and violently attacked peaceful protesters and opposition party supporters. Scores of people were killed by police during the year; some may have been extrajudicially executed. At least 74 people were sentenced to death. More than 750 people were under sentence of death at the end of the year.

Presidential and parliamentary elections, widely anticipated through much of the year, were finally held in late December. The government of President Daniel arap Moi was re-elected.

Ahead of the elections, a number of opposition groups, religious groups, human rights and non-governmental organizations (NGOs) came together in the National Convention Assembly to work for constitutional and legal reform. They challenged the impartiality of the Electoral Commission, restrictions on opposition parties – including lack of access to broadcast media – and the independence of the registration process.

Peaceful rallies calling for reform were violently broken up by police officers using tear-gas, batons, live ammunition and rubber bullets. Organizations engaged in civic education before the elections also had their meetings stopped or dispersed by police, sometimes violently.

In July the government announced that it would introduce legal reforms and set up a commission to look into constitutional reform, but that this commission would have up to two years to report its findings. In August the government published proposed amendments to several laws, including the Public Order Act, the Societies Act and the Chiefs' Authority Act, and in September the government and parliamentary opposition parties agreed on a number of legal reforms, including the outlawing of preventative detention, which were enacted in November. However, the authorities retained powers to restrict freedom of expression and to detain suspects. In November a number of unregistered political parties obtained registration.

In February the new Police Commissioner publicly ordered all police officers to stop beating suspects during interrogation and to stop harassing journalists. In February Kenya acceded to the UN Convention against Torture and Other Cruel, Inhuman or Degrading Treatment or Punishment.

In August political violence in the coastal region led to more than 70 deaths, with hundreds injured and tens of thousands of people displaced. The government was accused of failing to contain the violence, and was widely believed to have instigated it. There were numerous reports of ill-treatment by members of the security forces deployed to investigate the violence.

Human rights defenders, pro-democracy activists and journalists were harassed, threatened, arrested and detained or ill-treated on account of their non-violent activities.

Members of the Kenya Human Rights Commission (KHRC) were arrested in January during the launch of a campaign against police killings. Wafule Buke, a KHRC staff member, was arrested while giving out leaflets and held for six hours. When another member of staff went to protest, he was beaten by a senior police officer.

Wafule Buke was arrested again in July, with Morris Ochieng, while distributing leaflets calling for reforms. They were held for six days before being charged with publishing false statements "likely to cause fear and alarm". The case had not come to court by the end of the year.

In April police rounded up more than 80 people at a peaceful KHRC demonstration. Maina Kiai, the KHRC executive director, was questioned for about three hours before being released.

Three teachers who attended a civic education seminar in Loitokitok in April were arrested by administrative police, beaten and held for several hours.

In June President Moi accused the Pastoralists Forum, an NGO coalition, of being a front for an underground opposition organization. Some of the NGO's members were subsequently interrogated by the police.

In January G.G. Njuguna Ngengi and Charles Kuria Wamwere, both prisoners of conscience, were released on bail on medical grounds. In December charges against them and their co-accused, Koigi wa Wamwere, were dropped, as were all other outstanding charges against Koigi wa Wamwere and his fellow accused (see *Amnesty International Reports 1994* to *1997*).

In January charges of incitement and possession of a banned publication, *Inooro*, against Father Charles Kamori and three seminarians were withdrawn (see *Amnesty International Reports 1996* and *1997*).

In November and December politically motivated charges against a number of other people were also withdrawn. The charges of holding an illegal meeting and incitement to violence brought against members of the human rights organization Release Political Prisoners (RPP), the charge against Wang'ondu Kariuki of belonging to an illegal organization, and the sedition charge against Njehu Gatabaki (see *Amnesty International Reports 1996* and *1997*) were all withdrawn in November.

Journalists were attacked by the police for carrying out their duties. Susan Musoke, a photographer covering a story about delays and extortion in the issuing of new identity cards, was assaulted by armed administration police in February. They beat her, destroyed her film and briefly detained her and a colleague.

Evans Kanini, a journalist who had been repeatedly harassed by police (see *Amnesty International Report 1997*), was informed in March of an assassination plot against him. When he went to Eldoret police station to report it, the police locked him up for 12 hours.

In October Patrick Wangamati was arrested at Nairobi airport on his return from Ghana, and held incommunicado for nearly nine weeks before being released without charge. He had fled Kenya in 1994 after being accused of organizing a guerilla movement, and had been a recognized refugee in Ghana.

Police also rounded up the poor, women, street children and refugees in mass arrests. In July, for example, more than 600 Rwandese, Burundi and other foreign nationals were arrested, apparently arbitrarily. Some were ill-treated by the police. Most were released in August, but some were threatened with forcible return to countries where they would be at risk of human rights violations and many were transferred to Kakuma refugee camp in the north, where conditions are very harsh. At least four were held for over 70 days without charge.

Police routinely beat criminal suspects. In February, for example, three young people appeared in a court in Thika district bruised, bandaged and unable to walk without assistance. Their lawyer alleged that they had been tortured by a senior police officer.

In March Ali Hussein Ali died in Wajir, North Eastern province, after eight days' police interrogation. A post-mortem found evidence of severe beatings.

In May a 17-year-old herd boy died in police custody two days after his arrest in Turkana district. A police post-mortem conducted by the local medical officer failed to establish the cause of death, but a pathologist acting for the family concluded that he had been beaten and had died of strangulation and head injuries.

Action was rarely taken against those responsible for beatings and other torture and ill-treatment of detainees, but in March, three police officers from Embu were sentenced to 10 years' imprisonment for torturing a prisoner to death in 1994.

Police ill-treated peaceful protesters calling for constitutional reform. In early May, for example, about 2,000 heavily armed police and paramilitary officers attacked a crowd of more than 10,000 people attending a pro-democracy rally at Kamakunji, Nairobi. Many people in the crowd were beaten with whips and batons, and some were seriously injured. Later that month, police fired tear-gas into a crowd of several thousand people who were peacefully praying at a rally in Uhuru Park, Nairobi. Police and security force personnel later beat bystanders as well as protesters and looters. In July, 14 people, including a 17-year-old boy, died after pro-democracy rallies organized throughout the country were violently disrupted by the security forces, who used live ammunition as well as rubber bullets and tear-gas. Scores of people were injured. In August, one policeman was killed during a pro-democracy rally in Nairobi. Thirty men have been charged with his murder.

Opposition party supporters, including members of parliament, were ill-treated by police. In February riot police assaulted supporters of the then unregistered opposition party Safina at a market-place in Nyeri. Journalists and Safina activists were whipped and clubbed, while two members of parliament – Paul Muite and Kiraitu Mirungi – were chased and beaten. The police denied that the incident took place, despite numerous eye-witnesses.

Within one week in April, there was a series of incidents in which members of parliament were ill-treated by police. Raila Odinga of the National Development Party of Kenya, and Oburu Odinga of the Forum for the Restoration of Democracy (FORD)-Kenya, were injured by police who broke up a meeting in Eldoret. Charity Kariuki Ngilu, of the Democratic Party, who had been beaten by police in November 1996, was harassed in her home by police. The bodyguard of the FORD-Kenya Chairman Michael Kijana Wamalwa was shot and wounded by armed police who were trying to prevent the opening of a FORD-Kenya office in Kakamega.

Police failed to protect some prospective election candidates, especially women, who were attacked by supporters of the ruling Kenya African National Union party. Rhoda Fadhil, a prospective parliamentary candidate in the northwest, alleged that she had been harassed, intimidated and threatened with rape by the local member of parliament and his supporters, but had received no police protection despite her complaints.

Courts continued to impose sentences of caning, a cruel, inhuman or degrading punishment, for a variety of offences including robbery and rape. Many young men under 18 years were caned as an alternative, or in addition to custodial sentences, often after unfair trials.

Conditions in prisons were harsh and in many places amounted to cruel, inhuman or degrading treatment. Over 630 prisoners died during the year, the majority from infectious diseases resulting from severe overcrowding and shortages of food, clean water and adequate medical care.

Scores of people were killed by police during the year. Some were criminal suspects shot dead by police even though they appeared to have posed no threat. At least five people died in custody, apparently as a result of torture.

In March Anthony Chege, a student, was shot by police officers as he walked along the street with two friends. He died on the way to hospital. His two friends were severely beaten and held by police for seven days. It is not known if there has been an official investigation into his death.

Solomon Muruli, a student leader at the University of Nairobi, was burned to death in his room on campus in February. He had received death threats and believed that he was being followed. One week before his death he positively identified a senior police officer at an identification parade as one of the men who had allegedly abducted him in November 1996 (see *Amnesty International Report 1997*). An inquest into his death began in April.

At least 74 people were sentenced to death. More than 750 people were under sentence of death at the end of the year. No executions were reported, but prisoners on death row died as a result of extremely harsh prison conditions. Many prisoners under sentence of death were convicted after trials which failed to meet international standards. For example, not all defendants facing the death penalty had the right to a lawyer funded by the state, and some were therefore tried and sentenced to death without having had a lawyer. In addition some defendants have stated in court that they were tortured or ill-treated to make them plead guilty.

Amnesty International repeatedly appealed to the authorities to bring Kenya's laws and Constitution into line with international standards. It called on the government to protect people against torture, ill-treatment and extrajudicial executions by ensuring that all allegations of torture, ill-treatment and extrajudicial execution were investigated and those responsible brought to justice. It called for the abolition of the death penalty and cruel, inhuman or degrading punishments. It also urged the authorities to ensure that all those in Kenya were allowed to exercise their basic human rights, including freedom of expression, association and assembly.

In January Amnesty International published *Kenya: Detention, torture and health professionals.*

Amnesty International delegates visited Kenya five times during the year. In June delegates met representatives of the government, as well as opposition leaders, human rights activists, members of professional groups, business leaders and members of the international community. Alarmed by the potential for violent confrontation, the delegates called for meaningful dialogue within Kenya, but were accused by the government of "incitement". Amnesty International issued a *Human rights manifesto for Kenya*, aimed at all political parties in the run-up to elections and supported by numerous Kenyan NGOs. This called for systematic human rights reforms.

In September Amnesty International published *Kenya: The quest for justice*, and *Kenya: Violations of human rights.* It launched a worldwide campaign to support the local human rights community and to urge the government to stop violations of human rights. In November Amnesty International published *Kenya: Election monitors human rights brief.*

KOREA
(DEMOCRATIC PEOPLE'S REPUBLIC OF)

The country remained closed to human rights monitors. The government's decision to withdraw from the International Covenant on Civil and Political Rights (ICCPR) was not accepted by the UN.

Kim Jong Il was nominated as General Secretary of the ruling Korean Workers' Party (KWP) in October. This was the first major step taken by the Government of the Democratic People's Republic of Korea (DPRK), North Korea, to clarify institutional arrangements since the death in 1994 of former leader Kim Il Sung, Kim Jong Il's father. Although Kim Jong Il had apparently held effective power since before his father's death, the leadership of both the KWP and the state had remained vacant. The post of President of the DPRK remained unfilled at the end of the year. Kim Jong Il's nomination as KWP leader did not take place during a formal KWP Congress, as was believed to be required by KWP rules, but his name was reported to have been put forward at a series of regional KWP meetings and endorsed by the central leadership of the KWP.

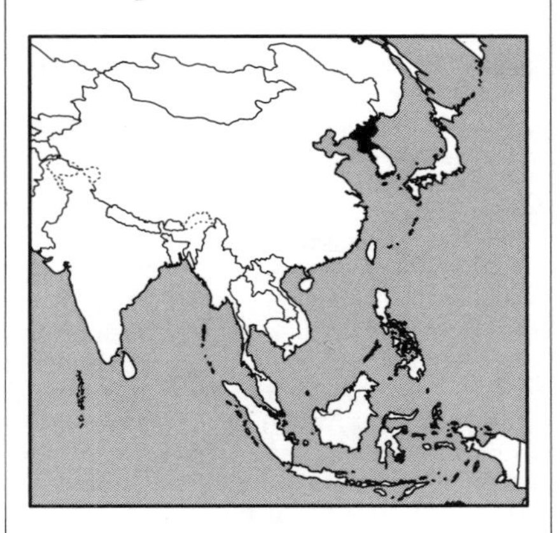

For the third consecutive year the population suffered severe food shortages. Few official statistics were available about the extent of the shortages but some observers from non-governmental organizations estimated that several thousand children had died every month as a result of malnutrition. Estimates also suggested that more than two million people had died in the last three years as a result of the food shortages, but the authorities' continued refusal to allow adequate monitoring of the situation hampered accurate evaluations. Official statements blamed the shortages on floods in 1995 and 1996 and on exceptional drought in 1997. However, it became increasingly clear during the year that longstanding agricultural practices and a lack of necessary materials such as fertilizer contributed to the loss of output, while the collapse of trade with former socialist states had removed a major source of imports.

In August the DPRK informed the UN that it had decided to withdraw from the ICCPR with immediate effect and to suspend its reporting to the UN Committee on the Rights of the Child. The DPRK stated that it had taken these steps in protest against a resolution critical of the human rights situation in the DPRK adopted in August by the UN Sub-Commission on Prevention of Discrimination and Protection of Minorities. This resolution criticized in particular the DPRK's failure to allow visits by human rights monitors and its failure to report in a timely manner to the UN Human Rights Committee on its implementation of the ICCPR. DPRK diplomats indicated that the DPRK viewed its withdrawal as a "defence" to protect its "sovereignty" and "dignity", while stating that the DPRK would "do its best" to "protect" human rights in accordance with the provisions of the ICCPR. For over 10 years, the DPRK had failed to report on its implementation of the ICCPR to the UN Human Rights Committee, a body of independent experts monitoring the implementation of the ICCPR by States Parties.

The DPRK's statement made it the first country ever to attempt to withdraw from the ICCPR – or from any other UN human rights treaty. In October the UN Human Rights Committee, which has authority to interpret ICCPR provisions, stated that countries which had ratified the ICCPR could not denounce (withdraw from) it. The Committee noted that the ICCPR contained no provision regarding its termination and did not provide for denunciation or withdrawal. It added that the rights enshrined in the ICCPR belonged to the people living in the territory of the State Party and that the drafters of the ICCPR "deliberately intended to exclude the possibility of denunciation" because the ICCPR "did not have a temporary character typical of treaties where a right of denunciation was deemed to be admitted". By the end of the year, the DPRK had not reacted to the comments of the UN Human Rights Committee.

In January Amnesty International released a report, *Democratic People's Republic of Korea: Public executions – converging testimonies*, detailing reports that at least 23 people, including one woman, had been publicly executed between 1970 and 1992. Among the cases reported to Amnesty International were those of four men executed for "banditry" in Chongjin City in the 1970s; two brothers convicted of stealing rice from a train, who were executed in Hamhung City in the 1980s; and a woman convicted of embezzlement, who was executed in the Sama Dong district of Pyongyang, the capital, in 1988. The authorities had indicated in 1993 that one execution had taken place in 1992. However, in 1995 North Korean officials had told Amnesty International that only one or two executions had taken place since 1985. In its January report, the organization called on the North Korean authorities to formally abolish the death penalty and to make public a complete list of all death sentences and executions carried out since 1970. No response was received from the authorities on these issues.

KOREA
(REPUBLIC OF)

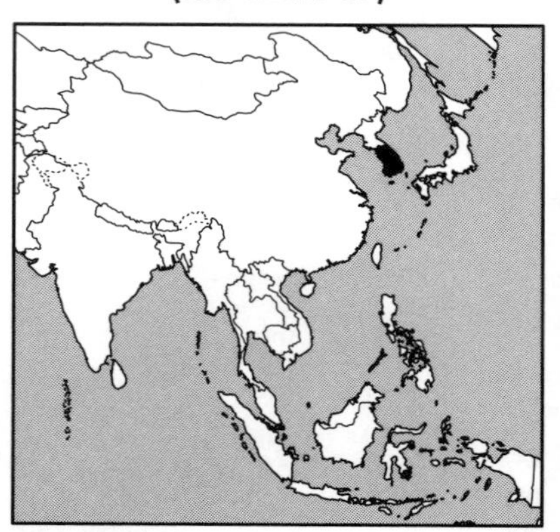

More than 650 people were arrested under the National Security Law, including prisoners of conscience. Dozens of political prisoners convicted in previous years remained in prison throughout the year, of whom at least 20 were imprisoned during the 1970s and 1980s after unfair trials. There were reports of ill-treatment of detainees during arrest and interrogation. Twenty-three people were executed and 36 others remained under sentence of death at the end of the year.

Throughout the year the government of President Kim Young-sam was weakened by the arrest and conviction of senior officials and businessmen on charges of corruption. Twenty-three businessmen convicted of corruption in previous years were released in a special amnesty in September. Former Presidents Chun Doo-hwan and Roh Tae-woo were released in December (see *Amnesty International Report 1997*).

Kim Dae-Jung was elected President in December. After the election he said he would release political prisoners when he took office in February 1998.

In early January thousands of trade unionists, led by the *Minju Nochong*, Korean Confederation of Trade Unions, took strike action to protest against new labour legislation adopted by the National Assembly in December 1996 (see *Amnesty International Report 1997*). The authorities responded by issuing arrest warrants for 20 trade union leaders on charges of organizing "illegal" strike action. Following mass public protest rallies throughout the country, the arrest warrants were withdrawn.

In March the National Assembly amended labour legislation to permit legal recognition of unauthorized trade union federations and to delay proposed mass lay-offs of workers. However several provisions continued to violate international standards, including a prohibition on the rights of teachers and thousands of public employees to form and join trade unions.

The defection to the Republic of Korea (South Korea) in April of a high-ranking official from the Democratic People's Republic of Korea (North Korea) increased tensions between the two countries. In July the Agency for National Security Planning announced an investigation into an unspecified number of alleged North Korean sympathizers, on the basis of information from the defector. Government opponents feared this information would be used to investigate people for their peaceful political activities.

In July the Constitutional Court ruled that an amendment to the Law on the Agency for National Security Planning, adopted in December 1996 (see *Amnesty International Report 1997*), was constitutional but declared that the railroading of the new law through the National Assembly had infringed the rights of lawmakers to review and vote on new laws.

More than 650 people, including prisoners of conscience, were arrested under the National Security Law which prohibits activities deemed to be pro-North Korean. Most were held under Article 7 on charges of "praising" and "benefiting" North Korea. After trial, most were sentenced to a short prison term or given a suspended sentence and released. They included 20 members of *Saminchong,* Union of Socialist Youth, arrested in March and April for holding study sessions and distributing information considered by the authorities to support North Korea's political ideas; they were prisoners of conscience. Others detained under provisions of the National Security Law included five members of *Pomminnyon,* Pan-National Alliance for the Reunification of Korea, arrested in July for using unofficial channels to send famine relief money to North Korea, and Yang Hyon-chu, a university student arrested in August after attempting to make an unauthorized visit to North Korea.

Arrests under the National Security Law peaked in June and July when 249 people were detained. The arrests took place in the context of student protests which escalated in late May when violent clashes resulted in the deaths of three men, two of whom were reportedly killed by students. Hundreds of students belonging to *Hanchongnyon,* National Association of University Student Councils, were arrested for participating in violent demonstrations and many were also charged under the National Security Law with belonging to an "enemy benefiting" (pro-North Korean) organization. Amnesty International did not condone student violence but was concerned that the confrontation with *Hanchongnyon* had led to a more general crack-down in which students and others were arrested for peaceful activities, unrelated to the demonstrations.

In November human rights activist Suh Jun-sik was arrested for alleged pro-North Korean activities, including the organization of a film festival by *Sarangbang,* a human rights organization. He was a prisoner of conscience. Five other festival organizers were arrested in Seoul, the capital, and Inchon as police attempted to obstruct the event; they were later released without charge. *Sarangbang* had refused to allow government censorship of 24 human rights films from 13 countries.

In February Kim Ha-ki was sentenced to three and a half years' imprisonment for making an unauthorized visit to North Korea and passing on "state secrets" (see *Amnesty International Report 1997*). In a written response to Amnesty International in May, the South Korean Government defended the sentence, saying Kim Ha-ki had visited North Korea out of admiration for the country. It also claimed that "concerning the inevitable restriction of civil rights and freedoms, the National Security Law has its legal basis in the [Universal] Declaration of Human Rights". Kim Ha-ki was a prisoner of conscience. In September Seoul High Court sentenced Buddhist human rights activist Jin Kwan to three and a half years' imprisonment under the National Security Law (see *Amnesty International Report 1997*).

Yun Sok-jin, a student arrested in 1996 for posting a "dangerous" opinion on a computer bulletin board (see *Amnesty International Report 1997*), was acquitted in April.

Dozens of political prisoners arrested in previous years remained in prison. They included prisoner of conscience Park Chang-hee, a university professor, sentenced to three and a half years' imprisonment under the National Security Law in February 1996 for allegedly leaking "state secrets" to North Korean sympathizers in Japan. He had been beaten, deprived of sleep and threatened by investigators from the Agency for National Security Planning after his arrest in April 1995. Another prisoner of conscience, 77-year-old Reverend Kang Hee-nam was serving a two-and-a-half-year prison sentence for alleged pro-North Korean activities. He was believed to be in poor health.

At least 20 political prisoners sentenced to long prison terms on charges of "espionage" during the 1970s and 1980s remained in prison. There was strong evidence that they had been convicted after unfair trials, largely on the basis of confessions obtained under torture. They included Kang Hui-chol, sentenced to life imprisonment in 1986 and held in Taejon Prison. He was reported to be suffering from psychological problems resulting from the effects of torture and long-term imprisonment in virtual isolation. Cho Sang-nok, also held in Taejon Prison, was believed to be in poor physical and mental health after 19 years in prison.

There were further reports that students and others were ill-treated by the police and the Agency for National Security Planning during arrest and interrogation. In February Choi Young-jun of Kyonggi University in Seoul claimed that he and other students were kicked and repeatedly hit by some 20 police officers wielding batons as they were arrested and transported to a police station, where the beatings continued. In May Kim Hye-jun of Hanyang University said she was hit in the face by police officers after she refused to show her identification to police officers who stopped her in the street close to the University. In June Kim Sun-il, a law student at Yonsei University, said he was gagged and beaten as he was arrested by three police officers. It was not known if investigations were initiated into these allegations.

Twenty-three people were executed in December – the first executions to be carried out in South Korea since November 1995. No advance warning of the executions was given to relatives. At the end of the year, 36 prisoners remained under sentence of death. They included Chon Jae-chon, a Chinese seaman of Korean descent, who had been sentenced to death in December 1996 for the murder of 11 other seamen on a Korean fishing vessel. Five other men who had also been sentenced to death in this case had their sentences commuted to life imprisonment after a high court ruling in April.

Throughout the year Amnesty International called for the release of prisoners of conscience and for the National Security Law and labour legislation to be amended in accordance with international standards. The organization called for a review of the cases of long-term political prisoners who had been convicted after unfair trials under past governments; for an end to torture and ill-treatment; and for the abolition of the death penalty. In May Amnesty International published a report, *South Korea: Hidden victims – the long-term political prisoners*. In October Amnesty International published an open letter, *A human rights agenda for the presidential election: open letter to all candidates*, in which it called on all candidates to commit themselves to taking specific steps to protect and promote human rights.

KUWAIT

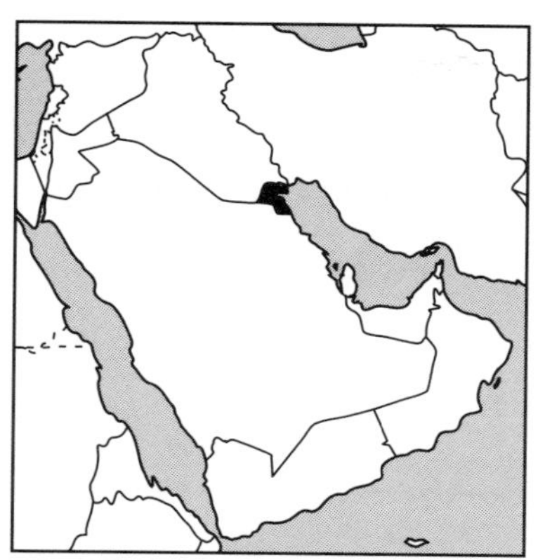

Over 120 people, including prisoners of conscience, continued to serve prison terms imposed after unfair trials since 1991. The status of scores of other political prisoners arrested at the same time remained unclear. Twelve political prisoners, including four prisoners of conscience, were released in an amnesty. There were allegations of ill-treatment of political prisoners. The fate and whereabouts of more than 70 detainees who "disappeared" in custody in 1991 remained unknown. Five people were sentenced to death, two people were executed and 17 others convicted in previous years remained under sentence of death at the end of the year.

A parliamentary committee charged with reviewing the status of over 100,000 stateless people, members of the *Bidun* community (see *Amnesty International Report 1997*), was reported to have stated in May that unless a solution was found, the number of *Bidun* in Kuwait could rise to 200,000 by the year 2006. The UN Special Rapporteur on contemporary forms of racism, racial discrimination, xenophobia and related intolerance presented his report on Kuwait to the 53rd session of the UN Commission on Human Rights. Among other things, he recommended that "...priority should be given to finding a definitive, humane and equitable solution to the problems of *Bidun*, some of whom appear to be stateless in their own country".

More than 120 political prisoners, including at least 12 prisoners of conscience, continued to serve prison terms in Kuwait Central Prison following their conviction on charges of "collaboration" with Iraqi forces during the occupation of Kuwait. They included nine women. The prisoners had been sentenced by the Martial Law Court and the State Security Court following unfair trials held since 1991 (see previous *Amnesty International Reports*). No information was available on scores of other political prisoners arrested in 1991 on suspicion of "collaboration" with Iraqi forces. A communication received from the Human Rights Committee of the Interior Ministry in August denied that there were any political prisoners in Kuwait. It also sought to justify the verdicts handed down by the Martial Law Court and the State Security Court following unfair trials, stating that the government offered legal safeguards for "fair and just trials in accordance with international standards".

Twelve political prisoners, including four prisoners of conscience of Jordanian nationality, were released in March following an amnesty granted by the Amir, al-Shaikh Jaber al-Ahmad al-Sabah. The four prisoners of conscience had been accused of "collaboration" as employees of the Iraqi occupation newspaper *al-Nida'*, and sentenced in 1991 by the Martial Law Court to terms of imprisonment ranging from 10 years to life (see *Amnesty International Report 1992*).

Hussein Qambar 'Ali, who had been declared an apostate and stripped of his civil rights by an Islamic court in May 1996 following his conversion to Christianity (see *Amnesty International Report 1997*), was reported to have returned to Kuwait and declared himself a Muslim.

According to reports, several political prisoners of Jordanian nationality held in Kuwait Central Prison were severely beaten on 22 January, apparently by Kuwaiti law enforcement officials wielding sticks. The beatings reportedly lasted several hours. The incident followed disturbances in the prison on 12 and 14 January, after tighter security measures were introduced in the wake of previous prison escapes and disturbances. At least four prisoners, including Zuhayr 'Omar Saleh and Ma'moun Mohammad Ahmed, were said to have been hospitalized with injuries consistent with beatings. There was no indication of an independent and impartial investigation into these allegations, as required by the UN Convention against Torture and Other Cruel, Inhuman or Degrading Treatment or Punishment, which Kuwait ratified in March 1996.

The fate and whereabouts of more than 70 detainees who "disappeared" in custody in 1991 remained unknown (see previous *Amnesty International Reports*). The Interior Ministry's August communication stated that the authorities were continuing to work towards establishing the whereabouts of these people, and that they would inform Amnesty International of any results.

Two Iranian nationals convicted of drug smuggling, a Saudi Arabian national convicted of murder and rape, and two Kuwaitis convicted of murder were sentenced to death. Two Egyptian nationals, Hassan Mohamed Helal and Hamdi 'Abdal Khalil, were executed in September. They had been convicted of premeditated murder. At least eight political prisoners convicted since 1993 by the State Security Court remained under sentence of death. Nine people convicted by criminal courts in previous years were also believed to be under sentence of death at the end of the year.

Amnesty International welcomed the release of 12 political prisoners, including four prisoners of conscience. Among other things, the organization urged the authorities to release all remaining prisoners of conscience and to carry out a judicial review of the cases of prisoners convicted after unfair trials before the Martial Law Court and the State Security Court. Amnesty International received a communication from the Interior Ministry, but this failed to provide detailed information about cases raised by the organization or to allay its continuing concerns about human rights violations in the country.

KYRGYZSTAN

Four prisoners of conscience were detained. There were allegations of torture and ill-treatment by law enforcement officials. At least four people were sentenced to death and 26 executions were reported.

In October President Askar Akayev signed into law a new Criminal Code to take effect in 1998 which reduced the number of crimes which carry the death penalty to six and decriminalized homosexual acts between consenting adult men.

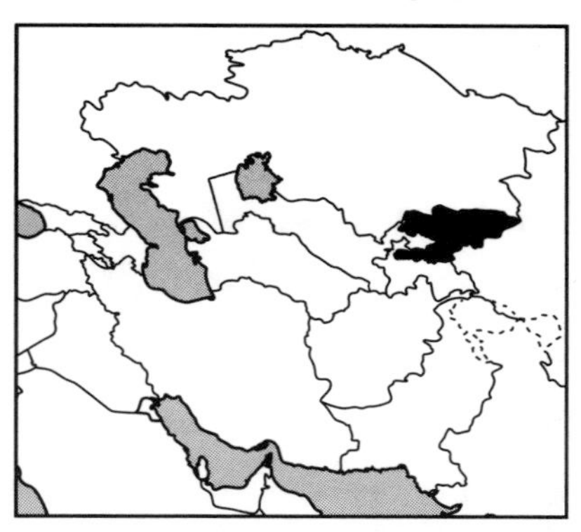

In February Kyrgyzstan acceded to the UN Convention on the Elimination of All Forms of Discrimination against Women, and in September to the UN Convention against Torture and Other Cruel, Inhuman or Degrading Treatment or Punishment.

Four prisoners of conscience were detained during the year. In January Topchubek Turgunaliyev, a leading opposition political activist, was sentenced to 10 years' imprisonment after being convicted of three offences relating to payments he authorized in 1994 as rector of the Humanities University in Bishkek, the capital. He had been detained since December 1996. On appeal in February only the charge of "abuse of authority" was upheld by the Supreme Court which replaced the 10-year prison term with a sentence of four years' confinement in a low-security penitentiary. Topchubek Turgunaliyev was apparently intended to be allowed to live in his home in Bishkek. In early March, however, Topchubek Turgunaliyev was taken to a low-security penitentiary in Arka, Osh Region, several hundred kilometres from Bishkek, apparently because he had taken part in opposition political gatherings in Bishkek following his release. Conditions at the penitentiary were believed to be harsh, and in June Topchubek Turgunaliyev was reported to be in very poor health. He was allowed to return to Bishkek in November. Topchubek Turgunaliyev had previously been held as a prisoner of conscience between December 1995 and April 1996 on charges which included "defaming" and "insulting" the President (see *Amnesty International Report 1997*).

During the February hearing of Topchubek Turgunaliyev's appeal, police detained Tursunbek Akunov, a well-known human rights defender, and Chynybek Aitkulov, an opposition political activist, for their involvement in a picket of the Supreme Court. Chynybek Aitkulov was quickly released on ill-health grounds, but Tursunbek Akunov was sentenced by a district court judge to 24 hours' administrative arrest for "organizing an unsanctioned meeting". The Supreme Court overturned the conviction in March.

Also in March journalist Yrysbek Omurzakov was detained and charged with criminal libel following publication of an article in the newspaper *Res Publika* which criticized the government's privatization policies and alleged corrupt practices in their implementation. The trial, which opened in May in a Bishkek district court, was halted after three days when the judge referred the case for reinvestigation. Yrysbek Omurzakov was released on bail in June after a hearing in the City Court, but the charges against him remained outstanding. At a retrial in a Bishkek district court in September he was sentenced to 30 months' imprisonment for criminal libel. Yrysbek Omurzakov had previously been held as a prisoner of conscience between April and July 1996 on a charge of "defamation" of the President (see *Amnesty International Report 1997*); the two-year suspended sentence passed on him in July 1996 became active as a result of his latest conviction and formed part of his current 30-month sentence. However, he remained at liberty pending appeal and in November he was amnestied by Bishkek City Court.

In May Zamira Sydykova, editor-in-chief of *Res Publika*, and Aleksandr Alyanchikov, a journalist on the paper, were each sentenced to 18 months' imprisonment for criminal libel. The charge related to articles published between 1993 and 1996 which criticized the president of the state-owned gold company and the Governor of Talas Region. In an appeal in June, Bishkek City Court suspended the sentence on Aleksandr Alyanchikov, ordering his release from custody, but banned him from journalism for 18 months. Zamira Sydykova's conviction was left unchanged. In August, she was released by order of the Supreme Court. The Court confirmed the earlier verdict on only one point, that Zamira Sydykova had libelled the Governor of Talas Region in 1993, an offence for which she had apparently already served a sentence imposed in 1995.

There were allegations of torture and ill-treatment by law-enforcement officials. Tursunbek Akunov stated that he was beaten by a police officer during arrest. It was not known whether the allegation was officially investigated. There were reports that four people had filed complaints in July 1996 against officers of the October District police department in Bishkek. The complainants alleged that they had been severely beaten while held in overnight custody. Medical examinations reportedly showed injuries consistent with the allegations, including concussion, cuts and bruising and, in one case, a fractured collar bone. The status of the investigation into the complaints was not known at the end of the year.

At least four death sentences were passed during the year and at least 26 executions were carried out. Full statistics on the application of the death penalty in 1996 became available: 51 death sentences were passed, of which two were commuted, and 15 executions were carried out.

In April Amnesty International wrote to Prime Minister Apas Dzhumagulov urging that human rights principles as set out in international standards be fully incorporated into any new state program on law and order. Also in April, Amnesty International wrote to the authorities expressing concern at a proposed extension in the scope of the death penalty to cover large-scale drug possession, arguing that there was no evidence to suggest that extending the death penalty would solve drug-related crime and calling for any such project to be dropped; the new criminal code adopted in October did not include this as a capital offence. The organization reiterated its calls for commutation of all death sentences and for total abolition of the death penalty.

In May Amnesty International published a report, *Kyrgyzstan: Prisoners of conscience back on trial*, in which it called for the immediate and unconditional release of Topchubek Turgunaliyev and Yrysbek Omurzakov, and for criminal proceedings against Yrysbek Omurzakov to be dropped. The organization expressed concern that charges of defamation continued to be used inappropriately to stifle criticism of public officials, or to intimidate those who voiced legitimate concerns about the actions of public officials (see *Amnesty International Report 1997*).

Amnesty International also expressed concern at continuing reports of serious human rights violations by law enforcement officials, including alleged torture and ill-treatment of criminal suspects.

LAOS

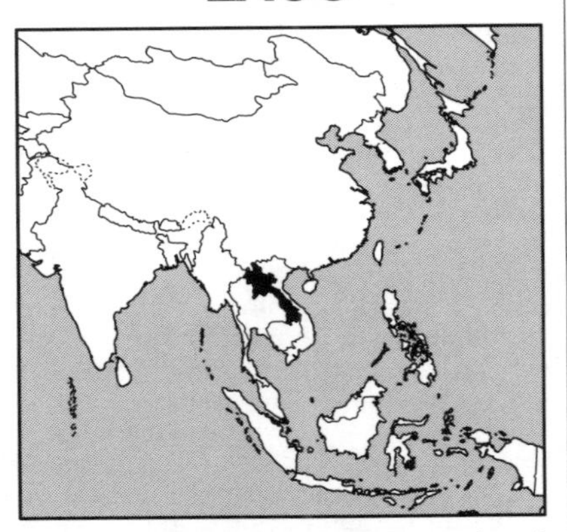

Three prisoners of conscience continued to be held. Three political prisoners continued to serve prison sentences imposed after unfair trials.

The government of President Nouhak Phoumsavan retained severe restrictions on freedom of expression and association. Information about human rights violations was difficult to obtain owing to the lack of official information and censorship of the news media.

In July the Association of South East Asian Nations (ASEAN) granted Laos full membership of the grouping.

Three prisoners of conscience continued to be held together with criminal prisoners in "Re-education" Camp 7 in a remote area of the northeastern province of Houa Phanh. Thongsouk Saysangkhi, Latsami Khamphoui and Feng Sakchittaphong had been sentenced to 14 years' imprisonment in November 1992 after a grossly unfair trial. Despite the official charges against them, it was believed that they had been detained for peacefully criticizing the political and economic system and for advocating a multi-party system (see *Amnesty International Report 1997*). Conditions in the camp remained harsh, with no medical facilities and irregular access to visitors. The three men continued to suffer from ill health requiring medical treatment.

Three political prisoners sentenced to life imprisonment after an unfair trial in 1992 continued to be held at "Re-education" Camp 7. Pangtong Chokbengboun, Bounlu Nammathao and Sing Chantakhoummane had previously been detained for 17 years without charge or trial (see *Amnesty International Report 1997*).

Amnesty International continued to call for the immediate and unconditional release of Thongsouk Saysangkhi, Latsami Khamphoui and Feng Sakchittaphong and urged that while they remained in detention they be treated in accordance with internationally recognized standards, particularly with regard to provision of medical treatment. In May a provincial official was reported to have told journalists that the prison sentences of the three men might be reduced if they "repented".

The organization also continued to call for the fair trial or release from prison of other long-term political prisoners. No response had been received from the authorities by the end of the year.

LEBANON

Scores of political prisoners, including prisoners of conscience, were arrested by the security forces. Some were released without charge after a few days, but most were charged and tried. Several political detainees received trials which fell short of international standards. At least 17 people were sentenced to death and five were executed. A militia allied to Israel continued to hold at least 150 prisoners in south Lebanon. Scores of civilians were killed in military attacks in south Lebanon, some of which appeared to be deliberate attacks on civilian targets or attacks in which no attempt was made to distinguish between civilians and military targets. The fate of thousands of people abducted by armed groups in previous years remained unknown.

In August a cabinet meeting chaired by President Elias al-Hrawi charged the army, the internal security forces, and the Public Prosecutor's office with the task of pursuing "those who call for revolts and civil disobedience". This decision apparently followed a demonstration in the Beqaa' Valley in July organized by Sheikh Subhi al-Tufayli, former Secretary General of *Hizbullah*, Party of God – the main armed group fighting Israel's presence in south Lebanon – who called for a "hunger revolt" and "civil disobedience". Lebanese troops were deployed in the central and northern valleys of the Beqaa' for the first time since the mid-1970s.

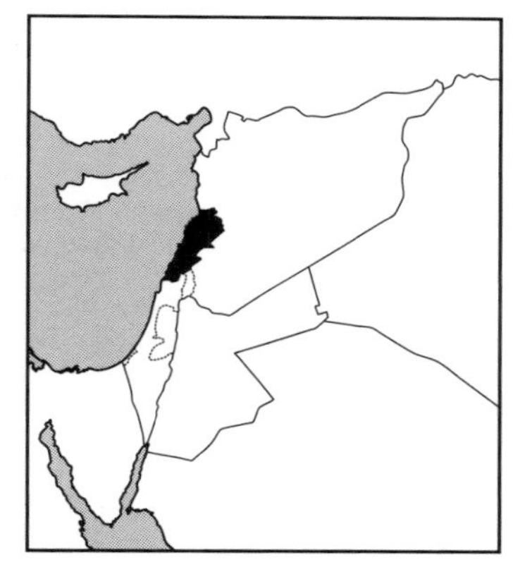

The government granted additional licences to television and radio stations in July bringing the total number authorized under the 1996 law regulating audio-visual media (see *Amnesty International Report 1997*) to six private television and 15 radio stations. However, in September a radio station, *Sawt Beirut* (Voice of Beirut), owned by the opposition group the Lebanese Popular Congress, was closed down after the security forces surrounded the building. Two other stations, the *sawt al-haq* (Voice of Right) radio and *al-Hilal* (Crescent) television, belonging to the Islamic Unification Movement, were forcibly closed after the security forces stormed their building and clashed with protesters.

Conflict continued in south Lebanon in and around Israel's self-declared "security zone" between the Israeli Defence Force (IDF) and Israel's proxy militia, the South Lebanon Army (SLA) on the one hand, and *Hizbullah* on the other. Civilian casualties were reported on both sides of the conflict, but most resulted from attacks mounted by the IDF and SLA in retaliation for *Hizbullah* operations.

With the agreement of the Lebanese Government, Syrian forces remained deployed throughout most of the country.

The International Monitoring Group, formed in 1996 as a result of the "April Understanding" (see *Amnesty International Report 1997*) met 25 times throughout the year.

In April Lebanon acceded to the Convention on the Elimination of All Forms of Discrimination against Women.

In April the UN Human Rights Committee considered Lebanon's second periodic report on its implementation of the International Covenant on Civil and Political Rights (ICCPR). Among other things, the Committee expressed concern about arbitrary arrests, torture and ill-treatment; urged the government to review its capital punishment policy and legislation; and called on Lebanon to bring its legislation into full compliance with the provisions of the ICCPR.

Scores of people, including prisoners of conscience, were arrested on security grounds or for political reasons. Some were released without charge, but most were charged and tried or were standing trial at the end of the year. Elias Abu Rizq, former President of the General Trade Union Confederation (CGTL), was detained for nine days in May, charged with "impersonating" the current head of CGTL and "usurping authority". He was a prisoner of conscience. In July Elias Abu Rizq and Yassir Nehmeh, former Secretary General of the CGTL, were charged with "damaging the prestige of the state abroad and undermining its financial credibility". No date had been determined for their trial by the end of the year.

In December dozens of people were arrested in Beirut, the capital, in connection with a demonstration against the government's banning of a live television interview with the former military leader General Michel 'Aoun. Police and security forces used tear-gas, batons, and water canons to disperse the demonstrators, at least seven of whom were injured. Those detained included Hikmat Dib, an engineer who had been detained in 1994 and reportedly tortured (see *Amnesty International Report 1995*). They were possible prisoners of conscience. All were released the following day.

More than 70 people were arrested in September when the security forces forcibly closed down television and radio stations belonging to the Islamic Unification Movement in Tripoli, north Lebanon. Two men, Khaled al-Wazze and 'Abd al-Hadi al-Masri, died in clashes between the security forces and the members and sympathizers of the Islamic Unification Movement who were protesting against the closure. The authorities launched an investigation into the circumstances of the deaths. Forty-eight of those arrested were charged with obstructing the security forces and appeared before the military court in Beirut in September. The court acquitted 17, fined six, and transferred one to a juvenile court. 'Abd al-Nasser Qaddur and Bilal al-Zu'bi were sentenced to prison terms of two and three weeks, respectively, and the remaining 22 were sentenced to up to five days' imprisonment.

Derar al-Karmi, a Jordanian national working for a Beirut hotel, was reportedly arrested by Syrian military intelligence in January and taken to Syria where he was held incommunicado for three weeks before being released without charge or trial. The reasons for his arrest were not disclosed by the Lebanese or the Syrian authorities.

Ahmad Hamad, a medical doctor and suspected member of the pro-Iraqi wing of the Arab Socialist *Ba'th* Party, was believed to have been arrested in 'Akkar, north Lebanon, by Syrian military intelligence and subsequently transferred to Syria. His whereabouts remained unknown at the end of the year.

Rafiq Abu Younes, who had been detained in Syria since 1994 for his alleged links with the pro-Iraqi wing of the Arab Socialist *Ba'th* Party, was released in April. Hassan Gharib, Zafer al-Muqadam and Hani Shu'aib, Lebanese nationals detained in Syria for alleged links with the pro-Iraqi wing of the Arab Socialist *Ba'th* Party, remained in detention (see *Amnesty International Reports 1996* and *1997*). About 200 Lebanese detained in Syria in previous years remained held at the end of the year (see **Syria** entry).

Several political prisoners were sentenced after trials which fell short of international fair trial standards. In January Antoinette Chahin, a student who was alleged to have been involved in the assassination of the priest Sam'an al-Khoury in 1992, was sentenced to death, commuted to life imprisonment with hard labour. According to the court's verdict, the killing of Sam'an al-Khoury had been planned and carried out by the Lebanese Forces, of which Antoinette Chahin was allegedly a member. Other defendants, including Sa'd Jibra'il, Jihad Abi Ramia, and Rashid Daw, were each sentenced to 12 years' imprisonment with hard labour. Two others, Antoinette Chahin's brother, Jean Chahin, and George Bakhous, were sentenced to death *in absentia*. The trial was seriously flawed. The convictions were apparently based on confessions by some of the defendants which were allegedly extracted under torture and were retracted in court. An appeal filed by the lawyers of Antoinette Chahin and other defendants was upheld by the Court of Cassation. A retrial scheduled to start in November was postponed to February 1998.

The trial of 20 people charged with the killing of Sheikh Nizar al-Halabi, leader of the *al-Ahbash* movement (see *Amnesty International Reports 1996* and *1997*) concluded in January before the Justice Council. The Justice Council, whose verdicts are final, sentenced four people to death and 16 others to sentences ranging from one year to life imprisonment. Of those sentenced to death, three were executed (see below). The fourth, Ahmad 'Abd al-Karim al-Sa'di (also known as Abu Mahjan), leader of *'Usbat al-Ansar*, the group which allegedly perpetrated the killing, was sentenced *in absentia*. Twenty members of *'Usbat al-Ansar* were also referred to the military court on charges "of terrorist attacks and blowing up businesses selling alcohol in Sidon since 1993".

In April the Military Court of Appeal upheld the verdict, passed in 1995 by the military court in Beirut, on Hanan Yasin and her co-defendants for their role in a 1994 bombing which killed three people, including two members of *Hizbullah* (see *Amnesty International Reports 1996* and *1997*), but reduced the sentence imposed on Hanan Yasin from 15 to 12 years' imprisonment.

The trials of seven people accused of collaboration with Israel took place in May before the military court in Beirut. Among the defendants were Tony Shamieh, a journalist arrested in March; the brothers Wisam, Marwan, and Jirjis Khawand; Tony Abu Musa; Elias al-Halit; and Jean Saliba, who was tried *in absentia*. Most were former members of the Guardians of the Cedar Party. Sentences imposed ranged from one to 15 years' imprisonment. Most of the defendants claimed that they had been beaten by the military intelligence interrogators to extract confessions. No independent investigation was initiated into these or other allegations of torture reported during the year.

At least 17 people were sentenced to death, most convicted of murder, including Ahmad Rida Yasin, who was sentenced to death for murder by the Court of Cassation in October. Five people were executed. Two Palestinians, Munir 'Abbud and Khalid Muhammad Hamid and a Lebanese, Ahmad al-Kasm, were executed in March after being convicted of the killing of Sheikh Nizar al-Halabi (see above). Muhammad Mahmoud Kour and Hasan Jamal 'Attiyah, an Egyptian, were executed in March and April respectively; both had been convicted of murder.

In south Lebanon dozens of people were arrested by the SLA or the IDF and were either held without charge or trial at the Khiam detention centre, or transferred to Israel (see **Israel and the Occupied Territories** entry). Some were released after weeks or months in detention in Khiam. Ahmad Kamil Sa'id, a student, was arrested by the IDF and held in Khiam for a month before being released. Roger Nahra, a journalist, and three of his relatives were arrested by the IDF in July. Roger Nahra and two of his relatives were released after five weeks in Khiam, but Michel Nahra, a retired policeman, remained detained at the end of the year. Other Lebanese detainees in Khiam included 12-year-old Mazen 'Abdallah. A total of 53 detainees were released from Khiam during the year. At least 150 prisoners, most of them suspected members of armed groups opposed to the Israeli presence in Lebanon, or their relatives, continued to be held by the SLA outside any legal framework in Khiam at the end of the year. Visits by the International Committee of the Red Cross and by prisoners' families were suspended by the SLA in September.

During the year scores of Lebanese civilians were killed in military attacks in south Lebanon, some of which appeared to be deliberate attacks on civilian targets or attacks in which no attempt was made to distinguish between civilians and military targets. In August three civilians were killed, including two children of an SLA commander, in Jezzine, south Lebanon, as a result of bombardment and shelling; *Hizbullah* denied responsibility. Seven civilians were killed and 36 wounded when a Jezzine-based militia allied to the SLA retaliated by shelling residential areas of Sidon in what appeared to be a deliberate attack on civilian areas. In November at least seven civilians were killed and others wounded when mortar shells were fired at the village of Beit Lif in south Lebanon in an attack for which no group had claimed responsibility by the end of the year. Scores of civilians were killed in south Lebanon throughout the year, mostly as a result of IDF and SLA shelling.

The fate of thousands of people, including Palestinians, Lebanese and other nationals abducted in Lebanon by armed groups since 1975, remained unknown.

Amnesty International delegates visited Lebanon and raised the organization's concerns with government. In April Amnesty International received a response from the Lebanese authorities to its memorandum, submitted in September 1996 (see *Amnesty International Report 1997*), which provided information on specific cases, but did not address the organization's substantive concerns.

Amnesty International published *Israel/South Lebanon: Israel's forgotten hostages – Lebanese detainees in Israel and Khiam Detention Centre* in July; and *Lebanon: Human rights developments and violations* in October, which highlighted human rights violations since the end of the war in 1990. In December Amnesty International received an official response to its report from the Lebanese Government which addressed some aspects of the report and stressed that Lebanese laws and the Constitution provide for "fundamental human rights guarantees". However, the response failed to address the organization's substantive concerns.

Throughout the year Amnesty International urged the authorities to release prisoners of conscience, guarantee fair trial for political prisoners, investigate allegations of torture, and commute death sentences.

LESOTHO

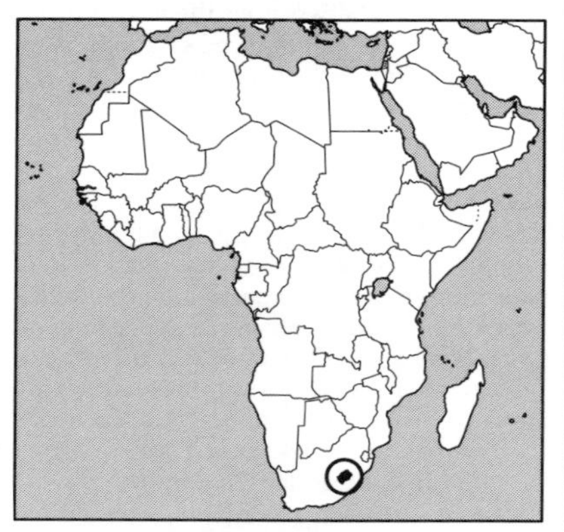

Journalists were threatened and harassed. Two police officers were killed in circumstances suggesting extrajudicial execution. There were allegations of torture and ill-treatment of criminal suspects by police. One prisoner was sentenced to death. There were no executions.

A power struggle between two factions of the ruling Basotholand Congress Party (BCP) culminated on 7 June in Prime Minister Ntsu Mokhehle and his supporters splitting from the BCP. The resulting breakaway Lesotho Congress for Democracy (LCD) formed a new government, retaining Ntsu Mokhehle as Prime Minister. The remaining BCP members of parliament disputed the constitutionality of their opponents' action, but *de facto* became the minority party in parliament.

On 16 February a police mutiny in support of nine colleagues facing arrest in connection with the fatal shootings in Maseru Central Police Station in 1995 (see *Amnesty International Report 1996*) was suppressed when the government deployed the army. Scores of police officers were arrested. Most were released without charge (see below).

To mark the coronation of King Letsie III in October, 387 prisoners were released under a royal pardon.

Some journalists covering political developments were publicly criticized by officials and subjected to other forms of harassment by members of the security forces. They included Candi Ramainoane, editor-in-chief of the privately owned Sesotho-language newspaper *MoAfrika*, Khutliso Sekoati of *Mopheme* and Christopher Shale of *Mleletsi oa Basotho*. In September armed police enforced a two-week ban on coverage of parliamentary proceedings.

Sergeant Monyatsi Senekane – one of the nine police officers wanted in connection with the Maseru Central Police Station shootings – and another police officer were killed in circumstances suggesting they may have been extrajudicially executed. Sergeant Senekane was shot dead on the night of 15 February by soldiers who reportedly ambushed his vehicle in a Maseru suburb. Earlier, on 31 January, Trooper Nthako, reportedly a sympathizer of the nine, had been shot dead at his home by unknown assailants. The outcome of any investigations into the circumstances surrounding these deaths was not known by the end of the year.

In June the brother of Sergeant Senekane, army private Mokitimi Senekane, and police sergeant Thabo Tsukulu were charged with treason, in connection with an alleged petition calling upon the King to resolve conflict between the police and the army and obtain the release of the police mutineers. In the weeks preceding his arrest, Mokitimi Senekane had been pressing the police authorities for information concerning the death of his brother. In December Attorney Haae Phoofolo, the lawyer representing the two accused, was arrested and charged with conspiring with his clients to commit treason. He was later released on bail. There was concern that the charges against Attorney Phoofolo might be politically motivated, aimed at hampering the defence of Mokitimi Senekane, Thabo Tsukulu and other police officers whom he was representing. No trial date had been set by the end of the year.

Thirty-three police officers were scheduled to be tried in February 1998 on charges relating to the mutiny. By the end of the year, six of the accused, whose imminent arrests had provoked the mutiny, had still not been furnished with details of the charges against them nor committed for trial in relation to the 1995 killings.

Allegations of the torture and ill-treatment of criminal suspects persisted. In one incident in the middle of the year, Leabua Thaabe, who was mistakenly identified as a wanted suspect, was taken to Maseru police cells where police stripped him naked and subjected him to beatings and torture by suffocation. He was released when police realized that he had been wrongly arrested.

Of four prisoners sentenced to death in 1996 (see *Amnesty International Report 1997*), two had their convictions overturned and two had their sentences reduced on appeal. One prisoner convicted of murder in August and sentenced to death was awaiting the outcome of his appeal at the end of the year. There were no executions.

Amnesty International made appeals on behalf of journalists subjected to harassment or threats. The organization also called for investigations into cases from previous years which remained unresolved, including those involving excessive and at times lethal use of force by police, and cases of torture and deaths in custody.

LIBERIA

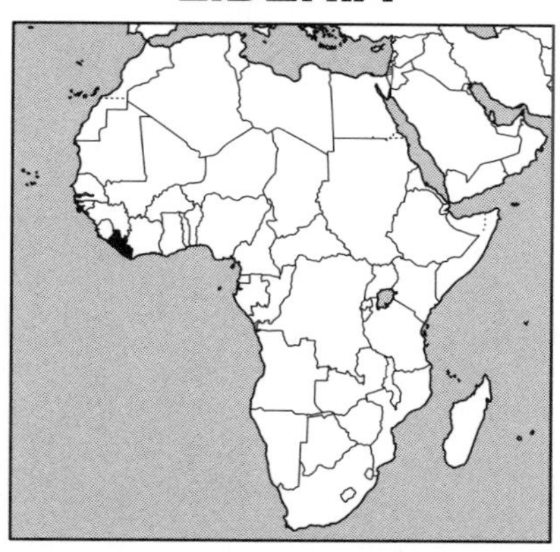

At least nine possible prisoners of conscience were briefly detained. There were reports of torture and ill-treatment by both Liberian police and regional peacekeeping forces. At least one person died in custody, allegedly as a result of ill-treatment. An opposition figure and three relatives were reportedly extrajudicially executed.

The security situation in the country improved during the year and there was a corresponding decline in human rights abuses committed by warring factions. However, outside the capital, Monrovia, there were no judicial institutions in place.

The peace agreement which ended Liberia's seven-year civil war laid down a timetable for disarmament, demobilization and general elections (see *Amnesty International Reports 1996* and *1997*). Although there was progress in each of these areas, the timetable was not maintained. To support the implementation of the agreement, the Economic Community of West African States (ECOWAS) Cease-fire Monitoring Group (ECOMOG) deployed about 11,000 troops in most parts of the country.

Elections originally scheduled for May were postponed until July. Thirteen political parties contested the elections, three led by former leaders of warring factions. During the election campaign, there were numerous reports of intimidation and harassment by former combatants, particularly in the north and the southeast of the country and by former members of the National Patriotic Front of Liberia (NPFL). Both were accused of threatening civilians and some returning refugees. Former NPFL leader Charles G. Taylor and his party, the National Patriotic Party, won more than two thirds of the vote. In August he was sworn in as President, replacing Ruth Perry, who had been Chairperson of the Council of State. Liberia's third National Transitional Government was dissolved. The 1985 Constitution was reinstated and the Supreme Court reconstituted.

Voluntary disarmament, which had started in November 1996, was completed on 7 February 1997. However, several caches of weapons were found after the deadline. More than 20,300 combatants, including 4,306 minors, were disarmed from an estimated total of 33,000. ECOMOG had originally estimated the number of combatants to be 60,000 (see *Amnesty International Report 1997*), but it later claimed that the total had been exaggerated by former faction leaders.

The repatriation of refugees, due to be completed by 21 January, was also delayed. In the southeast, ECOMOG reported that former NPFL combatants were hampering the return of refugees. During the election campaign, the various political parties assisted in the repatriation of about 50,000 refugees from neighbouring West African countries to participate in the elections. According to the UN High Commissioner for Refugees (UNHCR), there were still about 600,000 Liberian refugees in neighbouring

West African countries at the end of the year. The majority came from Lofa and Nimba counties in northern Liberia. In May UNHCR embarked on an 18-month voluntary repatriation program. However, adequate legal structures were not yet in place to address human rights issues which might arise from their return.

In October the government established a National Human Rights Commission to promote and protect human rights in Liberia. It had not started work by the end of the year. There was concern that the Commission had no powers to initiate investigations and that it was specifically prohibited from influencing legislation.

The mandate of the UN Observer Mission in Liberia (UNOMIL) expired in September; all UNOMIL military observers and all but one of the human rights monitors left the country. The UN agreed with President Taylor that it would provide advisory and technical assistance to the Liberian government on issues relating to post-conflict peace building; two human rights officers were assigned to a UN Peace-building Support Office.

ECOMOG continued to perform the function of maintaining law and order, but was responsible for abuses (see below). In August ECOWAS extended ECOMOG's peacekeeping role in Liberia until August 1998, although it was not clear whether President Taylor had agreed to this extension.

Relations with neighbouring Sierra Leone deteriorated during the year. In October the government sealed its borders with Sierra Leone and sent troops to the border area.

Journalists were harassed and subjected to short-term arrest (see below) after covering stories of a politically sensitive nature. One newspaper with a reputation for critical analysis, *New Democrat*, was refused permission to relaunch itself, apparently on the grounds that it had not submitted its request in time.

At least nine possible prisoners of conscience were arrested and held without charge. In September Philip Wesseh, managing director of an independent newspaper, *The Inquirer*, questioned police methods in dealing with alleged armed robbers. He was arrested and interrogated for several hours. In December, seven journalists with *The Inquirer* were taken to the President's residence, the Executive Mansion, in connection with an article about the killing of Samuel Dokie (see below). They were questioned for two hours by members of the Special Security Services, who reportedly told them that some journalists might be killed if they did not improve their work. Later in December Alex Redd, a journalist with *Radio Ducor*, was abducted by plainclothes security officials, apparently in connection with interviews he had carried out while covering Samuel Dokie's funeral. He was abducted some 150 kilometres outside the capital, Monrovia, but was found two days later in police custody in the city. He had reportedly been beaten and bore knife wounds. His captors had apparently abandoned him in the capital with his arms still tied behind his back and he had been handed over to the police. He was held for questioning and charged with treason, but after six days in formal police custody the charges were reduced to felony and he was released on bail.

There were reports of torture and ill-treatment by both Liberian police and ECOMOG soldiers. Between February and May, ECOMOG forces undertook cordon-and-search operations to find hidden weapons. More than 70 people were arrested and held in secret detention camps on suspicion of possessing weapons. Most of them were tortured or ill-treated. In February an ECOMOG patrol arrested 25 suspected former combatants in Grand Cape Mount county, took them to Monrovia and held them in a secret cell at the ECOMOG base. They were reportedly beaten with electric wire. Also in February, four dock workers suspected of being former United Liberation Movement of Liberia for Democracy–Johnson branch (ULIMO-J) fighters were arrested in Sayontown and taken to the ECOMOG base in Monrovia. There, three ECOMOG soldiers reportedly beat them with wire on the back, shoulders and legs and kicked them. All those detained were believed to have been released after 14 March, when Alhaji Kromah, former leader of the defunct ULIMO–Kromah Branch (ULIMO-K), apologized for an arms cache found in his home.

In May ECOMOG soldiers based in Fendu travelled to Grand Cape Mount county to conduct a cordon-and-search operation at Lajoy goldmine. During interrogation, six former fighters and three civilians were reportedly beaten with wooden sticks and electric wire and one civilian was reportedly slashed with razor blades. One former combatant died during the night following the beating. The other victims reportedly had swollen faces, injured eyes, slash wounds and hearing problems.

In September Liberian police and ECOMOG soldiers assaulted a group of some 500 employees of the Firestone plantation company in Harbel, near Monrovia, who were demonstrating peacefully for the release of four colleagues held by the company's security staff. Police and soldiers reportedly beat the workers with batons and gun butts, then opened fire, injuring seven people.

Four people were killed in circumstances which suggested that they may have been extrajudicially executed. In November Samuel Dokie, former deputy speaker of the recently dissolved transitional legislative assembly and a former minister of Internal Affairs, his wife, Janet Dokie, and two other relatives were arrested by officials of the Special Security Service. In early December their bodies were found in a burned car; Samuel Dokie had reportedly been beheaded. Five people, including two senior security officials, were arrested in connection with the deaths and were in custody at the end of the year awaiting charges. Samuel Dokie had been a close associate of Charles Taylor within the NPFL until 1994, when they became political rivals.

In May Amnesty International delegates visited Liberia and met the Council of State, ministers of the National Transitional Government, leaders of political parties, and of former warring factions, and representatives from UN agencies and non-governmental organizations. Amnesty International expressed concern about human rights issues, including the future of human rights in Liberia, both during and after the elections, and impunity. They stressed the necessity of bringing to justice those responsible for past human rights abuses.

In October Amnesty International delegates again visited Liberia, where they launched a report, *Liberia: Time to take human rights seriously – placing human rights on the national agenda*. The report made specific recommendations which the organization believed could form the basis of long-term protection of human rights in Liberia, by creating a human rights culture and building institutions to uphold the rule of law and international human rights standards. In particular, the report urged the new government to investigate as a matter of urgency human rights abuses which took place during the civil war.

LIBYA

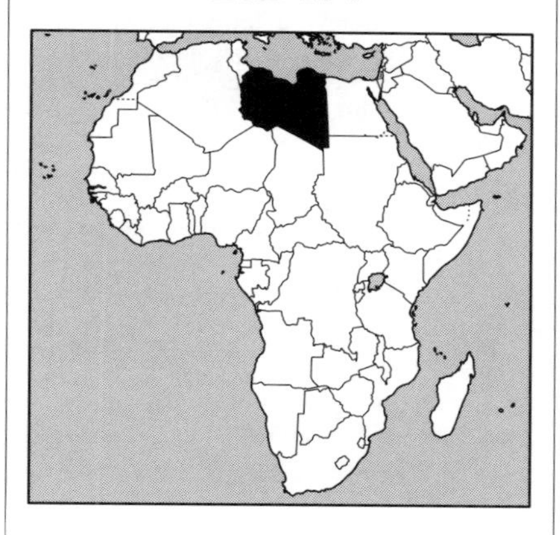

Five prisoners of conscience arrested in 1973 continued to serve life sentences. Hundreds of political prisoners, including possible prisoners of conscience, remained in detention. Some were detained without charge or trial, others continued to be held despite acquittal by courts or following grossly unfair trials. Scores of people were arrested in connection with their religious or political activities. Torture and ill-treatment were reported. At least eight people were executed.

The UN sanctions on Libya (see previous *Amnesty International Reports*), imposed in 1992 in connection with the 1988 bombing of a US passenger airline, remained in force.

In March a new law came into force authorizing collective punishment for communities deemed to have protected or helped those responsible for "terrorism", acts of violence, unauthorized possession of weapons or sabotaging "people's power". Under the new law, which also provides for the punishment of those who fail to report such "criminals", the authorities could cut off water and electricity supplies, deprive villages or tribes of subsidized food, petrol and public services, and transfer development projects to other parts of the country.

An investigation into the bombing of a plane over Niger in 1989, which resulted in the deaths of all 170 passengers, was concluded in May. Six Libyan nationals, including the brother-in-law of Colonel Mu'ammar al-Gaddafi, Head of State, were charged in connection with the bombing and were due to be tried *in absentia* in France in 1998. In November, five people – two Palestinians, a former Libyan diplomat and two Germans – went on trial in Berlin for their role in the 1986 bomb attack on a West Berlin discotheque frequented by off-duty US servicemen in which three people were killed and about 230 injured. Prosecutors in the case stated that the attack had been carried out on direct orders from the Libyan intelligence service and was aimed at US military personnel.

In April Libyan soldiers dismantled a camp on the border between Libya and Egypt, where around 250 Palestinian refugees had been stranded since they were forcibly expelled from Libya in 1995 (see *Amnesty International Reports 1996* and *1997*). The Palestinians were believed to have been forcibly relocated to another camp near Tubruq inside Libya.

Five prisoners of conscience, who were arrested in 1973 and convicted of membership of the prohibited Islamic Liberation Party, continued to serve life sentences in Abu Salim Prison in Tripoli (see previous *Amnesty International Reports*). They included 'Ali Muhammad al-Qajiji and Muhammad al-Sadiq al-Tarhouni.

Hundreds of political prisoners arrested in previous years, including possible prisoners of conscience, remained held without charge or trial. Rashid 'Abd al-Hamid al-'Urfia, a law graduate, remained held without charge or trial in Abu Salim Prison in Tripoli. He was reportedly arrested with 20 others in 1982 on suspicion of founding an Islamist opposition group. All those arrested with him were released following a general amnesty in 1988.

Muhammad Suleiman al-Qaid, a university lecturer, remained in detention in Abu Salim Prison without charge or trial. He had been arrested in 1991 along with three other suspected opponents of the government; all were possible prisoners of conscience.

Scores of other detainees remained held despite having been tried and acquitted by courts. Others continued to serve prison sentences imposed in previous years after grossly unfair trials. They included Fakhri Younis al-Fitouri, his father, Younis 'Issa al-Fitouri, and his brother, 'Omran al-Fitouri, who were among a group of 23 men accused of opposition activities and sentenced to life imprisonment in 1991 following trials which failed to meet basic requirements for fair trial as set out in international standards and despite having previously been acquitted of the charges against them owing to lack of evidence.

Jum'a Ahmad 'Ateyqa, a possible prisoner of conscience who had been arbitrarily detained despite his acquittal in 1990 (see *Amnesty International Report 1997*), was released in April.

There were unconfirmed reports that Nurya Ahmad al-Firjani, a possible prisoner of conscience who had been arrested in 1995 along with her six-month-old daughter, was released at the end of 1996 (see *Amnesty International Report 1997*).

Scores of people, including possible prisoners of conscience, were detained during the year in connection with their political or religious beliefs or activities. Many were believed to have been arrested in connection with their suspected involvement with Islamist opposition groups and were thought to remain detained at the end of the year. They included Mohammad Salem, a mechanical engineer, and Salem Mu'ammar, a businessman, who were arrested in Benghazi in June. Their whereabouts remained unknown at the end of the year.

Torture and ill-treatment were reported. Reports suggested that conditions inside Abu Salim Prison amounted to cruel, inhuman or degrading treatment. For example, political prisoners and detainees were said to have frequently been subjected to sleep deprivation by the repeated, loud and prolonged broadcast of political speeches. No investigations were known to have been carried out into the killings which resulted from the mutiny in Abu Salim Prison in July 1996 (see *Amnesty International Report 1997*) or into allegations of torture and ill-treatment or into deaths in custody in previous years.

The fate and whereabouts of Ayman Salim Mohammad Dababish, a Palestinian who "disappeared" following his arrest in September 1996, remained unknown (see *Amnesty International Report 1997*).

In September Egyptian and Libyan government officials denied any responsibility in the "disappearance" of Mansur Kikhiya despite continuing allegations that Egyptian agents had staged his abduction in 1993. Mansur Kikhiya was handed over to the Libyan authorities and allegedly executed in January 1994. The Egyptian authorities stated that they were prepared to reopen the investigation if any new or additional information was made available. Mansur Kikhiya, a prominent Libyan opposition leader and human rights activist, "disappeared" in Egypt in December 1993 (see previous *Amnesty International Reports*). No new information came to light regarding the fate of Jaballah Hamed Matar and 'Izzat Youssef al-Maqrif, who both "disappeared" in Cairo, Egypt, in March 1990.

In June an inquest held in the United Kingdom into the murder in London of 'Ali Mohammad 'Abu-Zaid, a well-known Libyan opposition activist, recorded a verdict of unlawful killing. 'Ali Muhammad 'Abu-Zaid was found stabbed to death in his shop in London in November 1995 in circumstances suggesting that he may have been extrajudicially executed by agents working for, or on behalf of, the Libyan authorities.

At least eight people were executed. Six senior army officers, including Colonel Miftah Qarrum al-Wirfalli, and two civilians were executed in January. All had been arrested in the aftermath of a rebellion by army units around the cities of Misrata and Bani Walid in October 1993 (see previous *Amnesty International Reports*) and charged with "passing defence secrets to foreign states [the United States of America]" and membership of the National Front for the Salvation of Libya, an opposition group in exile. At least five others tried in the case were sentenced to prison terms ranging from five to 20 years.

In April there were reports that at least 10 Tunisian nationals, including the families of four, all suspected members or supporters of *al-Nahda*, an Islamist group banned in Tunisia, were forcibly returned to Tunisia, allegedly as a result of their suspected anti-Tunisian Government activities, where most faced serious human rights violations.

Amnesty International continued to call for the immediate and unconditional release of all prisoners of conscience and for all other political prisoners to be granted fair and prompt trials or released. The organization also called on the Egyptian authorities to carry out a new inquiry into the "disappearance" of Mansur Kikhiya in light of the new allegations of Egypt's involvement.

Amnesty International publicly condemned the execution of eight men in January and urged the authorities to work towards the total abolition of the death penalty. In June Amnesty International published a report, *Libya: Gross human rights violations amid secrecy and isolation*, which detailed the wide range of human rights violations and called on the authorities to implement the recommendations set out in the report. No response had been received by the end of the year.

MACAO

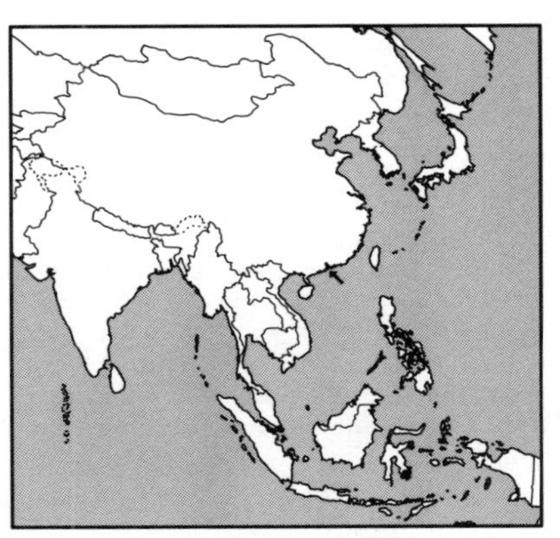

There was continuing uncertainty about nationality arrangements for residents, including refugees, after the handover to China.

The handover to China of the neighbouring territory of Hong Kong in June highlighted the need for the Portuguese administration to pursue administrative reforms ahead of Macao's own return to Chinese control on 20 December 1999. In May Chinese officials expressed concern at the slowness of some of the preparations for the handover. In particular they were concerned that many of Macao's laws and official documents had not yet been translated into Chinese or made available in bilingual form. There were also continuing delays in ensuring that court proceedings could be bilingual. Also in May China highlighted its concern over the slow rate at which senior civil service positions held by colonial administrators were being devolved to Macao residents.

The year was marked by an upsurge in violent crime, attributed mainly to conflicts among criminal gangs. In July the *Leal Senado* (legislative assembly) passed legislation reinforcing penalties for gang membership and creating new offences aimed at curbing gang activities.

In April the UN Human Rights Committee considered a report presented by Portugal on the implementation in Macao of the International Covenant on Civil and Political Rights (ICCPR). The Committee reaffirmed that it expected to receive and review reports on the implementation of the ICCPR in Macao beyond the 1999 handover, even though China had not yet ratified it. The Committee welcomed the formal abolition of the death penalty in the 1996 Criminal Law; it expressed concern that "firm arrangements" on the nationality of Macao residents after 1999 had not yet been agreed with China.

Uncertainty remained about the situation of immigrants after the handover, including people granted asylum in Macao and illegal immigrants from China. In particular, it was unclear whether East Timorese refugees in Macao, most of whom were eligible to apply for a Portuguese passport, would be authorized to remain in Macao after 1999. Despite a policy of returning illegal Chinese immigrants to China, many remained in Macao for long periods; they had no entitlement to social services. Two Chinese immigrants were briefly detained in March when an illegal school for immigrant children was closed.

MACEDONIA
(THE FORMER YUGOSLAV REPUBLIC OF)

A man sentenced to three years' imprisonment for "insulting" the national symbols of the state was a prisoner of conscience. Four ethnic Albanians were sentenced to long terms of imprisonment after unfair trials but they remained free pending appeal; at least two might be prisoners of conscience if imprisoned. Hundreds of people, mainly ethnic Albanians, were tortured or ill-treated by police. One man died as a result of ill-treatment and two others may also have been unlawfully killed by police.

Early in the year a number of municipal councils in the west of the country passed regulations making it obligatory to display the flags of the national minorities, mainly Albanian and Turkish, on municipal buildings. The opposition Albanian Party of Democratic Prosperity had taken control of the councils in local elections of November 1996. During the year, the party was renamed the *Partia Demokratike Shqiptare* (PDSH), Democratic Party of Albanians. The government challenged the regulations and referred them to the Constitutional Court, which held that the regulations were unconstitutional. On 8 July the government passed a new law regulating the use of the flags of the national minorities. Although it allowed the use of the flags for private purposes, the new law restricted their use on public buildings to public holidays. That night, police removed the flags from the municipal building in Gostivar and detained the mayor. Violent confrontations followed on 9 July between police and demonstrators.

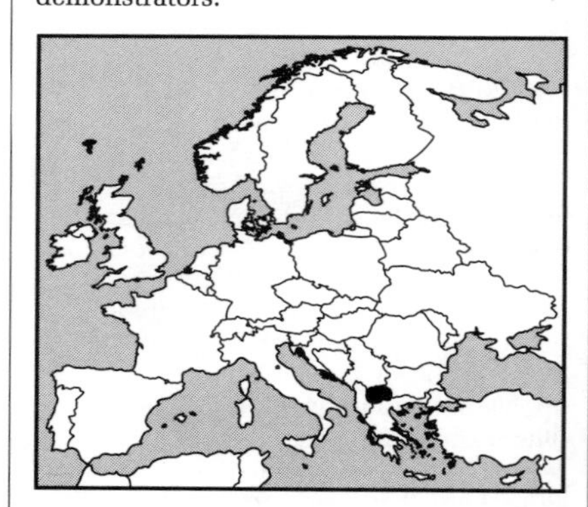

In March a law was passed establishing the National Ombudsman, whose mandate included the investigation of human rights violations. However, the Ombudsman's office was not fully in operation by the end of the year. In April a new Code of Criminal Procedure came into effect which strengthened the rights of those detained or questioned by police, but these were not respected in practice.

In April Macedonia ratified the European Convention for the Protection of Human Rights and Fundamental Freedoms, and Protocol No. 6 concerning abolition of the death penalty. In June Macedonia ratified the European Convention for the Prevention of Torture and Inhuman or Degrading Treatment or Punishment and its Protocols Nos. 1 and 2.

The mandate of the peacekeeping force, the UN Preventive Deployment Force (UNPREDEP), was extended twice during the year to expire in August 1998. The mandate of the Organization for Security and Co-operation in Europe Spillover Mission was also extended.

In August Ičo Gavrilov was sentenced to three years' imprisonment for "damaging the reputation of the Republic of Macedonia" under Article 178 of the Criminal Law. He deliberately trod on the national flag at National Day celebrations on 2 August. He was a prisoner of conscience.

In September, two leaders of the local authorities in Gostivar, both ethnic Albanians, were convicted of "failing to carry out a judicial decision" following the removal of the national minorities' flags from municipal buildings on 9 July and the clashes that ensued. The trial was unfair. Defence lawyers were denied unsupervised communication with their clients during much of their time in custody, and were denied adequate opportunity to prepare the defence. Refik Dauti, President of the municipal council, was sentenced to three years' imprisonment and, if imprisoned, might be a prisoner of conscience. Rufi Osmani, the mayor, who was also convicted of further more serious charges of "inciting national hatred" and "organizing resistance", was sentenced to 13 years and eight months' imprisonment. They remained free pending appeal at the end of the year. In October the President of Tetovo Municipality was sentenced to two and a half years' imprisonment on similar charges. He would be a prisoner of conscience if imprisoned.

Hundreds of people were tortured or ill-treated by police. Most of the victims were ethnic Albanians and some were ethnic Turks who were beaten in the town of Gostivar during or following the 9 July protests. The protests were violent, involving the use of firearms, petrol-bombs, bricks and metal bars by the demonstrators, causing injuries to police officers, nine of whom needed hospital treatment. However, the police severely beat or otherwise ill-treated many people who were not using violence, who had no connection with the demonstration, or who were not offering any resistance at the time of the ill-treatment. The victims included minors as young as 13 and elderly men and women. One of the victims, Milaim Dauti, died in hospital as a result of head injuries sustained during beating by the police. The beatings generally occurred in the streets, in police stations and during house searches. Among those beaten was 61-year-old Adem Rexhepi, whose injuries included concussion and several broken ribs. His wife Latifi was also hit on the head in their home and his son was also beaten during arrest and detention. A smaller number of people were arrested in Tetovo in connection with the demonstrations. Some men from both Gostivar and Tetovo, mainly political activists, were taken to police stations in other towns and ill-treated. For example, Arsim Sinani, president of the youth branch of the PDSH, was arrested in Tetovo and taken to Skopje where he was systematically beaten during several hours of interrogation. He was released without charge. Relatives and a lawyer were denied information about his whereabouts following his detention.

At least 200 people received hospital treatment following the 9 July protests, the majority as a consequence of ill-treatment by police.

There were other reports of ill-treatment by police of Macedonians and members of minorities other than the ethnic Albanians. In July Pepi Krstanov, who declared himself to be an ethnic Bulgarian, was reportedly beaten in Struga. His teeth were broken and he sustained other injuries.

Two ethnic Albanian demonstrators died of bullet wounds during the July demonstrations. They may have been unlawfully killed, but the authorities appeared not to have investigated their deaths fully or that of Milaim Dauti (see above).

In July Amnesty International appealed to the authorities to carry out thorough, impartial and independent investigations into the deaths and injuries of demonstrators in Gostivar. It asked the authorities to remind police of international standards on the use of force and firearms and to ensure that detainees were treated in accordance with international human rights standards.

MALAWI

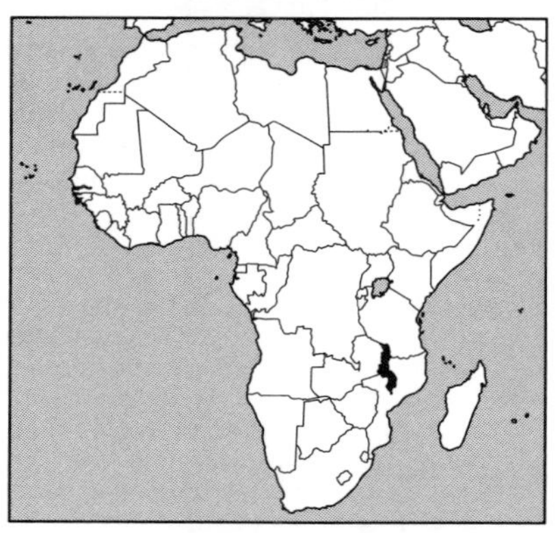

Trade unionists were arrested during a nationwide strike, many of whom were prisoners of conscience. Harsh prison conditions led to more than 100 deaths in custody. The President commuted all death sentences in July and pledged not to carry out any executions.

In February Malawi's former President for life Hastings Kamuzu Banda, his companion Cecilia Kadzamira, opposition Malawi Congress Party (MCP) figure John Tembo, and two others were charged with defrauding the government of MK137 million (US$9.13 million). The High Court of Malawi ruled in May that charges against them should be dropped. In April the opposition MCP and Alliance for Democracy (AFORD) ended their nine-month parliamentary boycott.

In July Malawi's Supreme Court upheld the 1995 acquittal of former President Banda on charges of conspiring to murder four politicians in 1983. In November former President Banda died and was buried with state honours. President Bakili Muluzi demanded a public apology from the MCP for the atrocities committed during its rule.

In July trials began of 64 prisoners charged with murder, which carries a mandatory death penalty. By the end of the year, at least 10 had been sentenced to death, but their sentences were scheduled to be commuted to life imprisonment. A review process cleared a court backlog of about 1,000 outstanding cases of murder, at least one dating back to 1984.

In April civil servants – including doctors, nurses, teachers and police – went on a six-week strike in protest at the government's failure to implement an agreed pay increase. The strike was declared illegal by the government, and police used teargas, truncheons and police dogs to break up peaceful gatherings of striking civil servants, resulting in injuries to some. More than 30 trade union leaders were arrested, including Civil Servants Trade Union Vice-President Mike Gondwe, on charges of breaching the peace or using language likely to cause violence. Many were prisoners of conscience. By the end of the year they had all been released pending trial.

In July the government disclosed that, on average, three prisoners were dying every day at Malawi's main prison in Zomba town. According to the authorities, lack of medical care contributed to almost 150 deaths, which were mainly due to tuberculosis and other infectious diseases. Some 5,500 prisoners were held in other prisons, many in equally poor conditions.

President Muluzi announced in July, after meeting an Amnesty International delegation, that he had commuted all 10 existing death sentences and that he would not sign any orders of execution while in power.

In August the Malawian authorities announced a voluntary repatriation exercise to encourage refugees from Rwanda and the Democratic Republic of the Congo (DRC) to return to their countries. A heavy police presence at Dzaleka refugee camp near Lilongwe created panic among the Rwandese refugees, causing many to flee. Officials from the UN High Commissioner for Refugees and the Malawian Government began individual screening of up to 100 Rwandese refugees, many of whom did not want to return. The main objective of the screening seemed to be to identify any who had participated in the genocide in Rwanda in 1994. Amnesty International was concerned that the unwillingness to return on the part of some refugees may have been misinterpreted.

Amnesty International wrote to President Muluzi in April about the excessive use of force by police breaking up demonstrations by striking civil servants and the arrests of prisoners of conscience. In July an Amnesty International delegation met President Muluzi to discuss abolition of the death penalty. In August Amnesty International visited Dzaleka refugee camp and spoke with Rwandese and Congolese refugees, as well as Malawian Government officials. Some refugees said that they felt intimidated into signing voluntary repatriation forms. Malawian officials conducted a further review of refugee status and assured Amnesty International that refugees who did not want to return would not be forcibly repatriated.

In August Amnesty International sent President Muluzi its recommendations on draft National Human Rights Commission legislation. The organization also expressed concern about legislation limiting the Ombudsman's activities and allowing government officials to restrict access to information. Amnesty International asked the government to ensure the safe repatriation of Zambian opposition politicians John Chinula and William Banda.

MALAYSIA

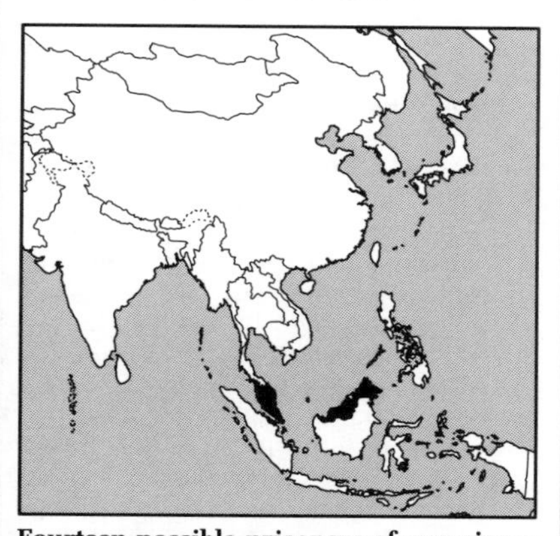

Fourteen possible prisoners of conscience held under the Internal Security Act (ISA) were released in February; all but one reportedly remained under orders restricting their freedom of association, speech and movement. Ten possible prisoners of conscience were detained without trial under the ISA in November. Members of the Dayak Iban indigenous community were detained and reportedly ill-treated in connection with protests over land rights. An opposition member of parliament found guilty of sedition and publishing "false news" faced a possible prison sentence, as did the head of a women's non-governmental organization on trial for publishing a report on ill-treatment in camps for detained migrant workers. Caning was inflicted for a range of crimes. At least seven people were sentenced to death and at least two people were executed.

Although the government of Prime Minister Mahathir Mohamad reiterated its intention to amend the Internal Security Act (ISA), (see *Amnesty International Report 1997*), it had not done so by the end of the year. The ISA allows detention for up to two years, renewable indefinitely, of any person suspected of threatening the national security or economic life of Malaysia. In September the police threatened to use the ISA to detain local financial traders suspected of "economic sabotage" by assisting foreign financial speculators.

In June, in relation to a libel case, the High Court of Malaysia ruled that the UN Special Rapporteur on the independence of judges and lawyers, Param Cumaraswamy, did not enjoy full immunity from Malaysia's legal process, as guaranteed by the UN Convention on the Privileges and Immunities of the Specialized Agencies.

In August the government announced that the application of *Shari'a* law would be standardized in all states. The announcement followed earlier calls by the government of Kelantan state, headed by the opposition *Parti Islam Sa-Malaysia*, Islamic Party of Malaysia, for punishments of amputation and stoning, and the arrest by Selangor state religious authorities of three Muslim contestants in a beauty pageant.

In February, 14 former members of the banned *Al Arqam* Islamic sect, who were possible prisoners of conscience, were released after being held without trial under the ISA for between six and nine months (see *Amnesty International Report 1997*). The government had claimed that the detentions were necessary to curb "deviant" religious teaching. Only one of the 14 was reported to have been released unconditionally. The others were reportedly banished to remote districts and placed under orders restricting their freedom of expression, movement and association.

In July the government identified at least 24 other Islamic groups it regarded as "deviant". In November, 10 possible prisoners of conscience, including Lutpi Ibrahim, a university professor, and Paharuddin Mustapha, a scrapyard dealer and former activist with the opposition Malaysian People's Party, were detained under the ISA for alleged "activities prejudicial to national security and Muslim unity". Lutpi Ibrahim and Fadzullah Shuib, a college lecturer, filed a writ of *habeas corpus* and the High Court ordered their release. They were rearrested under the ISA on leaving the court-house. Two of the 10 detainees were released in late December but remained under restriction orders.

In June, 42 members of the Dayak Iban indigenous community in the state of Sarawak were detained in connection with a dispute over their native customary land with a private company working with a state government agency. They were possible prisoners of conscience. The Iban were arrested without being shown warrants during an apparently lawful, peaceful protest and were beaten, kicked and assaulted with gun butts by police officers. A local magistrate ordered them to sign a six-month "bond to keep the peace", but they refused on the grounds that they had not committed any criminal offence. The magistrate then ordered their detention. Nine women were released in early July and the remaining men were released in mid-July after relatives paid bail. In August the High Court in Miri granted their appeal and quashed the magistrate's order. At least two similar cases involving Iban were reported during the year. In December three Iban were shot and injured, one fatally, by police during a demonstration against land developers. Several others were injured by police wielding batons, and six Iban were detained for up to 10 days.

In April the Malacca High Court found Lim Guan Eng, deputy leader of the opposition Democratic Action Party, guilty of sedition and "spreading false news". Lim Guan Eng had been charged after he publicly criticized the government's handling of allegations of statutory rape made against a former Chief Minister of Malacca (see *Amnesty International Reports 1996* and *1997*). Lim Guan Eng was fined a total of US$6,000 and consequently faced being disbarred from parliament. Before Lim Guan Eng lodged his appeal, the Attorney General filed an appeal on the grounds that the sentence was inadequate, provoking concern that the government was seeking a custodial sentence. The appeals had not been heard by the end of the year. If imprisoned, Lim Guan Eng would be a prisoner of conscience.

The trial of Irene Fernandez, director of the non-governmental organization *Tenaganita,* Women's Force, had not been completed by the end of the year. She was charged in 1995 with maliciously publishing "false news" in a report detailing allegations of ill-treatment, sexual abuse and denial of medical care in camps for detained migrant workers (see *Amnesty International Reports 1996* and *1997*). If convicted, Irene Fernandez faced up to three years' imprisonment or a fine, or both. If imprisoned, she would be a prisoner of conscience.

Caning, a form of cruel, inhuman or degrading punishment, was imposed throughout the year as an additional punishment to imprisonment. In July, in the first such case under the amended Immigration Act, six Indonesian migrant workers who returned to Malaysia following deportation, and their Malaysian boat captain, each received jail sentences and two strokes of the cane.

During the year at least seven people were sentenced to death and at least two were executed. Most had been convicted of drug-trafficking offences, for which a death sentence is mandatory.

Amnesty International urged the government to withdraw all charges against Irene Fernandez and to halt her trial. It urged the government to set up a full, impartial inquiry into the deaths of migrant workers in detention camps and into other allegations of ill-treatment. In March Amnesty International issued a report, *Malaysia: The trial of opposition parliamentarian Lim Guan Eng,* and called on the government to ensure that those peacefully exercising their right to freedom of expression could do so free from intimidation and the threat of imprisonment. In April the organization urged the authorities to revoke the fine imposed on Lim Guan Eng and not to deprive him of his parliamentary seat. In July and December Amnesty International expressed concern at the arrest, ill-treatment and fatal shooting of members of the Dayak Iban indigenous people, and called for impartial inquiries into the incidents and for the release of detainees held solely on account of peaceful protests. In November Amnesty International expressed concern at the detention without charge or trial of 10 men under the ISA and urged that they be charged or released. Throughout the year the organization appealed to the authorities to end the punishment of caning and to commute all death sentences.

MALDIVES

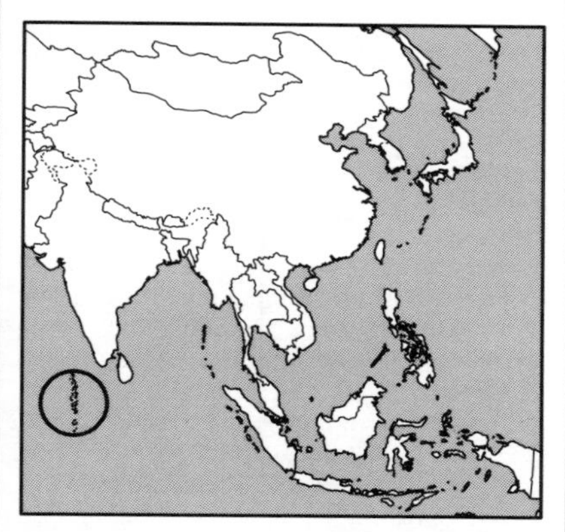

Several prisoners of conscience and possible prisoners of conscience were held in detention. There were reports of torture or ill-treatment of detainees. Conditions of detention amounted to cruel, inhuman or degrading treatment.

Tight restrictions imposed on the right to freedom of expression by the government of President Maumoon Abdul Gayoom made information on human rights violations difficult to gather and verify.

In late September, three types of new lower court were established, dealing with civil, criminal and family cases. In November a new Constitution was adopted which for the first time permits rival candidates to compete in the 48-member Citizen's *Majlis* (parliament) to obtain its nomination for the presidency.

Several prisoners of conscience and possible prisoners of conscience were held in detention. Among them were intellectuals, who were subjected to severe retaliatory measures for criticizing the government. Mohamed Shaheeb, a journalist writing for the newspaper *Haveeru*, was arrested in January, reportedly in connection with a fictional short story he had written about the treatment of a young woman detained in solitary confinement in police custody. He was held as a prisoner of conscience until his release in March.

In January Ilyas Ibrahim, a possible prisoner of conscience held under house arrest since March 1996 (see *Amnesty International Report 1997*), was reportedly released from restrictions on his movements.

Also in January, possible prisoners of conscience Mohamed Didi, Hussain Shareef and Ahmed Saeed were reportedly released. They were among a group of people arrested in early 1996 in connection with a demonstration about a rise in electricity prices in Fuvahmulaku Island (see *Amnesty International Report 1997*). There was no news about the other possible prisoners of conscience, including Hussain Shakir, Ibrahim Musthafa and Mohamed Rasheed, who had been arrested with them.

In April it came to light that Wu Mei De, a Chinese national, had been held for over three years in Gaamadhoo Prison without charge or trial. His arrest in November 1993 followed a court case in the Maldives in which Wu Mei De was suing a Maldivian national on grounds of alleged irregularities in a business partnership. His continued detention without charge or trial appeared to be due to official connivance in attempts by his business partner to prevent him from pursuing the court case.

Possible prisoner of conscience Ismail Saadiq, a Maldivian businessman who had been held in detention or under house arrest for various periods since July 1996, remained in detention without charge or trial at the end of the year. His detention, for alleged business irregularities, appeared to have been prompted by his support for a candidate in the 1993 presidential elections who was defeated and subsequently tried for "unconstitutional behaviour". Ismail Saadiq was reported to be passing blood in his urine and suffering from other health problems, for which he was being denied adequate medical care.

There were reports that detainees were subjected to torture or ill-treatment. Methods included leaving detainees for long periods on chairs with their hands handcuffed to their feet, and forcing detainees to stand on a chair for hours with arms outstretched and a coconut in each palm.

Conditions in most detention centres amounted to cruel, inhuman or degrading treatment. Seventeen Turkish asylum-seekers were reportedly held in a space meant for 10 people, under a metal roof which caused very high temperatures in the cell. They had to drink brackish sea water, food was inadequate, and men and women had to share the same toilets, with no privacy. The 17, students of Kurdish ethnicity, had been detained on arrival in Malé, the capital, in mid-March, and were held in Gaamadhoo Prison without charge or trial. Fifteen of them were released in May. There was no news about the remaining two.

Amnesty International urged the government to release unconditionally all prisoners of conscience, expressed concern about conditions of detention which amounted to cruel, inhuman or degrading treatment, and repeatedly appealed to the government to ratify major human rights instruments. In November Amnesty International asked the government to provide adequate medical care for Ismail Saadiq. No responses were received.

MALI

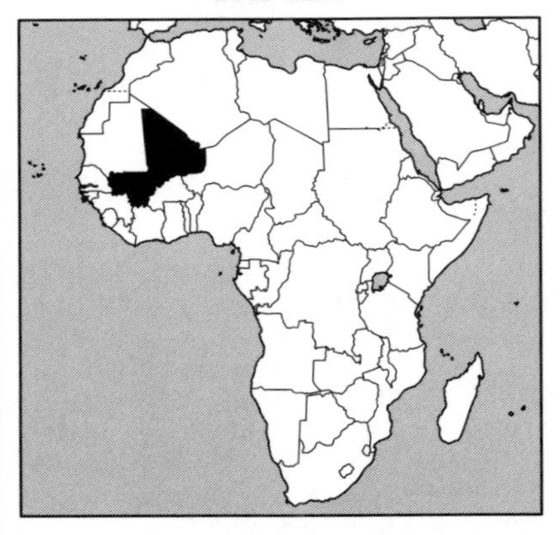

Dozens of opposition party supporters were detained, some of whom were prisoners of conscience. There were reports of torture and ill-treatment by police. All death sentences were commuted to life imprisonment.

In March President Alpha Oumar Konaré dissolved the National Assembly, leading to parliamentary elections in April which were marred by considerable organizational problems. The elections were eventually annulled by the Constitutional Court. In May presidential elections were boycotted by the opposition. President Konaré was re-elected with a large majority. Parliamentary elections held in July were also boycotted by the opposition. A new government, led by the *Alliance pour la démocratie au Mali* (ADEMA), Alliance for Democracy in Mali, was formed in September.

Opposition parties repeatedly protested about the electoral process, demanding the resignation of the government and the dissolution of the electoral commission supervising the elections. Widespread demonstrations were broken up by the security forces and many degenerated into violence. In May the authorities prohibited all demonstrations, but the wave of protests continued. At least four people lost their lives in the political unrest.

Dozens of members and supporters of the opposition were arrested, some of whom were prisoners of conscience.

In June, five opposition party leaders were arrested after a demonstration organized in Bamako, the capital, was dispersed by the security forces. They included Almamy Sylla, President of the opposition coalition and of the *Rassemblement pour la démocratie et le progrès*, Rally for Democracy and Progress; and Moussa Koné, President of the youth section of the opposition coalition. All five, including Mountaga Tall, President of the *Congrès national d'initiative démocratique* (CNID), National Congress of Democratic Initiative, were charged with security offences and provisionally released after one week. They appeared to be prisoners of conscience.

A second wave of arrests of opposition leaders occurred in August, shortly after a plainclothes police officer was beaten to death following his ejection from an opposition rally. Those detained included Mohamed Lamine Traoré, National Secretary of the *Mouvement pour l'indépendance, la renaissance et l'intégration africaine*, Movement for Independence, Renewal and African Integration, and former Minister of the Interior. Some were released but 10, including Fanta Mantchini Diarra, a leading member of the CNID, were charged and held for two months before being provisionally released. They were prisoners of conscience.

Journalists attending a press conference organized by the opposition in August were detained for two hours in a police camp, where they were questioned and several were beaten (see below).

Mady Diallo, a former minister in the government of former President Moussa Traoré, who was allowed to leave the country for medical treatment abroad, remained in detention at the end of the year. Mady Diallo and six soldiers were arrested in October 1996 (see *Amnesty International Report 1997*) and charged with "attack against the lawful government of the Republic of Mali with the intention of overthrowing it by force".

Five members of the *Association des travailleurs volontaires partant à la retraite*, Association of Voluntarily Retired Workers, were released in July (see *Amnesty International Report 1997*).

There were reports of torture and ill-treatment by police. Opposition party supporters arrested in May were alleged to have been systematically tortured by police in the presence of senior police officers. Police disrupted an opposition press conference in August, indiscriminately beating participants, including women, with truncheons and pieces of wood. Many were rounded up and allegedly forced into a sealed room into which tear-gas canisters were thrown. Yero Diallo, publishing manager of the independent magazine *Le Tambour*, was badly beaten on his head and back by police.

In December President Konaré commuted to life imprisonment all death sentences passed in previous years. Former President Moussa Traoré was among those who benefited from this measure.

In November Amnesty International published a report, *Mali: Basic liberties at risk*, in which it appealed to the authorities to release all prisoners of conscience; to end prolonged political detention without trial; to ensure that all allegations of torture or ill-treatment were impartially investigated and those responsible brought to justice; and to control the use of force by members of the security forces. In a letter published in a national newspaper, the government responded that after investigation, it had concluded that torture did not take place in detention centres and added that no complaints alleging torture had been registered. However, the government acknowledged that excessive force had been used when the police disrupted a press conference organized by the opposition.

MAURITANIA

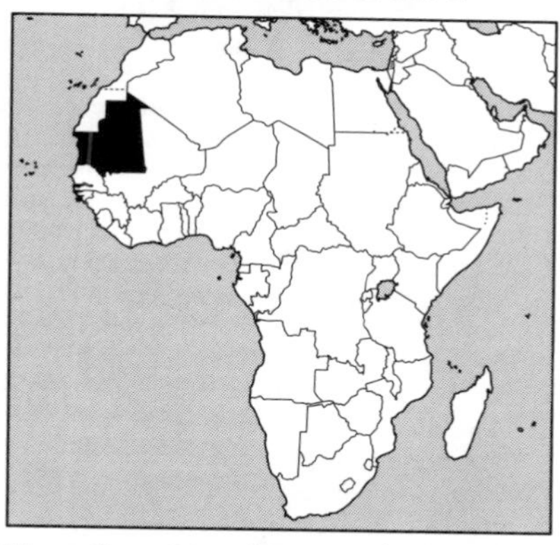

More than 90 prisoners of conscience, many of them students and teachers, were detained for periods of up to three months. There were still no investigations into past human rights violations.

The presidential election on 12 December was contested by five candidates, including Kane Amadou Moctar, the first black Mauritanian to stand for president. Many opposition parties boycotted the election as their demands for an independent electoral commission were not met and some of their members were arrested (see below). President Maaouya Ould Sid'Ahmed Taya won the election with 90 per cent of the vote.

Freedom of the press was again attacked. *Le Calame* newspaper was banned until February. *Mauritanie nouvelles* was banned for one month in April and for three months in October, preventing it from covering the election period. This ban was challenged by lawyers on the basis that it violated freedom of expression, but the Supreme Court confirmed the ban in November. Other newspapers had individual issues seized. When the Presidents of France and Mauritania held a joint press conference in September, about 14 members of the independent press were expelled from it.

The situation of some Mauritanians who returned to the country after going into exile in 1989 as a result of intercommunal violence and human rights violations (see *Amnesty International Reports 1990* to *1997*) remained uncertain. They were denied identity papers and had limited access to their own lands. There were reports of arbitrary detention and ill-treatment in southern Mauritania. The authorities claimed that all Mauritanians were free to return, but many still remained outside the country, demanding guarantees for their safety and access to land.

In April Mauritania hosted a session of the African Commission on Human and Peoples' Rights. Official attempts to prevent some local human rights activists from attending the session were thwarted by non-governmental organizations (see below). In November, at the next session of the Commission in Gambia, the Mauritanian authorities reportedly called upon the Gambian authorities to arrest a Mauritanian human rights activist. Aldiouma Cissoko, a spokesperson for a non-governmental organization representing Mauritanian refugees in Senegal, had held a press conference in Gambia. He was briefly held in police custody in Gambia.

At least 10 prisoners of conscience were arrested in January, apparently on account of their political activities. They included Messaoud Ould Boulkheir, President of the political party *Action pour le Changement*, Action for Change, who was questioned about the party's links with Libya. He and most others were released one week later, but at least five, all members of the *Alliance populaire progressiste*, Popular Progressive Alliance, remained held until their trial in February. They were questioned about links with Libya and Arab organizations and charged with "collective illegal acts". All received prison sentences of between three and six months, but for two the sentence was suspended. On appeal, all were acquitted, except for Abdallahi Al Atiq Ould Iyahi, who served a six-month prison sentence.

More than 70 students and teachers, all prisoners of conscience, were arrested between March and May. Mohamed Fadel Ould Bahaidda, deputy secretary general of the *Syndicat indépendant des professeurs de l'enseignement secondaire* (SIPES), Independent Union of Secondary Teachers, was arrested in March, the day before a press conference about a strike planned for early April. He and at least 12 other teachers, mostly leading members of SIPES, were held for a week in prison in the capital, Nouakchott, before being sent to their home villages, where they had to report to the police daily. More than 60 students were also first held in custody in Nouakchott then sent home and required to report daily to the police. Two of them – Abdallahi Ould Hormatallah and Mohamed Ould Bilal – escaped from Boutilimit, where they were restricted, to attend the session of the African Commission on Human and Peoples' Rights in Nouakchott in April. With the support of non-governmental organizations, the two testified before the Commission, and the Mauritanian government representative assured the two men that their safety would be guaranteed. However, less than two weeks later, these two students and many others were arrested. Some were reportedly beaten, and most were sent to their home areas. Abdallahi Ould Hormatallah and Mohamed Ould Bilal were held in Boumdeid prison. All were released without charge on 19 June.

At least 10 political activists were arrested in December. They were all members of parties which were boycotting the elections and were prisoners of conscience. They were held for less than 24 hours and some were reportedly beaten.

The Mauritanian authorities continued to prevent investigations into past human rights violations, including the suspected extrajudicial executions of more than 500 black Mauritanians held in military custody between 1990 and 1991.

Amnesty International appealed to the authorities to ensure that all detainees were protected from ill-treatment and were released promptly if no recognizably criminal charges were to be brought against them. In April, at the time of the session of the African Commission on Human and Peoples' Rights in Nouakchott, Amnesty International criticized the recent deterioration in respect for human rights and called on the government to comply with its obligations under the African Charter on Human and Peoples' Rights.

MEXICO

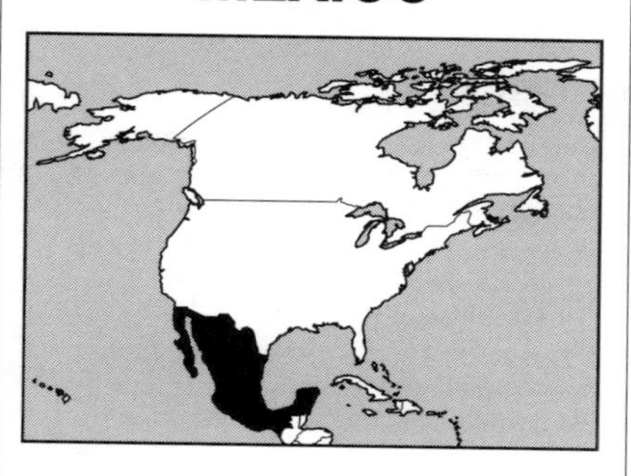

Scores of prisoners of conscience were detained. Human rights defenders and journalists were victims of death threats, attacks and other forms of harassment. Torture and ill-treatment by the army and police were widespread. At least 30 people "disappeared" and scores of people were extrajudicially executed.

President Ernesto Zedillo increased the participation of the army in law enforcement, anti-narcotics and counter-insurgency operations. There was a marked increase in the number of human rights violations, including torture, "disappearances" and extrajudicial executions, by members of the security forces and paramilitary groups.

In July the ruling *Partido Revolucionario Institucional* (PRI), Institutional Revolutionary Party, lost its absolute majority in the Chamber of Deputies for the first time, while Cuauhtémoc Cárdenas Solórzano, of the opposition *Partido de la Revolución Democrática* (PRD), Democratic Revolutionary Party, won the governorship of Mexico City, a post formerly appointed by the President. Allegations of vote-rigging by the PRI in Campeche State led to protests, during which scores of PRD activists were beaten by the police.

Peace talks between the government and the *Ejército Zapatista de Liberación Nacional* (EZLN), Zapatista National Liberation Army, an armed opposition group, remained suspended throughout the year (see *Amnesty International Report 1997*). In May the *Ejército Popular Revolucionario* (EPR), Popular Revolutionary Army, another armed opposition group, launched new attacks on military targets. Serious human rights violations continued to be reported in the context of the conflict with the EZLN and EPR.

In June the UN Committee against Torture concluded that torture "continued to be practised systematically" in Mexico. The Committee criticized the impunity benefiting perpetrators and the courts' persistence in admitting as evidence statements extracted under torture. In August the UN Special Rapporteur on torture visited Mexico for the first time.

In January the Inter-American Commission on Human Rights called for the immediate release of Brigadier General José Francisco Gallardo, but he remained in prison at the end of the year (see below and *Amnesty International Report 1997*).

Scores of prisoners of conscience were held. Benigno Guzmán, a leader of the *Organización Campesina de la Sierra del Sur*, Southern Sierra Peasant Organization, was arrested in January in Mexico City and imprisoned in Acapulco, Guerrero State, following unsubstantiated accusations that he had links with the EPR. Bertoldo Ramírez Cruz, a leading human rights and PRD activist in Guerrero State, was arrested in Acapulco in February. Chinantec Indian leaders Juan Zamora González and Marcos Zamora González were arrested, tortured and imprisoned in Veracruz, Veracruz State, because of their peaceful activism over community land rights. Ignacio García Muñiz, a human rights and PRD activist, was arrested and tortured by soldiers in Guerrero State, and imprisoned on false drug charges. They all remained in prison at the end of the year.

Prisoners of conscience detained in previous years continued to be held. They included Manuel Manríquez San Agustín (see *Amnesty International Reports 1994* to *1996*), Brigadier General José Francisco Gallardo, and six members of the *Sindicato de Trabajadores Petroleros de la República Mexicana*, the Mexican oil workers' union (see *Amnesty International Report 1997*). Gerardo Demesa Padilla, a leader of the *Comité de Unidad de Tepoztlán*, Committee of Unity of Tepoztlán, was sentenced in August to eight years' imprisonment (see *Amnesty International Report 1997*). His appeal had not been heard by the end of the year.

Some prisoners of conscience were released during the year. Cecilia Elizalde Mora and Maximina Excobar Sánchez were released in May, Hilario Mesino

Acosta was released in June, and former trade union leader Joaquín Hernández Galicia was released in December (see *Amnesty International Report 1997*).

Scores of human rights defenders and journalists investigating human rights violations or official corruption received death threats. The authorities consistently failed to bring those responsible to justice (see *Amnesty International Report 1997*). Among those targeted were dozens of leading members of non-governmental organizations (NGOs), such as María Luisa Mussot, of the *Coordinadora de Mujeres en Defensa de la Seguridad Social*, Women's Coordinating Committee for Social Security; Father Miguel Concha Malo, a Jesuit priest from the *Centro de Derechos Humanos Fray Francisco de Vitoria*, Centre for Human Rights Fray Francisco de Vitoria, in Mexico City; Fathers Javier Ávila and Camilo Daniel, Roman Catholic priests from the *Comisión de Solidaridad y Defensa de los Derechos Humanos*, Commission for the Defence of Human Rights and Solidarity, in Chihuahua; and Cleotilde Porras from the *Coordinación de Organismos No Gubernamentales por la Paz*, Coalition of NGOs for Peace, in Chiapas.

In November Roman Catholic Bishops Raúl Vera and Samuel Ruiz survived an armed attack by members of a paramilitary group while visiting Indian communities in Chiapas State. Bishop Samuel Ruiz had suffered previous death threats for his human rights advocacy.

Journalist Daniel Lizarraga, investigating police corruption for the daily *Reforma*, was detained, beaten and threatened with death in early September by plainclothes policemen in Mexico City. René Solorio and Ernesto Madrid, television news reporters investigating police killings, were detained, beaten and threatened in mid-September by members of the Federal District police in Mexico City.

Hundreds of politicians, civil rights activists, and witnesses or relatives of victims of human rights violations also suffered death threats and other abuses. Víctor Quintana Silveyra, federal deputy for the PRD, was abducted in Mexico City in June by unidentified men who beat and threatened to kill him. María Estela García Ramírez and Riquilda Hernández Martínez, who had witnessed the murders of their husband and father, respectively, by members of the Oaxaca State police, had to flee their homes with their families, following repeated death threats by the authorities to make them withdraw their complaints.

Foreign human rights monitors faced restrictions on their work, and at least three were expelled from the country on charges of having infringed immigration laws. In April Benjamín Cuéllar, a Salvadorean, and Vilma Núñez de Escorcia, a Nicaraguan, members of a delegation from the International Federation of Human Rights, were expelled after visiting prisoners in Guerrero State.

Hundreds of detainees were allegedly tortured or ill-treated by the security forces, including the army and paramilitary groups. The victims were denied medical treatment. The courts continued to accept confessions extracted under torture, and no perpetrators were convicted of torture.

In March Gerónimo Hernández López and Gonzalo Rosas Morales, Jesuit priests and leading members of local human rights and indigenous organizations in Palenque, Chiapas State, were detained with at least five Indian community leaders by the state police. All were tortured by being beaten, burned and subjected to mock executions before being released without charge days later. In May Alberto Gómez García, a public prosecutor, and six members of the judicial police in San Luis Río Colorado, Sonora State, were arrested and then held in unacknowledged detention for two weeks. During interrogation they were beaten, given electric shocks and nearly suffocated with plastic bags.

Martín Barrientos Cortés, a peasant activist, was abducted by soldiers on 28 May, near his community in El Cucuyachi, Guerrero State. The army denied holding him and he remained "disappeared" until 9 June, when he was released without charge. He was beaten, given electric shocks and semi-asphyxiated, and accused of links with the EPR. He complained to the local authorities to no avail.

Between late May and early June at least 14 street children in Mexico City were arbitrarily arrested and beaten, and at least two were raped by policemen. They were also threatened with death to deter them from complaining to the authorities.

In September César Guzmán Santiago, a local PRI leader, was arrested by police in Cunduacán, Tabasco State. Despite forensic evidence that his confession to a robbery had been extracted under torture, the courts admitted it as evidence. He remained in pre-trial detention at the end of the year. In September Gloria Roque Bautista, a human rights activist, was raped and tortured by two soldiers who interrogated her about her human rights activities.

At least 20 people, including children, reportedly died as a result of torture. Erik Cárdenas Esqueda, aged 16, was detained in January by the municipal police in Nuevo Laredo, Tamaulipas, then transferred to a local police station. He was beaten to death for insulting the police. Alberto Alonso Salmerón, a renowned environmental, human rights and indigenous leader arrested in July in Aranza, Michoacán State, was tortured and died in a local police station. He had received previous death threats. Víctor Hernández Martínez, a journalist, was detained and beaten to death in July behind the headquarters of the federal judicial police in Mexico City. He had repeatedly accused the police of corruption. Those responsible for the death of Valentín Carrillo Saldaña in 1996 (see *Amnesty International Report 1997*) were not brought to justice.

At least 30 people "disappeared" following detention by members of the security forces, including the army, mostly in the context of anti-narcotics and counterinsurgency operations. Most were held in unacknowledged detention for short periods, tortured and then released following campaigns on their behalf. However, at least 10 remained "disappeared" at the end of the year. Among those who "disappeared" after arrest by anti-narcotics agents were Raúl Berber Campos, Cecilio Beltrán Campos and Rogelio Berber Campos, who were detained in January in Tijuana, Baja California Norte State. Alejandro Enrique Hodoyán Palacios, a US citizen, "disappeared" following his detention in March in Tijuana, Baja California Norte State. Also in March, José Guadarrama García, a former policeman who specialized in anti-kidnap operations, was abducted by former colleagues and "disappeared". Wilfredo Guinea, a Jesuit priest, was abducted in Mexico City in June, and "disappeared".

Political activists also "disappeared", including 16-year-old Freddy Nava Ríos, a community activist arrested in May by the army in El Cucuyachi, Guerrero State. He remained "disappeared" at the end of the year. The whereabouts of hundreds who "disappeared" in previous years remained unknown.

Scores of people, including children, were extrajudicially executed by the security forces and paramilitary groups. In most cases the perpetrators were not brought to justice. Guadalupe Valentino López Carrasco and his wife Nicasia Hernández Petatán, PRD members, were shot dead in front of their grandchildren by gunmen linked to local authorities, who raided their home in Tlapa de Comonfort, Guerrero State, in March. In April Gerardo Hurtado Arias, a human rights and peasant activist, was gunned down at close range by members of the security forces in Tepetixtla, Guerrero State. Twelve-year-old Benito Juárez Gutiérrez was killed in June by members of the paramilitary group *Paz y Justicia*, Peace and Justice, who opened fire on a group of unarmed peasant supporters of the PRD in Sabanilla, Chiapas State.

Juan Carlos Romero Peralta, aged 17, and five other young men were seized in September by members of a combined army and police unit operating in Mexico City. Their bodies, discovered days later, revealed that they had all been shot dead after being tortured. In December, 45 men, women and children were gunned down in the village of Acteal, Chenalhó, Chiapas State. Members of a paramilitary group widely reported to have links with the authorities were accused of the massacre. Days later, following a national and international outcry, 39 people, including the PRI mayor of Chenalhó, were charged with murder and other criminal offences.

A high-level Amnesty International delegation visited Mexico in September. The delegates addressed a memorandum to the government stressing the need to halt gross human rights violations, bring an end to impunity, and implement reforms to the administration of justice. They were unable to meet some relevant officials, but held talks with the Attorney General and the presidents of the Chamber of Deputies and of the Supreme Court of Justice. In October the organization met President Zedillo during his visit to France and presented the memorandum to him.

In April the organization published *Amnesty International's concerns regarding torture and ill-treatment in Mexico.* In December Amnesty International called for those responsible for the Acteal massacre to be brought to justice and urged President Zedillo to ensure a public and independent investigation into allegations that paramilitary groups were involved in this and previous killings. The authorities rejected the appeal as "unacceptable interference in Mexico's internal affairs". Amnesty International issued scores of appeals on behalf of victims of human rights violations throughout the year. The authorities replied to many of those appeals but failed to respond satisfactorily to the concerns raised by the organization.

MOLDOVA

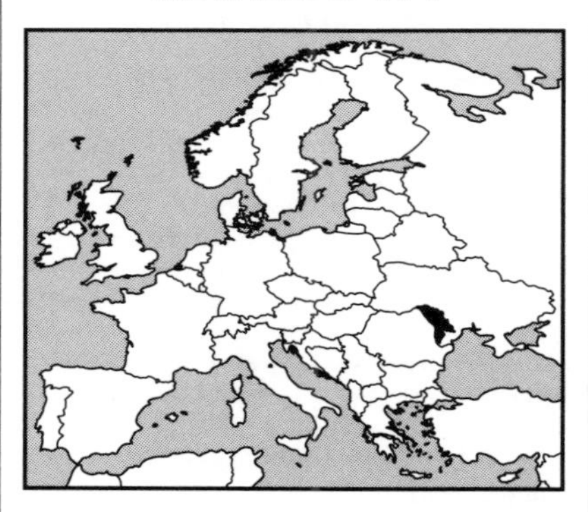

There were allegations of ill-treatment by police. Conditions of detention remained inadequate. At least four political prisoners remained imprisoned in the self-proclaimed Dnestr Moldavian Republic (DMR).

Leaders from Moldova and the DMR signed an agreement in May which moved towards ending the seven-year dispute over the status of the DMR. The agreement did not specify what constitutional status would eventually be granted to the DMR region, but included a pledge that it would remain part of Moldova.

In September, in fulfilment of its commitments on joining the Council of Europe, Moldova ratified the European Convention for the Protection of Human Rights and Fundamental Freedoms and Protocol No. 6 to the Convention, concerning the abolition of the death penalty. In October Moldova also ratified the European Convention for the Prevention of Torture and Inhuman or Degrading Treatment or Punishment. The Moldovan parliament said, however, that Moldova was unable to ensure the implementation of the Conventions in the DMR. The Moldovan Government also said that it would need one year in which to amend existing legislation that contradicts the two Conventions.

In April President Petru Luchinschi issued a decree creating a special police department to combat corruption and organized crime. The department was reportedly given wide powers to monitor personal correspondence, to tap telephones and to collect information using modern technology. The decree contained no mention of the duty of the Office of the Procurator to order and monitor such police investigations.

In the DMR, a presidential decree introducing a state of emergency continued to be enforced. It allowed law enforcement officials to detain suspects for up to 30 days without charge and allegedly without access to a defence lawyer. There were reports that the DMR authorities continued to use the provisions of the decree to detain political opponents.

There were allegations of ill-treatment by police. In January a group of seven Roma were allegedly beaten about the head by police, who also fired guns into the air, in a Romani neighbourhood in the town of Soroca. Igor Cerari and Artur Preida reportedly suffered serious head injuries as a result. The two men filed a formal complaint. The chief of the Soroca Police Department reportedly claimed that an investigation into the incident had been carried out by the Office of the Procurator, and had concluded that the two police officers had acted within legal bounds. However, other sources stated that there was no record of the case at the Soroca Office of the Procurator.

Prison conditions remained inadequate, with serious overcrowding. Conditions were especially harsh in pre-trial detention centres. Members of the Moldovan Helsinki Committee were reportedly denied access to pre-trial detention centres on several occasions. The incidence of malnutrition and disease, especially tuberculosis, was high in all penal institutions. The Moldovan Ministry of Justice took over responsibility for prisons from the Ministry of the Interior in 1995, but reform of the system was said to be progressing slowly.

Ilie Ilaşcu, Alexandru Leşco, Andrei Ivanţoc and Tudor Petrov-Popa from the so-called "Tiraspol Six", who had been convicted of murder in 1993 by a court in the DMR (see previous *Amnesty International Reports*) remained in prison at the end of the year, although their release was reportedly discussed during negotiations between Moldovan and DMR leaders. Their trial had apparently failed to meet international standards of fairness, and the men had allegedly been prosecuted for political reasons, because of their membership of the Christian Democratic Popular Front, a Moldovan party favouring reunification with Romania.

Alexandru Leşco, Andrei Ivanţoc and Ilie Ilaşcu were reported to be seriously ill but not receiving adequate medical care. The DMR authorities repeatedly refused to allow independent medical examination of the prisoners by outside experts, including representatives of the International Committee of the Red Cross. In an unprecedented move in November, the DMR authorities allowed an independent medical commission access to Ilie Ilaşcu in detention. However, the commission did not have access to the equipment necessary to examine him. Amnesty International continued to call for a review of the case, and for the prisoners to receive all appropriate medical care.

Amnesty International urged the authorities to conduct prompt, impartial and effective investigations into all allegations of ill-treatment by police and to bring those responsible to justice.

MOROCCO AND WESTERN SAHARA

Over 50 political prisoners and prisoners of conscience continued to serve long prison sentences imposed after unfair trials in previous years. Dozens of members of an opposition organization were sentenced to terms of imprisonment: they were prisoners of conscience. Scores of political opposition activists were imprisoned after unfair trials. Torture and ill-treatment continued to be reported, particularly of people charged with criminal offences. Hundreds of Sahrawis and Moroccans who "disappeared" in previous years remained unaccounted for. A former prisoner of conscience forcibly exiled in 1991 remained unable to return to Morocco. At least three people were sentenced to death and at least 40 others reportedly remained on death row at the end of the year. No executions were carried out.

Municipal elections were held in June, followed by parliamentary elections in November. The four parties grouped in the *Koutla Addimocratia* (democratic bloc) won 102 of the 325 seats in the parliamentary elections. The three parties representing the *Wifaq* (consensus bloc) won 100 seats, the centre bloc 97, and other smaller parties 26. An interim cabinet was appointed by King Hassan II in July.

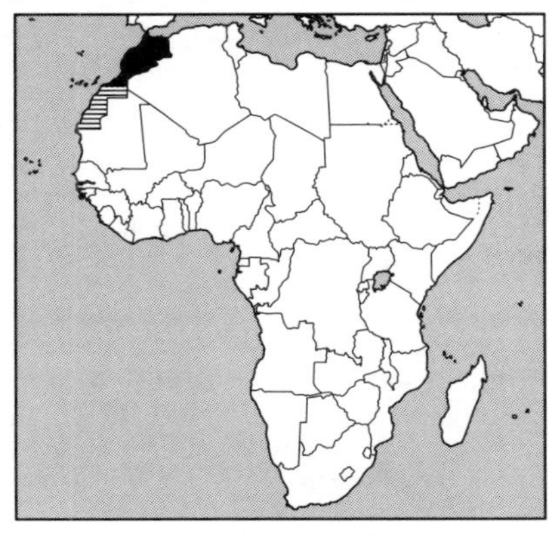

Under the auspices of the newly appointed personal envoy of the UN Secretary-General to Western Sahara, talks resumed between the Moroccan Government and the *Frente Popular para la Liberación de Saguia el-Hamra y Rio de Oro*, Popular Front for the Liberation of Saguia el-Hamra and Rio de Oro (known as the Polisario Front). In September the two parties were reported to have agreed a "code of conduct" for the planned referendum on the international status of Western Sahara. The agreement led to the resumption in December of the voter identification process by the UN Mission in Western Sahara (MINURSO), a process which had been suspended by the UN Security Council in May 1996 as a result of a dispute between the two parties. In October the UN Security Council extended the mandate of MINURSO. It was announced that the referendum would take place in December 1998.

More than 50 prisoners of conscience and political prisoners imprisoned after unfair trials in previous years continued to be detained. The prisoners of conscience were 'Ahmed Haou, 'Abdelkader Sfiri, Mustapha Marjaoui and Youssef Cherkaoui-Rbati, who continued to serve life sentences. They had been arrested in 1983 with other supporters and sympathizers of unauthorized Islamist groups and accused of putting up anti-monarchist posters, distributing leaflets and participating in demonstrations (see previous *Amnesty International Reports*). Prisoner of conscience 'Abdessalem Yassine, the spiritual leader of the banned Islamist association *al-'Adl wa'l 'Ihsan* (Justice and Charity), remained under administratively imposed house arrest for the seventh consecutive year.

More than 130 supporters of the *Parti de l'avant-garde démocratique socialiste* (PADS), Socialist Democratic Vanguard Party, were arrested in June and November in various towns following calls by the PADS to boycott the municipal and parliamentary elections. Dozens of them were tried and sentenced to up to five months' imprisonment on charges of inciting voters to abstain from voting. They were prisoners of conscience.

Scores of political opposition activists were imprisoned after unfair trials. In June, 45 people were reportedly arrested in the Sidi Bettach constituency near Rabat, the capital, following protests at alleged ballot rigging by the authorities during the municipal elections. Nineteen of those arrested were tried in June on various charges, including assault and insulting public authority, and sentenced to two years' imprisonment after a summary trial. The court allegedly refused to hear all the defence witnesses and did not investigate claims by some defendants that they had been ill-treated by the police. There were also reports of violence by the police in court against supporters of the defendants. The sentences were reduced to one year's imprisonment on appeal in August.

Scores of Islamist students were reportedly arrested during the year in several towns following protests against their university conditions. A few were subsequently sentenced after unfair trials to up to one year's imprisonment on various charges, including taking part in unauthorized demonstrations and using insulting and violent behaviour. They were possible prisoners of conscience. Scores of members of the *Association des chômeurs diplômés*, Association of Unemployed Graduates, were reportedly arrested during demonstrations and sentenced to up to six months' imprisonment after unfair trials. They too were possible prisoners of conscience. Allegations by the Islamist students and members of the *Association des chômeurs diplômés* that they had been beaten by the police or tortured were not investigated by the courts during the trials.

Other reports of torture and ill-treatment were received during the year. At least three of nine Sahrawis reportedly arrested in connection with their alleged support for the independence of Western Sahara were said to have been tortured. Among them was Hammad 'Ali Hamad, who was reportedly arrested in May in Laayoune and held incommunicado for 11 days. Some of the political opposition activists arrested during the year at protests were reportedly beaten by the police and in some cases tortured. For example, El Hayouni Ossama, who was arrested in January during a student protest at Hassan II University in Casablanca, was reportedly tortured for two days by having a cloth soaked in dirty water, chemicals and urine inserted into his mouth, and by being beaten and deprived of sleep.

People arrested on criminal charges were also reported to have been tortured or ill-treated. The authorities failed to investigate complaints made in previous years of torture and ill-treatment of detainees during incommunicado detention, sometimes illegally prolonged for weeks, and the acceptance as evidence by courts of confessions allegedly extracted under torture (see previous *Amnesty International Reports*).

Hundreds of Sahrawis and Moroccans who "disappeared" after arrest in previous years remained unaccounted for (see previous *Amnesty International Reports*). They included 'Abdelhaq Rouissi, a trade unionist who "disappeared" in 1964; 'Abdallah Cherrouk, a student who "disappeared" in 1981; and Mohamed-Salem Bueh-Barca and Tebker Ment

Sidi-Mohamed Ould Khattari, who "disappeared" in Laayoune in 1976.

No steps were taken to investigate the "disappearance" of hundreds of Sahrawis and Moroccans who were released in 1991 after up to 18 years in secret detention, or the deaths in secret detention of scores of others. Neither those released in 1991 nor the families of those who died in secret detention received any compensation.

There was no information at the end of the year on the investigations being carried out into the deaths in custody in 1996 of Houssein Al-Mernissi (see *Amnesty International Report 1997*) and Mohamed Feddaoui.

Abraham Serfaty, a former prisoner of conscience who was forcibly expelled to France on his release in 1991, remained unable to return to Morocco.

At least three people were sentenced to death and at least 40 others reportedly remained on death row at the end of the year. No executions were carried out.

Amnesty International wrote to the authorities requesting information about cases of alleged human rights violations and calling for independent investigations to be carried out. The organization also called on the authorities to release all prisoners of conscience. No response was received.

In November an Amnesty International delegation met the Minister of Justice and discussed the organization's concerns.

MOZAMBIQUE

There were dozens of reports of torture of criminal suspects and witnesses by police. One person died in custody, apparently as a result of torture. Four policemen were convicted of torturing prisoners. Two people reportedly "disappeared" and one person was apparently extrajudicially executed in police custody.

Mozambique enjoyed its fifth year of peace but the government, led by President Joaquim Chissano, still faced problems caused by the war. Several large caches of weapons and ammunition were unearthed but large quantities were believed to be still in criminal hands. Landmine clearance continued, but it was estimated that about one million remained undiscovered. In February the government banned the use, production and transfer of anti-personnel land-mines.

Despite improvements in the economy, poverty and high levels of crime persisted. In January the Interior Minister, appointed in late 1996, announced new measures to control crime, including the opening of police stations closed down during the war. A project to restructure the police, using the Spanish *Guardia Civil* as a model, and to retrain police was agreed in June.

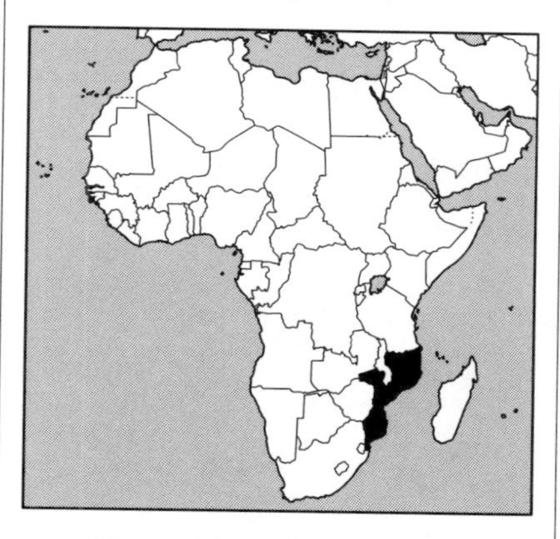

In May and June the main opposition political party, *Resistência Nacional Moçambicana* (RENAMO), Mozambique National Resistance, formerly the armed opposition movement, organized a series of demonstrations, some involving acts of violence, against the high cost of living. At least 60 people were detained for a few days and 14 were convicted in September of orga-nizing illegal demonstrations. Their two-year prison sentences were suspended.

A policeman was given a one-year prison sentence in December for firing the shot which killed Spanish aid worker Inmaculada Vieira in November 1996. Friends of the deceased who had initiated a private prosecution had to engage a new lawyer after their first legal counsel complained of receiving threats.

Prisons remained overcrowded although some efforts were made to improve conditions. For example, in Gaza Province prisoners who had been detained for longer than the law allowed were released on bail. Professor E.V.O. Dankwa, Special Rapporteur on prisons and conditions of detention in Africa of the African Commission on Human and Peoples' Rights visited Mozambique in December. The report of his visit had not been published by the end of the year.

A law on compulsory military service for men aged between 18 and 35 was passed in November. There was no provision allowing for conscientious objection.

In April Mozambique acceded to the UN Convention on the Elimination of All Forms of Discrimination against Women.

Dozens of people were reportedly tortured in police custody. In January police arrested Alice Luís on suspicion of prostitution and drug offences. Police beat her as they escorted her in handcuffs to the 4th Police Station in Maputo, the capital, and they beat and whipped her in the cell before releasing her in the early hours of the following morning.

Two minors, Abdul Bernardo and Abubacar Tauzene, were severely beaten in a Maputo police station in February. They had been arrested for failing to supply proof of their identity and were released the next day, after inquiries had been made by the *Liga Moçambicana dos Direitos Humanos* (LMDH), Mozambique Human Rights League.

Maria José Camacho was severely beaten by police in Maputo in March. A neighbour had accused her of building a wall across a road; four policemen, acting without any judicial authority, arrived at her house and began to destroy the wall. When she protested, they handcuffed her and beat her until she fainted. The police took her to hospital but did not let her daughter accompany her.

Three people suspected of stealing car spares were tortured at the Esquadra da Liberdade police station in Matola, Maputo, in June. They were beaten with the tail of a ray fish, which tore their flesh with its serrated edge.

In August Intepa Faque died in a police cell in Nacala-Porto, Nampula Province. He and other members of his family had been arrested and beaten after one of them was accused of stealing a video machine. Police then reportedly thrust a stick down Intepa Faque's throat, causing severe bleeding. He died two hours later. There was an investigation but at the end of the year none of those responsible had been brought to justice.

Four policemen each received seven-year prison sentences in January for torturing Franque Luís Tchembene in 1996. The victim died as a result of the torture (see *Amnesty International Report 1997*). One of the defendants continued to fulfil police functions pending the result of his appeal. The trial of police accused of torturing 19-year-old triplets in 1995 (see *Amnesty International Report 1997*) was scheduled for 1998.

Two people apparently "disappeared". Issufo Aly and Carlos Cossa were detained in June and accused of stealing a motorbike. Issufo Aly's wife said that a week later four members of the Criminal Investigation Police brought him home in handcuffs at midnight and demanded a sum of money, which she gave them in the belief that it might save her husband's life. During the following 10 days, his wife tried to see him but was not given permission to do so. Nearly three weeks after his arrest, members of the LMDH made inquiries about the two men and were told that they had died in a traffic accident. The police subsequently told the press that they had escaped from a police vehicle which had been taking them to court. By the end of the year the LMDH had not received a detailed explanation of what happened to the two men.

In October Crescêncio Sergio Muchanga was reportedly shot dead by police who had earlier tortured him. He had been detained in the 1st Police Station in Matola in connection with the theft of a government vehicle, along with about 14 other people, including women and children. At least five of the detainees were severely beaten and at least two of them were taken at night to the banks of the Matola River where they were buried up to the neck in sand and had shots fired near their heads. In addition, Crescêncio Sergio Muchanga was dragged behind a moving vehicle by a rope attached to his wrists. He was still alive when police returned him to the 1st Police Station. Representatives of the LMDH subsequently saw his body in the morgue, bearing what appeared to be bullet holes in the neck and chest.

The fate and whereabouts of Abdul Mota, who "disappeared" in police custody in 1996 (see *Amnesty International Report 1997*), remained unknown.

Amnesty International expressed concern about cases of torture and the "disappearance" of detainees in police custody. It welcomed the bringing to justice of the police officers responsible for the torture and death of Franque Luís Tchembene. Amnesty International called on the government to ensure that police training programs included thorough training in the protection of human rights. It received no response from the government.

MYANMAR

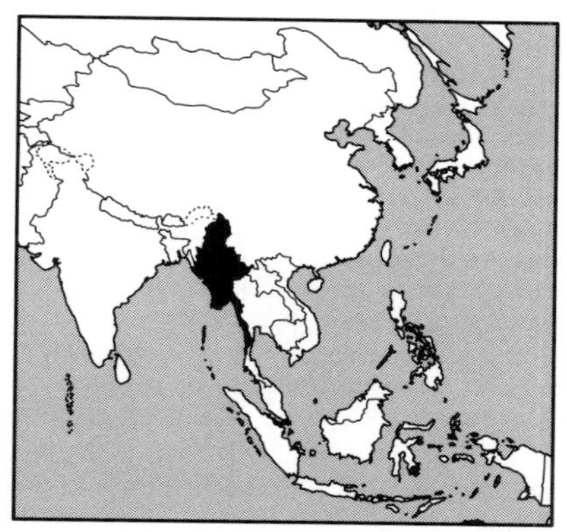

More than 1,200 political prisoners arrested in previous years, including 89 prisoners of conscience and hundreds of possible prisoners of conscience, remained in prison throughout the year. Hundreds of people were arrested for political reasons; although most were released, 31 – five of them prisoners of conscience – were sentenced to long terms of imprisonment after unfair trials. Political prisoners were ill-treated and held in conditions that amounted to cruel, inhuman or degrading treatment. Members of ethnic minorities continued to suffer human rights violations, including extrajudicial executions and ill-treatment during forced labour and portering, and forcible relocations. Two people were sentenced to death.

Military leaders reorganized the State Law and Order Restoration Council (SLORC) and changed its name to the State Peace and Development Council (SPDC). The SPDC continued to be chaired by General Than Shwe, and ruled by decree in the absence of a constitution. Martial law decrees severely restricting the rights to freedom of expression and assembly remained in force.

The National Convention, convened by the SLORC in 1993 to agree principles for a new constitution and adjourned in March 1996, did not meet during the year. Throughout the year the National League for Democracy (NLD), the legal opposition party led by Daw Aung San Suu Kyi, appealed to the SLORC to enter into a dialogue. In July the SLORC held a meeting with senior NLD leaders; however, Daw Aung San Suu Kyi was not invited. When the SLORC called another meeting in September, again excluding her, the NLD refused to meet. The SLORC permitted the NLD to hold a party congress of 700 people in September.

Cease-fire talks between the SLORC and the armed opposition group the Karen National Union (KNU) broke down in January, and in February the SLORC launched a major offensive against remaining KNU positions in the Kayin (Karen) State. Some 20,000 Karen civilians fled to Thailand to escape the fighting and human rights violations (see **Thailand** entry). Skirmishes between the Karenni National Progressive Party (KNPP) and the government in the Kayah State continued throughout the year. Fighting between the SLORC and the Shan United Revolutionary Army, an armed Shan opposition group, also continued in the Shan State.

Some 20,500 Rohingyas (Burmese Muslims from the Rakhine State) remained in camps in Bangladesh. Repatriation stopped in April, but resumed briefly in July when 399 Rohingyas were forcibly returned to Myanmar after the SLORC agreed to accept 7,500 returnees (see **Bangladesh** entry). There were no further repatriations during the year. Thousands of other Rohingyas, fleeing poverty and ill-treatment during forced labour in the Rakhine State, sought refuge in Bangladesh during the first half of the year, but were not allowed to enter refugee camps there. Rohingyas and other ethnic minorities, including the Arakanese and Mro, were forced to work on roads and bridges by the security forces in the Rakhine State.

In March, the UN Special Rapporteur on Myanmar submitted his report to the UN Commission on Human Rights. In April, the Commission adopted by consensus a resolution extending the Special Rapporteur's mandate for another year and expressed grave concern at the extremely serious human rights situation in

Myanmar. A similar resolution was adopted by consensus by the UN General Assembly in December. The Special Rapporteur continued to be denied access to Myanmar, although officials in the UN Secretary-General's office visited Myanmar in February and May.

In July Myanmar acceded to the UN Convention on the Elimination of All Forms of Discrimination against Women.

At an International Labour Organisation (ILO) conference in June, Myanmar's failure to implement Convention No. 87 with regard to freedom of association, which it has ratified, was identified as a situation of particular gravity. The ILO was also carrying out a Commission of Enquiry into Myanmar's failure to implement the provisions of Convention No. 29 on forced labour, to which it has been a party since 1955.

In March the Council of Ministers of the European Union suspended preferential tariffs to Myanmar under the Generalized System of Preferences. In May the US Government implemented 1996 legislation which prohibits any new US investment in Myanmar. In July the Association of South East Asian Nations (ASEAN) granted Myanmar full ASEAN membership.

Over 1,200 political prisoners arrested in previous years, including 89 prisoners of conscience and hundreds of possible prisoners of conscience, remained in detention. Hundreds of people were arrested for political reasons during the year, although most of them were later released uncharged.

Prisoners of conscience and NLD leaders Dr Aung Khin Sint, U Win Htein, U Aye Win and U Win Tin (see *Amnesty International Report 1997*) were reported to be in poor health. Dr Aung Khin Sint, U Win Tin and U Aye Win were hospitalized for cardiac problems.

It became known that Nay Min, a prisoner of conscience arrested in 1988, had been released in November 1996.

In May over 300 NLD party members were either arrested or threatened with arrest when attempting to attend a party conference. Those arrested were released in June without charge.

At least 64 people, 31 of whom had been arrested during the year, were sentenced to prison terms for their political activities after unfair trials. Five of the 31 were prisoners of conscience. In April and May respectively NLD activists Dr Than Aung and U Myo Khin, who had been arrested in February and May, were sentenced to four years' imprisonment on criminal charges which were politically motivated. They were both prisoners of conscience.

In August the government sentenced Cho Aung Than, a cousin and former assistant of Daw Aung San Suu Kyi, his sister Nge Ma Ma Than and her husband U Myint Swe to 10 years' imprisonment for allegedly passing money to the NLD from foreign sources and helping to smuggle a videotape of Daw Aung San Suu Kyi to Thailand. The three, who had been arrested in June, were prisoners of conscience. Cho Aung Than was hospitalized in September for hypertension.

In January the SLORC sentenced 34 possible prisoners of conscience to seven years' imprisonment for their involvement in the December 1996 demonstrations led by university students in support of human rights and a higher quality of education (see *Amnesty International Report 1997*).

In August Myo Aung Thant, a member of the Federation of Trade Unions–Burma, was sentenced to "transportation for life" – defined in the 1957 Burmese Penal Code as equivalent to transportation for 20 years – for committing "High Treason" and to 10 years' additional imprisonment. He had been arrested in June and accused of passing money to the NLD and assembling explosives in order to assassinate an unnamed SLORC member. His trial was reportedly held *in camera* and lasted only 10 days.

Reports of torture and ill-treatment of prisoners in prisons and labour camps continued. Prisoner of conscience Khin Zaw Win, arrested in 1994 (see *Amnesty International Report 1995*), was reported to have been badly tortured in early 1996, and remained in poor health.

Prison conditions for political prisoners often amounted to cruel, inhuman or degrading treatment. Prisoners suffered from lack of proper medical care and an inadequate diet. In April and May at least 51 political prisoners, including Khin Zaw Win, were transferred to prisons far from their homes, making it extremely difficult to receive supplementary food and medicine from their families.

U Tin Shwe, a 67-year-old lawyer, writer and NLD founding member imprisoned since 1990, died of a heart attack in

April in Insein Prison. Requests for proper medical care had reportedly been ignored. He was one of 29 political prisoners who had been placed in tiny cells meant for dogs and deprived of food and medical care during 1995 and 1996 (see *Amnesty International Report 1997*).

The military continued to commit widespread human rights violations against ethnic minorities, including extrajudicial executions, forcible relocations, torture and ill-treatment. In April Pa Nya Paw, a Karen villager, was tortured to death by the army during interrogation about the whereabouts of KNU soldiers. From January onwards, thousands of people were randomly seized by the army and forced to carry supplies and ammunition during the offensive against the KNU. Porters were held in army custody for periods ranging from a few days to several months. They usually received little food and no medical treatment, and were beaten if they were unable to carry their loads.

Civilians of all ethnicities were routinely seized by the military for forced labour duties on infrastructural projects such as roads, quarries and railways. Conditions often amounted to cruel, inhuman or degrading treatment. Members of ethnic minorities, particularly the Karen, Karenni, Mon and Shan, were most at risk. A group of 400 Mon refugees sent back to Myanmar by the Thai army were subjected to forced portering and labour on army bases by the Burmese army. All of them had fled back to Thailand by July.

In January Burmese soldiers crossed into Thailand and attacked two Karenni refugee camps. They opened fire, deliberately killing two Karenni refugees and seriously wounding nine others (see **Thailand** entry).

Forcible relocations, apparently carried out solely because of ethnic origin or perceived political beliefs, continued, particularly in the Shan State, but also in other areas, including the Kayin, Kayah, Rakhine, and Mon States. Relocations were often accompanied by death threats, ill-treatment, and restrictions on freedom of movement. From March onwards, tens of thousands of Shan civilians were forcibly evicted from their villages by the army. Tens of thousands fled to Thailand. There were widespread reports of troops killing scores of villagers who attempted to return to their homes to retrieve their belongings. In June and July 300 Shan civilians were reportedly killed by the army in retaliation for the killing of 25 ethnic Burman civilians by an unknown Shan armed opposition group. In March Muslims in the Kayin State were forcibly evicted from their villages under threat of death and, beginning in February, thousands of Karen civilians in Papun District, northern Kayin State, were also evicted by the army. Ninety-three villages were destroyed and at least nine Karen civilians shot dead.

In May two convicted drug-traffickers were sentenced to death for heroin possession after having been arrested in August 1996 in the Shan State. No executions were known to have taken place.

The Democratic Kayin Buddhist Army (DKBA), a Karen armed opposition group, continued to attack Karen refugees in Thailand; at least five refugees were killed and several injured. In January the DKBA destroyed two refugee camps in Thailand, leaving 7,000 Karen civilians homeless.

In February and October Amnesty International published reports about the continuing repression of students and members of the NLD. In July the organization published *Myanmar: Ethnic minority rights under attack*, which detailed human rights violations against the Mon, Karen, Karenni and Shan ethnic minorities.

Amnesty International continued to call for the release of prisoners of conscience and for an end to torture and ill-treatment.

NEPAL

Scores of people arrested for political reasons in 1996, including possible prisoners of conscience, remained in detention without trial. Torture by police and forest guards was widespread; at least three people were reported to have died as a result. Nine people were killed in alleged "encounters" by police. A Supreme Court ruling confirmed the abolition of the death penalty for all offences. An armed opposition group was responsible for serious human rights abuses, including deliberate and arbitrary killings of civilians.

Increasing political instability contributed to a lack of decisive action by the authorities in the field of human rights.

Three different coalition governments held power during the year. Members of the *Rastriya Prajatrantra Party*, National Democratic Party, held the balance of power between the Communist Party of Nepal–United Marxist Leninist and the Nepali Congress Party (NCP) and occupied key posts in each coalition. Consecutive governments failed to appoint members to the National Human Rights Commission established in October 1996 (see *Amnesty International Report 1997*).

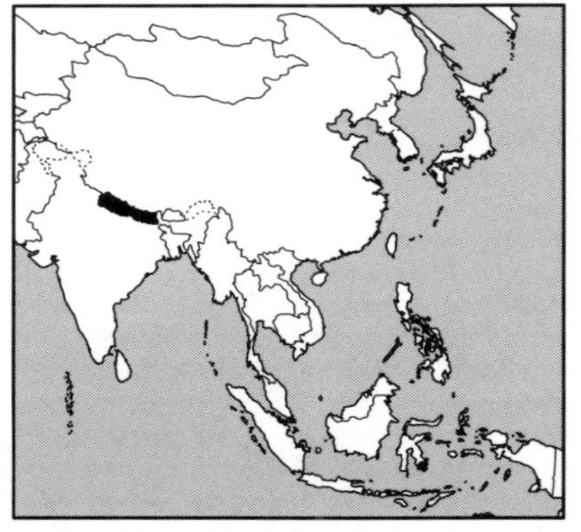

Armed conflict between the Communist Party of Nepal (CPN) (Maoist) and the security forces after the declaration of "people's war" in February 1996 (see *Amnesty International Report 1997*) continued, particularly in the Mid-Western Region.

Initially, the government of Prime Minister Lokendra Bahadur Chand, which came to power in March, took various measures to address the deteriorating human rights situation, including setting up a Task Force to make recommendations for the protection of human rights. However, after a few months, the government adopted a more hard-line approach. In August it approved the Terrorist and Disruptive Crimes (Control and Punishment) Bill allowing, among other things, trials before special courts. However, the Bill was dropped after a change of government in early October. The government also deployed several hundred army personnel in Rukum, Salyan, Jajarkot and Rolpa districts and reactivated the Public Security (Second Amendment) Act, 1991, which allows for people to be detained for up to 12 months on vague grounds such as "the interest of the common people". Several members of the Task Force, including its Chairman, resigned in August in protest over the government's measures.

On 4 June, 28 members of non-governmental organizations were arrested during a peaceful demonstration to commemorate the massacre in China in June 1989. Twenty others were arrested the following day during a demonstration calling for the release of Rongthong Kunley Dorji, a Bhutanese refugee detained in India awaiting the outcome of extradition proceedings to Bhutan. All were released without charge after several hours.

Scores of people arrested in 1996 on suspicion of being members or sympathizers of the CPN (Maoist), including possible prisoners of conscience, remained in detention without trial. Among them were several juveniles, including Bir Bahadur Gosain, reported to have been 13 years old at the time of arrest in December 1996. In August, 731 people were reported to be in detention or awaiting trial in connection with the "people's war", including 38 held under the Public Security Act. Jhakku Prasad Subedi, Chairman of the District Development Committee of Rolpa, who had been tortured while detained in February 1996 (see *Amnesty International Report 1997*), was released on bail on 24 March. His trial was still continuing at the end of the year.

Torture by police and forest guards was widespread. In February, 12 people, including an 11-year-old boy, were arrested by forest guards at Kamdi, Kohalpur district, on suspicion of theft. Four were tortured with electric shocks through a wire attached to the palms of their hands or to their ears. Bir Bahadur Gosain (see above) was also allegedly tortured at Chaurjhari police station, Rukum district, during the initial 30 days of his detention. He was beaten with sticks, including on the soles of his feet, and thrown into a water tank.

At least three people were reported to have died in police custody as a result of torture. Among them was Kabiraj Dangi, who was arrested in August in Simle, Rukum district, on suspicion of being a member of the CPN (Maoist). He was allegedly beaten in detention at Simle police station and during transfer to Musikot police station. He died at Machimi village, apparently as a result of torture, while being taken to Musikot police station. Several contradictory statements were made about the circumstances of his death. According to police at Simle, Kabiraj Dangi died from injuries sustained when he fell during an escape attempt, while police at Musikot alleged that he died in an "encounter". According to the post-mortem, he died due to heart and lung problems.

At least nine people were reportedly killed by police during alleged "encounters" in the context of the "people's war". They included those killed in five cases reported from Rolpa district.

In September the Supreme Court ruled that all existing provisions in several laws allowing for the imposition of the death penalty had *ipso facto* become inoperative one year after the Constitution was promulgated in 1990 (see *Amnesty International Report 1991*).

At least 18 people were reported to have been deliberately and arbitrarily killed by members of the CPN (Maoist). Among them were seven candidates and voters killed by the CPN (Maoist) in the run-up to local elections in May; the CPN (Maoist) had called for a boycott of the elections. Among those killed was Sita Ram Thapa, an NCP member from Amale in Sindhuli district. He was hacked to death at his home in May.

Amnesty International requested information from the government about Jhakku Prasad Subedi and several juveniles reportedly held without charge or trial on suspicion of being sympathizers of the CPN (Maoist). Amnesty International also called for investigations into several cases of torture and deaths in custody. The authorities did not respond. In March Amnesty International published a report, *Nepal: Human rights violations in the context of a Maoist "people's war"*, which included details of 52 cases of alleged extrajudicial executions by police and 13 deliberate and arbitrary killings by the CPN (Maoist). In May, in the run-up to local elections, Amnesty International called upon the government and the CPN (Maoist) to fully respect human rights.

NIGER

Scores of opposition party supporters were detained, many of them prisoners of conscience. Prisoners of conscience were sentenced to prison terms after unfair trials. The security forces were reportedly responsible for torture and extrajudicial executions. An armed opposition group took unarmed civilians as hostages.

The political deadlock stemming from the 1996 military coup that overthrew the government of elected President Mahamane Ousmane (see *Amnesty International Report 1997*) continued throughout the year. Negotiations between the government and the opposition started in late January but soon reached an impasse after one of the conditions demanded by opposition leaders – the dissolution of the National Assembly – was rejected by President Ibrahim Baré Maïnassara. There were also sporadic clashes in the east between the security forces and an armed opposition group, the *Front démocratique révolutionnaire* (FDR), Democratic Revolutionary Front.

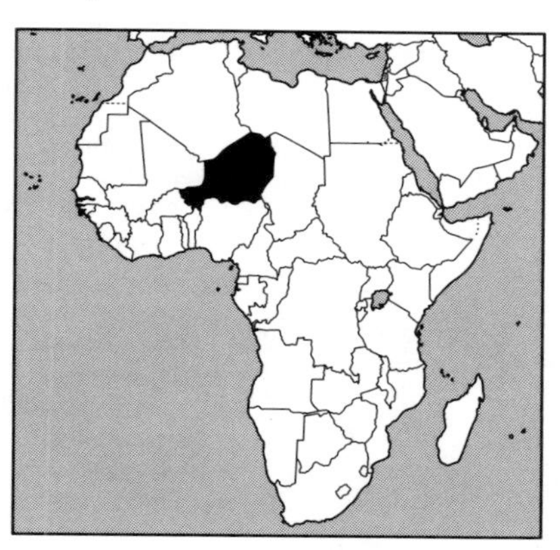

The opposition coalition, the *Front pour la restauration et la défense de la démocratie* (FRDD), Front for the Restoration and Defence of Democracy, organized several demonstrations. A demonstration in the capital, Niamey, in January, was violently dispersed by the security forces. Tear-gas was used and at least 20 people were beaten. A few hours later, leaders of the three main opposition parties were arrested: former President Ousmane, of the *Convention démocratique et sociale*, Democratic Social Convention; Mahamadou Issoufou, of the *Parti nigérien pour la démocratie et le socialisme*, Party for Democracy and Socialism of Niger; and Mamadou Tandja of the *Mouvement national pour la société de développement*, National Movement for the Society of

Development. Over the following days, the security forces arrested at least 100 more opposition party supporters and the government announced the reintroduction of the State Security Court, established in 1974 but unused since 1990. The procedures of this court allow incommunicado pre-trial detention (*garde à vue*) for up to two months, and defendants have no right of appeal to a higher court. In the event, the government did not re-establish the State Security Court, and released without charge all those detained in connection with the demonstration after about 10 days. Most or all of them were prisoners of conscience.

The authorities also detained people who criticized the government. Souleye Oumarou, a lawyer, was detained for three days in January on fraud charges. He was one of a group of lawyers who planned to bring a suit against President Maïnassara for overthrowing the elected President in January 1996. El Hadj Bagnou Bonkoukou, President of the *Ligue nigérienne de défense des droits de l'homme*, Human Rights Defence League of Niger, was sentenced to two years' imprisonment in October for criticizing the President of Niger in an interview published in a newspaper in Burkina Faso. He was provisionally released in December.

Two unfair and politically motivated trials led to the conviction of several prisoners of conscience. In March, nine people were sentenced to two months' imprisonment for "unlawful armed assembly" after an unfair trial held *in camera* using summary procedures. They had been arrested after an opposition demonstration that had been banned by the authorities, but most had not participated in the demonstration.

In April, 22 trade unionists were tried on charges of sabotage. Several were arrested after an anti-privatization strike in March that deprived Niamey of electricity. Two trade unionists were sentenced to two years' imprisonment and two others were sentenced to two months' imprisonment. Although acquitted, the other 18 trade unionists remained in detention following a prosecution appeal against the verdict.

In March military personnel wrecked the premises of an independent radio station, *Radio Anfani*. Two weeks later, five of the radio station's employees, including its general manager, Gremah Boucar, were arrested. Three were released, but Gremah Boucar and Harouna Issoufou, the night-watchman who had witnessed the attack, were charged with fraud and accused of ransacking the radio station themselves. They were conditionally released and Gremah Boucar publicly apologized to the army for having lodged a complaint.

Uniformed members of the security forces, acting under orders or on their own initiative, seized and tortured political opponents of the government. In February Elhadj Oumarou Oubandawaki, an FRDD member, was seized by six uniformed police officers, who beat him and then abandoned him outside Niamey. He lost several teeth in the attack and suffered a broken arm. In April Souley Adji, an academic, was seized by four men, one of whom was in military uniform. He was stripped naked and beaten unconscious. There were apparently no investigations into these incidents.

The security forces were reported to have extrajudicially executed unarmed civilians in eastern regions where the FDR armed opposition group was active. The victims were apparently killed because they belonged to the Toubou ethnic group. For example, Hassane Ali, a former local government official, was arrested by gendarmes on 27 May, released, then seized by soldiers a day later. He died shortly afterwards, apparently as a reult of torture. There was apparently no inquiry into his death.

The FDR reportedly took unarmed civilians hostage, including a Canadian aid worker who was held for four months

In May Amnesty International published *Niger: Harassment of government opponents has become systematic*, in which it urged the authorities to put an end to human rights violations committed with impunity by its security forces. Amnesty International also called on the government not to reactivate the State Security Court and to ensure that trials by ordinary courts met international standards for fair trial.

NIGERIA

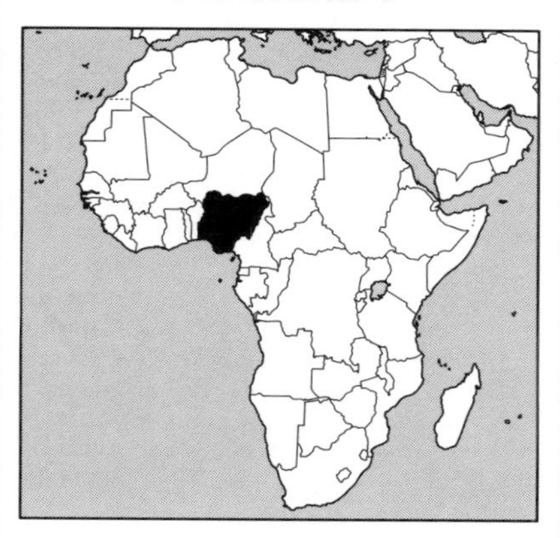

Hundreds of prisoners of conscience and possible prisoners of conscience, including human rights defenders, were imprisoned during the year. Most were detained without charge or trial; others had been convicted in unfair political trials. There were reports of torture and ill-treatment of prisoners, and at least two prisoners of conscience died as a result of prison conditions so harsh as to amount to cruel, inhuman or degrading treatment. People with links to the political opposition or human rights groups were attacked and threatened, allegedly by government agents. At least 43 prisoners were sentenced to death and 33 executed.

Local government and state assembly elections took place as part of the transition to civilian rule promised by the military government of General Sani Abacha and scheduled for completion by October 1998. However, the new Constitution recommended by a part-elected Constitutional Conference in 1995 had still not been published by the end of the year. Local government elections in March were marred by the disqualification, before and after election, of candidates perceived to support the excluded pro-democracy opposition, and by fraud, vote-rigging and corruption. Security police again screened candidates for state assembly elections in December. Elections for state governors were postponed until 1998.

The government continued to obstruct fact-finding visits by intergovernmental organizations (see *Amnesty International Report 1997*). In March the UN Commission on Human Rights adopted a critical resolution, appointing a Special Rapporteur to keep the human rights situation in Nigeria under scrutiny. The Commonwealth Heads of Government Meeting in October maintained the suspension of Nigeria's membership of the Commonwealth which was imposed after the 1995 Ogoni executions (see *Amnesty International Report 1996*). The African Commission on Human and Peoples' Rights sent a fact-finding delegation to Nigeria in March, but by the end of the year had not made known any of its findings or recommendations.

There were sporadic bomb attacks by unidentified perpetrators, directed mainly at military targets, in which several people were killed. The authorities accused the opposition grouping, the National Democratic Coalition (NADECO), of responsibility and in March charged 16 people with treason, including pro-democracy and human rights activists (see below). The relocation of two local government headquarters led to scores of deaths in communal unrest between March and July around Warri, where oil-workers were taken hostage and a military taskforce sent in; and from August in Osun State where hundreds were displaced. In December the government announced that it had thwarted a coup attempt by the Deputy Head of State and other senior armed forces officers (see below).

Numerous meetings organized by human rights or pro-democracy groups were forcibly broken up by the security police. The authorities imposed restrictions on government critics and human rights activists by seizing their passports or briefly detaining them.

Hundreds of prisoners of conscience and possible prisoners of conscience were detained, many without charge or trial. They included human rights defenders, journalists, members of pro-democracy and Islamist opposition groups, trade unionists, politicians, soldiers and relatives of political prisoners.

Among the prisoners of conscience held without trial was Moshood Abiola, winner of the 1993 presidential elections. He had been imprisoned since June 1994, ostensibly awaiting trial for treason, and denied access to his family and lawyers (see previous *Amnesty International Reports*).

In March the authorities charged 16 people, including leading pro-democracy and human rights activists, with treason, a capital offence. The 12 imprisoned in Nigeria included Dr Frederick Fasehun, Acting Chairman of the Campaign for Democracy (CD), and Olu Falae, a former government minister and member of NADECO. Four exiles were charged including writer and Nobel laureate Wole Soyinka and NADECO leader retired General Alani Akinrinade. Relatives and employees of General Akinrinade were arrested in January and February and detained without charge for several weeks. Among them was Dr Adegbenga Adebusuyi who was subsequently charged with treason and was reported to have been hung by his feet and kicked in the head.

Leading members of the Muslim Brotherhood, an Islamist opposition group in northern Nigeria, were charged in July with inciting public disaffection and sedition; they had been detained incommunicado for 10 months (see *Amnesty International Report 1997*). Their trial started in October but had not concluded by the end of the year. They included Ibrahim Yakub Al-Zakzaky, an Islamic scholar and preacher, whose family were reportedly driven from their home by the security forces, and Hamid Danlami, publisher of the Muslim Brotherhood's newspaper.

A group of 20 Ogoni prisoners continued to be held without trial on identical murder charges to those used to execute Ken Saro-Wiwa and eight other Ogoni in November 1995. Many said they had been tortured or severely beaten after their arrests in 1994, and all were ill, some seriously, as a result of insanitary prison conditions and lack of food or medical treatment (see previous *Amnesty International Reports*).

Other prisoners of conscience and possible prisoners of conscience were held without charge.

Two oil workers' leaders remained detained without charge for their involvement in a two-month strike by oil workers in 1994. Frank Ovie Kokori and Milton G. Dabibi were denied visits by lawyers or union colleagues, and in May 1997 Frank Kokori's home was reportedly looted and his wife and son threatened by unidentified assailants after his wife made a public appeal for his release. Prison doctors recommended that Frank Kokori receive medical treatment for a spinal injury, but the authorities refused to allow it. Chief Olabiyi Durojaiye, a 63-year-old lawyer and founding member of NADECO who had been arrested in December 1996, was held incommunicado throughout the year without explanation. He was held in solitary confinement, and was reported to have become haggard and disoriented as a result of the harsh conditions.

Scores of journalists were detained, usually for short periods, throughout the year. Moshood Fayemiwo, publisher of the *Razor* news magazine, was reportedly abducted by Nigerian security agents from neighbouring Benin in February and subsequently detained in an underground cell at a Directorate of Military Intelligence detention facility in Lagos.

In October and November, some 30 journalists were arrested in a crack-down on the opposition press. Those who were still detained, incommunicado and without charge or trial, at the end of the year included Soji Omotunde, editor of the *African Concord* magazine, and Babafemi Ojudu, managing editor of the newspaper group *The News*.

Foday Sankoh, leader of the Revolutionary United Front, an armed political group in Sierra Leone, was arrested in Lagos in March, reportedly for possession of arms and ammunition. He was still detained under house arrest without charge or trial at the end of the year.

In December the Deputy Head of State, Lieutenant-General Oladipo Diya, was arrested with 10 other officers and a civilian. The government said that they had plotted to overthrow the government. They had not been charged and were still held incommunicado at the end of the year. Officials warned journalists not to speculate about whether there really had been a coup plot, making reference to the imprisonment for treason in 1995 of four journalists who had reported the fabrication of evidence and grossly unfair trials of treason suspects.

Prisoners of conscience convicted of treason in secret and grossly unfair military trials in 1995 continued to be held (see *Amnesty International Report 1996*). Those sentenced to long prison terms included political leaders, such as retired General Olusegun Obasanjo, Head of State from 1976 to 1979, and human rights campaigners Dr Beko Ransome-Kuti and Shehu Sani, CD Chairman and Deputy Chairman respectively. Four editors and journalists were among this group; they included Kunle Ajibade and Chris Anyanwu.

Eleven soldiers continued to be held despite an announcement by the military authorities that they had been released (see *Amnesty International Report 1997*), and despite an order for the release of seven of them in July by the Federal High Court in Lagos. They had been convicted of involvement in a 1990 coup attempt following unfair and secret military trials.

Torture and ill-treatment of political and criminal suspects by soldiers and police at the time of arrest and to extract confessions were routine.

Scores of supporters of the Movement for the Survival of the Ogoni People (MOSOP) were allegedly arrested, beaten and briefly detained by officers of the Rivers State Internal Security Task Force for commemorating Ogoni Day on 4 January. Two journalists were reportedly beaten by soldiers at the State Military Administrator's offices in Owerri, Imo State. One, Chief Oni Egbunine, publisher of the newspaper *The Horn*, was reportedly arrested and beaten unconscious in July after his newspaper published allegations of corruption among state officials. The other, Oby Eke-Aghbai, a leading member of the Nigeria Union of Journalists, was reportedly whipped with a belt in September. Also in September Chris Ikwunze, Rivers State correspondent of the *Vanguard* newspaper, was reportedly horsewhipped by soldiers for smuggling out a note while he was detained without charge for several days for reporting a press statement by MOSOP.

Conditions for most prisoners were so injurious to health as to amount to cruel, inhuman or degrading treatment. Medical care was virtually non-existent and political prisoners were frequently refused access to treatment. In December former Deputy Head of State retired Major-General Shehu Musa Yar'Adua, a critic of the government's transition program, died in unexplained circumstances after becoming ill in Abakaliki prison. Neither his death nor that of Staff Sergeant Patrick Usikekpo, another prisoner of conscience imprisoned after the grossly unfair treason trials in 1995, were the subject of independent investigations. Patrick Usikekpo was reported to have died in a typhoid fever epidemic in December which killed six prisoners at Uyo prison.

Attacks and death threats against Nigerians associated with the pro-democracy and human rights movements continued, some allegedly carried out by government agents. In January Abraham Adesanya, then Vice-President of NADECO, escaped injury when unidentified gunmen fired at his car from another vehicle. Human rights lawyers Chief Gani Fawehinmi and Femi Falana, and journalists at the magazine *Tell* reported death threats during the year.

At least 33 people were executed during the year, including a 17-year-old minor who had sought an urgent injunction from the Federal High Court to prevent his execution. Chidiebere Onuoha was shot dead in front of a crowd of thousands in July after being convicted by a Robbery and Firearms Tribunal, a special court directly appointed by the military authorities which allows no right of appeal.

In July, six men were publicly executed by firing-squad in Abia State, the first executions in the state since its creation in 1991. Their identities were not published but they had reportedly been under sentence of death for armed robbery since 1979.

At least 43 prisoners were sentenced to death; as many as 800 prisoners were under sentence of death at the end of the year. In November the High Court in Zaria sentenced 24 prisoners to death for a mob killing during an industrial dispute in 1995.

Throughout the year, Amnesty International appealed for the release of prisoners of conscience, for the prompt and fair trial of all political prisoners, for an end to torture and the death penalty, and for investigations into deaths in custody and attacks and threats against human rights defenders and opponents of the government.

Amnesty International urged the UN Commission on Human Rights, which met in March, to appoint a Special Rapporteur on Nigeria after its Special Rapporteurs on extrajudicial, summary or arbitrary executions and on the independence of judges and lawyers continued to be denied access to key political prisoners. In April and July Amnesty International provided written and verbal submissions on Nigeria to the Commonwealth Ministerial Action Group, urging the Commonwealth to set specific goals on human rights for the Nigerian authorities to achieve.

In September Amnesty International published *Nigeria: No significant change – human rights violations continue,* and called on the government to commit itself to establishing respect for human rights in Nigeria and to cooperating with the international community in this endeavour – in particular by implementing the recommendations of the UN Secretary-General, the UN Human Rights Committee, the UN Commission on Human Rights and the Commonwealth Ministerial Action Group.

Amnesty International protested at restrictions on its activities in Nigeria. These included the seizure of the passports of two officers of Amnesty International's Nigerian Section, which were returned in October.

OMAN

At least 12 possible prisoners of conscience were detained; five of them were reportedly sentenced to prison terms after a secret trial.

In June the Government of Sultan Qaboos Bin Sa'id issued a decree allowing women to stand for election to the *Majlis al-Shura,* Consultative Council. Two women were later elected to the Consultative Council, which comprises 82 seats. Four women were appointed to the State Council (senate), which was established in December.

At least 12 possible prisoners of conscience were detained at the end of August or the beginning of September. They were reportedly suspected of being Shi'a activists. Most of them were released after several weeks in detention, but at least five were still held at the end of the year, reportedly serving prison sentences ranging from 18 months to three years. No details were available regarding the trial proceedings or the exact charges on which they were convicted. The five, all said to be members of the Shi'a community, reportedly included Dr Hassan Muhsan, a physician, and Jum'a Abd al-Reda Jum'a, a manager at the Ministry of Civil Services, who were said to be serving sentences of 18 months' and three years' imprisonment, respectively.

PAKISTAN

Hundreds of political prisoners, including prisoners of conscience, were detained without charge or trial; others received unfair trials. Torture and ill-treatment continued to be widespread, leading to some 35 deaths in custody. At least two people were flogged. At least 50 possible extrajudicial executions were reported. At least 88 people were sentenced to death and at least six were executed. Armed opposition groups were responsible for deliberate and arbitrary killings of civilians.

In general elections in February, the Pakistan Muslim League, led by Prime Minister Nawaz Sharif, obtained a two-thirds majority. Parliament amended the Constitution in April to remove the President's powers to dissolve parliament and dismiss elected governments, and again in July to curtail parliamentarians' right to vote against party policy.

In December Rafiq Tarar was elected President, following the resignation of Farooq Leghari.

In Punjab province some 200 people were killed in sectarian violence between the majority Sunni and the minority Shi'a communities. In Sindh province, scores of people were injured and about 400 killed in political and ethnically-motivated violence. The government responded with mass arbitrary arrests and detentions. In August parliament passed the Anti-Terrorism Act which gave police sweeping powers to use lethal force against anyone "committing, or believed to be about to commit, a terrorist offence" and established special courts to summarily try people charged with "terrorist" offences. The special courts, set up in Sindh and Punjab, suspend several legal safeguards available in regular proceedings; trials before such courts must conclude within seven days. At the end of the year several petitions challenging the constitutionality of the new courts were pending in the Supreme Court and the four high courts; the higher judiciary had explicitly warned against instituting a new parallel court system. Existing Special Courts for the Suppression of Terrorist Activities were closed in Sindh and Punjab provinces and thousands of pending cases were transferred to the new courts.

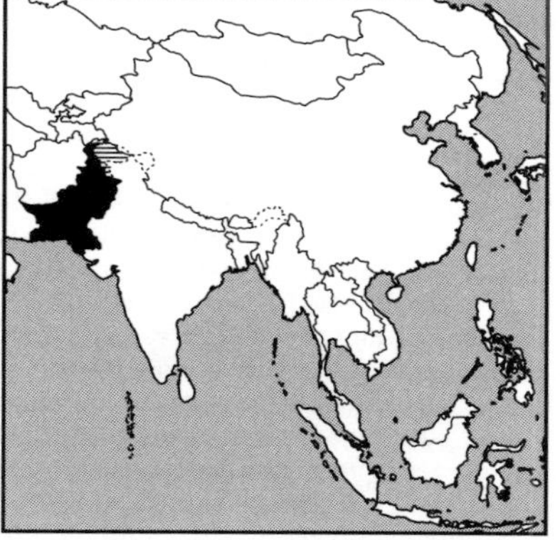

In February police were reportedly involved in an attack by several hundred Muslims on a Christian community in Shantinagar, Punjab province, following rumours that some Christians had desecrated the *Qur'an*. One man was killed in the attack and over 300 homes were burned down. The incident was apparently instigated by police in retaliation for the suspension of three police officers disciplined after being found guilty of desecrating the *Bible* in January. A judicial inquiry submitted its report to the government in July, but it was not made public.

In June the Prime Minister announced that a judicial inquiry under a Supreme Court judge was to investigate alleged extrajudicial executions committed in Karachi under the previous government; it had not submitted its findings by the end of the year. A senate committee, authorized to trace 28 members of the Muttahida Qaumi Movement who allegedly "disappeared" in 1995 and 1996, questioned police and examined police records but failed to trace them.

In July the Chief Justice initiated hearings into the sectarian and politically motivated killings in Karachi and in Punjab province, under the Supreme Court's powers to investigate questions of fundamental rights which are of public importance.

In August the Commission of Inquiry for Women set up in 1994 submitted its recommendations to the government. These included the repeal of the *Zina* law relating to "unlawful fornication", which contravenes constitutional safeguards and provisions of the UN Convention on the Elimination of All Forms of Discrimination against Women (the Women's Convention) ratified by Pakistan in 1996. However, no action to implement these recommendations was known to have been taken.

At least 32 members of the Ahmadiyya community were charged with religious offences during the year, including two who were charged with blasphemy under section 295-C of the Pakistan Penal Code which carries a mandatory death sentence. They were prisoners of conscience.

Riaz Ahmed Chowdhury and his three relatives from Mianwali in Punjab province (see *Amnesty International Report 1997*), who were detained in November 1993 and charged with blasphemy, continued to be held without trial. Their bail application had been pending in the Supreme Court since 1994.

In September a 16-year-old Ahmadi boy from Sanghar district, Sindh province, was charged with blasphemy for reciting Muslim words of belief. He was also charged with possessing a gun, and consequently his case was to be tried by a special anti-terrorist court. He went into hiding before he could be arrested.

The trial of Ayub Masih, a Christian, on blasphemy charges (see *Amnesty International Report 1997*) was continuing at the end of the year. He escaped unhurt when attackers shot at him in Sahiwal court in November.

Dozens of prisoners of conscience were held on false charges or without charge or trial, often incommunicado and in undeclared places of detention. During a surprise visit to a Shikarpur police station in July, a Sindh provincial minister found 11 detainees held in an adjacent mosque, clamped in bar fetters. They had not been charged and their arrest had not been recorded.

Throughout the year police arbitrarily detained hundreds of people without charge, usually for short periods. In July police arrested and detained for several days some 175 students from a Shi'a religious school in Lahore where a criminal suspect was believed to be hiding. In Sindh province, following the deliberate and arbitrary killing in July of Shahid Hamid, director of the Karachi Electric Supply Corporation, over 2,000 people, including workers for all the opposition parties, were arrested. Most were released after a few hours or days.

Dozens of people were held under preventive detention provisions, apparently because criminal charges could not be framed against them. In July the Lahore High Court declared the detention of Tahir Khan Niazi under the Maintenance of Public Order Ordinance of 1960 to be unlawful, stating that a person could not be detained under preventive detention laws solely on the likelihood that a case would be registered against them. Tahir Khan Niazi had been detained since May, despite having obtained pre-arrest bail, and was interrogated by the Federal Investigation Agency in its undeclared detention centre in Islamabad. A corruption charge was being prepared against him but had not been finalized when he was arrested.

Scores of political prisoners were denied fair trials and legal safeguards were often ignored. Humayun Far, a journalist, was arrested in June. Local police denied holding him but, during the hearing of a *habeas corpus* petition filed by his son before the Lahore High Court, state representatives admitted that he was being detained by military intelligence, allegedly for anti-state activities. Despite court orders, Humayun Far was not brought before the court, nor were charges against him made known to his family. In July the court dismissed the petition when it was told that Humayun Far was already being tried *in camera* by court martial for espionage. In September Humayun Far was sentenced to five years' imprisonment by a military court for anti-state activities. On 2 October he was transferred to hospital with hepatitis, where he was held in fetters despite the fact that he was in a coma. He was unconditionally released on 7 October.

Torture, including rape, and ill-treatment in police custody continued to be widespread, leading to at least 35 deaths. In July a 15-year-old girl was reportedly raped by three police officers in Mithi, Sindh province. Although a complaint was filed, police delayed arrest of the alleged perpetrators who remained at liberty on pre-arrest bail at the end of the year. In August, police in Faisalabad reportedly cut off the tongue of a criminal suspect, Ghulam Murtaza, who refused to pay a bribe. Police claimed that he had maimed himself to escape punishment. Detainees continued to be placed in iron leg-fetters when brought to court in some parts of the country.

Chanesar Palari died in custody at Bhitai Nagar police station in Hyderabad in August, allegedly after torture. He and seven of his relatives had been detained by police officers nine days earlier and robbed of a large amount of money. There were numerous burns on his body and the skin on his hands had peeled off. Five days after his death, another detainee, Finyas Masih, died after allegedly being tortured in the same police station. Complaints against the police were registered in both cases but all the accused remained free on bail. The family of Chanesar Palari agreed a compromise with the accused in October and the charges were dropped.

In May, 14-year-old Famidullah and Zaman Shah were publicly flogged in Bara Bazaar in Khyber Agency after a tribal council found them guilty of sexual intercourse. The area has its own legal and judicial system. Although flogging is banned for all offences except for those for which it is a mandatory punishment under Islamic provisions of the penal code, dozens of people convicted of drug offences in various parts of the country were sentenced to flogging. It was not known if these punishments were carried out.

The whereabouts of four members of the Ansari family who "disappeared" in May 1996 remained unknown as no further steps were taken by the authorities to trace them (see *Amnesty International Report 1997*).

At least 50 possible extrajudicial executions were reported. In most cases the authorities claimed that the victims had died in exchanges of fire with police. In

June, 17-year-old Yar Mohammad Makrani was reportedly shot dead in Tando Jam, Sindh province, by paramilitary Shahbaz Rangers who opened fire on local people when they refused to hand over criminal suspects. Three Ranger personnel were charged with murder, but no one had been arrested by the end of the year.

A tribunal investigating the killing of Mir Murtaza Bhutto and his associates (see *Amnesty International Report 1997*) said in June that the killings had been extrajudicial and presupposed clearance from high-level political authorities. In July Asif Zardari, husband of former Prime Minister Benazir Bhutto, and 18 former officials were charged with murder and several were arrested. The trial was continuing at the end of the year.

At least 88 people were sentenced to death, most for murder after summary trials by special courts. In April, the death penalty was extended to the offence of gang-rape. Prime Minister Sharif announced that convicted rapists would be hanged in front of the victims' homes. At least six people were executed, including Shamoun Masih, sentenced to death for a murder committed in 1988 when he was only 14 years old. The execution of Maqsud Ahmad, sentenced to death for a murder committed in 1989 to which two other men had confessed, was stayed one day before the scheduled date, pending a review by the Supreme Court. The review had not been completed by the end of the year.

In September, a tribal *jirga* (council) in Hyderabad imposed "death sentences" on a newly-wed couple for the alleged abduction of the bride by the groom and executed them. Police filed murder charges against the *jirga* members.

Members of opposition groups committed dozens of human rights abuses. In Punjab province, civilians were victims of deliberate and arbitrary killings by members of religious groups. Seven lawyers were deliberately killed in June alone. Places of worship were indiscriminately attacked by members of religious groups leading to the deaths of dozens of men, women and children. Retired Lahore High Court Judge Arif Iqbal Bhatti was shot dead by unidentified members of religious groups in October. His death was believed to be linked to his role in the acquittal in 1995 of Salamat Masih and Rehmat Masih who had been sentenced to death for blasphemy (see *Amnesty International Report 1996*). In Sindh province, prominent citizens, including administrators and relatives of government officials, were killed or injured in deliberate attacks. In August members of the Sindh National Front attacked and injured journalist Shakeel Naich of the *Awami Awaz* newspaper apparently because they objected to his reports.

In March Amnesty International published a report, *Pakistan: Women's human rights remain a dead letter*, highlighting the government's failure to end discrimination against women in law or practice one year after ratification of the UN Women's Convention. On the occasion of the 50th anniversary of Pakistan's creation in August, Amnesty International published a report, *Pakistan: Time to take human rights seriously*, and urged the new government to commit itself to the promotion and protection of the range of fundamental rights guaranteed in the Constitution. In a report published in October, *Pakistan: Legalizing the impermissible – the new anti-terrorism law*, Amnesty International urged the government not to suspend legal safeguards in its pursuit of law and order and to repeal the act which facilitates police abuse and unfair trials.

PALESTINIAN AUTHORITY
(AREAS UNDER THE JURISDICTION OF THE)

At least 400 suspected opponents of the Palestinian Authority were arrested; they included prisoners of conscience and possible prisoners of conscience. More than 115 political detainees arrested in previous years, including possible prisoners of conscience, remained in detention without charge or trial. At least one person "disappeared". Trials of detainees charged with political offences frequently failed to meet international fair trial standards; at least 30 people received grossly unfair trials before the State Security Court. Torture of detainees remained widespread. Seven detainees died in custody. Unlawful killings, including possible extrajudicial executions, continued to be reported. Seven people were

sentenced to death; no one was executed and one death sentence was commuted.

In January Israel withdrew from 80 per cent of Hebron, leaving the main towns in the West Bank, except East Jerusalem, under the sole jurisdiction of the Palestinian Authority. After suicide bombings by *Hamas* and Islamic *Jihad*, two Islamist opposition groups, killed 24 people, including seven suicide bombers, the Israeli Government carried out large-scale arrests of Palestinians in areas partly or solely under Israeli control. The Israeli authorities imposed repeated border closures, preventing inhabitants of areas under the sole control of the Palestinian Authority from entering other areas (see **Israel and the Occupied Territories** entry).

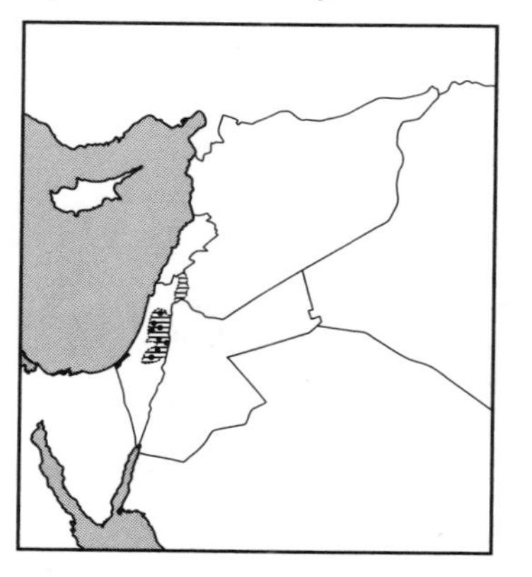

The Basic Law, which passed its first reading in the Legislative Council in 1996 (see *Amnesty International Report 1997*), had not been approved by President Yasser Arafat by the end of the year. The Palestinian Independent Commission for Citizens' Rights, set up by President Arafat in 1993, published a number of reports on human rights issues and stated in its annual report that human rights violations were still widespread but that the authorities and security forces showed greater willingness to respond to its inquiries. A new Attorney General, Fayez Abu Rahma, was appointed in July and promised to re-examine the files of 185 political detainees held since May 1994 and to release those who had not been involved in any criminal act. In August he ordered the release of 11 detainees held for up to two years without charge or trial. They were released the same day but were immediately rearrested by the Preventive Security Service (*amn al-wiqa'i*) (PSS). All of the detainees remained held at the end of the year.

At least 11 different security services continued to operate, although unpublished orders attempted to define more precisely their spheres of operation, giving the police force sole responsibility for interrogating common law suspects. However, the guidelines were frequently not implemented and families of those arrested frequently had difficulty in locating and gaining access to detained family members.

Prisoners of conscience arrested during the year for peaceful opposition activities included Da'ud Kuttab, Head of the Modern Communications Centre at al-Quds University. He was arrested in May and held in Ramallah police station for one week, reportedly for televising Legislative Council debates concerning its Human Rights and Monitoring Committee's report on corruption. He was released without charge. Fathi Subuh, Assistant Professor of Education at al-Azhar University in Gaza, was arrested in July after setting an examination paper which contained questions relating to corruption in the Palestinian Authority and the university administration. While held by the PSS in Tel al-Hawa' Prison in Gaza he was beaten and forced to sit in painful positions for long periods. He held a number of hunger-strikes, lasting up to 26 days. Fathi Subuh's lawyer brought a *habeas corpus* petition before the High Court in Gaza. The High Court repeatedly postponed the case before ruling in October that the case did not come under its jurisdiction, as it was before the State Security Court. The High Court failed to examine allegations that Fathi Subuh was tortured in detention. In discussions with an Amnesty International delegate, the head of the PSS in Gaza did not deny the allegations of torture and stated that Fathi Subuh had been arrested on charges of "collaboration" and "illicit sex". In October Fathi Subuh collapsed in prison and was transferred to hospital. He was released on bail in November.

At least 300 suspected supporters of Islamist opposition groups, including prisoners of conscience, were arrested by the Palestinian Authority following the suicide bombings in Israel in March, July and September. Those arrested in September included members of the *Hizb al-Khalas*, Salvation Party, a political party opposed to the peace process which does not advocate violence. Some reports of torture or ill-treatment of *Hamas* supporters were received; for instance nine suspected members of *Hamas* were allegedly tortured in Dhahariya detention centre. Most supporters of Islamic groups arrested during the year were released after several months' detention without charge or trial, but at least 140 arrested in 1997 and in previous years remained in prison at the end of the year. Shaykh Mahmud Muslah, a *Hamas* activist arrested in September and held without charge or trial, whose release was ordered by the Palestinian High Court in November after a test case, remained in prison.

More than 115 other political detainees arrested in previous years remained in detention without charge or trial; some had no access to families or the outside world. They included Faruq Abu Hassan, detained incommunicado by the military intelligence (*istikhbarat*) in Gaza Central Prison since November 1994. Others detained throughout the year for political reasons included up to 100 people suspected of "collaboration" with Israel or selling land to Israelis, offences defined as treason.

Two students from Bir Zeit University whose release had been ordered in August 1996 by the High Court of Justice, were eventually released in January (see *Amnesty International Report 1997*).

There was at least one "disappearance". In July Shafiq Muhammad Hassan 'Abd al-Wahhab, a former inspector for the Israeli Department of Land Administration, was summoned to the *istikhbarat* headquarters in Ramallah. When he failed to return, his wife visited all the branches of the Palestinian security services and submitted formal *habeas corpus* requests through her lawyer, but the security services did not admit holding him.

At least 30 Palestinians received grossly unfair trials before State Security Courts. Three members of the al-Bheisi family were sentenced to death and seven members of the same family given terms of imprisonment in a pre-dawn trial in March. The trial, for the murder of Isma'il Hasuna, a PSS officer accused by the al-Bheisi family of killing a relative alleged to have "collaborated" with Israel during the Palestinian *intifada* between 1987 and 1993, took place before the Gaza State Security Court less than 48 hours after the murder. The trial was closed to the public and the defendants were represented by state-appointed military lawyers and had no time to prepare their defence. Trials of political detainees before military courts also failed to respect international fair trial standards.

Torture of detainees remained widespread, especially by the intelligence services (*mukhabarat*), the *istikhbarat* and the PSS. Methods reported included beatings, sometimes while hanging by the wrists, and prolonged sleep deprivation while sitting or standing in painful positions. Seven detainees died in custody, including two who died in circumstances where torture was believed to be the cause of death. Yusef Mahmud al-Baba died in January, a month after his arrest by the *istikhbarat* in Nablus. His body showed severe burns, bruises and rope marks. Five people, including the head of the *istikhbarat* in Nablus and the deputy governor, were arrested in connection with his death. However, they were not brought to justice and it was not clear whether any of them remained detained at the end of the year. After the death of Yusef Mahmud al-Baba, orders not to use violence against detainees were reportedly issued to Palestinian security services. In June Nasser Radwan was arrested in Beit Hanun by Force 17, one of the 11 Palestinian security forces, and severely beaten. He was taken to hospital brain-dead and died a week later. Eight members of Force 17 were tried before a special military court on charges of "unintentionally killing" Nasser Radwan and so "inciting the masses to rebel" against the Palestinian Authority. In July, three days after the death of Nasser Radwan, three officers of Force 17, including a colonel, were sentenced to death and three others to up to five years' imprisonment, in a summary trial before a special military court. Two were acquitted.

Two detainees, who had reportedly been tortured during detention, allegedly committed suicide. Torture after arrest and lack of medical treatment in prison may have hastened the deaths of three other detainees. No autopsy reports on these deaths were available to their families or to human rights organizations.

Torture of those accused of "collaboration" with Israel or selling land to Israelis appeared to be systematic. Muhammad Bakr, accused of "collaboration" with Israel and land-dealing, was arrested in June and beaten while hung by the wrists in detention centres in Qalqilya and Nablus. Torture or ill-treatment of criminal detainees appeared to be widespread in Gaza.

Unlawful killings, including possible extrajudicial executions, continued to occur. Three land-dealers were found dead during May after the Minister of Justice, Freih Abu Middein, announced that the Palestinian Authority would begin applying a Jordanian law which provided for the death penalty for those convicted of selling land to Jews. There were fears that statements by the Minister of Justice and the failure to condemn the killings appeared to constitute permission to security services to carry out extrajudicial executions with impunity. In June the Palestinian Authority made a public statement supporting the death sentence for land-dealers but rejecting any killing without trial and conviction. The Palestinian Authority announced that it was setting up a commission to investigate the deaths, but no results had been made public by the end of the year.

Seven people were sentenced to death, mostly on charges of murder or unlawful homicide. No one was executed. In a trial of four defendants, three of whom were members of Force 17, Fawzi Sawalha, a member of Force 17, was sentenced to death plus 22 years' imprisonment by a military court in Nablus in August on charges of "terrorizing civilians under the orders of the Israeli intelligence service". The other defendants received sentences of between five years and life plus 15 years' imprisonment. The trial fell short of international fair trial standards. Defence lawyers were not allowed free access to their clients and all defendants stated that they had been tortured to make confessions. Fawzi Sawalha stated that he had been taken by the *mukhabarat* into an olive grove where he was hit with a hammer on his head and knees, subjected to prolonged sleep deprivation, forced to remain in contorted positions, and threatened with reprisals against his family. No investigations were ordered by the judge into these allegations. The sentence was upheld by the military cassation court in Gaza, but commuted to life imprisonment by the President in October.

Amnesty International raised all its concerns, including torture, prolonged detention without trial and unfair trials, with members of the Palestinian Authority and heads of security forces. The organization also called for the death penalty to be abolished and all death sentences to be commuted. Amnesty International delegates made several visits to discuss issues of human rights protection and promotion with members of the Palestinian Authority and leading officers of Palestinian security services. Amnesty International continued to call on the USA and Israel not to put pressure on the Palestinian Authority to arrest and detain people without recognizably criminal charges and fair trials.

PANAMA

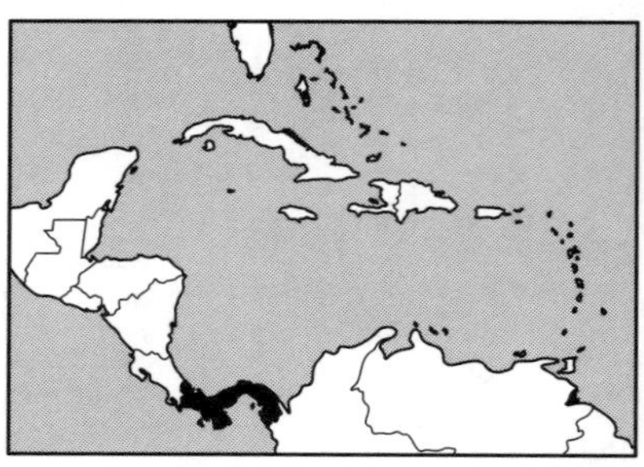

More than 300 Colombian refugees were forcibly returned. Ill-treatment by prison guards was reported and prison conditions were harsh.

Several hundred Colombian refugees fleeing persecution by Colombian paramilitary groups entered Panama in the Darién jungle region between March and April. Despite promises to the UN High Commissioner for Refugees (UNHCR) that they would not take immediate action, Panamanian authorities began the forcible return of more than 300 refugees in mid-April. In May the Panamanian Government accepted UNHCR intervention in the crisis. After conducting visits to refugee communities, UNHCR stated that the refugees' claims for asylum were fully justified.

In April more than 200 members of a Colombian paramilitary group crossed into Panama, reportedly attacking and killing at least four people, including Colombian refugees and Panamanian nationals. In June and July paramilitaries again crossed over the border into Darién province and "disappearances" and further killings were reported.

Ill-treatment by prison guards was reported. In March Jorge Luis Alvarado Guerra died of a heart attack after being beaten by prison guards at the prison of Tinajitas, in San Miguelito, Panama Province. Three guards were detained and accused of causing his death. At the end of the year, legal proceedings against them were continuing. In July prisoners at Renacer Prison in Colón, 55 of whom were on hunger-strike, were reportedly tied up and beaten. Overcrowding in prisons became more severe after the closure of Modelo Prison, Panama City, in late 1996. In mid-September riots were reported at the prisons of La Joyita and La Joya, on the outskirts of Panama City, and hunger-strikes were reported at various prisons throughout the country in protest at deteriorating conditions. These included lack of medical treatment, insanitary conditions as well as ill-treatment by prison guards.

In June Amnesty International produced a report, *Panama/Colombia: Refugees – the right to escape from death.* The report focused on human rights violations against Colombians on both sides of the border fleeing escalating violence in the northwest of Colombia.

PAPUA NEW GUINEA

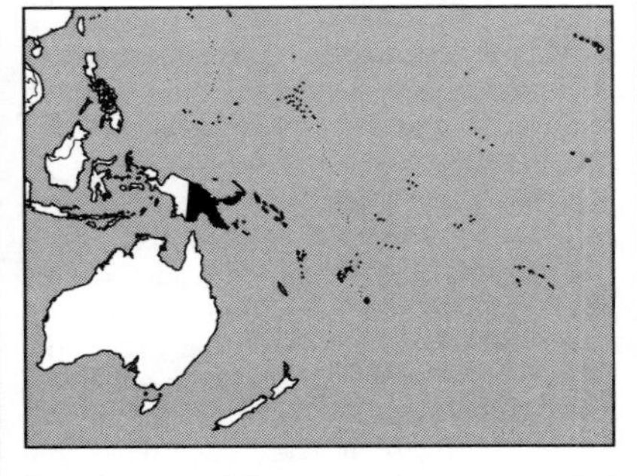

Four human rights activists were arrested and charged for their non-violent role in anti-government demonstrations. Ill-treatment by police continued to be reported. Possible extrajudicial executions continued to be reported on the island of Bougainville. In other parts of the country, at least five people were killed by police in suspicious circumstances or died in police custody. Three men were sentenced to death. No executions were carried out during the year. An armed secessionist group committed human rights abuses, including hostage-taking and deliberate and arbitrary killings.

In February it emerged that the government had recruited foreign mercenaries for deployment on the island of Bougainville, where the Papua New Guinea Defence Force (PNGDF) and government-backed paramilitary Resistance Forces continued fighting against the secessionist Bougainville Revolutionary Army (BRA). In March domestic opposition to the planned use of mercenaries culminated in the PNGDF Commander, Brigadier-General Jerry Singirok, calling on Prime Minister Sir Julius Chan to step down, and in large-scale protests, backed by PNGDF soldiers loyal to the PNGDF Commander, outside the National Parliament. In late March, the Prime Minister stepped down pending an inquiry into the hiring of the foreign mercenaries. The Prime Minister resumed power following completion of the inquiry, but national elections in June brought a new government, led by Prime Minister Bill Skate, to power. Brigadier-General Jerry Singirok was sacked as PNGDF Commander and at the end of the year was facing charges of sedition; five soldiers were convicted on charges of mutiny in December and sentenced to prison terms ranging from five to 10 years.

In October a truce was agreed by the government, the PNGDF, the Bougainville Resistance Forces, the government-funded Bougainville Transitional Government, and the military leaders of the BRA and its political party, the Bougainville Interim Government. The truce called for the respect of human rights and for neutral regional monitors of the cease-fire. In December defence and civilian personnel from neighbouring countries began arriving in Bougainville to monitor the truce which was holding at the end of the year. Plans for peace talks in 1998 made progress.

The new government announced that it would establish a National Commission on Human Rights, legislation for which had been prepared the previous year. Prime Minister Bill Skate stated that the proposed National Commission would consider human rights violations on Bougainville as a priority. In November, the Justice Minister announced that plans for the Commission had been postponed. He gave no indication of when the Commission would be established.

Restrictions on freedom of movement in Bougainville were lifted following the truce. It was not known whether previous restrictions on international human rights monitors would also be lifted.

In May a human rights lawyer and three human rights activists were detained and charged following their participation in demonstrations against the deployment of foreign mercenaries on Bougainville. The four men – Powes Parkop, Jonathan O'ata, John Kawowo and John Napu – were charged with unlawful assembly. At least one of the men was arrested without a warrant. All four appeared to have been charged for their non-violent role in protests against the government and the use of foreign mercenaries. The charges against the men were dropped in August, but in October, the charges were reinstated against Powes Parkop, John Napu and Jonathan O'ata. However, hearings related to the case were repeatedly postponed and the prosecution's case against the three men had still not been completed by the end of the year.

There were further reports of ill-treatment by the police, at times resulting in death. In February Guba Kevau was reportedly beaten in police custody in Boroko following his arrest for a curfew violation in the capital, Port Moresby. He was allegedly hit, punched and beaten with rifle butts. In May Jashihe Waniholo was awarded compensation after the National Court found that he had been beaten by police in custody in Boroko, Port Moresby, following his arrest in December 1995. Jashihe Waniholo was repeatedly beaten and thrown down on a concrete floor, as a result of which he suffered broken teeth, cuts and a dislocated shoulder. In March four police officers were suspended after allegedly beating to death a man arrested for suspected sorcery. It was not known if there had been an independent inquiry into the beating by police of William Tanka, Michael Peterson and Steve Pokua in June 1996 (see *Amnesty International Report 1997*).

There was a significant drop in the number of reports of "disappearances" on Bougainville. There was no information as to the whereabouts of Peter Ugua who "disappeared" after arrest by the PNGDF in 1996 (see *Amnesty International Report 1997*).

There was a dramatic decline in the number of extrajudicial executions reported on Bougainville. In February a man linked to the BRA, who allegedly shot dead a member of the Resistance Forces and a civilian, was arrested and then reportedly shot dead by the security forces in Kokopau.

The police announced that they were intending to investigate several incidents in which people were reportedly shot dead by police in other areas of the country. In March, police in Chimbu Province announced that they would investigate the death of a man reportedly shot by police. The outcome of the inquiry was not known by the end of the year. In May Golden Sasaviro was reportedly shot dead by police in the Asaro Valley, Eastern Highlands. The police announced an investigation into the incident but the outcome was not known by the end of the year.

While investigations appeared to have been initiated into some cases of possible human rights violations, others remained unresolved. There was no information concerning progress in the investigation into the death of Mathew Fugo who was shot by police in 1996, despite the announcement of a police inquiry (see *Amnesty International Report 1997*). Nor was there any information about inquiries initiated into "disappearances" and killings by the security forces on Bougainville in previous years.

There was no progress in the investigation into the killing of former Bougainville Transitional Government Premier, Theodore Miriung. No member of the security forces had been charged by the end of the year, despite a coroner's inquiry which concluded that Theodore Miriung had been killed by members of the Resistance Forces and the PNGDF. No other investigations were conducted into past violations on Bougainville, such as the killing of 14 civilians, including children, by the security forces in southwest Bougainville in December 1996.

Three men – Steven Ima Loke, Charles Kaona and Greg Wawa Kavoa – were sentenced to death in February for the rape and wilful murder of a woman in December 1995. The men appealed to the Supreme Court, but the outcome of their appeal was not known by the end of the year. No executions were carried out during the year.

On Bougainville, the BRA committed human rights abuses, including hostage-taking and deliberate and arbitrary killings. In July five members of the security forces taken hostage by the BRA in September 1996 were released unharmed (see *Amnesty International Report 1997*). In June John Momis, a representative for Bougainville in the National Parliament, was taken hostage by the BRA which demanded a large ransom and the withdrawal of government soldiers from Bougainville for his release. The BRA dropped their demands and he was released two weeks later. In June the BRA reportedly killed one of their own commanders who advocated disarmament on Bougainville.

In February Amnesty International launched a major report, *Papua New Guinea: Bougainville – the forgotten human rights tragedy*, which documented human rights violations by the government security forces and abuses by the BRA. The report called on the government and the BRA to take immediate steps to prevent further abuses. In March Amnesty International wrote an open letter to the then Prime Minister, Sir Julius Chan, expressing concern that the deployment of foreign mercenaries on Bougainville could contribute to human rights violations. In May Amnesty International called on the authorities to drop the charges against four men detained and facing trial for their non-violent role in demonstrations against the government.

PARAGUAY

Peasant leaders were arrested and intimidated in the context of land disputes; one was shot dead. There were continued reports of torture and ill-treatment of criminal suspects, including minors, by police. Prosecutions for past human rights violations continued, although little progress was made in investigating more recent abuses.

The political crisis which followed an attempted coup in 1996 by General Lino Oviedo, who was subsequently forced to resign, resurfaced in 1997 (see *Amnesty International Report 1997*). In September Lino Oviedo claimed victory in the internal elections of the ruling Colorado Party as candidate for the 1998 presidential elections. However, his eligibility to stand as candidate was placed in doubt by a number of legal proceedings opened against him. In November the Supreme Court announced that proceedings against Lino Oviedo for his part in the 1996 military uprising were being reactivated. President Juan Carlos Wasmosy, as supreme commander of the armed forces, ordered former General Oviedo to undergo 30 days' disciplinary arrest for allegedly insulting him. In December, after several weeks in hiding, Lino Oviedo gave himself up.

In its consideration of Paraguay's second periodic report in May the UN Committee against Torture stated: "The Committee has been informed by reliable sources that, although the infliction of torture and ill-treatment is no longer, as in the past, an official State policy, it is still practised by public officials, particularly in police stations and primary detention centres, in order to obtain confessions or information which are accepted by judges as grounds for instituting proceedings against the victims. The Committee is also concerned about information received from the same sources concerning the frequent physical ill-treatment of soldiers during their compulsory military service." Commenting on the Committee's findings, the then commander of the National

Police, General Mario Sapriza Nunes, accepted that there had been some instances of torture in police stations, but insisted that it was not a widespread practice.

There were renewed reports of serious confrontations between hundreds of landless peasant families and specialist police units in several areas of the country. Peasant communities attempting to establish land claims were violently expelled from land they had occupied by police personnel, frequently operating in conjunction with armed civilians reportedly paid by landowners. In many cases forcible expulsions, sometimes without judicial order, were accompanied by mass arrests, and the ill-treatment of detainees. The majority of detainees were released without charge or trial after weeks or months in custody.

Peasant leaders were again targeted for attack by groups of armed civilians who reportedly operated with the support or acquiescence of the local authorities and police. Peasant leader Felipe Benítez was shot dead by armed civilians in the 3 de Mayo community, municipality of Yuty, department of Caazapá, in July. Felipe Benítez was Vice-President of the *Comisión Vecinal de Puente Kué*, Puente Kué Association. For over two months prior to his killing, members of the Association had been camped in the entrance of the Metropolitan Cathedral in Asunción as part of their campaign to secure the expropriation of land in their favour. Two men were arrested and charged in connection with the killing. Trial proceedings continued at the end of the year. Following Felipe Benítez' killing, Epifanio Cantero, another leader of the *Comisión Vecinal de Puente Kué*, reportedly received anonymous death threats.

Reports of torture and ill-treatment of detainees, including minors, by the police continued and conditions of detention remained harsh in police stations and prisons. Although in several cases formal criminal complaints of ill-treatment were lodged and, in some, judicial investigations opened, those responsible were not brought to justice. Three youths arrested in May on suspicion of stealing a motorcycle were reportedly tortured in a police station in the town of San Antonio, Central department. While held in the police station they were allegedly subjected to torture including beatings on the soles of their feet and having plastic bags placed over their heads to the point of near-asphyxiation. One of the youths was reportedly threatened with death if he complained about the torture.

Judicial investigations continued into torture and deaths in custody of political prisoners under the government of General Stroessner (see previous *Amnesty International Reports*). In May a custody order was issued against retired General Ramón Duarte Vera, a police chief in the 1950s and 1960s. He faced several trials on charges of serious human rights violations against former political prisoners.

Paraguayan judicial officials cooperated in the investigation of "disappearances" in Argentina during the period of military rule between 1976 and 1983. In March, a former Argentine army major, Norberto Blanco, and his wife, Susana, were extradited to Argentina to face charges in connection with the illegal adoption of two children whose parents were believed to have "disappeared" after arrest by the Argentine security forces. The couple had moved to Paraguay with the children in 1987 after an Argentine court ordered the children to undergo genetic tests to determine their real identity.

In March, Amnesty International informed the UN Committee against Torture of its concerns in Paraguay. The Committee addressed many of these concerns in its recommendations to the Government of Paraguay (see above).

In July, Amnesty International expressed concern to the government about the killing of Felipe Benítez and repeated death threats received by other peasant leaders.

PERU

Hundreds of prisoners of conscience and possible prisoners of conscience remained imprisoned. At least 3,000 prisoners accused of terrorism were serving sentences or awaited trial under procedures which fell short of international standards. Critics of the government and human rights defenders suffered intimidation, including armed attacks and death threats. Cases of torture were frequently reported. Prison conditions amounted to cruel, inhuman or degrading treatment. Four people were reported to have been extra-

judicially executed. Past human rights violations affecting thousands of people remained unpunished. Armed groups continued to commit human rights abuses.

The number of reported armed attacks by the clandestine *Partido Comunista del Perú (Sendero Luminoso)* (PCP), Communist Party of Peru (Shining Path), and *Movimiento Revolucionario Túpac Amaru* (MRTA), Túpac Amaru Revolutionary Movement, declined for the fifth year running. However, armed attacks by the PCP increased in the second half of the year, especially in the rainforest Alto Huallaga region. The proportion of the population under a state of emergency decreased from 44 per cent in January to 22 per cent in December.

The MRTA hostage crisis was brought to an end in April when President Alberto Fujimori ordered a military assault on the residence of the Japanese Ambassador in Lima, the capital (see *Amnesty International Report 1997* and below).

In response to the hostage crisis, in January the government suspended prison visits "of any kind" to some 400 MRTA prisoners. The suspension, which remained in place for 11 weeks and effectively rendered these prisoners incommunicado, contravened international standards. Permission for the International Committee of the Red Cross to visit prisons, suspended by the authorities in December 1996 also in response to the hostage crisis, was renewed in December.

In May Congress removed from office three Constitutional Tribunal judges who declared that it would be unconstitutional for President Fujimori to stand as a presidential candidate for a third term of office. The Inter-American Commission on Human Rights (IACHR) expressed concern that this undermined the independence and impartiality of the judiciary and the protection of human rights.

The mandate of the *ad hoc* Commission charged with recommending that the President pardon prisoners falsely accused of terrorism was extended to August 1998 (see *Amnesty International Report 1996*). The Commission received requests from at least 2,300 prisoners claiming that they had been falsely accused of terrorism. Since the Commission started its work, 360 of these prisoners had benefited from a presidential pardon.

The government suffered a series of political crises, following revelations about human rights violations by members of the *Servicio de Inteligencia del Ejército* (SIE), Army Intelligence Service, and acts of intimidation against critics of the government (see below). The crises reflected claims that Peru was administered by an "authoritarian civilian-military government".

In August new regulations designed to ease the harsh conditions faced by prisoners accused of terrorism came into force. The regulations improved family visits and extended daily exercise from 30 to 60 minutes. However, the new regulations explicitly excluded prisoners held in military prisons.

In September and November respectively, the Inter-American Court of Human Rights ruled that Peru had violated the rights of María Elena Loayza Tamayo and Ernesto Castillo Páez, in contravention of the American Convention on Human Rights. María Elena Loayza was first acquitted by a military court in 1993 but then sentenced by a civilian court in 1994 to 20 years' imprisonment for the same terrorism-related crimes. The Court also ruled that María Elena Loayza had been tortured while in police custody. In October she was released. In the case of Ernesto Castillo Páez, who "disappeared" in 1991 (see *Amnesty International Reports 1992* and *1993*), the Court ruled that Peru had violated the rights to liberty, integrity and life, and the right to judicial protection for him and his family. The government continued to ignore the request made by the Court and the IACHR to compensate the relatives and bring to justice those responsible for the "disappearance" of three El Frontón prisoners in June 1986 and the "disappearance" or killing of 21 peasants from Chumbivilcas in April 1990.

In October provisions allowing for terrorism suspects to be tried by "faceless judges" were allowed to lapse (see *Amnesty International Reports 1993* to *1997*). However, legislation which undermined internationally recognized fair trial standards continued to be used (see below).

In December a congressional commission received a bill which proposed making torture, "disappearances" and genocide criminal offences.

Thirty-one prisoners of conscience and at least 550 possible prisoners of conscience, all accused of terrorism, remained in prison at the end of the year. For example, prisoner of conscience Marco Antonio Monge Hoyos, an agricultural worker from the hamlet of Cruz del Sur, near the city of Iquitos, Loreto department, was detained in March 1993. Despite a police inquiry concluding that Marco Antonio Monge was "not implicated in subversive activities", a provincial attorney charged him with collaboration. He had not been brought to trial by the end of the year, despite spending almost five years in prison.

In August former prisoner of conscience Zacarías Merma Farfán was detained again. A High Court had acquitted him of terrorism in 1995 and ordered his release, but the Supreme Court of Justice overturned the High Court ruling and ordered a retrial. Prisoners of conscience Marco Antonio Ambrosio Concha and Carlos Florentino Molero Coca, arrested in April 1992, remained in prison.

Seventeen prisoners of conscience and at least 233 possible prisoners of conscience, all falsely accused of terrorism, benefited from a presidential pardon in 1997 and were released. They included prisoner of conscience Juan Alberto Huapaya Palomino, who was released in June (see *Amnesty International Report 1993*). However, none of the pardoned prisoners had their charges or convictions quashed, nor did they receive compensation for their arbitrary detention.

Although prisoners accused of terrorism continued to be released following acquittals by special courts, at least 3,000 prisoners were serving sentences or awaited trial under procedures which fell short of international standards for fairness. For example, until October prisoners continued to be tried by "faceless judges". Thereafter, they continued to be denied a public trial and defence lawyers were prohibited from cross-examining members of the security forces involved in arrests and interrogations.

A pattern of intimidation directed at critics of the government and independent human rights defenders continued. Victims suffered armed attacks, death threats, and short-term abduction. In March Patricia Valdez, a human rights activist, together with a chauffeur and bodyguard, were abducted in Lima. Armed men wearing bullet-proof vests opened fire on their car, and then drove them to another part of Lima, where they were interrogated and later released. The authorities claimed the attack was the work of common criminals but independent sources alleged that the incident was intended to intimidate opposition congressman Javier Diez Canseco, the owner of the car. Anonymous death threats were received by journalists Edmundo Cruz and César Hilderbrandt in April, human rights lawyer Heriberto Benítez Rivas in July, and the staff and director of APRODEH, an independent human rights organization, in September.

Numerous cases of torture continued to be reported. In January and February SIE agent Leonor La Rosa Bustamante, suspected of leaking security plans to the press, was tortured in the basement of a military installation in Lima, a place where she claimed alleged members of the armed opposition were also tortured. Leonor La Rosa was subsequently diagnosed as having suffered a serious spinal injury. Four SIE officers accused of torturing her were each found guilty by a military court of "abuse of authority" and sentenced to eight years' imprisonment. In March the dismembered body of Mariela Lucy Barreto Riofano, another SIE agent, was found in plastic bags on the outskirts of Lima. Her death and the torture of Leonor La Rosa were widely believed to have been connected.

During a single counter-insurgency operation spanning February and March in the Alto Yurinaki region, province of Chanchamayo, Junín department, the army claimed to have captured 38 members of an MRTA unit and an unspecified number of "subversives" who had infiltrated a nearby army base. The Ministry of Defence stated that the army had respected the detainees' human rights. However, many of the detainees testified that they had been beaten, repeatedly immersed in a water-tank, and subjected to electric shocks. Inés Marilú Avila Gálvez, one of the detainees, claimed that two officers attempted to rape her. All those detained and transferred into police custody were subsequently released without charge. However, Jorge Quispe Montalván, one of those detained, was shot dead by soldiers in circumstances suggesting that he had been extrajudicially executed. A complaint was filed before the Public Ministry about these allegations of torture and extrajudicial execution, but by the end of the year those responsible had not been brought to justice.

Prison conditions were reported to be harsh, amounting to cruel, inhuman or degrading treatment. The conditions endured by prisoners accused of terrorism were especially harsh in the maximum security Yanamayo Prison, near the city of Puno, and in the prison in the Callao Naval Base, near Lima, where a handful of MRTA and PCP leaders have been held since 1992 in underground cells.

Amnesty International and other human rights organizations expressed concern about the adverse effects on the health of prisoners, should they be transferred to the newly constructed Challapalca Prison in the Andean highlands. The authorities claimed that Challapalca Prison was between 4,600 and 5,000 metres above sea level. According to medical opinion, holding prisoners at an altitude in excess of 4,500 metres for prolonged periods of time could lead to serious illness or even death. Despite an appeal by Peru's Ombudsman's Office for the prison authorities to review the decision to bring Challapalca Prison into operation, 51 prisoners accused of common crimes were transferred there in August.

The authorities continued to disregard the recommendation made in 1996 by the UN Human Rights Committee to repeal amnesty laws passed in 1995 which legally sanctioned impunity (see *Amnesty International Reports 1996* and *1997*). Thousands of human rights violations committed between 1980 and 1995, including cases of torture, "disappearance" and extrajudicial execution, thus remained unpunished, as did most human rights violations committed after the 1995 amnesty laws were passed. An exception to this pattern of impunity was the eight-year prison sentence imposed by the Supreme Court of Justice on a non-commissioned army officer for the homicide of Víctor Ramírez Arias in 1994 (see *Amnesty International Report 1995*).

The armed opposition continued to commit abuses. Seventy-two of the 81 hostages held by the MRTA in the Japanese Ambassador's residence remained captive until April; nine were released in January and February (see *Amnesty International Report 1997*). On 22 April an armed assault by the security forces ended the 126-day hostage crisis with the rescue of 71 of the hostages. One hostage, two members of the security forces and all 14 MRTA hostage-takers died. There were allegations that possibly three of the MRTA hostage-takers had been extrajudicially executed.

In August members of the PCP were reported to have taken hostage 29 workers based at a remote oil exploration plant in the department of Junín. The hostages, who were threatened with death, were released after two days in exchange for livestock and equipment. In September and October members of the PCP were reported to have deliberately and arbitrarily killed some 20 villagers and local officials whom they took captive in Los Milagros, Mohena, and other hamlets near the river Alto Huallaga, Huánuco department. The victims were accused of being army informers.

Amnesty International repeatedly appealed to the authorities to immediately and unconditionally release all prisoners of conscience. In April an Amnesty International delegation visited Peru. At the end of the visit the delegation expressed concern about allegations that critics of President Fujimori's administration suffered intimidation, including armed attacks and death threats, and concluded that the protection of human rights in Peru was in jeopardy. The delegation publicly appealed to the authorities to have the allegations investigated and bring those responsible to justice.

In March Amnesty International published *Peru: Women's human rights – in memory of María Elena Moyano*. The report outlined the organization's concerns about abuses of women's human rights and recalled the deliberate and arbitrary killing by the PCP of María Elena Moyano and other women activists (see *Amnesty International Reports 1993* and *1997*). The report called on the authorities and the armed opposition to respect international human rights and humanitarian standards. In August the organization published *Peru: Prisoners of conscience – every day in prison is one day too many*, which expressed concern about the prolonged imprisonment of hundreds of prisoners of conscience and possible prisoners of conscience.

In February and March Amnesty International repeated calls on the MRTA to immediately and unconditionally release the remaining 72 hostages. In June the organization wrote to President Fujimori requesting a full and independent investigation into the deaths of all 17 people killed at the end of the MRTA crisis. However, no such investigation would appear to have been ordered.

In August, and again in October, the organization reiterated previous appeals to repeal those elements of the anti-terrorism legislation which undermined the right to a fair trial.

PHILIPPINES

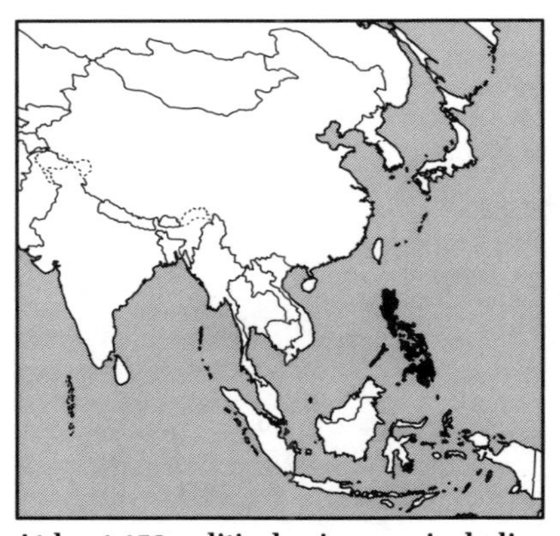

At least 150 political prisoners, including possible prisoners of conscience, remained in detention. Reports of torture and ill-treatment by police continued. Human rights violations occurring in the context of counter-insurgency continued to decline, but at least three possible "disappearances" were reported, and at least 10 people were allegedly extrajudicially executed. At least 170 people were sentenced to death and the way was cleared for executions to resume in February 1998. Armed opposition groups committed human rights abuses, including deliberate and arbitrary killings and hostage-taking.

Proposals to amend the Constitution to allow President Fidel Ramos to stand for a second six-year term in 1998 sparked domestic controversy. In September, after large-scale public protests, a congressional motion in favour of the constitutional amendment was withdrawn, the Supreme Court ruled against a plebiscite on the issue, and President Ramos announced that he would not stand for re-election.

Peace talks continued between the government and the National Democratic Front, representing the Communist Party of the Philippines (CPP) and its armed wing, the New People's Army (NPA). Negotiators reached a tentative agreement on the first stage of a four-stage agenda for the peace process. In August the first stage agreement, covering respect for human rights and international humanitarian law during military operations, was initialled. Negotiations, interrupted by outbreaks of military conflict, were held between the government and the Moro Islamic Liberation Front (MILF) on the southern island of Mindanao in an attempt to agree a general cease-fire as a prelude to a formal peace accord. No comprehensive cease-fire had been announced by the end of the year.

In January President Ramos ordered the release of 19 political prisoners and extended from April 1994 to June 1995 the period during which crimes could be considered as having been "politically motivated", and therefore eligible for consideration by the National Amnesty Commission. In March Juanito Ecal, a former labour leader accused of being a member of the NPA and of killing a company security guard in 1984, was released after 13 years in detention. Juanito Ecal was allegedly tortured by soldiers during interrogation and convicted of murder mainly on the strength of evidence which had reportedly been planted by police. At least 150 political prisoners, including possible prisoners of conscience, continued to be held for offences which allegedly occurred in the context of CPP-NPA insurgency. Most were held on criminal charges, particularly illegal possession of firearms, robbery and murder, and had not been convicted by the end of the year.

There were continued reports of torture and ill-treatment by police of criminal suspects and of those accused of involvement in insurgency, in order to coerce confessions and extract the names of suspected accomplices. The Philippine National Police (PNP) practice of arresting suspects without warrants remained widespread. Patterns of ill-treatment and torture were most often reported during "administrative detention" – the period between arrest and the laying of formal charges which, under Philippine law, is permitted for between 12 and 36 hours, depending on the seriousness of the charge. Prisoners in Manila, the capital, charged with criminal offences alleged that PNP and National Bureau of Investigation (NBI) officers punched them with fists, at times with bullets held between the interrogator's fingers, and beat them with rifle butts or batons. Pistol barrels were reportedly placed against the head or in the mouth and suspects threatened with death. Plastic bags were allegedly put over the suspects' heads and held tightly at the back, or water was dripped on cloths placed over the face. Electric shocks were also reportedly applied to the genitals, lips, ears, arms or legs.

Instances of harassment, ill-treatment and use of excessive force by police and other law enforcement officials were reported within the context of labour disputes, and of the forced eviction and demolition of poor residential areas and indigenous communities. Some human rights abuses were carried out by private security guards with the apparent connivance and collusion of local officials and police. In July community leader Jonathan Mana-ay was shot dead, allegedly by private security guards, after more than 30 people were injured during violent confrontations between armed demolition teams and the residents of a poor residential area at Sitio Mendez, Barangay Bahay Toro in Manila. In July, three members of the Suminao clan of the Higaonon indigenous people were shot dead by PNP officers during a violent forced eviction in Bukidnon province, Mindanao. One clansman was reportedly kicked and beaten and four other people, including the clan chieftain and an eight-year-old girl, were taken to hospital with gunshot wounds. The incident followed earlier reports of harassment of clan members, including death threats and the burning of houses, by unidentified men. The Suminao clan had been in dispute with a prominent local political family over ownership of ancestral lands.

Despite the continued fall in the number of grave human rights violations perpetrated by members of the security forces in the context of counter-insurgency operations, at least three possible "disappearances" were reported. In an incident reminiscent of past patterns of "disappearances" carried out by members of the security forces, Romeo Cortez was abducted in Pampanga province, Luzon, by unidentified armed men in April as he returned home, apparently because of his activities as a peasant leader. His whereabouts remained unknown at the end of the year.

At least 10 possible extrajudicial executions were reported. In May a militia unit in Misamis Oriental province, Mindanao, opened fire on a family house which they suspected was occupied by NPA sympathizers. Carmelita Lauron and her three children were killed, and four other relatives wounded. In August members of an Armed Forces of the Philippines (AFP) unit in Misamis Oriental province asked the wife of Lito Aslag about the whereabouts of her husband. After the soldiers were directed to nearby woods, shots were heard. The following day Lito Aslag and his two companions, 16-year-old twin brothers Roy and Rey Loreno, were found in a Cayayan de Oro City mortuary. Witnesses stated that the bodies had been brought to the mortuary by soldiers. In early 1997 a series of death threats were sent to two senior judges, a senator and human rights lawyers linked to the prosecution of 27 PNP officers allegedly involved in the extrajudicial execution of 11 suspected members of a bank robbery gang in 1995 (see *Amnesty International Report 1997*).

Thousands of people were displaced following intermittent military offensives against MILF forces, some in response to reported attacks and kidnappings by armed groups. In June over 40,000 civilians fled their homes after AFP attacks on a MILF camp and surrounding areas in North Cotabato province during which scores of people were killed or wounded.

At least 170 people were sentenced to death. In September the Supreme Court, which automatically reviews all death sentences, ruled that Leo Pilo Echegary, the first prisoner to have his sentence confirmed (see *Amnesty International Report 1997*), could be executed by lethal injection between February and August 1998. Over 410 people had been sentenced to death since capital punishment was restored in December 1993. Reports of torture and ill-treatment to coerce confessions from some suspects accused of involvement in capital crimes increased concern over the risk of judicial error in death penalty cases.

Armed opposition groups were responsible for human rights abuses. Muslim armed groups in Mindanao, including the MILF, *Abu Sayyaf* and renegade units of the Moro National Liberation Front continued to take civilians hostage and to carry out deliberate and arbitrary killings. In October the MILF publicly executed two men accused of murder and robbery.

In February Amnesty International called for adequate protection for the judges and lawyers involved in the prosecution of PNP officers linked to the extrajudicial execution of 11 bank robbers. The organization called for investigations into reports of possible "disappearances" and possible extrajudicial executions. In October Amnesty International released a report, *Philippines: The death penalty – criminality, justice and human rights*, detailing its concerns over the application of the death penalty, calling for investigations into allegations of torture and ill-treatment by police, and urging President Ramos to exercise clemency in the cases of those prisoners whose sentences have been confirmed by the Supreme Court, and to suspend executions with a view to completely abolishing the death penalty.

PORTUGAL

Law enforcement and prison officers were the subject of fresh allegations of ill-treatment. Judicial inquiries into such allegations and into a number of deaths that occurred in or immediately subsequent to police custody in previous years, were slow. The trials of several law enforcement officers accused of ill-treatment and of homicide were held.

In March, in the context of an inter-party agreement to revise the Constitution, the two major political parties proposed an amendment which would have allowed people to be extradited who were accused of crimes which carried the death penalty under the law of the requesting state. However, the amendment was abandoned. Under the revised Constitution, approved in September, extradition is not allowed for crimes which carry the death penalty in the law of the requesting state.

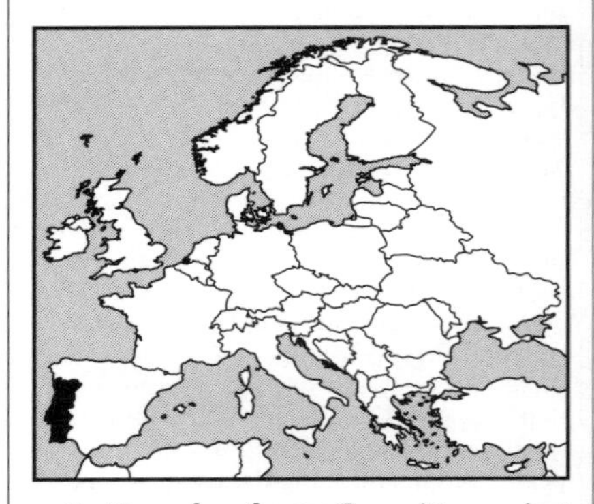

In November the UN Committee against Torture considered Portugal's second periodic report on its implementation of the UN Convention against Torture and Other Cruel, Inhuman or Degrading Treatment or Punishment. The Committee welcomed several new penal and administrative measures taken by the government to safeguard against torture and ill-treatment by law enforcement officers. However, it expressed its "grave concern about recent cases of ill-treatment and torture and, in some instances, of suspicious deaths allegedly involving law enforcement officers... as well as an apparent absence of appropriate reaction by the competent authorities." The Committee urged the government to make greater attempts to bridge the gap between the law and its application, to apply appropriate punishment where due, and to clarify the laws governing torture or ill-treatment by law enforcement officers in order to ensure that inquiries were "automatically and systematically" opened into all cases where there was reason to believe torture had occurred.

There were further allegations of ill-treatment by law enforcement and prison officers. In February Vítor Manuel Santos was arrested in a bar by officers of the Public Security Police after he spilled beer over them. He complained that the officers beat him in transit to, and inside, the police station in the town of Vila Franca de Xira. A medical report from the hospital he visited the next day stated that he was in a state of great anxiety and that he repeated constantly that he had been assaulted by the police. He was later found shot through the head in the family vegetable plot. An autopsy report concluded that the cause of death was suicide, but press reports stated that marks on his body indicated he could have been beaten shortly before his death. A disciplinary inquiry, carried out immediately afterwards by the General Inspectorate of Internal Administration (IGAI), found no evidence of assault by the police officers, and affirmed that, contrary to reports, the autopsy had not discovered any external signs of violence. IGAI also stated that Vítor Santos had only been held for 15 minutes at the police station. The officers were nevertheless disciplined for falsely stating that they had been responding to a call when they had in fact been in the bar as customers. The judicial inquiry into the circumstances surrounding the death was closed in August, but reopened by the public prosecutor of Vila Franca de Xira in November. The prosecutor was reported to have decided that certain avenues of inquiry were still to be explored.

In June Belmiro Santana reported that he had been severely beaten by five prison guards in Caxias Prison. He claimed he had been kicked and beaten on the arms and body, that two of his teeth had been broken and that the rings on his pierced nipples and navel had been torn out leaving deep gashes in the flesh. He also claimed he had been left in solitary confinement, without medical treatment, for the rest of the night. He was subsequently taken to S. Francisco Xavier Hospital before being transferred back to the prison infirmary. An inquiry into the incident was opened by the General Prison Services Directorate and was continuing at the end of the year.

A number of judicial inquiries relating to alleged ill-treatment and deaths in custody in previous years remained opened; in some cases officers were tried. Judicial and disciplinary inquiries continued into the death of Olívio Almada, whose body was found in the Tagus river in 1996 following his arrest by police officers. His arrest had not been registered at any police station. Inquiries also continued into the death of Carlos Manuel Gonçalves Araújo, who died in 1996, shortly after being taken into custody of a gunshot wound sustained in the course of arrest. According to IGAI, disciplinary proceedings were being taken against a police officer for unjustifiably assaulting Carlos Araújo and two other men while they were held at Évora police station for attempted robbery.

In September the trial opened of seven officers of the National Republican Guard (GNR) in connection with the killing of Carlos Rosa (see *Amnesty International Report 1997*). Defence lawyers acting for the sergeant accused of shooting, beheading and concealing the remains of the detainee attempted to reduce the charge against the officer from murder to one of manslaughter. However, in December the court found the sergeant guilty of murder and sentenced him to a total of 17 years' imprisonment: 12 for the killing itself, and the remainder for breach of official duty and for concealing and mutilating the corpse. A second GNR officer was sentenced to six years' imprisonment for breach of official duty and assisting with concealment of the body, and a third to a prison term of two and a half years, suspended for five years. Four other GNR officers were acquitted.

The trial of Joaquim Teixeira and of two police officers concluded in November (see *Amnesty International Reports 1996* and *1997*). Joaquim Teixeira alleged he had been assaulted in 1995 by the officers, who in turn alleged that he had assaulted them. Unable to decide who had initiated the dispute between the computer technician and the police officers, the judge found both Joaquim Teixeira and one of the officers guilty of common criminal assault and sentenced them to a fine.

Amnesty International urged the authorities to ensure full and prompt investigations into all allegations of ill-treatment and into deaths in or immediately after police custody, and sought information from the authorities on the progress of judicial and disciplinary inquiries into such allegations. In many cases replies were received regarding the status of inquiries.

In May the organization launched an urgent appeal against the proposed amendment to the Constitution regarding extradition to countries where the death penalty could be applied.

In information submitted to the UN Committee against Torture, Amnesty International raised its concerns not only about specific cases, but also about the slowness of judicial procedures investigating allegations of torture and ill-treatment, the questionable effectiveness of that section of the penal code relating to torture and ill-treatment, and the nominal sentences given in those exceptional cases in which offenders were found guilty.

QATAR

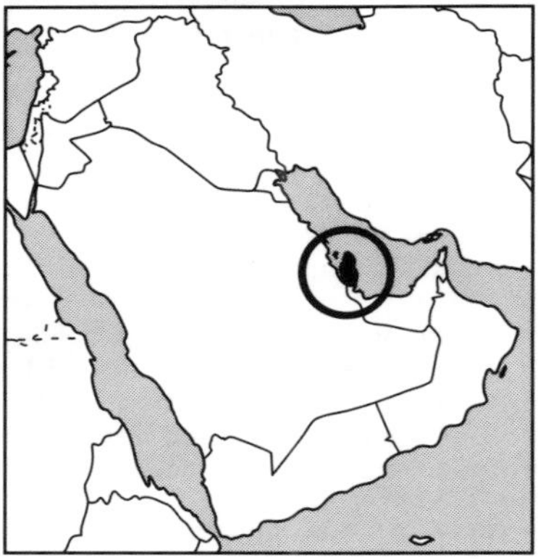

At least 117 people were charged in connection with the coup attempt of February 1996. Forty of them were charged *in absentia*; the other 77 were held incommunicado and without access to a lawyer until trial hearings began at the end of the year. Some of the detainees alleged that they were tortured. In a separate case, a man was reported to have died in custody, allegedly as a result of torture.

The government of the Amir, al-Shaikh Hamad Ibn Khalifa Al-Thani, stated that Qatar would abide by all international human rights treaties. However, no steps were known to have been taken by the government to accede to the International Covenant on Civil and Political Rights or to the UN Convention against Torture and Other Cruel, Inhuman or Degrading Treatment or Punishment.

At least 117 people were charged in connection with the attempt to overthrow the government in February 1996 (see *Amnesty International Report 1997*). They were tried in two separate groups before a criminal court in Doha. The hearings involving a first group of 110 defendants, 40 *in absentia*, began on 26 November; the trial was then postponed until February 1998. Approximately 12 of the 70 defendants who appeared before the court had been detained during the year, including Hassan Hilal Hassan al-Muhandi, a police officer, who was reportedly arrested in March in Doha. The remaining defendants before the court had been arrested in 1996. Among them were reported to be a number of foreign nationals, including Palestinians, Saudi Arabians, Bahrainis and Egyptians. They included Brigadier Bakhit Marzug, Lieutenant-Colonel 'Abd al-Hadi Rashid Sihabi and Lieutenant-Colonel Rashid 'Ali. The trial of the second group, comprising seven Qatar nationals, started on 17 December and was continuing at the end of the year. Until their court appearances all 77 detainees had been held incommunicado and denied access to lawyers. Some of the defendants claimed that they had been tortured in order to force them to make a confession.

In a separate case, Musfir al-Marri, a businessman, was reported to have died in custody days after his arrest in July or August, allegedly as a result of torture. The Amir reportedly undertook to carry out a thorough investigation into the circumstances of Musfir al-Marri's death. It was not known whether such an investigation had been carried out.

Amnesty International delegates visited Qatar in May and raised with members of the judiciary and government officials concerns about the lengthy incommunicado detention without trial of those held in connection with the coup attempt of February 1996. The officials maintained that these conditions of detention were justified on the grounds of continuing investigation. However, they offered Amnesty International delegates access to some of the detainees and undertook to give the defendants a fair trial. On 25 November Amnesty International received an invitation to attend the trial of the first group of defendants. The organization was intending to send observers when the trial resumed in 1998.

Amnesty International delegates also raised the case of an Iraqi asylum-seeker, Ghanima Nimr, who had been detained with her two children following entry into Qatar during the year. The government assured the organization that she would not be forcibly returned to Iraq, where she would have been at risk of grave human rights violations. Ghanima Nimr and her two sons were subsequently released and resettled in the United Kingdom.

ROMANIA

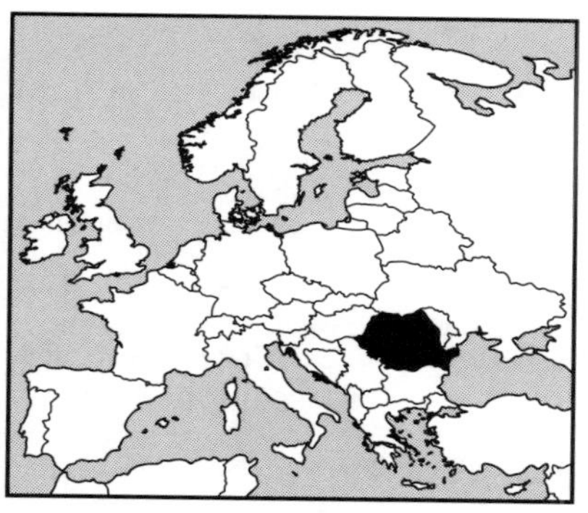

At least one prisoner of conscience was held. There were reports of torture and ill-treatment, and of shootings by police officers in disputed circumstances. Some of the victims of human rights violations were Roma.

In April the Parliamentary Assembly of the Council of Europe adopted a resolution suspending the procedure for monitoring Romania's compliance with the obligations and commitments accepted on admission to the Council of Europe in 1993. The resolution, however, urged Romania to ensure the independence of the judiciary and to amend certain provisions of the Penal Code which "seriously imperil the exercise of fundamental freedoms", especially those concerning homosexuality and provisions which interfere with the right to freedom of speech. The Parliamentary Assembly noted "deplorable conditions in Romanian prisons" and regretted that the country had made "all too few efforts to improve these conditions and to end the overcrowding of prisons". It also called on Romania to fight racism, xenophobia and intolerance, particularly in respect of the Romani community.

The authorities failed to initiate a legislative revision of the Penal Code and to bring it into line with international human rights standards. Article 200, paragraph 1, criminalizes homosexual relations between consenting adults "if the act is committed in public or has produced public scandal", and continues to permit imprisonment of adults solely for engaging in consensual homosexual relations in private. Paragraph 5, which prohibits "enticing or seducing a person to practise same-sex acts, as well as forming propaganda associations or engaging in other forms of proselytizing with the same aim", can also lead to imprisonment of individuals solely for exercising their rights to freedom of expression and freedom of peaceful assembly and association. Similarly, no amendments were proposed to provisions of the Penal Code proscribing dissemination of false news, defamation of the state or nation, "offences against the authorities" and "outrage", which impose excessive restrictions on the right to freedom of expression.

It came to light in December that Mariana Cetiner had been arrested in October 1995 and sentenced to three years' imprisonment under Article 200, paragraph 5, of the Penal Code, for attempting to seduce another woman. In January Alba Court upheld Mariana Cetiner's appeal and acquitted her. She was released from prison where she had been held since her arrest. In May, however, following an appeal by the public prosecutor, Alba Iulia Appellate Court reversed the acquittal and ordered Mariana Cetiner to serve the remainder of the three-year prison sentence. Ten days later she was rearrested and held in the Târșor penitentiary.

Although in the past the authorities occasionally disclosed information about the number of people currently imprisoned under Article 200, paragraphs 1 and 5, of the Penal Code, no information was made available on the total number of prosecutions and convictions, some of which might have resulted in criminal sanctions other than imprisonment. It has never, therefore, been possible to determine the full extent to which this law is enforced.

Reports of torture and ill-treatment were widespread. Investigations into complaints of ill-treatment continued to be prolonged, often lasting two or more years. An investigation into the ill-treatment of Virgiliu Ilieş, a 15-year-old who was arrested in Craiova in January 1994 and reportedly beaten by police officers to force him to confess to a series of thefts from cars, had still not been completed. In March he was sentenced to two and a half years' imprisonment, reportedly on the basis of the statement made at the police station.

Prompt investigations were an exception. In February in Ungureni, Bacău county, the local police chief and his deputy reportedly severely beat Daniel Neculai Dediu during the 24 hours he was held on suspicion of burglary. The officers reportedly beat and kicked him in the abdomen and hit him on the back with a truncheon and a metal chair. In August, following an investigation, the officers were reportedly charged with illegal arrest and abusive conduct.

Dozens of people were beaten with truncheons and otherwise ill-treated by guards in the Jilava Penitentiary in Bucharest, the capital, following a mass hunger-strike organized by the detainees in February. A colonel in charge of security in penitentiaries was reportedly responsible for the guards' action, in the course of which tear-gas was used in enclosed spaces. In one incident, the colonel reportedly led a group of masked officers into a room where they beat detainees indiscriminately with wooden batons. An hour later a number of detainees were ordered to leave the room via a corridor lined on both sides with officers, who beat them all over the body. An inquiry into the beatings was initiated by the Senate Commission for Human Rights. A representative of the Ministry of the Interior denied at a Commission hearing that police officers had participated in the incident. The results of this inquiry had not been made public by the end of the year.

Also in February, in Târgu Mureş, two public guards (security officers employed by municipal authorities) beat 16-year-old Zóltan Herman and László Bernad, whom they had reportedly caught cutting telephone wires. After the police had found no grounds on which to charge them, they were held for three hours in the public guards' office and reportedly beaten with truncheons on the palms of their hands. Zóltan Herman was slapped on the face and kicked, and forced to perform squat thrusts while counting aloud the number of repetitions performed. He was then made to dance while singing a Hungarian folk song, and to sing the Romanian national anthem.

In May, two police officers came to take Ioana Enuţă to the police station in Berceni for an unpaid fine against which she had promptly appealed to the municipal court. Outside her house one officer reportedly grabbed her, making her fall to the ground, and kicked her as they pulled her towards the police car. A number of villagers called on the officers to stop the beating and Ioana Enuţă ran into a nearby house. She complained about the ill-treatment to the appropriate authority, the Bucharest Military Prosecutor, and there were no further attempts to apprehend her.

In June a 10-year-old boy was apprehended in a closed sales kiosk in a small town on the Black Sea. He was detained for over five hours and reportedly brutally beaten by three officers who questioned him about the break-in. The boy was ordered to take his pants off and bend over, and was repeatedly beaten on the buttocks with a truncheon. He was also beaten on the palms, punched and kicked. One officer threatened to kill him and pointed a gun at his head. Following his release he was hospitalized for three days and treated for head injuries and bruising all over the body. In the course of an investigation the police officers, who had not been suspended, denied the allegations of torture and reportedly claimed that the boy's mother had inflicted the injuries after his release from their custody.

Victims of ill-treatment included Roma. In July, Belmondo Cobzaru, the son of a Romani leader in Mangalia, went to the police station following an incident in which he broke into the flat of his former girl-friend. Two officers reportedly punched him in the head until his nose bled. He was then thrown to the ground and kicked. Later, a newspaper was placed on the back of his neck and he was hit with a wooden stick. Before his release he was reportedly forced to sign a statement to the effect that he had been injured in a fight with his girl-friend's brother-in-law. A forensic medical certificate issued following three days of hospital treatment described bruising around the eyes, on the right hand, chest, and right leg.

There were shootings by police officers in disputed circumstances. In February in Bucharest two police officers reportedly saw Laurențiu Ciobanu, a Rom from Găneasa, take a radio-cassette player from a parked car. When the officers attempted to apprehend him he reportedly swung a screwdriver at one of the officers and started to run; the officers called on him to stop, fired two warning shots, and then shot at him three times, bringing him to the ground. He was taken to hospital, where he reportedly underwent several operations for injuries to the lungs and kidneys caused by the bullets. Investigations into similar incidents reported in the past two years have been suspended on the grounds that Law No. 26/1994 permits the use of firearms "to apprehend an offender caught in the act who is attempting to escape and does not obey orders to stop". However, in September officials of the Military Prosecutor's Office told an Amnesty International representative that the officer responsible for the killing of Mircea Muresul Mosor (see *Amnesty International Report 1997*) had been discharged from the police force and indicted for murder.

In March Amnesty International published a report, *Romania: Unlawful use of firearms by law enforcement officials*. In May, July and August the organization urged the General Prosecutor to initiate investigations into seven cases of torture and ill-treatment. It subsequently called for investigations into further cases of torture and ill-treatment. Amnesty International also wrote to the Minister of Justice in August requesting information about all prosecutions and convictions which had taken place in 1995 and 1996 under Article 200, paragraph 1, of the Penal Code. In December Amnesty International urged President Emil Constantinescu to release Mariana Cetiner.

In March the Ministry of the Interior published a report on cases Amnesty International had raised with the authorities in 1996. In a reply Amnesty International explained in detail why it considered that the reported investigations had not been carried out promptly and impartially, and requested specific information on individual cases. No response had been received from the Ministry of the Interior by the end of the year. In December the Minister of Justice informed Amnesty International that he intended to propose the abolition of Article 200, paragraph 1, and thus decriminalize consensual homosexual relations between adults.

RUSSIAN FEDERATION

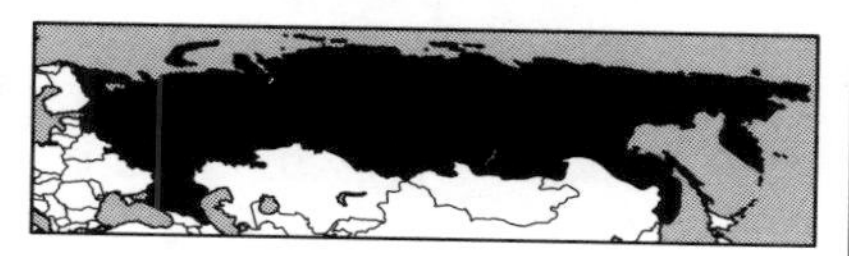

Two prisoners of conscience were held during the year. Two others released in 1996 were awaiting trial. Conscientious objectors were forcibly conscripted. Torture and ill-treatment by law enforcement officers and within the armed forces continued to be reported. Conditions in penitentiaries and pre-trial detention centres amounted to cruel, inhuman or degrading treatment. At least 846 prisoners remained under sentence of death. Refugees and asylum-seekers received inadequate protection. In the Chechen Republic-Ichkeriya at least five people were publicly executed following trials by *Shari'a* courts and at least seven journalists were taken hostage.

In April President Boris Yeltsin issued a decree pronouncing 1998 a year of human rights in the Russian Federation to mark the 50th anniversary of the Universal Declaration of Human Rights.

In January the Parliamentary Assembly of the Council of Europe condemned continuing executions during 1996 as a violation of the Russian Federation's commitment to institute a moratorium on executions, and threatened to expel it from the Council of Europe should more executions be carried out. In February the Chairman of the Presidential Clemency Commission stated that no executions had been carried out since August 1996 and urged parliament to pass legislation providing for a moratorium on executions. President Yeltsin reportedly instructed the government to take steps towards abolishing the death penalty.

In April the Russian Federation signed Protocol No. 6 to the European Convention for the Protection of Human Rights and Fundamental Freedoms concerning the abolition of the death penalty.

Responsibility for drafting a law on alternative service was transferred in April to the parliamentary committee dealing with public associations and religious organizations. However, conscientious objectors to military service continued to be at risk of imprisonment or forcible conscription.

In March an amnesty law relating to the armed conflict in the Chechen Republic was adopted by parliament. There were fears that the amnesty law could create serious obstacles to the exchange of prisoners of war and others detained on both sides. According to reports in January, 1,058 Russian soldiers and officers were still detained by Chechen fighters who were willing to release them in exchange for members of Chechen armed groups detained by the Russian authorities on criminal charges.

People charged with treason, espionage and terrorism were also excluded from the amnesty, which cast serious doubt on the procedure for resolving the cases of servicemen who evaded service in the Chechen Republic, including conscientious objectors to military service who might have been charged with such offences by the Russian military authorities.

In September President Yeltsin signed a law banning all religions which had not formally existed in Russia for 15 years from actively seeking converts. Religions that fail to meet the requirement would be prevented from opening schools, distributing religious material, and owning printing works or media outlets.

In June President Yeltsin rescinded the 1994 and part of the 1996 presidential decrees on fighting organized crime which allowed for incommunicado detention for up to a month. In July the Constitutional Court ruled that a similar presidential decree on fighting organized crime in the Republic of Mordovia violated citizens' constitutional rights.

In August President Yeltsin submitted legislation to parliament proposing an amnesty for nearly half a million prisoners to help alleviate overcrowding in jails. The law, covering 445,000 people in pre-trial detention and prison colonies, was adopted by the State *Duma* in December. In October President Yeltsin signed a decree, in accordance with the recommendations of the Council of Europe and the UN Committee against Torture, which envisaged step-by-step reform of the penitentiary system. President Yeltsin also instructed the government to create a commission to draw up proposals before 1 December 1997 to deal with any problems that might occur during the transfer of the penitentiary system from the jurisdiction of the Ministry of the Interior to that of the Ministry of Justice. The government was also instructed to submit to the State *Duma* corresponding federal draft laws before the end of 1997. In December the State *Duma* formed a special commission to deal with violations in pre-trial detention centres.

Two prisoners of conscience were held during the year. In May Oleg Pazyura, a human rights defender and retired naval officer, was arrested by officers from Oktyabrsky District Department of Internal Affairs in the city of Murmansk. His family were not informed of his whereabouts for four days. He was reportedly charged with "slander" and "threatening or assaulting a procurator, investigator, interrogator or other official". Shortly before his arrest Oleg Pazyura had reportedly spoken publicly about allegations of violations of the judicial process by local courts and corruption in the procuracy. Oleg Pazyura's family was not allowed to visit him during pre-trial detention, and initially he was without a defence lawyer after the lawyer he requested declined to represent him, allegedly fearing persecution by the authorities. Oleg Pazyura reportedly remained in detention at the end of the year.

Rafail Usmanov, a member of the Magadan group of the International Society for Human Rights, was arrested in April. He had been reporting on allegations of torture of detainees by police in the Magadan Region. He was released later in April reportedly without charge. Shortly afterwards, six law enforcement officers from Magadan were detained and charged in connection with allegations of torture.

During the year two former prisoners of conscience, Yury Shadrin and Aleksandr Nikitin (see *Amnesty International Report 1997*), were at liberty awaiting trial. In September Aleksandr Nikitin was presented with a new indictment by the Federal Security Service (FSB), the fifth since his arrest in February 1996. Yury Shadrin was still confined to the city of Omsk.

Following the failure of the courts in several cases to enforce the conscription of conscientious objectors, the Military Conscription Committee appeared to resort to forcibly removing conscientious objectors to military camps. In June Nikolay Moschukhin was taken to an army base in the Yaroslavl Region, despite a court judgment in November 1996 upholding his right to an alternative service. He was released from the army in early September.

There were continued reports of widespread torture and ill-treatment of detainees by law enforcement officers. In July during a raid on the "Chance" nightclub, frequented by homosexuals, armed police officers from the South East region of Moscow allegedly beat and otherwise ill-treated 40 people and forced them to sign pre-prepared statements containing falsified drug test results.

Larisa Kharchenko, a former employee of the St Petersburg city administration who was arrested in July, was reportedly denied essential medical treatment for chronic high blood pressure and heart disease while held incommunicado in pre-trial detention centre No. 6 in Moscow. She remained in detention at the end of the year.

There were continued reports of torture and ill-treatment of soldiers by their superiors and fellow soldiers. In January Sergey Odinokov was found guilty of "offending his subordinate" and sentenced to a fine and a one-year limit on his military service. He reportedly admitted hanging a conscript in front of other soldiers and only releasing his neck from the noose when he promised not to absent himself without leave in the future.

Conditions in penitentiaries and pre-trial detention centres continued to amount to cruel, inhuman or degrading treatment. The Procurator General expressed concern at serious overcrowding and revealed that some 2,000 people had died of tuberculosis in prisons in 1996, a death rate 10 times the rate in the general population.

Official statistics published in October revealed that 846 prisoners remained under sentence of death. No executions were reported in 1997, with the exception of at least five public executions in the Chechen Republic (see below).

Asylum-seekers continued to be detained in contravention of international standards, to be denied access to asylum procedures and to face possible *refoulement* to countries where they might be subjected to human rights violations. In January two ethnic Somalis were detained in Moscow and reportedly threatened with deportation on the grounds that they had been living in Moscow for three years without registering with the passport office, despite the fact that they were registered with the office of the UN High Commissioner for Refugees (UNHCR) and the Federal Migration Service. It was not known whether they had been deported by the end of the year. In October an African asylum-seeker was reportedly subjected to *refoulement* to his country of origin where he was at risk of human rights violations.

In June the President of the Chechen Republic, Aslan Maskhadov, stated that only *Shari'a* courts would function in the Republic. A new Criminal Code, adopted by presidential decree at the end of 1996, included provisions for cruel, inhuman or degrading punishments, including amputations and caning. A large number of offences, including heterosexual or homosexual anal intercourse on third conviction, carried the death penalty. President Maskhadov was reported to have demanded of the *Shari'a* courts "severe verdicts" and their "immediate enforcement".

In the Chechen Republic, at least five people were executed following conviction by *Shari'a* courts, and more than 30 were believed to be in imminent danger of execution. It was not known whether the five had had access to a defence lawyer or the opportunity to appeal against their sentence to a higher court. Ibrahim, an ethnic Chechen, was publicly executed in April by having his throat slit; relatives of the victims of his crime were reportedly among the executioners and the execution was televised. He was believed to have been tried by a *Shari'a* court and found guilty of committing murder while under the influence of drugs and alcohol. In September a man and a woman were publicly executed by firing-squad after being sentenced to death for murder by the Chechen Supreme *Shari'a* Court. Their co-defendant, Assa Larsanova, was not executed during 1997 because she was pregnant, but there were fears that she might be executed after giving birth. Also in September, Rasul Doshukayev and Said Khasiyev were publicly executed in Grozny, after having been found guilty of murder. According to reports, three of the victims' relatives were among the six executioners.

In October President Maskhadov issued a decree dismissing the Supreme Court panel of judges responsible for applying Islamic law, reportedly because of the public executions.

Continuing abductions of journalists and media employees in the Chechen Republic called into question the ability of both the Russian and Chechen authorities to guarantee the safety of journalists in this region. Among the seven media employees abducted in the Republic were prominent Russian television journalist Yelena Masyuk, her cameraman and her sound technician. They were ambushed by gunmen in May. Yelena Masyuk had allegedly suffered persecution by agents of the FSB while covering the conflict in the Chechen Republic from 1994 to 1996. All three were released in August. It was not disclosed who had held them.

Amnesty International called for the immediate and unconditional release of prisoners of conscience and expressed concern that the restrictions imposed by the new law on freedom of conscience and religion could allow for the imprisonment of prisoners of conscience.

In April Amnesty International issued a report, *Russian Federation: The right to conscientious objection to military service*, and launched a Europe-wide campaign on conscientious objection in Moscow. The organization urged the Russian authorities, among other things, to enact legislation creating an alternative civilian service of non-punitive length.

Amnesty International urged the authorities to launch thorough and impartial investigations into allegations of torture and ill-treatment. The organization published a report, *Torture in Russia: "This man-made hell"*, in April, which documented the torture of criminal suspects in police custody, in prisons and during the conflict in the Chechen Republic. Also in April Amnesty International published *Russian Federation: Torture, ill-treatment and death in the army*, which called on the authorities to eradicate the torture of soldiers by fellow soldiers or their superior officers.

In April Amnesty International published a report, *Russian Federation: Failure to protect asylum seekers – 'We don't want refugees here – go back to your own country'*, urging the Russian Government to take immediate steps towards establishing a fair and satisfactory refugee determination procedure, and to ensure that no one was forcibly returned to a country where he or she risked serious human rights violations.

Amnesty International called on President Yeltsin to grant clemency to all those sentenced to death and to publicly announce a moratorium on executions.

The organization condemned the public executions in the Chechen Republic and called for revision of the Chechen Criminal Code to exclude the death penalty and corporal punishment.

Amnesty International called on the Russian and Chechen authorities to condemn the abductions of journalists, to undertake all necessary measures to locate them and bring them to safety, and to take immediate steps to ensure the safety of all journalists working in the Chechen Republic.

RWANDA

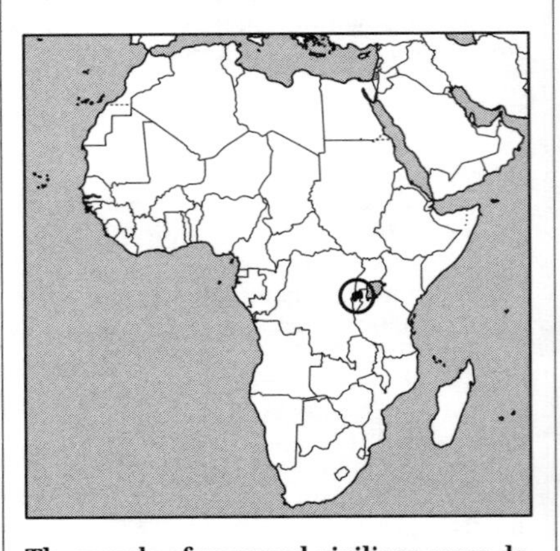

Thousands of unarmed civilians were deliberately killed; some were extrajudicially executed by government soldiers, others were deliberately and arbitrarily killed by armed opposition groups. Critics of the government were arrested and

harassed, or killed in circumstances suggesting extrajudicial executions. More than 130,000 people were detained, most in connection with the 1994 genocide. Most were held without trial. Many of the trials that were held were unfair. Most were held in conditions amounting to cruel, inhuman or degrading treatment; many died as a result. Torture or ill-treatment of detainees, leading to scores of deaths, were reported. Scores of people "disappeared". At least 111 people were sentenced to death, but no executions were reported. The government forcibly returned hundreds of refugees to Burundi.

The government of President Pasteur Bizimungu faced intensified armed conflict, particularly in the northwest. Government soldiers of the Rwandese Patriotic Army (RPA) fought against armed opposition groups believed to include members of the former Rwandese armed forces and *interahamwe* militia responsible for many massacres during the 1994 genocide. Both sides committed gross human rights abuses.

Growing insecurity forced the UN Human Rights Field Operation for Rwanda (UNHRFOR) to withdraw staff from western areas. Five of its members were deliberately killed (see below). Other agencies, including the UN High Commissioner for Refugees, were also forced to reduce their programs.

Despite reports from UNHRFOR on the significant increase in killings of unarmed civilians, little action was taken by the international community to address the deteriorating human rights situation.

The UN Commission on Human Rights replaced the mandate of the Special Rapporteur on Rwanda with that of Special Representative, who visited Rwanda in July.

Following a visit to Rwanda in December, the UN High Commissioner for Human Rights issued a statement highlighting the gravity of the human rights situation, in particular the substantial increase in killings by armed opposition groups and by the RPA, arbitrary arrests and inhumane conditions of detention.

In December the UN General Assembly adopted a resolution reaffirming the need to complete a case file for every detainee in Rwanda and to improve conditions of detention.

The third report of a UN commission of inquiry into transfers of arms and *matériel* to the former Rwandese government forces (see *Amnesty International Report 1996*), which had been submitted in October 1996, was finally made public in December. It included a series of recommendations on preventing further arms transfers to these forces and recommended that the UN Security Council urge Rwanda to take all possible measures to create a climate conducive to the harmonious reintegration of refugees in order to encourage their return in safety and dignity. The UN Security Council did not follow up on the work of the commission of inquiry or implement its recommendations.

Thousands of people were extrajudicially executed by government soldiers. Unarmed civilians, including young children and elderly people, were often killed by RPA soldiers in reprisal for armed opposition attacks, especially in the northwest. In January, 28 unarmed local residents were killed by RPA soldiers during a military search operation in Nyamugali, Ruhengeri. Twenty-four reportedly died after being herded into a building into which soldiers threw a grenade.

Between 9 and 11 May, at least 1,430 unarmed civilians, including more than 90 children, were reportedly killed by RPA soldiers in Nkuli, Ruhengeri, after clashes between soldiers and armed opposition fighters. Around the same period, 423 people were reportedly killed in neighbouring Nyamutera, 123 of whom allegedly burned to death in houses which were deliberately set on fire. In late October many unarmed civilians, estimated to number several thousand, were reportedly killed by RPA soldiers in a large cave at Nyakimana, in Kanama, Gisenyi. The total number of victims could not be confirmed as there were no independent investigations at the site.

Scores of unarmed civilians were killed in churches. In June RPA soldiers reportedly killed at least 120 people inside a Protestant church in Karago, Gisenyi. They went on to attack the houses of two community leaders and reportedly killed a further 38 people in their homes, including an 85-year-old man and a 90-year-old woman.

Many of those killed were former refugees who had been forcibly returned from the former Zaire and Tanzania in late

1996. They included soldiers of the former Rwandese army and their families. Jean de Dieu Bizabarimana, a major in the former Rwandese army, his wife, their children and several neighbours – 16 people in all – were killed in their home in Nyarutovu, Ruhengeri, in January.

Scores of detainees were killed by members of the security forces, who often claimed the victims had been shot while trying to escape. In several incidents witnesses reported that soldiers took detainees away and shot them dead. At least 95 detainees at Rubavu detention centre in Gisenyi were reportedly killed by the security forces in August.

Two men accused of murdering a local official were publicly and summarily executed by RPA soldiers in Karengera, Cyangugu, in January.

Hundreds of unarmed civilians were deliberately and arbitrarily killed by armed opposition groups. In January a group of armed men reportedly killed at least 24 Tutsi civilians in Kinigi, Ruhengeri. Most of the victims were reportedly killed in their homes. They included a 70-year-old man and at least five children. In April a group of armed men attacked several educational institutions in Satinsyi, Gisenyi, killing 22 people; 16 were female students shot dead in a school dormitory. In August at least 130 refugees from the Democratic Republic of the Congo (formerly Zaire) were killed during an attack by members of an armed opposition group on Mudende camp, in Mutura, Gisenyi; the victims included young children who were killed as they slept. Most were killed with machetes and clubs. Around 300 refugees were killed in a second attack on Mudende camp in December.

In many other cases, those responsible for killing unarmed civilians remained unidentified. In February four men, including Vincent Nkezabaganwa, President of the Council of State and Vice-President of the Supreme Court, were killed by armed men in military uniform in Kigali, the capital.

Several government critics were killed in circumstances suggesting that they may have been extrajudicially executed; others were arrested and harassed. In January Evariste Burakali, a National Assembly member for the *Parti libéral*, Liberal Party, was shot by soldiers in Rutare, Byumba; he died from his injuries the same night. In April Appollos Hakizimana, a journalist working for an independent newspaper, *Intego*, was shot dead by unidentified gunmen in Nyamirambo, in Kigali. He had previously been arrested, ill-treated and threatened on several occasions because of the critical views he had expressed as a journalist (see *Amnesty International Report 1997*). Amiel Nkuriza, director of *Intego*, was arrested a few days after the murder of Appollos Hakizimana. He was held in prison in Kigali awaiting trial at the end of the year. He had been arrested and threatened with death on several previous occasions (see *Amnesty International Report 1997*).

Several employees of international organizations were killed. In January three Spanish employees of the non-governmental organization *Médicos del Mundo* (Doctors without borders) were shot dead at their home in Ruhengeri. In February five members of UNHRFOR were ambushed and killed by armed men in Karengera, Cyangugu. In June two employees of the World Food Program (WFP), Jean de Dieu Murwanashyaka and Didace Nkezagera, and Didace Nkezagera's wife, young child and another relative were killed in Ruhengeri. Circumstances suggested that they had been killed by RPA soldiers. Didace Nkezagera had reportedly been questioned by soldiers about the WFP's work in the region on three consecutive days prior to his death. Jean de Dieu Murwanashyaka was taken by soldiers to an unknown destination; his mutilated body was found four days later.

In September four RPA officers were sentenced to 28 months' imprisonment by a military court for their role in the massacre of at least 110 civilians in Kanama, Gisenyi, in September 1995 (see *Amnesty International Report 1996*). In November, four RPA soldiers were sentenced to life imprisonment for their role in the assassination in October of Captain Théoneste Hategekimana, a member of the former Rwandese armed forces who had been integrated into the RPA. In December six RPA officers were given sentences ranging from 44 months to five years' imprisonment for their role in the killing of several hundred people during a military operation in Kigombe, Ruhengeri, in March.

More than 130,000 people, most accused of participating in the 1994 genocide, were held in civilian prisons and detention centres throughout the country; an unknown number were held in military detention centres, to which human rights and humanitarian organizations were usually denied access. Many were held without charge and most without trial. Many of those arrested were returned refugees. Among them were around 97 former Rwandese soldiers forcibly returned from Gabon in August, who were held in military custody at an undisclosed location and denied access to humanitarian organizations. Some people appeared to have been arrested because their relatives had served in the former government or army; others were held in the context of property disputes. In many cases, accusations that detainees had been involved in the genocide remained unsubstantiated. Many arrests appeared to be arbitrary and many detainees did not have case files. More than 2,000 prisoners were reportedly released following the government's announcements that it would release minors, the elderly and the sick.

Trials of people accused of participating in the 1994 genocide continued (see *Amnesty International Report 1997*). At least 320 people were tried of whom at least 111 were sentenced to death. Many of the earlier trials were grossly unfair; some defendants were denied defence lawyers and many were denied adequate time to prepare their defence. The conduct of trials improved in some respects during the year; a greater number of defendants had access to lawyers, requests for adjournments were granted more frequently, and witnesses began appearing in the courts. However, in at least one trial a defence witness failed to return to court after being threatened following her initial appearance. Other defence witnesses asked to submit their testimonies in writing as they were afraid of appearing in court, but their requests were rejected. Most defendants in trials in the western regions did not have access to legal counsel as widespread insecurity prevented lawyers from travelling there.

The trials of four individuals accused of participating in the genocide began at the International Criminal Tribunal for Rwanda (ICTR) in Arusha, Tanzania. By the end of the year the ICTR had issued 22 indictments against 35 individuals and was holding 23 detainees at its detention centre in Arusha, but no trials had been completed. Despite some changes in personnel, there were continued concerns about delays in proceedings, weaknesses in the protection of witnesses and lack of experienced staff. The first ever charges relating to sexual violence were laid against a defendant at the ICTR. The UN Special Rapporteur on violence against women visited Rwanda and Arusha in October to study gender issues relating to the ICTR.

Detainees in Rwanda were frequently beaten with sticks during arrest or soon after while held in detention centres. Scores of deaths in detention as a result of torture or ill-treatment were reported. In February, 12 detainees died in Rusumo detention centre, Kibungo; they had allegedly been beaten and then denied water and medical care. Many detention centres and prisons were seriously overcrowded and lacked basic hygiene and medical facilities. Many deaths in custody as a result of conditions which amounted to cruel, inhuman or degrading treatment were reported.

Scores of people were reported to have "disappeared". In January around 20 people, including refugees who had returned from Tanzania, "disappeared" in Rusumo, Kibungo, after being arrested by a local government official. Innocent Murengezi, a lawyer, "disappeared" in Kigali in January. He had reportedly been threatened several times because of his work defending some of those accused in genocide trials. His whereabouts were unknown at the end of the year and he was feared dead. Many refugees who had returned from the former Zaire in late 1996 were reported "disappeared" or missing.

At least 111 people were sentenced to death. The Court of Appeal rejected several appeals, including those of Deogratias Bizimana and Egide Gatanazi, the first two people to be tried for participating in the genocide (see *Amnesty International Report 1997*); their sentences were confirmed. No judicial executions were carried out.

Hundreds of refugees returned to Burundi, where their lives were at grave risk. Many appeared to have returned under duress. Refugees in Musange transit centre in Butare were reportedly threatened by Rwandese security officials to make them leave. Many of the more than 1,700 refugees in Kigeme, Gikongoro, who returned to Burundi in late August and early September were reportedly coerced into returning.

Throughout the year, Amnesty International appealed to the authorities to ensure respect for human rights. In January Amnesty International published *Rwanda: Human rights overlooked in mass repatriation*, which called for long-term monitoring of the human rights situation in Rwanda and an end to forcible repatriations until the country was safe.

In April it published a report analysing the genocide trials, *Rwanda: Unfair trials – justice denied*, to which the Ministry of Justice issued a public response. Amnesty International published *Rwanda: Ending the silence*, documenting the escalation of killings and other human rights abuses, and appealing for action by the Rwandese authorities, armed opposition groups, foreign governments and the international community, in September; and *Rwanda: civilians trapped in armed conflict*, which documented the further increase in killings of unarmed civilians, in December.

Amnesty International delegates undertook research in Rwanda and observed trials of those accused of participation in the genocide.

In July Amnesty International called on the South African Government not to resume the supply of light weapons and related military equipment to Rwanda, as such equipment would be likely to contribute to further human rights abuses.

Amnesty International repeatedly appealed to the Rwandese Government not to forcibly return refugees to Burundi where their lives would be at grave risk.

SAUDI ARABIA

Scores of suspected political or religious opponents of the government were detained; most were possible prisoners of conscience. Hundreds of others arrested in previous years remained held without trial. About a dozen political prisoners were serving prison sentences imposed after grossly unfair trials in previous years. There were continued allegations of torture and ill-treatment. The judicial punishment of flogging continued to be imposed. At least 122 people, most of them foreign nationals from developing countries, were executed after trials which fell short of international standards. At least six others had their death sentences lifted moments before they were due to be executed.

In September Saudi Arabia acceded to the UN Convention against Torture and Other Cruel, Inhuman or Degrading Treatment or Punishment (Convention against Torture) with two limiting reservations. One reservation related to Article 3(1) which prohibits the forcible return of anyone to another state where she or he would be at risk of torture. The other reservation was a refusal by the government to recognize the authority of the UN Committee against Torture to investigate allegations of systematic torture, as stipulated in Article 20.

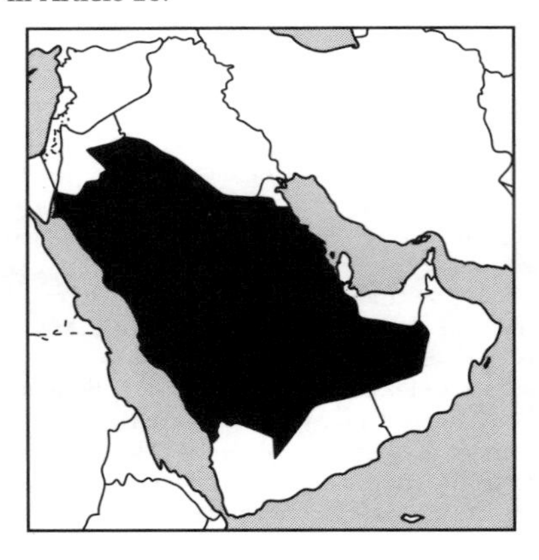

The government of King Fahd bin 'Abdul-'Aziz took the apparently unprecedented judicial step of allowing two British nurses, Deborah Parry and Lucille McLauchlan, to appoint and have access to lawyers. The two nurses had been arrested and charged with murder at the end of December 1996. The right of access to, and defence by, lawyers in criminal and political trials was neither recognized by law nor allowed in practice in Saudi Arabia. The government did not clarify whether the granting of access to lawyers to the two nurses was introduced as an exception or as a universal rule applicable in all cases. However, this right was not extended to other prisoners during the year.

The government's ban on political parties and trade unions remained in place. Press censorship continued to be strictly enforced. Information on human rights violations remained severely limited. The government continued to impose restrictions on access to the country by international human rights organizations, and failed to respond to communications by Amnesty International.

Scores of suspected political or religious opponents of the government, most of them possible prisoners of conscience, were detained. Most were members of the Shi'a community and were detained following sporadic arrests in various parts of the country, particularly the Eastern Province, during the first half of the year. Those detained included Shi'a clerics such as Sheikh Hassan Muhammad Nimr who was arrested in March by the *al-Mabahith al-'Amma* (General Intelligence) in al-Dammam. He reportedly remained held incommunicado at the headquarters of the *al-Mabahith al-'Amma* at the end of the year. Bander Fahd al-Shihri, who was detained on political grounds, was reportedly held without charge or trial in al-Ha'ir Prison in Riyadh at the end of the year. He had been forcibly returned to Saudi Arabia in May by the Canadian Government, which refused his asylum claim, and was arrested upon arrival in Riyadh. He was held incommunicado for weeks before being allowed family visits. He was a possible prisoner of conscience.

Hundreds of political prisoners, including possible prisoners of conscience, arrested in previous years continued to be held without trial. Scores of others arrested with them were released during the year. The detainees included the so-called Arab Afghan veterans – who had returned to Saudi Arabia after taking part in the armed conflicts in Afghanistan and Bosnia – and Shi'a and Sunni Muslim critics or opponents of the government, some of whom had been detained since their arrest in 1994. Sheikh Ja'far 'Ali al-Mubarak, who was detained following mass arrests in 1996 targeting Shi'a Muslim critics or opponents of the government (see *Amnesty International Report 1997*), continued to be held incommunicado and in solitary confinement in the headquarters of *al-Mabahith al-'Amma* in al-Dammam. Sheikh Salman bin Fahd al-'Awda and Sheikh Safr 'Abd al-Rahman al-Hawali, both arrested in 1994, and Dr Nasser 'Umr, arrested in 1995, remained held in al-Ha'ir Prison (see *Amnesty International Report 1997*).

Among those released during the year were Anmar al-Mas'ari, son of Mohammad al-Mas'ari, a government opponent living in exile, and three of his relatives (see *Amnesty International Report 1997*). They also included 'Abdullah 'Abbas al-'Ahmad, an employee of the Saudi Arabian national oil company (ARAMCO), who had been detained together with his brother, Kamil 'Abbas al-'Ahmad, a student, following the wave of arrests targeting members of the Shi'a community in July 1996. 'Abdullah 'Abbas al-'Ahmad was released without charge in November, but his brother continued to be held without charge or trial (see below).

About a dozen possible prisoners of conscience convicted in previous years were serving prison sentences imposed after grossly unfair trials; the trials were held in secret and defendants were denied an effective opportunity to defend themselves. They included 'Ali al-'Utaybi, who was serving a three-year prison sentence imposed in 1996 following his conviction on charges which reportedly included having contact with the Committee for the Defence of Legitimate Rights, an illegal organization. However, at least seven other possible prisoners of conscience who were serving prison terms imposed following their convictions on charges of membership of the *Hizb al-Tahrir al-'Islam*, Islamic Liberation Party, were released. They included 'Uthman Bakhash, a Lebanese national, who was serving a 30-month prison sentence (see *Amnesty International Report 1997*). New information was received that Donato Lama, a Philippine national previously reported to have been detained without trial since his arrest in 1995 on suspicion of preaching Christianity (see *Amnesty International Report 1997*), had in fact been sentenced in December 1996 to one and a half years' imprisonment and 70 lashes (see below). He was released in April or May following completion of his sentence and was deported to the Philippines.

There were allegations of torture and ill-treatment and reports that one prisoner died as a result of torture in December 1996. Methods of torture to which the prisoners were allegedly subjected included beatings, suspension from the ceiling and use of shackles. Those reported to have been tortured and ill-treated during the year included more than 40 Indian children aged between six and 14, and Kamil 'Abbas al-'Ahmad who had been in detention since his arrest in July 1996 (see above). The children were allegedly beaten and deprived of food while in the custody of the police in Jeddah. They were arrested at the beginning of the year apparently for begging and because their visas had expired. They were deported to India in February. Kamil 'Abbas al-'Ahmad was reported to have been suspended upside-down from a fan and beaten with cables and sticks. Maitham al-Bahr, a student from al-Qatif, was reported to have died as a result of torture after his detention during the mass arrests which followed the bombing of the al-Khobar military complex in June 1996 (see *Amnesty International Report 1997*). He was initially held incommunicado in the headquarters of the *al-Mabahith al-'Amma* in al-Dammam and was subsequently admitted to al-Dammam Central Hospital, where he died. A post-mortem examination reportedly revealed that he suffered from, among other things, renal failure and swellings on various parts of his body, which were said to be consistent with the allegations of torture.

The judicial punishment of flogging continued to be imposed. For example, Donato Lama (see above) was subjected to 70 lashes carried out in a single session in February in the courtyard of Malaz Prison in full view of other prisoners, and was barely able to walk as a result.

At least 122 people were executed and at least six others had their death sentences lifted moments before they were due to be executed. Most of those executed were migrant workers, notably from Afghanistan, Chad, India, Nigeria, Pakistan and the Philippines. All had been sentenced after grossly unfair trials conducted in secret and without legal assistance; most were convicted of drug-trafficking or murder. At least three women were executed, including Soleha Anam Kudiran, an Indonesian domestic worker who was executed in September. She had been sentenced to death, possibly in 1994, for the murder of her Saudi Arabian employer. According to reports, neither her family in Indonesia nor the Indonesian Embassy in Saudi Arabia were aware that she had been sentenced to death; they learned about her fate only after her execution had been carried out and made public in a Ministry of the Interior statement. The six who had their sentences lifted had all been convicted of murder and pardoned by heirs of the victims who, under *Shari'a* (Islamic) Law, have the right to settle for *Diyya* (blood money) instead of the execution of the murderer. In one case, that of Muhammad Salah 'Obeid, who was convicted of murdering Muhammad Hamid Khider, the heirs pardoned him on the day of his scheduled execution, reportedly in exchange for payment of a large sum of money.

The exact number of prisoners who remained under sentence of death at the end of the year was not known as such information was kept secret, but included at least one woman, Sarah Dematera, a Philippine national who had been convicted of murdering her employer in 1992 (see *Amnesty International Report 1997).*

In November Amnesty International published a report, *Behind closed doors: unfair trials in Saudi Arabia*, which highlighted the areas of the justice system that violate the right to fair trial and put forward a set of recommendations designed to redress the situation. In response to press questions about the report, the Minister of Foreign Affairs was quoted in November as having said: "It's nothing new. We are sure we are on the right path, preserving the interests of the nation and its citizens... We don't care what it says."

Amnesty International welcomed Saudi Arabia's accession to the International Convention on the Elimination of All Forms of Racial Discrimination and the UN Convention against Torture, and urged the government to take further steps to accede to other human rights treaties and to implement them fully. The organization requested clarification of the reasons for the arrest and detention of political detainees and called for the immediate and unconditional release of all prisoners of conscience and for fair trials in accordance with international standards for all others held on political grounds. Amnesty International also called for reports of torture to be investigated, for anyone found responsible to be brought to justice, and for the commutation of all sentences of flogging and death. No response was received from the government.

In April Amnesty International updated its previous submissions on Saudi Arabia for UN review under a procedure established by Economic and Social Council Resolutions 728F/1503, for confidential consideration of communications about human rights violations.

SENEGAL

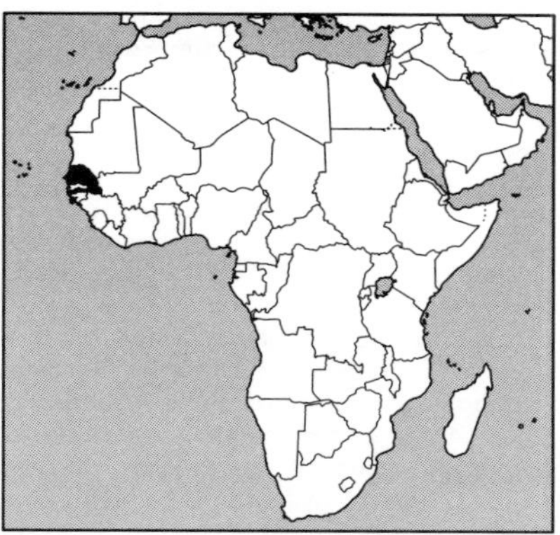

More than 120 alleged supporters of an armed separatist organization arrested in 1995 were still detained without trial. Most of them appeared to be prisoners of conscience. The army was responsible for "disappearances" and extrajudicial executions. Armed separatists in the Casamance region also committed human rights abuses, including deliberate and arbitrary killings of civilians.

Hopes that peace talks would start between the government and the armed separatist *Mouvement des forces démocratiques de Casamance* (MFDC), Democratic Forces of Casamance Movement, were quashed by the resumption in July of clashes between government forces and the MFDC.

More than 120 suspected MFDC sympathizers continued to be held without trial throughout the year. Most had been tortured during their first days of detention. They had been rounded up and arrested by the army from April 1995 onwards. Most of them appeared to be prisoners of conscience, arrested because they were members of the Diola community, and held without any evidence of individual responsibility for acts of violence (see *Amnesty International Reports 1996* and *1997*).

Many people arrested in Casamance after the resumption of fighting in July were tortured and ill-treated by the security forces. A number of people were reported to have been burned with petrol-filled plastic bottles. One was allegedly forced to drink the blood of one of his friends who had been killed by soldiers and another, before being killed himself, was said to have been forced to eat his own lips after they had been cut off by a soldier. None of these allegations were investigated.

Despite official promises, there was no sign of any readiness on the part of the authorities to put an end to the impunity of the security forces. Nine police officers and gendarmes charged in 1995 and 1996 with torturing prisoners remained at liberty, on provisional release, and none had been tried by the end of the year (see *Amnesty International Reports 1996* and *1997*).

The army was responsible for "disappearances" and extrajudicial executions in Casamance. In response to the renewed fighting in July and the death of 25 soldiers in Mandina Mancaye, near Ziguinchor, in August, the army arrested scores of civilians suspected of supporting the separatist movement in various towns and villages. At least 30 of those arrested subsequently "disappeared". For example, on 24 August Edgar Diédhiou was arrested at a party in his village of Siganar Boulou, Department of Oussouye. He was tortured by soldiers, who broke his leg. He was then taken in a military vehicle in the direction of the National Training Centre for Agricultural Technicians in Ziguinchor and has not been seen since. On 25 August Edmond Sékou Sadio, a barman in Tilène, a district of Ziguinchor, was arrested by soldiers at his place of work in the presence of a number of witnesses. He then "disappeared".

One of four members of the MFDC executive committee, Sarani Manga Badian, was arrested at his home on 24 August by a group of soldiers in front of his family and other witnesses. He then "disappeared".

The majority of the "disappeared" were feared to have been killed and buried in communal graves not far from military camps such as those at Nyassia and near the airport at Ziguinchor.

The MFDC was also responsible for human rights abuses, including deliberate and arbitrary killings of civilians, some targeted because of their ethnic origin. During the night of 7 to 8 September, armed MFDC combatants burst into the youth hostel in the village of Djibanar, Department of Sédhiou, and killed nine young people. The victims included two young girls: Timinadya Diatta, aged six, and Nakéba Diatta, aged nine.

In January Amnesty International delegates visited Senegal and met President Abdou Diouf, senior ministers and judicial and security officials. The delegates raised Amnesty International's concerns about the widespread use of torture and the apparent reluctance to investigate allegations of torture and bring those responsible to justice. The delegates also met the MFDC Secretary General, Father Diamacoune Senghor, in Ziguinchor, and expressed their concerns about abuses committed by the MFDC, including deliberate and arbitrary killings of civilians.

In May Amnesty International sent a memorandum asking the authorities to investigate allegations of torture and extrajudicial executions. It also called for the immediate and unconditional release of any prisoners of conscience detained in the context of the conflict in Casamance.

In September Amnesty International delegates visited Senegal to investigate human rights abuses committed by both parties in Casamance.

SIERRA LEONE

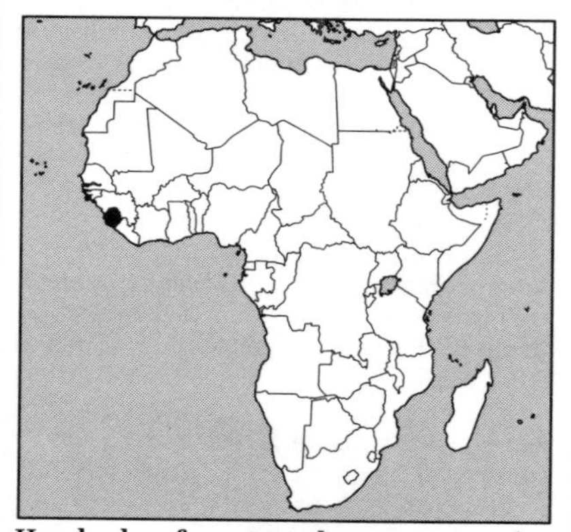

Hundreds of suspected opponents of a military coup were arbitrarily detained. They included supporters of the ousted government, journalists, students and human rights activists. Most, if not all, were prisoners of conscience. Many were tortured or ill-treated. Dozens of extrajudicial executions of political opponents were reported. Thirty-five people sentenced to death by military courts were executed. Armed opposition groups were responsible for deliberate and arbitrary killings and torture.

On 25 May President Ahmad Tejan Kabbah's government, in power since elections in 1996, was overthrown in a military coup. The Armed Forces Revolutionary Council (AFRC) which took power was subsequently joined by the armed opposition Revolutionary United Front (RUF) which had fought government forces for five years until a peace agreement in November 1996. The AFRC cited the failure to implement this agreement as one of the reasons for seizing power. The Constitution was suspended, political parties banned and demonstrations prohibited. The AFRC assumed extensive powers of detention, without safeguards against arbitrary arrest or indefinite detention without charge or trial.

The AFRC was headed by Lieutenant-Colonel (formerly Major) Johnny Paul Koroma who, with hundreds of other prisoners, was freed from the Central Prison, Pademba Road, in Freetown, on the day of the coup. He had been among nine soldiers charged in December 1996 with conspiring to overthrow the government, but not yet tried (see *Amnesty International Report 1997*).

Almost all sectors of society opposed the coup which was also strongly condemned by the international community – including the UN, the Organization of African Unity (OAU), the Commonwealth and the European Union. West African (predominantly Nigerian) troops present in Sierra Leone clashed repeatedly with AFRC and RUF forces. There was also fighting between a civilian militia of *kamajors* (traditional hunters) loyal to President Tejan Kabbah and AFRC and RUF forces. Nigerian forces used shelling to enforce an embargo on oil and arms imposed by the international community. Fighting and shelling resulted in hundreds of civilian casualties.

In October representatives of the AFRC and five other West African countries agreed on President Tejan Kabbah's return to power by April 1998. However, implementation of this agreement, which included cessation of hostilities, disarmament and demobilization, encountered serious set-backs. Fighting between soldiers and *kamajors* intensified in December and disarmament had not begun by the end of the year.

The reintegration within Sierra Leone agreed in November 1996 of hundreds of thousands of returning refugees and internally displaced people – nearly half the population – was thwarted by violence and insecurity following the coup. Thousands of civilians throughout the country were again forced to flee their homes. Many fled to other West African countries, where some encountered rejection at the frontier (see **Gambia** and **Liberia** entries), while others became internally displaced.

Following the coup, many people associated with the ousted government or suspected of opposing the AFRC were arbitrarily detained. An accurate assessment of their number was impossible but it appeared to be several hundred.

Immediately after the coup, several members of the ousted government and senior military officers were detained briefly at Cockerill military headquarters in Freetown. In June at least 15 senior military officers and civilians, including Dr Sama Banya, a prominent political figure, and Abu Aiah Koroma, former Minister for Parliamentary and Political Affairs, were arrested and accused of conspiring to overthrow the AFRC. Most were released in the following weeks, but Dr Sama Banya and five others remained in detention until late July and under house arrest until October.

A radio station began broadcasting in July, transmitting messages supporting the ousted government. Many people suspected of either knowing the location of the transmitter or of passing information to the radio station were arrested.

In October Mohamed B. Sesay, a former government minister, was among several people arrested and accused of subversive activities. He was held at police Criminal Investigation Department (CID) headquarters in Freetown before being released uncharged.

Those speaking out against human rights violations were arbitrarily detained. Some fled Sierra Leone and threats against those who remained severely restricted their activities. The president of a human rights organization, the Civil Liberties Congress, Sulaiman Banja Tejan-Sie, was arrested in August and forced at gunpoint to appear on television to call on students not to proceed with planned demonstrations. He was severely beaten, had his arms tied tightly and was locked in the boot of a car for several hours. He was again beaten at Cockerill military headquarters before being transferred to Pademba Road prison where he was denied food and washing facilities for several days. He was released without charge after 11 days.

In October soldiers and RUF members attempted to arrest the Secretary General of the Sierra Leonean Section of Amnesty International. Isaac Lappia, apparently suspected of opposing the AFRC and passing information outside Sierra Leone, escaped arrest; however, family members and others at his house were beaten and briefly detained.

Many students were vocal in their opposition to the AFRC. More than 120 people, mostly students, were arrested in August after attempting to stage a march for democracy. Most of those arrested were released after 12 days; others, however, were believed to have been held until October. Some students, including Juliet Jones, remained missing; it was unclear whether they had been arrested or had gone into hiding.

The AFRC's stated commitment to press freedom on coming to power was short-lived. In July the Sierra Leone Association of Journalists condemned unprecedented harassment and intimidation of journalists. That month four members of staff of *The Democrat* newspaper, and three others at its premises, were arrested by soldiers searching for the clandestine radio transmitter. Although four were released a few days later, Jeff Bowley Williams, Salomon Conteh and Fatmata Kamara were held for 12 days. Two journalists on their way to cover the students' demonstration in August were arrested with their driver and taken to Cockerill military headquarters. Kelvin Lewis, a correspondent for *Radio France Internationale* and *Voice of America*, and Winston Ojukutu Macaulay, a *British Broadcasting Corporation* (BBC) correspondent previously arrested in June, sustained serious injuries from beatings by soldiers who also threatened to kill them. Both journalists and their driver were released the following day. During October and November the crack-down on the press intensified; at least 20 journalists, including Jon Z. Foray, editor of *New Storm*, and Jonathan Leigh, editor of the *Independent Observer*, were detained without charge for up to two weeks.

Before the coup, in March, three journalists of the *Expo Times* newspaper were arrested on charges of spying, following an article criticizing the detention of RUF leader Foday Sankoh in Nigeria (see below). Released on bail, their trial was scheduled for May but the coup intervened and in July the charges against them were effectively dropped.

At least 15 people, both soldiers and civilians, were arrested in November, accused of conspiring to overthrow the AFRC and abort the return to civilian rule agreed the previous month. They included Stephen Bio, a businessman and close relation of the former Head of State who ceded power to President Tejan Kabbah, and Gibril Massaquoi, a prominent RUF member. None had been tried by the end of the year.

Following the coup, torture and ill-treatment by both soldiers and RUF members were widespread. In June Ansu Bockarie, a student leader, was reportedly beaten and cut with a razor blade by a prominent AFRC member. Students arrested in August were beaten, cut with machetes or stabbed with bayonets. Some women students were reported to have been sexually assaulted while held at the residences of AFRC members.

Many journalists detained during the year were tortured or ill-treated. In October Umaru Fofanah, a freelance journalist suspected of providing information to the clandestine radio station, was reportedly tortured and shot in the leg by soldiers.

Some of those arrested in Freetown were held in conditions amounting to cruel, inhuman or degrading treatment. For example, Sam Goba, arrested in September because of his close association with President Tejan Kabbah, was held with others in a freight container at Cockerill military headquarters for several months. His health seriously deteriorated as a result and his fate was unclear at the end of the year.

There were also reports of torture and ill-treatment by soldiers and RUF members in areas of the country affected by fighting with *kamajors*, in particular around Kenema in the east and Zimmi in the south. Villagers accused of supporting the *kamajors* were beaten and had their arms tied tightly behind their backs, causing serious injuries; women and girls were raped and forced into sexual slavery.

Many civilians died in the violence following the coup, some of whom were deliberately killed for political reasons by soldiers and RUF members. Soldiers searching for *kamajors* in Southern Province in June were reported to have killed about 25 people in the villages of Telu Bongor and Sembehun, as well as Albert Sandy Demby, father of the ousted Vice-President and a traditional leader, who was shot dead at his home in Gerihun. Also in June more than 10 people, including women and children, were reported to have been deliberately and arbitrarily killed when armed men, believed to be RUF members, attacked the town of Moyamba; a student, Sheku Kabbah, was reported to have had his eyes gouged out, ears cut off and throat slit. Many civilians were deliberately killed during fighting around Zimmi, Southern Province, in June. In December about 100 villagers were reportedly shot dead by soldiers posing as *kamajors* in the east of the country.

At least six students were shot dead in August by security forces. They included Morie Momoh, shot when soldiers entered his hostel room. In late August, six men suspected of involvement with the clandestine radio station were reportedly shot dead at Cockerill military headquarters.

Following the coup, several people were summarily executed by soldiers in Freetown following repeated AFRC warnings that suspected looters would be shot on sight.

In October, November and early December, 35 people, mostly soldiers but including some civilians, were executed by firing-squad following conviction for murder and other offences by military courts. Reports suggested, however, that in some cases no trial had taken place. In late November the AFRC passed retroactive legislation providing for the death penalty for looting or commandeering vehicles.

Despite the November 1996 agreement providing for immediate cessation of hostilities, unarmed civilians continued to be tortured and killed by RUF forces in the months before the coup, particularly in Tonkolili District, Northern Province. In January dozens of civilians were reported to have been killed and young girls raped in RUF attacks on several villages. According to reports, when soldiers moved into forest areas in Kailahun District, an RUF stronghold in Eastern Province, in February, they found more than 100 young children separated from their families, including three girls whose hands had been deliberately cut off and another child with an ear cut off. Similar atrocities by the RUF were reported during attacks on villages, including Kalangba and Pendembu, north of Makeni, in May before the coup; dozens of civilians were killed and others mutilated by having their arms or feet cut off.

In late March RUF members abducted at least five of their own members, a Sierra Leonean diplomat and members of the Guinean security forces in Kailahun District shortly after an announcement by prominent RUF members that Foday Sankoh had been removed as leader because he had obstructed the peace process. Foday Sankoh had been detained on arrival in Lagos, Nigeria, in early March, apparently for possession of arms and ammunition; he remained under house arrest in Nigeria at the end of the year. Two of those abducted, Fayia Musa and Ibrahim Deen-Jalloh, were RUF representatives on the Commission for the Consolidation of Peace established by the peace agreement. Although the diplomat was freed shortly after the coup, five RUF members remained held at the end of the year.

There were also reports that *kamajors* fighting AFRC and RUF forces deliberately killed, tortured and ill-treated civilians. In September four people, including a woman, who were suspected of being soldiers or AFRC supporters, were reportedly summarily executed by being beheaded when the vehicle in which they were travelling from Bo to Makeni was stopped by *kamajors*.

In February Amnesty International received a response from the Minister of Justice to its request for clarification of the death in custody of a soldier among those arrested with Major Johnny Paul Koroma (see *Amnesty International Report 1997*). The reply included a post-mortem report, rejected allegations of ill-treatment during interrogation and stated that he had died after attempting to escape by jumping from a window. In March Amnesty International called for the humane treatment and release of RUF members held hostage. Following the coup Amnesty International repeatedly called for an end to arbitrary arrest and detention, torture and ill-treatment, and extrajudicial executions, and in October published a report documenting these violations, *Sierra Leone: A disastrous set-back for human rights.* It called on the international community to give priority to the protection of human rights in efforts to resolve the political crisis in Sierra Leone. Amnesty International strongly condemned executions in October, November and December, called for the repeal of retroactive legislation extending the scope of the death penalty and urged that no further executions take place.

SINGAPORE

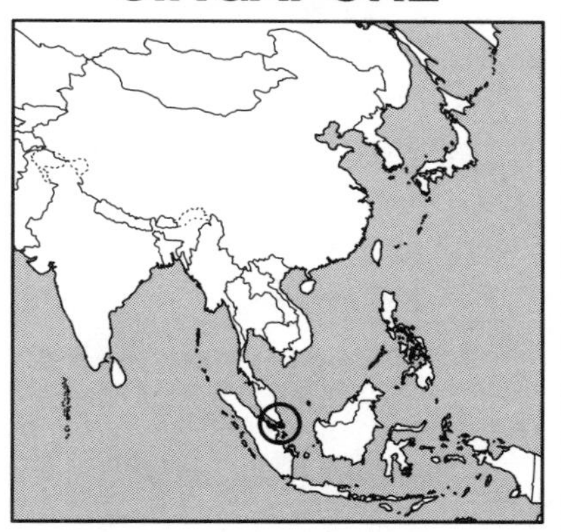

Civil suits were brought by government leaders against two members of an opposition party. At least 38 prisoners of conscience were held throughout the year for their conscientious objection to military service. One former prisoner of conscience continued to be subject to government orders restricting his freedom of expression and association. Criminal offenders continued to be sentenced to caning. At least eight death sentences were passed and at least 14 executions were reported.

Following elections in January the ruling People's Action Party (PAP), headed by Prime Minister Goh Chok Tong, was returned to parliament with an overwhelming majority, winning 81 of the 83 seats.

In an apparently politically motivated move to restrict freedom of expression, government leaders lodged civil defamation suits against two members of the opposition Workers' Party, claiming large amounts of damages. The suits appeared to be designed to bankrupt the opposition members, thereby preventing them from participating in public life.

During the campaign preceding the January elections, senior PAP members publicly accused opposition Workers' Party candidate Tang Liang Hong of being an "anti-Christian Chinese chauvinist", a serious charge given Singapore's sensitivity to issues of racial and religious harmony. Tang Liang Hong, who subsequently received death threats, filed two police reports against 11 members of the PAP, accusing them of making false statements and of inciting religious groups against him. Following the elections, Prime Minister Goh Chok Tong, Senior Minister Lee Kuan Yew and nine other PAP members lodged a series of civil suits against Tang Liang Hong claiming that he had defamed them through the police reports. In March the High Court found Tang Liang Hong – who had left Singapore in January following the death threats – liable for damages, and in May ordered him to pay a total of US$5.65 million. In November the Court of Appeal reduced the amount of damages to US$2.3 million.

In January Prime Minister Goh Chok Tong lodged a claim for US$130,000 damages against Workers' Party leader J.B. Jeyaretnam for allegedly defaming him during an election rally by saying the words, "finally, Mr Tang Liang Hong has just placed before me two reports he has made to police against, you know, Mr Goh Chok Tong and his people".

Ten other PAP politicians, whose names had been listed in the police reports filed by Tang Liang Hong, also lodged claims for damages against J.B. Jeyaretnam. In August the High Court heard the case lodged by the Prime Minister and in September the court found J.B. Jeyaretnam liable for defamation and ordered him to pay US$13,000 in damages, plus 60 per cent of costs. An appeal by the Prime Minister for the award to be increased was pending at the end of the year. The related defamation cases lodged by 10 other PAP members were also pending at the end of the year. J.B. Jeyaretnam faced possible bankruptcy and the subsequent loss of his parliamentary seat.

At least 38 conscientious objectors to military service were imprisoned during the year. They were prisoners of conscience. All were members of the Jehovah's Witnesses, a religious group which has been banned in Singapore since 1972. All refused to perform military service on religious grounds. There is no alternative civilian service for conscientious objectors to military service in Singapore. In September Bay Poh Heng was court-martialled and sentenced to two years' detention for refusing for the second time to comply with military orders. He had already served one year in prison for his objection to military service.

Government restriction orders against Chia Thye Poh, a former prisoner of conscience, continued to curtail his freedom of association and expression.

Caning, which constitutes a cruel, inhuman or degrading punishment, remained mandatory for some 30 crimes, including attempted murder, rape, armed robbery, drug-trafficking, illegal immigration and vandalism. It remained an optional penalty for a number of other crimes, including extortion, kidnapping and causing grievous injury. In August Alan Loo Pei Xiang, aged 16, was sentenced to 24 strokes of the cane and a 15-year prison sentence for trafficking in cannabis. It was not known how many sentences were carried out during the year.

At least eight death sentences were reported to have been passed during the year for murder or drugs offences.

At least 14 executions by hanging were reported to have been carried out, the majority for drug-related offences. Despite the lack of official information, there were reliable indications that the real figure was much higher. In July an Indonesian national, La Abuhari bin La Ode Hamid, and Singaporean Abdul Raman bin Yusof were executed for trafficking in cannabis. Three other men, including two Thai nationals convicted of murder, were reported to have been executed on the same day.

Amnesty International observers attended the defamation trial of J.B. Jeyaretnam and the appeal hearing of Tang Liang Hong. In October the organization published a report, *Singapore: J.B. Jeyaretnam – the use of defamation suits for political purposes*. In its response to the report, the government maintained the legitimacy of defamation suits as a means for leaders to defend their reputation and integrity.

In January Amnesty International reiterated its concerns about the use of the death penalty in Singapore in a report, *Against the tide: The death penalty in Southeast Asia.*

Amnesty International continued to urge the government of Prime Minister Goh Chok Tong to release all prisoners of conscience and to lift the restrictions on Chia Thye Poh. The organization also urged the authorities to end the punishment of caning, to commute all death sentences and publish statistics on the use of the death penalty.

SLOVAKIA

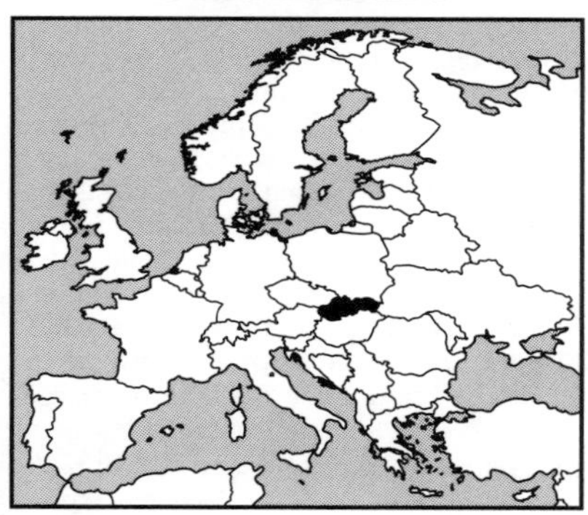

At least four conscientious objectors to military service were imprisoned. They were prisoners of conscience.

In April the government authorized the publication of the report of the European Committee for the Prevention of Torture and Inhuman or Degrading Treatment or Punishment on its visit to places of detention in Slovakia in June and July 1995. The Committee stated that it heard numerous allegations of ill-treatment by the police and concluded that persons suspected of a criminal offence run a significant risk of being ill-treated by the police at the time of apprehension and during the first hours in police custody, and that on occasion such persons may be subjected to severe ill-treatment. The Committee also expressed concern about the apparent lack of access to a lawyer and to a doctor for persons in detention. The government acknowledged the findings of the Committee and undertook to put into practice its recommendations.

In July the UN Human Rights Committee met to consider Slovakia's initial report on its compliance with the International Covenant on Civil and Political Rights. In its concluding remarks, the Committee "noted with concern that the remnants of the former totalitarian rule have not yet been completely overcome and that further steps remain to be undertaken in consolidating and developing democratic institutions and strengthening the implementation of the Covenant". The Committee noted the persistence of political and social attitudes adverse to the promotion and full protection of human rights. It expressed concern that insufficient steps had been taken to implement various provisions of the Slovak Constitution concerning fundamental rights, and provisions of the Covenant, including Article 18, concerning the right to alternative service of non-punitive length for conscientious objectors to military service; that Roma, who were often victims of racist attacks, reportedly did not receive adequate protection from law enforcement officials; about cases of excessive use of force by law enforcement officials, and ill-treatment of detainees during police custody; and about freedom of expression, including the excessive restrictions on this right imposed by Article 98 of the Penal Code, which makes it an offence to "disseminate false information abroad which harms the interest" of Slovakia (see *Amnesty International Report 1997*).

In February Martin Bednár, a conscientious objector, was imprisoned for refusing to perform military service. He was conditionally released in September after serving half of his one-year sentence. In May Erik Kratmüller and Martin Badin, who had been imprisoned in June and August 1996 respectively (see *Amnesty International Report 1997*), were released. Miroslav Albert began serving a one-year prison sentence in September. At least four other conscientious objectors to military service were prosecuted for evading military service and faced imprisonment. In most of these cases the defendants had not submitted their application for alternative service within 30 days of being declared fit for service, as required by the Law on Civilian Service.

Amnesty International urged the authorities to release the prisoners of conscience immediately and to stop criminal proceedings against conscientious objectors to military service. In April Amnesty International published a report, *Slovak Republic: Restrictions on the right to conscientious objection*. The organization also urged the authorities to revise the Law on Civilian Service, to bring it into line with internationally recognized principles.

SOMALIA

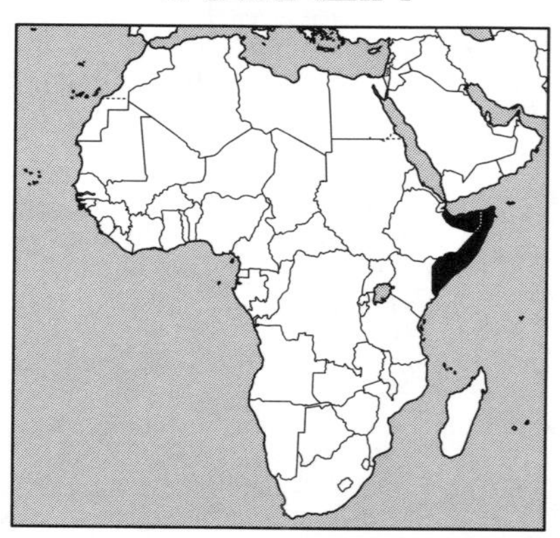

Human rights abuses against unarmed civilians, including women and children, were carried out by militias of clan-based factions. Abuses included scores of deliberate and arbitrary killings, as well as hostage-taking and rape. Several prisoners of conscience who were imprisoned in 1996 and early 1997 were released. An Islamic court imposed two sentences of amputation and many floggings. Several people were believed to have been executed after being condemned to death by Islamic and clan courts.

Efforts continued towards peace, reconciliation and the establishment of a transitional government for the former Somali Republic, but at the end of the year there was still no central or recognized government in the collapsed state. Nor was there any consistent, effective or fair criminal justice system (see *Amnesty International Report 1997*). The Sodere agreement, signed in Ethiopia in January by 26 Somali factions, created a National Salvation Council but this was boycotted by Hussein Aideed's Somali National Alliance and by the self-declared, but still unrecognized, Somaliland Republic in the northwest. Two inter-faction agreements reached in Cairo, Egypt, and Sanaa, Yemen, in May similarly failed to include all parties. However a meeting in Cairo in December, which included Hussein Aideed's group, agreed to convene a reconciliation conference in Somalia in 1998 to form a transitional government, elect its leaders and a constituent assembly, and set up an independent judiciary.

The level of faction fighting was lower than in any year since civil war started in 1991, but in certain areas casualties included unarmed civilians. In Mogadishu there were several outbreaks of fighting between the militia forces of Hussein Aideed and Ali Mahdi, both of whom claimed to be president of Somalia. There were also clashes between Hussein Aideed's forces and those of Osman Ali Atto, and in July between Ali Mahdi's forces and Islamic court militias. There were several periods of intensive fighting in the central Bay and Bakol regions, where the Rahanweyn Resistance Army (RRA) sought to dislodge Hussein Aideed's forces from Baidoa town. In Gedo region, the Marehan clan-based Somali National Front, reportedly supported at times by Ethiopian army units, fought with Islamist *Al-Itihad* militias. Tensions between Marehan and Majerten clans in Kismayu port and between pro-Aideed and pro-Ali Mahdi factions in other central regions also occasionally erupted into violence. Meanwhile, Somaliland and Bari and Nugal regions in the northeast remained mainly peaceful.

The UN Security Council in February made further appeals to all Somali political factions for peace and reconciliation. In April the UN Commission on Human Rights, having received a report from the UN Independent Expert on the situation of human rights in Somalia, called for all parties to respect human rights and international humanitarian law. The Commission called on them to support the re-establishment of the rule of law by applying internationally accepted criminal justice standards, and to protect UN and other humanitarian workers. It called on the international community to incorporate human rights principles and objectives into humanitarian and development work. In July the UN Secretary-General appointed a Special Envoy for Somalia to further the peace process.

In the Somaliland capital of Hargeisa in February, the National Conference of the Clans elected Mohamed Ibrahim Egal for a further three-year term as President of Somaliland and the National Assembly approved a provisional Constitution. The Constitution maintains the independence of Somaliland and contains a number of human rights provisions relating to the independence of the judiciary and protection against arbitrary imprisonment.

There were new allegations of human rights violations by some of the foreign troops during the 1993 UN operation in Somalia. Fresh allegations of abuses including torture, sexual abuse and unlawful killings were levelled at Belgian and Italian troops. These allegations were the subject of various investigations and criminal proceedings in those countries (see **Belgium** and **Italy** entries).

Human rights abuses by clan-based militias continued throughout the year. There were several cases of hostage-taking accompanied by death threats, although it was rarely clear which group was responsible. Several people, both Somalis and foreign nationals, working for non-governmental and intergovernmental organizations, including the UN, were kidnapped, but all were apparently released within a few days. Somali journalists and human rights activists frequently received death threats on account of their professional activities. A Portuguese doctor working for *Médecins sans Frontières* was killed in Baidoa in June and two Somali staff of World Concern were killed in Kismayu in August. The victims were deliberately targeted on account of their humanitarian work, although it was not clear who was responsible. In February and October there were several revenge killings of prominent people in the rival factions of Osman Atto and Hussein Aideed in Mogadishu.

Scores of unarmed civilians were deliberately and arbitrarily killed by armed militias, some in artillery bombardments. Few details were available of these incidents and the perpetrators were rarely identified. In March, 17 members of the Bantu minority, including four women and eight children, were killed by faction militias in Jamiya Misra village in Middle Shebelle region, and seven women were raped. There were reports that as many as 200 civilians had been killed in September by Hussein Aideed's forces in and around Baidoa.

In Somaliland, Mahmoud Abdi Shidde, publisher of the *Jamhuriya* newspaper which had been critical of the Somaliland administration, was detained twice. He was held briefly in April, until a court ordered his release, and for a week in September. He was a prisoner of conscience. All political prisoners and captured clan fighters imprisoned in Somaliland in 1996, including about 20 prisoners of conscience jailed after a peaceful demonstration (see *Amnesty International Report 1997*), were released in an amnesty in January.

It was difficult to establish whether any political prisoners were held by faction militias in Mogadishu or elsewhere, although there were reports that captured RRA fighters and possibly civilian opponents were held by Hussein Aideed's forces in Baidoa.

An Islamic court imposed floggings and amputations, punishments which are cruel, inhuman and degrading, and so prohibited by international law. In North Mogadishu in May, an Islamic court imposed two sentences of amputation, which were carried out immediately. Abshir Mohamed Ahmed, convicted of theft, had his right hand amputated, and Qasim Beshir Mohamed, convicted of armed robbery, had his right hand and left foot amputated. They did not have fair trials – the proceedings were arbitrary and summary, and they were denied legal representation and the right of appeal. Subsequently, after criticism by Somali lawyers and a local human rights organization, the Dr Ismail Centre for Human Rights, the court agreed to review its procedures and no more amputations were imposed during the year.

Several executions were believed to have taken place after trials by Islamic and clan courts but details were not available.

There was a new development in June regarding gross violations of human rights committed by the former government of Siad Barre (1969 to 1991). Mass graves were discovered in Hargeisa of some 200 political prisoners extrajudicially executed in May 1988.

Amnesty International called throughout the year on all factions to respect human rights and control their militias. In June it welcomed the inquiries and prosecutions of those allegedly responsible for torture or extrajudicial executions during the UN operation, and gave evidence to an Italian commission of inquiry. In July Amnesty International published a report on a human rights training workshop it held for Somali organizations, *Somalia: Putting human rights on the agenda.*

SOUTH AFRICA

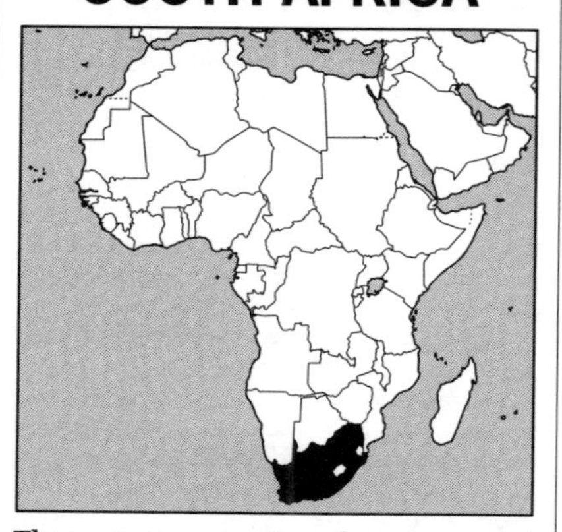

There were reports of torture and ill-treatment in police custody and in prisons. More than 100 deaths in custody were reported. Members of the security forces and right-wing paramilitaries were implicated in killings of trade unionists, local councillors and other activists. Evidence continued to emerge of systematic violations of human rights under the former government.

In December President Nelson Mandela was succeeded as president of the African National Congress (ANC) by Deputy President Thabo Mbeki. Talks between the ANC and the Inkatha Freedom Party (IFP) about a "peace deal" for KwaZulu Natal included proposed amnesties for those implicated in the political violence. Towards the end of the year there were reports of political tensions and violence between ANC supporters and supporters of the newly formed United Democratic Movement. There was an increasing number of apparently targeted killings of white farmers, and a high level of violence between organized criminal gangs and anti-crime vigilantes in the Cape Town area.

During the year the national parliament passed a number of laws with significance for human rights. The Correctional Services Amendment Act, which established a judicial inspectorate of prisons and permitted the construction and management of prisons by private businesses, inadequately protected the rights of prisoners. The Criminal Law Amendment Act provided for the resentencing of 453 prisoners whose death sentences had been declared unconstitutional in 1995, and deleted provisions in other statutes which had allowed for capital punishment. The Abolition of Corporal Punishment Act repealed statutory provisions permitting judicial and other forms of corporal punishment. The Criminal Procedure Second Amendment Act, which restricted the right to bail for people accused of serious offences, appeared to unnecessarily restrict the rights of the accused. The State of Emergency Act empowered the President to declare a state of emergency and make regulations suspending certain rights subject to Section 37 of the Constitution.

The Commission on Gender Equality, which began operating in April, focused initially on violations of women's rights in rural and other marginalized sectors.

Human rights monitors and the statutory Independent Complaints Directorate (ICD) received reports of torture and ill-treatment by police officers. In January police officers allegedly tortured and ill-treated a number of suspects held in police and prison cells in connection with violence in the Lusikisiki area of the Eastern Cape. The provincial Minister of Health and Welfare confirmed that the prisoners, who had apparently been beaten on their backs and buttocks with a *sjambok* (whip), suffered "severe injuries" and had been denied food, medication and toilet facilities. Four required hospitalization for severe dehydration, blood in their urine and *sjambok* wounds. An investigation ordered by the provincial Commissioner of Police had not concluded by the end of the year.

Between April and November the ICD reported receiving seven complaints of rape of criminal suspects by police officers. In April the Attorney-General for KwaZulu Natal withdrew charges against a police officer due to be retried for the rape of Thokozani Nzama in a cell at Stanger police station two years earlier. His previous conviction and 10-year prison sentence for the rape had been overturned by the High Court on a technicality in 1996. The police officer had remained on duty pending his successful 1996 appeal hearing. During that period he had allegedly threatened the life of the complainant. In June Thokozani Nzama was raped, beaten and shot dead by four unidentified men.

Eight members of the Umfolozi Public Order Policing Unit, based at Mtubatuba in the North Coast region of KwaZulu Natal, appeared in court in July charged with assaulting Kevin Kunene, Chairperson of the KwaMbonambi Environmental Group, and four other local community activists in February 1996. The court heard evidence that police officers abducted the five activists and subjected them variously to beatings, electric shocks and suffocation. The trial was due to conclude in February 1998. In another development, prosecution proceedings were instituted against police officers from the Middleburg Murder and Robbery Unit following the seizure of torture equipment from their office in 1996 (see *Amnesty International Report 1997*).

The ICD, which has a statutory responsibility to investigate every death in police custody, received reports of 134 such deaths between April and November, the majority in Gauteng Province, KwaZulu Natal, and the Eastern and Western Capes. Investigations continued into the circumstances of these deaths. In June, 17-year-old Angelo Asia died in hospital following his arrest by Ravensmead police officers. They allegedly beat, choked and used teargas on him, before throwing him in their van and then dumping him, unconscious, in a police cell. The ICD had nearly completed its investigation by the end of the year. Also in June a Burundi refugee, Jean-Pierre Kanyangwa, died within hours of being arrested by Cape Town police. When the police brought him to the refugee section of the Department of Home Affairs, he was in pain, but the officers allegedly refused to take him to hospital. An immigration official called an ambulance, but Jean-Pierre Kanyangwa died before reaching the hospital. A preliminary post-mortem examination showed that he died as a result of injury to his spleen. An inquest was scheduled for 1998.

In July the ICD recommended disciplinary action against a Potchefstroom police officer in connection with the death in custody in February of a criminal suspect, Swartland Dails. Independent post-mortem examinations revealed that the detainee had died of unnatural causes. The ICD were investigating possible causes of death, including electro-shock torture. The police officer involved was already under investigation in connection with other allegations of torture and ill-treatment.

A number of serious incidents of torture and ill-treatment of prisoners were investigated by the statutory Human Rights Commission. In one incident in February, warders at Helderstroom Maximum Prison allegedly beat, kicked, punched and used electric shields on more than 50 prisoners when moving them from communal to isolation cells. Apparently, no disciplinary action was taken following the Commission's investigation. Some of the same warders were reportedly also involved in an incident at Pollsmoor Maximum Prison in May, when 150 warders recruited from different prisons allegedly assaulted prisoners with batons, fists and pistols during a search for weapons. A ministerial inquiry found, among other things, that 155 prisoners sustained injuries requiring medical attention, and that the prison doctor failed to provide medical care for many of them. In December police investigators recommended to the Attorney-General that 132 warders be prosecuted for assault and other offences.

Prisoners transferred to a new maximum security prison which opened in September, the CMAX, were held in solitary confinement in 3.5m x 2m cells, with one hour's daily exercise in a 4m x 2m outdoor cage. The Minister of Correctional Services denied that the conditions were potentially damaging to prisoners' mental health.

The Human Rights Commission investigated allegations that prisoners were being held in leg irons at Victor Verster Prison, and confirmed that in one case a prisoner had been held in leg irons for as long as 60 consecutive days.

Political violence in the province of KwaZulu Natal resulted in more than 300 deaths, according to the non-governmental Human Rights Committee. One of the worst affected areas was Richmond, where in May Rodney van der Bijl, a member of the Transitional Local Council, was shot dead outside his home. Less than two weeks earlier, other councillors had resigned, allegedly under pressure from a self-styled local "warlord", provincial member of parliament and leading member of the newly formed National Consultative Forum (NCF) who had been expelled from the ANC after his alleged links with the former police Security Branch emerged. In July, after the NCF was defeated by ANC candidates in a council by-election, two new councillors, Bhekamusa Mchunu and Alpheus Mchunu, and three other ANC members were dragged from their homes and shot dead. The previous day, they had reported seeing the "warlord" with police officers distributing weapons. In September police from combined national task forces arrested him and 23 others. They were remanded in custody to stand trial in 1998. In October a national investigating officer indicated that the role of senior police in the Richmond killings was under investigation. The same month, the national government deployed hundreds of police and soldiers in the Richmond area.

In the rural areas of Tsolo and Qumbu in the Eastern Cape, at least 151 people were killed during the first nine months of the year. There were indications of police acquiescence in the killings. In one attack in August, gunmen killed seven women and injured another, before setting their home alight. The attack followed the refusal by the house-owner to join an anti-crime vigilante group. Government intervention leading, for instance, to the deployment of non-local police and soldiers failed to stop the killings.

At least six National Union of Mineworkers (NUM) officials and their relatives were victims of targeted killings by alleged members of a rival union, the Workers' Mouthpiece Union, in violence which started near Rustenburg but spread to the Eastern Cape. Other senior NUM officials and shop stewards received death threats. There were indications that a white right-wing paramilitary group and police officers were implicated in the killings.

In March the Durban High Court convicted 13 IFP supporters on 18 counts of murder and six counts of attempted murder in connection with the December 1995 attack on Shobashobane (see *Amnesty International Report 1996*).

In May an inquest court ruled that Dr Henry Vuka Luthuli, who had been shot dead in his Esikhawini surgery in 1990, had been killed by a police constable from Vlakplaas, the base of the former security police counter-insurgency unit. The court referred the case to the Attorney-General for a decision on prosecution.

In September a former agent of the covert Civil Cooperation Bureau was remanded in custody to stand trial for the 1989 murder of human rights activist David Webster (see *Amnesty International Report 1990*).

The judicial inquest into the death of eight IFP members outside the ANC's Shell House headquarters in March 1994 (see *Amnesty International Report 1995*) concluded in the Johannesburg High Court in December. The presiding judge was unable to establish criminal responsibility for the deaths, but stated that there was no *prima facie* justification for the ANC guards to shoot at the crowd, and that "the barrage of fire was in any event grossly excessive".

Further information on past human rights violations emerged through Truth and Reconciliation Commission (TRC) investigations. The life-span of the Human Rights Violations, and Reparations and Rehabilitation Committees was extended by Parliament until 30 April 1998, and that of the Amnesty Committee until 30 June 1998. In October the Reparations and Rehabilitation Committee recommended financial compensation for the estimated 22,000 people whose complaints have been corroborated by the TRC by June 1998.

The TRC held hearings on the role of the health and business sectors, the judiciary, religious institutions and the media in creating a climate which encouraged human rights violations. There were also hearings on "events" or patterns of human rights violations, including a hearing on the role of state structures in the June 1986 destruction of "KTC" squatter camp in Cape Town, and a special hearing on women's experiences of political and state violence, and torture, including sexual assault and rape.

Public hearings on amnesty applications from former security police officers resulted in important admissions of their involvement in the torture and murder of government opponents. For instance, former security police officer Jeff Benzien demonstrated how he had used torture by suffocation to extract information. One of his commanding officers acknowledged having endorsed this method of interrogation. Former security officials admitted abducting and murdering three Port Elizabeth Black Civic Organization leaders who "disappeared" in 1985 (see *Amnesty International Report 1986*).

The TRC's investigations led to the identification of secret graves and the exhumation of the bodies of a number of ANC members who had apparently been extrajudicially executed by the security forces in the 1980s.

Despite the emerging evidence, former National Party government leaders denied having authorized security force abuses.

The TRC also heard evidence on human rights abuses committed by former opposition organizations, for instance, in amnesty application hearings involving members of the armed wing of the Pan Africanist Congress and during Section 29 subpoena hearings on alleged abuses committed by the so-called Mandela United Football Club in the late 1980s.

The TRC sought a High Court review of the Amnesty Committee's decision to grant amnesties to a group of ANC members, including currently serving cabinet ministers. The Committee denied amnesty to a former security police officer for the torture of Mkhuseli Jack, an activist from Port Elizabeth, in 1985, but granted amnesties to former Vlakplaas security police unit members Dirk Coetzee, Almond Nofomela and David Tshikalange, for the 1981 murder of human rights lawyer Griffiths Mxenge. The latter's family announced that they would seek a High Court review of the decision.

Amnesty International representatives visited South Africa on five occasions, meeting government officials, human rights monitors and others to investigate the problem of impunity, the functioning of the criminal justice system, and allegations of human rights violations in prisons and torture and deaths in police custody. Representatives also attended TRC hearings, presenting written and oral submissions on human rights violations and recommendations for their prevention. In October the organization submitted recommendations to the government and national parliament on the draft National Prosecuting Authority Bill, and made a further submission on South Africa's arms trade with central African countries, appealing for government support for measures to protect human rights in the region.

SPAIN

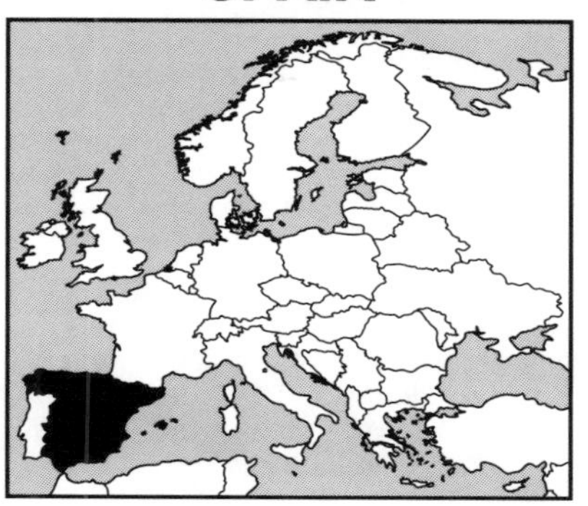

Judicial inquiries continued into allegations of a clandestine "dirty war" waged in the 1980s against the armed Basque group *Euskadi Ta Askatasuna* (ETA), Basque Homeland and Freedom. There were fresh allegations of torture and ill-treatment by law enforcement officers. Several law enforcement officers charged with torture were tried and sentenced. ETA continued to commit human rights abuses, which included deliberate and arbitrary killings and hostage-taking.

Judicial investigations continued into acts of kidnapping, torture and murder during a "dirty war" between 1983 and 1987 against presumed ETA members, waged by the *Grupos Antiterroristas de Liberación* (GAL), Anti-Terrorist Liberation Groups (see *Amnesty International Reports 1996* and *1997*). In September the Supreme Court ordered the committal for trial of a former interior minister, a former secretary of state for security and 10 others, including a former leading politician, senior officials and senior police officers, for involvement in the kidnapping by GAL of Segundo Marey (see *Amnesty International Report 1997*). Judicial investigations also continued into the kidnapping, torture and murder by GAL of two ETA members, José Antonio Lasa and José Ignacio Zabala, and into the killing of a presumed ETA member, Ramón Oñederra, in the 1980s.

In November the UN Committee against Torture considered Spain's third periodic report on its implementation of the UN Convention against Torture and Other Cruel, Inhuman or Degrading Treatment or Punishment. The Committee welcomed the measures taken by the government to implement the core safeguards set out in the Convention, including the definitive abolition of the death penalty and the introduction into the new Penal Code of articles prohibiting torture and ill-treatment. However, it observed that the long delays in legal proceedings relating to torture, both at the investigation and trial stages, were "absolutely incompatible" with the promptness required by the Convention and that sentences passed by the courts on officials accused of torture were often nominal. The Committee affirmed that it continued to receive frequent allegations of torture and ill-treatment, many of which "appeared to reveal signs of racial discrimination". It also expressed concern at the way in which the continuing practice of extended incommunicado detention facilitated the practice of torture. The Committee urged the authorities to take the necessary measures to address its concerns.

In December the 23 members of the National Board of the Basque nationalist coalition party *Herri Batasuna* (HB), People's Unity Coalition, were each sentenced by the Supreme Court to seven years' imprisonment for "collaboration with an armed band". They were acquitted of "belonging to an armed band" and "defence of terrorism". In its ruling, the Court stated that its decision related to an incident during the 1996 general election when HB ceded its free television broadcasting time to ETA by showing an ETA-made video. This featured three hooded men, who were seated at a table on which they had placed their guns, as they set out ETA's conditions for peace negotiations and a cease-fire. The defence lawyers presented an appeal to the Constitutional Court.

A reform of the law on conscientious objection to military service, proposed in 1996 (see *Amnesty International Report 1997*), was still under consideration by Congress at the end of the year.

Allegations of torture and ill-treatment by law enforcement officers continued to be reported. In January Iván González Polanco formally accused a municipal police officer in Badajoz of inflicting serious injuries on him after he had been arrested in connection with a traffic incident. A medical report confirmed that his nose was fractured and that the bone structure had been shifted towards the left side of his face. The police officer, who denied the charge of ill-treatment, lodged a counter-complaint against Iván González.

Allegations of torture were made by an ETA member detained in connection with the killing in March of a prison psychologist in San Sebastian. Fernando Elejalde Tapia, alleged to have fired the fatal shot, was taken into custody by officers of the national police after a short chase and held under anti-terrorist legislation. Two days later he was taken to hospital semi-conscious, with a perforated eardrum, four broken vertebrae, bruising all over his body, blackened eyes and a kidney malfunction. An inquiry ordered by the Ministry of the Interior concluded that his injuries were not the result of police ill-treatment but of collision with a stationary car during the chase and of a violent struggle during arrest. A judicial inquiry into the allegations of torture was continuing.

Mamadou Kane, a Senegalese resident in Spain, alleged that in March he had been illegally detained, ill-treated and racially abused by municipal police officers at Vigo. The officers, who remain in active service, were subsequently charged with illegal detention and ill-treatment. Other cases of assault by municipal police officers in Vigo, on both African immigrants and Spanish citizens, were reported.

Naia Zuriarrain, arrested in Bilbao in April for alleged collaboration with ETA, claimed that while under interrogation at Indautxu police station she was beaten repeatedly, particularly on the back of the head, and was subjected to death threats and sexual harassment. She reportedly lodged a complaint of ill-treatment with the judge of the National Criminal Court in Madrid, before whom she appeared the next day, and was released without charge.

José Amado Capote Martín, a resident of Santa Cruz de la Palma in the Canary Islands, lodged a judicial complaint, according to which in October he was beaten in a patrol car by four municipal police officers. He alleged that he was transferred to the custody of the national police, who took him to hospital after blood was found in his urine, and remained at the hospital for three days, 12 hours of which were spent in intensive care. The municipal police officers denied any ill-treatment occurred.

In June a Moroccan student was shot dead in Madrid by a Civil Guard reservist. Mourad El Abedine, who was walking with his girlfriend, had reportedly bent down to tie his shoelace when he was shot in the shoulder. According to a statement made by the police, the reservist opened fire with his revolver after he had been drinking. The family of Mourad El Abedine claimed that the killing was racially motivated.

Several law enforcement officers charged with torture were tried. In March a Madrid court sentenced four national police officers to three months' imprisonment for the torture of Enrique Erreguerena, who was arrested in 1982 in connection with an inquiry into ETA activities. He had been beaten, plunged in a bath and given electric shocks to his penis. The officers' trial had been postponed on numerous occasions.

In November, three Civil Guards were each sentenced to four years, two months and one day's imprisonment and six years' disqualification from public office for the illegal detention and torture of ETA member Kepa Urra Guridi following his arrest in 1992. Three other officers were acquitted. The Provincial Criminal Court of Vizcaya found that the three convicted officers had tortured Kepa Urra after taking him to a deserted area, but did not consider that Kepa Urra had been ill-treated at the Civil Guard barracks in Bilbao or in the hospital of Basurto (see *Amnesty International Reports 1993* and *1996*). The prosecuting authorities attached to the Court at once appealed against the sentence to the Supreme Court, partly on technical grounds and partly on the grounds that there was a "huge disproportion between the deed and the punishment". The lawyers defending the police officers, and the private prosecutors for Kepa Urra, also appealed to the Supreme Court.

ETA continued to commit human rights abuses against both security forces and civilians, and was widely believed to be responsible for 13 deaths, a significant increase on the previous year. Two ETA hostages were freed. In July Cosme Delclaux Zubiria was released by ETA and found tied to a tree (see *Amnesty International Report 1997*). Hours later José Antonio Ortega Lara was also discovered, in wretched conditions in a cell beneath an abandoned warehouse (see *Amnesty International Report 1997*). Days afterwards ETA kidnapped and killed Miguel Ángel Blanco Garrido, a local town councillor. A further killing by ETA of a town councillor, José Luis Caso, in December was widely seen as a riposte to the Supreme Court judgment on the members of the HB National Board (see above).

Amnesty International sought information on new allegations of illegal detention and ill-treatment; it urged the authorities to ensure that all such allegations were thoroughly and impartially investigated. The organization wrote to the Ombudsman, expressing concern about the fatal shooting of Mourad El Abedine and requesting confirmation that administrative and judicial inquiries had been set up to look into the circumstances of his death. The Ombudsman's office replied that inquiries were under way. Amnesty International submitted information to the UN Committee against Torture about specific cases of torture and ill-treatment. It also expressed concern at the long delays before judgments in such cases were reached and at the continuing effective impunity of law enforcement officers charged with or convicted of ill-treatment or torture.

Amnesty International repeatedly condemned abuses by armed opposition groups, such as deliberate and arbitrary killings and hostage-taking, as contraventions of international humanitarian law. The organization publicly called on ETA to release its hostages immediately and without conditions.

SRI LANKA

Thousands of Tamil people were arrested, including scores of possible prisoners of conscience. Torture and ill-treatment in army and police custody were widespread. Approximately 80 Tamil civilians were reported to have "disappeared". There were several reports of alleged extrajudicial executions. Three

detainees were killed in prison. The Liberation Tigers of Tamil Eelam (LTTE), an armed opposition group, was responsible for grave human rights abuses, including the killing of two members of parliament.

Armed conflict between the LTTE and the government continued. Hundreds of combatants died in heavy fighting during an army offensive started in May to open a land supply route to the northern peninsula of Jaffna through the "Vanni", an area largely controlled by the LTTE. Tens of thousands of people were displaced by the fighting.

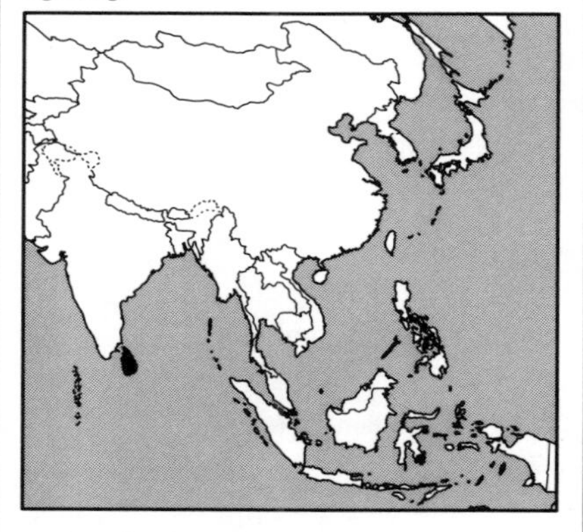

In July the state of emergency, which had been in force throughout the country, was confined to the north and east, and to the capital, Colombo, and surrounding areas. In August, September and October, it was further extended to several areas bordering the north and east.

In March members of the newly-created Human Rights Commission (HRC) were appointed. The functions of the Human Rights Task Force (see *Amnesty International Reports 1995* to *1997*) were transferred to the HRC from July onwards.

In October Sri Lanka ratified the (first) Optional Protocol to the International Covenant on Civil and Political Rights. The UN Special Rapporteur on extrajudicial, summary or arbitrary executions visited the country, including the north and east, in September.

The three commissions of inquiry established in late 1994 to look into past human rights violations, particularly "disappearances", (see *Amnesty International Reports 1995* to *1997*) presented their final reports to President Chandrika Bandaranaike Kumaratunga in September. They had reportedly found evidence of 16,742 "disappearances" since 1 January 1988. The government announced it would make the reports public and initiate legal proceedings in those cases where the commissions found *prima facie* evidence against members of the security forces.

A Board of Investigation, set up in late 1996 within the Ministry of Defence to investigate "disappearances" reported in Jaffna, received complaints concerning 760 people. Of these, 180 were found to be in detention or to have been released; the others remained unaccounted for at the end of the year.

In July the President reissued directives, initially introduced in 1995, aimed at safeguarding the welfare of detainees. Among the provisions were requirements to issue "arrest receipts" and to report all arrests and detentions to the HRC within 48 hours (see *Amnesty International Reports 1996* and *1997*).

Thousands of Tamil people, including scores of possible prisoners of conscience, were arrested during security operations in all parts of the country. According to official figures, 8,652 people were arrested in Colombo alone between July 1996 and July 1997. After an attack on the World Trade Centre in Colombo in October, apparently by the LTTE, 965 Tamil people were arrested, including 139 women. Approximately 50 of them were detained for further investigation. At the end of the year, an estimated 1,200 people were detained without charge or trial under the Emergency Regulations or Prevention of Terrorism Act, of whom 400 had been held for more than two years. The security forces also held relatives of LTTE members as hostages in order to put pressure on LTTE suspects to give themselves up. Sinnathamby Kanmany, whose daughter was suspected of being an LTTE member, was arrested in March in Vavuniya and held without charge or trial for four months by the Crime Detection Bureau in Colombo. She was finally released in July on the order of the Supreme Court.

Full implementation of safeguards for the welfare of detainees remained a concern. There were reports of the use of unauthorized places of detention, particularly in the north and east but also in Colombo. Some of them were run by Tamil armed groups fighting alongside the security forces.

Torture and ill-treatment in army and police custody were widespread. Kumaru Selvaratnam was arrested in March on suspicion of involvement with the LTTE. During the first eight days of his detention at Slave Island police station in Colombo, he was assaulted with a broomstick. He suffered injury to the testicles as a result of which they had to be surgically removed. In Jaffna, torture was widespread. Methods included near-suffocation with plastic bags filled with petrol; beatings with wire and plastic pipes; electric shocks; and suspension by the thumbs or ankles. The Supreme Court awarded compensation to a 14-year-old girl who had been tortured by police in Hungama in 1995. No prosecutions were initiated under the Convention against Torture and other Cruel, Inhuman or Degrading Treatment or Punishment Act (see *Amnesty International Report 1995*).

There were several allegations of rape by members of the security forces, particularly in the north and east. In March Velan Rasamma, a widow, and her sister, Velan Vasantha, were reportedly raped by four soldiers in Mayilampaveli Colony, Batticaloa district. The soldiers allegedly involved were arrested, but later released after the women failed to identify them at an identification parade, apparently because of fear of reprisals.

Approximately 80 Tamil civilians reportedly "disappeared" after arrest by the army, most in Jaffna, Batticaloa, Mannar and Killinochchi. Further evidence emerged about approximately 600 "disappearances" reported in Jaffna in 1996 (see *Amnesty International Report 1997*). As many as 190 "disappearances" were reported in July 1996 alone, apparently in reprisal for attacks by the LTTE at the beginning of that month. Among those who "disappeared" during 1997 in Batticaloa were Somanadan Dharmalingam, a village headman, and Perinpam Prabaharan, who were last seen talking to soldiers at the Sittandy army camp in September. Despite appeals to the Deputy Minister of Defence, their fate and whereabouts remained unknown at the end of the year.

There were several reports of alleged extrajudicial executions, particularly in Vavuniya and the "Vanni", where internally displaced people trying to return to their homes were killed by the army. In September the bodies of the Reverend Arulpalan and two labourers, Joseph and his 16-year-old son Surendran, were found in Shalom Nagar, their home village, in the security zone around Killinochchi town. They had "disappeared" after they were seen being arrested by soldiers when they went to cut some palmyrah leaves in August. According to reports, the Reverend Arulpalan had been shot in the head and Surendran's head had reportedly been severed and placed between his legs. The army denied responsibility for the killings and blamed the LTTE. In Vavuniya members of the People's Liberation Organization of Tamil Eelam, an armed Tamil group working alongside the security forces, were suspected of being responsible for the deliberate killing of several civilians, including internally displaced people. Murugesupillai Koneswary was killed when police officers attached to the Central Camp police station in Batticaloa district allegedly threw a grenade at her genitals. In September police officers from the Central Camp area, together with Home Guards, were accused of the deliberate killing of five civilians in reprisal for the killing of a constable by the LTTE the previous day.

One Muslim and two Tamil detainees were killed at Kalutara prison in December by a group of Sinhalese criminal prisoners in an apparently premeditated attack. There were reports that prison staff and army personnel failed to take measures to protect the detainees, and that some were actively involved in the attack. A presidential commission of inquiry was appointed to investigate the killings.

Police officers charged with murdering 12 prisoners in Nittambuwa, Gampaha district, in 1990 (see *Amnesty International Reports 1991, 1992* and *1996*) were acquitted in April owing to lack of evidence. The trial of nine soldiers charged with the rape and murder of Krishanthy Kumarasamy and the murder of her mother, brother and neighbour in 1996 started in November (see *Amnesty International Report 1997*). Little progress was reported in the inquiries into the deaths of people whose bodies were found during exhumations in 1994, or those found in lakes and rivers around Colombo in mid-1995 (see *Amnesty International Report 1996*). Three police officers were charged with the abduction and murder of Richard de Zoysa in February 1990 (see *Amnesty International Reports 1991* and *1992*).

The trial of a school principal and eight army personnel charged in connection with the "disappearance" of a group of young people at Embilipitiya in late 1989 and early 1990 continued throughout the year (see *Amnesty International Reports 1995* to *1997*).

The LTTE was responsible for grave human rights abuses, including the killing of two members of parliament – Arunasalam Thangathurai of the Tamil United Liberation Front and Mohamed Maharoof of the United National Party – in the Trincomalee area in July. At least nine civilians were killed in an attack on the World Trade Centre in Colombo in October. In Jaffna several people were detained and killed on suspicion of being army informants. In June Kugathasan Sritharan, a farmer from Udupiddy, Jaffna, was shot dead and a hand grenade was thrown at his body. A leaflet left on his body stated that he had been punished by the LTTE because he was an army informant.

The LTTE was also responsible for taking hostages. In July, 35 Muslim and four Sinhalese villagers from Irakkakandy, Trincomalee district, were abducted by members of the LTTE. When villagers made representations to the local LTTE leader, they were told to negotiate with the army for the release of five members of the LTTE who had been handed over to the army by local residents. All the villagers had been released by the end of November. Nine crew members of the passenger ferry *Misen* were taken prisoner in July off the coast of Mannar district. Two Indonesian nationals were released after a few days, but seven Sri Lankans remained held at the end of the year. They had not been given access to the International Committee of the Red Cross (ICRC) nor had they been allowed to communicate with their relatives. The LTTE stated that they were being held because the ship was "trespassing within Tamil Eelam's maritime limits". The fate of several prisoners of conscience and Tamil and Muslim prisoners held for several years remained unclarified.

In August an Amnesty International delegation visited the country, including Jaffna, and met with government officials. This was the first visit to Jaffna by the organization since 1982. An Amnesty International delegation met President Chandrika Bandaranaike Kumaratunga at the time of the Commonwealth Heads of Government meeting in Edinburgh, Scotland, in October.

In November Amnesty International published a report, *Sri Lanka: Government's response to the widespread "disappearances" in Jaffna during 1996*. It acknowledged the action taken by the government to curb "disappearances" in Jaffna but pointed to the need to address underlying structures and practices in the security forces. Throughout the year, Amnesty International called for a halt to "disappearances" and other human rights violations; for the prosecution of alleged perpetrators; and for a review of the Emergency Regulations and the Prevention of Terrorism Act. It also urged the government to establish an independent inquiry into the killing of three detainees at Kalutara prison.

Amnesty International appealed to the leadership of the LTTE for the unconditional release of hostages and for all prisoners to be given immediate access to the ICRC, to be treated humanely and to be given the opportunity to communicate with their relatives. The organization also appealed for a halt to deliberate and arbitrary killings of civilians. In May, it asked for information about nine members of the security forces taken prisoner by the LTTE in the course of armed confrontations and feared to have been deliberately killed in custody. No response was received to a memorandum setting out longstanding concerns about human rights abuses by the LTTE submitted in 1996 (see *Amnesty International Report 1997*).

SUDAN

Hundreds of suspected opponents of the government, including prisoners of conscience, were detained without charge or trial for periods ranging from a few weeks to several months. More than 50 political prisoners received unfair trials. Torture and ill-treatment by security officials and police remained common; at least two prisoners died after being tortured. Courts imposed judicial punishments of flogging and amputation. Hundreds of women and children were

abducted by paramilitary forces; the fate of hundreds of children abducted in previous years remained unknown. Scores of people were extrajudicially executed in the war zones. At least 11 prisoners were sentenced to death. Armed opposition groups were responsible for human rights abuses.

The government of President Omar Hassan Ahmad al-Bashir faced intensified armed opposition from the military wing of the National Democratic Alliance (NDA), an umbrella grouping of banned political parties and trade unions. In January the Sudan Alliance Forces (SAF) led by Abdel Aziz Khalid and the Sudan People's Liberation Army (SPLA) led by John Garang de Mabior captured territory in eastern Sudan, close to a dam that provides Khartoum, the capital, with most of its electricity. Between March and May the SPLA gained hundreds of kilometres of territory and encircled Juba, the largest city in southern Sudan. Meanwhile, the SPLA, SAF and the Beja Congress, another armed opposition group, captured territory along the Eritrean border. The Sudanese Government accused the Eritrean, Ethiopian and Ugandan governments of mounting an invasion. The Sudanese authorities continued to support Ugandan armed opposition movements responsible for gross human rights abuses and to allow them to use bases in Sudan (see **Uganda** entry).

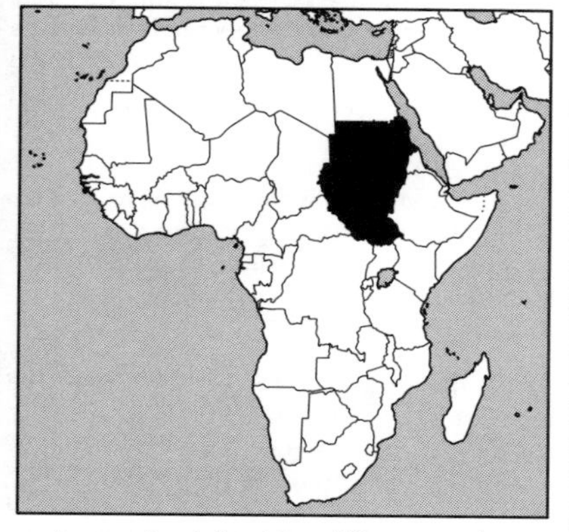

Approximately 4.5 million people remained internally displaced. Tens of thousands fled the fighting in eastern Sudan in January; approximately 5,000 crossed into Ethiopia. Over 60,000 refugees in Uganda returned to southern Sudan in April, after their camps were attacked and the Sudan authorities refused to allow food rations to be distributed in surrounding towns and villages.

In April the government followed the peace charter signed in 1996 by concluding a peace agreement with the South Sudan Independence Army, a group calling itself the SPLA led by Kerubino Kuanyin Bol that had been operating as a government militia in Bahr al-Ghazal, and four little-known southern Sudanese groups. The southern signatories merged their armed forces into a new organization, the South Sudan Defence Force. In November peace talks in Nairobi between the government and the SPLA, mediated by the Inter-Governmental Authority on Development (IGAD) countries (Eritrea, Ethiopia, Kenya and Uganda), adjourned without progress.

In January the UN Special Rapporteur on Sudan arrived in Khartoum just as a clamp-down on political opponents began (see below). The authorities indicated that they were unable to guarantee his safety, as a result of which he was forced to leave the country. However, he was able to return to Khartoum in September. In April the UN Commission on Human Rights expressed deep concern at continuing grave human rights violations and abuses in Sudan and alarm at the large numbers of forcibly displaced in the country. For the third year running, the Commission recommended the placement of international human rights field officers. Once again they were not in place by the end of the year.

In May a commission of inquiry established by the government in 1992 into events in Juba in which over 200 people "disappeared" reported that five employees of foreign organizations, including the UN, had been executed after being tried by military tribunals. The trials did not conform to international standards of fair trial. Eighty-nine others brought before the tribunals were either executed or given prison sentences; 11 men were acquitted. However, the report, which contained a number of internal inconsistencies, failed to account for the remaining 135 people who "disappeared" (see *Amnesty International Report 1997*).

Hundreds of suspected opponents of the government, including prisoners of conscience, were arrested during the year and detained without charge or trial for periods ranging from a few weeks to several months. In Khartoum most prisoners were held in a section of Kober prison run by the security services. However, secret detention centres notorious for torture, known as "ghost houses", were also in use. Many suspected political opponents, including recently released prisoners, had to report daily to security offices where they were made to wait until sunset.

Within hours of the military incursion by the SPLA and SAF in January, scores of suspected political opponents in Khartoum and other northern Sudanese cities were detained. President al-Bashir described the arrests as a precautionary measure that would "end when the foreign threat is removed". Among the first to be arrested were former members of the banned organizations that made up the NDA in exile. They included Abdel Mahmud Haj Saleh, a former Minister of Justice and member of the Umma party; Sid Ahmad al-Hussein, a former Deputy Prime Minister and member of the Democratic Unionist Party; and Awad al-Karim Mohamed Ahmad, a trade unionist and member of the Sudan Communist Party (SCP).

In the days and weeks that followed, hundreds of less well-known people were arrested. They included adherents of traditional *Sufi* orders of Islam, former members of banned political parties, students, workers, trade unionists, doctors, lawyers, businessmen, engineers, civil servants and Eritrean and Ethiopian nationals. By the end of February, more than 250 suspected political opponents were in detention.

Although at least 100 further arrests took place in March and April, the authorities also began to release prisoners. For example, Saudi Darraj, a former member of the banned SCP, and nine other trade unionists and left-wing activists were released in Khartoum in March. However, at the end of the month Jalal Ismail Awadallah, 'Abd al-Rahman al-Amin and two other trade unionists were detained in Port Sudan.

In May the authorities announced the release of all political detainees and issued a list of 71 men freed in the middle of the month. Most detainees held in Kober prison in Khartoum had been released by the start of June.

However, as with similar announcements in previous years, not all political detainees were actually released. George Berhane Kidane, a Sudanese of Ethiopian origin, and Abubakr Abbas al-Zein, an engineer in the eastern town of Damazin, who were both originally detained in January, remained in prison with at least 17 other suspected left-wing activists, including Awad al-Karim Mohamed Ahmad.

There were further arrests within days of the announced releases. For example, Abdelbasit Abbas, a paediatrician, and more than 20 other men were arrested at the start of June. Abdelbasit Abbas was released without charge in October, but Mauwia Ali al-Shafie, a doctor, and Kamal Abdulrahman, a lawyer, were among 13 men brought to trial in December on diverse treason-related charges.

More than 50 political prisoners arrested in previous years received unfair military trials in which their rights to a defence and to appeal were infringed. The military trial of Colonel Awad al-Karim Omar Ibrahim al-Naqar and 30 others accused of waging war against the state, which began in August 1996, concluded in mid-1997. Nineteen defendants received prison sentences ranging from one month to 15 years; nine others were acquitted (see *Amnesty International 1997*). Twenty soldiers and civilians arrested in Port Sudan in August 1996 and accused of an attempted coup were court-martialled in proceedings that began in February and concluded in April. Six men were given prison sentences ranging from five to 20 years, five were given administrative sentences and nine were acquitted.

Torture and ill-treatment by security officials and police remained common; detainees held in security offices and secret detention centres on suspicion of plotting against the government or having information about opposition activities were particularly at risk. Anti-government demonstrators were frequently beaten at the moment of arrest and on arrival at a security office. At least two detainees died after being tortured. In June Mauwia Awad Khojali died of burns sustained in a secret detention centre in May. In October Amin Bedawi Mustapha died in detention after torture.

Courts imposed sentences of flogging and amputation. Flogging was common for offences against "public order" or "public decency", the latter an offence that was particularly applied to women. For example, in December, 25 women received 10 lashes each after they demonstrated against the conscription of secondary-school leavers into the armed forces. They received an unfair summary trial before a Public Order Court and were among 38 women arrested and beaten with batons and rubber hosepipes as they attempted to deliver a petition to UN offices. One woman received a further 30 lashes for wearing trousers and a shirt, which the court defined as indecent dress.

In August, three men convicted of *hiraba* (armed robbery) were sentenced to amputation of the right hand and left foot by courts in Darfur. In November the Minister of Justice reported to the National Assembly that five sentences of limb amputation had been carried out since 1989.

In March and April Popular Defence Force (PDF) paramilitary forces and other militia abducted hundreds of women and children during military operations in Bahr al-Ghazal and the Nuba Mountains. For example, in March over 100 women and children were abducted by PDF troops sent to reinforce Kerubino Kuanyin Bol's forces around Wun Rog. Hundreds of children abducted in Bahr al-Ghazal and the Nuba Mountains in previous years remained unaccounted for. Although the government continued to deny the existence of slavery, in July the Deputy Chairman of the National Assembly's Human Rights Committee said that children from northern Bahr al-Ghazal were being abducted for use as slaves.

A Ugandan armed opposition group, the Lord's Resistance Army (LRA), armed and supplied by the Sudanese authorities, abducted hundreds of Ugandan children, who were then held captive along with thousands of children abducted in previous years, for use as child soldiers. They were held in bases in Sudan, next to Sudanese army positions and were frequently tortured and ill-treated. The Sudanese authorities made no attempt to intervene to free children held by the LRA on Sudanese territory (see **Uganda** entry).

Scores of unarmed civilians were extrajudicially executed by the regular army and the PDF and other militia. For example, in a military campaign starting in February, the army and PDF burned down homes and granaries in villages along the fringes of Jebel Limon in a sustained assault that was apparently aimed at depopulating one of the more fertile parts of the Nuba Mountains under SPLA control. At least six people were extrajudicially executed after they failed to escape, among them an elderly woman who was burned to death in her hut. Dozens of extrajudicial executions took place around Wun Rog and Gogrial in fighting in February and March.

At least 11 people convicted of criminal offences were sentenced to death. In November the Minister of Justice announced that since 1989, out of 894 death sentences passed for murder and armed robbery, 112 executions had been carried out.

Armed opposition groups were responsible for human rights abuses, including torture, abducting and ill-treating children for use as soldiers, and deliberate and arbitrary killings. The victims included some government officials captured during fighting. For example, in May the SPLA tortured and deliberately and arbitrarily killed Samuel Mabor Malek, a retired Major-General of Prisons, after they captured the southern town of Rumbek.

Amnesty International urged both the government and armed opposition groups to end human rights abuses. The organization called on the government to release prisoners of conscience, to end detention without charge or trial and torture and to commute death sentences.

In April Amnesty International published a report, *Sudan: A new clampdown on political opponents*, which described the arrest of political opponents since the start of the year. A report published in May, *In search of safety: the forcibly displaced and human rights in Africa*, contained a chapter describing human rights abuses against the 4.5 million people internally displaced by war in Sudan and called for action from government, armed opposition groups and international organizations to secure their protection.

In September Amnesty International published a report, *Uganda: Breaking God's commands – the destruction of childhood by the Lord's Resistance Army*, which described the Sudanese authorities' use of the LRA as a militia and said that the Sudanese Government could be held responsible for many of the armed group's human rights abuses. Amnesty International called on the government to end its supply of weapons, bases and other support to the LRA and to intervene to free abducted children. The government denied that it had links with the LRA.

In December Amnesty International received a letter from the Minister of Justice inviting the organization to send a delegation to Sudan (see *Amnesty International 1997*).

SWAZILAND

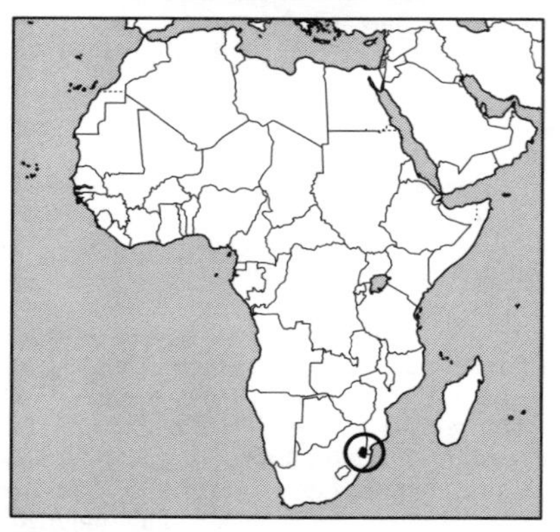

Prisoners of conscience were arbitrarily detained. Law enforcement officers ill-treated detainees and unarmed demonstrators. Eight prisoners remained under sentence of death.

Political activity continued to be banned and the rights of freedom of assembly and expression were restricted. A number of demonstrations and strikes took place, including a month-long national strike in February, in protest at these restrictions. The Constitutional Review Commission appointed by King Mswati III in 1996 had produced few results by the end of the year, and the state of emergency imposed in 1973 remained in force.

In November the Minister of Information and Broadcasting introduced a bill in parliament which would permit the imprisonment of journalists for violations of a government-drafted code of ethics.

Prisoners of conscience were arbitrarily detained. They included senior Swaziland Federation of Trade Unions (SFTU) officials Jabulani Nxumalo, Richard Nxumalo, Jan Sithole (see *Amnesty International Report 1997*) and Themba Msibi, who were detained on 31 January, prior to the planned national strike. On 3 February they were charged under Section 12 of the 1963 Public Order Act with acting in common purpose to "intimidate" and "molest" bus owners into suspending bus services. Bail was denied as the Minister of Justice had, on the day of their arrest, announced that their offence fell within the scope of the Non-Bailable Offences Act. On 26 February the trial magistrate acquitted the trade unionists of the charges and ordered their release, after strongly criticizing the police evidence as lacking any credibility.

In another incident, police officers detained Simon Noge, Secretary of the Human Rights Association of Swaziland and Chairperson of the Swaziland Democratic Alliance, on 5 February. When his lawyer challenged the legality of the police officers' action, they threatened to arrest him too. Simon Noge was released without charge the following day. In October police officers who dispersed a peaceful demonstration by striking teachers and their supporters reportedly detained several hundred demonstrators for several hours before releasing them without charge.

Some detainees were ill-treated by police officers. In one case Mxolisi Mbatha, an SFTU official arrested with other trade union colleagues on 3 February, was kicked, beaten and dragged across the ground before being put in a cell with other detainees at Manzini Regional Police Headquarters. The police then allegedly sprayed tear-gas into the cell. Mxolisi Mbatha, who is paraplegic as a result of a previous accident, was denied access to medical care while in detention. Following his release without charge some two days later, he required emergency and then prolonged treatment in hospital. He instituted legal proceedings against the government, who denied liability. The case was expected to reach the courts in 1998.

On a number of occasions the security forces ill-treated unarmed demonstrators and striking workers. In a case in October, police officers used tear-gas and batons to disperse peaceful demonstrators who had gathered near the national airport to petition the King on his return to the country. Among those ill-treated was a schoolteacher who ran into a police patrol while trying to escape the tear-gas. They allegedly verbally insulted her, beat her severely and smashed her glasses. When she fled she was set upon by soldiers, who allegedly beat her and threw her into a ditch. Legal proceedings instituted against the government on her behalf were under way at the end of the year.

Eight prisoners remained under sentence of death, of whom four had appeals pending before the appeal court. The other four had exhausted all channels of appeal except clemency appeals to the King. No new death sentences were imposed and there were no executions. However, the possibility of renewed executions had been raised by the Minister of Justice.

An Amnesty International representative visited the country in February to investigate reports of ill-treatment in police custody and other concerns. The organization called on the government to release prisoners of conscience; expressed concern about the misuse of laws to harass, detain and ill-treat government opponents and critics; and called for the rights of freedom of expression and association to be fully respected.

SWEDEN

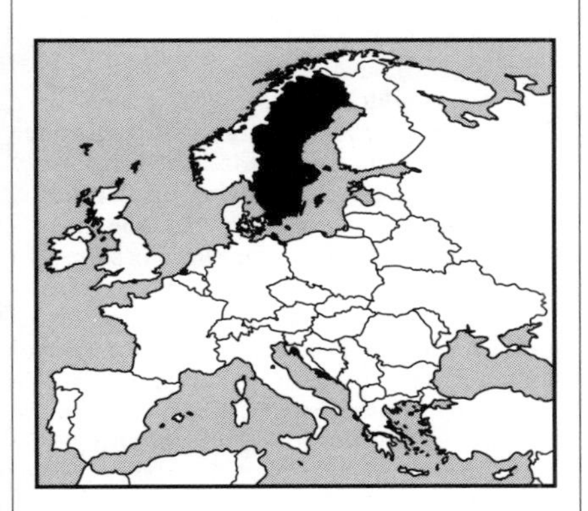

The death of a man in police custody revealed flaws in the investigative system. Information emerged about other deaths in custody since 1992. There were reports of ill-treatment by police officers.

In May the UN Committee against Torture and Other Cruel, Inhuman or Degrading Treatment or Punishment expressed concern about people being held in solitary confinement for prolonged periods of time during pre-trial detention; isolated cases of ill-treatment by the police; and methods used by the police with regard to crowd control.

The investigation by the regional public prosecutor into the death of Osmo Vallo, who died in May 1995 while in police custody in Karlstad, was closed in April after a second post-mortem examination. Police who had been called to investigate a disturbance approached Osmo Vallo, who was reportedly under the influence of drugs and alcohol. Eye-witnesses stated that police officers kicked him in the back, unleashed a police dog which bit him many times, and stamped on his back as he lay handcuffed, face down on the ground. Once police officers realized that he had collapsed, they made no attempt to resuscitate him; instead they drove him, face down and still handcuffed, to a hospital. There he was pronounced dead. Two post-mortem examinations failed to identify the exact cause of death. Of various reports issued following these examinations, one indicated that he might have died from the combined effects of alcohol, drugs and severe physical exertion; another indicated that he might have died from the combined effects of alcohol, drugs and postural asphyxia. The first examination recorded signs of 39 wounds and bruises on Osmo Vallo's face, arms and legs.

Following the first examination, the two arresting police officers were convicted in 1996 in connection with their failure to control the dog and were fined. No criminal proceedings were brought in connection with the other reports of ill-treatment, and no disciplinary proceedings were initiated.

During the year it emerged that in the past five years there had been about a dozen deaths in custody in similar circumstances. Some of these deaths had been caused by postural asphyxia, or postural asphyxia combined with the effects of drugs or alcohol.

Three men alleged that they were ill-treated and subjected to racist abuse by police officers, following the arrest of one of them for driving offences in Stockholm in November. The three men made formal complaints about their treatment; they were subsequently charged with making a false complaint.

In April Amnesty International raised its concerns about the circumstances of

Osmo Vallo's death with the government. The organization also expressed its concerns about his death to the UN Committee against Torture. In October Amnesty International issued a report, *Sweden: Osmo Vallo – action needed to prevent more deaths in custody,* which highlighted a number of areas of concern. The organization urged the authorities to reopen the case for further investigation. Amnesty International also urged the government to initiate a comprehensive review of all recent deaths of people in the custody of law enforcement officials in which restraint methods may have contributed to the cause of death, and to make the findings public.

In October the Minister of Justice requested the Chancellor of Justice to examine how the authorities acted in the case of Osmo Vallo and other similar cases. The Prosecutor General initiated a review of the prosecution authorities' decisions in these cases. In addition, the National Police Board issued instructions on the dangers of certain restraint methods.

In December Amnesty International wrote to the government about allegations of ill-treatment and racist abuse by police officers.

SWITZERLAND

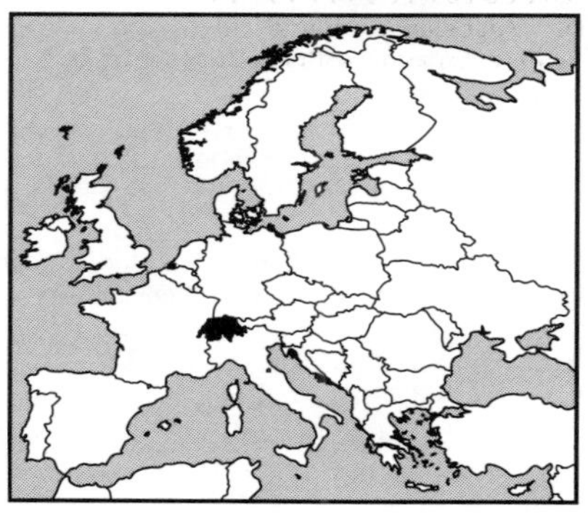

There were further allegations of ill-treatment of detainees by police officers.

The findings of a visit of inspection carried out in February 1996 by the European Committee for the Prevention of Torture and Inhuman or Degrading Treatment or Punishment were published in June, together with the federal government's interim response. The Committee examined the treatment of people held in various places of detention in the cantons of Bern, Geneva, Ticino, Valais, Vaud and Zurich.

The great majority of detainees interviewed indicated that they had been correctly treated by the police. However, the Committee stated that it had met "a certain number of people, in particular foreign nationals and people arrested in connection with drugs-related offences, who alleged having been subjected to ill-treatment, consisting mainly of insults, slaps and blows, by police officers at the time of arrest". It said that the delegation had also heard some isolated allegations of ill-treatment inflicted during police interrogation.

The Committee noted that the situation regarding the implementation of the core recommendations on safeguards against ill-treatment in police custody made following its first visit of inspection in 1991 had "scarcely developed". The Committee recommended that the Swiss authorities re-examine their position on these matters.

In November the UN Committee against Torture considered Switzerland's third periodic report on its implementation of the UN Convention against Torture and Other Cruel, Inhuman or Degrading Treatment or Punishment. It expressed concern about "frequent" allegations of ill-treatment by police and a lack of independent mechanisms for registering and investigating such allegations. It recommended the introduction of such mechanisms in all cantons. The Committee regretted the non-existence in some cantons of certain legal guarantees providing safeguards against ill-treatment for detainees in police custody, "especially for foreigners" . It recommended the harmonization of the 26 cantonal codes of penal procedure, "particularly with regard to the granting of fundamental guarantees" in police custody. It stressed the need to allow criminal suspects to contact a lawyer or their family and to be examined by an independent doctor, immediately after arrest, after each interrogation and before being brought before an investigating magistrate or being released. The Committee said it was "seriously concerned about the absence of appropriate reaction" by the competent authorities to complaints of police ill-treatment. It recommended that Switzerland pay "the greatest possible attention" to such cases so as to ensure the opening of investigations and, in proven cases, the imposition of adequate sanctions.

In March Switzerland ratified the Convention on the Elimination of All Forms of Discrimination against Women.

New allegations of police ill-treatment often concerned foreign nationals. Clement Nwankwo, a prominent Nigerian lawyer and human rights activist, said that in April Geneva police officers stopped him on the street, without explanation. He stated that he presented his identity papers, as requested, but that police officers then kicked and punched him, racially abused him, beat him with their fists and batons, and put a baton across his neck, exerting such pressure that he lost consciousness. He claimed that after transfer to a police station he was slapped, forced to strip naked and then left in his underpants, handcuffed painfully to a table leg in an interview room, for around an hour. A medical certificate issued the day after his release, recording injuries to his wrists and left eye, stated that "in all probability" they could have been caused by the ill-treatment he alleged. He was released after about 72 hours' detention, after being tried under a summary procedure and found guilty of shoplifting and resisting the police. He entered a formal challenge against the conviction and was committed for full trial in June when he was acquitted of shoplifting, but again convicted of resisting the police. His appeal against the conviction was examined by a Geneva court in September. In December the court confirmed the conviction and Clement Nwankwo lodged an appeal with the Federal Court.

Following an administrative investigation into the alleged incidents, the Geneva cantonal authorities informed Clement Nwankwo that his "strong resistance" to arrest had led the police officers to use force. However, they apologized for "the conditions" of his detention in the interview room and promised sanctions against the officers concerned. Clement Nwankwo maintained all his allegations against the police and lodged a criminal complaint against them in July. It was still under consideration by the Geneva Prosecutor General at the end of the year.

There were delays in several judicial proceedings relating to alleged police ill-treatment. In September the Ticino cantonal authorities stated that investigations were still continuing into a criminal complaint lodged three years earlier by two Turkish Kurds. They alleged that Ticino police had punched and kicked them and beaten them with a chair during their detention in June 1994.

In March a Ticino court rejected an appeal lodged by Turkish Kurds Abuzer Tastan and Ali Doymaz against a ruling by the Procurator General. He had ruled that there were no grounds to prosecute Chiasso police officers whom the complainants had accused of ill-treating them in April 1995 (see *Amnesty International Reports 1996* and *1997*). In their appeal, Abuzer Tastan and Ali Doymaz protested that the procurator had closed his investigation without questioning or contacting them, and also without questioning the accused officers or their colleagues, or any of three possible witnesses. He had questioned only an interpreter who had assisted them during police interviews, but who had not been present at the time of the alleged incidents. In July the federal court rejected their appeal against the Ticino court's decision, but stated that it was not competent to examine their complaint that the procurator had not questioned them or corresponded directly with them.

In July the Lugano Public Prosecutor stated that the allegations which A.S., an asylum-seeker from the Kosovo province of Yugoslavia, made in a complaint against Lugano police officers in January 1996 were unfounded (see *Amnesty International Report 1997*). A.S. had claimed that, following his arrest for theft, officers had ill-treated him, causing serious injuries described in medical certificates issued within hours of his release from police custody. He stated that police denied his requests for medical treatment and coerced him into signing a document written in Italian – a language he did not understand – withdrawing his asylum application. The prosecutor stated that it appeared that A.S. had tried to escape during questioning, slightly injuring a policewoman, and had assaulted other police officers who were obliged to use "coercive methods proportionate to the situation". The prosecutor did not comment on the apparent failure to provide A.S. with medical treatment during his detention or on the withdrawal of his asylum application, but said that, according to the police officers' statements, A.S. was not pressurized or threatened and made "no requests of any kind during his detention". She also indicated that on release A.S. was informed that the injured officer reserved the right to lodge a complaint against him for causing bodily harm.

In May the Geneva Procurator General informed Marc Guerrero that no further action would be taken on the complaint which he had lodged against Geneva police officers in March 1996, after his arrest for theft (see *Amnesty International Report 1997*). He had accused Geneva police officers of ill-treating him and depriving him of necessary medical assistance for several hours. The Procurator indicated that he agreed with the conclusions of the investigating magistrate that Marc Guerrero's allegations had been "contradicted by the inquiries carried out".

In June and September Amnesty International observers attended the court hearings in the case of Clement Nwankwo.

Amnesty International sought information from the authorities on the steps taken to investigate new allegations of ill-treatment and the outcome of inquiries opened into such allegations in previous years. In response the authorities provided information about the status of investigations and court proceedings: in some cases they stated that the allegations were unfounded or that injuries sustained by detainees were the result of police officers using the degree of force necessary to subdue a person violently resisting arrest.

In November Amnesty International issued a report, *Switzerland: Comments relating to the submission of the Third Periodic Report to the UN Committee against Torture,* which described some of the organization's concerns about alleged ill-treatment by police as well as official initiatives aimed at strengthening safeguards against ill-treatment.

SYRIA

Dozens of people were arrested on political grounds, and hundreds of political prisoners, including prisoners of conscience, continued to serve prison sentences or were held without charge or trial. At least six political prisoners, including prisoners of conscience, continued to be held beyond the expiry of their sentences. The fate of scores of prisoners who "disappeared" in previous years remained unknown. Information came to light about the sentencing to death of one political prisoner in previous years.

Dozens of people were arrested during the year on suspicion of involvement in political activities. They included Zubayda Muqabel, a press officer at the office of former Vice-President Rif'at al-Assad, who was arrested in Damascus by *al-Amn al-Khass* (special security) in July and held in incommunicado detention. Her whereabouts remained unknown at the end of the year.

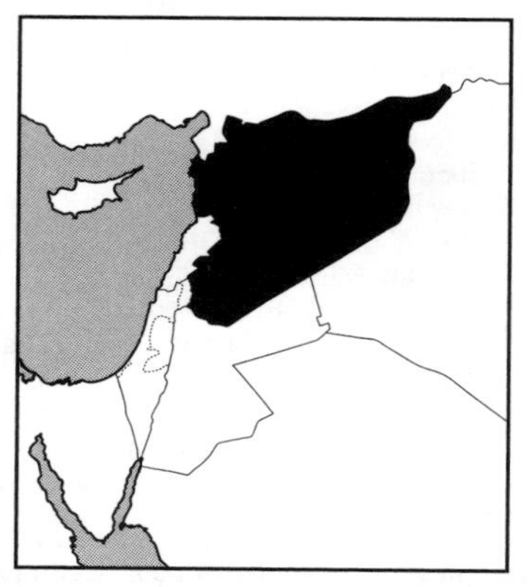

At least 20 Kurds were arrested in al-Haska and Aleppo districts between January and March in connection with organizing Kurdish cultural activities. At least 15 were arrested in March on the eve of the Kurdish *Nawruz* (New Year) celebrations. They were arrested by the Syrian security service and reportedly detained in Aleppo, Far' Falastin and 'Adra prisons. Among them were Khaled Daoud Sheikhu, 'Umar Ayoub Hamu and Mahdi al-'Ali, who were reportedly arrested for circulating cassettes of a Kurdish nationalist song. Most were still in detention at the end of the year. They were possible prisoners of conscience. Most of the Kurds who were arrested in 1996 (see *Amnesty International Report 1997*) were reportedly released.

Hundreds of political prisoners, including prisoners of conscience, remained held without charge or trial, or serving prison sentences imposed mostly after unfair trials.

At least 130 prisoners of conscience remained held in connection with *Hizb al-'Amal al-Shuyu'i*, Party for Communist Action (PCA). They included Doha 'Ashur al-'Askari, a student who was arrested in 1993 and sentenced to six years' imprisonment by the Supreme State Security Court (SSSC). 'Abd al-'Aziz al-Khayyir, who was arrested in Damascus in February 1992 and sentenced by the SSSC to 22 years' imprisonment in August 1995, remained in detention.

At least 10 prisoners of conscience sentenced by the SSSC to terms of imprisonment of up to 15 years in connection with the PCA, were released during the year. They included 'Abbas 'Abbas, who was released in March after completing his 15-year prison sentence (see *Amnesty International Report 1997*), and Munif Mulhim, who was released in April after "disappearing" for two months following the expiry of his 15-year prison term.

About a dozen prisoners of conscience continued to serve prison sentences for alleged activities in connection with *al-Hizb al-Shuyu'i al-Maktab al-Siyassi*, Communist Party–Political Bureau (CPPB). Riad al-Turk, a leading member of the CPPB, who was arrested in 1980 continued to be detained incommunicado at the *Far' al-Tahqiq al 'Askari* (Military Interrogation Branch) in Damascus, without charge or trial. He was reportedly in poor health (see *Amnesty International Report 1997*). Of the 29 prisoners of conscience who were transferred to Tadmur military prison in 1996, apparently to punish them for refusing to sign an undertaking dissociating themselves from all past political activities (see *Amnesty International Report 1997*), five were released. Those released included Yasin al-Hajj Salih, who spent one year in Tadmur prison beyond the expiry of his 15-year sentence in connection with the CPPB. The other 24 remained in detention.

Four prisoners of conscience held in connection with the Committees for the Defence of Democratic Freedoms and Human Rights in Syria (CDF) were released during the year, after the expiry of their sentences. These were Jadi' Nawfal, Ya'qub Musa, Hasan 'Ali and Husam Salama. Six other prisoners of conscience – Aktham Nu'aysa, Thabit Murad, Muhammad 'Ali Habib, Nizar Nayyuf, 'Afif Muzhir and Bassam al-Sheikh – continued to serve prison sentences ranging from eight to 10 years. Aktham Nu'aysa, a lawyer, was reported during the year to be in poor health and in need of specialist medical care (see previous *Amnesty International Reports*).

There were new political trials before the SSSC, whose procedures fell seriously short of international fair trial standards (see previous *Amnesty International Reports*). At least 25 suspected members of the Kurdish Workers' Party (PKK) were brought to trial before the SSSC accused of "secession", and "terrorist acts". Most were sentenced to three years' imprisonment.

Hundreds of people held in connection with the unauthorized *al-Ikhwan al-Muslimun*, the Muslim Brotherhood, remained in detention. Most had been held incommunicado since the late 1970s and early 1980s without charge and trial or after summary and secret trials (see previous *Amnesty International Reports*). They included Hassan Farahat, a student who was arrested in Damascus in September 1982, and Taisir Lutfi and Salah Halawi, both brigadiers in the Syrian army who were arrested in 1982 and reportedly tried by a military tribunal.

News emerged during the year that more than 20 prisoners of conscience – medical personnel and engineers – detained since 1980 had been released in previous years. They included Talal Sufi, Sami Walid, Hassan Sa'id and Taisir Samsam. Dozens of doctors and engineers remained held who had been arrested following a one-day general strike in March 1980 led by members of the Medical, Bar and Engineers' Associations (see previous *Amnesty International Reports*). They included Ahmad Faris, an engineer who was arrested in November 1980 in Lataqiyya. It was not known whether any of them had been tried.

Scores of Palestinians arrested in Lebanon or Syria on political grounds in previous years continued to be held incommunicado (see previous *Amnesty International Reports*). In most cases, their whereabouts were unknown. They included Salama George Kila, arrested in 1992 and sentenced to eight years' imprisonment for "anti-revolutionary activities" against the Syrian Government; and Muhammad 'Abdallah Abu Nar who was arrested in June 1985 and was reportedly tried by a military court in Tadmur prison in July 1988. No information was available about the trial of Muhammad 'Abdallah Abu Nar or his sentence.

About 200 Lebanese nationals continued to be held in Syrian prisons. Scores had been arrested in Lebanon during the Lebanese war from 1975 to 1990 and transferred to Syria. Others were arrested and taken to Syria after 1990. For example Bashir al-Khatib, a chef, was arrested in July 1996 by Syrian military intelligence in Lebanon and transferred to Syria where he remained held, reportedly without charge or trial, in al-Mezze prison. (See **Lebanon** entry.)

At least six political prisoners, including prisoners of conscience, remained in custody despite having completed their prison sentences. They included Mustafa Fallah, a former army officer in his sixties who was arrested in 1970 and sentenced in a mass trial by the SSSC in 1971 to a 15-year sentence. By the end of the year, he had been held for 12 years beyond the expiry of his prison term, and was reportedly in poor health. Three prisoners of conscience – Bassam Budur, Taisir Hassoun, and 'Adib al-Jani – remained held in Tadmur military prison, three years beyond the expiry of their eight-year sentences imposed by the SSSC in connection with the PCA. Fateh Jamus, a prisoner of conscience arrested in 1982 and sentenced in 1994 to 15 years' imprisonment in connection with the PCA, was reportedly transferred during the year to the Military Interrogation Branch, and was still in detention at the end of the year.

The health of a number of prisoners of conscience, mainly held in Tadmur prison, gave cause for concern. At least seven of them were reportedly suffering from serious health problems, including cancer and diabetes. The health of these prisoners had apparently deteriorated owing to the harsh conditions in Tadmur, where torture and ill-treatment were routine. There were reports that these prisoners were not receiving adequate medical care.

Information came to light during the year about the death in custody of at least four political prisoners held in connection with the one-day general strike in March 1980 (see above). They included 'Adnan al-'Adawi, Zahi 'Abbadi, 'Abd al-Majid 'Abd al-Qadir Bitar and Muhammad Shakir Bismar. Scores of other political prisoners arrested in previous years remained unaccounted for and it was feared that they had "disappeared".

During the year the authorities stated that two "disappeared" prisoners – 'Adnan Murad, a Syrian Kurd held apparently in connection with the *al-Ikhwan al-Muslimun* (Muslim Brotherhood), and Muhammad 'Adnan Qassar – were tried and sentenced in 1981 and 1993 respectively. According to this information, 'Adnan Murad was sentenced to death in November 1981 in connection with "a terrorist armed group which carried out assassinations and explosions inside Syria", and Muhammad 'Adnan Qassar was sentenced to life imprisonment in December 1993 for "carrying out terrorist acts and attempting to bomb shops using an explosive device". No details were given of their trials or whether the death sentence was carried out.

In March an Amnesty International delegation visited Syria to discuss its concerns with the government, and asked for information about approximately 500 cases. These included prisoners of conscience, cases of torture, deaths in custody, and "disappearances". No substantive progress appeared to have been made to address the concerns raised by the organization on this and previous occasions.

During the year the government responded to some of Amnesty International's communications, and provided information on some "disappearance" and refugee cases.

In April Amnesty International submitted information about its concerns in Syria for UN review, under a procedure established by Economic and Social Council Resolutions 728F/1503 for confidential consideration of communications about human rights violations.

TAIWAN

Several people detained in police custody allegedly suffered ill-treatment and at least two detainees died. There were renewed calls for human rights safeguards in the military as further information emerged on suspicious deaths of conscripts. The use of the death penalty increased markedly with at least 29 people executed.

President Lee Teng-hui, under pressure from public opinion over allegations of government corruption and gang violence, appointed a new Prime Minister. Vincent Siew took office with a reshuffled cabinet in September. In July the National Assembly adopted amendments to the Constitution which reinforced presidential powers, gave the Legislative *Yuan* (the main law-making body) the right to hold votes of confidence in the cabinet, and trimmed the powers of the Taiwan Provincial Government, an intermediate tier of administration.

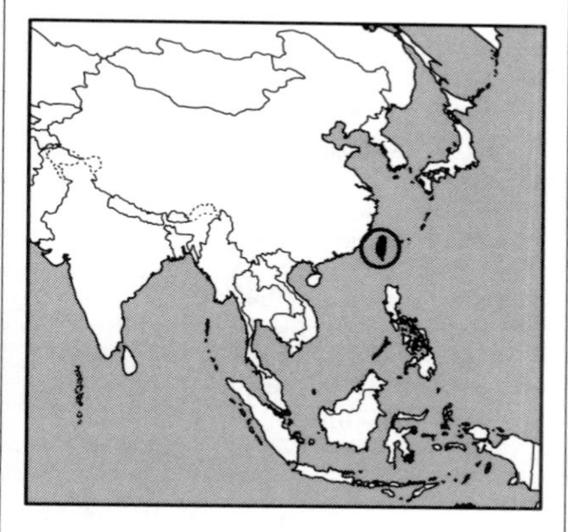

The anniversary of a massacre of mainly Taiwanese civilians by government troops in February 1948 was made a national holiday. A government proposal to "pardon" the Taiwanese leaders of the protests which led to the massacre was opposed by survivors on the grounds that the protesters had committed no offence and therefore needed no pardon.

In May the Minister of Justice stated that his administration was considering the reintroduction of whipping as a punishment for certain offences committed by juveniles. However, no such measures had been implemented by the end of the year. In October and December the Legislative *Yuan* passed legislation increasing the number of offences carrying a mandatory death penalty to at least 60.

In October the Council of Grand Justices (CGJ), a constitutional tribunal, ruled that several aspects of the law governing military tribunals were unconstitutional because the law did not allow for appeals before civilian tribunals and did not adequately safeguard judicial independence. Under constitutional provisions, the government was given a two-year period to amend the relevant legislation. The Ministry of National Defence (MND) agreed to amend the legislation to allow appeals before civilian courts when the death penalty had been imposed by a military court. However, the MND did not accept all the CGJ's findings in relation to the independence of judges in military tribunals. The law had not been amended by the end of the year.

A member of the Jehovah's Witness religious group was reportedly detained in January for refusing to undergo military service. The MND stated that there were no plans to introduce alternative forms of military service or to recognize conscientious objection to military service.

Several detainees were allegedly ill-treated by police and at least two died in police custody. In May the death in police custody of Li Yao-hsi, a farmer from Taipei County, led to violent protests by residents of Juifang Township, where Li had been detained. Police initially claimed that Li Yao-hsi had committed suicide. However, an autopsy suggested that he had died of suffocation after water had been forced down his throat. Seven police officers were held for questioning and were released on bail in late May. In October Ai Han-ching died in police custody in Taichung County. Five policemen suspected of having beaten Ai Han-ching to death were suspended and briefly detained for questioning, while some of their superiors were given administrative punishments. Criminal proceedings against the policemen involved in the two cases were still pending at the end of the year.

Concern continued to be expressed throughout the year over alleged human rights violations against military conscripts. There was no progress in investigations into the deaths of conscripts given disciplinary punishments (see *Amnesty International Reports 1996* and *1997*). In November Lei Tzu-wen, a respected surgeon, was charged with arson after he set fire to his own surgery in a suicide attempt. Dr Lei's attempted suicide followed his repeated protests at the alleged inadequacy of official investigations into the causes of the death of his son, Lei Cheng-ju, who was found dead during his military service in 1994. The military alleged that Lei Cheng-ju had hanged himself.

However, there were indications that he had been killed as a result of bullying or arbitrary punishment. Hours before his death, Lei Cheng-ju had phoned his parents to seek help, stating that an officer "wanted to harm" him. Forensic experts who examined photographs of his body suggested that he was strangled and that water was poured down his throat before his body was hanged to simulate suicide. The MND denied that officers had committed any wrongdoing in this case, and refused requests for a new inquiry.

The death penalty continued to be widely used, and the number of people executed rose to at least 29. Following the legalization of the use of lethal injections to execute prisoners, the first execution by lethal injection was reportedly carried out in May. Prisoners sentenced to death continued to be at risk of ill-treatment in detention: the practice of permanent shackling of the hands and feet of these prisoners continued.

Prisoners awaiting execution included people about whose guilt there were strong doubts. Su Chien-ho, Liu Ping-lang and Chuang Lin-hsiung, sentenced to death in 1991 for a double murder despite strong indications that they were innocent, remained in prison (see *Amnesty International Reports 1996* and *1997*). They were liable to be executed at any time once their execution warrant was signed by the Minister of Justice. They had exhausted all legal appeals and the courts refused to grant them a retrial.

In one case during the year, a death sentence was stayed on appeal. In January the Supreme Court ordered a retrial for Chang Fang-tien, sentenced to death in 1996 for murder. The Supreme Court accepted Chang Fang-tien's allegation that his original confession to the police had been made under duress. The retrial had not been completed by the end of the year, but a police officer convicted of ill-treating Chang Fang-tien during interrogation was given a suspended prison sentence in July.

In February and July Amnesty International renewed its appeals for the commutation of the death sentences passed against Su Chien-ho, Liu Ping-lang and Chuang Lin-hsiung. In November, following a visit to Taiwan by Amnesty International delegates, the organization sought further information from the authorities about the case of Chang Fang-tien.

TAJIKISTAN

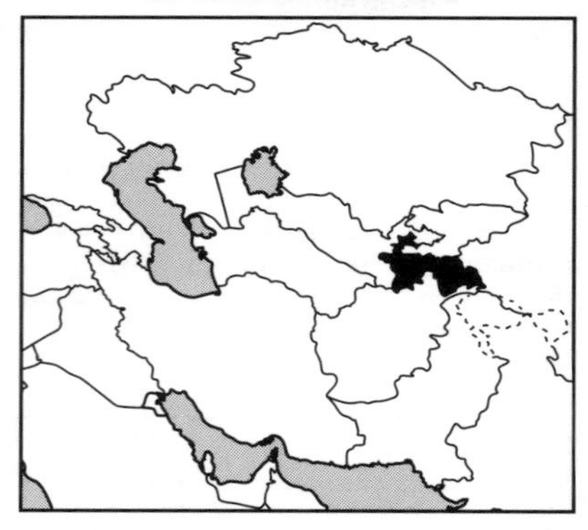

At least 13 possible prisoners of conscience were detained following an assassination attempt on the President. One possible prisoner of conscience was extradited from Russia at the request of the Tajik authorities. At least one opposition supporter and his brother allegedly "disappeared"; the brother later reappeared. There were reports of possible extrajudicial executions during the suppression of a prison riot. Progress in bringing to justice those responsible for past human rights abuses stalled. The death penalty was extended and at least four people were sentenced to death.

More than five years of civil war formally ended in late June when President Imomali Rakhmonov and United Tajik Opposition (UTO) leader Sayed Abdullo Nuri signed a General Agreement on Peace and National Accord. The agreement, signed in Moscow, Russia, provided for a National Reconciliation Commission, to be made up of an equal number of government and UTO representatives. The Commission was to be in charge of preparing new parliamentary elections in 1998, supervising the merger of UTO armed forces into the national army and the return of refugees, and implementing a general amnesty.

A general amnesty for people imprisoned for crimes in connection with the civil war was signed into law by President Rakhmonov in July and approved by parliament in August. It reportedly allowed people convicted of violent crimes in connection with the civil war to petition for a review of their cases if they believed they had been punished for political actions.

The two sides carried out several prisoner exchanges as part of the peace accord. There was opposition, some of it violent, to the peace accord from various groups which had been excluded from the National Reconciliation Commission.

At least 13 possible prisoners of conscience were detained following an assassination attempt on President Rakhmonov in the Leninabad regional capital, Khujand, in April. A hand grenade was thrown at the President, causing minor injuries to his legs. Two people died in the attack and more than 70 were injured. Officials reported the arrest of Firdavs Dustboyev, who they claimed had thrown the grenade. Within days, at least 11 more people were reportedly detained in connection with the incident. The day after the attack a shoot-out was reported in a village near Khujand between police and a group of people suspected of involvement in the assassination plot. Five of the group were killed. Arrests in Leninabad region continued through May. According to reports, those detained included people who had no connection with the assassination attempt, but had been identified as government opponents because of their participation in anti-government protests in Leninabad a year earlier (see *Amnesty International Report 1997*). Firdavs Dustboyev was said to have been an organizer of these protests. In late May police in Khujand arrested Abdukhafiz Abdullayev, younger brother of Abdumalik Abdullojanov, a former Prime Minister and head of the secular opposition National Revival Bloc. He was apparently first held on a charge of illegal narcotics possession, but it was subsequently reported that he had been charged in connection with the assassination attempt. His supporters claimed that the charge was a fabrication, and that the motive of the arrest was to intimidate the Khujand-based opposition.

In June authorities in the Russian Federation extradited Akhmajon Saidov, a former deputy speaker of Tajikistan's parliament who had been living in Russia since 1994, to Tajikistan. A warrant for his arrest had been issued in Tajikistan in August 1996 on charges of abuse of authority and embezzlement, and in February 1997 he was arrested in Moscow. There were suspicions that the true motive for bringing the charges was to punish Akhmajon Saidov for his connection with the National Revival Bloc, the formation of which had been announced at a press conference in Moscow days before the warrant was issued.

There were at least two possible "disappearances". Rizoali Ojiyev was detained for questioning on 28 February by police in Khujand, where he ran a business. Early the following day witnesses saw him being brought home in a police car, and moments later a group of armed masked men who had been waiting in another car outside Rizoali Ojiyev's home seized him and drove him away. Rizoali Ojiyev's younger brother, Gadoali Ojiyev, also "disappeared" on 28 February after being detained in the town of Kanibadam, near Khujand. He reappeared five weeks later, and stated that he had been held by law enforcement officials in Uzbekistan, ostensibly on suspicion of involvement in an incident in mid-February when an Uzbek customs post on the Tajikistan-Uzbekistan border had been attacked by armed men crossing from Tajikistan. However, Gadoali Ojiyev claimed that he had been repeatedly questioned not about that incident, but about the activities of his brother Rizoali. He was driven back to Khujand from Uzbekistan in April and was reportedly released without charge. He subsequently went into hiding.

There was concern that law enforcement officials may have used excessive force when they stormed a penitentiary in Khujand to suppress a riot in April. The official death toll among inmates was put at 21, with over 30 wounded, but unofficial sources put the casualty figures considerably higher.

The escape from custody of a man accused of committing extrajudicial executions in 1993 cast doubt on the commitment of the authorities to ending impunity for past human rights abuses. Khoja Karimov, a former member of parliament and former field commander of the paramilitary People's Front (see *Amnesty International Report 1996*), had escaped from detention by the start of the year. Arrested in November 1995, he had been held pending trial for the July 1993 "disappearance" and murder of member of parliament Saidsho Shoyev and his brother Siyarsho Shoyev, and the murder of member of parliament Tagkhoykhon Shukurov.

The July general amnesty for people imprisoned for crimes connected with the civil war also gave rise to concern about impunity for members of formerly pro-government paramilitary groups and opposition armed forces suspected of having committed human rights abuses.

In August the authorities stated that criminal investigations into the alleged "disappearances" in 1992 and 1993 of Democratic Party activist Ayniddin Sadykov (see *Amnesty International Report 1994*) and several others had been opened, but that they had failed to identify the perpetrators or to establish the whereabouts and fate of the victims.

A report in May indicated that the death penalty had been extended to the offence of "hooliganism" (Article 220 of the Criminal Code), raising the number of capital crimes to 42. At least four death sentences were passed during the year. Twelve people were sentenced to death in 1996, according to official figures obtained by the International Helsinki Federation for Human Rights. Two members of pro-government paramilitary forces, Safarqul Samadov and Abdurauf Urunov, were sentenced to death in 1995 after being convicted of multiple murder and other offences committed in late 1992 and early 1993. It was unclear whether provisions in the general amnesty of July extended to people convicted of capital offences. It was also unclear whether a moratorium on carrying out death sentences connected with the civil war, declared by the government in June 1995 (see *Amnesty International Report 1996*), was still in force.

Amnesty International sought further information about arrests of suspected government opponents in Leninabad region, including the arrest and detention of Abdukhafiz Abdullayev. Amnesty International called on the Russian authorities not to extradite Akhmajon Saidov on the grounds that he might become a prisoner of conscience. It also called on authorities in Tajikistan to provide more information about the charges against him. Amnesty International appealed for information about the whereabouts of Rizoali Ojiyev to authorities in both Tajikistan and Uzbekistan. In June Uzbek authorities replied, denying involvement in Rizoali Ojiyev's alleged "disappearance". In September the Tajik authorities informed Amnesty International that a criminal investigation had been opened into his "disappearance" under Article 135 of the Tajik Criminal Code (hostage-taking).

Amnesty International sought further information about the conduct of law enforcement personnel during the storming of the Khujand prison. Amnesty International continued to call for complete abolition of the death penalty, and appealed for the commutation of each death sentence which came to its attention.

TANZANIA

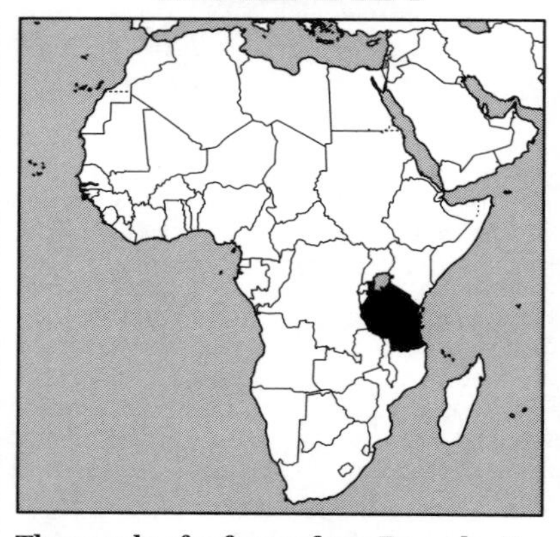

Thousands of refugees from Rwanda, Burundi and the Democratic Republic of the Congo (formerly Zaire) were forcibly returned, although Tanzania continued to host over 200,000 refugees from Burundi. Journalists were harassed; one was briefly held as a prisoner of conscience. Fourteen possible prisoners of conscience were charged with treason on the island of Zanzibar.

Relations with Burundi remained tense. Burundi accused the Tanzanian authorities of allowing Burundi refugees from the Hutu ethnic group to mount attacks on Burundi, and Tanzania accused the Burundi authorities of carrying out armed attacks along the border. In the first four months of the year thousands of refugees fled from fighting in Zaire between the government of Zairian President Mobutu Sese Seko and the *Alliance des forces démocratiques pour la libération du Congo-Zaïre* (AFDL), Alliance of Democratic forces for the Liberation of Congo-Zaire, led by Laurent-Désiré Kabila. In August, three months after the AFDL captured Kinshasa, Tanzania concluded an agreement for the return of refugees with the new government of the renamed Democratic Republic of the Congo.

The islands of Pemba and Zanzibar remained politically tense. The opposition Civic United Front (CUF) maintained that the 1995 elections to the islands' government, won by the ruling *Chama cha Mapinduzi*, led on the islands by Salmin Amour, had been rigged. CUF members elected to the Zanzibar House of Representatives refused to take their seats.

The government continued to have an uneasy relationship with independent media, especially on the island of Zanzibar. In March the Zanzibar authorities threatened to order the arrest of practising journalists who were not in possession of a licence required under largely unenforced legislation dating from 1988. In July the work ban imposed in January 1996 on a Zanzibar journalist working for the independent newspaper *Majira* (see *Amnesty International Report 1997*) was lifted. However, the newspaper itself, published on the mainland, remained banned from circulation on the island.

In January, 126 Burundi refugees were forcibly expelled by the Tanzanian army from Kitale camp to Burundi, where 122 were extrajudicially executed by Burundi soldiers in Kobero, on the border. In a separate incident 48 other refugees were similarly expelled and then arrested by the Burundi authorities. The Tanzanian authorities had accused the refugees of being involved in factional fighting within the refugee camp. Although the authorities promised there would be no further expulsions of Burundi refugees, in October over 2,000 Burundi nationals accused of entering the country illegally were expelled. The border with Burundi remained officially closed throughout the year, in contravention of Tanzania's obligations under international and regional treaties. However, thousands of refugees were allowed to flee into Tanzania, so long as they remained in areas officially designated for refugees.

The situation of Rwandese nationals was also insecure. Thousands of them, including refugees, were expelled. Over the first four months of the year over 700 Rwandese officially described as having entered the country illegally were deported. In October and November, over 2,000 Rwandese nationals, some of whom had been in Tanzania since 1951, were rounded up by the Tanzanian army and expelled. Some were reported to have been beaten and raped by Tanzanian soldiers.

Journalists suffered harassment. In February, for example, Adam Mwaibabile, a freelance journalist, was sentenced to one year's imprisonment for possession of a "secret government document" – a letter from a public official directing that he be refused a business licence because of his "hostile" writing. After three weeks in detention he was freed pending appeal. He was a prisoner of conscience. The High Court quashed the conviction in April.

In December, 14 possible prisoners of conscience on Zanzibar were charged with treason and refused bail. The men, supporters of the CUF, were arrested and initially charged with sedition in November and December, during the week the CUF won a by-election to the Zanzibar House of Representatives. They included two opposition members of the Zanzibar House of Representatives and CUF Deputy Secretary General Nassor Seif Amour.

Amnesty International criticized Tanzania for betraying its international obligations not to forcibly return refugees who were at risk of human rights violations in their own countries. In January, after the expulsion and subsequent killing of Burundi refugees, an Amnesty International delegation led by a former Canadian minister of external affairs visited Tanzania and met President Benjamin Mkapa and other government officials. The President stated that there would be no forced repatriation of Burundi refugees.

In January an Amnesty International report on refugees in the Great Lakes region expressed concern about the continuing risk of *refoulement* facing refugees from Rwanda, Zaire and Burundi in Tanzania. In June Amnesty International published a report on refugees in Africa which included criticism of the Tanzanian authorities for forcibly returning refugees to Rwanda. The report also criticized other governments for failing to support and adequately assist Tanzania's efforts to host hundreds of thousands of refugees. In December Amnesty International wrote to the President expressing renewed concern at the forcible expulsion of refugees.

In April Amnesty International's continuing concerns about the death penalty in Tanzania were described in a report about the death penalty in Africa. In response to a letter received in August from the Minister of Foreign Affairs, Amnesty International was investigating further the alleged killing in August 1996 of 50 goldminers in Bulyanhulu, Shinyanga region (see *Amnesty International Report 1997*).

THAILAND

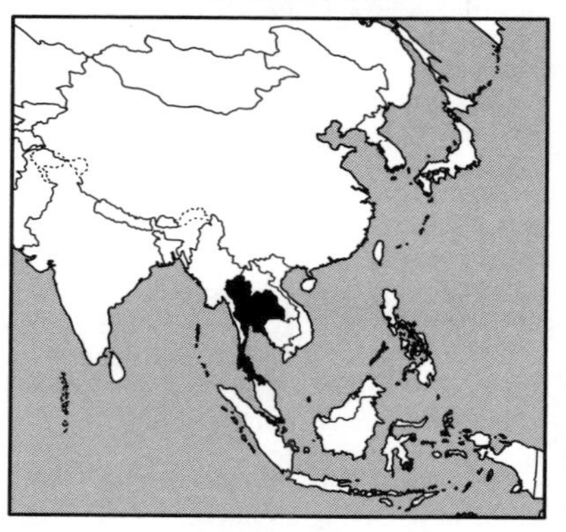

A new Constitution was adopted with strong human rights provisions. Three Cambodian children were killed by Thai border guards in disputed circumstances. Thirty-seven death sentences were passed and two people were executed. At least 6,000 refugees were forcibly repatriated to Myanmar. Burmese asylum-seekers continued to be arrested for "illegal immigration" and detained in harsh conditions.

In November Chuan Leekpai formed a new coalition government after General Chaowalit Yongchaiyudh resigned as Prime Minister in the midst of a serious economic crisis. In October the Parliament adopted a new Constitution, the first of Thailand's 16 constitutions to have been drafted with public participation. The Constitution included provisions for the formation of a national human rights commission and guaranteed the rights to freedom of association, movement, religion, and speech. The death penalty was retained, although torture and cruel, inhuman or degrading treatment were prohibited. Criminal suspects could be detained without a court order for only 48 hours. The Constitution also aimed to eliminate vote-buying and other forms of corruption, to decentralize the government, and to strengthen the democratic process.

In February 20,000 ethnic Karen asylum-seekers fled from Myanmar into Thailand during a Burmese army offensive against the armed ethnic minority opposition group, the Karen National Union (KNU). This brought the number of Karen refugees in Thai camps to over 100,000. At least 30,000 asylum-seekers from the Shan State in Myanmar fled into Thailand from massive forcible relocations and extrajudicial executions by the Burmese army. Unlike the Karen and Karenni groups, the Shan were not allowed by the authorities to establish camps on the Thai/Myanmar border (see **Myanmar** entry).

In January Burmese soldiers crossed into Thailand and attacked two Karenni refugee camps, killing two Karenni refugees and wounding nine others. Also in January the Democratic Kayin Buddhist Organization (DKBO), an armed ethnic minority group allied with the Burmese army, burned down two Karen refugee camps in Tak Province, leaving about 7,000 refugees homeless and killing one Thai civilian.

In January, three Cambodian children were shot dead by Thai security forces in Sa Kaew Province after they had been abducted by three Cambodian adults. Thai military sources claimed that the three adults had opened fire first, but other sources indicated that the children were shot dead when Thai border guards opened fire on the group, who were crossing the border into Cambodia.

In June the families of six suspected amphetamine traffickers who were shot dead by police in November 1996 (see *Amnesty International Report 1997*) filed lawsuits against the police department and nine police officers.

Thirty-seven death sentences were passed during the year and 158 people were believed to be under sentence of death. The death penalty was imposed for murder, rape and murder, and drug-trafficking. In November Boonchot Pongprom and Panom Thaweesuk, who had both been convicted of rape and murder in the early 1990s, were executed by firing-squad.

More than 6,000 refugees from the Karen, Mon, and Pa'O ethnic minority groups were forcibly sent back to Myanmar by Thai security forces during the year. In February and March more than 4,000 refugees who had recently fled to Thailand were forcibly returned by the Ninth Infantry Division of the First Army. In November the Fourth Infantry Regiment Task Force forcibly returned 1,100 Karen refugees who had recently fled from forced labour and relocations by the Burmese army. Troops entered the refugee settlement, fired mortars and shots in the air, and beat several refugees after dragging them out of their shelters. After a group of 400 Mon refugees were returned in June, they were subjected to forced portering and labour on army bases by the Burmese army. All of them had fled once again to Thailand by July. Thousands of Karen asylum-seekers were prevented by the Thai authorities from crossing into Thailand and remained at risk of human rights violations inside Myanmar. The UN High Commissioner for Refugees continued to be denied a permanent presence on the Thai/Myanmar border, although officials were able to conduct monitoring visits there.

Immigration officials and police continued to detain asylum-seekers and refugees from Myanmar and other countries in harsh conditions, including severe overcrowding and inadequate access to medical care. Detained asylum-seekers were not given an opportunity to challenge the legality of their detention as required by international standards.

In October the police commissioner's office, which supervises immigration activities, admitted publicly that the Immigration Detention Centre (IDC) in Bangkok was seriously overcrowded, with barely enough room for detainees to sit or sleep. There were also reports of severe overcrowding and insufficient sanitation and medical care at Mahachai Police Station, Samut Sakhon Province, where hundreds of Burmese nationals, some of whom were refugees, were detained for "illegal immigration".

In April a group of prisoners raped three young Lao women who had been arrested for "illegal immigration" and detained at a police station in Rayong Province. The young women were kept in an adult police lock-up with men, in violation of international standards. Eight of the prisoners were brought to trial but the three police officers responsible, although transferred to another police station, were not known to have been prosecuted.

In January and February Amnesty International delegates visited Thailand and met government officials and parliamentarians. In February and throughout the year Amnesty International condemned the forcible return of asylum-seekers to Myanmar. In May the organization published *Kingdom of Thailand: Human rights in transition* and in September it published *Kingdom of Thailand: Erosion of refugee rights.*

TOGO

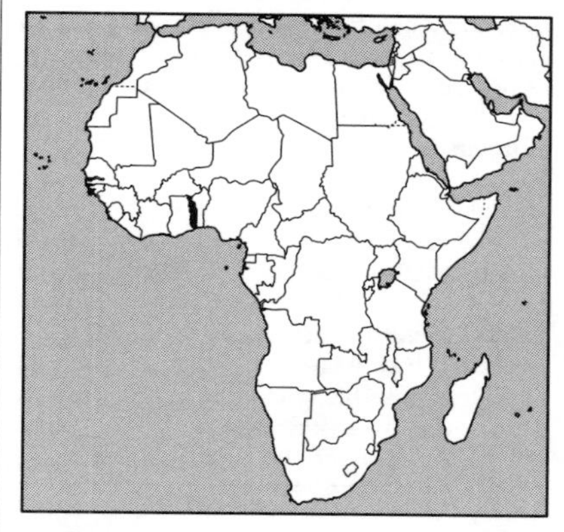

At least seven people were alleged to have been extrajudicially executed by the security forces, who continued to enjoy total impunity for widespread human rights violations. Opposition party supporters, including prisoners of conscience, were detained for short periods. There were new allegations of torture and ill-treatment.

In September Parliament adopted a new electoral law intended to ensure greater independence for the National Electoral Commission responsible for supervising presidential elections due to be held in August 1998. Under this law, eight members were elected, from both the ruling party and opposition parties. However, the main opposition party did not participate in the vote.

Perpetrators of human rights violations were rarely brought to justice. However, two soldiers responsible for the death of a German diplomat in March 1996 (see *Amnesty International Report 1997*) were sentenced to 10 years' imprisonment by the Assizes Court in December.

The *Forces armées togolaises* (FAT), Togolese Armed Forces, were alleged to have committed at least seven extrajudicial executions in two incidents. The victims were mainly people who had returned to Togo after fleeing in January 1993 when the security forces opened fire on a peaceful opposition demonstration. In February the FAT were reported to have extrajudicially executed Apetse Koffi Amen, known as "Miky", a former soldier, and Agbemoa, a Ghanaian national who was accompanying him. The two men were reportedly seized by soldiers in an ambush at Agbadjankin, between Assahoun and Batoume, before being killed. In June in Assahoun, FAT soldiers stopped a car travelling from Ghana to Togo's capital, Lomé. The five occupants of the car, including Amoussou Koffi and Amah Messan, were later killed. There appeared to be no investigation into these killings.

Dozens of people, including journalists and opposition supporters, were arrested by the security forces in Lomé and other places. Many of them were tortured or ill-treated. Most were not formally charged and were possible prisoners of conscience. Some were released after a short period, but by the end of the year at least three people remained in detention without charge or trial.

At least four journalists were detained during the year. Among them was Augustin Assiogbo, managing director of the privately-owned weekly *Tingo-Tingo*. He was arrested in February after the family of former Minister of Foreign Affairs Alasounouma Boumbera filed a complaint. He was released in May after being sentenced to four months' imprisonment, two of them suspended. Also in February, Gabriel Agah, publisher of *Forum Hebdo*, was sentenced *in absentia* to a one-year prison term and a heavy fine. The court also issued an order suspending the newspaper from publication for six months. In December Kodjo Afatsao, the publishing director of the weekly newspaper *Le nouveau journal* was detained for four days. He was accused of propagating false information offensive to the Head of State, by referring to an article in a French-based magazine accusing the Togolese authorities of assisting Zairian soldiers loyal to the former Zairian President, Mobutu Sese Seko.

In February Segla Atchikiti, an opposition member, was arrested in Atakpame and detained for at least four days without charge or trial. During his detention he was transferred to the palace of the Head of State in Kara.

In October at least eight people were arrested in the village of Akato, considered to be an opposition stronghold. Some were released but at least three, including Masseme Kodjo, were still in detention without charge or trial at the end of the year. In December Jean-Pierre Fabre, Secretary General of the *Union des forces de changement*, Union of the Forces of Change, an opposition party, was arrested and accused of ordering a group of young people to take pictures of dead bodies in certain hospitals. He was released without charge after one day.

Adjété Ako and Djekpo Jolevi, two army officers arrested in 1995 on their return from Benin, remained in detention without charge or trial (see *Amnesty International Report 1997*). However, Folly Dagnon Koffi, another soldier held with them, was apparently released, although his release was not confirmed. Claude Gumedzoe and Sergeant Augustin Ihou, who were arrested in 1996 (see *Amnesty International Report 1997*), remained in detention without charge or trial.

There were further reports of torture and ill-treatment. Many of those held by the security forces were tortured and ill-treated and at least two people died in custody, allegedly as a result. In July Danklou Dosseh and Agbodjinshie Yakanou, who had been arrested a month earlier in Akato, reportedly died as a result of torture and ill-treatment in Lomé prison.

TRINIDAD AND TOBAGO

About 104 people remained under sentence of death, including 17 who were sentenced to death during the year. At least seven people were sentenced to corporal punishment.

In October the government issued instructions setting strict time limits on death-row prisoners' petitions to the Inter-American Commission on Human Rights and to the UN Human Rights Committee. If the time limits are not met by the prisoner or the international body, the instructions permit the government to proceed with execution, even while the petition remains pending.

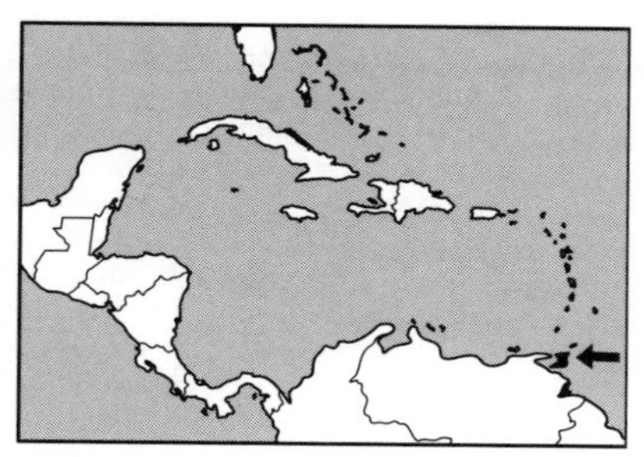

About 104 people remained under sentence of death, including 17 who were sentenced to death during the year. Although no executions took place, a warrant was issued for the execution of Gerald Wilson in May; the execution was stayed pending his further appeal. Gerald Wilson, however, died in prison in October. The government commissioned reports on the possibility of extending the death penalty as a sentence for drug-trafficking and rape.

At least seven people were sentenced to corporal punishment, in addition to terms of imprisonment. Reports indicated that several people sentenced to corporal punishment in previous years were flogged or whipped. After a retrial ordered by the Court of Appeal, Myra Bhagwansingh – who was the first woman to have received a sentence of corporal punishment (see *Amnesty International Report 1997*) – was again convicted of causing grievous bodily harm. She was sentenced to 12 years' imprisonment, but not to corporal punishment.

There were reports of fatal shootings by police in disputed circumstances. In August Marcus Antoine, Lawrence Jobity and Stephan Perreira were killed by members of the police Anti-Kidnapping Squad. The incident was investigated by an Assistant Police Commissioner; inquest hearings were scheduled to begin in 1998.

There were developments in cases of fatal shootings by police in disputed circumstances in previous years. In July the inquest into the death in 1990 of Njisane Omowale, a student, concluded. He was killed during a police raid on the home of a relative of Yasin Abu Bakr a few days after the unsuccessful attempt to overthrow the government by members of the *Jamaat-al-Muslimeen* in 1990. The inquest found that a felony had been committed, but could not determine by whom and sent the case back to the Police Commissioner for further investigation.

In August, following an inquest which had lasted more than six years, a coroner recommended that a member of the police be indicted for the unlawful killing in 1990 of Franklyn John.

Amnesty International expressed concern about sentences of corporal punishment – a cruel, inhuman or degrading punishment. It asked for information about the imposition of sentences, urged the government to ensure that no sentences of corporal punishment were carried out in future, and called on the government to repeal legislation allowing corporal punishment. In November the organization urged the authorities not to extend the scope of the death penalty. It reminded the authorities of their obligation, under the American Convention on Human Rights, not to extend the scope of the death penalty. It expressed concern about the time limits imposed on death-row prisoners' petitions to the Inter-American Commission on Human Rights and the UN Human Rights Committee, which denied prisoners the effective recourse to redress for alleged human rights violations which such petitions are intended to afford. It also asked for information about developments in the cases of Njisane Omowale, Franklyn John, Marcus Antoine, Lawrence Jobity and Stephan Perreira and urged the government to submit its overdue third periodic report to the UN Human Rights Committee.

TUNISIA

Hundreds of prisoners of conscience were detained, including human rights defenders and people suspected of supporting unauthorized political opposition groups. The wives and relatives of imprisoned or exiled opponents were detained and harassed. Up to 2,000 political prisoners arrested in previous years, most of them prisoners of conscience, remained

imprisoned. Political trials frequently violated international standards for fair trial. Torture and ill-treatment remained widespread, especially during incommunicado detention, and at least six people died in custody. Several people remained under sentence of death, although no executions were reported.

The crack-down by the government of President Zine el 'Abidine Ben 'Ali against human rights defenders and critics and non-violent political opponents of the government continued. Further restrictions were imposed on the activities of local and international human rights organizations and the media.

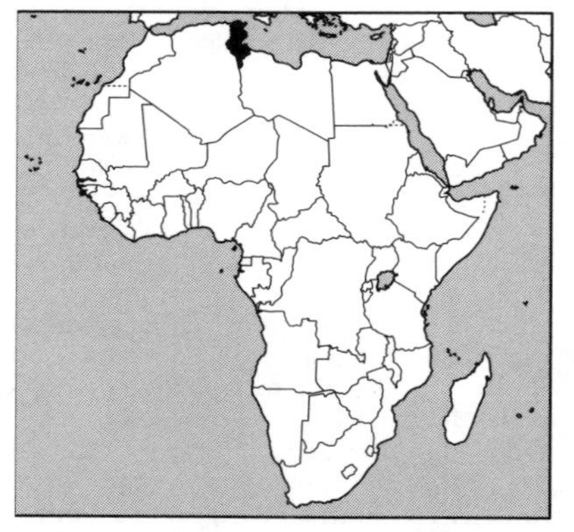

An amendment to the law on the external security of the state was approved by the government in September and was awaiting ratification by parliament at the end of the year. The amendment proposed making contacts with agents of foreign or international organizations a crime punishable by between five and 12 years' imprisonment.

Human rights defenders were increasingly targeted and intimidated. Hechmi Jegham, a lawyer and President of the Tunisian Section of Amnesty International, was arrested without a warrant on two consecutive days in March and interrogated at the Central Police Station in Sousse about his participation in a legal conference which was scheduled to take place in Tunisia, and about his contacts with non-governmental organizations abroad. He was released without charge on both occasions.

Khemais Ksila, Vice-President of the *Ligue tunisienne des droits de l'homme* (LTDH), Tunisian League for Human Rights, was arrested at his home in September after he issued a communique condemning human rights violations in Tunisia and announcing that he was beginning an unlimited hunger-strike to protest against the harassment to which he and his family were subjected. He was charged with undermining public order, spreading false information and inciting the population to violate the law. He remained detained awaiting trial at the end of the year.

Former LTDH President Moncef Marzouki and human rights lawyer Najib Hosni, both former prisoners of conscience (see *Amnesty International Reports 1995* to *1997*), and Khemais Ksila were subjected to constant harassment. They were prevented from working, their telephone lines were disconnected, their mail intercepted, and their passports confiscated. They were prevented from leaving the country to attend a meeting on the human rights situation in Tunisia at the European Parliament in June.

Hundreds of prisoners of conscience suspected of links with unauthorized political groups were arrested. Many were released without charge or trial, but scores were sentenced to prison terms, including people who had previously been imprisoned on similar charges. Most were accused of links with the unauthorized Islamist group *al-Nahda*, and others of links with the *Parti communiste des ouvriers tunisiens*, Tunisian Workers' Communist Party, or the *Union de la jeunesse communiste*, Union of Communist Youth.

'Abdelmoumen Belanes, detained in 1995 and 1996 (see *Amnesty International Reports 1996* and *1997*), was rearrested in March, accused of having complained, during a previous period of imprisonment, that Tunisian newspapers carried too many photographs of government officials. He was sentenced in April to one year's imprisonment. The sentence was upheld on appeal in May.

Lazhar No'man, a high-school teacher and father of five, was arrested in August, less than two weeks after his release from prison. He had previously been imprisoned on political charges in 1991 and 1994 for a total of four years. He was accused of links with *al-Nahda* and remained detained awaiting trial at the end of the year.

At least nine senior members of the *Union générale des travailleurs tunisiens*,

Tunisian General Workers' Union, were arrested in April, and accused of involvement in the issuing of several petitions criticizing the increasing restrictions on civil liberties, trade union rights and human rights. Five were promptly released, but four – Rachid 'Ennajar, Monji Sou'ab, Jilali Hammami and 'Ahmed Berramila – were detained for up to five weeks and charged with distributing leaflets, spreading false information aimed at disturbing public order and insulting an official institution. They were released on bail in May. No trial had taken place by the end of the year.

Scores of wives and relatives of imprisoned or exiled supporters of *al-Nahda* were detained as prisoners of conscience and interrogated about their contacts with their exiled husbands and relatives, and about any financial assistance given to, or received from, families of prisoners. Dozens of women reported having been ill-treated, threatened with torture, including rape, and asked to divorce their exiled or imprisoned husbands.

Rachida Ben Salem was arrested in May as she prepared to leave Tunisia with her two children to join her husband, an *al-Nahda* supporter and refugee in the Netherlands who had fled Tunisia in 1992. In September she was sentenced to two years and three months' imprisonment on charges of belonging to an unauthorized association and unauthorized border crossing. The sentence was increased to two years and nine months' imprisonment on appeal in November. Radhia Aouididi, who had been arrested in 1996 as she attempted to leave Tunisia on a false passport in order to join her fiancé, an *al-Nahda* supporter exiled in France, remained detained awaiting trial at the end of the year. Both women had been subjected to repeated detention and harassment in previous years and were banned from leaving the country. 'Aicha Dhaouadi and Tourkia Hamadi (see *Amnesty International Report 1997*), were allowed to leave Tunisia with their children in June. In October more than 40 wives of exiled political opponents were allowed to leave Tunisia with their children to join their husbands abroad.

Tunisians living outside the country were arrested and interrogated about their activities abroad when they returned to Tunisia. Lazhar Belgacem, a Tunisian worker resident in Austria and father of two, was arrested in July when he visited his family and was accused of unauthorized political activities abroad. He remained detained awaiting trial at the end of the year. 'Ali Hadfi, who was arrested in 1996 (see *Amnesty International Report 1997*), was released in February but was required to report to the police daily and could not leave the country.

Up to 2,000 political prisoners, most of them prisoners of conscience, arrested in previous years remained detained. They included 'Imed 'Ebdelli and Sou'ad Charbati who were serving sentences of three and six years' imprisonment, respectively, and Salwa Dimassi and Ahlam Garat-'Ali, who were arrested in 1996 and remained detained without trial at the end of the year, in violation of the maximum 14-month period allowed by Tunisian law for pre-trial detention (see *Amnesty International Report 1997*). 'Ali Ba'azaoui, who was imprisoned in 1995, was conditionally released in May (see *Amnesty International Report 1997*).

Political trials continued to violate international standards for fair trial. The courts routinely failed to investigate allegations of torture and ill-treatment and accepted as evidence confessions retracted in court by defendants who stated that they had been forced to sign them under torture. Courts often convicted defendants even though no convincing evidence was produced to substantiate the charges. For example, Habib Hemissi, a teacher in Saudi Arabia and father of four who was arrested in 1996 when he returned to Tunisia to visit his family, was sentenced in May to 10 years' imprisonment on charges of links with *al-Nahda*. The charges, which he denied, were based on his contacts with his sister and her husband, both supporters of *al-Nahda* and refugees in the United Kingdom (UK).

Torture and ill-treatment continued to be reported, including on the premises of the Ministry of the Interior and in prisons. 'Abdelwahab Memmichi, a British national of Tunisian origin living in the UK, was arrested in January on arrival in Tunisia. He was beaten, kicked and threatened in the Ministry of the Interior, where he was questioned about his contacts with exiled Tunisian political opponents in the UK. He was released the same day without charge. 'Abdelmoumen Belanes (see above) was tortured and ill-treated by guards in Nadhor Prison in April and May.

At least six people died in detention, reportedly as a result of torture, ill-treatment and lack of medical care. Mabrouk Zran died in May after the amputation of a leg. He had been tortured after arrest in 1991 and had not received adequate medical care. Ridha Khimri, a teacher, died in Jendouba Prison in July, after having been on hunger-strike for more than 50 days. He had been detained without trial on political charges since his arrest in January, only days after having been released on expiry of an eight-year prison sentence, and had reportedly been tortured. No investigations were carried out into complaints of torture and deaths in custody in the previous year (see *Amnesty International Report 1997*).

Several people remained under sentence of death, but no executions were reported.

An Amnesty International researcher continued to be excluded from Tunisia.

In June, Amnesty International issued a report, *Tunisia: A widening circle of repression,* highlighting the continuing and widespread human rights violations. In July it issued a joint statement with the *Fédération internationale des droits de l'homme*, Human Rights Watch, the Lawyers Committee for Human Rights and *Reporters Sans Frontières*, expressing concern at the increasing intimidation and harassment of human rights defenders and urging the Tunisian Government to respect human rights and honour international human rights treaties ratified by Tunisia. No response was received from the government and no measures were taken by the government to address the concerns raised.

TURKEY

Hundreds of people were detained because of their non-violent political activities; most were released after a short period of police detention but others were sentenced to terms of imprisonment. Torture continued to be widespread and systematic in police stations and gendarmeries, although new legislation on detention procedures had some impact. There were at least six reported deaths in custody. At least nine people reportedly "disappeared" in security force custody and at least 20 people were killed in circumstances suggesting that they had been extrajudicially executed. There were no judicial executions, although courts continued to pass death sentences. Armed opposition groups committed deliberate and arbitrary killings of prisoners and civilians.

The government headed by Necmettin Erbakan of the Islamist Welfare Party in coalition with the right-wing True Path Party ended with his resignation in June, largely as a result of pressure from the armed forces. Later that month, a new coalition headed by Motherland Party leader Mesut Yılmaz was formed together with the Democratic Left Party and Democratic Turkey Party. State of emergency legislation was lifted in three provinces in October, but remained in force in six provinces of the southeast, where the 13-year conflict between government forces and armed members of the Kurdish Workers' Party (PKK) claimed the lives of 6,000 people, including civilians, during the year.

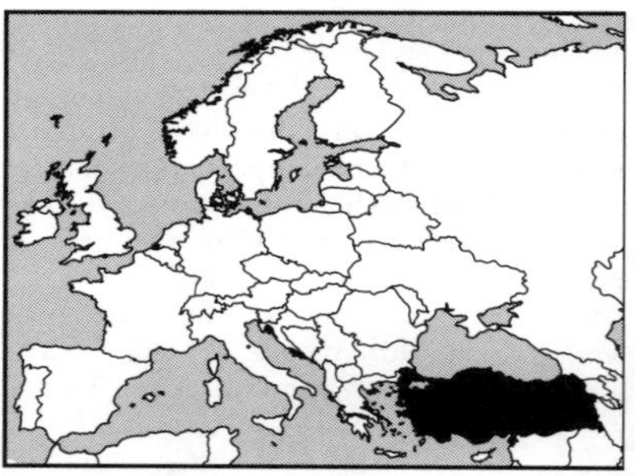

Trade unionists, students and demonstrators were frequently taken into custody at peaceful public meetings or at their organizations' offices, and were held in police detention for hours or days because of their non-violent political activities.

The trial under Article 8 of the Anti-Terror Law, which outlaws any advocacy of "separatism", of 184 members of Turkey's literary and cultural elite for publishing a book entitled *Freedom of Thought* (see *Amnesty International Report 1997*) was halted in October under the terms of a law which suspended judicial proceedings against editors for three years.

Other articles of the Turkish Penal Code (TPC) were also used against writers, journalists and political activists whose statements criticized the Turkish state. In June the writer and lawyer Ahmet Zeki Okçuoğlu was imprisoned under Article 159 of the TPC for "insulting the institutions of the state", after the Supreme Court upheld a 10-month sentence handed down in 1993 by Istanbul Criminal Court No. 2 for his article published in the newspaper *Azadi* (Freedom). He was released in October. The trials under Article 159 continued against Münir Ceylan, a trade unionist; Ercan Kanar, president of the Istanbul branch of the Turkish Human Rights Association (HRA); and Şanar Yurdatapan, spokesperson for the Together for Peace initiative (see *Amnesty International Report 1997*). They had publicly accused the Chief of General Staff of covering up the Güçlükonak massacre, in which state forces allegedly detained and killed 11 civilians and village guards. The security forces presented the killings as having been committed by the PKK.

Prisoners of conscience Hatip Dicle, Orhan Doğan, Selim Sadak and Leyla Zana, former parliamentary deputies for the Democracy Party, continued to serve 15-year sentences, imposed in 1994 for alleged membership of the PKK, at Ankara Closed Prison. No conclusive evidence was presented to support the charges against them during the course of a blatantly unfair trial and they appeared to have been imprisoned because of their criticism of state policy in the predominantly Kurdish southeastern provinces.

People expressing political beliefs from an Islamic point of view were also held as prisoners of conscience. Former parliamentary deputy Hasan Mezarcı was serving an 18-month sentence imposed in 1996 under Law 5816 for insulting Mustafa Kemal Atatürk, founder of the Turkish Republic. He was released in October. In April members of the Aczmendi religious order detained in October 1996 were sentenced to prison terms by Ankara State Security Court (SSC) for appearing in public in Ankara in turbans and cloaks – garments which contravened the Dress and Hat Laws instituted by Mustafa Kemal Atatürk. Ilyas Eldi, Yakup Akkuş, Ahmet Arslan, Ömer Faruk, Bülent Baykal, and Servet Dündar were sentenced to four years' imprisonment after conviction under Article 7/1 of the Anti-Terror Law for "membership of an organization founded to transform the Republic by means of intimidation or threats." In fact, the Aczmendi order does not advocate violence. Another 110 Aczmendi defendants received sentences of three years' imprisonment.

The HRA was subjected to intense harassment. Three branches were shut down including the Diyarbakır branch, which was closed on the grounds that "its activities threaten the unity of the state." Aziz Durmaz, president of the Şanlıurfa branch, was detained and reportedly tortured in June. He was committed to prison on apparently bogus charges of membership of an armed organization. He was a prisoner of conscience. Aziz Durmaz was released in November.

Turkey does not recognize the right of conscientious objection to military service and there is no provision for alternative civilian service. In January the General Staff Military Court in Ankara sentenced Osman Murat Ülke, chairperson of the Izmir War Resisters' Association (ISKD) (see *Amnesty International Report 1997*), to six months' imprisonment and a fine for "alienating the public from the institution of military service" by publicly declaring his conscientious objection and burning his call-up papers in 1995. In February the General Staff Military Court opened a new trial against Osman Murat Ülke and a further 11 defendants from the HRA and ISKD on charges of "alienating the public from the institution of military service" in speeches that they had given during Human Rights Week in 1995. Osman Murat Ülke was conditionally released in May, but was rearrested in October at Eskişehir Military Court after being convicted of "persistent insubordination", for which he received a five-month prison sentence, and "desertion", for which he received a further five-month sentence.

In March detention procedures were amended for people held under the Anti-Terror Law (which includes non-violent offences). The Turkish Government announced this as a measure to combat torture. The new law shortened the maximum terms of police detention from 30 to 10 days in provinces under state of emergency legislation, and from 14 to seven days throughout the rest of the country. The new provisions were a substantial improvement but still failed to meet international standards. The law provides for four days' incommunicado detention, described by the European Committee for the Prevention of Torture and Inhuman or Degrading Treatment or Punishment as "unacceptable". Incommunicado detention is widely recognized as being conducive to torture.

The revised detention procedures appeared to have some inhibiting effect on the practice of torture. Nevertheless, there were many well-documented reports of torture by police and gendarmes (soldiers carrying out police duties, mainly in rural areas) in many parts of the country. Male and female detainees frequently complained that they were sexually assaulted. The victims included those detained for common criminal offences as well as for offences under the Anti-Terror Law. Children and juveniles were again among the victims. Sixteen-year-old Murat Yiğit reported that he was tortured at a police station in Ankara while detained in January. He stated that he was blindfolded and stripped naked, drenched with cold water, beaten on the soles of his feet and given electric shocks to his penis and feet by police officers who wanted him to sign a confession to a series of burglaries. He was later released without charge. A medical report issued by Ankara Forensic Medicine Institute recorded injuries consistent with his statement.

Hatun Temuzalp, a reporter for a left-wing journal, stated that she was tortured while held for interrogation at Istanbul Police Headquarters for seven days during March. Police officers insulted and threatened her, and pulled some of her clothes off. Her arms were tightly bound to a wooden bar and two people grabbed her, lifted her onto a chair, hung her up, and pulled the chair away. This happened repeatedly. After a period of intense pain she started to lose consciousness. A radiography report indicated a fractured shoulder blade. When brought before a judge, Hatun Temuzalp made a complaint of torture. She was released, but her interrogators were not prosecuted.

In a judgment in September the European Court of Human Rights found that Turkish security forces had tortured Şükran Aydın while she was detained at Derik Gendarmerie Headquarters in Mardin in 1993. She was 17 years old at the time. The Court found that Şükran Aydın had been raped, paraded naked in humiliating circumstances and beaten, and that the Turkish authorities had failed to conduct an adequate investigation into her complaint. The Court ordered the Turkish Government to pay Şükran Aydın compensation of approximately US$41,000.

There were at least six deaths in custody apparently as a result of torture. Fettah Kaya died at Aksaray Police Station in May, after being detained by vice-squad officers at the music hall where he worked. Police authorities reportedly claimed that the 23-year-old man had died of a heart attack, but a detainee who was in custody with him stated that both of them had been tortured by police, who struck them with sandbags.

At least nine people were reported to have "disappeared" in the custody of police or soldiers. In February witnesses saw four armed men, apparently plainclothes police officers, stop Fikri Özgen outside his house in Diyarbakır, check his identity and drive him away. His family made inquiries with all the relevant authorities, who denied that he was detained. In common with several other victims of "disappearance", Fikri Özgen had relatives reported to have PKK connections.

At least 20 people were reported to be victims of political killings, many of which may have been extrajudicial executions. In January Murat Akman was killed during a house raid in Savur, Mardin province, shortly after two security force officers had been killed by the PKK. According to a family member who witnessed the killing, members of the Special Operations Team (a special heavily armed police force unit) came to the door, asking for Murat Akman. When he appeared and showed his identity card, they opened fire, killing him instantly. The family made an official complaint, but by the end of the year those responsible for the killing had not been brought to justice.

The forcible return to their country of origin of recognized refugees and asylum-seekers, including Iraqi and Iranian nationals, continued throughout the year. On several occasions, Amnesty International expressed grave concern to the Turkish Government about these *refoulements*. No response was received.

For the 13th consecutive year there were no judicial executions, although courts continued to pass death sentences.

Armed separatist, leftist and Islamist organizations were responsible for at least 13 deliberate and arbitrary killings of civilians and prisoners. Armed members of the PKK were allegedly responsible for at least 10 of the killings. According to reports, in July PKK members killed Mehmet Özdemir at Üzümlü village, near Eruh in Siirt province, and also abducted Abdullah Teymurtaş from the same village before killing him. In October Merka Akay was taken from her home in Nusaybin, Mardin province, and strangled by PKK members. The Turkish Workers and Peasants' Army (TIKKO) reportedly claimed responsibility for the killing in June of Devrim Yasemin İldırten and Behzat Yıldırım in Istanbul, claiming that they were "traitors and collaborators". The Islamic Raiders of the Great East–Front claimed responsibility for the bombing of a sewage treatment plant in Istanbul in June. Mehmet Şahin Duran, a worker at the plant, was wounded in the blast and subsequently died of his injuries. Amnesty International condemned these grave abuses and publicly called on armed opposition groups to ensure that their members were instructed to respect international humanitarian law and human rights standards.

Throughout the year Amnesty International appealed for the release of prisoners of conscience and urged the government to initiate prompt and independent investigations into allegations of torture, extrajudicial executions and "disappearances". Reports published during the year included *Turkey: Refoulement of non-European refugees – a protection crisis.*

Amnesty International delegates observed several trial hearings, including the January hearing in the trial at Izmir SSC of a group of juveniles who had been tortured at Manisa Police Headquarters in 1996 and subsequently accused of membership of an armed organization, and the final hearing in May of a trial at Adana Primary Court in which Dr Tufan Köse, an employee of a rehabilitation centre for torture victims, was sentenced to a fine for refusing to give officials access to treatment records.

TURKMENISTAN

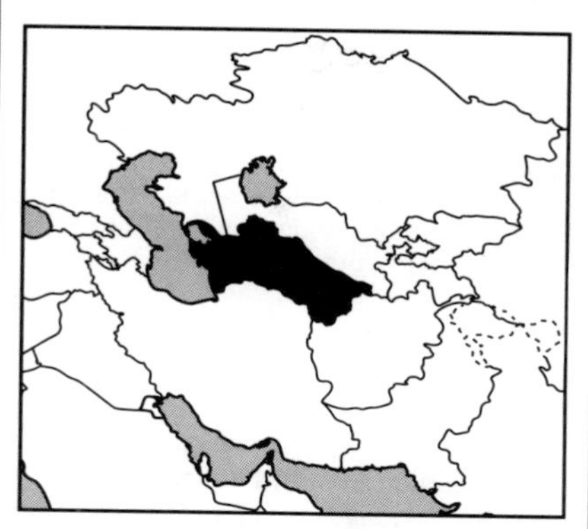

At least three possible prisoners of conscience were serving long prison sentences. One possible prisoner of conscience was detained without charge. Eight political prisoners serving sentences imposed in previous years may have received unfair trials. Cruel, inhuman or degrading prison conditions and other ill-treatment continued to be reported. A government opponent was under threat of forcible repatriation. At least 10 people were executed and at least 35 people were under sentence of death at the end of the year.

In April President Saparmurad Niyazov publicly stated that Turkmenistan's courts often prosecuted "innocent people" instead of real criminals. Announcing the dismissal of the Procurator General, the President complained of widespread incompetence and corruption among law enforcement officials. Further officials were dismissed in July, including the procurator of Lebap Region, who was accused of allowing "the complete merging of law-enforcement agencies with the criminal underworld".

In June the President issued an amnesty decree reportedly covering over 2,000 prisoners. This was believed to be an attempt to address the problem of serious overcrowding and appalling conditions in the country's penitentiaries. The amnesty was reported to include commutation of 222 death sentences, the first official indication that the number of people on death row was as high as had been alleged by unofficial sources.

Also in June a new Criminal Code was approved by the *Majlis* (parliament). It provided for the death penalty for 17 offences, including murder, genocide, various anti-state crimes and a number of drug-related crimes.

In May Turkmenistan acceded to the International Covenant on Civil and Political Rights and its (first) Optional Protocol, to the UN Convention on the Elimination of All Forms of Discrimination against Women and to the International Covenant on Economic, Social and Cultural Rights.

At least three possible prisoners of conscience were serving long sentences, including Mukhametkuli Aymuradov and Khoshali Garayev (see *Amnesty International Reports 1996* and *1997*). There were fears that a charge of drug-trafficking made against Ashirgeldy Syadiyev, serving a 15- or 20-year prison sentence, could have been politically motivated, and that he may be a prisoner of conscience. Taxi driver Ashirgeldy Syadiyev, a relative of a prominent dissident, was living in Ashgabat, the capital, where he and his family were the sole focus of contact between the exiled Khalmurad Soyunov and his relatives. In March a passenger, who had reportedly deliberately chosen Ashirgeldy Syadiyev's taxi from a number of others waiting for fares, left luggage at Ashirgeldy Syadiyev's house. Police searched the house and allegedly discovered narcotics in the passenger's luggage. Ashirgeldy Syadiyev was arrested the same day. The police reportedly made no efforts to trace his passenger. In May Ashirgeldy Syadiyev was tried in Ashgabat City Court and sentenced to death for drug-trafficking after a witness testified to having bought narcotics from him. The witness was not prosecuted. In June the death sentence was commuted under the presidential amnesty.

Yovshan Annakurban, an independent journalist, was arrested in October at Ashgabat airport by members of the Turkmen Committee of National Security (KNB), reportedly to prevent him from attending a training seminar with *Radio Liberty* in Prague, Czech Republic. KNB officials claimed to have found materials by the underground political opposition in his luggage. He was detained for two weeks before being released without charge following international pressure. Yovshan Annakurban had been detained for six months following an anti-government demonstration in July 1995 (see *Amnesty International Reports 1996* and *1997*).

Reports suggested that the "Ashgabat Eight", serving prison sentences in connection with an anti-government demonstration in July 1995 (see *Amnesty International Reports 1996* and *1997*), may have received an unfair trial. Seven – Amanmyrat Amandurdyyev, Khudayberdi Amandurdyyev, Gulgeldi Annanyyazov, Charymyrat Gurov, Begmyrat Khojayev, Kakamyrat Nazarov and Batyr Sakhetliyev – were reported to have received prison sentences in December 1995 or January 1996 of between four and 15 years for a range of crimes, including drug and firearms offences, "malicious hooliganism" and "preparation to commit murder". The trial appeared to have been held in secret, in violation of international fair trial standards. The eighth man, Charymyrat Amandurdyyev, was believed to have been arrested in February 1996. It was not known whether he was subsequently charged or tried, but he was reportedly still held at the end of the year.

There was concern that the "Ashgabat Eight" might have been coerced into testifying against themselves by means of ill-treatment and threats. There were widespread allegations that law enforcement officials beat participants in the 1995 demonstration both at the time of arrest and during preliminary detention (see *Amnesty International Report 1996*).

There was also concern for the current physical well-being of the "Ashgabat Eight". Gulgeldi Annanyyazov was reportedly deliberately held among violent criminals in order to put him at risk of assault, a practice common in the former Soviet Union, of which Turkmenistan was a part. In addition, prisoners routinely suffer overcrowding and severe food shortages, and outbreaks of diseases such as cholera have been reported.

In November former Deputy Prime Minister Nazar Soyunov was detained in Moscow, Russia, by officers of the Russian Federal Security Service and questioned for four hours about criminal charges brought against him in Turkmenistan. There were allegations that the charges, which related to corruption during his time in office, had been fabricated in order to punish him for an interview he had given to *Radio Liberty* in October which was critical of President Niyazov.

At least 10 people were reported to have been executed, although the true figure was believed to be much higher. At the end of the year at least 35 people were believed to remain under sentence of death. Three death sentences – all for alleged drug offences – passed on Gulsere Dzhumayeva, Dunyagozel Ovezdurdyyeva and Ashirgeldy Syadiyev were commuted, the latter two under the presidential amnesty in June. It was not possible to ascertain which other prisoners under sentence of death benefited from the amnesty.

In September Amnesty International expressed concern that Ashirgeldy Syadiyev may have been detained solely because he was related to Khalmurad Soyunov and maintained contact with him. The organization called for a full judicial review of the case and in particular investigation of allegations that the evidence against him was fabricated.

In November the organization urged the authorities to clarify the charges against Yovshan Annakurban and to protect him from any form of ill-treatment.

In a report issued in July, *Turkmenistan: The "Ashgabat Eight" – two years on, time for the truth*, Amnesty International called on the authorities to provide detailed information about the fate of all those arrested following the July 1995 demonstration in Ashgabat and about the conduct of the trial of all those still serving sentences in connection with the demonstration. It also sought assurances that the "Ashgabat Eight" had not been tortured or ill-treated, or placed at risk of violence from fellow inmates.

In April, following the President's admission of widespread judicial error and malpractice in Turkmenistan, Amnesty International reiterated its calls for a judicial review of the criminal convictions of Mukhametkuli Aymuradov and Khoshali Garayev, and asked whether the cases of people arrested after the 1995 demonstration would be re-examined. In November the organization called on the Russian authorities not to extradite Nazar Soyunov to Turkmenistan. Amnesty International renewed calls for a moratorium on the death penalty, arguing that if some of the "innocent people" to whom the President had referred were executed, these mistakes could never be undone. There was no response from any Turkmen official to Amnesty International's appeals and statements.

UGANDA

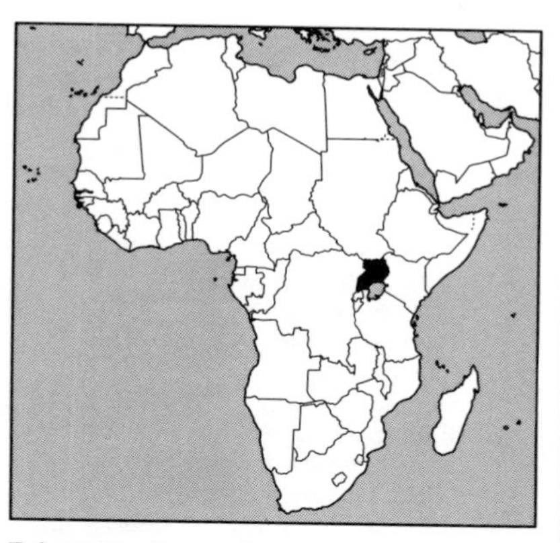

Prisoners of conscience were among hundreds of prisoners detained for short periods without charge or trial. Over 900 alleged members of armed opposition groups were charged with treason, but there was little progress in bringing them to trial. Torture, including rape, and ill-treatment were widespread, resulting in at least seven deaths. Prison conditions were harsh; more than 60 prisoners died as a result. Courts imposed sentences of caning. Soldiers and police were responsible for extrajudicial executions. More than 1,000 prisoners were under sentence of death, including 15 sentenced during the year. Armed opposition groups were responsible for abuses of human rights, including the abduction of hundreds of children, torture including rape, and hundreds of deliberate and arbitrary killings.

Fighting between the Uganda People's Defence Forces (UPDF) and armed opposition movements backed by the Sudanese Government caused the internal displacement of more than 400,000 people in the north, northwest and west. In January more than 60,000 people in the northern district of Kitgum fled assaults by the armed opposition Lord's Resistance Army (LRA), joining 200,000 others already displaced. In the west, the Allied Democratic Front (ADF) attacked both military and civilian targets from bases in the Democratic

Republic of the Congo; more than 170,000 people were displaced. In the northwest, there was a reduction in fighting after military action in February and March against bases in Sudan used by the West Nile Bank Front (WNBF) and the Uganda National Rescue Front-Two (UNRF-II).

Prisoners of conscience were among hundreds of people briefly detained without charge or trial. Most, but not all, detentions took place in the war zones and involved suspected members of armed opposition movements or "rebel collaborators". Kagwe Lawrence p'Owot, a teacher, was detained in Gulu military barracks between February and April, when he was released without charge. In the north detainees were periodically detained in army bases in remote rural areas. In May, three men were detained for two weeks in a pit dug in an army base in Paicho in Gulu District. The men, one of whom had been tortured by having a plastic jerrycan melted onto his body, were freed after the intervention of a visiting Amnesty International team. The soldiers alleged to be responsible were arrested.

Hundreds of alleged members of the WNBF and UNRF-II captured in March and April were detained without charge for several weeks. In June, 234 alleged former members of the WNBF were released. More than 900 other alleged combatants were charged with treason, but trials had not begun by the end of the year. In the past, treason charges – which preclude the granting of bail for 360 days – have been used to hold suspected opponents of the government for long periods without trial.

Torture and ill-treatment were common, especially immediately after arrest; those responsible included police, soldiers, prison warders and government militia. In at least seven cases, torture resulted in death. In May Paulo Kolo died in police custody in Gulu 24 hours after he was arrested and beaten by soldiers. In July Sabiiti Ivan Kisembo died after he was beaten by police. His body was dumped in a Kampala mortuary without identification. In August, nine men were hospitalized in Gulu after soldiers, who were subsequently arrested, beat 21 civilians while searching for a UPDF deserter. In September police and soldiers in Gulu beat and ill-treated at least 20 men during identity checks, including a journalist whose ears were cut with a bayonet.

In northern Uganda soldiers were responsible for raping dozens of women. For example, in March and April soldiers in Awach raped five women, one of whom was forced into marriage with the rapist. Most incidents of rape went unreported because of the social consequences for women.

Courts imposed sentences of caning – a cruel, inhuman or degrading punishment. In February a man received 12 strokes after being convicted of sexually abusing children.

Prison conditions continued to be harsh, with serious overcrowding in many jails. Food shortages, overcrowding and inadequate medical services led to the deaths of 57 prisoners in Arua Prison during the year. An investigation was ordered in December. Nine prisoners in Marokatipe prison died of starvation in July and August. One starving prisoner in the jail died after he was beaten for stealing groundnuts from a prison warder's garden.

Police and soldiers were responsible for at least 20 extrajudicial executions. In July police in Kampala arrested two suspected thieves and shot them dead a few hours later. In August police in Lira tortured Alex Okello, who they claimed was an armed robber, to make him reveal where he had hidden his weapon. They then took him outside the town and shot him dead. In September, four civilians in Omoro, who soldiers claimed were LRA members, were shot dead.

Fifteen men were sentenced to death, including a soldier convicted of murdering a civilian detained in Lubiri military barracks in 1995. By the end of the year more than 1,000 prisoners were under sentence of death.

Armed opposition groups were responsible for gross abuses of human rights, including child abduction, torture including rape, and deliberate and arbitrary killings. In the north, the LRA abducted hundreds of children and forced them to become soldiers; many were held in camps in Sudan. Children were beaten and forced to kill unarmed civilians and captured government soldiers. Hundreds of abducted girls were raped in forced marriages. In January the LRA deliberately and arbitrarily killed more than 490 civilians in Lamwo as punishment for lack of support. Hundreds of civilians were killed in other incidents, in which scores of women were raped. The ADF was also responsible for killings and abductions. For example, in July at least 60 unarmed villagers were killed in villages around Bundibugyo. Nineteen boys studying in a seminary in Kasese were abducted in August and taken to ADF bases in the Democratic Republic of the Congo.

In May an Amnesty International delegation visited northern Uganda to research human rights abuses in the northern war zone. In meetings with military officers and government officials, the delegates raised concerns about the detention without charge or trial and torture of suspected rebel collaborators in rural military outposts. In July a second Amnesty International delegation visited the north to participate in a meeting organized by Ugandan human rights organizations. In September Amnesty International issued a report, *Uganda: 'Breaking God's commands' – the destruction of childhood by the Lord's Resistance Army*, which condemned gross abuses by the LRA and called on it to respect international humanitarian law and international human rights standards. The report also called on the Sudanese Government to end its military and logistical support for the LRA and to intervene to free abducted children. Amnesty International lobbied the UN Committee on the Rights of the Child meeting to discuss Uganda's report on its progress towards implementing the UN Convention on the Rights of the Child. In December Amnesty International raised its human rights concerns in northern Uganda with Ugandan exiles, including government opponents, in the United Kingdom.

UKRAINE

At least 13 prisoners were executed and more than 260 remained under sentence of death at the end of the year. Ill-treatment and torture in detention continued to be reported.

In January the Parliamentary Assembly of the Council of Europe adopted a resolution condemning the continuing executions and threatening Ukraine with eventual expulsion from the Council of Europe should more executions be carried out. Ukraine had committed itself to an immediate moratorium on executions on joining the Council of Europe in November 1995 (see *Amnesty International Reports 1996* and *1997*). In January the Ministry of Justice released figures showing that 167 prisoners were executed in 1996.

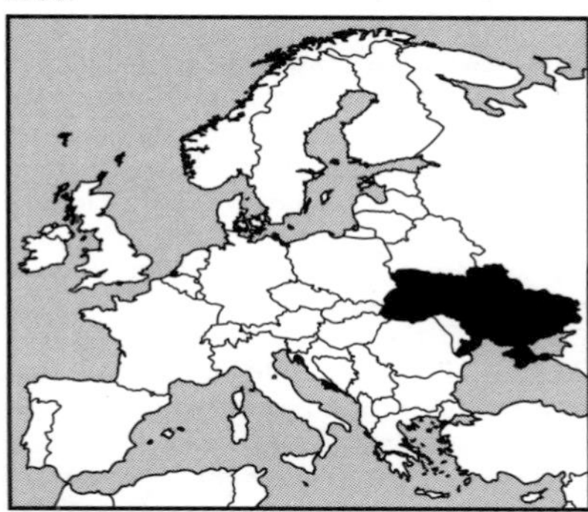

In May Ukraine fulfilled one of the commitments made on joining the Council of Europe by signing Protocol No. 6 to the European Convention for the Protection of Human Rights and Fundamental Freedoms, which provides for the abolition of the death penalty in peacetime. Ukraine ratified the European Convention for the Prevention of Torture and Inhuman or Degrading Treatment or Punishment in May, and the European Convention for the Protection of Human Rights and Fundamental Freedoms in July.

In April the UN Committee against Torture considered Ukraine's third periodic report. The Committee expressed concern at Ukraine's failure to institute an immediate moratorium on executions and warned the government of the consequences should it continue to violate its obligations. The Committee also found that law enforcement officials in Ukraine had tortured and ill-treated detainees, in some cases causing their death. It said that the lack of an effective system for independent scrutiny of complaints and for compensating victims; the lack of provisions for court review of arrest and detention; and the absence of the crime of torture in national legislation, all contributed to these violations. Ukraine was also criticized for the systematic torture of new recruits in the armed forces; inhuman or degrading conditions of pre-trial detention; and failure to ensure access to a lawyer of the detainee's choice. The Committee made specific and extensive recommendations for a comprehensive plan to stop torture in Ukraine.

In November an official Council of Europe fact-finding mission to Ukraine was told that 13 prisoners had been executed between 1 January and 11 March; their petitions for clemency had been rejected by President Leonid Kuchma in November 1996. Officials stated that no further petitions for clemency were rejected and no further executions carried out. Other sources, however, maintained that executions continued beyond March. The mission was informed that 264 prisoners were under sentence of death.

In April the Ukrainian delegation told the UN Committee against Torture that over the previous three years, 529 people had been sentenced to death and 73 had had their sentences commuted. Among those believed to be on death row at the end of the year was Sergey Romanov, who was sentenced to death in July 1997 for premeditated, aggravated murder. There were allegations of serious irregularities in the conduct of pre-trial investigations in his case and reports of ill-treatment in police custody.

Death sentences on Sergey Vysochansky and Andrey Yevtemy were commuted in March and April respectively. Other prisoners under sentence of death, including Vitaly Gumenyuk, were awaiting the outcome of petitions for clemency. Following the Council of Europe fact-finding mission to Ukraine, the Rapporteur of the Committee on Legal Affairs and Human Rights of the Council of Europe issued a report stating that the procedure for carrying out executions "is shrouded in secrecy". In particular, "relatives of executed prisoners are not informed where their sons, husbands or fathers are buried". The report also criticized the conditions in pretrial detention centres where prisoners under sentence of death were held, citing, in particular, lights being left on continuously, the lack of daylight in prisoners' cells, and prisoners not being able to leave their cells except to have a shower once every five to 10 days.

Ill-treatment and torture in detention continued to be reported. In March, Sergey Valkovanysh was reportedly tortured while in police custody in the Donetsk region. He was reportedly beaten, suffering broken ribs, and had a plastic bag placed over his head and filled with gas. Following an official investigation, the Procurator General reportedly refused to open criminal proceedings against the police officers involved because of lack of evidence.

Maksim Pyatigorsky, a 14-year-old boy, was reportedly denied adequate medical care and refused access to his parents while held in pre-trial detention in Lukiyanovska prison from October 1996 to June 1997. The parents of two other boys reportedly lodged complaints that police officers beat their sons until they agreed to testify against Maksim Pyatigorsky.

In August there were reports that Aleksandr Barketov, a prisoner in Krivoy Rog region, was suffering from a wasting condition and skin ulcers, and was passing blood; his health was said to be prejudiced by poor prison conditions. He was serving a two-year prison sentence for deserting from the army, allegedly following incidents of ill-treatment.

In January an Interior Ministry official reported that two of its employees in the Transcarpathian region "carried out illegal actions... during which they caused bodily harm to persons of Gypsy nationality... Information regarding rape of Eva H. by the above members of staff was not confirmed" (see *Amnesty International Report 1997*). The officers were dismissed.

The Procurator General reportedly opened criminal cases against 10 law enforcement officials from the Lviv investigation isolation prison allegedly responsible for the death in custody of Yury Mozola in 1996 (see *Amnesty International Report 1997*). However, during a trial which took place in February and March, the cases were reportedly closed and further investigation requested. No further information was available at the end of the year.

In September Amnesty International wrote to President Kuchma, urging him to take action to stop all executions. In January the organization wrote to the Secretary-General of the Council of Europe conveying its concerns about the continuing use of the death penalty and urging that the Ukrainian Government issue public orders to all prison governors that no further executions be carried out.

Amnesty International submitted a report to the members of the UN Committee against Torture, and met the Ukrainian delegation to discuss implementation of the Committee's recommendations.

The organization asked the Ukrainian authorities to ensure that a full and comprehensive inquiry was instigated into all allegations of torture and ill-treatment.

UNITED ARAB EMIRATES

A prisoner of conscience held beyond the expiry of his sentence was released. At least three possible prisoners of conscience were held throughout the year. Torture and ill-treatment were reported and the use of cruel judicial punishments increased significantly. At least 15 people were sentenced to death and six executions were reported.

The punishment of flogging was extended to traffic offences and reportedly to begging in the Emirate of Ras al-Khaimah.

Prisoner of conscience Elie Dib Ghalib, a Lebanese Christian, was released in July – more than six months after the expiry of his sentence. He had been sentenced to one year's imprisonment and 39 lashes after his marriage to a Muslim United Arab Emirates national was ruled null and void and his relationship therefore a criminal offence under the country's law. No investigation was known to have been carried out into reports that he was tortured and ill-treated in prison. It was not known whether the sentence of flogging was carried out (see *Amnesty International Report 1997*).

Three possible prisoners of conscience detained in June 1996 – brothers Jassim and Yassir 'Issa al-Yassi and Ahmad 'Abdullah Makki – remained held without trial and possibly without charge (see *Amnesty International Report 1997*).

Torture and ill-treatment of detainees continued to be reported.

Cruel, inhuman or degrading punishments, including flogging and amputation, continued to be imposed. At least 19 sentences of flogging were reported for a range of offences – including theft and sexual offences such as adultery – often in conjunction with prison sentences. In April, a Sri Lankan woman and an Indian man were reportedly sentenced to 130 and 90 lashes respectively, and deportation, by a court in Ras al-Khaimah. Also in April, three men convicted of drinking alcohol, assaulting a woman and threatening to kill her, were reportedly each sentenced to 680 lashes and six years' imprisonment by a court in Khawr Faqqan. In June, a court in the Emirate of Fujairah reportedly sentenced two men to 80 lashes and 10 years' imprisonment each for rape; a third defendant was sentenced to 180 lashes and 10 years' imprisonment. It was not known if the sentences had been implemented by the end of the year.

Sentences of amputation were also reported. In April, two men convicted of robbery were sentenced by a court in Fujairah to have their right hands and feet amputated. It was not known whether the sentence had been carried out by the end of the year.

At least 15 death sentences were reported – a significant increase over previous years – and two death sentences imposed in previous years were confirmed. In April, Ahmad Mohammad Amin Bada'u and Mohammad 'Abdullah 'Abdul 'Aziz were reportedly sentenced to death for the kidnap, rape and murder of an eight-year-old girl in October 1996. The outcome of their appeal was not known at the end of the year. In June, Nur Ibrahim, a Pakistan national, was reportedly sentenced to death for drug smuggling by a court in Ras al-Khaimah. Two other men tried in the same case were each sentenced to 80 lashes and life imprisonment.

In April, the Federal Supreme Court in the town of al-'Ain upheld the death sentence imposed on Zad Khan Shah, a Pakistan national, for murder in December

1993. The sentence was awaiting ratification by the President, Al-Sheikh Zayed bin Sultan Al-Nahyan, at the end of the year.

In February the Federal Supreme Court in Abu Dhabi upheld the death sentence against John Aquino, a Philippine national (see *Amnesty International Reports 1996* and *1997*). In September, the Court agreed to allow him until December to seek clemency from the victim's family. At the end of the year he remained under sentence of death.

It was not known whether the death sentence on Mashal Badr al-Hamati, a Yemeni national, had been commuted (see previous *Amnesty International Reports*).

At least six people, including a woman, were executed. In July, three Indian nationals, convicted of murder and sentenced to death in December 1996, were executed by firing-squad in a Dubai prison. The death sentences had been confirmed by the Court of Appeal in April, despite reports that blood money had been paid to the families of the victims, who subsequently waived the punishment against the three men. In September, Majid Fakher Hussain Majid and 'Abdul Mehdi Karim Mushtaq, an Iranian national, were publicly executed by firing-squad in the town of al-'Ain. They had been convicted earlier in the year of the murder of five people during a series of robberies and sentenced to be crucified before being executed. However, the sentence of crucifixion was not carried out. In December Zainab Ramdhan Zaki, an Egyptian national convicted by a court in Ras al-Khaimah of murdering her husband, was executed.

Amnesty International appealed for the release of prisoners of conscience and for the fair trial or release of detainees held for political or religious reasons. It also called for investigations into allegations of torture and ill-treatment. Amnesty International expressed concern at the increased use of the death penalty and called for the commutation of all death sentences and sentences of flogging and amputation. No responses were received from the authorities.

UNITED KINGDOM

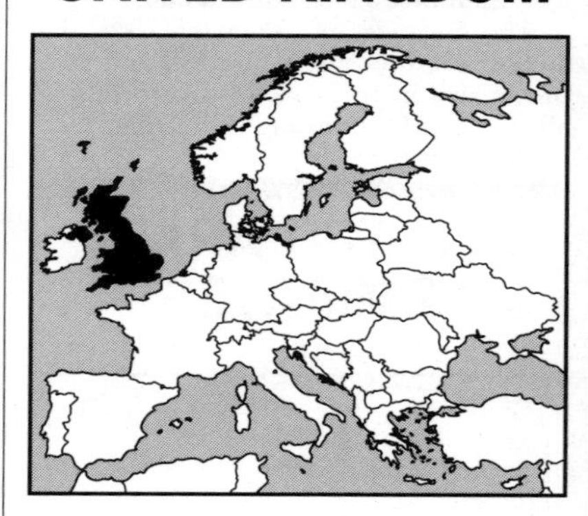

Inquests into deaths in custody underlined the dangers of certain methods of restraint used by law enforcement officers. There were allegations of ill-treatment by police officers, and reports of human rights violations by the security forces during the "parade" season in Northern Ireland. Conditions in Special Security Units constituted cruel, inhuman or degrading treatment. Armed political groups were responsible for human rights abuses.

In September multi-party talks aimed at a political settlement began in Northern Ireland. The inclusion of the Republican political party, *Sinn Féin*, in the talks followed a declaration by the Irish Republican Army (IRA) of a second cessation of military activities in July. Prior to the cessation, the IRA was responsible for a number of bomb attacks and the killing of three members of the security forces. The Continuity Army Council, a Republican armed group, claimed responsibility for several bombings. There were acts of violence by Loyalist armed groups despite the cease-fire. Divisions emerged among the Loyalists, resulting in the disbanding of the Combined Loyalist Military Command – which linked the Ulster Defence Association and the Ulster Volunteer Force – and in the creation of the Loyalist Volunteer Force (LVF), which was responsible for a number of attacks and killings.

In October the new government, which was elected in May, published a bill setting out provisions for the incorporation of the European Convention for the Protection of Human Rights and Fundamental

Freedoms (European Convention) into national law.

Inquests into deaths in custody in England revealed that certain methods of restraint used by law enforcement officers can lead to positional asphyxia. In January the inquest into the death of Kenneth Severin in Belmarsh Prison in November 1995 returned an "open verdict". The post-mortem stated that the most likely cause of death was positional asphyxia. The jury was told that Kenneth Severin died shortly after being forcibly held face down by prison officers. The officers denied applying a neckhold or placing their knees on his back, and kicking and punching him; they could not account for the bruises to his upper back and neck. In October an inquest jury ruled that Ibrahima Sey had been unlawfully killed while in police custody in March 1996. Ibrahima Sey had been handcuffed, sprayed in the face with CS gas, and then held face down for about 15 minutes by several police officers (see *Amnesty International Report 1997*). The coroner recommended an urgent review of police use of CS gas and warned chief constables of "grave public concerns" about methods of restraint and the dangers of positional asphyxia. In December an inquest jury ruled that Dennis Stevens' death in Dartmoor Prison in October 1995 was accidental (see *Amnesty International Report 1996*).

The decisions of the Director of Public Prosecutions (DPP) not to prosecute police officers involved in the deaths in custody of Shiji Lapite and Richard O'Brien (see *Amnesty International Reports 1996* and *1997*) were challenged in the High Court in July. The DPP admitted that the decision-making process had been flawed and agreed to review those decisions. The Police Complaints Authority also stated that its handling of the Shiji Lapite case was "flawed" and that it would reinvestigate. In addition, the Attorney General initiated an independent inquiry into the handling by the prosecution authorities of serious complaints against the police, including cases of death in custody.

In England damages were awarded to many people for ill-treatment by police officers. The European Committee for the Prevention of Torture sent a delegation to the United Kingdom (UK) in September to examine, among other matters, legal remedies in cases involving allegations of ill-treatment by police officers.

During 1997, a large volume of evidence emerged concerning the 1972 Widgery Inquiry into the killing of 13 unarmed people and the wounding of 15 others by British soldiers in Northern Ireland on 31 January 1972 (known as "Bloody Sunday"). The evidence showed that the findings of the inquiry had been seriously flawed. By the end of the year, the government had not made a decision on whether to institute a new inquiry.

Internal inquiries were initiated by the police into several incidents in Northern Ireland involving undercover members of the security forces. In March Gareth Doris was shot and wounded by undercover soldiers shortly after an explosion at a police station in Coalisland. Eye-witnesses alleged that no warning was given before he was shot. He was unarmed. Also in March, masked men, later identified as undercover police officers, reportedly attacked staff and customers in the Derryhirk Inn in Aghagallon near Lurgan; 93 complaints were lodged about the officers' conduct.

There were continued reports of ill-treatment by the security forces in Northern Ireland. The report of an independent review of police complaints procedures in Northern Ireland, published in January, recommended the appointment of a Police Ombudsman to investigate complaints using a staff of independent investigators. The recommendations were incorporated into a police bill which was proposed in December.

In October the installation of video-recording cameras began in the three special interrogation centres in Northern Ireland where suspects arrested under emergency legislation are questioned, and an amended emergency provisions bill was issued proposing that audio-recording should also be installed. The UN Special Rapporteur on the independence of judges and lawyers visited the UK in October to investigate the effects of emergency legislation on lawyers' ability to practise in Northern Ireland, including complaints about police intimidation of lawyers.

Reports were received indicating a continued lack of even-handed policing in Northern Ireland (see *Amnesty International Report 1997*). Robert Hamill, a Catholic, died in May, 11 days after being severely beaten by a large crowd of Protestants in Portadown. Relatives who were with him claimed that Royal Ulster Constabulary (RUC) officers sitting in a parked vehicle at the scene of the beating had not intervened to protect them, despite requests.

During the parades in Northern Ireland in July and August, the security forces fired a large number of plastic bullets, at times indiscriminately, at protesters. Fourteen-year-old Gary Lawlor was in a coma for several days after being hit by a plastic bullet in West Belfast and 13-year-old Maire Walsh, who was standing next to him, was injured in the mouth. It was also reported that the security forces beat and kicked peaceful protesters, resulting in many injuries. Some 200 civil actions were lodged concerning the security forces' conduct in policing a parade in Garvaghy Road, Portadown.

Large stocks of plastic bullets were withdrawn twice during the year, because of faults in their velocity and weight. The publication in August of guidelines on the use of plastic bullets revealed that the RUC guidelines were less stringent than those of the British Army and of police forces in the rest of the UK. A review of the guidelines was initiated by the Association of Chief Police Officers.

Independent medical reports indicated that conditions in Special Security Units, where "exceptional escape risk" Category A prisoners are held, led to a serious deterioration of prisoners' physical and psychological health. In January a trial judge refused to send six prisoners, charged with attempted escape from a maximum security prison in England, for retrial on the grounds that "medical evidence suggests five of the defendants have deteriorated mentally" after being held in such units for lengthy periods of time.

Róisín McAliskey, who was four months pregnant at the time of her arrest in November 1996 (see *Amnesty International Report 1997*), continued to be held in custody pending extradition to Germany for questioning about an IRA attack on an army base. As a Category A prisoner, she was subjected to frequent strip-searches, "closed visits" and severe restrictions throughout her pregnancy on her rights to associate with other prisoners and to exercise. Some restrictions were eased towards the end of her pregnancy, and she gave birth in May in a civilian hospital. She was subsequently transferred on bail to a mother-and-baby secure unit in a London hospital because of her medical condition.

The Chief Inspector of Prisons published thematic reports which were critical of prison conditions for women and young offenders.

The Criminal Cases Review Commission, an independent body responsible for reviewing alleged miscarriages of justice, began work in March. In August the Commission referred the case of Danny McNamee to the Court of Appeal. Danny McNamee had been convicted in 1987 of a bomb attack in London and sentenced to 25 years' imprisonment, solely on the basis of forensic evidence which was reportedly subsequently discredited.

The convictions of four men (known as the "Bridgewater Four") for the murder of 13-year-old Carl Bridgewater in 1978 were quashed in July. Three had been released in February on bail after 17 years' imprisonment; the fourth had died in prison in 1981. The Appeal Court was told that the police had falsified one suspect's confession and then applied undue pressure, including ill-treatment, on another to force a confession.

Patrick Kane was released in June after the Court of Appeal quashed his 1990 conviction in connection with the murder of two army corporals. The convictions of his co-defendants, Sean Kelly and Michael Timmons, had still not been reviewed by the end of the year (see *Amnesty International Report 1994*).

In December the Court of Appeal quashed the conviction of Christopher Sheals for murder in connection with the killing of Margaret Wright, but upheld other convictions. Margaret Wright had been beaten and shot dead in 1994 by a group of men in a hall which displayed insignia of the Red Hand Commando, a Loyalist armed group. The Court rejected the "common purpose" basis for his conviction.

Colin Duffy, whose conviction for murder was quashed by the Court of Appeal in September 1996 (see *Amnesty International Report 1997*), claimed that he continued to be subjected to systematic harassment by the security forces. In June he was charged with the murder of two police officers and detained until October, despite the existence of detailed alibi evidence. In November he was charged with grievous bodily harm of a police officer, although witnesses to the incident stated that Colin Duffy and others had in fact been ill-treated by the police; he was released on bail.

Nineteen people were killed by members of armed political groups in Northern Ireland; 14 deaths were attributed to Loyalists, three to the IRA, and two to the Irish National Liberation Army (INLA). In March John Slane, a Catholic, died after being shot in his home by Loyalists. Sean Brown, a Catholic, was abducted by Loyalists and shot in the head in May. Bernadette Martin, an 18-year-old Catholic, was shot dead by Loyalists at her Protestant boyfriend's house in July. In the same month 16-year-old James Morgan, a Catholic, was found dead. He had been killed by Loyalists and his body mutilated. In December the INLA shot dead Billy Wright, a leader of the LVF, in the Maze prison. The LVF subsequently attacked two bars, killing Seamus Dillon and Eddie Treanor, both Catholics, and wounding eight other people.

Some people died as a result of "punishment" beatings and shootings. Among those allegedly killed by Loyalists were David Templeton, a Presbyterian minister, and Robert Bates, a former Loyalist prisoner. Armed groups were responsible for 150 "punishment" shootings and at least 72 "punishment" beatings of members of their own communities in Northern Ireland. In February, 16-year-old Judith Boylan was tied to a lamp post, beaten, and threatened with an iron bar; her attackers, allegedly members of the IRA, then threw paint on her and hacked off her hair. Sean McNally was shot at close range through the knee by alleged IRA members in June; his right leg had to be amputated at the knee.

In June Amnesty International published a report, *United Kingdom: An agenda for human rights protection*. In October Amnesty International welcomed the government's decision to incorporate the European Convention into national law as a first step towards implementing a much broader range of international obligations. The organization called on the government to ensure that human rights protection would be effective by, among other things, establishing an independent Human Rights Commission.

Amnesty International sent observers to court hearings in connection with the deaths in custody of Shiji Lapite and Richard O'Brien and to the inquests of Ibrahima Sey and Alex Patterson, killed by undercover soldiers in Northern Ireland in 1990. Amnesty International observers attended appeal hearings in other cases in England and Northern Ireland in which the organization had concerns about unfair trial procedures.

Amnesty International repeatedly urged the government to quash the findings of the 1972 Widgery Tribunal and to establish an immediate and full inquiry into the events of "Bloody Sunday". The organization continued to urge the government to investigate the circumstances of the killing of Diarmuid O'Neill in September 1996 (see *Amnesty International Report 1997*).

Amnesty International sent an observer to monitor the policing of some of the parades in Northern Ireland in July.

In March Amnesty International published *United Kingdom: Special Security Units – cruel, inhuman or degrading treatment*, which urged the government to carry out a review of the treatment of Category A prisoners; and in April *United Kingdom: Cruel, inhuman or degrading treatment – detention of Róisín McAliskey*.

Throughout the year, Amnesty International was concerned at reports of human rights abuses by armed political groups in Northern Ireland.

UNITED STATES OF AMERICA

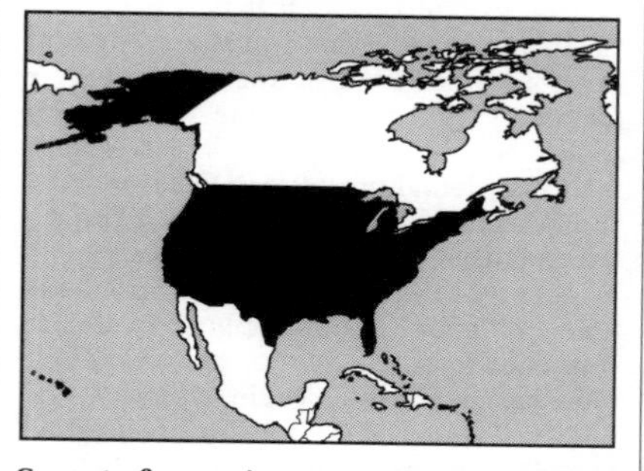

Seventy-four prisoners were executed in 16 states and more than 3,300 remained on death row. There were reports of

shootings in disputed circumstances and torture and ill-treatment by police and prison officers, sometimes resulting in deaths in custody. A prisoner whose prosecution was found to have been politically motivated was released.

In September the UN Special Rapporteur on extrajudicial, summary or arbitrary executions visited the USA.

The death penalty continued to be used extensively. Seventy-four people were executed, bringing the number executed since the end of the moratorium on the death penalty in 1977 to 432.

In Texas, 37 prisoners were executed, including Terry Washington, who was said to have had the mental age of a seven-year-old. The jury which sentenced him to death for murder in 1987 was unaware of his mental illness. Irineo Tristán Montoya, a Mexican national, was executed in Texas in June. He had reportedly signed a four-page confession in English – a language he did not read, speak or understand – after lengthy police interrogation without the presence of a lawyer or the assistance of the Mexican Consulate, in contravention of the UN Vienna Convention on Consular Relations, which the USA has ratified. Of 62 foreign nationals known to be under sentence of death, most had effectively been denied access to consular assistance.

Harold McQueen was the first person to be executed in Kentucky for 35 years. He was executed in July although the jury which sentenced him to death was unaware of crucial mitigating factors, including medical evidence of brain damage. Flint Gregory Hunt, a black man, was executed in July in the first execution to take place in Maryland without the prisoner's consent for 36 years. Of the 17 people on death row in Maryland at the end of the year, 14 were from ethnic minorities. In Colorado the first execution for 30 years took place when Gary Lee Davies was executed by lethal injection in October.

Three men were executed on 8 January in Arkansas. According to reports, Kirt Wainwright, who was awaiting the outcome of a last-minute appeal to the US Supreme Court, lay strapped to a mobile stretcher, with the needle which would administer the lethal dose in his arm, for over 45 minutes before being executed.

Pedro Medina, a Cuban refugee with a history of mental illness, was executed in Florida in March. A malfunction in the 74-year-old electric chair caused Pedro Medina's black leather face mask to burst into flames during his execution.

Joseph O'Dell was executed in July in Virginia despite continuing doubts about the safety of his conviction. He had been convicted of murder in 1986 on the basis of the testimony of a prosecution witness who subsequently testified that he had lied in the hope of receiving a reduced sentence himself. DNA test results which had not been available during the trial contradicted evidence presented by the prosecution. In 1994 the US Supreme Court ruled that juries in capital cases should be told if defendants would have no possibility of parole if sentenced to life imprisonment, but the ruling was not made retroactive. This information had not been given to the jury at Joseph O'Dell's original trial.

In August William T. Boliek Jr was granted a stay of execution. The Governor of Missouri appointed a three-member board of inquiry to investigate claims that William T. Boliek Jr had received inadequate legal representation during his original trial for murder in 1984.

There were further reports of torture and ill-treatment and shootings in disputed circumstances by police. In April Kevin Cedeno, a black teenager, was shot in the back by a New York City Police Department (NYPD) officer. Initial police reports stated that Kevin Cedeno had threatened the officer with a machete. However, other witnesses raised doubts about whether Kevin Cedeno had posed an immediate danger to the officer or to others.

In August Abner Louima, a Haitian, was allegedly tortured and racially abused by NYPD officers. According to reports, he was kicked and beaten in the police car and, on arrival at the station, an officer thrust the handle of a toilet cleaner into his rectum and then jammed it into his mouth. Despite serious injuries, including a punctured small intestine and damage to his bladder, Abner Louima was not taken to hospital for two and a half hours. Two officers were charged with aggravated sexual abuse and another two with beating Abner Louima. Investigations continued at the end of the year and the trials of the police officers were pending.

Allegations of police brutality caused widespread protests in Chicago in several cases, including that of Jeremiah Mearday, a black teenager who suffered serious injuries, including a broken jaw, after he was beaten and allegedly subjected to racial slurs by two white police officers in September. The police department's Office of Professional Standards recommended that both officers be dismissed. A Justice Department investigation was pending at the end of the year.

In June Mexican immigrants Leticia González and Enrique Funes Flores agreed to accept substantial damages in an out-of-court settlement of their claim alleging ill-treatment by the Los Angeles County Sheriff's Department (see *Amnesty International Report 1997*). One of the two deputies involved was dismissed and the other suspended for a month; both were appealing against those decisions at the end of the year.

There were concerns about the use by police of OC spray, a form of pepper spray, which many US police departments permit for the temporary disablement of combative suspects. In June police wearing gas masks reportedly sprayed OC spray at non-violent demonstrators for prolonged periods in Eugene, Oregon. One protester was reportedly beaten and sprayed on various parts of the body, including the face and genitals. He required hospital treatment for burns. An investigation by the Eugene Police Department had not been completed by the end of the year.

In October a police videotape showed sheriff's deputies in Humboldt County, California, swabbing liquid pepper spray directly into the eyes of anti-logging demonstrators. A 17-year-old protester, whose eyelids were prised apart to apply the spray, described acute pain and burning in the eyes. A federal district judge refused to grant a temporary injunction banning police from using pepper spray against non-violent demonstrators. A civil action seeking a permanent injunction and a federal Justice Department civil rights investigation were pending at the end of the year. In November the Attorney General of California announced that he was conducting a state-wide review of the use of the spray by law enforcement officers.

In June Sammy Marshall, a prisoner in San Quentin Prison, California, died of heart failure after prison officers sprayed him periodically with OC spray for more than an hour. A coroner found that the most likely cause of death was an allergic reaction to OC spray.

The case of 15-year-old Frank Arzuega, who was shot dead in January 1996 by an NYPD officer, was closed in March on the grounds that there was insufficient evidence of police misconduct to refer the case to a grand jury (see *Amnesty International Report 1997*).

In April the judge considering the request for a retrial of two police officers from the Pittsburgh area of Pennsylvania – whose trial on charges of the involuntary manslaughter of Johnny Gammage in October 1995 had ended in a mistrial in 1996 – ruled that they could not be retried on the same charges. Another officer, acquitted of manslaughter in the case in November 1996 (see *Amnesty International Report 1997*), was promoted.

In May a New York police officer was convicted of the manslaughter of Nathaniel Gaines Jr, an unarmed black man shot in the back in 1996 (see *Amnesty International Report 1997*), and sentenced to between 18 months' and four and a half years' imprisonment.

In February the federal Justice Department charged the City of Pittsburgh with tolerating a longstanding pattern of civil rights abuses, including brutality, by the Pittsburgh Police Department against citizens, especially members of the black community. While denying allegations of systematic abuses, the city entered into a Consent Decree (a court-supervised agreement), under which it agreed to implement wide-ranging reforms within the police department, including detailed procedures for monitoring officers' behaviour and for improving the investigation of complaints as well as revised policies on the use of force.

This was the first case brought by the Justice Department under legislation passed by Congress in 1994 enabling it to bring civil actions against police departments accused of a "pattern and practice" of abuses. At the end of the year the Justice Department was actively investigating at least three other police departments under these powers.

In November a former NYPD police officer convicted of slapping and choking a teenager in September 1993 was sentenced to seven and a half months' imprisonment. The officer had previously been acquitted of criminally negligent homicide in the death of Anthony Baez in December 1994 (see *Amnesty International Reports 1996* and *1997*), but had subsequently been expelled from the police.

In December an NYPD officer received a sentence of 20 years to life following conviction for the murder of Charles Campbell in 1996 (see *Amnesty International Report 1997*).

There were further reports of cruel, inhuman or degrading treatment in prisons and jails, including the abusive use of restraints such as specially designed chairs with arm and leg shackles (four-point restraint chairs), which completely immobilize the prisoner. In Utah, mentally ill inmates in state prisons were reportedly held in such chairs for several hours or even several days. In March Michael Valent died after being held in a four-point restraint chair for 16 hours. He was reported to have died of a blood clot caused by prolonged immobilization. The Department of Corrections stopped using the restraint chair.

In March the federal Justice Department filed lawsuits against the Departments of Corrections in Arizona and Michigan for failing to protect female inmates from sexual misconduct and invasion of privacy, after a series of complaints by women inmates about abuses by prison guards, including rape and sexual assault.

In July pre-trial hearings were held in the federal lawsuit brought by inmates at Hays State Prison, Atlanta, Georgia, against the Commissioner of Prisons and others. The Commissioner was alleged to have supervised the beating of inmates during a "shakedown" (search) at the prison in July 1996 (see *Amnesty International Report 1997*). Eight prison employees testified in support of the inmates' complaints.

A videotape, apparently compiled for training purposes, showed guards in a privately-run section of Brazoria County Detention Center, Texas, kicking and beating inmates, coaxing dogs to bite prisoners and using stun guns. An investigation by the Federal Bureau of Investigation into the allegations had not been completed by the end of the year. The federal authorities announced an investigation into conditions in other privately-run county jails in Texas which housed hundreds of inmates from Montana and Hawaii, following complaints by inmates about strip searches and the use of warning shots by guards when giving orders.

In October the federal authorities announced that there would be no criminal charges brought following their investigation into the death of Kenneth Trentadue, who allegedly committed suicide in a federal prison in Oklahoma in August 1995 (see *Amnesty International Report 1997*). The District Attorney of Oklahoma County stated that he would continue to investigate whether Kenneth Trentadue's death was a homicide or a suicide.

An Amnesty International observer attended the court hearing in March of Elmer "Geronimo" Pratt, former leader of the Black Panther Party (BPP), who was released in June. His retrial followed the discovery of evidence supporting his allegations that his prosecution had been politically motivated because of his BPP activities (see previous *Amnesty International Reports*). Amnesty International had called for an inquiry into the case since 1981.

Amnesty International continued to call for clemency for prisoners on death row. In October and November two high-level Amnesty International delegations visited Texas and Pennsylvania. They visited death row facilities and raised awareness of death penalty issues, particularly among minority communities.

Amnesty International reiterated its call for an independent inquiry into allegations of brutality and excessive use of force by New York City police.

Amnesty International wrote to the authorities in Eugene, Oregon and Humboldt County expressing concern about the use of pepper spray by police. In a public statement issued in November, Amnesty International called for a national review of the use of pepper spray by law enforcement agencies. The organization said that police departments should either cease using the spray or introduce strict limits on its use.

Amnesty International expressed grave concern about ill-treatment in prisons and jails. In June Amnesty International delegates visited several jails and met officials and others in Maricopa County, Arizona. Among the issues raised in subsequent correspondence were the death of Scott Norberg in Madison Street Jail in June 1996 after a struggle with guards in which he sustained numerous contusions, was repeatedly hit with a stun gun and strapped into a restraint chair; allegations that other inmates in the same jail had been ill-treated; misuse of the restraint chair in other cases; the conditions for female juvenile detainees; and poor conditions in a facility in which jail inmates were housed in tents. Sheriff Joseph Arpaio replied to Amnesty International in October stating, among other things, that any instances of excessive force were adequately dealt with by the jail authorities, and defending the use of the restraint chair and stun devices. However, in October Maricopa County reached an agreement with the federal Justice Department to improve conditions in the tents and to revise its procedures on the use of restraints, stun guns and force.

In July Amnesty International called on the Governor of Utah to ensure that multipoint restraints were used only as a last resort, within strict time limits and under the direct supervision of adequately trained staff. The organization expressed concern to the Texan authorities about the death of Daniel Avellaneda, who was shot and killed by a corrections officer at French Robertson Unit in July 1996. The authorities replied that he was shot while trying to escape and that such use of lethal force was lawful in Texas. A grand jury had previously exonerated the officer involved.

In November Amnesty International wrote to the California Department of Corrections expressing concern about the death of Sammy Marshall and to the California Attorney General, welcoming his announcement of a review of the use of OC spray by state law enforcement agencies and urging him to include in the review the use of OC spray in prisons and jails.

URUGUAY

Two former prisoners of conscience had not yet had their release upheld by the Supreme Court of Justice. Prisoners were reportedly ill-treated during a prison protest. Human rights violations committed in past years remained unclarified.

In March Senator Rafael Michelini filed a complaint before a judge claiming that a retired army general had informed him that some detainees who "disappeared" under previous military governments had died under interrogation, and were secretly buried (see *Amnesty International Reports 1974* to *1986*). In April the judge ordered an investigation into the complaint. However, in June an appeal court overturned the judge's decision by invoking the 1986 Expiry Law. This law exempts all military and police personnel responsible for human rights violations committed between 1973 and 1985 from being punished (see *Amnesty International Report 1987*). The ruling by the appeal court was issued despite observations made by the Inter-American Commission on Human Rights in 1992, and by the UN Human Rights Committee in 1993, that the Expiry Law contravened the American Convention on Human Rights and the International Covenant on Civil and Political Rights. The authorities had failed to implement the recommendation of the UN Human Rights Committee that the government adopt legislation correcting the effects of the Expiry Law. However, in December the government annulled by decree rulings that had been made against 41 army officers who had been tried, imprisoned and expelled from the army during the period of military rule for their political opinions.

In May Congress received a bill on the right to seek asylum in Uruguay from President Julio María Sanguinetti and other members of the government. The bill states that "all foreign nationals whose situation complies with international treaties and conventions on asylum-seekers and refugees will have their refugee status recognized and, therefore, may be granted asylum". However, the bill denies asylum to people who commit a range of acts, including acts "against a country's sovereignty or contrary to its fundamental interests", or who come from a country defined as "safe". Amnesty International believed the provisions of the bill would weaken the right to seek asylum and contravene international standards on refugees. By the end of the year the bill had not been debated by Congress.

The Supreme Court of Justice had yet to decide whether to uphold or quash the conditional release in 1996 of former prisoners of conscience Federico and Carlos Fasano (see *Amnesty International Report 1997*).

In June prisoners in Libertad Prison in Montevideo, the capital, protested against having their exercise time curtailed. Guards ordered the prisoners out of their cells while firing weapons at the ceiling. At least 24 prisoners were reported to have been beaten and one prisoner was shot in the leg. A Congressional human rights commission received a complaint about the prisoner shot in the leg, but was not known to have conducted an investigation into the incident.

Members of the security forces accused of human rights violations committed under past governments, including the "disappearance" and subsequent extrajudicial execution of Eugenio Berrios, remained unpunished (see previous *Amnesty International Reports*).

In May Amnesty International reiterated previous calls on the authorities to ensure a full and independent investigation into human rights violations committed under past military governments, and to bring those responsible to justice.

UZBEKISTAN

Two imprisoned Islamic leaders were possible prisoners of conscience. Scores of possible prisoners of conscience were detained and ill-treated following the murder of several officials. One human rights activist was beaten by police. One Islamic activist reportedly "disappeared" and three others remained "disappeared". At least two executions took place. Further death sentences were believed to have been passed and carried out, but no reliable information was available.

In January the Ministry of Justice refused registration to the Human Rights Society of Uzbekistan. The Society, which had formerly operated underground and in exile, had been officially invited to submit a registration application (see *Amnesty International Report 1997*, which mistakenly reported actual registration). In May the Independent Human Rights Organization of Uzbekistan applied to the city government of Tashkent, the capital, to hold a founding congress; this was one of the procedures required for registration. The city government failed to respond to the application ahead of the congress's scheduled date, thereby effectively denying registration to the organization. In December the Ministry of Justice refused to register the organization, stating that the address on the application form was incomplete.

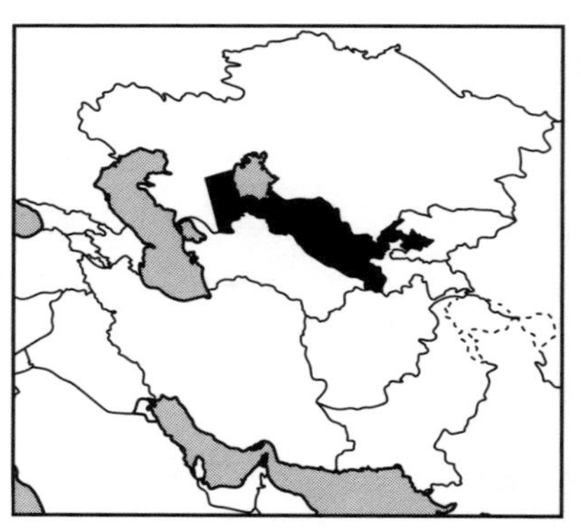

In May, following military action in northern Afghanistan, the Uzbek authorities closed the border crossing point on the Amu Darya river which provided the safest route back to Tajikistan for thousands of Tajiks who sought refuge in Afghanistan in 1992, at the height of Tajikistan's civil war, and who were returning as part of a UN High Commissioner for Refugees (UNHCR) repatriation program. Refugees and distributors of humanitarian aid were permitted to cross by barge following talks between President Islam Karimov and senior UN officials, but the bridge over the river remained closed.

Two leaders of Islamic congregations not affiliated to the state-regulated Muslim Spiritual Directorate were possible prisoners of conscience. Abdurauf Gafurov, formerly the elected *kazi* (Muslim judge) of the Fergana Valley, was serving a two-year prison sentence for "disobeying the legal demands of the penitentiary administration" imposed in December 1996. The charge had been brought one week before a previous three-year term of imprisonment for "embezzlement of state and social property through misuse of official position" was due to expire. In 1994 he had been convicted of possession of narcotics and so failed to qualify for release under an amnesty; this charge was brought only three weeks before the amnesty was due to come into effect.

It appeared possible that the charges against Abdurauf Gafurov had been fabricated, and that the real motive for his continuing imprisonment was to prevent him from playing a prominent role in the unregistered Islamic community. At the end of the year he was held in Kyzyl-tepe corrective labour colony in Navoiy region, which was said to have some of the worst prison conditions in Uzbekistan.

In June Rakhmat Otakulov, a religious teacher, was sentenced to three and a half years' imprisonment for possession of illegal weapons and narcotics. He had been detained for questioning in April – ostensibly about a road traffic accident – but after a search of his car and home, police claimed to have discovered bullets and narcotics. According to reports, the arresting officers' evidence, which formed the basis for the charges against him, was not seriously scrutinized in court, and two civilians enlisted by the police as witnesses to the searches of Rakhmat Otakulov's car and home gave contradictory evidence under cross-examination. It was feared that the charges against Rakhmat Otakulov may have been fabricated and that the incriminating evidence had been planted by police; this was an established practice used against political opponents of the government, particularly during 1993 and 1994.

In December more than 100 people were reported to have been arbitrarily detained in the eastern town of Namangan following the murder of several police officers and regional officials. Police reportedly detained young men with beards arbitrarily, calling them "Wahhabists" (members of a strict Islamic sect). All those detained were reported to have been beaten and ill-treated in detention. It was alleged that weapons and narcotics were openly planted on some detainees in order to fabricate a criminal case against them. Abdumalik Nazarov, the youngest brother of independent Islamic leader Obidkhon Nazarov, was detained in late December at the Uzbek-Kyrgyz border together with his father and an older brother. He was held in pre-trial detention in Fergana and later charged with possession of narcotics. It was alleged that the narcotics were planted by police officers during a search of the car. Abdumalik Nazarov and his brother Umarkhon had been detained for questioning in Namangan several days earlier.

In December Mikhail Ardzinov, chairman of the Independent Human Rights Organization of Uzbekistan, was detained by police in Samarkand for 20 hours, badly beaten, and forcibly returned to Tashkent. He had travelled to Samarkand with Jomol Mirsaidov, a member of the Independent Human Rights Organization and leader of the Tajik minority in Uzbekistan, to attend a constituent meeting of the National Culture Centre of ethnic Tajiks. Jomol Mirsaidov was also detained and sentenced to 10 days' administrative arrest. It was alleged that the two men were detained in order to prevent the constituent meeting of the National Culture Centre of ethnic Tajiks from taking place.

Albert Musin, a journalist and monitor of human rights developments in central Asia living in exile, was detained in February by Moscow police but released in early March, shortly after Uzbek Embassy officials in Moscow stated that his extradition to Uzbekistan was not being sought.

In September Nematjon Parpier, an Islamic activist from Andizhan, reportedly "disappeared". He was an assistant to Abduvali Mirzoyev (see below) and was apparently involved in an independent investigation into the "disappearance" of Abduvali Mirzoyev when he himself reportedly "disappeared".

There was no further information concerning Abdullo Utayev and Abduvali Mirzoyev, two Islamic religious activists who "disappeared" in 1992 and 1995, respectively (see previous *Amnesty International Reports*). In February 1997 the Internal Affairs Directorate of the city of Andizhan placed a "missing person's" appeal in the local newspaper on behalf of Ramazan Matkarimov, who "disappeared" in 1995 with Abduvali Mirzoyev.

Death sentences were believed to have been passed and carried out, but no official information was available. At least two executions took place. The true figure was believed to be much higher.

Information came to light of five death sentences passed in 1996 in addition to the 12 reported in *Amnesty International Report 1997*. Tuychi Akhtamov, Khusnitdin Kasymov, Saitniyaz Sharipov and Yodgor Toshpulatov had been convicted of drug-trafficking; Aleksandr Korneyev had been sentenced to death for murder. There were fears that they faced imminent execution. The organization also learned that Jahongir Gofurov, sentenced to death in 1995, had been executed in May 1996. His death certificate, however, was only issued in January 1997 and then passed to his mother.

A clemency petition in the case of Shokir Davronov, sentenced to death in 1994, was still outstanding in early 1997. However, it was feared that he may have been executed but the information withheld from his family.

Amnesty International called for a full judicial review of the cases of Abdurauf Gafurov and Rakhmat Otakulov. The organization called for the disclosure of the charges against all those arrested in Namangan and for a full and impartial inquiry into the allegations of beatings and ill-treatment. It sought further information about the charges against Abdumalik Nazarov and called for investigations into the beating of Mikhail Ardzinov and the administrative arrest of Jomol Mirsaidov.

Amnesty International called for clarification of the whereabouts of Nematjon Parpier and the organization continued to seek information concerning the three missing Islamic activists. It called on the President to commute all death sentences and to abolish the death penalty.

VENEZUELA

At least 10 prisoners of conscience were detained during the year. Torture by the security forces was widespread, in some cases leading to death. Prison conditions amounted to cruel, inhuman or degrading treatment. Scores of people, including children, were extrajudicially executed by the security forces.

In January President Rafael Caldera declared 1997 to be human rights year. However, constitutional guarantees, including the right not to be arrested without a warrant, remained suspended in areas bordering Colombia (see *Amnesty International Report 1997*).

In October the Supreme Court annulled the *Ley de Vagos y Maleantes,* Law of Vagrants and Crooks, which permitted administrative detention by the police without judicial review. However, hundreds of people detained previously under that law remained in prison.

The report of the UN Special Rapporteur on torture about his 1996 visit to Venezuela was presented in March (see *Amnesty International Report 1997*). It documented the prevalence of torture and impunity for perpetrators, and included significant recommendations. However, most perpetrators of human rights violations continued to benefit from impunity. Seven officials imprisoned for the massacre of 14 fishermen by soldiers in El Amparo in 1988 were released on bail by military courts in November (see *Amnesty International Report 1997*).

At least 10 prisoners of conscience were detained for short periods. All alleged that they had been tortured or ill-treated. In March Félix Faría Arias, a student and human rights activist, was detained by members of the *Dirección de los Servicios de Inteligencia y Prevención* (DISIP), Directorate of Intelligence and Prevention Services, in Baruta, near Caracas, the capital. He was interrogated and tortured with beatings, electric shocks, burns and death threats. He was released without charge the next day, but continued to receive threats, and was detained once more in October by members of the DISIP. He was again tortured for hours with electricity, beatings and death threats.

In April Wilma Rauseo, a trade union activist, was arrested without warrant in Caracas by members of the DISIP, who also arrested her colleagues Graciela Aguirre García and Marisela Baoda Medina two days later. They were all held incommunicado for several days, interrogated and threatened with death. They were then held in military prisons. Wilma Rauseo and Marisela Baoda Medina were released without charge in August, but Graciela Aguirre García remained in detention until October.

In October Yonny Orlando Mora, a trade union and community activist, was arbitrarily detained by members of the *Guardia Nacional,* National Guard, in Cantón, Apure state, for having helped a human rights advocate to document gross human rights violations by the army in the region (see below). He was held incommunicado for several days and told that he and his family would be killed. He was released without charge in mid-November.

Torture by the security forces, including the army, continued to be widespread. No perpetrator was convicted of torture. Victims included children and community activists. Beatings, electric shocks, suspension from wrists or ankles for prolonged periods of time, near-asphyxiation with plastic bags and mock executions were used to extract confessions from suspects and to intimidate detainees. Confessions extracted under torture continued to be accepted as evidence by the courts. State attorneys regularly failed to act effectively on complaints of torture and official forensic doctors frequently avoided documenting cases of torture. Medical treatment for detainees who had suffered torture continued to be unavailable. Torture was widespread and systematic in the region bordering Colombia, where the Venezuelan security forces responded to incursions by Colombian armed opposition groups with widespread repression against the civilian population, whom they suspected of collaborating with such groups.

In June, 16-year-old Rafael Guillén Dugarte was arrested by members of the DISIP and the National Guard in Mérida, Mérida state, and tortured with beatings and electric shocks to force him to confess to a robbery he did not commit. He was released for medical treatment for his serious injuries. Wilfredo Alvarado Baldaggio, a community activist, was arbitrarily arrested by members of the National Guard in Barquisimeto, Lara state, in July and held incommunicado in a local state police station. He was hung from the wrists and subjected to beatings, electric shocks and mock executions while being interrogated and threatened about his role in local land disputes. He was released after six days, but was forced to leave his town following threats and harassment by local authorities. In October Yuraima Lara, a student activist, was arbitrarily detained by members of the *Policía Municipal de Sucre*, Sucre Municipal Police, in Caracas. She was transferred to local DISIP headquarters, where she was interrogated, beaten and subjected to electric shocks, mock executions and threats of rape. She was released six days later and required urgent hospital treatment for her injuries.

Those who died as a result of torture included 16-year-old Jimmy Canelón Durán, who was arrested without warrant by the Metropolitan Police at his home in Caracas in April. His mother, who witnessed the arrest, was informed the next morning that he had died in a shoot-out with the police, despite evidence that he had been tortured. Those responsible were not brought to justice.

Prison conditions remained extremely harsh, often amounting to cruel, inhuman or degrading treatment. Despite the government's acknowledgment of poor conditions in prisons throughout the country, they were not improved. Serious overcrowding, insanitary conditions and inadequate medical care led to dozens of protests by inmates. In March inmates in El Dorado prison, Bolívar state, staged a peaceful protest against human rights violations by warders, including torture, but no action was taken by the authorities. In August, 29 inmates were killed and at least 10 wounded in the prison, during a clash between rival gangs. Warders failed to intervene to prevent or stop the killings, despite warnings from local officials and relatives that tensions were reaching crisis point. In October hundreds of inmates in La Planta prison in Caracas went on hunger-strike to demand improved conditions and an end to systematic beatings by warders. In November, 16 inmates died and 32 were badly injured when a fire broke out inside the seriously overcrowded prison of Sabaneta, in Maracaibo, Zulia state. Previous demands from inmates to improve the appalling conditions in that prison, including serious fire hazards which led to the tragedy, had been largely ignored by the relevant authorities.

Scores of people, including children, were extrajudicially executed by the security forces. Those responsible were rarely brought to justice, and the relatives of victims had no effective recourse before the law to seek redress and compensation. In March Rubén Darío González was arbitrarily detained in Barcelona, Anzoátegui state, by members of the *Dirección de Inteligencia Militar*, Military Intelligence Directorate, who forced him into a vehicle and shot him in the head in front of several witnesses, including relatives. The officials claimed he had been caught committing a crime, but witnesses disputed this. In May, 16-year-old Erick Jean Lucena was arbitrarily detained, badly beaten and shot at point-blank range in Caracas by members of the *Policía Metropolitana*, Metropolitan Police, who reportedly mistook him for a criminal. Witnesses prevented the police from planting a weapon on the victim, but those responsible for the killing were not brought to justice. Seventeen-year-old Jean Carlos Camacho Delgado died in similar circumstances in May, when he was shot at point-blank range by a member of the Metropolitan Police in Caracas.

In May, eight-year-old Yasser Smith Guzmán Luzón was killed by members of the Metropolitan Police who fired their weapons indiscriminately into a neighbourhood, apparently in order to intimidate petty criminals. In June Eduardo Richard Aristigueta Peña was stopped by members of the Metropolitan Police near his home in Caracas, and shot in the face in front of relatives. The police later claimed he was a criminal, despite lack of evidence.

The perpetrators of dozens of extrajudicial executions in 1996, including that of 13-year-old Lian Jonathan Cáseres Herrera, were not brought to justice (see *Amnesty International Report 1997*).

In October Amnesty International published a report, *Venezuela: The silent cry – gross human rights violations against children*, documenting the widespread but under-reported pattern of human rights violations against children in Venezuela, and their lack of means to seek redress and compensation for such abuses. During the year, Amnesty International appealed on behalf of dozens of victims of human rights violations.

VIET NAM

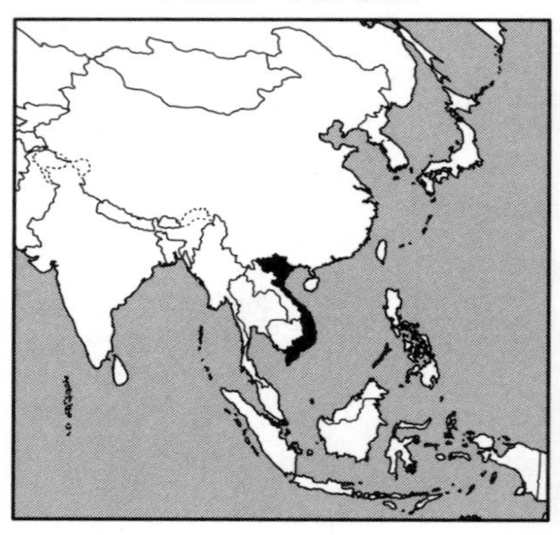

At least 49 prisoners of conscience and possible prisoners of conscience continued to be held throughout the year. One prisoner of conscience was tried. Two prisoners of conscience were released. One political prisoner was known to have been arrested. At least 56 people were sentenced to death. Nine people were officially reported to have been executed, but the actual number was believed to be much higher.

In September members of the National Assembly elected in July approved the appointment of a new President, Tran Duc Luong, Prime Minister Phan Van Khai, and other ministerial changes. In December General Le Kha Phieu replaced Do Muoi as Secretary General of the Communist Party of Viet Nam. New legislation was introduced in April providing for restrictions, including up to two years' monitoring, on people alleged to have acted unlawfully who are not formally prosecuted. Restrictive regulations limiting freedom of expression were issued throughout the year on the use of the media, cooperation with foreign media and the activities of foreign journalists. The government ran national campaigns against corruption and "social evils" such as drug abuse. Serious social unrest provoked by economic difficulties and alleged fraud and corruption by local officials in the northern province of Thai Binh was reported in May and June, and again in November. Allegedly violent demonstrations involving thousands of people were reported in southern Dong Nai province in November, reportedly instigated by local corruption and the confiscation of land. Lack of official information and restrictions on freedom of expression made obtaining details of human rights violations difficult.

At least 49 prisoners of conscience and possible prisoners of conscience arrested in previous years continued to be detained. Dr Nguyen Dan Que, sentenced to 20 years' imprisonment in 1991 after founding the High Tide of Humanism movement, an unauthorized organization calling for peaceful political and economic change, was reported to be in deteriorating health. The charges against him included membership of Amnesty International (see *Amnesty International Reports 1991* and *1992*). Suffering from severe dental problems, he was unable to eat solid foods and had recurrent duodenal ulcers (see *Amnesty International Report 1996*). The health of Dong Tuy, sentenced to 11 years' imprisonment for his membership of the Movement to Unite the People and Build Democracy, continued to give cause for concern (see *Amnesty International Reports 1996* and *1997*). Six other members of the Movement imprisoned with Dong Tuy included its leader, Nguyen Dinh Huy, a professor of English and history sentenced to 15 years' imprisonment in 1995.

Prisoners of conscience held for their religious beliefs remained in detention. They included two leaders of the unofficial Unified Buddhist Church of Viet Nam (UBCV): its Supreme Patriarch, Thich Huyen Quang, held without charge or trial for almost 13 years, and its Secretary-General, Thich Quang Do, serving a five-year sentence. Six members of the Catholic Congregation of the Mother Co-Redemptrix were reported to be suffering from poor health including general weakness, severe arthritis, high blood pressure and heart conditions (see *Amnesty International Report 1996*). Throughout the year the government denied that it held any political prisoners.

In October Nguyen Hoi was sentenced to three years' imprisonment for "abusing freedom and democratic rights and violating interests of the state and social organizations", after being detained without trial for two years. According to an official report, he had been arrested in October 1995 with newsletters containing articles which criticized the government and its policies on religion. He was accused of being a member of the unofficial UBCV. He was believed to be a prisoner of conscience.

Two prisoners of conscience were released during the year. Le Hong Ha, a former Interior Ministry official and senior member of the Communist Party of Viet Nam, had been arrested in December 1995 and sentenced to two years' imprisonment in August 1996 for divulging national secrets (see *Amnesty International Reports 1996* and *1997*). He was released in August, four months before the end of his sentence. Pham Duc Kham, co-author of *Freedom Forum*, a newsletter critical of the government, was arrested in 1990 and sentenced to 12 years' imprisonment in March 1993. He had been in poor health in detention (see *Amnesty International Report 1997*). He was released at the beginning of September, five years before the expiry of his sentence, and allowed to join his family in the USA. According to a Foreign Ministry official, his sentence was shortened under a presidential amnesty for National Day and because of his "good behaviour while serving his sentence". It was also learned that prisoner of conscience Brother Vu Thanh Dat (Hai) had been released in late 1996. A member of the Catholic Congregation of the Mother Co-Redemptrix, he had been sentenced to 10 years' imprisonment in 1987 (see *Amnesty International Reports 1996* and *1997*).

In October the editor of a business newspaper, Nguyen Hoang Linh, was arrested for allegedly violating laws relating to national secrets. The precise charges against him were not known. He had been demoted from his post as editor-in-chief in September after he had written a series of articles alleging that customs officials were corruptly involved in purchasing four patrol boats. At the end of the year he remained in detention without trial. He was a possible prisoner of conscience.

At least 56 people were sentenced to death. In January, six men were sentenced to death in two separate trials for the economic offences of embezzlement and corruption. Both trials were widely publicized as part of the government campaign against corruption. In March Nguyen Thi Hiep, a Canadian woman of Vietnamese origin, was sentenced to death for drug-trafficking. In another showcase trial, seven men and two women, some of them public officials, were sentenced to death in May and June for involvement in drug-trafficking. Nine people were officially reported to have been executed, but it was believed that the actual number of executions was much higher. Duong The Tung was executed in April; he had been sentenced to death in 1996 for the murder of a policeman and was reportedly tortured in custody (see *Amnesty International Report 1997*). In June, six men found guilty of murder and armed robbery were executed in Ho Chi Minh City, in front of thousands of people. Another man, Nguyen Nhan Tai, was executed in June in An Giang province for embezzlement. In August Phan Huu Ha was executed for murder in front of hundreds of people in Lao Cai province.

Throughout the year Amnesty International appealed for the release of all prisoners of conscience, and for an improvement in conditions of detention. The organization expressed concern at reported executions and called for the commutation of all death sentences and the abolition of the death penalty. In October the organization expressed concern about the arrest of newspaper editor Nguyen Hoang Linh and asked for further information about his detention. By the end of the year Amnesty International had received no response from the government.

YEMEN

One prisoner of conscience remained under sentence of death for the 15th year. Scores of suspected political or religious opponents of the government, including possible prisoners of conscience, were detained during the year; at least 27 of them were on trial, some on charges carrying the death penalty. Twenty political prisoners, most of them sentenced to death, remained in prison. Torture and ill-treatment continued to be reported and at least two people were reported to have died in custody, possibly as a result of torture. The judicial punishment of flogging was widely imposed and at least three sentences of amputation were passed. The fate and whereabouts of hundreds of people who "disappeared" in previous years remained unknown. At least five people were executed and scores of others were sentenced to death. The cases of hundreds of people sentenced to death in previous years were at different stages of the appeal process.

The second legislative elections since the unification of Yemen were held in April. The ruling General People's Congress (GPC) of President 'Ali 'Abdullah Saleh won 187 of the 301 seats of the Council of Deputies (parliament). Its former coalition partner, the Islamic Yemeni Congregation for Reform (*al-Islah*) party, won 53 seats. The remaining seats were won by independent candidates and smaller opposition parties. The Yemeni Socialist Party (YSP), a member of the ruling coalition until the civil war of 1994, and a number of smaller parties boycotted the elections following disagreement with the government on election procedures.

One prisoner of conscience, Mansur Rajih, remained under sentence of death in Tai'z Central Prison for the 15th year (see *Amnesty International Reports 1996* and *1997*). His sentence had not been ratified by the President at the end of the year.

Scores of suspected political or religious opponents of the government, including possible prisoners of conscience, were detained during the year following waves of arrests, particularly at the end of July after a series of bomb explosions in Aden. They were arrested without warrants and denied access to family and lawyers. Those targeted for arrest included members and sympathizers of legally registered parties such as *Rabitat Abna' al-Yemen*, League of the Sons of Yemen, and the YSP, as well as people suspected of having links with *al-Jabha al-Wataniya Lilmu'ardha*, National Front for the Opposition, an opposition organization based abroad. Most of those arrested were released after short periods, but at least 27 of the detainees were charged in connection with the bombings in Aden and brought to trial in November before the Criminal Court of Sira in Aden. The defendants included Nabil Kanakli Kasaybati, a Spanish national of Syrian origin, who was charged with planning acts of sabotage and assassination which are punishable by death. Some of the defendants reportedly alleged that they had been tortured to force them to confess. The trial was in progress at the end of the year.

Twenty political prisoners, suspected members of the former *al-Jabha al-Wataniya al-Dimuqratiya*, National Democratic Front (NDF), an opposition organization in the former Yemen Arab Republic, continued to serve their sentences. Most of them were under sentence of death (see *Amnesty International Report 1997*). They included Muhammad Ahmad 'Abdullah al-Zahayj and Muhammad Mahdi Makhrouf, who remained in Dhamar Central Prison under sentence of death. Both were sentenced on charges of murder in 1986 following trials which fell short of international standards and despite having been previously acquitted of the charges against them. Their sentences had not been ratified by the President by the end of the year.

No information was available about the progress of the trial of Adam Salah al-Din Mansur, an Algerian national, and 20 Yemeni nationals that began in 1995 (see *Amnesty International Reports 1996* and *1997*).

Torture and ill-treatment continued to be reported and at least two people were reported to have died in custody in circumstances which suggested that torture may have been a contributory factor. Wadi' Sheibani and 'Adel al-Zabidi, who had been suspected of involvement in a series of explosions in Aden in July, died in Solaban Prison in October. The exact circumstances of their deaths were unclear. No investigation into their deaths was known to have been instigated by the end of the year.

The judicial punishment of flogging was widely imposed. Defendants often had no opportunity to appeal to a higher court as most punishments were carried out immediately after the sentence was passed. In some cases, however, the verdict was subject to appeal. In May 'Abd al-Jabbar Sa'ad and his brother 'Abdullah Sa'ad, editor of the weekly opposition newspaper *al-Shura*, were sentenced to 80 lashes each after they were convicted of writing and publishing a series of articles critical of Sheikh 'Abd al-Majid Zendani, a leading politician in *al-Islah*. An appeal was believed to be in progress at the end of the year.

At least three people were sentenced to amputation of limbs. In January a Court of First Instance in Hadramout province was reported to have sentenced three men to cross-amputation (severing of the right hand and the left foot) on charges of highway robbery. It was not clear whether these sentences or those passed in previous years were carried out or commuted upon appeal.

The fate and whereabouts of hundreds of people who "disappeared" in previous years remained unknown. Undertakings made by the government to investigate the cases of those who "disappeared" since 1994, including Farazdaq Fuad Qa'ied, were apparently not implemented (see *Amnesty International Report 1997*).

At least five people were executed during the year and scores of others were sentenced to death, often following trials which fell short of international norms for a fair trial in death penalty cases. For example, Muhammad Ahmad Mislah al-Nadhiri, a building contractor who reportedly suffered psychological problems, was publicly executed in April after he was convicted of multiple murder. He had been sentenced to death only a week earlier following a single trial hearing which lasted approximately four hours.

Yahya Hadi Jazilan, a police officer, and Faisal Saleh Adham al-'Amlisi were sentenced to death and public crucifixion on charges of murder. The two men were executed just two weeks later at the end of

July and their bodies were displayed in the crucifix position for one day.

Jalal 'Abdullah al-Rada'i and 'Abdullah 'Ali Idris al-Rada'i were sentenced to death and crucifixion in August on charges of highway robbery and murder following court hearings which appeared to breach international standards for fair trial. Both men were reported to have been denied access to legal assistance and were sentenced after three court sessions which appeared to have been summary. The sentences against them were upheld by a court of appeal and were believed to remain pending before the Supreme Court at the end of the year.

Hundreds of people sentenced in previous years remained under sentence of death. Among them was Muhammad Hussein 'Ali al-Zandani, whose sentence was upheld by the Supreme Court during the year and reportedly ratified by the President in August. He was reported to have been scheduled for execution three times between August and October, but was given a stay of execution on each occasion following appeals by his lawyer and family for a review of his case, including on grounds of age. Muhammad Hussein 'Ali al-Zandani, whose family and lawyer argued that he was aged 16 at the time of the crime, was sentenced to death on murder charges in 1995. The Penal Code prohibits the imposition of the death penalty on anyone who was under the age of 18 at the time of the offence.

The death sentences on Sabah al-Difani and 'Ali Ahmad Qassim al-Khubayzan (see *Amnesty International Report 1996*) were reportedly under appeal.

In March Amnesty International published a report, *Ratification without implementation: The state of human rights in Yemen*, which detailed the organization's human rights concerns and set out a series of recommendations designed to redress the situation. In August Amnesty International received a response to the report from the Attorney General, in which he referred to a unit to investigate reports of torture that had been established in his office as part of the undertakings made by the government during Amnesty International's visit to Yemen in 1996 (see *Amnesty International Report 1997*). However, he did not mention the working methods of the unit or whether it had investigated any cases of torture. The Attorney General did not address other undertakings made by the government to address the issues of arbitrary arrest, "disappearances" since 1994 and human rights violations against women (see *Amnesty International Report 1997*).

Amnesty International continued to call for the immediate and unconditional release of prisoners of conscience and for prompt and fair trials for all political prisoners. The organization called for an end to the arbitrary arrest and detention of political suspects and urged that all allegations of torture, "disappearances" and deaths in custody be investigated. Amnesty International also urged that all sentences of death, amputation and flogging be commuted.

YUGOSLAVIA
(FEDERAL REPUBLIC OF)

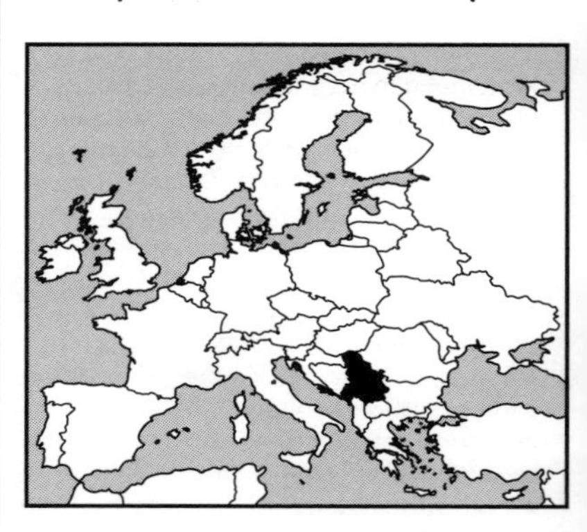

Approximately 34 ethnic Albanian political prisoners were convicted, mostly after unfair trials. Scores of others remained in prison. Some may have been prisoners of conscience. Police routinely tortured or ill-treated detainees and peaceful demonstrators. Most victims were ethnic Albanians from Kosovo province, but some were Serbs. At least three people died in police custody. At least three people were sentenced to death.

At the start of the year, demonstrations led by supporters of the *Zajedno* (Together) coalition of opposition parties continued in Belgrade and other towns, as the authorities refused to reinstate local election results which they had overturned in late 1996 (see *Amnesty International*

Report 1997). After continued international pressure, the authorities conceded the opposition victories in February.

In Kosovo province, ethnic Albanian political parties continued to demand independence for the province by peaceful means. However, violent attacks against police stations, police officers, Serb civilians and ethnic Albanians working for or with the authorities occurred throughout the year. Among dozens of victims were two police officers who were shot near Srbica in August and an ethnic Albanian civilian who was travelling in their car. Responsibility for many of the attacks was claimed by a clandestine organization called the *Ushtria Çlirimitare e Kosovës* (UÇK), Kosovo Liberation Army. Police responses to the violent attacks included what appeared to be indiscriminate arrests and house searches.

In July the President of Serbia, Slobodan Milošević, stood down. He was subsequently elected President of the Federal Republic of Yugoslavia (FRY) by the Federal Parliament. Milan Milutinović was elected President of Serbia in December. Some Serbian opposition parties and all ethnic Albanian parties from Kosovo province boycotted the election. In October students and opposition supporters staged demonstrations against the ousting of the Mayor of Belgrade. In October Milo Djukanović, an opponent of Slobodan Milošević, was elected President of Montenegro.

In October and December ethnic Albanian students from the unofficial Albanian-language university staged peaceful demonstrations demanding access to state university facilities in Priština.

The Federal and Serbian authorities continued to fail to cooperate fully with the International Criminal Tribunal for the former Yugoslavia. However, the authorities in Montenegro met Tribunal officials and expressed a desire to cooperate.

In February a Belgrade military court reportedly sentenced an adherent of the Jehovah's Witnesses, a religious group, to six months' imprisonment for refusing, on conscientious grounds, to do military service. He was a prisoner of conscience.

Courts in Kosovo province held a number of political trials during the year involving ethnic Albanians. Among the most significant cases was that of Avni Klinaku and 19 other ethnic Albanians who were sentenced in Priština in May to between two and 10 years' imprisonment. They were convicted of "conspiring to endanger the territorial integrity of the FRY" and other similar charges. Two were tried and sentenced *in absentia*. They were accused of belonging to a secret association called the *Levizje Kombëtare për Çlirimin e Kosovës* (LKÇK), National Movement for the Liberation of Kosovo. The trial was unfair: the conviction was based largely on self-incriminating statements which were not substantiated in court and 11 of the accused alleged that the statements had only been given as a result of torture in custody.

In a similar trial in July, 15 ethnic Albanian men were convicted – 12 *in absentia* – of having formed a terrorist organization – the UÇK – and of responsibility for attacks between 1993 and 1996 on police and civilians resulting in the death of four people. Twelve of the accused, including Besim Rama (see *Amnesty International Report 1997*), received the maximum sentence of 20 years' imprisonment. The trial was unfair. Statements from the three detained defendants were reportedly extracted by means of torture during unacknowledged detention. One of the defendants told the court that he was denied access to his defence lawyer for six months, only being allowed a brief private consultation with his lawyer three days before the trial. In December Nait Hasani and 16 other ethnic Albanians were sentenced to prison terms of up to 20 years after a similar unfair trial.

Scores of ethnic Albanians remained in prison after being convicted in largely unfair political trials between 1994 and 1997. Most of them had been charged with seeking the secession of Kosovo province by means of violence. However, evidence of the use or advocacy of violence was not presented in all cases and some may have been prisoners of conscience.

Incidents in which police beat and ill-treated ethnic Albanians, including women, children and elderly people, took place almost daily throughout the year. Victims were often beaten in their homes during searches for arms. The most severe ill-treatment took place in police stations where victims were often taken for questioning. Ethnic Albanians engaged in political parties or ethnic Albanian "parallel" institutions, such as Albanian-language schools, were often targeted.

Many of the instances of torture or ill-treatment occurred in the context of police operations in response to the violent attacks on police and Serbian civilians. For example, Nait Hasani (see above) was arrested by police on 28 January and was transferred the next day to hospital, reportedly to treat injuries sustained from torture during interrogation. On 31 January he "disappeared" after being taken from hospital by people who were later identified as police officers. Despite repeated requests from his family and lawyer, the police and judicial authorities refused to provide any information about his whereabouts or confirm that he was in detention until he was brought before an investigating magistrate on 28 February. He was reportedly further tortured during his time in unacknowledged detention.

In January and February police beat hundreds of opposition supporters who were demonstrating peacefully in Belgrade, Kragujevac and other towns in Serbia. For example, Zoran Simonović, a paediatrician and opposition member of the Federal Parliament, was reportedly beaten unconscious in Kragujevac when police beat demonstrators surrounding the town radio station. The new opposition-controlled authorities had appointed a new managerial board, but police reportedly stormed the radio station building in an attempt to overturn the decision. In February Vesna Pešić, leader of the political party *Gradjanski Savez*, Civic Alliance, was beaten by police along with other peaceful demonstrators on a bridge in Belgrade.

At least three people, all ethnic Albanians, died in police custody, allegedly as a result of torture, ill-treatment or shooting. For example, Ismet Gjocaj died after being shot by police in November. Despite police claims that he had been shot while participating in an armed attack on a police station, there was clear evidence that at the time of his death he was already in custody and had been tortured.

Despite the abolition of the death penalty in federal law in 1992, at least three people were sentenced to death during the year for aggravated murder under the criminal codes of the FRY's two constituent republics. No executions were reported to have been carried out during the year.

Refugees who had returned to the FRY from abroad, either voluntarily or under duress, were allegedly ill-treated by police. For example, in May Azem Hali Haxolli, who had returned voluntarily from Germany, was allegedly denied food and ill-treated after being held in detention by police in Belgrade. He was subsequently returned to Germany.

Amnesty International appealed repeatedly to the authorities for thorough, independent and impartial investigations into allegations of "disappearance", torture and ill-treatment and for the perpetrators to be brought to justice. The organization also appealed for the immediate and unconditional release of prisoners of conscience and for other political prisoners to receive fair and prompt trials.

ZAMBIA

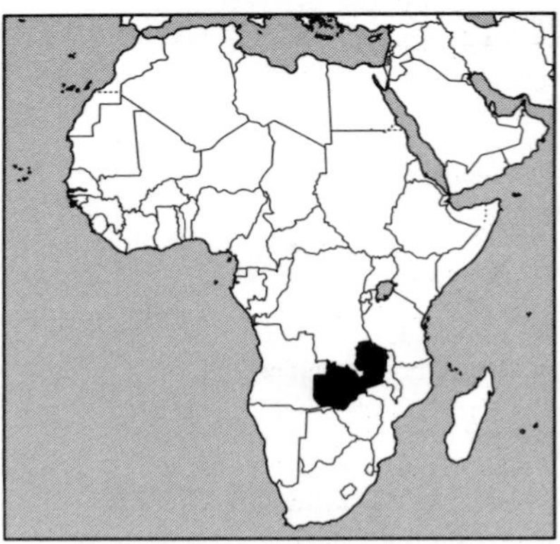

A newspaper journalist was a prisoner of conscience; several other journalists were detained for brief periods. More than 90 people were detained without charge or trial following an attempted coup; some were tortured and one may have died as a result of torture. There were allegations of ill-treatment, torture, shootings and unlawful killings by law enforcement officers. Two opposition politicians were shot and injured while driving away from police. Prison conditions remained harsh and amounted to ill-treatment. A former Rwandese cabinet minister, a refugee in Zambia, apparently "disappeared"; she later reappeared in a Rwandese prison. Eight prisoners were hanged in the first executions in eight years. Around 130 prisoners remained under sentence of death.

In January Home Affairs Minister Chitaulu Sampa reportedly ordered police to be "very brutal" in dealing with what he termed "arrogant members of the public" who disobeyed police instructions to demonstrators to disperse.

In April the government proposed a bill which would have created a government-appointed media council with powers to impose fines on and imprison journalists who did not conform to its rules. The bill was withdrawn following criticism from civic organizations, journalists, international human rights organizations and foreign governments.

An attempted coup took place in October, following which a three-month state of emergency was declared. Many rights guaranteed under the Constitution were suspended, allowing lengthy detention without charge or trial, and restrictions on freedom of conscience, expression, assembly and movement.

A newspaper journalist was detained as a prisoner of conscience. In February the Supreme Court of Zambia sentenced *The Post* newspaper editor Masautso Phiri to a three-month prison term for "contempt of court" for publishing a column containing allegations that members of the Supreme Court were offered bribes amounting to US$10.8 million by President Frederick Chiluba. Masautso Phiri was released in April, but was rearrested in August while covering a demonstration (see below).

Several other journalists were detained for brief periods. In February an editor and a reporter on the independent newspaper *The Chronicle* were detained for two days on charges of contempt of parliament, publishing false news and criminal libel against President Chiluba. The charges were later dropped in a court settlement that reportedly included printing a retraction. Another *Chronicle* reporter, George Jambwa, was charged with criminal trespass in February, after being arrested and held for four days in December 1996 at an army barracks in Lusaka, the capital, where he had gone to interview an army officer. Dismissing the charges in April, a magistrate noted that George Jambwa had been the victim of "a conspiracy to cover up the inefficiency of security at the gate". In January, April and August *Post* reporters were arrested and briefly detained.

In April a judge dismissed criminal defamation charges, pending since 1994, against four *Post* journalists who had published an article alleging an extra-marital affair by presidential press assistant Richard Sakala. In May a judge dismissed charges against three editors of *The Post* who had been accused of revealing a state secret when, in February 1996, they published details of a cabinet plan for a referendum over the 1996 draft constitution (see *Amnesty International Report 1997*).

Following the attempted coup in October, police and security forces indefinitely detained more than 90 suspects. Many of them were initially held incommunicado and without charge under the terms of the state of emergency. One detainee, Dean Mung'omba, President of the opposition Zambia Democratic Congress, was reportedly subjected to beatings, electric shocks, cigarette burns and sleep deprivation. Other detainees – mostly army officers – were also reportedly tortured or ill-treated by the police. One detainee allegedly died as a result of torture. Among those detained were Captain Stephen Lungu, Captain Jackson Chiti, Major Bilex Mutale, Major Musonda Kangwa and Staff Sergeant Kennedy Sinutala. All were still detained at the end of the year. None had been charged or tried.

Kenneth Kaunda, former President of Zambia and leader of the United National Independence Party (UNIP), who had been travelling abroad at the time of the coup, was arrested on 25 December after he returned. He was later put under house arrest, where he remained at the end of the year. The authorities accused him of conspiring with Dean Mung'omba, leader of the opposition Liberal Progressive Front, Roger Chongwe, Captain Stephen Lungu, Captain Jack Chiti and Major Musonda Kangwa to overthrow the government. Roger Chongwe remained outside the country. Hearings on the legality of this and other related detentions continued at the end of the year.

Police beat and otherwise ill-treated participants in opposition rallies scheduled without giving notice to the police, and other demonstrators. In February, for example, police fired tear-gas and used batons and whips to break up a peaceful demonstration by the UNIP in Ndola. Some demonstrators were injured. In July police broke up a peaceful UNIP rally in Lusaka. They then surrounded the UNIP headquarters, entered the building and fired tear-gas inside, in violation of international standards. Several people were injured in police beatings when they emerged from the building or later in police custody. In August police reportedly beat and kicked stall-holders who rioted after their stalls mysteriously burned down. Several stall-holders were injured in the beatings, and two allegedly died of their injuries.

Unarmed suspects were injured or killed in police shootings which appeared to involve excessive or unlawful use of force. In June, two police officers in the northern town of Kitwe allegedly shot a suspected robber in both legs after beating him with gun butts and tying his hands together. In a case in October police officers in Lusaka shot and killed a man who was urinating in public. The police officers later claimed that the man had grabbed for an officer's gun, but eye-witnesses dispute this. No disciplinary action was known to have been taken in either case.

In August police in Kabwe shot and wounded Kenneth Kaunda and Roger Chongwe. A bullet grazed Kenneth Kaunda's head and caused serious injury to Roger Chongwe's cheek and neck. That morning, police had used live ammunition to disperse people gathering for an unsanctioned opposition rally which the two were due to address, arresting journalist Masautso Phiri and reportedly beating him and smashing his camera. Police reportedly then cornered the two politicians in an office building, allegedly opening fire when the two attempted to flee. Two senior police officers were later suspended. Police officials claimed that officers mistakenly used live ammunition to disperse the rally. The authorities denied allegations that there had been an officially sanctioned attempt to assassinate Kenneth Kaunda and Roger Chongwe. By the end of the year no official investigation into the allegations appeared to have taken place.

Prison conditions remained harsh and amounted to ill-treatment. The number of prisoners was nearly double that which could be adequately housed, and clean water, food, blankets, clothing and medicines were in short supply. Up to 100 prisoners, weakened by malnourishment, died from diseases such as tuberculosis and AIDS. In a measure believed to be aimed at addressing the problem of overcrowding, President Chiluba pardoned 480 prisoners in May and another 300 in October.

In May, Agnes Ntamabyaliro Rutagwera, a former Rwandese government minister who had been living in Zambia as a refugee since 1995, was abducted from her house in the northern town of Mufalira. According to reports, her abductors wore the uniform of the Zambian Immigration Service and used a vehicle bearing Zambian government licence plates. She was later discovered to be in prison in Kigali, Rwanda. The Zambian Government, which denied any involvement in the incident, had apparently failed to initiate a promised investigation by the end of the year.

Eight prisoners were hanged in the first executions in eight years. There was particular concern about the secrecy surrounding the executions in January of Abraham Kasongo, Nelson Ngundano, Dennis Chisela Chembe, Robert Mulumbi, David Kapanga, John Gumbo, Joseph Masiti Chilanda, and Christopher Mwansa Oldfield, all of whom had been convicted of murder or aggravated robbery. The executions only came to light by March, and the government refused to confirm the names of those executed or the charges on which they had been convicted. There was concern at reports that one of the men – Nelson Ngundano – had been suffering from mental illness developed after nearly 15 years under sentence of death. Approximately 130 prisoners remained under sentence of death.

Amnesty International called for Kenneth Kaunda and the others detained in connection with the coup attempt to be charged with a recognizably criminal offence or released, and for the investigation and prosecution of those police officers responsible for the torture of detainees. The organization wrote to President Chiluba urging that an immediate, thorough and independent investigation take place into the shootings by police in June, August and October, including the incident involving Kenneth Kaunda and Roger Chongwe, as well as shootings which took place in previous years, and that the results of all such investigations be made public. Amnesty International wrote to the President calling for an immediate investigation into the circumstances surrounding Agnes Ntamabyaliro Rutagwera's "disappearance". The organization also wrote to the President to express its deep regret at, and condemnation of, the execution of the eight men in January.

In a report published in November, *Zambia: Forcible exile to suppress dissent*, Amnesty International described how investigations into the nationality of government critics had been used to intimidate them. The report detailed the cases of two UNIP politicians, William Stephen Banda and John Lyson Chinula, who had been deported in 1994 in circumstances amounting to forcible exile because of their political activities.

ZIMBABWE

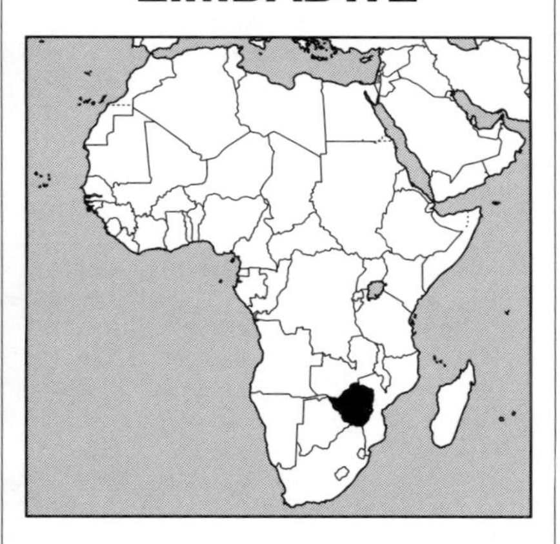

An opposition leader remained on trial for treason, punishable by death. At least 10 people were sentenced to death and 12 were executed.

In February the Supreme Court overturned the government's use of the controversial Private Voluntary Organisations (PVO) Act to dismiss the directors of a women's organization and replace them with government appointees. In September the Supreme Court declared unconstitutional a law that had provided the ruling Zimbabwe African National Union–Patriotic Front (ZANU-PF) with approximately US$3 million in state funding each year since 1992. The Supreme Court stated that excessively high thresholds for qualifying for funding meant that only ZANU-PF received funds, limiting freedom of expression and putting opposition political parties "at a severe disadvantage" in elections.

In March, two Zimbabwean human rights organizations presented President Robert Mugabe with a report entitled *Breaking the Silence*, which detailed atrocities carried out in the 1980s by forces of the army's 5th Brigade in the southwestern region of Matabeleland. Compiled over five years from testimony by more than 1,000 people, the report was leaked to a South African newspaper after months of silence from the government. The government did not respond to the report's recommendations, which included creating a public development fund as compensation.

Starting in April, war veterans carried out a series of public protests to demand their share of a war victims' compensation fund, which was allegedly defrauded of millions of dollars by senior government officials. In July the government imposed a two-week ban on all public demonstrations and strikes after a demonstration by veterans at the time of an investment conference of black US businessmen. In September, when President Mugabe promised the estimated 70,000 veterans a tax-free pay-out and a stipend for life, the World Bank froze balance of payments support, just after lifting its 1995 suspension on aid.

In December the authorities flouted a High Court order not to block a planned demonstration in Harare, the capital, to mark a one-day nationwide general strike. Police used tear-gas and batons to disperse tens of thousands of people who gathered peacefully to protest against proposed new taxes and violent clashes ensued. The Home Affairs Minister stated that police would shoot anyone demonstrating against the tax rises, and the Commissioner of Police reportedly said that the strike organizers, the Zimbabwe Congress of Trade Unions (ZCTU), would be crushed if the strike went ahead. Less than 48 hours later, several people assaulted and severely injured ZCTU Secretary-General Morgan Tsvangirai in an incident later condemned by President Mugabe. The ZCTU alleged ZANU-PF involvement in the attack.

In December, more than two years after his arrest, opposition leader the Reverend Ndabaningi Sithole was sentenced to two years' imprisonment for conspiring to assassinate President Mugabe (see *Amnesty International Reports 1996* and *1997*). He remained at liberty pending appeal. The High Court ruled in November that the Terrorism Act, under which the Reverend Ndabaningi Sithole had been charged, was unconstitutional because it forced a suspect to prove his or her innocence. The Reverend Ndabaningi Sithole maintained his innocence, alleging that the evidence against him had been fabricated by the state Central Intelligence Organisation.

In October Amnesty International received reports that the government had forcibly returned scores of refugees to the Democratic Republic of the Congo (DRC), formerly Zaire. Reports indicated they may have been returned because they were suspected of opposing DRC President Laurent Kabila.

More than 10 people were sentenced to death, and 12 were executed for murder, the largest number of executions in any single year since independence in 1980. No public notice was given before the hangings, and the last four were executed in September, just a year after the Supreme Court had dismissed their appeals.

In May Amnesty International wrote to President Mugabe to protest at the growing number of executions, as well as the apparent secrecy before the hangings.

Before President Mugabe assumed the chairmanship of the Organization of African Unity (OAU) in June, Amnesty International wrote an open letter to the President urging him to accept and implement recommendations in the report *Breaking the Silence*, and describing the documented atrocities as "tantamount to crimes against humanity". In October Amnesty International expressed concern about the possible deportation of Georges Bizimana back to Burundi, and of Jean Hubert Feruzi Mbayo to the DRC.

APPENDICES

AMNESTY INTERNATIONAL VISITS 1997

DATE	COUNTRY	PURPOSE
January	Palestinian Authority	Research/Talks with government
January	Pakistan	Research
January	Tanzania	Talks with government
January	Rwanda	Legal proceedings
January	Turkey	Legal proceedings
January	Kazakstan	Research
January/February	Thailand	Research
January/February	Rwanda	Research/Legal proceedings
January/February	Senegal	Research/Talks with government
February	Switzerland	Research on region
February	South Africa	Research/Talks with government
February	Hong Kong	Talks with government
February	Colombia	Talks with government
February	Swaziland	Research
February	Haiti	Research/Talks with government
February/March	Albania	Research
February/March	Colombia	Research on region
February/March	Kenya	Legal proceedings
February/March	Kenya	Research
February/March	Turkey	Research
February/March/May	Turkey	Legal proceedings
March	Syria	Talks with government/Legal proceedings
March	Germany	Research
March	USA	Research/Legal proceedings
March/April	Israel/Occupied Territories/ Palestinian Authority	Talks with government
April	Brazil	Legal proceedings
April	Guatemala	Talks with government
April	Russian Federation	Research/Campaigning
April	USA	Research/Talks with government
April	Peru	Research
April	United Kingdom	Research/Legal proceedings
April/May	Ecuador	Research
April/May	Turkey	Legal proceedings
April/May	Philippines	Research
April/May	Liberia	Talks with government
April/May	Brazil	Research/Talks with government
April/May	Slovak Republic	Research/Campaigning
April/May	Thailand	Research on region
April/May	Qatar	Research on region/Talks with government
May	Kenya	Research
May	South Africa	Legal proceedings
May	Uganda	Research/Talks with government
May	Turkey	Legal proceedings

DATE	COUNTRY	PURPOSE
May	Croatia	Research/Talks with government
May	United Kingdom	Research/Legal proceedings
May	Philippines	Research on region
May	USA	Research
May	Armenia	Research
May	France	Research
May	USA	Research
May	Turkey	Legal proceedings
May	USA	Research
May/June	Kenya	Talks with government
May/June	Bulgaria	Research/Talks with government
May/June	Japan	Research/Talks with government
May/June	Republic of the Congo	Research on region
May/June	Tunisia	Research
June	Federal Republic of Yugoslavia	Research
June	Switzerland	Legal proceedings
June	Spain	Research on region
June	South Africa	Research/Legal proceedings
June	Norway	Research on region
June	USA	Research/Talks with government
June	Germany	Research on region
June/July	Hong Kong	Research/Talks with government
July	United Kingdom	Research
July	South Africa	Talks with government
July	United Kingdom	Legal proceedings
July	Azerbaijan	Research
July	Ethiopia	Research
July	France	Research on region
July	Malawi	Talks with government
July	Uganda	Research/Talks with government
July	Turkey	Legal proceedings
July	Lebanon	Research/Legal proceedings
July	Egypt	Research/Legal proceedings
July	Germany	Campaigning/Talks with government
July	Jordan	Research on region
July	Thailand	Research on region
July	Malaysia	Research on region
July/August	Kenya	Research on region
August	Sri Lanka	Research/Talks with government
August	Singapore	Legal proceedings
August	USA	Research
August	USA	Research
August	USA	Research on region
August/September	Cambodia	Research/Talks with government
August/September	Mexico	Research
August/September	India	Research/Talks with government
August/September	Malawi	Research

DATE	COUNTRY	PURPOSE
August/October	USA	Research
September	Kenya	Research/Campaigning
September	Philippines	Research
September	El Salvador	Research
September	Honduras	Research
September	Senegal	Research
September	Israel/Occupied Territories/ Palestinian Authority	Research
September	Romania	Research/Talks with government
September	USA	Research
September	Georgia	Research
September	Switzerland	Legal proceedings
September	Portugal	Research on region
September	Singapore	Legal proceedings
September	Turkey	Legal proceedings
September	Brazil	Research/Talks with government
September	Egypt	Research on region
September	Macedonia	Research
September	Mexico	Talks with government
September	Russian Federation	Research/Talks with government
September/October	Lebanon	Research/Legal proceedings
October	Belarus	Research
October	Ukraine	Research
October	United Kingdom	Legal proceedings
October	South Africa	Research/Legal proceedings
October	Liberia	Research/Talks with government
October	Brazil	Talks with government
October	Turkey	Legal proceedings
October	USA	Research
October	Turkey	Legal proceedings
October	Romania	Talks with government
October	Angola	Research/Talks with government
October	Tanzania	Legal proceedings
October/November	Rwanda	Legal proceedings
October/November	Guatemala	Research
October/November	Bosnia-Herzegovina	Research
October/November	USA	Research/Talks with government
November	USA	Research/Talks with government
November	Russian Federation	Research
November	Germany	Research
November	Belgium	Research on region
November	Germany	Research on region
November	Kenya	Research
November	Japan	Talks with government
November	Guatemala	Research
November/December	France	Research on region
November/December	Russian Federation	Research
November/December	Cambodia	Research

DATE	COUNTRY	PURPOSE
November/December	Colombia	Research
December	Turkey	Research/Legal proceedings
December	South Africa	Research/Talks with government
December	Jordan	Research on region

STATUTE OF AMNESTY INTERNATIONAL

As amended by the 23rd International Council, meeting in Cape Town, South Africa, 12 to 19 December 1997

Articles 1 and 2

Object and Mandate

1. The object of AMNESTY INTERNATIONAL is to contribute to the observance throughout the world of human rights as set out in the Universal Declaration of Human Rights.

In pursuance of this object, and recognizing the obligation on each person to extend to others rights and freedoms equal to his or her own, AMNESTY INTERNATIONAL adopts as its mandate:

To promote awareness of and adherence to the Universal Declaration of Human Rights and other internationally recognized human rights instruments, the values enshrined in them, and the indivisibility and interdependence of all human rights and freedoms;

To oppose grave violations of the rights of every person freely to hold and to express his or her convictions and to be free from discrimination, and of the right of every person to physical and mental integrity, and, in particular, to oppose by all appropriate means irrespective of political considerations:

a) the imprisonment, detention or other physical restrictions imposed on any person by reason of his or her political, religious or other conscientiously held beliefs or by reason of his or her ethnic origin, sex, colour, language, national or social origin, economic status, birth or other status, provided that he or she has not used or advocated violence (hereinafter referred to as 'prisoners of conscience'; AMNESTY INTERNATIONAL shall work towards the release of and shall provide assistance to prisoners of conscience);

b) the detention of any political prisoner without fair trial within a reasonable time or any trial procedures relating to such prisoners that do not conform to internationally recognized norms;

c) the death penalty, and the torture or other cruel, inhuman or degrading treatment or punishment of prisoners or other detained or restricted persons, whether or not the persons affected have used or advocated violence;

d) the extrajudicial execution of persons whether or not imprisoned, detained or restricted, and "disappearances", whether or not the persons affected have used or advocated violence.

Methods

2. In order to achieve the aforesaid object and mandate, AMNESTY INTERNATIONAL shall:

a) at all times make clear its impartiality as regards countries adhering to the different world political ideologies and groupings;

b) promote as appears appropriate the adoption of constitutions, conventions, treaties and other measures which guarantee the rights contained in the provisions referred to in Article 1 hereof;

c) support and publicize the activities of and cooperate with international organizations and agencies which work for the implementation of the aforesaid provisions;

d) take all necessary steps to establish an effective organization of sections, affiliated groups and individual members;

e) secure the adoption by groups of members or supporters of individual prisoners of conscience or entrust to such groups other tasks in support of the object and mandate set out in Article 1;

f) provide financial and other relief to prisoners of conscience and their dependants and to persons who have lately been prisoners of conscience or who might reasonably be expected to be prisoners of conscience or to become prisoners of conscience if convicted or if they were to return to their own countries, to the dependants of such persons and to victims of torture in need of medical care as a direct result thereof;

g) provide legal aid, where necessary and possible, to prisoners of conscience and to persons who might reasonably be expected to be prisoners of conscience or to become prisoners of conscience if convicted or if they were to return to their own countries, and, where desirable, send observers to attend the trials of such persons;

h) publicize the cases of prisoners of conscience or persons who have otherwise been subjected to disabilities in violation of the aforesaid provisions;

i) investigate and publicize the disappearance of persons where there is reason to believe that they may be victims of violations of the rights set out in Article 1 hereof;

j) oppose the sending of persons from one country to another where they can reasonably be expected to become prisoners of conscience or to face torture or the death penalty;

k) send investigators, where appropriate, to investigate allegations that the rights of individuals under the aforesaid provisions have been violated or threatened;

l) make representations to international organizations and to governments whenever it appears that an individual is a prisoner of conscience or has otherwise been subjected to disabilities in violation of the aforesaid provisions;

m) promote and support the granting of general amnesties of which the beneficiaries will include prisoners of conscience;

n) adopt any other appropriate methods for the securing of its object and mandate.

The full text of the Statute of Amnesty International is available free upon request from: Amnesty International, International Secretariat, 1 Easton Street, London WC1X 8DJ, United Kingdom.

AMNESTY INTERNATIONAL AROUND THE WORLD

In 1997 there were more than 4,300 local Amnesty International groups registered with the International Secretariat and several thousand professional and other groups, including over 3,400 youth and student groups, in more than 105 countries and territories around the world. In 55 countries and territories these groups are coordinated by sections, whose addresses are given below. There are individual members, supporters, and recipients of Amnesty International information (such as the bimonthly *Amnesty International News*) in around 176 countries and territories. Amnesty International information is also available on the Internet on more than 100 websites worldwide.

SECTION ADDRESSES

Algeria:
Amnesty International,
Section Algérienne,
BP 377 Alger,
RP 16004

Argentina:
Amnistía Internacional,
Sección Argentina,
25 de Mayo 67, 4º Piso,
1002 Buenos Aires

Australia:
Amnesty International,
Australian Section,
Private Bag 23, Broadway,
New South Wales 2007

Austria:
Amnesty International,
Austrian Section,
Moeringstrasse 10/1 Stock,
A-1150, Wien

Bangladesh:
Amnesty International,
Bangladesh Section,
100 Kalabagan,
1st Floor, 2nd Lane,
Dhaka - 1205

Belgium:
Amnesty International,
Belgian Section (AI Vlaanderen),
Kerkstraat 156,
2060 Antwerpen

Amnesty International,
Section belge (francophone),
Rue Berckmans 9,
1060 Bruxelles

Benin:
Amnesty International,
BP 01 3536,
Cotonou

Bermuda:
Amnesty International,
Bermuda Section,
PO Box HM 2136,
Hamilton HM JX

Brazil:
Anistia Internacional,
Porto Alegre - RS,
CEP 90040-270

Canada:
Amnesty International,
Canadian Section
(*English-speaking branch*),
214 Montreal Rd, 4th Floor, Vanier,
Ontario, K1L 1A4

Amnistie Internationale,
Section canadienne francophone,
6250 boulevard Monk,
Montréal, Québec H4E 3H7

Chile:
Amnistía Internacional,
Sección Chilena,
Casilla 4062,
Santiago

Costa Rica:
Amnistía Internacional,
De la Casa Italia,
100 Sur, 300 Este,
50 Sur, Yoses Sur,
San José

Côte d'Ivoire:
Amnesty International,
Section ivoirienne,
04 BP 895,
Abidjan 04

Denmark:
Amnesty International,
Danish Section,
Dyrkoeb 3,
1166 Copenhagen K

Ecuador:
Amnistía Internacional,
Sección Ecuatoriana,
Casilla 17-15-240-C,
Quito

Faroe Islands:
Amnesty International,
Faroe Islands Section,
PO Box 1075, FR-110,
Tórshavn

Finland:
Amnesty International,
Finnish Section,
Ruoholahdenkatu 24 D,
00180 Helsinki

France:
Amnesty International,
Section française,
4 rue de la Pierre Levée,
75553 Paris, Cedex 11

Germany:
Amnesty International,
German Section,
53108 Bonn

Ghana:
Amnesty International,
Ghanaian Section,
Private Mail Bag,
Kokomlemle,
Accra - North

Greece:
Amnesty International,
Greek Section,
30 Sina Street,
106 72 Athens

Guyana:
Amnesty International,
Guyana Section,
c/o PO Box 10720,
Palm Court Building,
35 Main Street,
Georgetown

Hong Kong:
Amnesty International,
Hong Kong Section,Unit C 3/F,
Best-O-Best Commercial Centre,
32-36 Ferry Street,
Kowloon

Iceland:
Amnesty International,
Icelandic Section,
PO Box 618,
121 Reykjavík

India:
Amnesty International,
Indian Section,
13 Indra Prastha Building,
E-109 Pandav Nagar,
New Delhi - 110092

Ireland:
Amnesty International,
Irish Section,
Sean MacBride House,
48 Fleet Street,
Dublin 2

Israel:
Amnesty International,
Israel Section,
PO Box 14179,
Tel Aviv 61141

Italy:
Amnesty International,
Italian Section,
Viale Mazzini, 146,
00195 Rome

Japan:
Amnesty International,
Japanese Section,
Sky Esta 2f,
2-18-23 Nishi Waseda,
Shinjuku-ku,
Tokyo 165

Korea (Republic of):
Amnesty International,
Kyeong Buk RCO Box 36,
706 600 Daegu

Luxembourg:
Amnesty International,
Luxembourg Section,
Boîte Postale 1914,
1019 Luxembourg

Mauritius:
Amnesty International,
Mauritius Section,
BP 69 Rose-Hill

Mexico:
Sección Mexicana
de Amnistía Internacional,
Calle Aniceto Ortega 624,
(paralela a Gabriel Mancera,
esq. Angel Urraza-eje 6 Sur),
Col. del Valle,
México DF

Nepal:
Amnesty International,
Nepalese Section,
PO Box 135, Bagbazar,
Kathmandu

Netherlands:
Amnesty International,
Dutch Section,
Keizersgracht 620,
1017 ER Amsterdam

New Zealand:
Amnesty International,
New Zealand Section,
PO Box 793,
Wellington

Nigeria:
Amnesty International,
Nigerian Section,
PMB 3061, Suru-Lere,
Lagos

Norway:
Amnesty International,
Norwegian Section,
PO Box 702 Sentrum,
0106 Oslo

Peru:
Señores,
Casilla 659,
Lima 18

Philippines:
Amnesty International,
Philippines Section,
PO Box 286, Sta Mesa Post Office,
1008 Sta Mesa,
Manila

Portugal:
Amnistia Internacional,
Secção Portuguesa,
Rua Fialho de Almeida, Nº 13, 1º,
1070 Lisboa

Puerto Rico:
Amnistía Internacional,
Sección de Puerto Rico,
Calle Robles No. 54-Altos,
Oficina 11, Río Piedras,
Puerto Rico 00925

Senegal:
Amnesty International,
Senegalese Section,
BP 21910,
Dakar

Sierra Leone:
Amnesty International,
Sierra Leone Section,
PMB 1021,
Freetown

Slovenia:
Amnesty International,
Komenskega 7,
1000 Ljubljana

Spain:
Amnesty International,
Sección Española,
PO Box 50318,
28080, Madrid

Sweden:
Amnesty International,
Swedish Section,
PO Box 23400,
S-104 35 Stockholm

Switzerland:
Amnesty International,
Swiss Section,
Postfach,
CH-3001, Bern

Taiwan:
Amnesty International,
Room 525, No. 2, Section 1,
Chung-shan North Road,
100 Taipei

Tanzania:
Amnesty International,
Tanzanian Section,
PO Box 4331,
Dar es Salaam

Tunisia:
Amnesty International,
Section Tunisienne,
67 rue Oum Kalthoum,
3ème étage, Escalier B,
1000 Tunis

United Kingdom:
Amnesty International,
United Kingdom Section,
99-119 Rosebery Avenue,
London EC1R 4RE

United States of America:
Amnesty International of the USA (AIUSA),
322 8th Ave,
New York, NY 10001

Uruguay:
Amnistía Internacional,
Sección Uruguaya,
Tristan Narvaja 1624, Apto 1,
CP 11200 Montevideo

Venezuela:
Amnistía Internacional,
Sección Venezolana,
Apartado Postal 5110,
Carmelitas 1010-A,
Caracas

COUNTRIES AND TERRITORIES WITHOUT SECTIONS BUT WHERE LOCAL AMNESTY INTERNATIONAL GROUPS EXIST OR ARE BEING FORMED

Albania
Aruba
Azerbaijan
Bahamas
Barbados
Belarus
Bolivia
Botswana
Bulgaria
Burkina Faso
Cameroon
Chad
Croatia
Curaçao
Cyprus
Czech Republic
Dominican Republic
Egypt
Gambia
Grenada
Hungary
Jamaica
Jordan
Kuwait
Macao
Malaysia
Mali
Malta
Moldova
Mongolia
Morocco
Pakistan
Palestinian Authority/ Israeli Occupied Territories
Paraguay
Poland
Romania
Russian Federation
Slovakia
South Africa
Thailand
Togo
Turkey
Uganda
Ukraine
Yemen
Zambia
Zimbabwe

APPENDIX IV

INTERNATIONAL EXECUTIVE COMMITTEE

Colm Ó'Cuanacháin/Ireland
Mary Gray/United States of America
Habiba Hasan/Pakistan
Menno Kamminga/Netherlands
Robin Rickard/United Kingdom
Mahmoud Ben Romdhane/Tunisia
Cristina Sganga/International Secretariat
Susan Waltz/United States of America
Samuel Zan Akologo/Ghana

Update on Abolition of the Death Penalty

Highlights of 1997 included the adoption by the UN Commission on Human Rights of a resolution encouraging states to consider suspending executions, and the decision of the Parliamentary Assembly of the Council of Europe to insist that the Russian Federation and Ukraine halt executions or face expulsion from the Council. Georgia and Poland abolished the death penalty for all crimes in parliamentary votes (see **Georgia** entry).

In late 1996, reports emerged from the Russian Federation and Ukraine that executions were continuing despite the commitments made by the two states on joining the Council of Europe, in February 1996 and November 1995 respectively, to institute an immediate moratorium on executions. In an unprecedented move, the Parliamentary Assembly of the Council of Europe in January voted to condemn the two countries for violating their commitments to stop executions, and threatened them with ultimate expulsion from the Council of Europe should executions continue.

No executions were carried out in the Russian Federation after August 1996, according to Russian officials, except in the Chechen Republic-Ichkeriya, but at least 13 people were executed in Ukraine in the first half of 1997. In response to the continuing executions in Ukraine, the Committee on Legal Affairs and Human Rights of the Parliamentary Assembly of the Council of Europe voted in December to propose that the Parliamentary Assembly suspend the credentials of the Ukrainian delegation unless the Ukrainian authorities sent it an official notification of a moratorium on executions.

In April the UN Commission on Human Rights adopted resolution 1997/12 calling on "all States that have not yet abolished the death penalty to consider suspending executions, with a view to completely abolishing the death penalty". It was the first time that any UN political body had supported the idea of a worldwide moratorium on executions. The resolution was adopted by a vote of 27 in favour and 11 against, with 14 abstentions. The initiative had been supported by several non-governmental organizations including Amnesty International and Hands off Cain, an international organization of members of parliament and others opposed to the death penalty.

In Poland, following votes in parliament in April and June, President Aleksander Kwasniewski in July signed into law a new penal code abolishing the death penalty for all crimes with effect from 1 January 1998. A five-year moratorium on executions had come into force in November 1995. The last execution was in 1988.

During 1997, at least 2,375 prisoners were executed in 40 countries and 3,707 people were sentenced to death in 69 countries. These figures include only cases known to Amnesty International; the true figures are certainly higher. As in previous years, a small number of countries accounted for the great majority of executions. At least 1,644 executions had been reported by the end of the year in China alone; many more may have gone unreported.

By the end of 1997, 63 countries had abolished the death penalty for all offences and 16 for all but exceptional offences, such as wartime crimes. At least 25 countries which retained the death penalty in law were considered abolitionist in practice, in that they had not executed anyone for the past 10 years or more or had made an international commitment not to carry out executions.

During the year, Colombia and Greece became parties to the Second Optional Protocol to the International Covenant on Civil and Political Rights, aiming at the abolition of the death penalty, bringing the number of states parties to 31. Croatia, the former Yugoslav Republic of Macedonia and Moldova became parties to Protocol No. 6 to the European Convention for the Protection of Human Rights and Fundamental Freedoms (European Convention on Human Rights) concerning the abolition of the death penalty, bringing the number of states parties to 27. Four countries were parties to the Protocol to the American Convention on Human Rights to Abolish the Death Penalty. The Russian Federation and Ukraine signed Protocol No. 6 to the European Convention on Human Rights.

SELECTED INTERNATIONAL HUMAN RIGHTS TREATIES

States which have ratified or acceded to a convention are party to the treaty and are bound to observe its provisions. States which have signed but not yet ratified have expressed their intention to become a party at some future date; meanwhile they are obliged to refrain from acts which would defeat the object and purpose of the treaty.

(AS OF 31 DECEMBER 1997)

	International Covenant on Civil and Political Rights (ICCPR)	Optional Protocol to ICCPR	Second Optional Protocol to ICCPR, aiming at the abolition of the death penalty	International Covenant on Economic, Social and Cultural Rights	Convention against Torture and Other Cruel, Inhuman or Degrading Treatment or Punishment	Convention relating to the Status of Refugees (1951)	Protocol relating to the Status of Refugees (1967)	Convention on the Elimination of All Forms of Discrimination against Women
Afghanistan	x			x	x(28)			s
Albania	x			x	x	x	x	x
Algeria	x	x		x	x(22)	x	x	x
Andorra								x*
Angola	x	x		x		x	x	x
Antigua and Barbuda					x	x	x	x
Argentina	x	x		x	x(22)	x	x	x
Armenia	x	x		x	x	x	x	x
Australia	x	x	x	x	x(22)	x	x	x
Austria	x	x	x	x	x(22)	x	x	x
Azerbaijan	x			x	x	x	x	x
Bahamas						x	x	x
Bahrain								
Bangladesh								x

	International Covenant on Civil and Political Rights (ICCPR)	Optional Protocol to ICCPR	Second Optional Protocol to ICCPR, aiming at the abolition of the death penalty	International Covenant on Economic, Social and Cultural Rights	Convention against Torture and Other Cruel, Inhuman or Degrading Treatment or Punishment	Convention relating to the Status of Refugees (1951)	Protocol relating to the Status of Refugees (1967)	Convention on the Elimination of All Forms of Discrimination against Women
Barbados	x	x		x				x
Belarus	x	x		x	x(28)			x
Belgium	x	x	s	x	s	x	x	x
Belize	x				x	x	x	x
Benin	x	x		x	x	x	x	x
Bhutan								x
Bolivia	x	x		x	s	x	x	x
Bosnia and Herzegovina	x	x		x	x	x	x	x
Botswana						x	x	x
Brazil	x			x	x	x	x	x
Brunei Darussalam								
Bulgaria	x	x		x	x(22)(28)	x	x	x
Burkina Faso						x	x	x
Burundi	x			x	x	x	x	x
Cambodia	x			x	x	x	x	x
Cameroon	x	x		x	x	x	x	x
Canada	x	x		x	x(22)	x	x	x
Cape Verde	x			x	x		x	x
Central African Republic	x	x		x		x	x	x
Chad	x	x		x	x	x	x	x
Chile	x	x		x	x	x	x	x
China				s*	x(28)	x	x	x
Colombia	x	x	x*	x	x	x	x	x
Comoros								x

	International Covenant on Civil and Political Rights (ICCPR)	Optional Protocol to ICCPR	Second Optional Protocol to ICCPR, aiming at the abolition of the death penalty	International Covenant on Economic, Social and Cultural Rights	Convention against Torture and Other Cruel, Inhuman or Degrading Treatment or Punishment	Convention relating to the Status of Refugees (1951)	Protocol relating to the Status of Refugees (1967)	Convention on the Elimination of All Forms of Discrimination against Women
Congo (Democratic Republic of the)	x	x		x	x	x	x	x
Congo (Republic of the)	x	x		x		x	x	x
Costa Rica	x	x	s	x	x	x	x	x
Côte d'Ivoire	x	x*		x	x	x	x	x
Croatia	x	x	x	x	x(22)	x	x	x
Cuba					x			x
Cyprus	x	x		x	x(22)	x	x	x
Czech Republic	x	x		x	x(22)	x	x	x
Denmark	x	x	x	x	x(22)	x	x	x
Djibouti						x	x	
Dominica	x			x		x	x	x
Dominican Republic	x	x		x	s	x	x	x
Ecuador	x	x	x	x	x(22)	x	x	x
Egypt	x			x	x	x	x	x
El Salvador	x	x		x	x	x	x	x
Equatorial Guinea	x	x		x		x	x	x
Eritrea								x
Estonia	x	x		x	x	x*	x*	x
Ethiopia	x			x	x	x	x	x
Fiji						x	x	x
Finland	x	x	x	x	x(22)	x	x	x
France	x	x		x	x(22)	x	x	x
Gabon	x			x	s	x	x	x
Gambia	x	x		x	s	x	x	x

	International Covenant on Civil and Political Rights (ICCPR)	Optional Protocol to ICCPR	Second Optional Protocol to ICCPR, aiming at the abolition of the death penalty	International Covenant on Economic, Social and Cultural Rights	Convention against Torture and Other Cruel, Inhuman or Degrading Treatment or Punishment	Convention relating to the Status of Refugees (1951)	Protocol relating to the Status of Refugees (1967)	Convention on the Elimination of All Forms of Discrimination against Women
Georgia	x	x		x	x			x
Germany	x	x	x	x	x	x	x	x
Ghana						x	x	x
Greece	x*	x*	x*	x	x(22)	x	x	x
Grenada	x			x				x
Guatemala	x			x	x	x	x	x
Guinea	x	x		x	x	x	x	x
Guinea-Bissau				x		x	x	x
Guyana	x	x		x	x			x
Haiti	x					x	x	x
Holy See						x	x	
Honduras	x*	s	s	x	x	x	x	x
Hungary	x	x	x	x	x(22)	x	x	x
Iceland	x	x	x	x	x(22)	x	x	x
India	x			x	s*			x
Indonesia					s			x
Iran (Islamic Republic of)	x			x		x	x	
Iraq	x			x				x
Ireland	x	x	x	x	s	x	x	x
Israel	x			x	x(28)	x	x	x
Italy	x	x	x	x	x(22)	x	x	x
Jamaica	x	x		x		x	x	x
Japan	x			x		x	x	x
Jordan	x			x	x			x

	International Covenant on Civil and Political Rights (ICCPR)	Optional Protocol to ICCPR	Second Optional Protocol to ICCPR, aiming at the abolition of the death penalty	International Covenant on Economic, Social and Cultural Rights	Convention against Torture and Other Cruel, Inhuman or Degrading Treatment or Punishment	Convention relating to the Status of Refugees (1951)	Protocol relating to the Status of Refugees (1967)	Convention on the Elimination of All Forms of Discrimination against Women
Kazakstan								
Kenya	x			x	x*	x	x	x
Kiribati								
Korea (Democratic People's Republic of)	x			x				
Korea (Republic of)	x	x		x	x	x	x	x
Kuwait	x			x	x			x
Kyrgyzstan	x	x		x	x*	x	x	x*
Lao People's Democratic Republic								x
Latvia	x	x		x	x	x*		x
Lebanon	x			x				x*
Lesotho	x			x		x	x	x
Liberia	s			s		x	x	x
Libyan Arab Jamahiriya	x	x		x	x			x
Liechtenstein					x(22)	x	x	x
Lithuania	x	x		x	x	x*	x*	x
Luxembourg	x	x	x	x	x(22)	x	x	x
Macedonia (former Yugoslav Republic of)	x	x	x	x	x	x	x	x
Madagascar	x	x		x		x		x
Malawi	x	x		x	x	x	x	x
Malaysia								x
Maldives								x
Mali	x			x		x	x	x
Malta	x	x	x	x	x(22)	x	x	x
Marshall Islands								

	International Covenant on Civil and Political Rights (ICCPR)	Optional Protocol to ICCPR	Second Optional Protocol to ICCPR, aiming at the abolition of the death penalty	International Covenant on Economic, Social and Cultural Rights	Convention against Torture and Other Cruel, Inhuman or Degrading Treatment or Punishment	Convention relating to the Status of Refugees (1951)	Protocol relating to the Status of Refugees (1967)	Convention on the Elimination of All Forms of Discrimination against Women
Mauritania						x	x	
Mauritius	x	x		x	x			x
Mexico	x			x	x			x
Micronesia (Federated States of)								
Moldova	x			x	x			x
Monaco	x*			x*	x(22)	x		
Mongolia	x	x		x				x
Morocco	x			x	x(28)	x	x	x
Mozambique	x		x			x	x	x*
Myanmar								x*
Namibia	x	x	x	x	x	x		x
Nauru								
Nepal	x	x		x	x			x
Netherlands	x	x	x	x	x(22)	x	x	x
New Zealand	x	x	x	x	x(22)	x	x	x
Nicaragua	x	x	s	x	s	x	x	x
Niger	x	x		x		x	x	
Nigeria	x			x	s	x	x	x
Norway	x	x	x	x	x(22)	x	x	x
Oman								
Pakistan								x
Palau								
Panama	x	x	x	x	x	x	x	x
Papua New Guinea						x	x	x

	International Covenant on Civil and Political Rights (ICCPR)	Optional Protocol to ICCPR	Second Optional Protocol to ICCPR, aiming at the abolition of the death penalty	International Covenant on Economic, Social and Cultural Rights	Convention against Torture and Other Cruel, Inhuman or Degrading Treatment or Punishment	Convention relating to the Status of Refugees (1951)	Protocol relating to the Status of Refugees (1967)	Convention on the Elimination of All Forms of Discrimination against Women
Paraguay	x	x		x	x	x	x	x
Peru	x	x		x	x	x	x	x
Philippines	x	x		x	x	x	x	x
Poland	x	x		x	x(22)	x	x	x
Portugal	x	x	x	x	x(22)	x	x	x
Qatar								
Romania	x	x	x	x	x	x	x	x
Russian Federation	x	x		x	x(22)	x	x	x
Rwanda	x			x		x	x	x
Saint Kitts and Nevis								x
Saint Lucia								x
Saint Vincent and the Grenadines	x	x		x		x		x
Samoa						x	x	x
San Marino	x	x		x				
Sao Tome and Principe	s			s		x	x	x
Saudi Arabia					x*			
Senegal	x	x		x	x(22)	x	x	x
Seychelles	x	x	x	x	x	x	x	x
Sierra Leone	x	x		x	s	x	x	x
Singapore								x
Slovakia	x	x		x	x	x	x	x
Slovenia	x	x	x	x	x(22)	x	x	x

	International Covenant on Civil and Political Rights (ICCPR)	Optional Protocol to ICCPR	Second Optional Protocol to ICCPR, aiming at the abolition of the death penalty	International Covenant on Economic, Social and Cultural Rights	Convention against Torture and Other Cruel, Inhuman or Degrading Treatment or Punishment	Convention relating to the Status of Refugees (1951)	Protocol relating to the Status of Refugees (1967)	Convention on the Elimination of All Forms of Discrimination against Women
Solomon Islands				x		x	x	
Somalia	x	x		x	x	x	x	
South Africa	s			s	s	x	x	x
Spain	x	x	x	x	x(22)	x	x	x
Sri Lanka	x	x*		x	x			x
Sudan	x			x	s	x	x	
Suriname	x	x		x		x	x	x
Swaziland							x	
Sweden	x	x	x	x	x(22)	x	x	x
Switzerland	x		x	x	x(22)	x	x	x*
Syrian Arab Republic	x			x				
Tajikistan					x	x	x	x
Tanzania	x			x		x	x	x
Thailand	x							x
Togo	x	x		x	x(22)	x	x	x
Tonga								
Trinidad and Tobago	x	x		x				x
Tunisia	x			x	x(22)	x	x	x
Turkey					x(22)	x	x	x
Turkmenistan	x*	x*		x*				x*
Tuvalu						x	x	
Uganda	x	x		x	x	x	x	x
Ukraine	x	x		x	x(28)			x
United Arab Emirates								

	International Covenant on Civil and Political Rights (ICCPR)	Optional Protocol to ICCPR	Second Optional Protocol to ICCPR, aiming at the abolition of the death penalty	International Covenant on Economic, Social and Cultural Rights	Convention against Torture and Other Cruel, Inhuman or Degrading Treatment or Punishment	Convention relating to the Status of Refugees (1951)	Protocol relating to the Status of Refugees (1967)	Convention on the Elimination of All Forms of Discrimination against Women
United Kingdom	x			x	x	x	x	x
United States of America	x			s	x		x	s
Uruguay	x	x	x	x	x(22)	x	x	x
Uzbekistan	x	x		x	x			x
Vanuatu								x
Venezuela	x	x	x	x	x(22)		x	x
Viet Nam	x			x				x
Yemen	x			x	x	x	x	x
Yugoslavia (Federal Republic of)	x	s		x	x(22)	x	x	x
Zambia	x	x		x		x	x	x
Zimbabwe	x			x		x	x	x

s – denotes that country has signed but not yet ratified

x – denotes that country is a party, either through ratification, accession or succession

* – denotes that country either signed or became a party in 1997

(22) denotes Declaration under Article 22 recognizing the competence of the Committee against Torture to consider individual complaints of violations of the Convention

(28) denotes that country has made a reservation under Article 28 that it does not recognize the competence of the Committee against Torture to examine reliable information which appears to indicate that torture is being systematically practised, and to undertake a confidential inquiry if warranted

SELECTED REGIONAL HUMAN RIGHTS TREATIES

(AS OF 31 DECEMBER 1997)

ORGANIZATION OF AFRICAN UNITY (OAU)
AFRICAN CHARTER ON HUMAN AND PEOPLES' RIGHTS (1981)

Algeria	x
Angola	x
Benin	x
Botswana	x
Burkina Faso	x
Burundi	x
Cameroon	x
Cape Verde	x
Central African Republic	x
Chad	x
Comoros	x
Congo (Democratic Republic of the)	x
Congo (Republic of the)	x
Côte d'Ivoire	x
Djibouti	x
Egypt	x
Equatorial Guinea	x
Eritrea	
Ethiopia	
Gabon	x
Gambia	x
Ghana	x
Guinea	x
Guinea-Bissau	x
Kenya	x
Lesotho	x
Liberia	x
Libya	x
Madagascar	x
Malawi	x
Mali	x
Mauritania	x
Mauritius	x
Mozambique	x
Namibia	x
Niger	x
Nigeria	x
Rwanda	x
Saharawi Arab Democratic Republic	x
Sao Tome and Principe	x
Senegal	x
Seychelles	x
Sierra Leone	x
Somalia	x
South Africa	x
Sudan	x
Swaziland	x
Tanzania	x
Togo	x
Tunisia	x
Uganda	x
Zambia	x
Zimbabwe	x

x denotes that country is a party, either through ratification or accession

This chart lists countries which were members of the OAU at the end of 1997.

ORGANIZATION OF AMERICAN STATES (OAS)

	American Convention on Human Rights (1969)	Inter-American Convention to Prevent and Punish Torture (1985)	Inter-American Convention on the Forced Disappearance of Persons (1994)
Antigua and Barbuda			
Argentina	x(62)	x	x
Bahamas			
Barbados	x		
Belize			
Bolivia	x(62)	s	s
Brazil	x	x	s
Canada			
Chile	x(62)	x	s
Colombia	x(62)	s	s
Costa Rica	x(62)	s	x
Cuba			
Dominica	x		
Dominican Republic	x	x	
Ecuador	x(62)	s	
El Salvador	x(62)	x	
Grenada	x		
Guatemala	x(62)	x	s
Guyana			
Haiti	x	s	
Honduras	x(62)	s	s
Jamaica	x		
Mexico	x	x	
Nicaragua	x(62)	s	s
Panama	x(62)	x	x
Paraguay	x(62)	x	x
Peru	x(62)	x	
Saint Kitts and Nevis			
Saint Lucia			
Saint Vincent and the Grenadines			
Suriname	x(62)	x	
Trinidad and Tobago	x(62)		
United States of America	s		
Uruguay	x(62)	x	x
Venezuela	x(62)	x	s

s denotes that country has signed but not yet ratified

x denotes that country is a party, either through ratification or accession

(62) denotes Declaration under Article 62 recognizing as binding the jurisdiction of the Inter-American Court of Human Rights (on all matters relating to the interpretation or application of the American Convention)

This chart lists countries which were members of the OAS at the end of 1997.

COUNCIL OF EUROPE

	European Convention for the Protection of Human Rights and Fundamental Freedoms (1950)	Article 25	Article 46	Protocol No. 6*	European Convention for the Prevention of Torture and Inhuman or Degrading Treatment or Punishment (1987)
Albania	x	x	x		x
Andorra	x	x	x	x	x
Austria	x	x	x	x	x
Belgium	x	x	x	s	x
Bulgaria	x	x	x		x
Croatia	x	x	x	x	x
Cyprus	x	x	x		x
Czech Republic	x	x	x	x	x
Denmark	x	x	x	x	x
Estonia	x	x	x	s	x
Finland	x	x	x	x	x
France	x	x	x	x	x
Germany	x	x	x	x	x
Greece	x	x	x	s	x
Hungary	x	x	x	x	x
Iceland	x	x	x	x	x
Ireland	x	x	x	x	x
Italy	x	x	x	x	x
Latvia	x				s
Liechtenstein	x	x	x	x	x
Lithuania	x	x	x		s
Luxembourg	x	x	x	x	x
Macedonia	x	x	x	x	x
Malta	x	x	x	x	x
Moldova	x	x	x	x	x
Netherlands	x	x	x	x	x
Norway	x	x	x	x	x
Poland	x	x	x		
Portugal	x	x	x	x	x
Romania	x	x	x	x	x
Russian Federation	s			s	s
San Marino	x	x	x	x	x
Slovakia	x	x	x	x	x
Slovenia	x	x	x	x	x
Spain	x	x	x	x	x
Sweden	x	x	x	x	x
Switzerland	x	x	x	x	x
Turkey	x	x	x		x
Ukraine	x	x	x	s	x
United Kingdom	x	x	x		x

s — denotes that country has signed but not yet ratified

x — denotes that country is a party, either through ratification or accession

Article 25 — denotes Declaration under Article 25 of the European Convention for the Protection of Human Rights and Fundamental Freedoms, recognizing the competence of the European Commission of Human Rights to consider individual complaints of violations of the Convention

Article 46 — denotes Declaration under Article 46 of the European Convention for the Protection of Human Rights and Fundamental Freedoms, recognizing as compulsory the jurisdiction of the European Court of Human Rights in all matters concerning interpretation and application of the European Convention

* Protocol No. 6 to the European Convention for the Protection of Human Rights and Fundamental Freedoms concerning the abolition of the death penalty (1983)

This chart lists countries which were members of the Council of Europe at the end of 1997.

SELECTED STATISTICS

AMNESTY INTERNATIONAL MEMBERSHIP

In 1997 there were more than 1,000,000 Amnesty International members and subscribers in over 160 countries and territories. There were more than 4,300 local Amnesty International groups registered with the International Secretariat, plus over 3,400 youth and student groups, in more than 105 countries and territories. In addition, there were many hundreds of other coordinators, groups, specialized networks, individual members and supporters.

LONG-TERM GROUP WORK

At the end of 1997 Amnesty International groups were working on almost 1,600 different long-term assignments, concerning more than 4,100 individuals. These included prisoners of conscience and victims of other human rights violations such as torture and "disappearance". During the year, action began on 248 new Action Files on specific cases, plus more than 230 new and updated regional actions, many of which concerned more than one individual. In 1997 more than 200 actions involving the detention of prisoners of conscience and possible prisoners of conscience were closed.

URGENT ACTION APPEALS

During 1997 Amnesty International initiated 583 actions which required urgent appeals from the Urgent Action Network. There were also 350 calls for further appeals on actions already issued. Members of the Urgent Action Network were therefore asked to send appeals on 933 occasions. These actions were issued on behalf of people in 99 countries and territories.

The 583 new actions were issued on behalf of people who were either at risk or had been the victim of the following human rights violations: torture – 177 cases; "disappearance" – 74 cases; judicial execution – 133 cases; political killings and death threats – 173 cases; and legal concerns – 62 cases. (These categories are not mutually exclusive; more than one concern may have been featured in an action.) Other concerns included ill health, deaths in custody, *refoulement* (forcible repatriation) of asylum-seekers, corporal punishment and forcible exile.

REGIONAL ACTION NETWORKS

Amnesty International's 23 Regional Action Networks cover human rights abuses in every country of the world. During the year, approximately 1,800 Amnesty International local groups participated in one or more of the networks. They took action on more than 230 new and updated appeals on behalf of thousands of victims of human rights violations in 88 countries and territories.

AMNESTY INTERNATIONAL FUNDING

The international budget adopted by Amnesty International for the financial year April 1997 to March 1998 was £17,101,000. This sum represents approximately one quarter of the estimated income likely to be raised during the year by the movement's national sections to finance their campaigning and other activities. Amnesty International's national sections and local volunteer groups are primarily responsible for funding the movement. An international fund-raising program is being developed. No funds are sought or accepted from governments for Amnesty International's work investigating and campaigning against human rights violations. The donations that sustain this work come from the organization's members and the public.

RELIEF

During the financial year April 1997 to March 1998, the International Secretariat of Amnesty International distributed an estimated £240,000 in relief (financial assistance) to victims of human rights violations such as prisoners of conscience and recently released prisoners of conscience and their dependants, and for the medical treatment of torture victims. In addition, the organization's sections and groups distributed a further substantial amount, much of it in the form of modest payments by local groups to their adopted prisoners of conscience and dependent families.

Amnesty International's ultimate goal is to end human rights violations, but so long as they continue it tries to provide practical help to the victims. Relief is an important aspect of this work. Sometimes Amnesty International provides financial assistance directly to individuals. At other times, it works through local bodies such as local and national human rights organizations so as to ensure that resources are used as effectively as possible for those in most need. When Amnesty International asks an intermediary to distribute relief payments on its behalf, it stipulates precisely the intended purpose and beneficiaries, and requires the intermediary to report back fully on the expenditure of the funds.

AMNESTY INTERNATIONAL REPORT 98

ERRATA

Introduction/All human rights for all
Page 2, line 21: Lidiya Morozvona Puchayeva should read Lidiya Morozovna Puchayeva

Burundi
Page 116, column 2, line 27: Cabies district should read Kabezi district
Page 117, column 1, line 24: Muramyva province should read Muramvya province

Germany
Page 174, column 2, line 57: Aliu Bo should read Aliu B.

Iraq
Page 203, column 2, line 13 should read: ...inspecting suspected weapon sites in Iraq.

Thailand
Page 330, column 2, line 21 should read: ...killing three karenni refugees...

United States of America
Page 351, column 1, line 15: Los Angeles County Sheriff's Department should read Riverside County Sheriff's Department

Uzbekistan
Page 355, column 2, line 40: Nematjon Parpier should read Nematjon Parpiev
Page 356, column 1, line 40: Nematjon Parpier should read Nematjon Parpiev

Appendix IV — International Executive Committee
Page 380: Colm Ó'Cuanacháin/Ireland should read Colm Ó Cuanacháin/Ireland

Appendix V — Update on Abolition of the death penalty
Page 381, column 2, line 25 should read: By the end of 1997, 61 countries had...